D1315090

JUMP AT HOME

NEW EDITION

GRADE 5

Worksheets for the JUMP Math Program

JOHN MIGHTON

Copyright © 2004, 2007 John Mighton

All rights reserved. No part of this publication may be reproduced or transmitted in any form or by any means, electronic or mechanical, including photocopying, recording, or any information storage and retrieval system, without permission in writing from the publisher.

First published in 2004 by House of Anansi Press Inc.

Revised edition published in 2007 by House of Anansi Press Inc.
110 Spadina Avenue, Suite 801, Toronto, ON, M5V 2K4
Tel. 416-363-4343 Fax 416-363-1017 www.anansi.ca

Distributed in Canada by HarperCollins Canada Ltd.
1995 Markham Road, Scarborough, ON, M1B 5M8
Toll free tel. 1-800-387-0117

Distributed in the United States by Publishers Group West
1700 Fourth Street, Berkeley, CA 94710
Toll free tel. 1-800-788-3123

Some of the material in this book has previously been published by JUMP Math.

Every reasonable effort has been made to contact the holders of copyright for materials reproduced in this work. The publishers will gladly receive information that will enable them to rectify any inadvertent errors or omissions in subsequent editions.

11 10 09 08 07 1 2 3 4 5

Library and Archives Canada Cataloguing in Publication Data

Mighton, John, 1957–
JUMP at home grade 5 : worksheets for the JUMP math program / John Mighton. — New ed.

(JUMP at home workbooks)
ISBN 978-0-88784-771-4

1. Mathematics — Problems, exercises, etc. I. Title. II. Series: Mighton, John, 1957– JUMP at home workbooks.

QA139.M555 2008 j510.76 C2007-902653-2

Library of Congress Control Number: 2007908576

Acknowledgements

Authors – Dr. John Mighton (PhD Mathematics, Ashoka Fellow, Fellow of the Fields Institute for Research in Mathematical Sciences), Dr. Sindi Sabourin (PhD Mathematics, BEd), and Dr. Anna Klebanov (PhD Mathematics)
Consultant – Jennifer Wyatt (MA Candidate, BEd)
Contributors – Betony Main, Lisa Hines, and Sheila Mooney
Layout – Katie Baldwin, Rita Camacho, Tony Chen, Lyubava Fartushenko, and Pam Lostracco

This book, like the JUMP program itself, is made possible by the efforts of the volunteers and staff of JUMP Math.

Cover design: The Bang

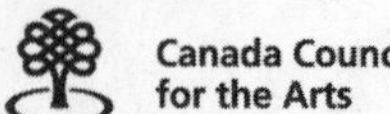

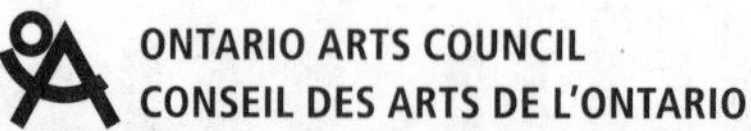

We acknowledge for their financial support of our publishing program the Canada Council for the Arts, the Ontario Arts Council, and the Government of Canada through the Book Publishing Industry Development Program (BPIDP).

Printed and bound in Canada

Contents

INTRODUCTION TO THE "JUMP AT HOME" WORKBOOKS

Based on my work with hundreds of elementary students, spanning fifteen years, I am convinced that all children can be led to think mathematically. Even if I am wrong, the results of JUMP suggest that it is worth suspending judgment in individual cases. A parent or teacher who expects a child to fail is almost certain to produce a failure. The method of teaching outlined in this book (or any method, for that matter) is more likely to succeed if it is applied with patience and an open mind.

If you are a parent and you believe that your child is not capable of leaning math, I recommend that you read *The Myth of Ability: Nurturing Mathematical Talent in Every Child* or *The End of Ignorance: Multiplying Our Human Potential*, and consult the JUMP website (at www.jumpmath.org) for testimonials from teachers who have tried the program and for a report on current research on the program.

You are more likely to help your child if you teach with the following principles in mind:

1) *If a child doesn't understand your explanation, assume there is something lacking in your explanation, not in your child.*

   When a teacher leaves a student behind, it is almost always because they have not taken responsibility for examining the way they teach. I often make mistakes in my lessons: sometimes I will go too fast for a student or skip steps inadvertently. I don't consider myself a natural teacher. I know many teachers who are more charismatic or faster on their feet than I am. But I have had enormous success with students who were thought to be unteachable because if I happen to leave a student behind I always ask myself: What did I do wrong in that lesson? (And I usually find that my mistake is neglecting one of the principles listed below.)

2) *In mathematics, it is always possible to make a step easier.*

   A hundred years ago, researchers in logic discovered that virtually all of the concepts used by working mathematicians could be reduced to one of two extremely basic operations, namely, the operation of counting or the operation of grouping objects into sets. Most people are able to perform both of these operations before they enter kindergarten. It is surprising, therefore, that schools have managed to make mathematics a mystery to so many students.

   A tutor once told me that one of her students, a girl in Grade 4, had refused to let her teach her how to divide. The girl said that the concept of division was much too hard for her and she would never consent to learn it. I suggested the tutor teach division as a kind of counting game. In the next lesson, without telling the girl she was about to learn how to divide, the tutor wrote in succession the numbers 15 and 5. Then she asked the child to count on her fingers by multiples of the second number, until she'd reached the first. After the child had repeated this operation with several other pairs of numbers, the tutor asked her to write down, in each case, the number of fingers she had raised when she stopped counting. For instance,

   15 5 3

   As soon as the student could find the answer to any such question quickly, the tutor wrote, in each example, a division sign between the first and second number, and an equal sign between the second and third.

   $15 \div 5 = 3$

   The student was surprised to find she had learned to divide in 10 minutes. (Of course, the tutor later explained to the student that 15 divided by five is three because you can add 5 three times to get 15: that's what you see when you count on your fingers.)

   In the exercises in the JUMP Workbook we have made an effort to break concepts and skills into steps that children will find easy to master. But the workbooks are far from perfect. Some pages are more cramped than we would have liked and some pages do not provide enough practice or preparation. The worksheets are intended as models for parents to improve upon: we hope you will take responsibility for providing your child with warm-up questions and bonus questions (see below for a discussion of how to create these questions), and for filling in any gaps our materials wherever you find them. We have made a serious effort to introduce skills and concepts in small steps and in a coherent order, so a committed parent should have no trouble seeing where they need to create extra questions for practice or where they need to fill in a missing step in the development of an idea.

3) *With a weaker student, the second piece of information almost always drives out the first.*

   When a teacher introduces several pieces of information at the same time, students will often, in trying to comprehend the final item, lose all memory and understanding of the material that came before (even though

No unauthorized copying

they may have appeared to understand this material completely as it was being explained). With weaker students, it is always more efficient to introduce one piece of information at a time.

I once observed an intern from teachers college who was trying to teach a boy in a Grade 7 remedial class how to draw mixed fractions. The boy was getting very frustrated as the intern kept asking him to carry out several steps at the same time.

I asked the boy to simply draw a picture showing the number of whole pies in the fraction 2 ½. He drew and shaded two whole pies. I then asked him to draw the number of whole pies in 3 ½, 4 ½ and 5 ½ pies. He was very excited when he completed the work I had assigned him, and I could see that he was making more of an effort to concentrate. I asked him to draw the whole number of pies in 2 ¼, 2 ¾, 3 ¼, 4 ¼, then in 2 1/3, 2 2/3, 3 1/3 pies and so on. (I started with quarters rather than thirds because they are easier to draw.) When the boy could draw the whole number of pies in any mixed fraction, I showed him how to draw the fractional part. Within a few minutes he was able to draw any mixed fraction. If I hadn't broken the skill into two steps (i.e. drawing the number of whole pies then drawing the fractional part) and allowed him to practice each step separately, he might never have learned the concept

As your student learns to concentrate and approach the work with real excitement (which generally happens after several months if the early JUMP units are taught properly), you can begin to skip steps when teaching new material, or even challenge your student to figure out the steps themselves. But if your student ever begins to struggle with this approach, it is best to go back to teaching in small steps.

4) *Before you assign work, verify that your student has the skills needed to complete the work.*

In our school system it is assumed that some students will always be left behind in mathematics. If a teacher is careful to break skills and concepts into steps that every student can understand, this needn't happen. (JUMP has demonstrated this in dozens of classrooms.)

Before you assign a question from one of the JUMP workbooks you should verify that your student is prepared to answer the question without your help (or with minimal help). On most worksheets, only one or two new concepts or skills are introduced, so you should find it easy to verify that your student can answer the question. The worksheets are intended as final tests that you can give when you are certain your student understands the material.

Always give a short diagnostic quiz before you allow your student to work on a worksheet. In general, a quiz should consist of four or five questions similar to the ones on the worksheet. The quizzes will help you identify whether your student needs an extra review before you move on.

5) *Raise the bar incrementally.*

Any successes I have had with weaker students are almost entirely due to a technique I use which is, as a teacher once said about the JUMP method, "not exactly rocket science." When a student has mastered a skill or concept, I simply raise the bar slightly by challenging them to answer a question that is only incrementally more difficult or complex than the questions I had previously assigned. I always make sure, when the student succeeds in meeting my challenge, that they know I am impressed. Sometimes I will even pretend I'm about to faint (students always laugh at this) or I will say "You got that question but you'll never get the next one." Students become very excited when they succeed in meeting a series of graduated challenges. And their excitement allows them to focus their attention enough to make the leaps I have described in *The Myth of Ability* and *The End of Ignorance.*

There is a growing body of evidence in cognition that suggests that the brain is plastic and that, through rigorous instruction, new abilities and forms of intelligence can emerge even in older students or in students who have struggled in a subject. The research has shown, however, that very little happens in the brain if a student's attention is not engaged. By raising the bar for your child — allowing them to succeed at a series of graduated challenges — you can help their brain work far more efficiently. (See *The End of Ignorance* for an account of new research in cognition.)

In designing the JUMP workbooks, I have made an effort to introduce only one or two skills per page, so you should find it easy to create bonus questions: just change the numbers in an existing question or add an extra element to a problem on a worksheet. For instance, if your child has just learned how to add a pair of three-digit numbers, you might ask your child to add a pair of four- or five-digit numbers. If you become excited when you assign more challenging questions, you will find that even a child who previously had trouble focusing will race to finish their work so they can answer a bonus question.

6) *Repetition and practice are essential.*

Even mathematicians need constant practice to consolidate and remember skills and concepts. Studies of chess players and other experts have shown that intuition, creativity and proficiency can develop out of rigorous practice and study. (See for instance the article "The Expert Mind" in *Scientific American*.) Practice doesn't have to be torture. By raising the bar, by allowing your child to make discoveries themselves, and by playing with subtle variations on patterns you can make practice fun.

7) *Praise is essential.*

We've found the JUMP program works best when teachers give their students a great deal of encouragement. Because the lessons are laid out in steps that any student can master, you'll find that you won't be giving false encouragement. (This is one of the reasons kids love the program so much: for many, it's a thrill to be doing well at math.)

We haven't observed a student yet – even among scores of remedial students – who couldn't learn math. When it is taught in steps, math is actually the subject in which children with attention deficits and learning disabilities can most easily succeed, and thereby develop the confidence and cognitive abilities they need to do well in other subjects. Rather than being the hardest subject, math can be the engine of learning for delayed students. This is one of JUMP's cornerstone beliefs. If you disagree with this tenet, please reconsider your decision to use JUMP. Our program will only be fully effective if you embrace the philosophy.

What Is JUMP Math?

JUMP Math is a philosophy and a set of materials and methods that aims to improve the teaching of mathematics and to help students enjoy and meet their potential in the subject.

The JUMP program is based on the belief that all children in the regular school system, even those diagnosed as having serious learning disabilities, or who are failing, can do well at math. Mathematics, rather than being the most difficult subject, is one in which children can most easily succeed, even at a young age, and can thereby develop the confidence and cognitive abilities they need to do well in other subjects.

JUMP is a registered not-for-profit organization and a charity.

About This Book

This book covers only part of the standard curriculum: it does not contain any material on Geometry, Probability, Statistics or Data Management and only partially covers the curriculum in Measurement. JUMP has published in-class versions of this book that cover the complete curriculum and that come with teacher manuals that have lesson plans for each worksheet. Significant discounts are available for teachers for class sets. For more information see the JUMP website (www.jumpmath.org).

The Fractions Unit

To prepare your child to use this book, you should set aside 40 to 50 minutes a day for three weeks to teach them the material in the JUMP Fractions Unit. You may print individual copies of the unit from the JUMP website at no charge The Fractions Unit has proven to be a remarkably effective tool for instilling a sense of confidence and enthusiasm about mathematics in students. The unit has helped many teachers discover a potential in their students that they might not otherwise have seen. In a recent survey, all of the teachers who used the Fractions Unit for the first time acknowledged afterwards that they had underestimated the abilities of some of their students. (For details of this study, see the JUMP website at www.jumpmath.org.)

Games

As much as possible make learning an adventure and a game for your child. Build lessons around the worksheets that allow your child to meet and overcome challenges, to solve puzzles and to make discoveries. For ways to turn your lessons into games see for instance the problem solving lesson in this introduction (pages viii-xii), the Modified Go Fish activity in Mental Math (page xxxv), and the activities with concrete materials (pages xiii-xxii). There are many standard games that help children develop a sense of numbers (like Cribbage or Monopoly) and an ability to reason and to make predictions and deductions (various card games and strategy games).

 No unauthorized copying

Sample Problem Solving Lesson

As much as possible, allow your child to extend and discover ideas on their own (without pushing them so far that they become discouraged). It is not hard to develop problem solving lessons (where your child can make discoveries in steps) using the material on the worksheets. Here is a sample problem solving lesson you can try with your child.

1. **Warm-up**
   Review the notion of perimeter from the worksheets. Draw the following diagram on grid paper and ask your child how they would determine the perimeter. (You may need to state that the drawings on the board are drawn to scale: 1 unit^2 = 1 cm^2.)

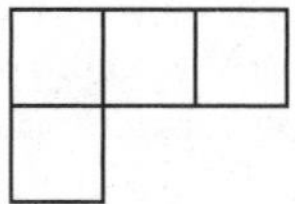

Allow your child to demonstrate their method (e.g., counting the line segments, or adding the lengths of each side).

2. **Develop the Idea**
   Draw some additional shapes on grid paper and ask your child to determine the perimeter of each.

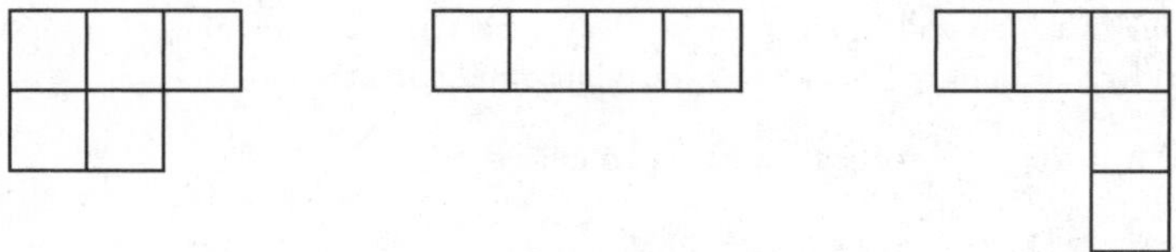

Check	Bonus	Try Again?
The perimeters of the shapes above are 10 cm, 10 cm and 12 cm respectively.	Have your child make a picture of a letter from their name on graph paper by colouring in squares. Then ask them to find the perimeter and record their answer in words.	Children may need to use some kind of system to keep them from missing sides. Suggest that your child write the length of the sides on the shape.

3. **Go Further**
   Draw a simple rectangle on the board and ask your child to again find the perimeter.

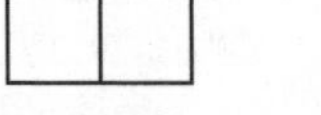

Add a square to the shape and ask your child how the perimeter changes.

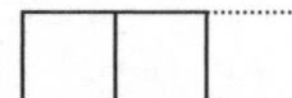

Draw the following polygons on the board and ask your child to copy the four polygons on their grid paper.

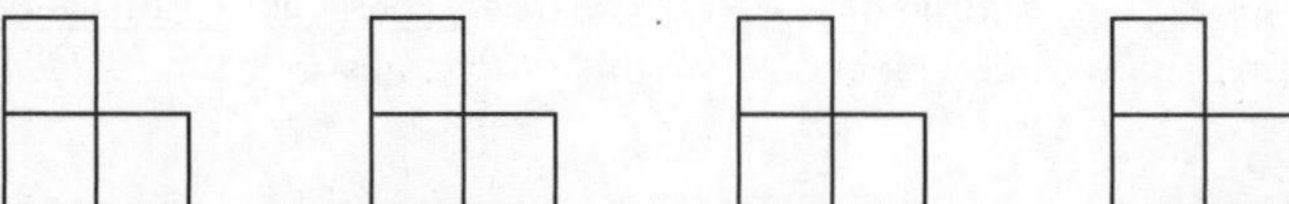

No unauthorized copying

Sample Problem Solving Lesson *(continued)*

Ask your child how they would calculate the perimeter of the first polygon. Then instruct them to add an additional square to each polygon and calculate the perimeter again.

Check	Bonus	Try Again?
Have your child demonstrate where they added the shapes and how they found the perimeter. Ask your child to discuss why they think the perimeter remains constant when the square is added in the corner (as in the fourth polygon above).	♣ Ask your child to calculate the greatest amount the perimeter can increase by when you add a single square. ♣ Ask them to add 2 (or 3) squares to the shape below and examine how the perimeter changes. ♣ Ask them to create a T-table where the two columns are labelled "Number of Squares" in the polygon and "Perimeter" of the polygon (see the Patterns section for an introduction to T-tables). Have them add more squares and record how the perimeter continues to change.	Ask your child to draw a single square on their grid paper and find the perimeter (4 cm). Then have them add a square and find the perimeter of the resulting rectangle. Have them repeat this exercise a few times and then follow the same procedure with the original (or bonus) questions.

4. **Another Step**
Draw the following shape on the board and ask your child, "How can you add a square to the following shape so the perimeter *decreases*?"

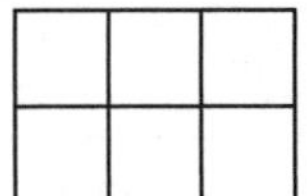

Check	Bonus	Try Again?
Discuss with your child why perimeter decreases when the square is added in the middle of the second row. You may want to ask them what kinds of shapes have larger perimeters and which have smaller perimeters.	Ask your child to add two squares to the polygons below and see if they can reduce the perimeter.	Have your child try the exercise again with six square-shaped pattern blocks. Have them create the polygon as drawn above and find where they need to place the sixth square by guessing and checking (placing the square and measuring the perimeter of the resulting polygon).

No unauthorized copying

Sample Problem Solving Lesson *(continued)*

5. **Develop the Idea**

Hold up a photograph that you've selected and ask your child how you would go about selecting a frame for it. What kinds of measurements would you need to know about the photograph in order to get the right sized frame? You might also want to show your child a CD case and ask them how they would measure the paper to create an insert for a CD/CD-ROM.

Show your child on paper how the perimeter of a rectangle can be solved with an addition statement (e.g., Perimeter = 14 cm is the sum of 3 + 3 + 4 + 4). Explain that the rectangle is made up of two pairs of equal lines and that, because of this, we only need two numbers to find the perimeter of a given rectangle.

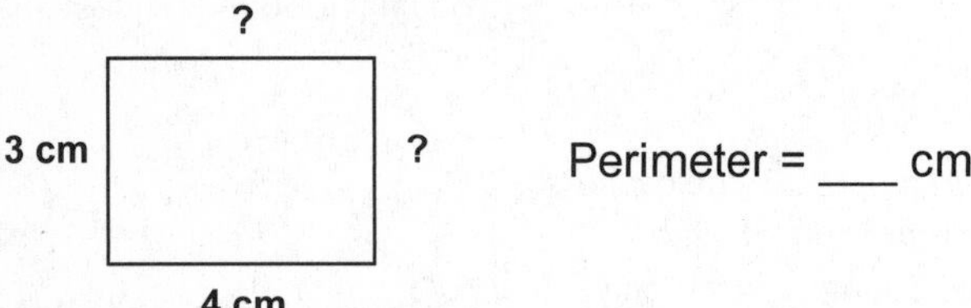

Show your child that there are two ways to find this:

a) Create an addition statement by writing each number twice: 3 cm + 3 cm + 4 cm + 4 cm = 14 cm
b) Add the numbers together and multiply the sum by 2: 3 cm + 4 cm = 7 cm; 7 cm × 2 = 14 cm

Ask your child to find the perimeters of the following rectangles (not drawn to scale).

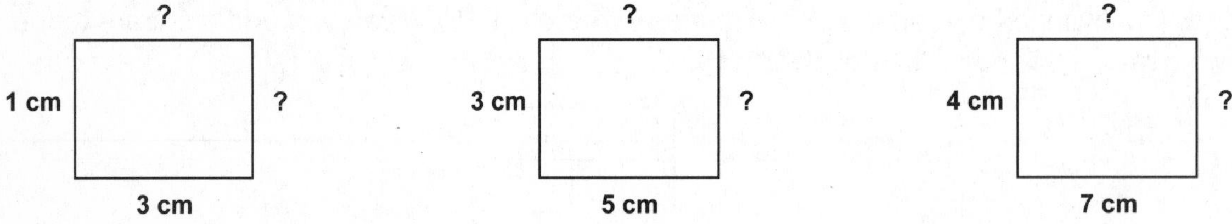

Check	Bonus	Try Again?
Take up the questions (the perimeters of the rectangles above, from left to right, are 8 cm, 16 cm and 22 cm).	Continue creating questions in this format for your child and gradually increase the size of the numbers.	Have your child draw a copy of the rectangle in a notebook and copy the measurements onto all four sides. Have them create an addition statement by copying one of the numbers and then crossing our the measurement: 4 cm 4 cm 1 cm + 1 cm

6. **Go Further**

Demonstrate on grid paper that two different rectangles can both have a perimeter of 10 cm.

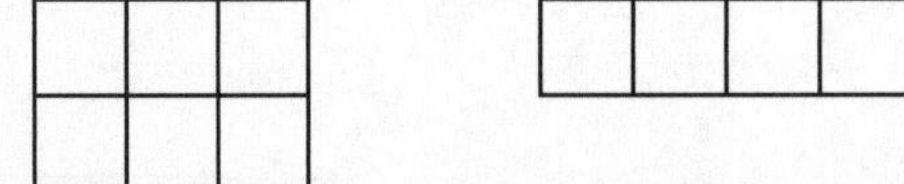

Sample Problem Solving Lesson *(continued)*

Ask your child to draw all the rectangles they can with a perimeter of 12 cm.

Check	Bonus	Try Again?
After your child has finished, ask them whether they were able to find one rectangle, then two rectangles, then three rectangles.	Ask your child to find (and draw) all the rectangles with a perimeter of 18 cm. After they have completed this, they can repeat the same exercise for rectangles of 24 cm or 36 cm.	If your child finds only one (or zero) rectangles, they should be shown a systematic method of finding the answer and then given the chance to practise the original question. On grid paper, have your child draw a pair of lines with lengths of 1 and 2 cm each. 1 cm 2 cm Ask them to draw the other three sides of each rectangle so that the final perimeter will be 12 cm for each rectangle, guessing and checking the lengths of the other sides. Let them try this method on one of the bonus questions once they accomplish this.

7. **Raise the Bar**

Draw the following rectangle and measurements on paper:

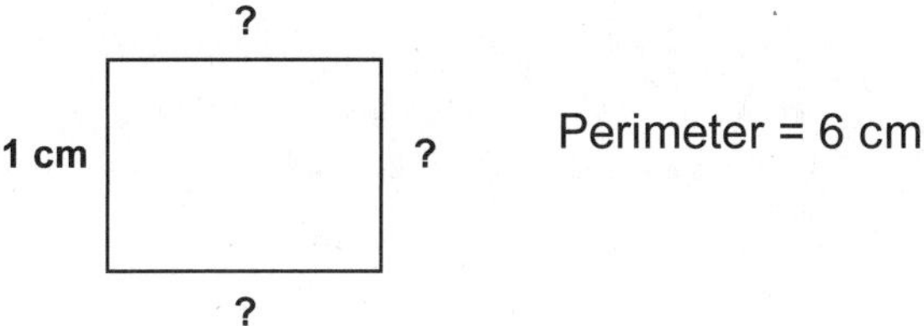

Ask your child how they would calculate the length of the missing sides. After they have given some input, explain to them how the side opposite the one measured will always have the same measurement. Demonstrate how the given length can be subtracted twice (or multiplied by two and then subtracted) from the perimeter. The remainder, divided by two, will be the length of each of the two remaining sides.

Draw a second rectangle and ask your child to find the lengths of the missing sides using the methods just discussed.

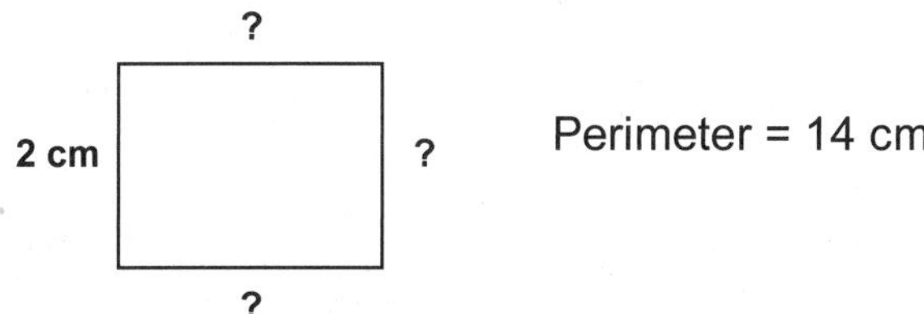

No unauthorized copying

Sample Problem Solving Lesson *(continued)*

Check	Bonus	Try Again?
Check that your child can calculate the length of the sides (2 cm, 2 cm, 5 cm and 5 cm).	Give your child more problems like above. For example: ♣ Side = 5 cm; Perimeter = 20 cm ♣ Side = 10 cm; Perimeter = 50 cm ♣ Side = 20 cm; Perimeter = 100 cm ♣ Side = 65 cm; Perimeter = 250 cm Be sure to raise the numbers incrementally on bonus questions.	Give your child a simple problem to try (similar to the first demonstration question). ? / 1 cm / ? / ? Perimeter = 8 cm Provide them with eight toothpicks (or a similar object) and have them create the rectangle and then measure the length of each side. Have them repeat this with more questions.

8. Assessment

Draw the following diagrams of rectangles and perimeter statements, and ask your child to complete the missing measurements on each rectangle.

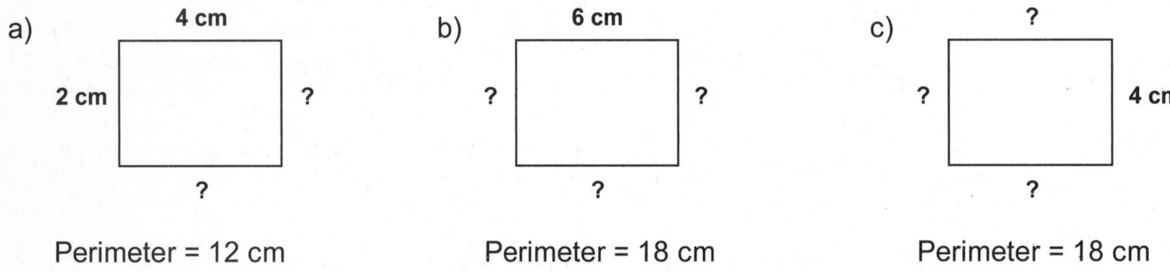

Perimeter = 12 cm   Perimeter = 18 cm   Perimeter = 18 cm

Check	Bonus
Answers for the above questions (going clockwise from the sides given): a) 2 cm, 4 cm b) 3 cm, 6 cm, 3 cm c) 5 cm, 4 cm, 5 cm	Draw a square and inform your child that the perimeter is 20 cm. What is the length of each side? (Answer: 5 cm.) Repeat with other multiples of four for the perimeter.

No unauthorized copying

Activities with Concrete Materials

When you teach the material in this book you should try, whenever possible, to illustrate and explore the ideas on a worksheet with concrete materials and models. For most exercises in the workbook you can use simple materials, such as coins, paper money, counters (such as buttons or poker chips), rulers, and so on.

The most common materials that are used in schools to make models of whole numbers and decimals are base ten blocks, which are made of 1 cm by 1 cm cubes.

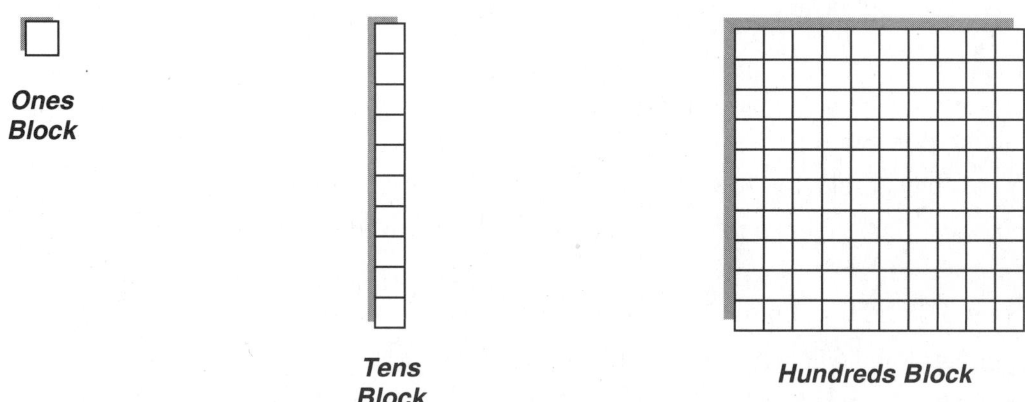

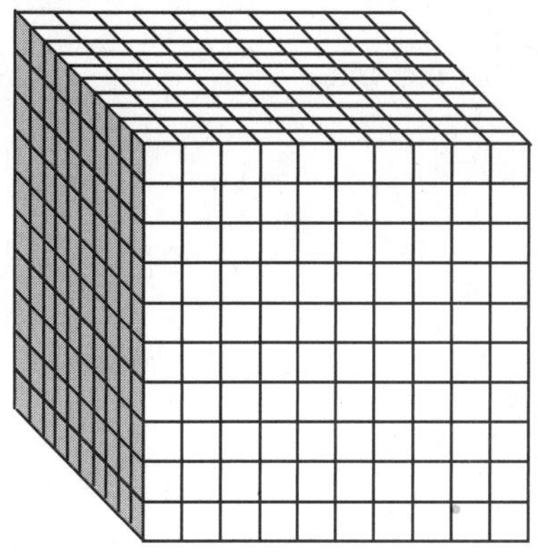

Thousands Block

We have provided blackline masters of the ones, tens, and hundreds blocks (see page xl) that you can copy and cut out. To make a model of the thousands block, tape six hundreds blocks together to make a cube.

Activities with Concrete Materials

1. Give your child ones, tens, and hundreds blocks.

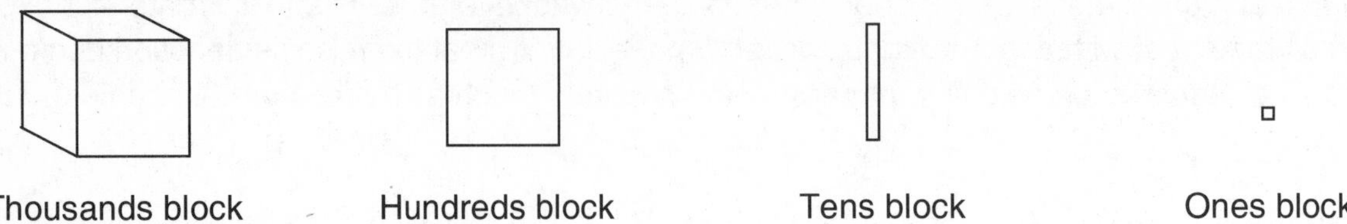

Instructions:

a) Show 17, 31, 252, etc. with base ten blocks.

b) Show 22 using exactly 13 blocks.

c) Show 31 using 13 blocks.

Harder: (You might want to wait until your child has finished more of the Number Sense section before you assign these questions.)

d) Show 315 using exactly 36 blocks.

e) I am a 2 digit number: Use 6 blocks to make me. Use twice as many tens blocks as ones blocks.

f) I am a greater than 20 and less than 30. My ones digit is one more than my tens digit.

g) I am a 3 digit number. My digits are all the same: use 9 blocks to make me.

h) I am a 2 digit number. My tens digit is 5 more than my ones digit: use 7 blocks to make me.

i) I am a 3 digit number. My tens digit is one more than my hundreds digit and my ones digit is one more than my tens digit: use 6 blocks to make me. What would I be if I was represented by 7 blocks?

j) Show 1123 using exactly 16 blocks. (There are 2 answers.)

k) I am a 4 digit number. My digits are all the same: use 12 blocks to make me.

2. *Wrap Up: Visualizing base ten materials*
Ask your child to imagine choosing some base ten blocks…

Instructions:

a) You have more tens than ones. What might your number be? (More than one answer is possible.)

b) You have the same number of ones and tens blocks. What might your number be? (Or give harder questions.)

c) You have twice as many tens blocks as ones blocks. What two digit numbers could you have?

d) You have six more ones than tens. What might your number be?

e) You have one set of blocks that make the number 13 and one set of blocks that make the number 22. Could you have the same number of blocks in both sets?

f) You have one set of blocks that make the number 23 and one set of blocks that make the number 16. Could you have the same number of blocks in both sets?

g) You have an equal number of ones, tens, and hundreds and twice as many thousands as hundreds. What might your number be?

NOTE: If some of the questions are too hard to solve by visualization, let your child sketch base ten models.

No unauthorized copying

Activities with Concrete Materials

3. Give your child a set of cards with the numbers 1 to 8 on them.

   a) Ask them to arrange the cards in two rows as shown so that the difference between the number is as small as possible.

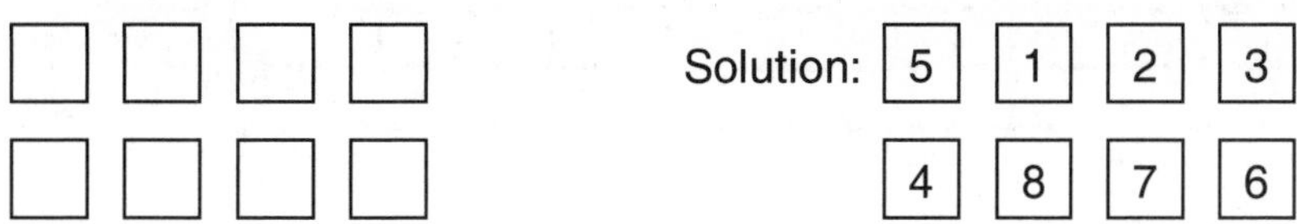

   b) Ask them to place the eight cards so that the three subtraction statements below are correct.

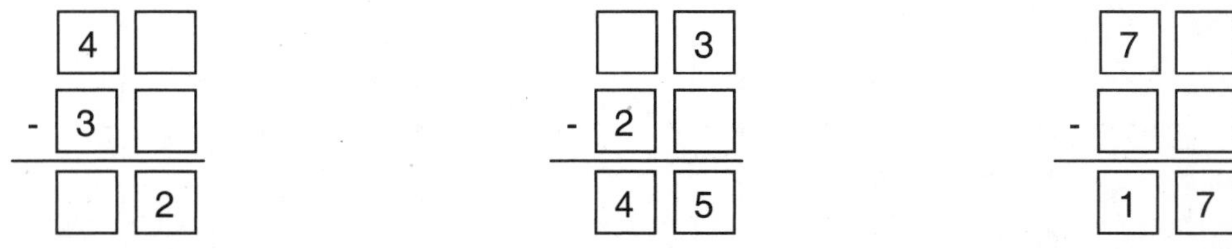

4. Your child can make base ten models to show how to break a product into smaller products. The picture at the top of worksheet NS5-18 on page 55 shows that $4 \times 23 = 4 \times 20 + 4 \times 3$. Ask your child to make a similar model to show that $4 \times 25 = 4 \times 20 + 4 \times 5$.

   Step 1:
   Make a model of 25 using 2 different colours of base ten blocks (one colour for the tens blocks and one colour for the ones blocks).

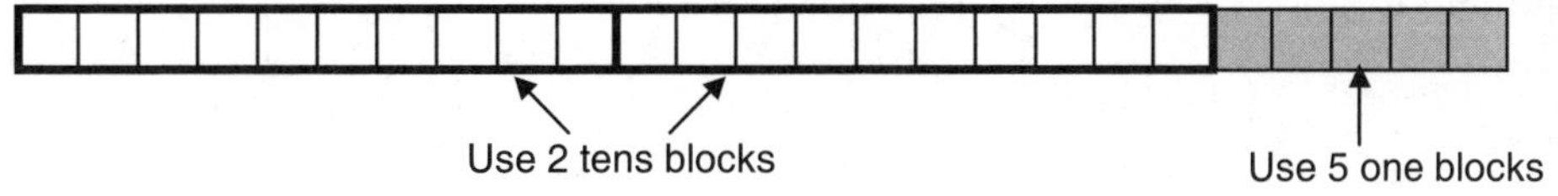

No unauthorized copying

Activities with Concrete Materials

Step 2:
Extend the model to show 4 × 25.

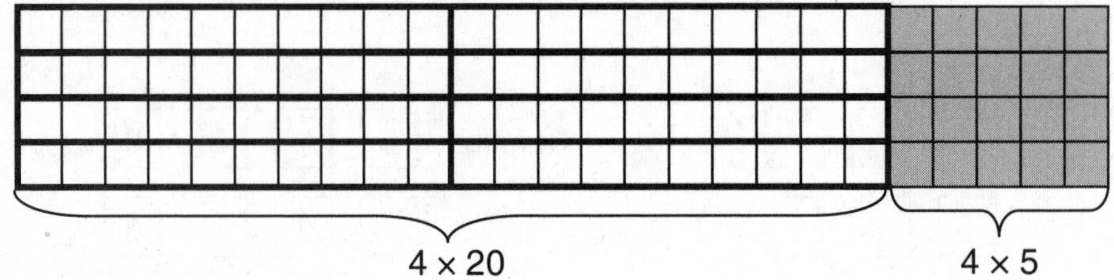

Step 3:
Break the array into two separate arrays to show 4 × 25 = 4 × 20 + 4 × 5.

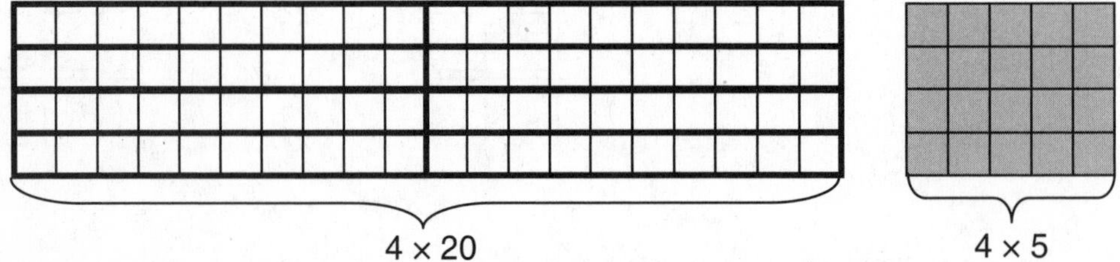

5. Give your child a set of base ten blocks and 3 containers large enough to hold the blocks. Ask them to make a model of 74 using the blocks. Point out that each of the tens blocks they used to make the model is made up of 10 smaller ones blocks. Then ask them to show how they would divide the 74 ones blocks in their model into the three containers as evenly as possible.

   Your child should see that they can solve the problem as follows:

   Step 1:
   Make a representation of 74.

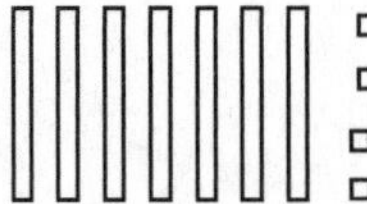

   Step 2:
   Divide the tens blocks among the three containers as evenly as possible.

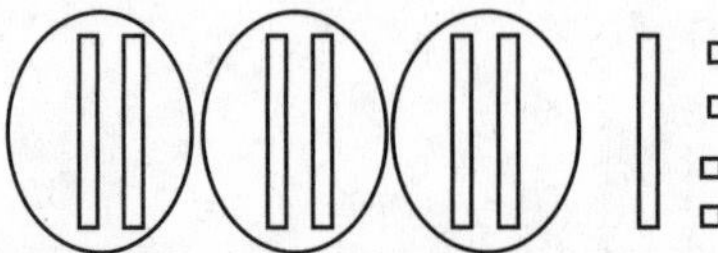

Activities with Concrete Materials

Your child should see that they can only place 2 tens blocks per container, with one left over (7 ÷ 3 = 2 R1). Point out to them that when they perform the standard long division algorithm, they are simply keeping track of the steps they followed in dividing up the tens blocks.

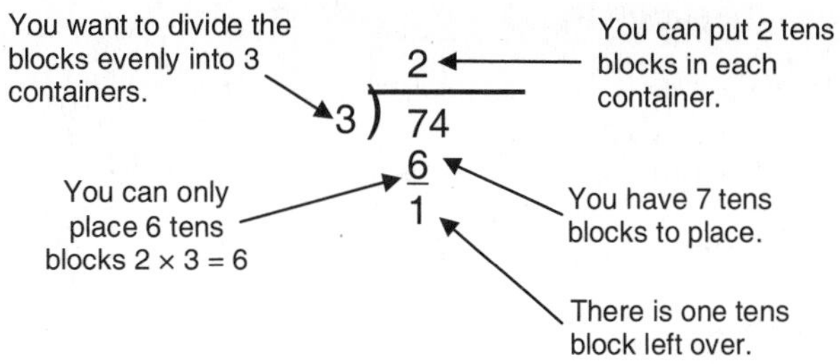
You want to divide the blocks evenly into 3 containers.
You can put 2 tens blocks in each container.
You can only place 6 tens blocks 2 × 3 = 6
You have 7 tens blocks to place.
There is one tens block left over.

Step 3:
Your child should recognize that they can only divide up the remaining units if they regroup the tens block as ten ones.

In the long division algorithm, this step is equivalent to brining down the number in the ones column.

```
     2
3 ) 74
    6↓
    14 ←
```

Regroup the tens block as 10 ones and put all your ones together – now you have 14 ones.

Step 4:
Divide the 14 ones among the 3 containers.

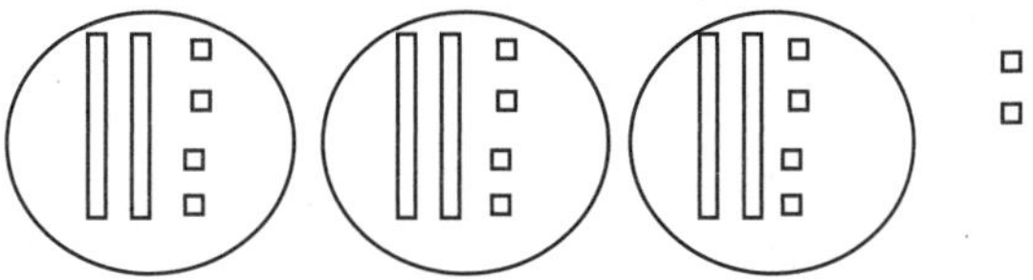

In the algorithm:

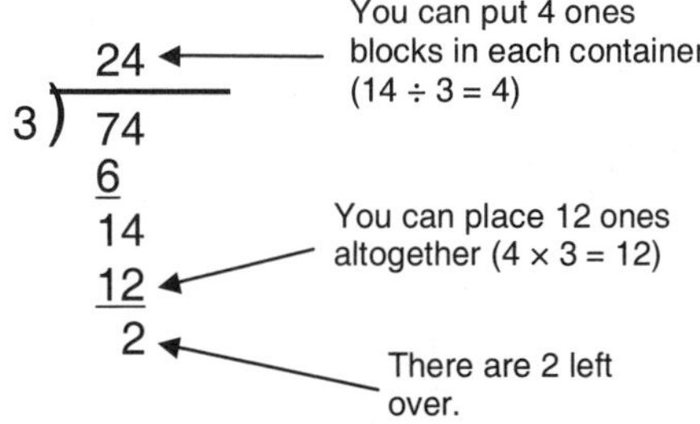
You can put 4 ones blocks in each container (14 ÷ 3 = 4)
You can place 12 ones altogether (4 × 3 = 12)
There are 2 left over.

Activities with Concrete Materials

After placing the 2 tens blocks and 4 ones blocks into each of the containers, you have placed 24 ones blocks altogether (and this is exactly the number you get on top of the division sign). Play the game with different numbers. Keep track of the steps your child takes with the blocks and write the equivalent step in the long division algorithm on a sheet of paper. Ask your child to explain on paper how the step they took matches the step in the algorithm.

6. Give your child a ruler and ask them to solve the following puzzles:

   a) Draw a line 1 cm long. If the line represents $\frac{1}{4}$ show what a whole line what look like.

   b) Line: 1 cm long. The line represents $\frac{1}{6}$ show the whole.

   c) Line: 2 cm long. The line represents $\frac{1}{3}$ show the whole.

   d) Line: 3 cm long. The line represents $\frac{1}{4}$ show the whole.

   e) Line: $1\frac{1}{2}$ cm long. The line represents $\frac{1}{2}$ show the whole.

   f) Line: $1\frac{1}{2}$ cm long. The line represents $\frac{1}{4}$ show the whole.

   g) Line: 3 cm long. The line represents $\frac{1}{4}$ show $\frac{1}{2}$.

   h) Line: 2 cm long. The line represents $\frac{1}{8}$ show $\frac{1}{4}$.

7. Give your child counters to make a model of the following problem:

   Postcards come in packs of 4. How many packs would you need to buy to send 15 postcards? Write a mixed and improper fraction for the number of packs you would use.

   Your child could use a counter of a particular colour to represent the post cards they have used and a counter of a different colour to represent the cards left over. After they have made their model, they could fill in the following chart:

Number of Postcards	15
Number of packs of 4 postcards (improper fraction)	$\frac{15}{4}$
Number of packs of 4 postcards (mixed fraction)	$3\frac{3}{4}$

Model:

4 postcards in each package

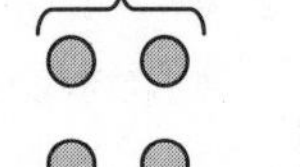

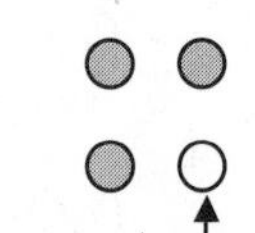

Here is another sample problem your child could try:

Juice cans come in boxes of 6. How many boxes would you bring if you needed 20 cans? What fraction of the boxes would you use?

No unauthorized copying

Activities with Concrete Materials

8. Give your child blocks of 2 colours and have them make models of fractions of whole numbers using the method described at the top of the worksheet. Here are some fractions they might try:

   a) $\frac{3}{4}$ of 15 b) $\frac{3}{4}$ of 16 c) $\frac{3}{5}$ of 20 d) $\frac{2}{7}$ of 21

9. Ask your child to draw 4 boxes of equal length on grid paper and shade 1 box:

Point out to them that $\frac{1}{4}$ of the area of the boxes is shaded. Now ask them to draw the same set of boxes, but in each box to draw a line dividing the box into 2 parts:

Now $\frac{2}{8}$ of the area is shaded. Repeat the exercise, dividing the boxes into 3 equal parts, (roughly: the sketch doesn't have to be perfectly accurate), then 4 parts, then five parts:

$\frac{3}{12}$ of the area is shaded

$\frac{4}{16}$ of the area is shaded

$\frac{5}{20}$ of the area is shaded

Point out to your child that while the appearance of the fraction changes, the same amount of area is represented:

$\frac{1}{4}, \frac{2}{8}, \frac{3}{12}, \frac{4}{16}, \frac{5}{20}$ all represent the same amount: they are equivalent fractions.

Ask your child how each of the denominators in the fractions above can be generated from the initial fraction of $\frac{1}{4}$:

Answer
Each denominator is a multiple of the denominator 4 in the original fraction:

$8 = 2 \times 4$ $12 = 3 \times 4$ $16 = 4 \times 4$ $20 = 5 \times 4$

Then ask them how each fraction could be generated from the original fraction.

Answer
Multiplying the numerator and denominator of the original fraction by the same number:

$\frac{1^{\times 2}}{4_{\times 2}} = \frac{2}{8}$ $\frac{1^{\times 3}}{4_{\times 3}} = \frac{3}{12}$ $\frac{1^{\times 4}}{4_{\times 4}} = \frac{4}{16}$ $\frac{1^{\times 5}}{4_{\times 5}} = \frac{5}{20}$

No unauthorized copying

Activities with Concrete Materials

Point out that multiplying the top and bottom of the original fraction by any given number, say 5, corresponds to cutting each box into that number of pieces:

$$\frac{1 \times 5}{4 \times 5} \begin{array}{l} \leftarrow \text{there are 5 pieces in each box} \\ \leftarrow \text{there are } 4 \times 5 \text{ pieces altogether} \end{array}$$

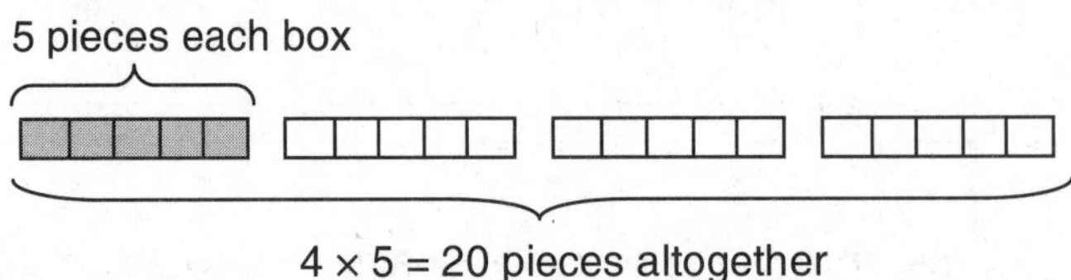

The fractions $\frac{1}{4}$, $\frac{2}{8}$, $\frac{3}{12}$, $\frac{4}{16}$ ... form a **family of equivalent fractions**. Notice that no whole number greater than 1 will divide into both the numerator and denominator of $\frac{1}{4}$: $\frac{1}{4}$ is said to be reduced to lowest terms. By multiplying the top and bottom of a reduced fraction by various whole numbers, you can generate an entire fraction family. For instance, $\frac{2}{5}$ generates the family

$$\frac{2 \times 2}{5 \times 2} = \frac{4}{10} \qquad \frac{2 \times 3}{5 \times 3} = \frac{6}{15} \qquad \frac{2 \times 4}{5 \times 4} = \frac{8}{20}$$

10. Children often make mistakes in comparing decimals where one of the decimals is expressed in tenths and the other in hundredths. (For instance, they will say that .17 is greater than .2.) The following activity will help your child understand the relation between tenths and hundredths.

Give your child a set of play-money dimes and pennies. Explain that a dime is a tenth of a dollar (which is why it is written as $0.10) and a penny is a hundredth of a dollar (which is why it is written as $0.01).

Ask your child to make models of the amounts in the left-hand column of the chart below and to write as many names for the amounts as they can think of in the right-hand columns (sample answers are provided in italics):

Amount	Amount in Pennies	Decimal Names (in words)	Decimal names (in numbers)
2 dimes	*20 pennies*	*2 tenths (of a dollar)* *20 hundredths*	*.2* *.20*
3 pennies	*3 pennies*	*3 hundredths*	*.03*
4 dimes and 3 pennies	*43 pennies*	*4 tenths and 3 hundredths* *43 hundredths*	*.43* *.43*

Activities with Concrete Materials

You should also write various amounts of money on a sheet of paper and have your child make models of the amounts (e.g., make models of .3 dollars, .27 dollars, .07 dollars, etc). Also challenge them to make models of amounts that have 2 different decimal representations (e.g., 2 dimes can be written as .2 dollars or .20 dollars).

When you feel your child is able to translate between money and decimal notation, ask them to say whether they would rather have .2 dollars or .17 dollars. In their answer, they should say exactly how many pennies each amount represents (e.g., they must articulate that .2 represents 20 pennies and so it is actually the larger amount).

Amount (in dollars)	Amount (in pennies)
.2	
.15	

For extra practice, ask your child to fill in the right-hand column of the chart and then circle the greater amount. (Create several charts of this sort for them.)

11. Your child can learn to count forwards and backwards by decimal tenths using dimes.

Ask them to complete the following patterns using dimes to help them count. (Point out that a number such as 2.7, while not standard dollar notation, can be thought of as "2 dollars and 7 dimes."

Ask them to practise saying the money amounts in the sequences below out loud as they count up. For instance, for the sequence "2.7, 2.8, ____, ____," they would say: "2 dollars and 7 dimes, 2 dollars and 8 dimes, 2 dollars and 9 dimes," etc. This will help them see that the next term in the sequence is 3 dollars.

a) .2 , .3 , .4 , ____, ____, ____
b) .7 , .8 , .9 , ____, ____, ____
c) 2.7 , 2.8 , 2.9 , ____, ____, ____
d) 1.4 , 1.3 , 1.2 , ____, ____, ____

No unauthorized copying

Activities with Concrete Materials

12. Give your child a set of base ten blocks and let them know that in the exercises below the hundreds block will represent the number 1 (the unit). This means that the tens block represents a tenth (0.1) and the ones block represents a hundredth (0.01).

According to this convention, the number 3.25 would be represented as:

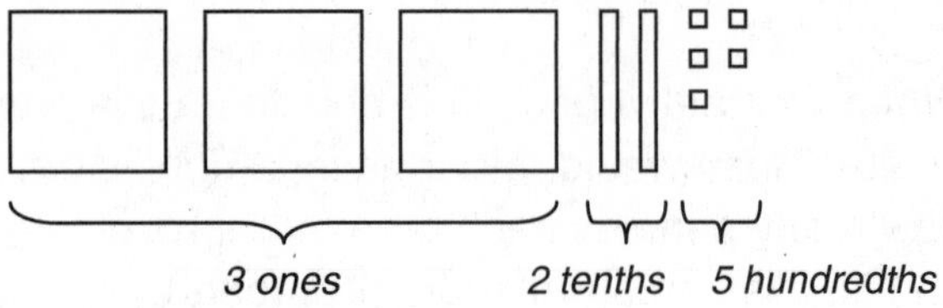

3 ones *2 tenths* *5 hundredths*

a) Start with these blocks:

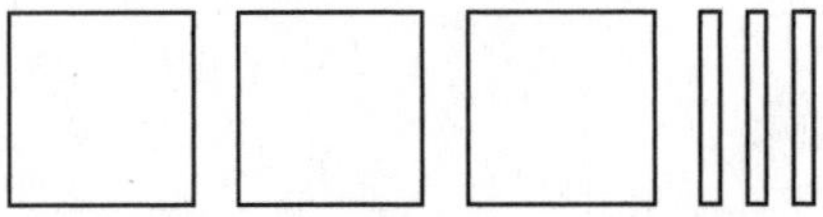

- Add 2 blocks so that the sum (or total) is between 3.4 and 3.48.
- Write a decimal for the amount you added.

b) Take these blocks:

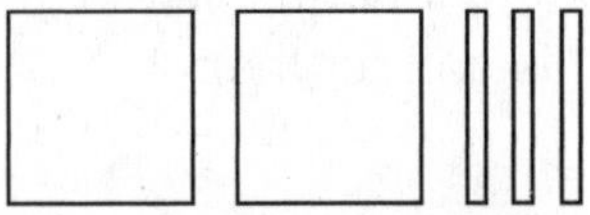

- Add 2 blocks so that the sum (or total) is between 2.47 and 2.63.
- Write a decimal for the amount you added.

c) Take these blocks:

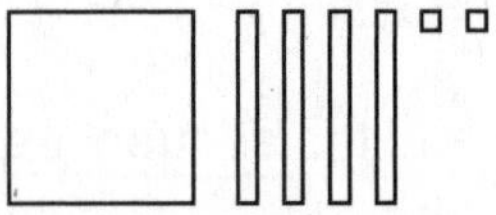

- Add 2 blocks so that the sum (or total) is between 2.51 and 2.6.
- Write a decimal for the amount you added.

13. Repeat the exercise of the preceding activity with the following instructions.
PARENT: Make up more problems of this sort.

a) Take these blocks:

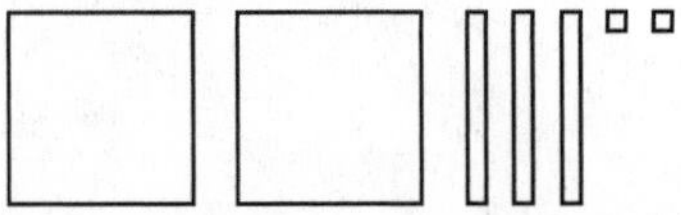

- Take away 2 blocks so the result (the difference) is between 1.21 and 1.35.
- Write a decimal for the amount you took away.

b) Take these blocks:

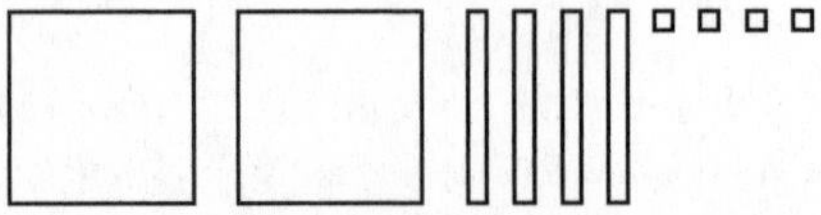

- Take away 3 blocks so the result (the difference) is between 2.17 and 2.43.
- Write a decimal for the amount you took away.

No unauthorized copying

Mental Math Skills: Addition and Subtraction

PARENT:
If your child doesn't know their addition and subtraction facts, teach them to add and subtract using their fingers by the methods taught below. You should also reinforce basic facts using drills, games and flash cards. There are mental math strategies that make addition and subtraction easier: some effective strategies are taught in the next section. (Until your child knows all their facts, allow them to add and subtract on their fingers when necessary.)

To **add** 4 + 8, Grace says the greater number (8) with her fist closed. She counts up from 8, raising one finger at a time. She stops when she has raised the number of fingers equal to the lesser number (4):

She said "12" when she raised her 4th finger, so: **4 + 8 = 12**

1. Add:

a) 5 + 2 = 7 b) 3 + 2 = 5 c) 6 + 2 = 8 d) 9 + 2 = 11

e) 2 + 4 = 6 f) 2 + 7 = 9 g) 5 + 3 = 8 h) 6 + 3 = 9

i) 11 + 4 = 15 j) 3 + 9 = 12 k) 7 + 3 = 10 l) 14 + 4 = 18

m) 21 + 5 = 26 n) 32 + 3 = 35 o) 4 + 56 = 60 p) 39 + 4 = 43

To **subtract** 9 – 5, Grace says the lesser number (5) with her fist closed. She counts up from 5 raising one finger at a time. She stops when she says the greater number (9):

She has raised 4 fingers when she stopped, so: **9 – 5 = 4**

2. Subtract:

a) 7 – 5 = 2 b) 8 – 6 = 2 c) 5 – 3 = 2 d) 5 – 2 = 3

e) 9 – 6 = 3 f) 10 – 5 = 5 g) 11 – 7 = 4 h) 17 – 14 = 3

i) 33 – 31 = 2 j) 27 – 24 = 3 k) 43 – 39 = 4 l) 62 – 58 = 4

PARENT:
To prepare for the next section (Mental Math), teach your child to add 1 to any number mentally (by counting forward by 1 in their head) and to subtract 1 from any number (by counting backward by 1)

 No unauthorized copying

Mental Math Skills: Addition and Subtraction *(continued)*

PARENT:
Children who don't know how to add, subtract or estimate readily are at a great disadvantage in mathematics. Children who have trouble memorizing addition and subtraction facts can still learn to mentally add and subtract numbers in a short time if they are given daily practice in a few basic skills.

SKILL 1 – Adding 2 to an Even Number

This skill has been broken down into a number of sub-skills. After teaching each sub-skill, you should give your child a short diagnostic quiz to verify that they have learned the skill. I have included sample quizzes for Skills 1 to 4.

i) *Naming the next one-digit even number:*

Numbers that have ones digit 0, 2, 4, 6 or 8 are called the even numbers. Using drills or games, teach your child to say the sequence of one-digit even numbers without hesitation. Ask them to imagine the sequence going on in a circle so that the next number after 8 is 0 (0, 2, 4, 6, 8, 0, 2, 4, 6, 8, ...). Then play the following game: name a number in the sequence and ask your child to give the next number in the sequence. Don't move on until they have mastered the game.

ii) *Naming the next greatest two-digit even number:*

Case 1 – Numbers that end in 0, 2, 4 or 6
Write an even two-digit number that ends in 0, 2, 4 or 6 on a piece of paper. Ask your child to name the next greatest even number. They should recognize that if a number ends in 0, then the next even number ends in 2; if it ends in 2 then the next even number ends in 4, etc. For instance, the number 54 has ones digit 4, so the next greatest even number will have ones digit 6.

QUIZ

Name the next greatest even number:

a) 52 : ______ b) 64 : ______ c) 36 : ______ d) 22 : ______ e) 80 : ______

Case 2 – Numbers that end in 8
Write the number 58 on a piece of paper. Ask your child to name the next greatest even number. Remind them that even numbers must end in 0, 2, 4, 6 or 8. But 50, 52, 54 and 56 are all less than 58 so the next greatest even number is 60. Your child should see that an even number ending in 8 is always followed by an even number ending in 0 (with a tens digit that is one higher).

QUIZ

Name the next greatest even number:

a) 58 : ______ b) 68 : ______ c) 38 : ______ d) 48 : ______ e) 78 : ______

iii) *Adding 2 to an even number:*

Point out to your child that adding 2 to any even number is equivalent to finding the next even number: e.g., 46 + 2 = 48, 48 + 2 = 50, etc. Knowing this, your child can easily add 2 to any even number.

Mental Math Skills: Addition and Subtraction *(continued)*

> **QUIZ**
>
> Add:
>
> a) 26 + 2 = ___ b) 82 + 2 = ___ c) 40 + 2 = ___ d) 58 + 2 = ___ e) 34 + 2 = ___

SKILL 2 – Subtracting 2 from an Even Number

i) *Finding the preceding one-digit even number:*

Name a one-digit even number and ask your child to give the preceding number in the sequence. For instance, the number that comes before 4 is 2 and the number that comes before 0 is 8. (Remember: the sequence is circular.)

ii) *Finding the preceding two-digit even number:*

Case 1 – Numbers that end in 2, 4, 6 or 8
Write a two-digit number that ends in 2, 4, 6 or 8 on a piece of paper. Ask your child to name the preceding even number. They should recognize that if a number ends in 2, then the preceding even number ends in 0; if it ends in 4 then the preceding even number ends in 2, etc. For instance, the number 78 has ones digit 8, so the preceding even number has ones digit 6.

> **QUIZ**
>
> Name the preceding even number:
>
> a) 48 : ______ b) 26 : ______ c) 34 : ______ d) 62 : ______ e) 78 : ______

Case 2 – Numbers that end in 0
Write the number 80 on a piece of paper and ask your child to name the preceding even number. They should recognize that if an even number ends in 0 then the preceding even number ends in 8 (but the ones digit is one less). So the even number that comes before 80 is 78.

> **QUIZ**
>
> Name the preceding even number:
>
> a) 40 : ______ b) 60 : ______ c) 80 : ______ d) 50 : ______ e) 30 : ______

ii) *Subtracting 2 from an even number:*

Point out to your child that subtracting 2 from any even number is equivalent to finding the preceding even number: e.g., 48 – 2 = 46, 46 – 2 = 44, etc.

> **QUIZ**
>
> Subtract:
>
> a) 58 – 2 = ___ b) 24 – 2 = ___ c) 36 – 2 = ___ d) 42 – 2 = ___ e) 60 – 2 = ___

No unauthorized copying

Mental Math Skills: Addition and Subtraction *(continued)*

SKILL 3 – Adding 2 to an Odd Number

i) *Naming the next one-digit odd number:*

Numbers that have ones digit 1, 3, 5, 7, and 9 are called the odd numbers. Using drills or games, teach your child to say the sequence of one-digit odd numbers without hesitation. Ask them to imagine the sequence going on in a circle so that the next number after 9 is 1 (1, 3, 5, 7, 9, 1, 3, 5, 7, 9, ...). Then play the following game: name a number in the sequence and ask your child to give the next number in the sequence. Don't move on until they have mastered the game.

ii) *Naming the next greatest two-digit odd number:*

Case 1 – Numbers that end in 1, 3, 5 or 7

Write an odd two-digit number that ends in 1, 3, 5, or 7 on a piece of paper. Ask your child to name the next greatest odd number. They should recognize that if a number ends in 1, then the next odd number ends in 3; if it ends in 3 then the next odd number ends in 5, etc. For instance, the number 35 has ones digit 5, so the next greatest odd number will have ones digit 7.

QUIZ

Name the next greatest odd number:

a) 51 : ______ b) 65 : ______ c) 37 : ______ d) 23 : ______ e) 87 : ______

Case 2 – Numbers that end in 9

Write the number 59 on a piece of paper. Ask your child to name the next greatest odd number. Remind them that odd numbers must end in 1, 3, 5, 7 or 9. But 51, 53, 55 and 57 are all less than 59. The next greatest odd number is 61. Your child should see that an odd number ending in 9 is always followed by an odd number ending in 1 (with a tens digit that is one higher).

QUIZ

Name the next greatest odd number:

a) 59 : ______ b) 69 : ______ c) 39 : ______ d) 49 : ______ e) 79 : ______

iii) *Adding 2 to an odd number:*

Point out to your child that adding 2 to any odd number is equivalent to finding the next odd number: e.g., 47 + 2 = 49, 49 + 2 = 51, etc. Knowing this, your child can easily add 2 to any odd number.

Add:

a) 27 + 2 = ___ b) 83 + 2 = ___ c) 41 + 2 = ___ d) 59 + 2 = ___ e) 35 + 2 = ___

Mental Math Skills: Addition and Subtraction *(continued)*

SKILL 4 – Subtracting 2 from an Odd Number

i) *Finding the preceding one-digit odd number:*

Name a one-digit odd number and ask your child to give the preceding number in the sequence. For instance, the number that comes before 3 is 1 and the number that comes before 1 is 9. (Remember: the sequence is circular.)

ii) *Finding the preceding two-digit odd number:*

Case 1 – Numbers that end in 3, 5, 7 or 9
Write a two-digit number that ends in 3, 5, 7 or 9 on a piece of paper. Ask your child to name the preceding odd number. They should recognize that if a number ends in 3, then the preceding odd number ends in 1; if it ends in 5 then the preceding odd number ends in 3, etc. For instance, the number 79 has ones digit 9, so the preceding odd number has ones digit 7.

QUIZ

Name the preceding odd number:

a) 49 : ______ b) 27 : ______ c) 35 : ______ d) 63 : ______ e) 79 : ______

Case 2 – Numbers that end in 1
Write the number 81 on a piece of paper and ask your child to name the preceding odd number. They should recognize that if an odd number ends in 1 then the preceding odd number ends in 9 (but the ones digit is one less). So the odd number that comes before 81 is 79.

QUIZ

Name the preceding odd number:

a) 41 : ______ b) 61 : ______ c) 81 : ______ d) 51 : ______ e) 31 : ______

iii) *Subtracting 2 from an odd number:*

Point out to your child that subtracting 2 from any odd number is equivalent to finding the preceding odd number: e.g., 49 – 2 = 47, 47 – 2 = 45, etc.

QUIZ

Subtract:

a) 59 – 2 = ___ b) 25 – 2 = ___ c) 37 – 2 = ___ d) 43 – 2 = ___ e) 61 – 2 = ___

SKILLS 5 and 6:

Once your child can add and subtract the numbers 1 and 2, then they can easily add and subtract the number 3: Add 3 to a number by first adding 2, then adding 1 (e.g., 35 + 3 = 35 + 2 + 1). Subtract 3 from a number by subtracting 2, then subtracting 1 (e.g., 35 – 3 = 35 – 2 – 1).

No unauthorized copying

Mental Math Skills: Addition and Subtraction *(continued)*

PARENT: All of the addition and subtraction tricks you teach your child should be reinforced with drills, flashcards and tests. Eventually they should memorize their addition and subtraction facts and shouldn't have to rely on the mental math tricks. One of the greatest gifts you can give your child is to teach them their number facts.

SKILLS 7 and 8

Add 4 to a number by adding 2 twice (e.g., 51 + 4 = 51 + 2 + 2). Subtract 4 from a number by subtracting 2 twice (e.g., 51 – 4 = 51 – 2 – 2).

SKILLS 9 and 10

Add 5 to a number by adding 4 then 1. Subtract 5 by subtracting 4 then 1.

SKILL 11

Your child can add pairs of identical numbers by doubling (e.g., 6 + 6 = 2 x 6). They should either memorize the 2 times table or they should double numbers by counting on their fingers by 2s.

Add a pair of numbers that differ by 1 by rewriting the larger number as 1 plus the smaller number (then use doubling to find the sum): e.g., 6 + 7 = 6 + 6 + 1 = 12 + 1 = 13; 7 + 8 = 7 + 7 + 1 = 14 + 1 = 15.

SKILLS 12, 13 and 14

Add a one-digit number to 10 by simply replacing the zero in 10 by the one-digit number: e.g., 10 + 7 = 17.

Add 10 to any two-digit number by simply increasing the tens digit of the two-digit number by 1: e.g., 53 + 10 = 63.

Add a pair of two-digit numbers (with no carrying) by adding the ones digits of the numbers and then adding the tens digits: e.g., 23 + 64 = 87.

SKILLS 15 and 16

To add 9 to a one-digit number, subtract 1 from the number and then add 10: e.g., 9 + 6 = 10 + 5 = 15; 9 + 7 = 10 + 6 = 16. (Essentially, your child simply has to subtract 1 from the number and then stick a 1 in front of the result.)

To add 8 to a one-digit number, subtract 2 from the number and add 10: e.g., 8 + 6 = 10 + 4 = 14; 8 + 7 = 10 + 5 = 15.

SKILLS 17 and 18

To subtract a pair of multiples of ten, simply subtract the tens digits and add a zero for the ones digit: e.g., 70 – 50 = 20.

To subtract a pair of two-digit numbers (without carrying or regrouping), subtract the ones digit from the ones digit and the tens digit from the tens digit: e.g., 57 – 34 = 23.

 No unauthorized copying

Mental Math – Further Strategies

Further Mental Math Strategies

1. Your child should be able to explain how to use the strategies of "rounding the subtrahend (i.e., the number you are subtracting) up to the nearest multiple of ten."

Examples:

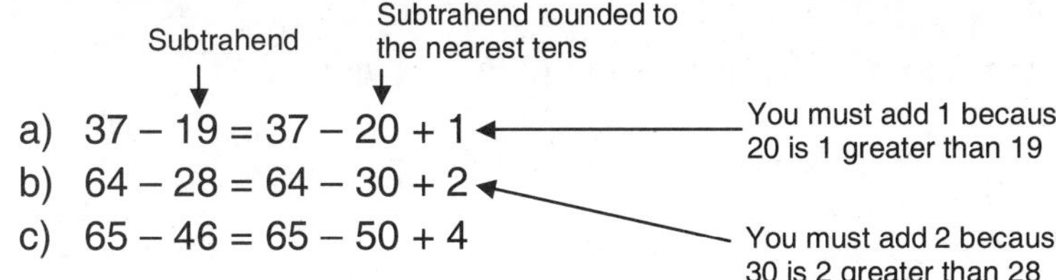

Subtrahend
Subtrahend rounded to the nearest tens
You must add 1 because 20 is 1 greater than 19
You must add 2 because 30 is 2 greater than 28

a) 37 – 19 = 37 – 20 + 1
b) 64 – 28 = 64 – 30 + 2
c) 65 – 46 = 65 – 50 + 4

Practice Questions:

a) 27 – 17 = 27 – ____ + ____
b) 52 – 36 = 52 – ____ + ____
c) 76 – 49 = 76 – ____ + ____
d) 84 – 57 = 84 – ____ + ____
e) 61 – 29 = 61 – ____ + ____
f) 42 – 18 = 42 – ____ + ____

PARENT: This strategy works well with numbers that end in 6, 7, 8 or 9.

2. Your child should be able to explain how to subtract by thinking of adding.

Examples:

Count by ones from 45 to the nearest tens (50)

Count from 50 until you reach the first number (62).

a) 62 – 45 = 5 + 12 = 17 ← The sum of counting up to the nearest ten and the original number is the difference.
b) 46 – 23 = 3 + 20 = 23
c) 73 – 17 = 6 + 50 = 56

← What method did we use here?

Practice Questions:

a) 88 – 36 = ____ + ____ = ____
b) 58 – 21 = ____ + ____ = ____
c) 43 – 17 = ____ + ____ = ____
d) 74 – 28 = ____ + ____ = ____
e) 93 – 64 = ____ + ____ = ____
f) 82 – 71 = ____ + ____ = ____

3. Your child should be able to explain how to "use doubles."

Examples:

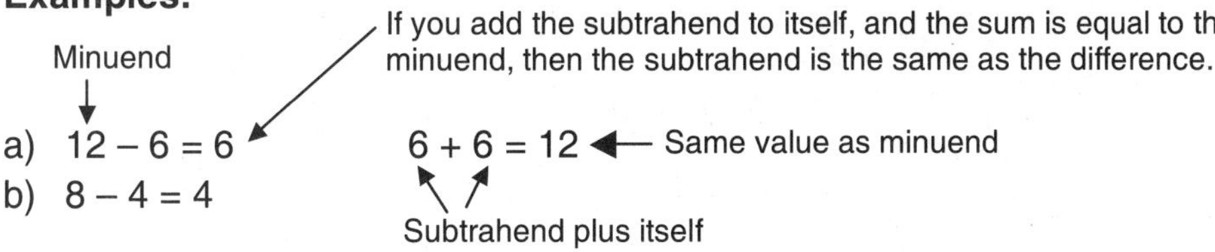

Minuend
a) 12 – 6 = 6
b) 8 – 4 = 4
If you add the subtrahend to itself, and the sum is equal to the minuend, then the subtrahend is the same as the difference.
6 + 6 = 12
Same value as minuend
Subtrahend plus itself

Practice Questions:

a) 6 – 3 = ____
b) 10 – 5 = ____
c) 14 – 7 = ____
d) 18 – 9 = ____
e) 16 – 8 = ____
f) 20 – 10 = ____

No unauthorized copying

Mental Math Exercises

PARENT: Teaching the material on these Mental Math worksheets may take several lessons. Your child will need more practice than is provided on these pages. These pages are intended as a test to be given when you are certain your child has learned the materials fully.

PARENT: Teach skills 1, 2, 3 and 4 as outlined on pages xxiv-xxvii before you allow your child to answer Questions 1 through 12:

1. Name the even number that comes after the number. Answer in the blank provided:

a) **32** ______ b) **46** ______ c) **14** ______ d) **92** ______ e) **56** ______

f) **30** ______ g) **84** ______ h) **60** ______ i) **72** ______ j) **24** ______

2. Name the even number that comes after the number:

a) **28** ______ b) **18** ______ c) **78** ______ d) **38** ______ e) **68** ______

3. Add:

REMEMBER: Adding 2 to an even number is the same as finding the next even number.

a) 42 + 2 = ______ b) 76 + 2 = ______ c) 28 + 2 = ______ d) 16 + 2 = ______

e) 68+ 2 = ______ f) 12 + 2 = ______ g) 36 + 2 = ______ h) 90 + 2 = ______

i) 70 + 2 = ______ j) 24 + 2 = ______ k) 66 + 2 = ______ l) 52 + 2 = ______

4. Name the even number that comes before the number:

a) **38** ______ b) **42** ______ c) **56** ______ d) **72** ______ e) **98** ______

f) **48** ______ g) **16** ______ h) **22** ______ i) **66** ______ j) **14** ______

5. Name the even number that comes before the number:

a) **30** ______ b) **70** ______ c) **60** ______ d) **10** ______ e) **80** ______

6. Subtract:

REMEMBER: Subtracting 2 from an even number is the same as finding the preceding even number.

a) 46 – 2 = ______ b) 86 – 2 = ______ c) 90 – 2 = ______ d) 14 – 2 = ______

e) 54 – 2 = ______ f) 72 – 2 = ______ g) 12 – 2 = ______ h) 56 – 2 = ______

i) 32 – 2 = ______ j) 40 – 2 = ______ k) 60 – 2 = ______ l) 26 – 2 = ______

7. Name the odd number that comes after the number:

a) **37** ______ b) **51** ______ c) **63** ______ d) **75** ______ e) **17** ______

f) **61** ______ g) **43** ______ h) **81** ______ i) **23** ______ j) **95** ______

8. Name the odd number that comes after the number:

a) **69** ______ b) **29** ______ c) **9** ______ d) **79** ______ e) **59** ______

Mental Math Exercises *(continued)*

9. Add:

REMEMBER: Adding 2 to an odd number is the same as finding the next odd number.

a) 25 + 2 = ______ b) 31 + 2 = ______ c) 47 + 2 = ______ d) 33 + 2 = ______

e) 39 + 2 = ______ f) 91 + 2 = ______ g) 5 + 2 = ______ h) 89 + 2 = ______

i) 11 + 2 = ______ j) 65 + 2 = ______ k) 29 + 2 = ______ l) 17 + 2 = ______

10. Name the odd number that comes before the number:

a) **39** ______ b) **43** ______ c) **57** ______ d) **17** ______ e) **99** ______

f) **13** ______ g) **85** ______ h) **79** ______ i) **65** ______ j) **77** ______

11. Name the odd number that comes before the number:

a) **21** ______ b) **41** ______ c) **11** ______ d) **91** ______ e) **51** ______

12. Subtract:

REMEMBER: Subtracting 2 from an odd number is the same as finding the preceding odd number.

a) 47 – 2 = ______ b) 85 – 2 = ______ c) 91 – 2 = ______ d) 15 – 2 = ______

e) 51 – 2 = ______ f) 73 – 2 = ______ g) 11 – 2 = ______ h) 59 – 2 = ______

i) 31 – 2 = ______ j) 43 – 2 = ______ k) 7 – 2 = ______ l) 25 – 2 = ______

PARENT:
Teach skills 5 and 6 as outlined on page xxvii before you allow your child to answer Questions 13 and 14.

13. Add 3 to the number by adding 2, then adding 1 (e.g., 35 + 3 = 35 + 2 + 1):

a) 23 + 3 = ________ b) 36 + 3 = ________ c) 29+ 3 = ________ d) 16 + 3 = ________

e) 67 + 3 = ________ f) 12 + 3 = ________ g) 35 + 3 = ________ h) 90 + 3 = ________

i) 78 + 3 = ________ j) 24 + 3 = ________ k) 6 + 3 = ________ l) 59 + 3 = ________

14. Subtract 3 from the number by subtracting 2, then subtracting 1 (e.g., 35 – 3 = 35 – 2 – 1):

a) 46 – 3 = ________ b) 87 – 3 = ________ c) 99 – 3 = ________ d) 14 – 3 = ________

e) 8 – 3 = ________ f) 72 – 3 = ________ g) 12 – 3 = ________ h) 57 – 3 = ________

i) 32 – 3 = ________ j) 40 – 3 = ________ k) 60 – 3 = ________ l) 28 – 3 = ________

15. Fred has 49 stamps. He gives 2 stamps away. How many stamps does he have left?

16. There are 25 minnows in a tank. Alice adds 3 more to the tank. How many minnows are now in the tank?

 No unauthorized copying

Mental Math Exercises *(continued)*

PARENT:
Teach skills 7 and 8 as outlined on page xxviii.

17. Add 4 to the number by adding 2 twice (e.g., 51 + 4 = 51 + 2 + 2):

a) 42 + 4 = ________ b) 76 + 4 = ________ c) 27 + 4 = ________ d) 17 + 4 = ________

e) 68 + 4 = ________ f) 11 + 4 = ________ g) 35 + 4 = ________ h) 8 + 4 = ________

i) 72 + 4 = ________ j) 23 + 4 = ________ k) 60 + 4 = ________ l) 59 + 4 = ________

18. Subtract 4 from the number by subtracting 2 twice (e.g., 26 – 4 = 26 – 2 – 2):

a) 46 – 4 = ________ b) 86 – 4 = ________ c) 91 – 4 = ________ d) 15 – 4 = ________

e) 53 – 4 = ________ f) 9 – 4 = ________ g) 13 – 4 = ________ h) 57 – 4 = ________

i) 40 – 4 = ________ j) 88 – 4 = ________ k) 69 – 4 = ________ l) 31 – 4 = ________

PARENT:
Teach skills 9 and 10 as outlined on page xxviii.

19. Add 5 to the number by adding 4, then adding 1 (or add 2 twice, then add 1):

a) 84 + 5 = ________ b) 27 + 5 = ________ c) 31 + 5 = ________ d) 44 + 5 = ________

e) 63 + 5 = ________ f) 92 + 5 = ________ g) 14 + 5 = ________ h) 16 + 5 = ________

i) 9 + 5 = ________ j) 81 + 5 = ________ k) 51 + 5 = ________ l) 28 + 5 = ________

20. Subtract 5 from the number by subtracting 4, then subtracting 1 (or subtract 2 twice, then subtract 1):

a) 48 – 5 = ______ b) 86 – 5 = ______ c) 55 – 5 = ______ d) 69 – 5 = ______

e) 30 – 5 = ______ f) 13 – 5 = ______ g) 92 – 5 = ______ h) 77 – 5 = ______

i) 45 – 5 = ______ j) 24 – 5 = ______ k) 91 – 5 = ______ l) 8 – 5 = ______

PARENT:
Teach skill 11 as outlined on page xxviii.

21. Add:

a) 6 + 6 = ______ b) 7 + 7 = ______ c) 8 + 8 = ______

d) 5 + 5 = ______ e) 4 + 4 = ______ f) 9 + 9 = ______

22. Add by thinking of the larger number as a sum of two smaller numbers. The first one is done for you:

a) 6 + 7 = 6 + 6 + 1 b) 7 + 8 = ______________ c) 6 + 8 = ______________

d) 4 + 5 = ______________ e) 5 + 7 = ______________ f) 8 + 9 = ______________

No unauthorized copying

Mental Math Exercises *(continued)*

PARENT:
Teach skills 12, 13 and 14 as outlined on page xxviii.

23. a) 10 + 3 = ______ b) 10 + 7 = ______ c) 5 + 10 = ______ d) 10 + 1 = ______
e) 9 + 10 = ______ f) 10 + 4 = ______ g) 10 + 8 = ______ h) 10 + 2 = ______

24. a) 10 + 20 = ______ b) 40 + 10 = ______ c) 10 + 80 = ______ d) 10 + 50 = ______
e) 30 + 10 = ______ f) 10 + 60= ______ g) 10 + 10 = ______ h) 70 + 10 = ______

25. a) 10 + 25 = ______ b) 10 + 67 = ______ c) 10 + 31 = ______ d) 10 + 82 = ______
e) 10 + 43 = ______ f) 10 + 51 = ______ g) 10 + 68 = ______ h) 10 + 21 = ______
i) 10 + 11 = ______ j) 10 + 19 = ______ k) 10 + 44 = ______ l) 10 + 88 = ______

26. a) 20 + 30 = ______ b) 40 + 20 = ______ c) 30 + 30 = ______ d) 50 + 30 = ______
e) 20 + 50 = ______ f) 40 + 40 = ______ g) 50 + 40 = ______ h) 40 + 30 = ______
i) 60 + 30 = ______ j) 20 + 60 = ______ k) 20 + 70 = ______ l) 60 + 40 = ______

27. a) 20 + 23 = ______ b) 32 + 24 = ______ c) 51 + 12 = ______ d) 12 + 67 = ______
e) 83 + 14 = ______ f) 65 + 24 = ______ g) 41 + 43 = ______ h) 70 + 27 = ______
i) 31 + 61 = ______ j) 54 + 33 = ______ k) 28 + 31 = ______ l) 42 + 55 = ______

PARENT:
Teach skills 15 and 16 as outlined on page xxviii.

28. a) 9 + 3 = ______ b) 9 + 7 = ______ c) 6 + 9 = ______ d) 4 + 9 = ______
e) 9 + 9 = ______ f) 5 + 9 = ______ g) 9 + 2 = ______ h) 9 + 8 = ______

29. a) 8 + 2 = ______ b) 8 + 6 = ______ c) 8 + 7 = ______ d) 4 + 8 = ______
e) 5 + 8 = ______ f) 8 + 3 = ______ g) 9 + 8 = ______ h) 8 + 8 = ______

PARENT:
Teach skills 17 and 18 as outlined on page xxviii.

30. a) 40 − 10 = ______ b) 50 − 10 = ______ c) 70 − 10 = ______ d) 20 − 10 = ______
e) 40 − 20 = ______ f) 60 − 30 = ______ g) 40 − 30 = ______ h) 60 − 50 = ______

31. a) 57 − 34 = ______ b) 43 − 12 = ______ c) 62 − 21 = ______ d) 59 − 36 = ______
e) 87 − 63 = ______ f) 95 − 62 = ______ g) 35 − 10 = ______ h) 17 − 8 = ______

 No unauthorized copying

Mental Math (Advanced)

Multiples of Ten

NOTE:
In the exercises below, you will learn several ways to use multiples of ten in mental addition or subtraction.

I 542 + 214 = 542 + 200 + 10 + 4 = 742 + 10 + 4 = 752 + 4 = 756

827 − 314 = 827 − 300 − 10 − 4 = 527 − 10 − 4 = 517 − 4 = 713

Sometimes you will need to carry:
545 + 172 = 545 + 100 + 70 + 2 = 645 + 70 + 2 = 715 + 2 = 717

1. Warm up:

a) 536 + 100 = b) 816 + 10 = c) 124 + 5 = d) 540 + 200 =

e) 234 + 30 = f) 345 + 300 = g) 236 − 30 = h) 442 − 20 =

i) 970 − 70 = j) 542 − 400 = k) 160 + 50 = l) 756 + 40 =

2. Write the second number in expanded form and add or subtract one digit at a time. The first one is done for you:

a) 564 + 215 = 564 + 200 + 10 + 5 = 779

b) 445 + 343 = ________ = ________

c) 234 + 214 = ________ = ________

3. Add or subtract mentally (one digit at a time):

a) 547 + 312 = b) 578 − 314 = c) 845 − 454 =

II If one of the numbers you are adding or subtracting is close to a number that is a multiple of ten, add the multiple of ten and then add or subtract an adjustment factor:

645 + 99 = 645 + 100 − 1 = 745 − 1 = 744

856 + 42 = 856 + 40 + 2 = 896 + 2 = 898

III Sometimes in subtraction, it helps to think of a multiple of ten as a sum of 1 and a number consisting entirely of 9s (e.g., 100 = 1 + 99; 1000 = 1 + 999). You never have to borrow or exchange when you are subtracting from a number consisting entirely of 9s.

100 − 43 = 1 + 99 − 43 = 1 + 56 = 57 ← *Do the subtraction, using 99 instead of 100, and then add 1 to your answer.*

1000 − 543 = 1 + 999 − 543 = 1 + 456 = 457

4. Use the tricks you've just learned:

a) 845 + 91 = b) 456 + 298 = c) 100 − 84 = d) 1000 − 846 =

Mental Math Game: Modified Go Fish

PURPOSE:

If children know the pairs of one-digit numbers that add up to particular **target numbers**, they will be able to mentally break sums into easier sums.

EXAMPLE:

As it is easy to add any one-digit number to 10, you can add a sum more readily if you can decompose numbers in the sum into pairs that add to ten. For example:

$$7 + 5 = \underbrace{7 + 3} + 2 = 10 + 2 = 12$$

These numbers add to 10.

To help children remember pairs of numbers that add up to a given target number, I developed a variation of "Go Fish" that I have found very effective.

THE GAME:

Pick any target number and remove all the cards with value greater than or equal to the target number out of the deck. In what follows, I will assume that the target number is 10, so you would take all the tens and face cards out of the deck (aces count as one).

The dealer gives each player six cards. If a player has any pairs of cards that add to 10 they are allowed to place these pairs on the table before play begins.

Player 1 selects one of the cards in his or her hand and asks Player 2 for a card that adds to 10 with the chosen card. For instance, if Player 1's chosen card is a 3, they may ask Player 2 for a 7.

If Player 2 has the requested card, Player 1 takes it and lays it down along with the card from their hand. Player 1 may then ask for another card. If Player 2 does not have the requested card, they say, "Go fish," and Player 1 must pick up a card from the top of the deck. (If this card adds to 10 with a card in Player 1's hand, they may lay down the pair right away.) It is then Player 2's turn to ask for a card.

Play ends when one player lays down all of their cards. Players receive 4 points for laying down all of their cards first and 1 point for each pair they have laid down.

PARENT: If your child is having difficulty, I would recommend that you start with pairs of numbers that add to 5. Take all cards with value greater than 4 out of the deck. Each player should be dealt only four cards to start with.

I have worked with several children who have had a great deal of trouble sorting their cards and finding pairs that add to a target number. I have found that the following exercise helps:

Give your child only three cards, two of which add to the target number. Ask them to find the pair that adds to the target number. After your child has mastered this step with three cards, repeat the exercise with four cards, then five cards, and so on.

PARENT: You can also give your child a list of the pairs that add to the target number. As your child gets used to the game, gradually remove pairs from the list so that they learn the pairs by memory.

No unauthorized copying

Hundreds Charts

1	2	3	4	5	6	7	8	9	10
11	12	13	14	15	16	17	18	19	20
21	22	23	24	25	26	27	28	29	30
31	32	33	34	35	36	37	38	39	40
41	42	43	44	45	46	47	48	49	50
51	52	53	54	55	56	57	58	59	60
61	62	63	64	65	66	67	68	69	70
71	72	73	74	75	76	77	78	79	80
81	82	83	84	85	86	87	88	89	90
91	92	93	94	95	96	97	98	99	100

1	2	3	4	5	6	7	8	9	10
11	12	13	14	15	16	17	18	19	20
21	22	23	24	25	26	27	28	29	30
31	32	33	34	35	36	37	38	39	40
41	42	43	44	45	46	47	48	49	50
51	52	53	54	55	56	57	58	59	60
61	62	63	64	65	66	67	68	69	70
71	72	73	74	75	76	77	78	79	80
81	82	83	84	85	86	87	88	89	90
91	92	93	94	95	96	97	98	99	100

1	2	3	4	5	6	7	8	9	10
11	12	13	14	15	16	17	18	19	20
21	22	23	24	25	26	27	28	29	30
31	32	33	34	35	36	37	38	39	40
41	42	43	44	45	46	47	48	49	50
51	52	53	54	55	56	57	58	59	60
61	62	63	64	65	66	67	68	69	70
71	72	73	74	75	76	77	78	79	80
81	82	83	84	85	86	87	88	89	90
91	92	93	94	95	96	97	98	99	100

1	2	3	4	5	6	7	8	9	10
11	12	13	14	15	16	17	18	19	20
21	22	23	24	25	26	27	28	29	30
31	32	33	34	35	36	37	38	39	40
41	42	43	44	45	46	47	48	49	50
51	52	53	54	55	56	57	58	59	60
61	62	63	64	65	66	67	68	69	70
71	72	73	74	75	76	77	78	79	80
81	82	83	84	85	86	87	88	89	90
91	92	93	94	95	96	97	98	99	100

No unauthorized copying

How to Learn Your Times Tables in 5 Days

PARENT:
Trying to do math without knowing your times tables is like trying to play the piano without knowing the location of the notes on the keyboard. Your students will have difficulty seeing patterns in sequences and charts, solving proportions, finding equivalent fractions, decimals and percents, solving problems etc. if they don't know their tables.

Using the method below, you can teach your students their tables in a week or so. (If you set aside five or ten minutes a day to work with students who need extra help, the pay-off will be enormous.) There is really no reason for your students not to know their tables!

DAY 1: Counting by 2s, 3s, 4s, and 5s

If you have completed the JUMP Fractions unit you should already know how to count and multiply by 2s, 3s, 4s, and 5s. If you do not know how to count by these numbers you should memorize the hands:

If you know how to count by 2s, 3s, 4s, and 5s, then you can multiply by any combination of these numbers. For instance, to find the product of 3 ⊆ 2, count by 2s until you have raised 3 fingers:

2

4

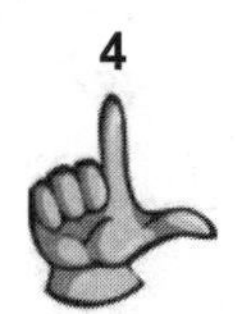

6

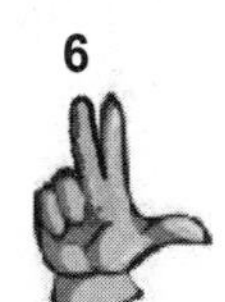

3 ⊆ 2 = 6

DAY 2: The 9 Times Table

The numbers you say when you count by 9s are called the **multiples** of 9 (0 is also a multiple of 9). The first ten multiples of 9 (after 0) are 9, 18, 27, 36, 45, 54, 63, 72, 81, and 90. What happens when you add the digits of any of these multiples of 9 (such as 1 + 8 or 6 + 3)? The sum is always 9!

Here is another useful fact about the 9 times table: Multiply 9 by any number between 1 and 10 and look at the tens digit of the product. The tens digit is always one less than the number you multiplied by:

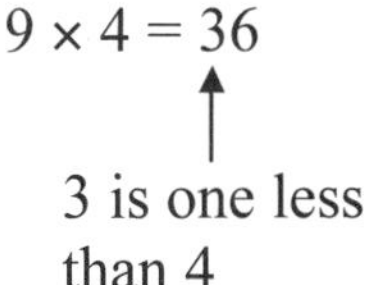

$9 \times 4 = 36$ — 3 is one less than 4

$9 \times 8 = 72$ — 7 is one less than 8

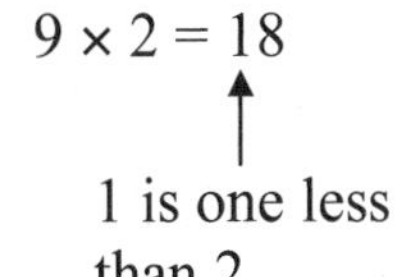

$9 \times 2 = 18$ — 1 is one less than 2

You can find the product of 9 and any number by using the two facts given above. For example, to find 9 × 7, follow these steps:

Step 1: 9 ⊆ 7 = __ __

Subtract 1 from the number you are multiplying by 9: **7 – 1 = 6**

9 ⊆ 7 = 6 __

Now you know the tens digit of the product.

Step 2: 9 ⊆ 7 = 6 __

These two digits add to 9.

9 ⊆ 7 = 6 3

So the missing digit is 9 – 6 = **3**.

(You can do the subtraction on your fingers if necessary.)

Practise these two steps for all of the products of 9: 9 × 2, 9 × 3, 9 × 4, and so on.

DAY 3: The 8 Times Table

There are two patterns in the digits of the 8 times table. Knowing these patterns will help you remember how to count by 8s.

Step 1: You can find the ones digit of the first five multiples of 8, by starting at 8 and counting backwards by 2s.

8
6
4
2
0

Step 2: You can find the tens digit of the first five multiples of 8, by starting at 0 and counting up by 1s.

08
16
24
32
40

(Of course you do not need to write the 0 in front of the 8 for the product 1 ⊆ 8.)

Step 3: You can find the ones digit of the next five multiples of 8 by repeating step 1.

8
6
4
2
0

Step 4: You can find the remaining tens digits by starting at 4 and counting by 1s.

48
56
64
72
80

Practise writing the multiples of 8 (up to 80) until you have memorized the complete list. Knowing the patterns in the digits of the multiples of 8 will help you memorize the list very quickly. Then you will know how to multiply by 8.

8 ⊆ 6 = 48

Count by 8 until you have 6 fingers up: 8, 16, 24, 32, 40, 48.

 No unauthorized copying

DAY 4: The 6 Times Table

If you have learned the 8 and 9 times tables, then you already know $6 \subseteq 9$ and $6 \subseteq 8$.

And if you know how to multiply by 5 up to $5 \subseteq 5$, then you also know how to multiply by 6 up to $6 \subseteq 5$! That is because you can always calculate 6 times a number by calculating 5 times the number and then adding the number itself to the result. The pictures below show how this works for $6 \subseteq 4$:

6 × 4 — 5 × 4 — plus one more 4

$6 \subseteq 4 = \mathbf{5} \subseteq 4 + 4 = 20 + 4 = 24$

5 fours — plus one more 4

$6 \subseteq 4 = 4 + 4 + 4 + 4 + 4 + 4$

Similarly: $6 \subseteq 2 = \mathbf{5} \subseteq 2 + 2$; $6 \subseteq 3 = \mathbf{5} \subseteq 3 + 3$; $6 \subseteq 5 = \mathbf{5} \subseteq 5 + 5$.

Knowing this, you only need to memorize 2 facts:

$\mathbf{6 \subseteq 6 = 36}$ $\mathbf{6 \subseteq 7 = 42}$

Or, if you know $6 \subseteq 5$, you can find $6 \subseteq 6$ by calculating $6 \subseteq 5 + 5$.

DAY 5: The 7 Times Table

If you have learned the 6, 8, and 9 times tables, then you already know $6 \subseteq 7$, $8 \subseteq 7$, and $9 \subseteq 7$.

And since you also already know $1 \subseteq 7 = 7$, you only need to memorize 5 facts:

$\mathbf{2 \subseteq 7 = 14}$ $\mathbf{3 \subseteq 7 = 21}$ $\mathbf{4 \subseteq 7 = 28}$ $\mathbf{5 \subseteq 7 = 35}$ $\mathbf{7 \subseteq 7 = 49}$

If you are able to memorize your own phone number, then you can easily memorize these 5 facts!

NOTE: You can use doubling to help you learn the facts above: 4 is double 2, so $4 \subseteq 7$ (28) is double $2 \subseteq 7$ (14); 6 is double 3, so $6 \subseteq 7$ (42) is double $3 \subseteq 7$ (21).

Try this test every day until you have learned your times tables.

1. $3 \subseteq 5 =$ _____	2. $8 \subseteq 4 =$ _____	3. $9 \subseteq 3 =$ _____	4. $4 \subseteq 5 =$ _____
5. $2 \subseteq 3 =$ _____	6. $4 \subseteq 2 =$ _____	7. $8 \subseteq 1 =$ _____	8. $6 \subseteq 6 =$ _____
9. $9 \subseteq 7 =$ _____	10. $7 \subseteq 7 =$ _____	11. $5 \subseteq 8 =$ _____	12. $2 \subseteq 6 =$ _____
13. $6 \subseteq 4 =$ _____	14. $7 \subseteq 3 =$ _____	15. $4 \subseteq 9 =$ _____	16. $2 \subseteq 9 =$ _____
17. $9 \subseteq 9 =$ _____	18. $3 \subseteq 4 =$ _____	19. $6 \subseteq 8 =$ _____	20. $7 \subseteq 5 =$ _____
21. $9 \subseteq 5 =$ _____	22. $5 \subseteq 6 =$ _____	23. $6 \subseteq 3 =$ _____	24. $7 \subseteq 1 =$ _____
25. $8 \subseteq 3 =$ _____	26. $9 \subseteq 6 =$ _____	27. $4 \subseteq 7 =$ _____	28. $3 \subseteq 3 =$ _____
29. $8 \subseteq 7 =$ _____	30. $1 \subseteq 5 =$ _____	31. $7 \subseteq 6 =$ _____	32. $2 \subseteq 8 =$ _____

No unauthorized copying

Base Ten Blocks

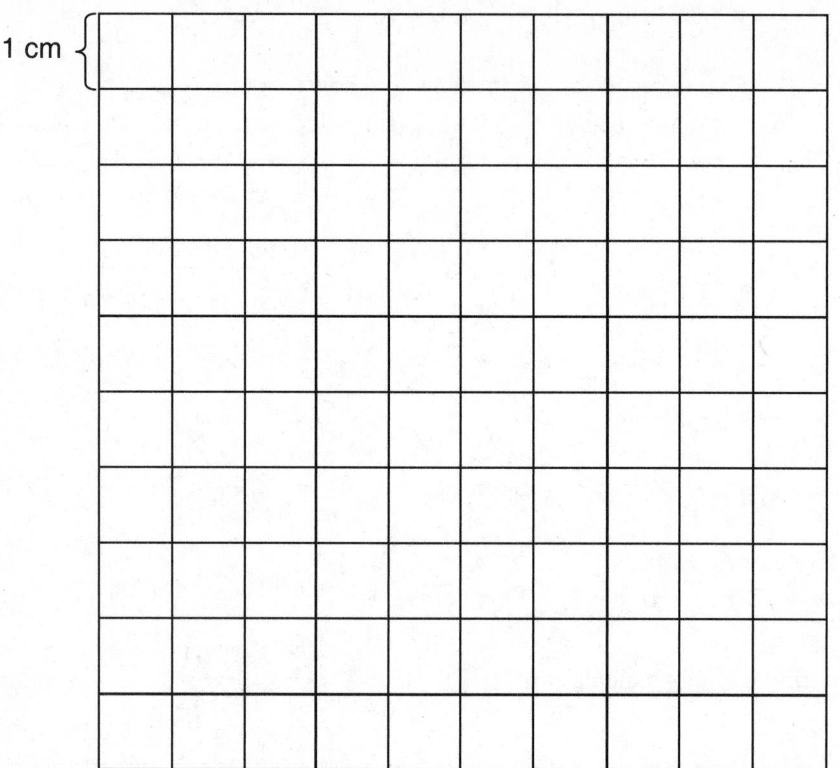

Hundreds Block

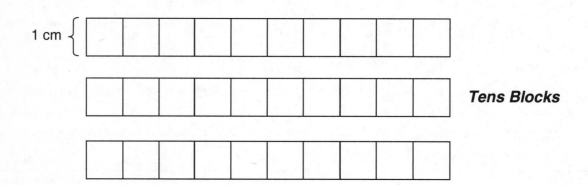

Tens Blocks

1 cm

1 cm

Ones Blocks

PA5-1: Counting

Jamie finds the **difference** between 15 and 12 by counting on her fingers.
She says "12" with her fist closed, then counts to 15, raising one finger at a time:

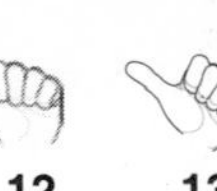

12 13 14 15

When she says "15," she has raised 3 fingers. So the difference or "gap" between 12 and 15 is 3.

---

1. Count the gap between the numbers. Write your answer in the circle:
HINT: If you know your subtraction facts, you may be able to find the answer without counting.

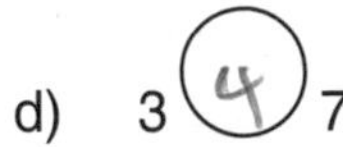

a) 2 ◯ 7 b) 5 ◯ 8 c) 3 ◯ 9 d) 3 ◯ 7 e) 2 ◯ 8

f) 11 ◯ 17 g) 11 ◯ 16 h) 22 ◯ 28 i) 36 ◯ 38 j) 31 ◯ 40

k) 32 ◯ 37 l) 43 ◯ 47 m) 49 ◯ 52 n) 85 ◯ 91 o) 67 ◯ 72

What number is 4 <u>more</u> than 16? (Or: 16 + 4 = ?)

Ravi finds the answer by counting on his fingers. He says 16 with his fist closed, then counts up from 16 until he has raised 4 fingers:

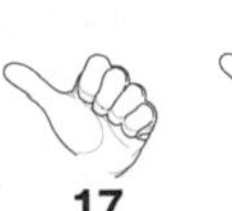

16 17 18 19 20

The number 20 is 4 more than 16.

2. Add the number in the circle to the number beside it. Write your answer in the blank:

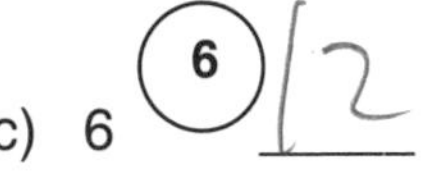
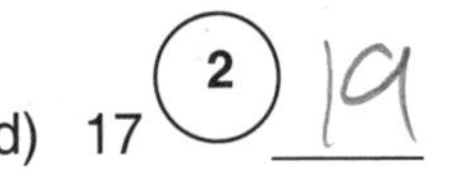
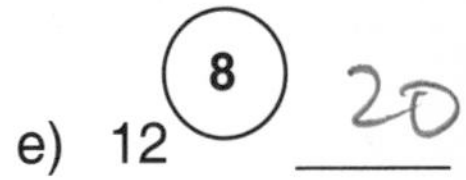

a) 5 ③ ___ b) 8 ④ ___ c) 6 ⑥ ___ d) 17 ② ___ e) 12 ⑧ ___

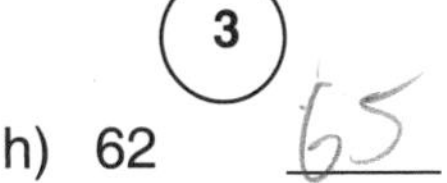
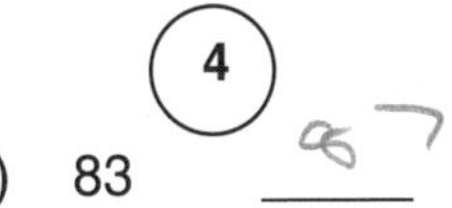
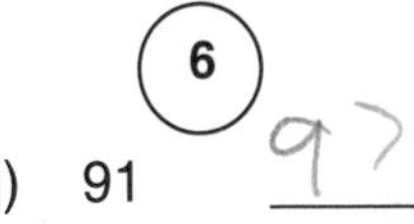

f) 25 ⑨ ___ g) 34 ⑦ ___ h) 62 ③ ___ i) 83 ④ ___ j) 91 ⑥ ___

3. Fill in the missing numbers:

a) ____ is 5 more than 6 b) ____ is 7 more than 26 c) ____ is 8 more than 17

d) ____ is 5 more than 29 e) ____ is 4 more than 38 f) ____ is 9 more than 65

No unauthorized copying

PA5-2: Increasing Sequences

In an **increasing sequence**, each number is greater than the one before it.

Deborah wants to continue the number pattern: 6 , 8 , 10 , 12 , ?

She finds the **difference** between the first two numbers:

6

7

8

(2) 6 , 8 , 10 , 12 , ?

She finds that the difference between the other numbers in the pattern is also 2. So the pattern was made by adding 2:

(2) (2) (2) 6 , 8 , 10 , 12 , ?

To continue the pattern, Deborah adds 2 to the last number in the sequence.

So the final number in the pattern is 14:

(2) (2) (2) (2) 6 , 8 , 10 , 12 , 14

---

1. Extend the following patterns by first finding the gap between the numbers.

a) 1 , 4 , 7 , 10 , 13 , 16

b) 1 , 5 , 9 , 13 , 17 , 21

c) 3 , 8 , 13 , 18 , 23 , 28

d) 3 , 6 , 9 , 13 , 14 , 24

e) 1 , 6 , 11 , 16 , 21 , 26

f) 4 , 10 , 16 , 22 , 28 , 34

g) 2 , 12 , 22 , 32 , 42 , 52

h) 7 , 13 , 19 , 25 , 31 , 37

i) 31 , 34 , 37 , 40 , 43 , 46

j) 82 , 88 , 94 , 100 , 106 , 112

k) 2 , 13 , 24 , 35 , 46 , 57

l) 8 , 17 , 26 , 35 , 54 , 63

m) 5 , 11 , 17 , 23 , 29 , 45

n) 0 , 4 , 8 , 12 , 16 , 20

No unauthorized copying

PA5-3: Counting Backwards

What number must you subtract from 43 to get 39? **43 – ? = 39**

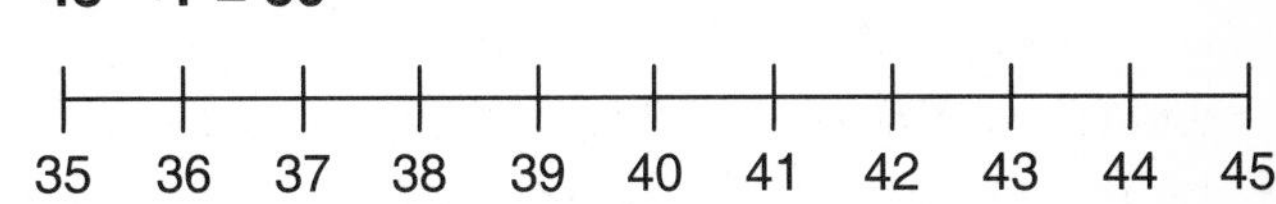
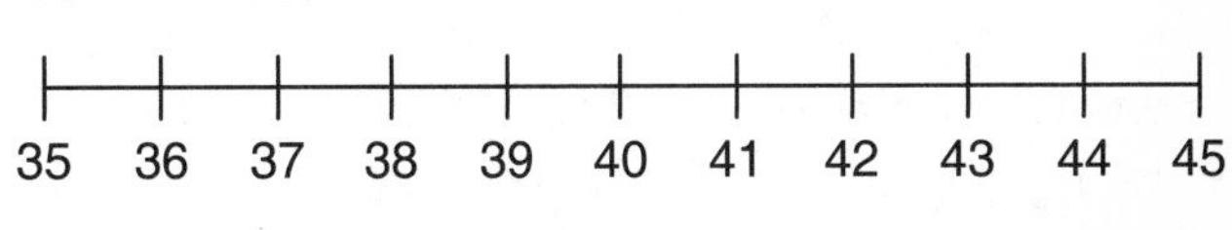

Jess finds the answer by counting backwards on her fingers. She uses the number line to help:

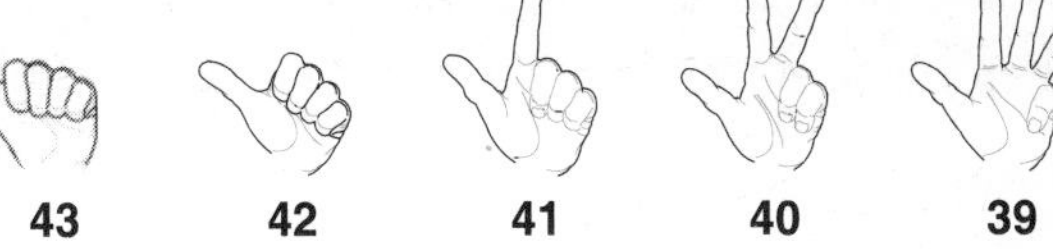

When Jess says 39, she has raised four fingers.
So 4 subtracted from 43 gives 39: **43 – 4 = 39**

---

1. What number must you <u>subtract</u> from the greater number to get the lesser number?

a) 43 (− 3) 40 b) 44 (5) 39 c) 41 (5) 36 d) 42 (7) 35

e) 44 (7) 37 f) 39 (3) 36 g) 42 (5) 37 h) 45 (6) 39

2. Find the gap between the numbers by counting backwards on your fingers.

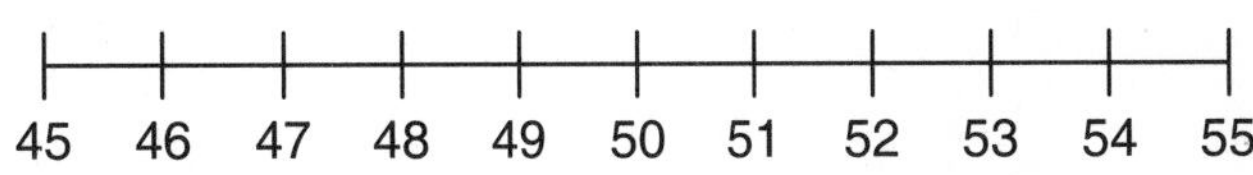

a) 52 (− 4) 48 b) 51 (2) 49 c) 52 (5) 47 d) 54 (7) 47

e) 51 (4) 47 f) 50 (4) 46 g) 52 (7) 45 h) 53 (8) 45

3. Find the gap between the numbers by counting backwards on your fingers (or by using your subtraction facts):

a) 87 (5) 82 b) 68 (9) 59 c) 40 (2) 38 d) 90 (2) 88

e) 51 (5) 46 f) 77 (4) 73 g) 55 (8) 47 h) 22 (6) 16

i) 78 (9) 69 j) 121 (5) 116 k) 102 (6) 96 l) 49 (10) 39

 No unauthorized copying

PA5-4: Decreasing Sequences

In a **decreasing sequence**, each number is less than the one before it.

What number is 3 less than 9? (Or: 9 – 3 = ?)

Jenna finds the answer by counting on her fingers.
She says 9 with her fist closed and counts backwards
until she has raised 3 fingers:

9
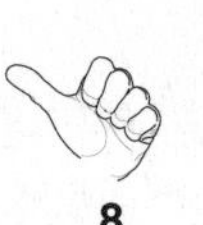
8

7

6

The number 6 is 3 <u>less than</u> 9: **9 – 3 = 6**

---

1. Follow the directions to the circle from the number given. Write your answer in the blank:

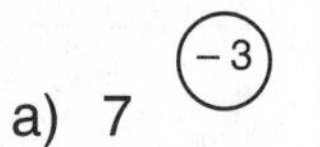

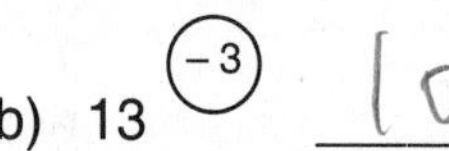
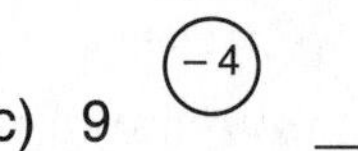

a) 7 (– 3) __4__ b) 13 (– 3) __10__ c) 9 (– 4) __5__ d) 17 (–1) __16__

e) 16 (– 5) __11__ f) 19 (– 4) __15__ g) 25 (– 1) __24__ h) 29 (– 2) __27__

i) 38 (– 4) __34__ j) 45 (– 6) __39__ k) 63 (– 8) __55__ l) 72 (– 4) __68__

2. Fill in the missing numbers:

a) __12__ is 5 less than 17 b) __16__ is 3 less than 19 c) __16__ is 2 less than 18

d) __20__ is 6 less than 26 e) __12__ is 8 less than 20 f) __25__ is 4 less than 29

g) __28__ is 7 less than 35 h) __33__ is 9 less than 42 i) __82__ is 8 less than 90

3. Extend the following <u>decreasing</u> patterns by first finding the gap between the numbers.

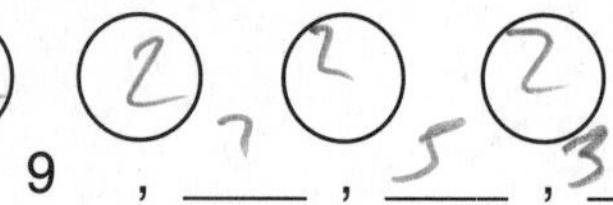
a) 13 , 11 , 9 , __7__ , __5__ , __3__

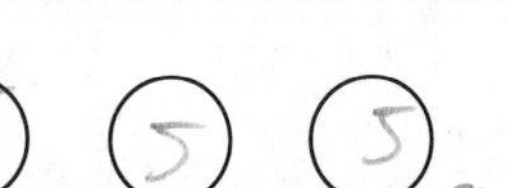
b) 33 , 28 , 23 , __18__ , __13__ , __8__

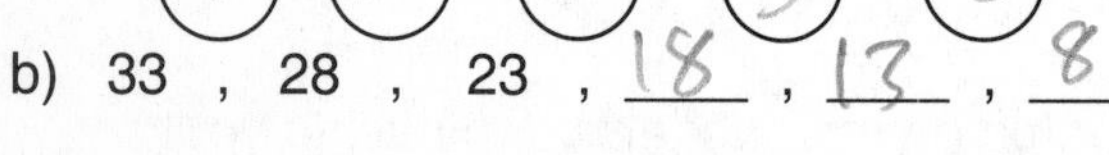
c) 64 , 61 , 58 , __55__ , __52__ , __49__

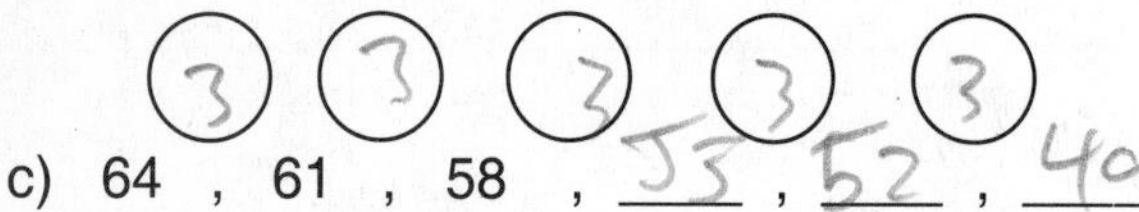
d) 55 , 46 , 37 , __28__ , __19__ , __10__

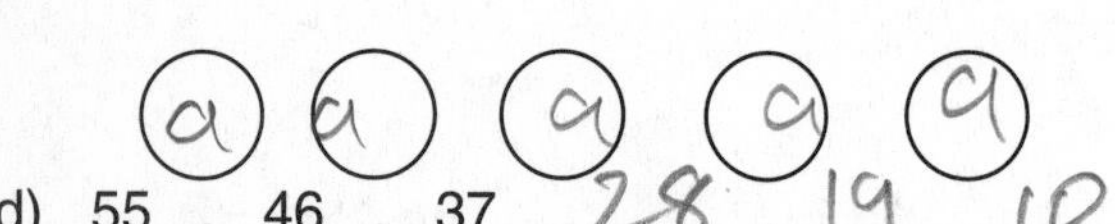
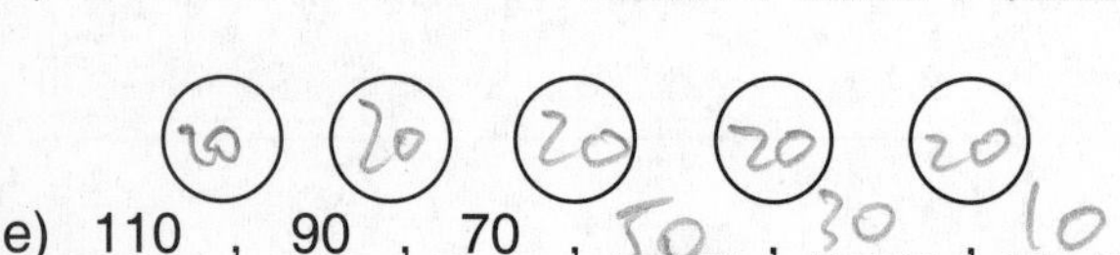
e) 110 , 90 , 70 , __50__ , __30__ , __10__

Example:

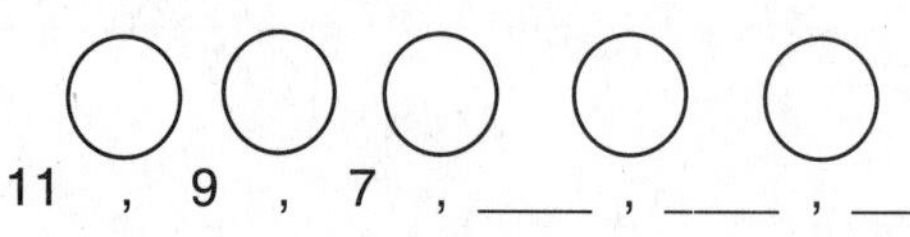
11 , 9 , 7 , ___ , ___ , ___

<u>Step 1</u>:

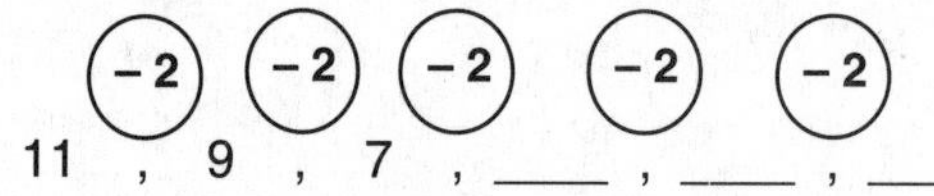
(– 2) (– 2) (– 2) (– 2) (– 2)
11 , 9 , 7 , ___ , ___ , ___

<u>Step 2</u>:

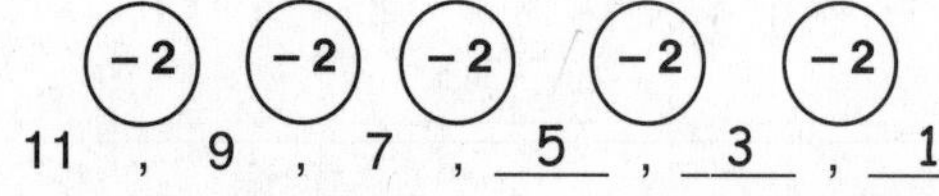
(– 2) (– 2) (– 2) (– 2) (– 2)
11 , 9 , 7 , __5__ , __3__ , __1__

No unauthorized copying

PA5-5: Increasing and Decreasing Sequences

1. Extend the following patterns, using the "gap" provided:

Example 1: 6 , 7 , 8 , 9 (+1)

Example 2: 8 , 6 , 4 , 2 (−2)

a) 5 , 11 , ____ , ____ , ____ (+6)

b) 1 , 5 , ____ , ____ , ____ (+4)

c) 3 , 7 , ____ , ____ , ____ (+4)

d) 6 , 9 , ____ , ____ , ____ (+3)

e) 36 , 31 , ____ , ____ , ____ (−5)

f) 10 , 17 , ____ , ____ , ____ (+7)

g) 17 , 13 , ____ , ____ , ____ (−4)

h) 19 , 15 , ____ , ____ , ____ (−4)

2. Extend the following patterns by first finding the "gap."

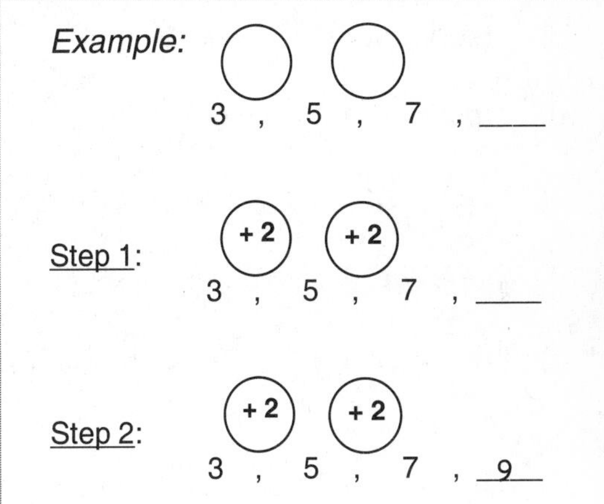

Example: 3 , 5 , 7 , ____

Step 1: 3 , 5 , 7 , ____ (+2) (+2)

Step 2: 3 , 5 , 7 , 9 (+2) (+2)

a) 4 , 8 , 12 , ____ , ____

b) 3 , 10 , 17 , ____ , ____

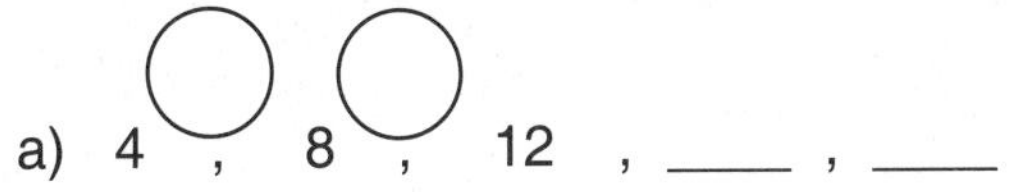

c) 1 , 4 , 7 , ____ , ____

d) 21 , 25 , 29 , ____ , ____

e) 11 , 16 , 21 , ____ , ____

f) 55 , 53 , 51 , ____ , ____

g) 79 , 73 , 67 , ____ , ____

3. Jameson has a roll of 52 stamps.
He uses 4 stamps each day for 6 days.
How many stamps are left? __________

4. Amy has saved $36. She saves $6 each day after that.
How much money has she saved after 5 days? ________________

No unauthorized copying

PA5-6: Extending a Pattern Using a Rule

1. Continue the following sequences by adding the number given:

a) (add 3) 41 , 44 , _______, _______, _______

b) (add 5) 60 , 65 , _______, _______, _______

c) (add 2) 74 , 76 , _______, _______, _______

d) (add 10) 20 , 30 , _______, _______, _______

e) (add 4) 61 , 65 , _______, _______, _______

f) (add 9) 31 , 40 , _______, _______, _______

g) (add 6) 20 , 26 , _______, _______, _______

2. Continue the following sequences by subtracting by the number given:

a) (subtract 2) 24 , 22 , _______, _______, _______

b) (subtract 3) 25 , 22 , _______, _______, _______

c) (subtract 5) 85 , 80 , _______, _______, _______

d) (subtract 10) 70 , 60 , _______, _______, _______

e) (subtract 4) 56 , 52 , _______, _______, _______

f) (subtract 7) 56 , 49 , _______, _______, _______

g) (subtract 11) 141 , 130 , _______, _______, _______

BONUS

3. Create a pattern of your own. Say what number you added or subtracted each time:

______ , ______ , ______ , ______ , ______ My rule: ______________________________

4. Which one of the following sequences was made by adding 4? Circle it.
HINT: Check all the numbers in the sequence.

a) 4, 8, 10, 14 b) 4, 8, 12, 16 c) 3, 9, 11, 15

5. **72, 63, 54, 45, 36, ...**

Yen says this sequence was made by subtracting 8 each time.
Hyun says it was made by subtracting 9. Who is right?

____

____

 No unauthorized copying

PA5-7: Identifying Pattern Rules

1. What number was added each time to make the pattern?

a) 2, 6, 10, 14 add ____ b) 2, 5, 8, 11 add ____

c) 18, 24, 30, 36 add ____ d) 40, 47, 54, 61 add ____

e) 81, 86, 91, 96 add ____ f) 69, 72, 75, 78 add ____

2. What number was subtracted each time to make each pattern?

a) 38, 36, 34, 32 subtract ____ b) 65, 60, 55, 50 subtract ____

c) 200, 199, 198, 197 subtract ____ d) 91, 88, 85, 82 subtract ____

e) 67, 64, 61, 58 subtract ____ f) 399, 397, 395, 393 subtract ____

3. State the rule for the following patterns:

a) 219, 212, 205, 198, 191 subtract ____ b) 11, 19, 27, 35, 43, 51 add ________

c) 301, 305, 309, 313 ____________ d) 210, 198, 186, 174 ____________

e) 633, 622, 611, 600, 589 ____________ f) 821, 830, 839, 848, 857 ____________

g) 407, 415, 423, 431 ____________ h) 731, 725, 719, 713 ____________

4. Find the rule for the pattern. Then continue the pattern:

a) 22, 27, 32, 37, 42, 47 The rule is: Start at 22 and add 5 each time

b) 38, 45, 52, _____, _____, _____ The rule is: ______________________

c) 124, 136, 148, _____, _____, _____ The rule is: ______________________

5. **5, 9, 13, 17, 21, ...**

Jonah says the pattern rule is: "Start at 5 and subtract 4 each time."
Pria says the rule is: "Start at 5 and add 5 each time."
Genevieve says the rule is: "Start at 5 and add 4 each time."

a) Whose rule is correct? ______________________

b) What mistakes did the others make? ______________________

____

____

PA5-8: Introduction to T-tables

Claude makes a **growing pattern** with squares.
He records the number of squares in each figure in a chart or T-table.

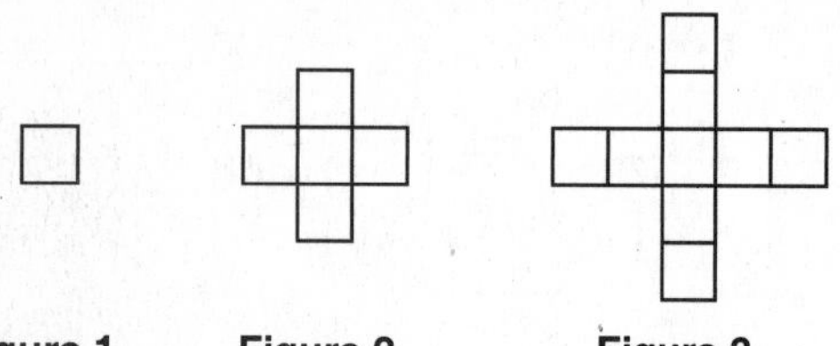

Figure	# of Squares
1	1
2	5
3	9

4
4
← Number of squares added each time.

The number of squares in the figures are 1, 5, 9, …
Claude writes a rule for this number pattern:

RULE: Start at 1 and add 4 each time.

---

1. Claude makes other growing patterns with squares.
How many squares does he add to make each new figure?
Write your answer in the circles provided. Then write a rule for the pattern:

a)

Figure	Number of Squares
1	2
2	7
3	12

Rule:
Start at 2 and add 5 each time

b)

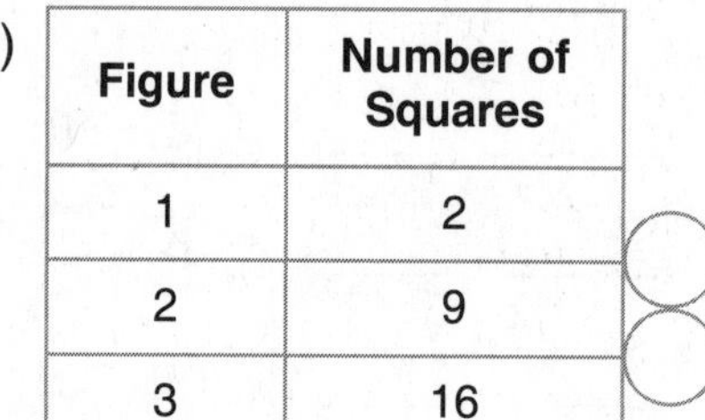

Figure	Number of Squares
1	2
2	9
3	16

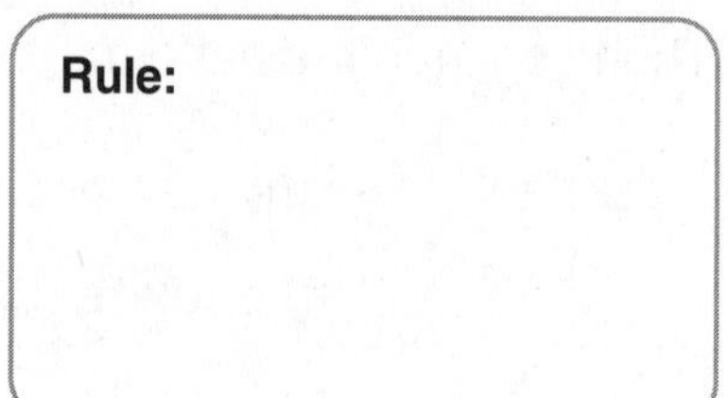

Rule:

c)

Figure	Number of Squares
1	1
2	4
3	7

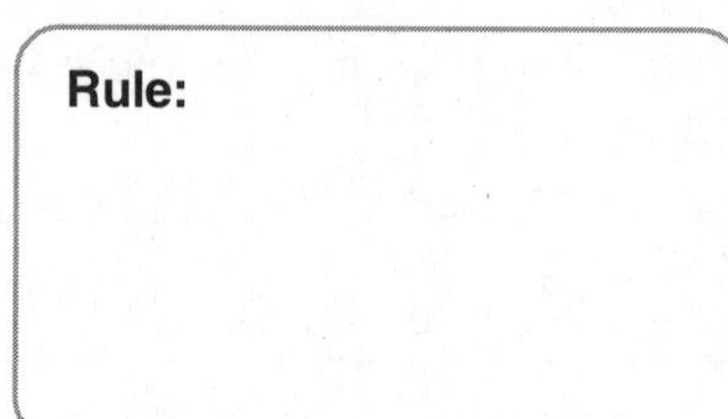

Rule:

d)

Figure	Number of Squares
1	1
2	7
3	13

Rule:

e)

Figure	Number of Squares
1	5
2	12
3	19

Rule:

f)

Figure	Number of Squares
1	13
2	21
3	29

Rule:

No unauthorized copying

g)

Figure	Number of Squares
1	3
2	11
3	19

Rule:

h)

Figure	Number of Squares
1	7
2	11
3	15

Rule:

i)

Figure	Number of Squares
1	8
2	14
3	20

Rule:

2. Extend the number pattern. How many squares would be used in Figure 6?

a)

Figure	Number of Squares
1	2
2	9
3	16

b)

Figure	Number of Squares
1	2
2	6
3	10

c)

Figure	Number of Squares
1	6
2	11
3	16

3. Trina makes the following growing patterns with squares.
After making Figure 3, she only has 16 squares left.
Does she have enough squares to complete Figure 4?

a)

Figure	Number of Squares
1	4
2	9
3	14

YES NO

b)

Figure	Number of Squares
1	5
2	9
3	13

YES NO

c)

Figure	Number of Squares
1	3
2	7
3	11

YES NO

4. Make a chart to show how many shapes will be needed to make the fifth figure in each pattern.

a) 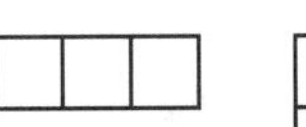 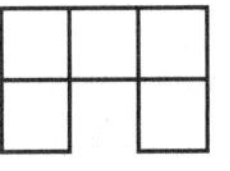 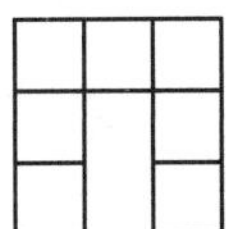

b)   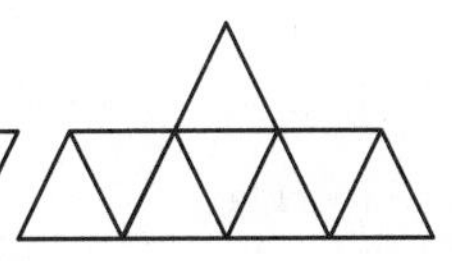

 No unauthorized copying

PA5-9: T-tables

1. Count the number of line segments (lines that join pairs of dots) in each figure.
HINT: Count around the outside of the figure first, marking line segments as you go.

Example:

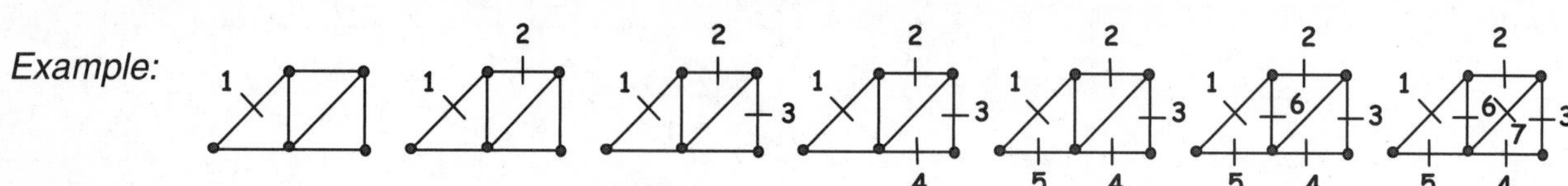

a) 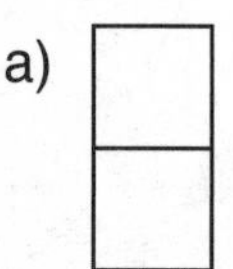 ____

b) 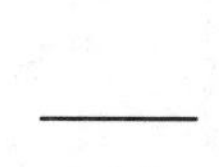 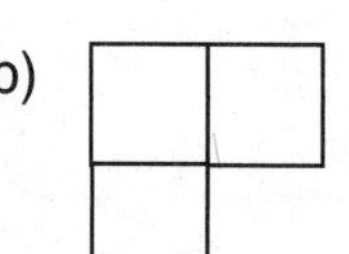 ____

c)  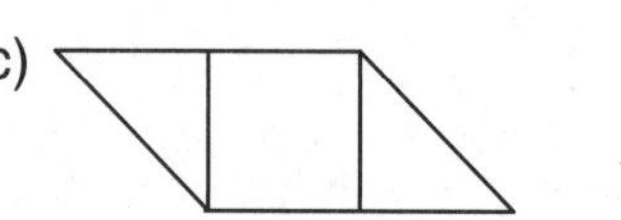 ____

d) 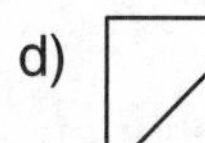 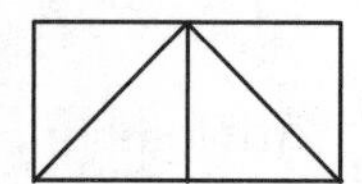 ____

e) 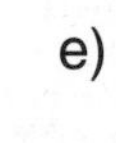 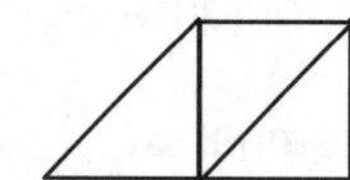 ____

f) 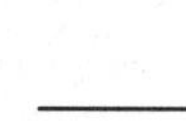 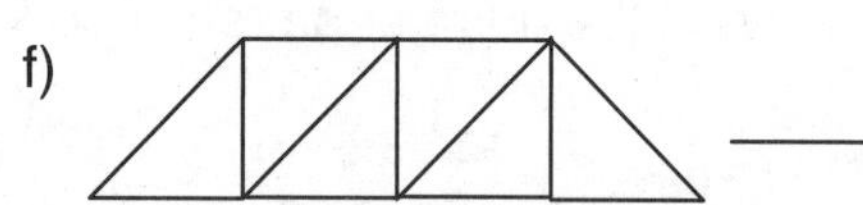 ____

2. Continue the pattern below, then complete the chart:

Figure 1

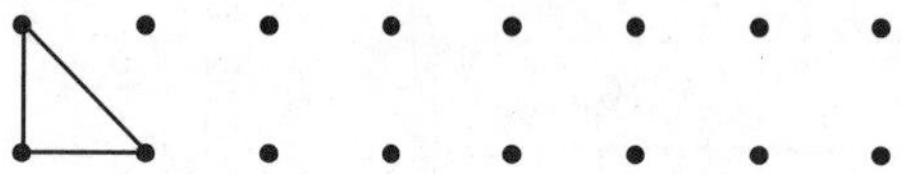

Figure 2

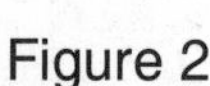

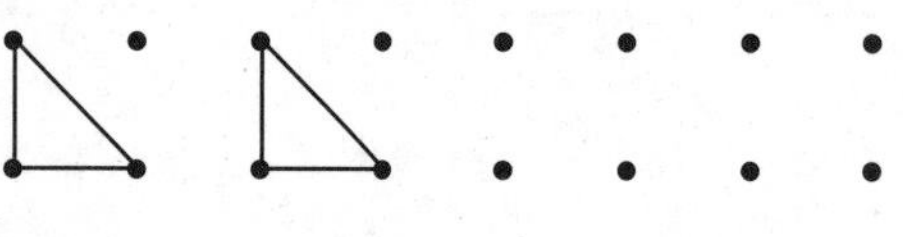

Figure 3

Figure 4

Figure	Number of Line Segments
1	
2	
3	
4	

How many line segments would Figure 5 have? ____________

3. Continue the pattern below, then complete the chart:

Figure 1

Figure 2

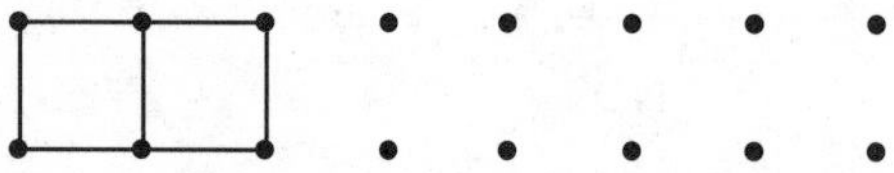

Figure 3

Figure 4

Figure	Number of Line Segments
1	
2	
3	
4	

How many line segments would Figure 7 have? ____________

No unauthorized copying

Continue the patterns below, then complete the charts.

4.

Figure 1

Figure 2

Figure 3

Figure 4

Figure 5

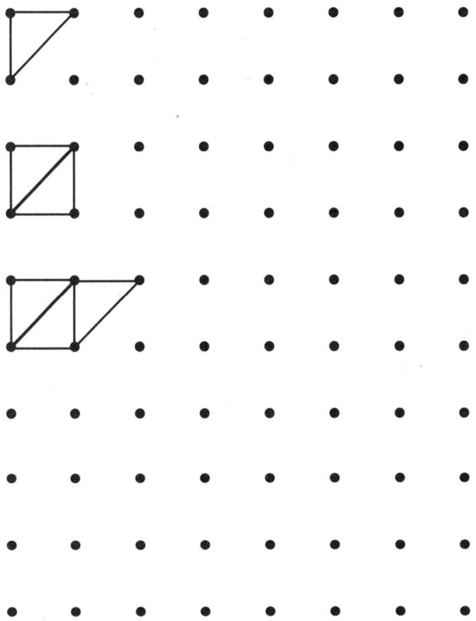

Figure	Number of Triangles	Number of Line Segments

a) How many line segments would Figure 6 have? ____________

b) How many triangles would Figure 6 have?

____

c) How many line segments would you need to make a figure with 7 triangles?

____

5.

Figure 1

Figure 2

Figure 3

Figure 4

Figure 5

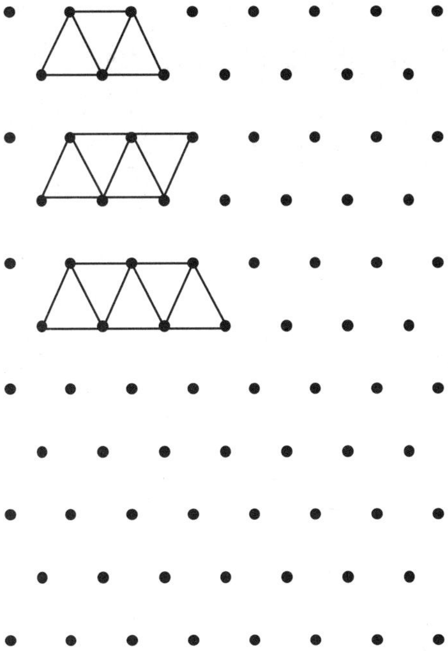

Figure	Number of Triangles	Number of Line Segments

a) How many line segments would Figure 6 have? ____________

b) How many triangles would Figure 6 have?

____

c) How many line segments would you need to make a figure with 9 triangles?

____

 No unauthorized copying

6.

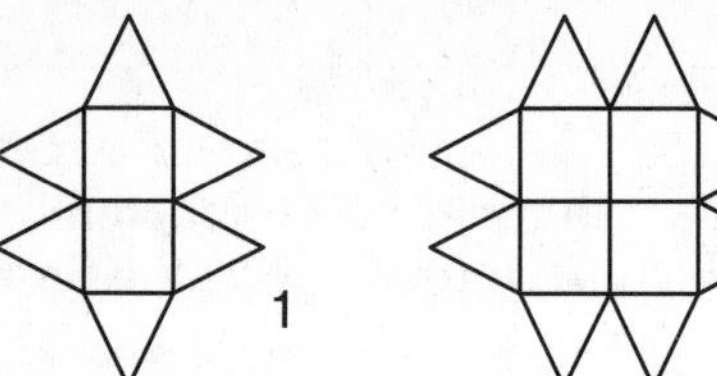

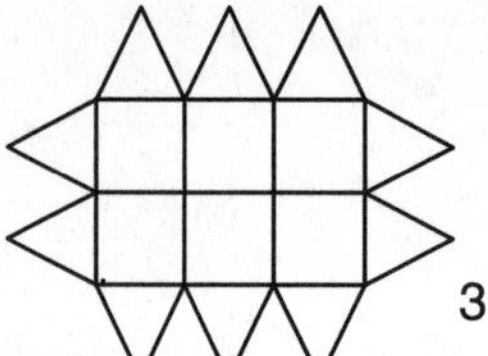

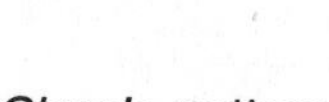

Clare's pattern

Figure	Number of Triangles	Number of Squares

a) State the pattern rule for the number of triangles:

Start at _____ and add _____ each time.

b) State the pattern rule for the number of squares:

____

c) How many squares would Clare need to make the fifth figure?

____

d) Clare says she needs 17 triangles to make the sixth figure. Is she correct?

____

e) How many triangles would Clare need to make a figure with 10 squares?

____

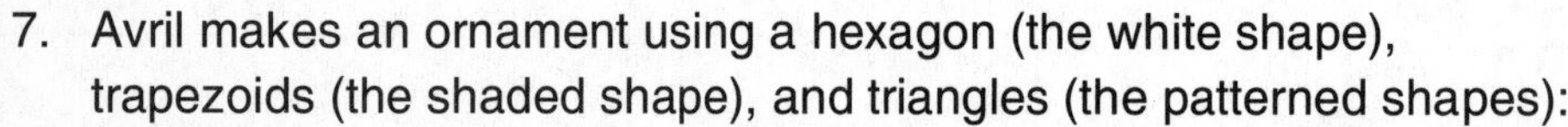

7. Avril makes an ornament using a hexagon (the white shape), trapezoids (the shaded shape), and triangles (the patterned shapes):

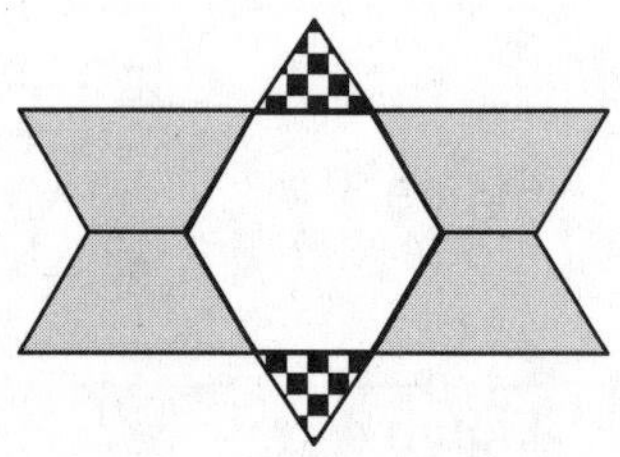

a) How many triangles would Avril need to make 9 ornaments?

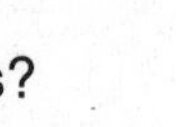

b) How many trapezoids would Avril need to make 5 ornaments?

c) Avril used 6 hexagons to make ornaments.
How many triangles and how many trapezoids did she use?

d) How many trapezoids would Avril need to make ornaments with 14 triangles?
HINT: Use skip counting or division to find out how many ornaments 14 triangles would make.

 No unauthorized copying

PA5-10: Problems Involving Time

1. Sarah's fish tank is leaking.
   At 6 pm, there are 21 L of water in the tank.
   At 7 pm, there are 18 L.
   At 8 pm, there are 15 L.

Hour	Amount of water in the tank
6 pm	21 L
7 pm	18 L
8 pm	15 L
9 pm	
10 pm	

   a) How many litres of water leak out each hour?

   ____

   b) How many litres will be left in the tank at 10 pm?

   ____

   c) How many hours will it take for all the water to leak out?

   ____

2. Maral has $28 in his savings account at the end of March.
   He saves $7 each month.
   How much does he have in his account at the end of June?

Month	Savings
March	$28

3. Reema has $42 in her savings account at the end of October.
   She spends $7 each month.
   How much does she have at the end of January?

Month	Savings
October	$42

4. Jane plants a 30 cm tall rose bush on May 1st.
   It grows 25 cm every month.
   What is its height on August 1st?

Date	Height
May 1st	30 cm

5. A white cedar tree seedling grows about 9 cm in a year.
   How tall will it be after 3 years?

Years	Height
0	0 cm

No unauthorized copying

PA5-11: T-tables (Advanced)

The **terms** of a sequence are the numbers or items in the sequence.

A **term number** gives the position of each item.

*This is **term number 4** since it is in the fourth position.*

4, 7, 10, 13, 16

1. Extend the T-table to find the 5th term in the sequence:

   3, 5, 7, …

Term Number	Term
1	3
2	5
3	7
4	
5	

2. Draw a T-table for each sequence to find the given term:

   a) Find the 6th term: 2, 5, 8, 11, …

   b) Find the 7th term: 21, 26, 31, 36, …

3. Travis says that the 6th term of the sequence 5, 7, 9, … is 17. Is he correct? Explain.

4. Using blocks or other shapes, make a model of a sequence of figures that could go with each T-table:

a)

Term Number	Term
1	2
2	5
3	8
4	11

b)

Term Number	Term
1	1
2	5
3	9
4	13

5. A marina rents sailboats at $6 for the first hour and $5 for every hour after that. How much does it cost to rent a sailboat for 6 hours?

6. Zoe saves $65 in August. She saves $6 each month after that. Adrian saves $62 in August. He saves $7 each month after that. Who has saved more money by the end of January?

7. A newborn elephant weighs about 77 kg. It drinks about 11 litres of milk a day and gains about 1 kg every day.

   a) How much weight does the baby gain in a week?

   b) How many litres of milk does the baby drink in a week?

   c) How many days does it take for the baby to double its weight?

No unauthorized copying

PA5-12: Repeating Patterns

Marco makes a **repeating** pattern using blocks:

*This is the **core** of Marco's pattern.*

The **core** of a pattern is the part that repeats.

---

1. Circle the core of the following patterns. The first one is done for you:

a) 

b) 

c) 

d) 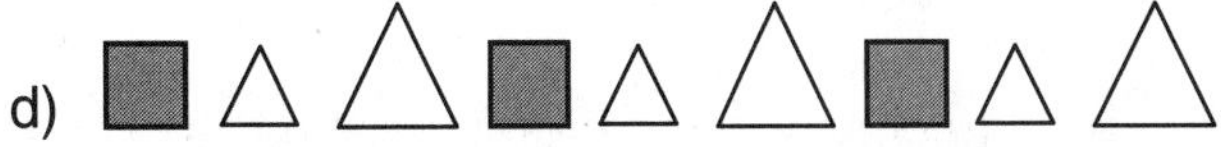

e) 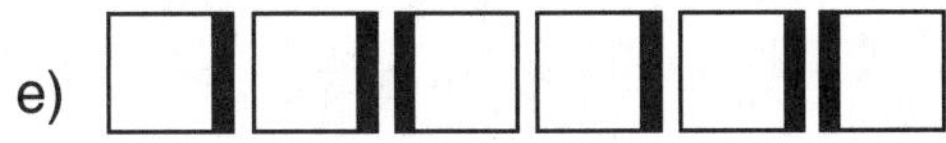

f) 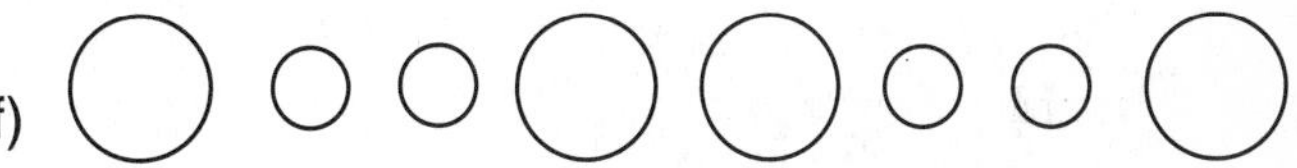

g) 

h) 

i) C B B C B B C B B C

j) 1 2 4 1 2 4 1 2 4

k) 1 2 3 4 8 1 2 3 4 8

l) 9 8 7 8 9 8 7 8 9 8

m) 

n) X Y Z X Y Z X Y Z X Y

2. Circle the core of the pattern. Then continue the pattern:

a) 

b) 

c) A B C A B C A ____ ____ ____ ____ ____

d) 2 8 9 6 2 8 9 6 ____ ____ ____ ____ ____

e) 3 0 0 4 3 0 0 4 3 0 ____ ____ ____ ____

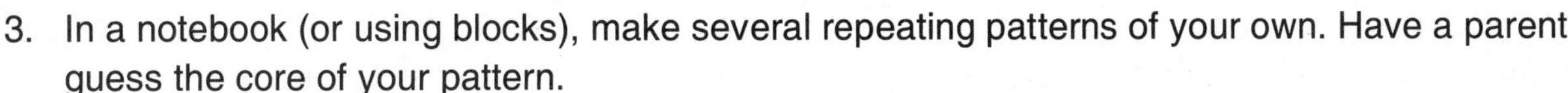

3. In a notebook (or using blocks), make several repeating patterns of your own. Have a parent guess the core of your pattern.

No unauthorized copying

PA5-13: Extending Patterns & Predicting Positions

1. Angela makes a repeating pattern using blue (**B**) and yellow (**Y**) blocks.
   The box shows the core of her pattern. Continue the pattern by writing Bs and Ys:

a) 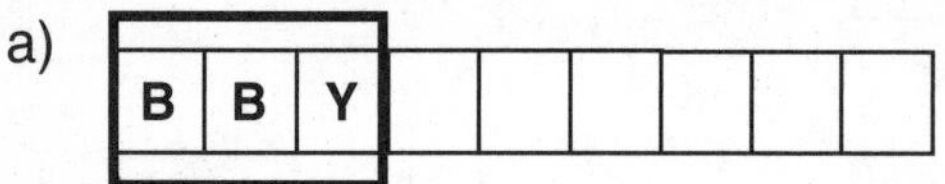

b) 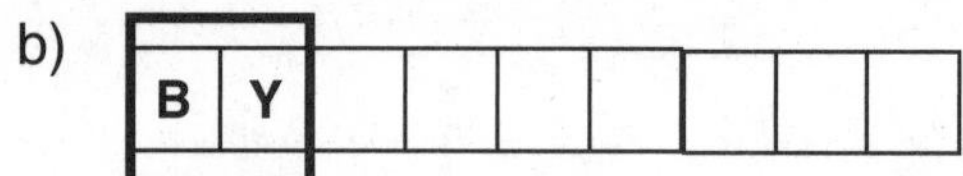

c) 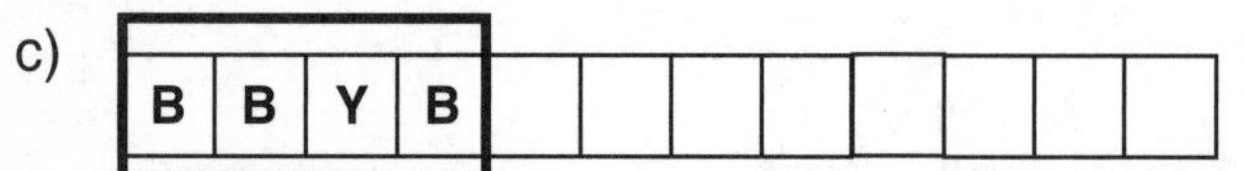

d) 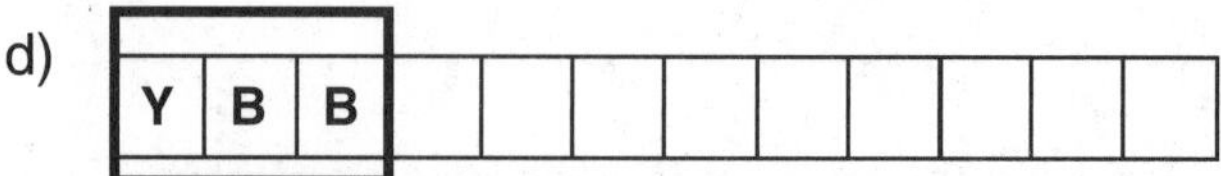

e) 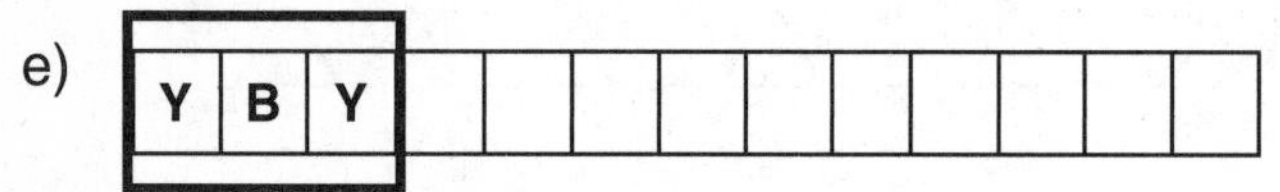

f) 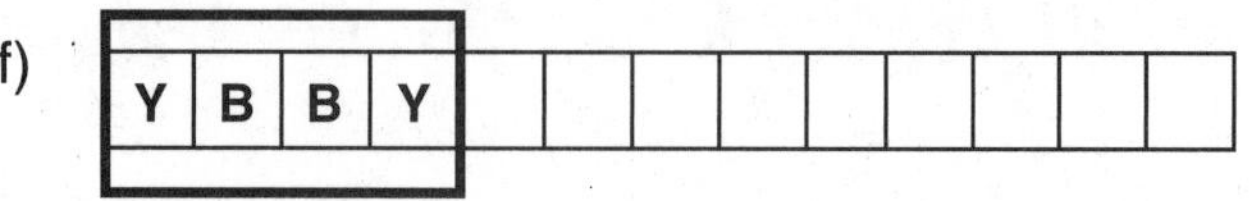

2. Barry tried to continue the pattern in the box. Did he continue the pattern correctly?
   HINT: Shade the yellows (Y) if it helps.

a) 

YES NO

b) 

YES NO

c) 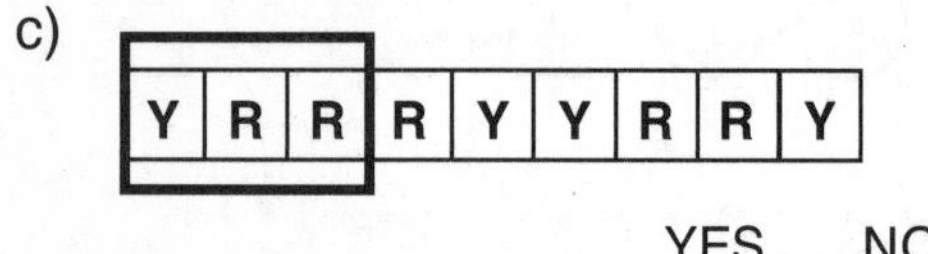

YES NO

d) 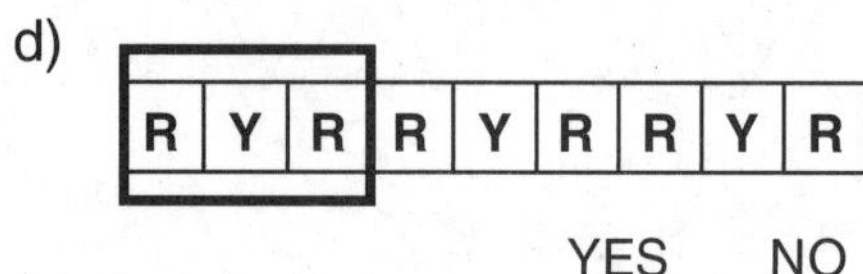

YES NO

e) 

YES NO

f) 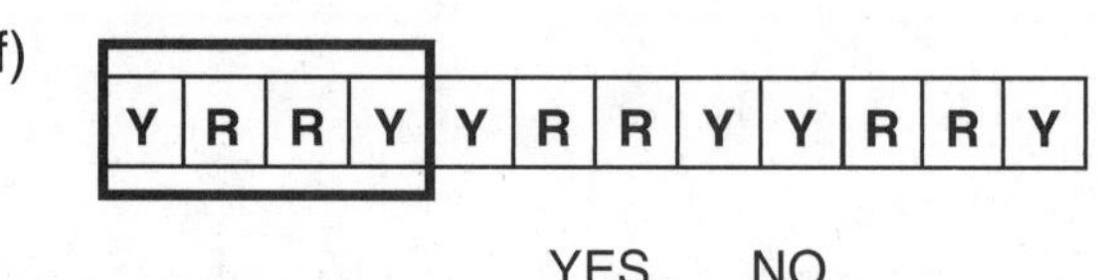

YES NO

3. For each pattern below, say whether the blocks in the rectangle are the core of the pattern:

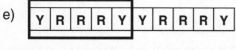

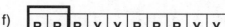

a) 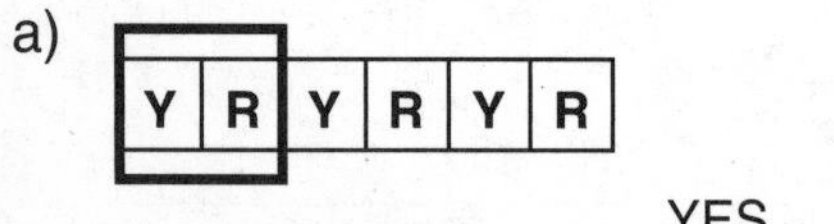

YES NO

b) 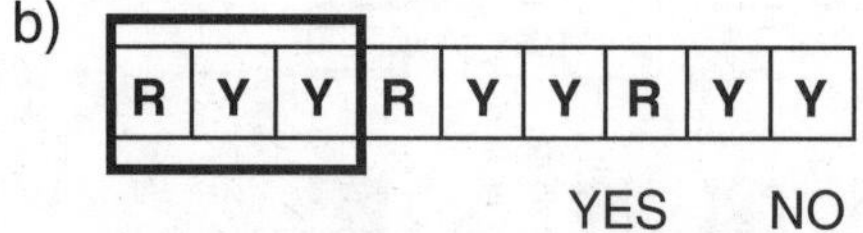

YES NO

c) 

YES NO

d) 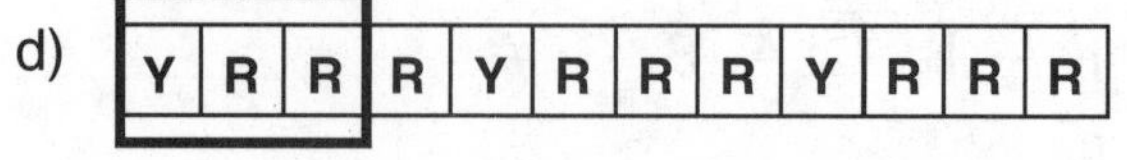

YES NO

e) Y R R R Y Y R R R Y

YES NO

f) 

YES NO

 No unauthorized copying

Sally wants to predict the colour of the 17th block in the pattern. First she finds the core of the pattern:

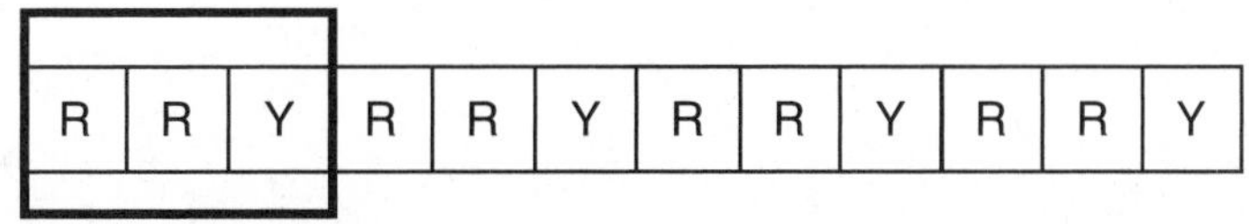

The core is 3 blocks long. Sally marks every <u>third</u> number on a hundreds chart.

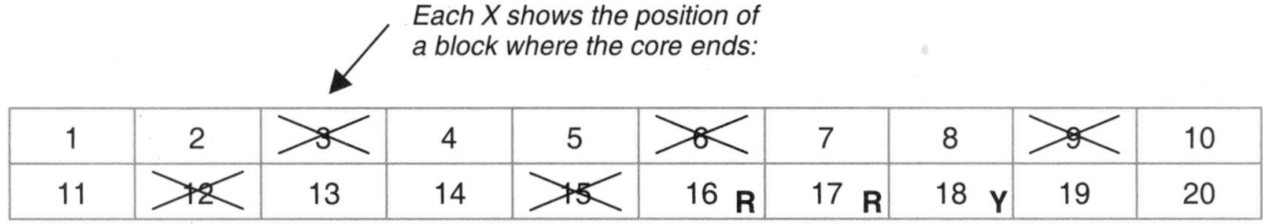

Each X shows the position of a block where the core ends:
1 2 3 4 5 6 7 8 9 10
11 12 13 14 15 16 R 17 R 18 Y 19 20

The core ends on the 15th block.
Sally writes the letters of the core on the chart, starting at 16.
The 17th block is red.

---

4. In the patterns below, put a rectangle around the blocks that make up the core:

a) | Y | R | R | Y | R | R | Y | R | R |

b) | R | Y | R | Y | R | Y | R | Y |

c) | Y | Y | R | R | Y | Y | R | R | Y | Y | R | R |

d) | Y | R | R | Y | Y | R | R | Y | Y |

e) | R | Y | R | Y | Y | Y | R | Y | R | Y | Y | Y |

f) | R | R | R | Y | R | R | R | Y | R | R |

5. Predict the colour of the 18th block using Sally's method:
NOTE: Start by finding the core of the pattern.

| R | Y | Y | Y | R | Y | Y | Y |

1	2	3	4	5	6	7	8	9	10
11	12	13	14	15	16	17	18	19	20

Colour: _______________

6. Predict the colour of the 19th block:

| R | R | Y | Y | R | R | Y | Y |

1	2	3	4	5	6	7	8	9	10
11	12	13	14	15	16	17	18	19	20

Colour: _______________

7. Predict the colour of the 17th block:

| R | R | Y | Y | Y | R | R | Y | Y | Y |

1	2	3	4	5	6	7	8	9	10
11	12	13	14	15	16	17	18	19	20

Colour: _______________

 No unauthorized copying

PA5-13: Extending Patterns & Predicting Positions *(continued)*

8. Draw a box around the core of the pattern. Then predict the colour of the 35th block:

Y	R	Y	Y	R	Y	Y	R	Y

Colour: _______________

1	2	3	4	5	6	7	8	9	10
11	12	13	14	15	16	17	18	19	20
21	22	23	24	25	26	27	28	29	30
31	32	33	34	35	36	37	38	39	40

9. Carl makes a pattern with red, green, and yellow beads:

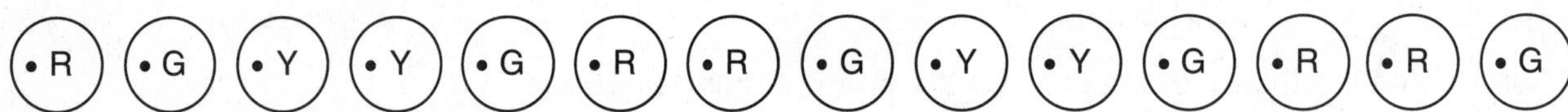

What colour will the 43rd bead be?

10. Megan plants a row of daisies and pansies in the pattern shown:

D P P D P P D

Is the 37th flower a daisy or a pansy?

11. Explain how you could find the colour of the 48th block in this pattern without using a hundreds chart.

R	R	Y	Y	Y	R	R	Y	Y	Y

12. Design a repeating pattern that has a core that is ten squares long. What is the colour of the 97th square? How do you know?

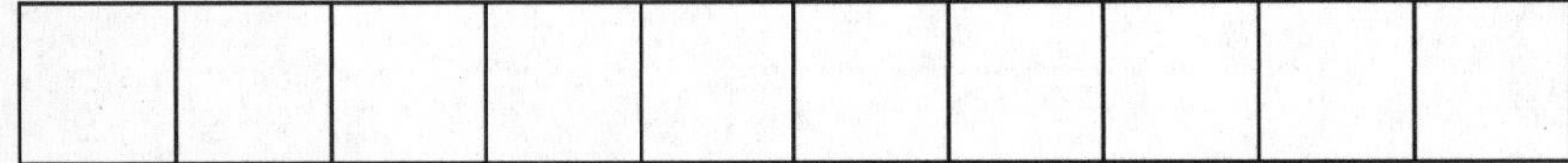

13. a) What is the 15th coin in this pattern? Explain how you know.

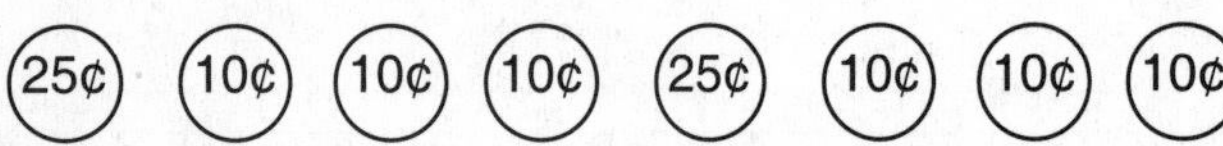

BONUS

b) What is the total value of the first 20 coins?

No unauthorized copying

PA5-14: Number Lines

On Monday morning, Olivia is 600 kilometres from Winnipeg.
Her solar-powered car can travel 150 km per day.
How far from Winnipeg will she be by Wednesday evening?

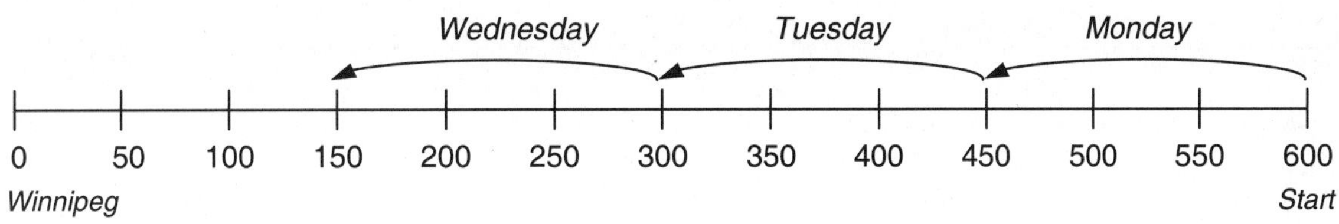

On Wednesday evening, Olivia will be 150 km from Winnipeg.

---

1. On Thursday morning, Eduardo's campsite is 19 km from Great Bear Lake.
   He plans to hike 6 km towards the lake each day.
   How far from the lake will he be on Saturday evening? ________________

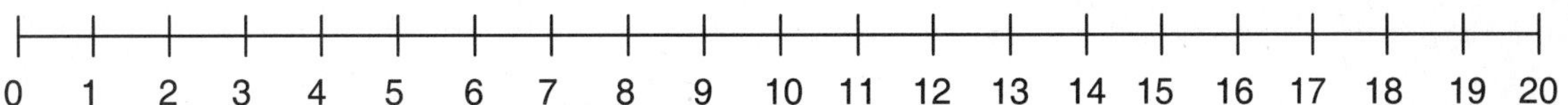

2. On Sunday morning, Nandita is on a bicycle tour 400 km from her home.
   She can cycle 75 km each day.
   How far from home will she be on Wednesday evening? ______________

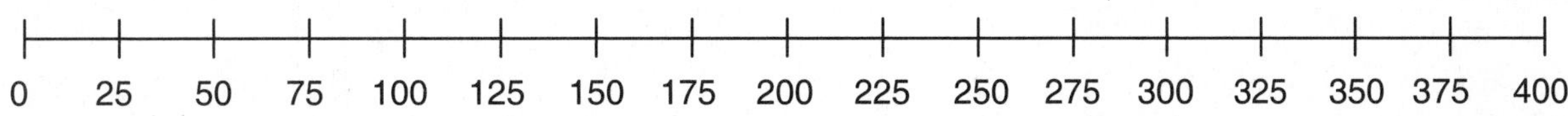

Draw and label a number line in the grid to solve.

3. Helen is 14 blocks from home. She can run 2 blocks in a minute.
   How far from home will she be in 3 minutes?

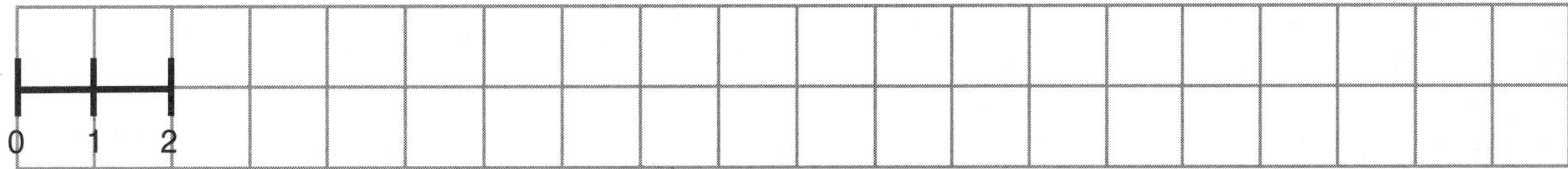

4. Ravi is 15 blocks from the store. He can cycle 4 blocks in a minute.
   How far from the store will he be after 3 minutes?

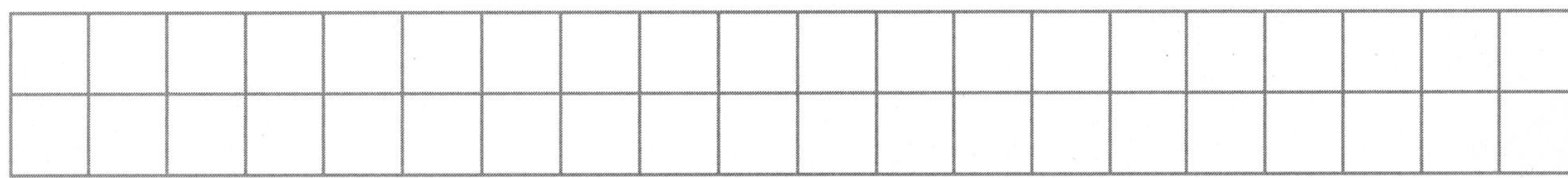

 No unauthorized copying

PA5-15: Number Lines (Advanced)

In each of the problems below you will have to decide on a scale for your number line.

1. Kristal has entered a 250 km bike race. He can cycle 75 km each day.
How far from the finish will he be after 3 days?

0 25 50 75

2. Wendy has to climb 5 walls in an obstacle course.
The first wall is 100 metres from the start.
After that, each wall is 75 metres farther than the last.
How far from the start is the 3rd wall?

3. Six telephone poles are placed 50 m apart.
Alan wants to string a wire between the first and last pole.
What length of wire will he need?

4. Peter plants 4 rosebushes in a row.
The nearest bush is 8 metres from his house.
The bushes are 3 metres apart.
How far away from Peter's house is the last rosebush?
HINT: Put Peter's house at zero on the number line.

5. Jill's house is 20 metres from the sidewalk.
A dog is tied to a tree halfway between the house and the sidewalk.
The dog's leash is 8 m long.
How close to the sidewalk can the dog come?

No unauthorized copying

PA5-16: 2-Dimensional Patterns

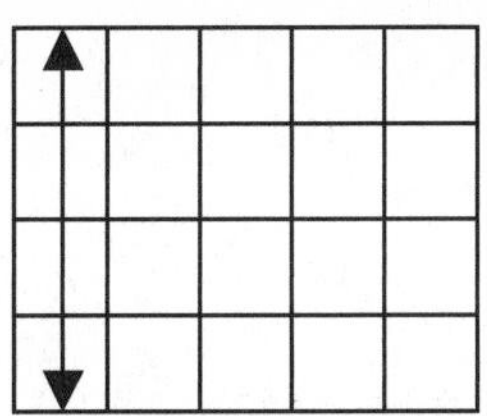

Columns run up and down.

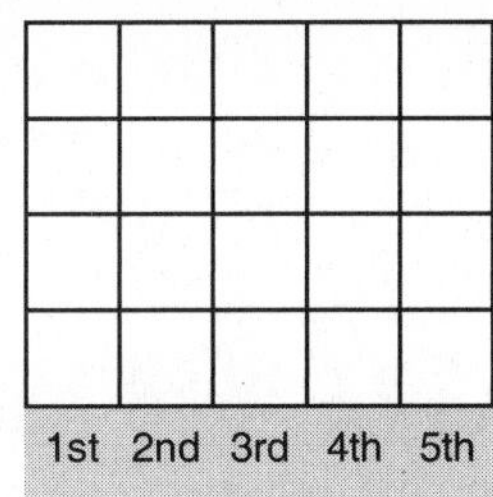

Columns are numbered left to right.

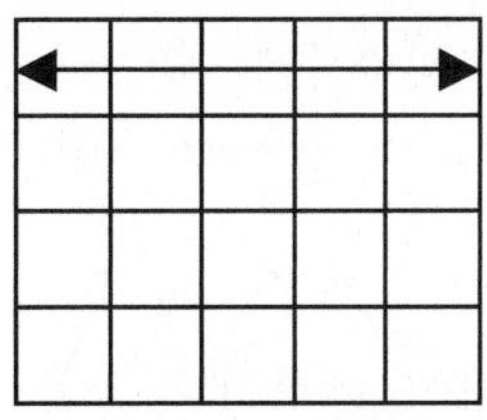

Rows run sideways.

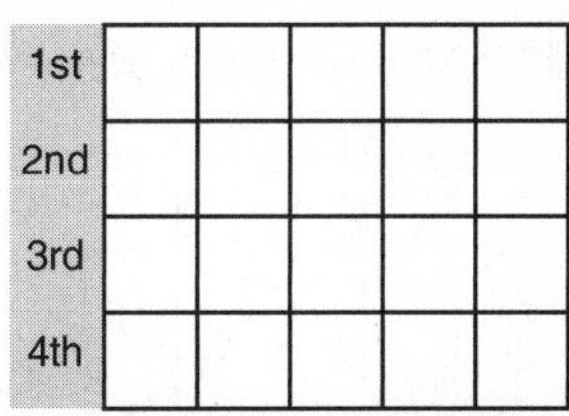

Rows are numbered top to bottom (in this exercise).

TEACHER: Review ordinal numbers before beginning this page.

---

1. Shade ...

a) 

the 1st column.

b) 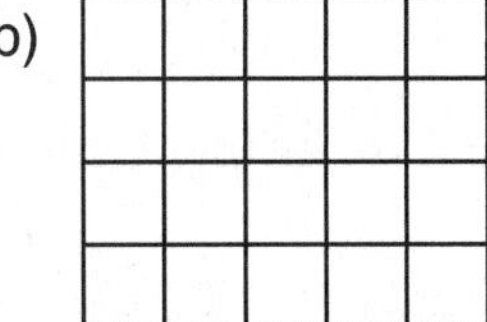

the 5th column.

c) 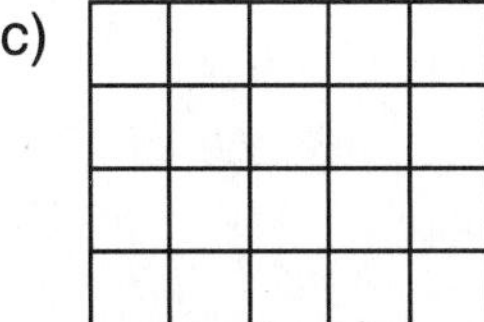

the 3rd column.

d) 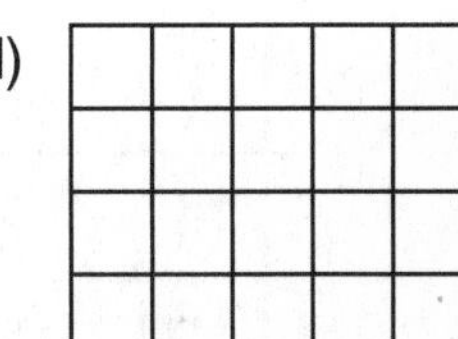

the 4th column.

2. Shade ...

a) 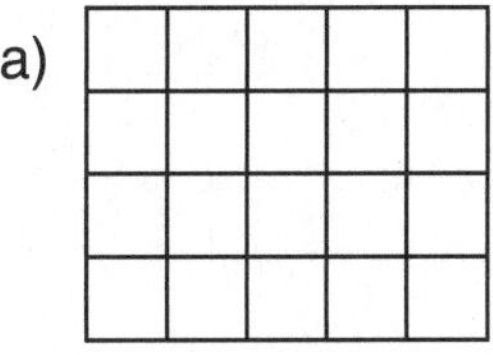

the 2nd row.

b) 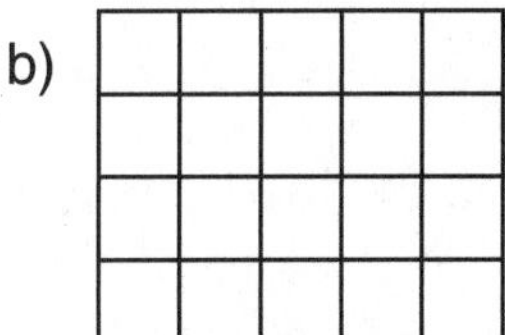

the 4th row.

c) 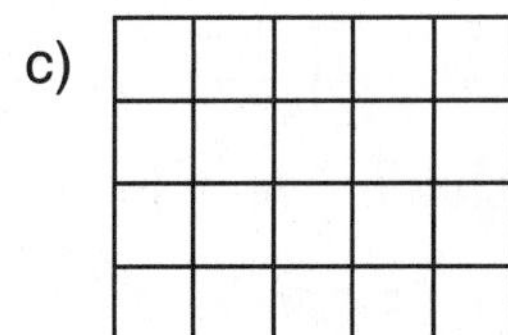

the 1st row.

d) 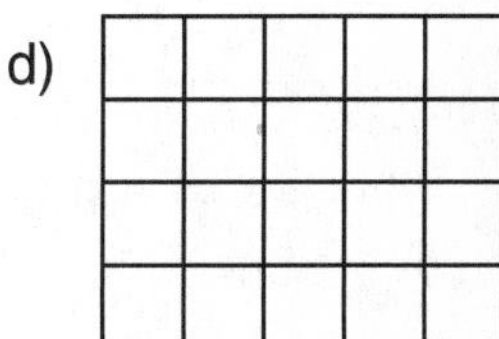

the 3rd row.

3. Shade ...

a) 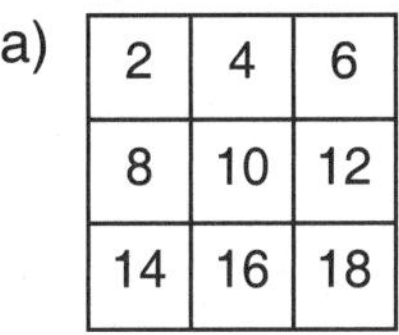

2	4	6
8	10	12
14	16	18

the 2nd row.

b)

2	4	6
8	10	12
14	16	18

the 1st column.

c)

2	4	6
8	10	12
14	16	18

the 3rd column.

d)

2	4	6
8	10	12
14	16	18

the diagonals *(one is shaded)*.

4. Describe any patterns you see in each chart below.
NOTE: You should use the words "rows," "columns," and "diagonals" in your answer.

a) 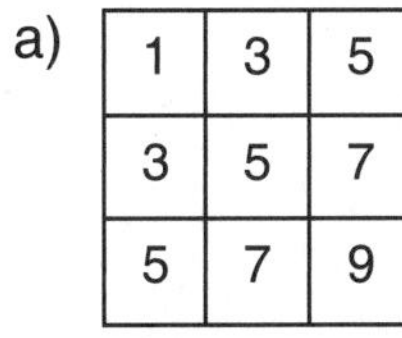

1	3	5
3	5	7
5	7	9

b)

5	10	15	20
10	15	20	25
15	20	25	30
20	25	30	35

c)

12	15	18	21
9	12	15	18
6	9	12	15
3	6	9	12

No unauthorized copying

5. Make up your own pattern and describe it.

6.

0	5	10	5	0
6	7	8	4	10
12	9	6	3	0
18	11	4	2	10
24	13	2	1	0

a) Which row of the chart has a decreasing pattern (looking left to right)?

____

b) Which column has a repeating pattern?

____

c) Write pattern rules for the first and second column.

____

d) Describe the relationship between the numbers in the third and fourth columns.

____

e) Describe one other pattern in the chart.

____

f) Name a row or column that does not appear to have any pattern.

____

7. Place the letters A and B so that each row and each column has two As and two Bs in it:

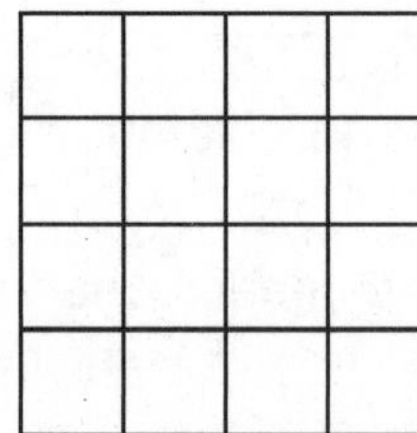

8. Fill in the blanks so the numbers in every row and column add to 15:

2		6
9		
	3	

PA5-17: Patterns in Times Tables

1. a)

1	2	3	4	5	6	7	8	9	10
11	12	13	14	15	16	17	18	19	20

Look at the ones digit in the multiples of 2.
How can you tell whether a number is a multiple of two?

b) The multiples of two (including zero) are called even numbers. Circle the even numbers:

17 3 418 132 64 76 234 89 94 167 506

2. a) Write out the first 12 multiples of 5 greater than zero:

5 , 10 , ____ , ____ , ____ , ____ , ____ , ____ , ____ , ____ , ____ , ____

b) How can you tell whether a number is a multiple of five?

c) Without counting up, circle the numbers that are multiples of 5:

83 17 45 37 150 64 190 65 71 235 618 1645

3.

1	2	3
11	12	13
21	22	23

Example

Shade all the multiples of 3 on a hundreds chart.
You should find that the shaded squares lie in diagonal lines.
Now add the ones digit and the tens digit of each number along any diagonal line.
Describe what you notice below. (Try this for each shaded diagonal.)

4. A number is a multiple of 3 if the sum of its digits is a multiple of 3. Fill in the chart below:

Number	**28**	**37**	**42**	**61**	**63**	**87**	**93**	**123**
Sum of digits	2 + 8 = 10							
Multiple of 3?	No							

 No unauthorized copying

PA5-18: Patterns in the Eight Times Table

1. On a hundreds chart, shade every eighth number (i.e., shade the numbers you would say when counting by eights: 8, 16, 24, ...).

   The numbers you shaded are the multiples of eight (up to 100).

2. Complete the following:

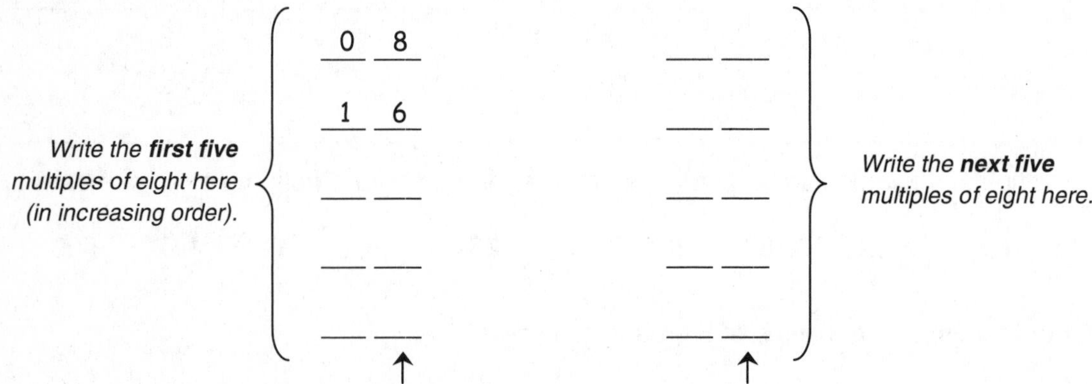

0 8
1 6
Write the **first five** multiples of eight here (in increasing order).
Write the **next five** multiples of eight here.

   Look down the columns marked by the arrows. What pattern do you see in the ones digits?

3. What pattern do you see in the number of tens?

PARENT:
Review the answers to Questions 2 and 3 before allowing your child to go further.

4. Use the pattern you found in Questions 2 and 3 to write out the multiples of 8 from 88 to 160:

 No unauthorized copying

PA5-19: Times Tables (Advanced)

PARENT:
Review Venn diagrams with your child before assigning the questions below.

1. a) Sort the numbers below into the Venn diagram.
The first number has been done for you:

~~10~~	20	15	27	74	39	5	27	34
70	4	19	63	60	50	75	6	66

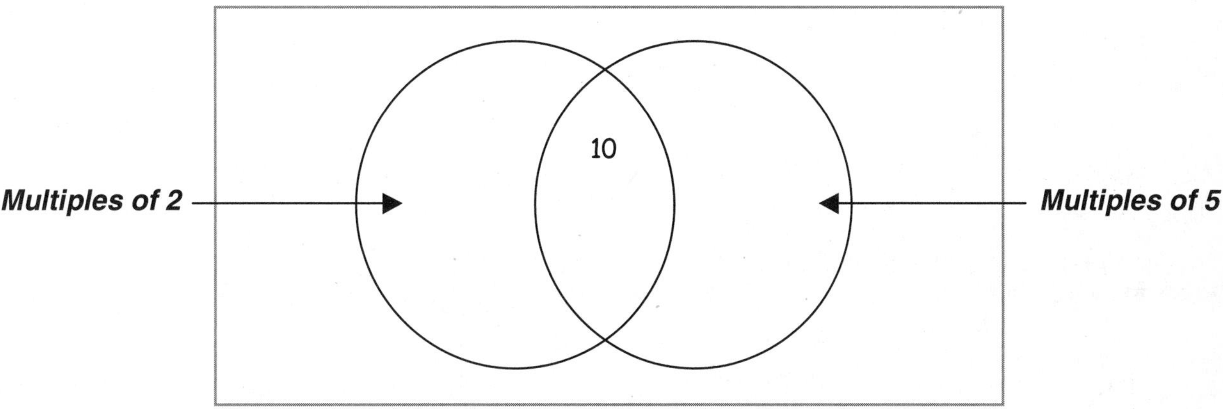

b) Think of two numbers from 50 to 100 that would go in the middle of the diagram: _____, _____

c) Think of two numbers from 50 to 100 that could not be placed in either circle: _____, _____

2. Sort the numbers below into the Venn diagram.
REMEMBER: A number is a multiple of 3 if the sum of its digits is a multiple of 3.

24	30	47	21	26	60	80	13	11
48	35	56	72	10	75	16	40	6

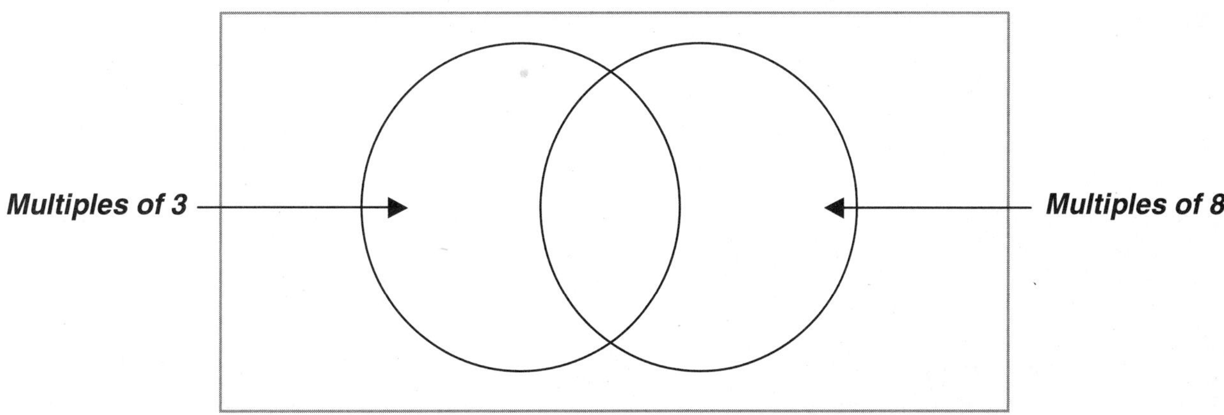

 No unauthorized copying

NS5-1: Place Value

1. Write the place value of the underlined digit.

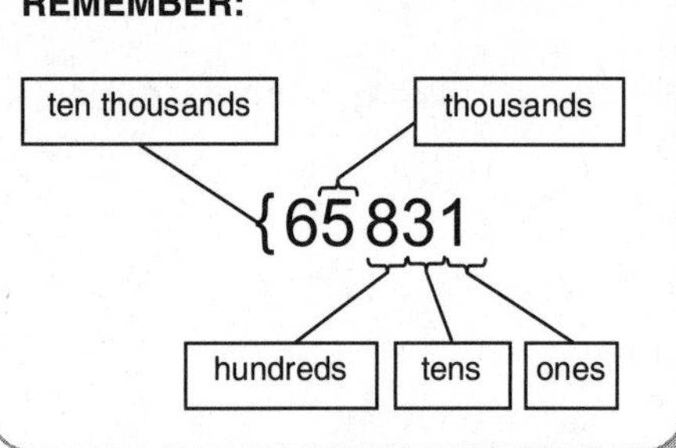

a) 23 862 tens　　b) 1 336

c) 2 378　　d) 67 225

e) 18 230　　f) 45 100

g) 6 214　　h) 21 813　　i) 20 745

j) 3 576　　k) 45 009　　l) 9 192

2. Give the place value of the number 5 in each number below.
HINT: First underline the 5.

a) 15 640　　b) 358　　c) 45 636

d) 2 415　　e) 51 188　　f) 451

g) 1 512　　h) 125　　i) 35 380

3. You can also write numbers using a place value chart.

Example:

In a place value chart, the number 52 953 is:

ten thousands	thousands	hundreds	tens	ones
5	2	9	5	3

Write the following numbers into the place value chart. The first one has been done for you.

	ten thousands	thousands	hundreds	tens	ones
a) 12 305	1	2	3	0	5
b) 45 001					
c) 3 699					
d) 19 053					
e) 546					
f) 20 127					

No unauthorized copying

NS5-1: Place Value *(continued)*

The number 23 967 is a **5-digit number.**

- The **digit** 2 stands for 20 000 – the **value** of the digit 2 is 20 000.
- The **digit** 3 stands for 3 000 – the **value** of the digit 3 is 3 000.
- The **digit** 9 stands for 900 – the **value** of the digit 9 is 900.
- The **digit** 6 stands for 60 – the **value** of the digit 6 is 60.
- The **digit** 7 stands for 7 – the **value** of the digit 7 is 7.

---

4. Write the **value** of each digit.

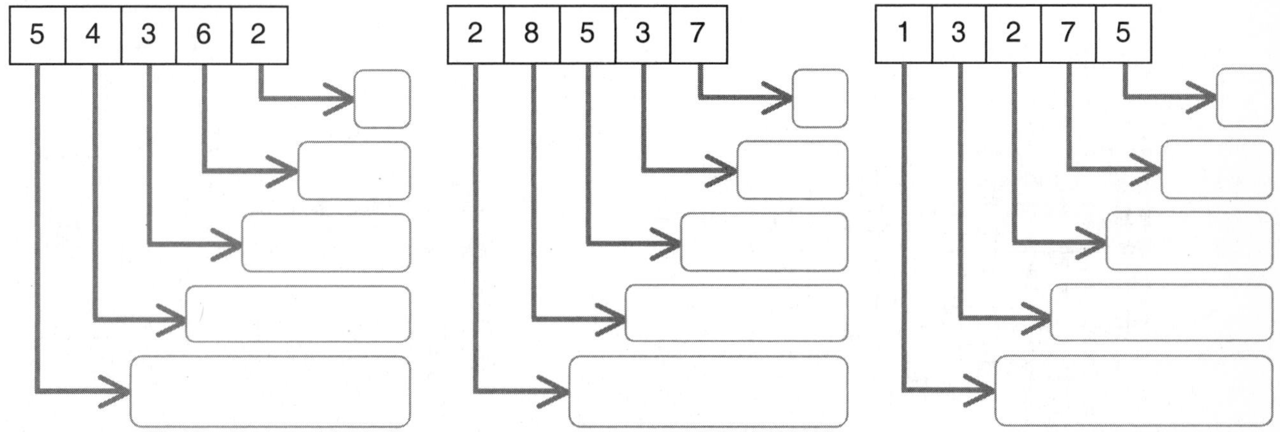

5. What does the digit 4 stand for in the number? The first one is done for you.

a) 847 — 40
b) 5243
c) 16423
d) 43 228
e) 4207
f) 3 742
g) 43092
h) 54283

6. Fill in the blank.

a) In the number 36 572, the **digit** 5 stands for ________________ .

b) In the number 24 236, the **digit** 3 stands for ________________ .

c) In the number 62 357, the **digit** 6 stands for ________________ .

d) In the number 8 021, the **value** of the digit 8 is ________________ .

e) In the number 26 539, the **value** of the digit 2 is ________________ .

f) In the number 7 253, the digit ________ is in the **thousands place**.

g) In the number 57 320, the digit ________ is in the **ten thousands place**.

No unauthorized copying

NS5-2: Representation with Base Ten Materials

1. Write the number in expanded word form (numerals and words).

Example:

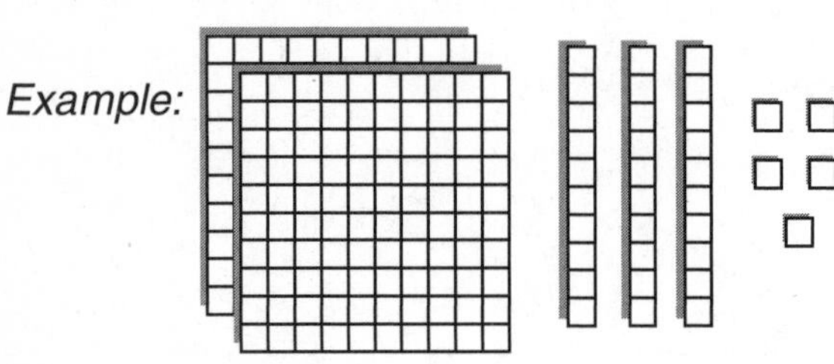

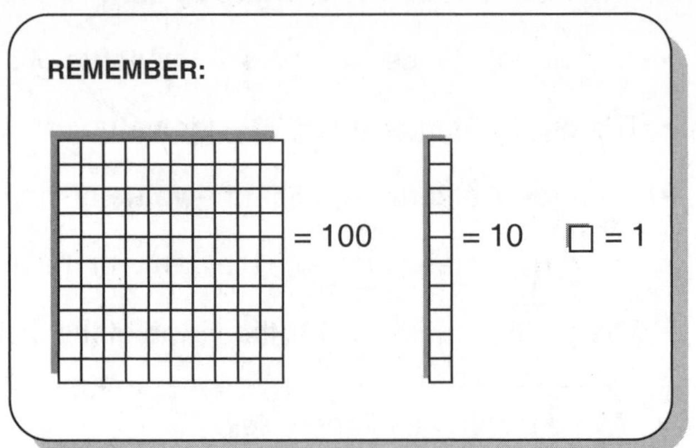

2 hundreds + 3 tens + 5 ones = 235

a)

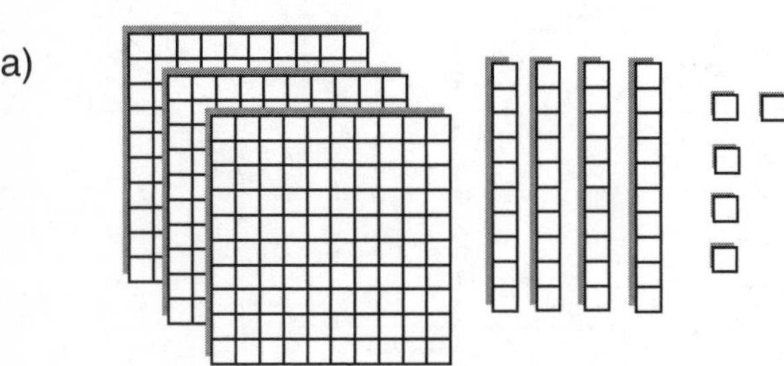

___ hundreds + ___ tens + ___ ones =

b)

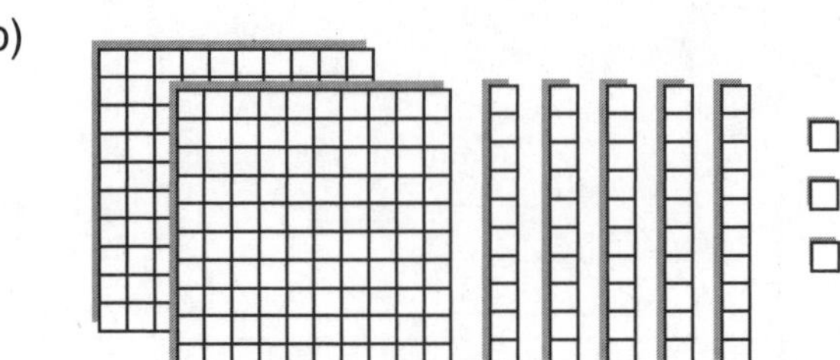

___ hundreds + ___ tens + ___ ones =

c)

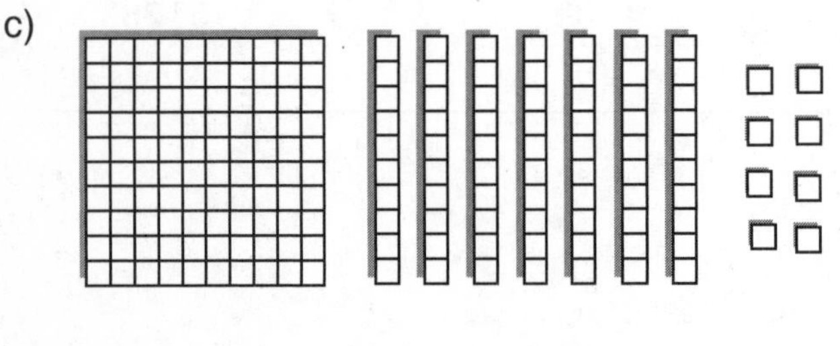

___ hundreds + ___ tens + ___ ones =

d)

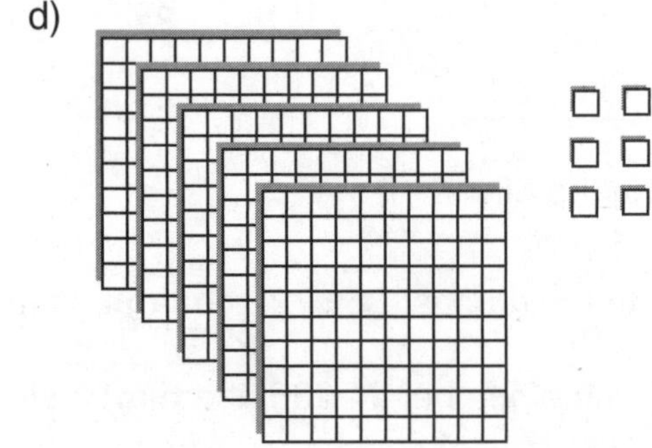

___ hundreds + ___ tens + ___ ones =

2. On grid paper, draw the base ten model for the number.

a) 114 b) 87 c) 68 d) 350 e) 249

No unauthorized copying

3. Write the number in expanded word form (numerals and words) and then as a numeral.

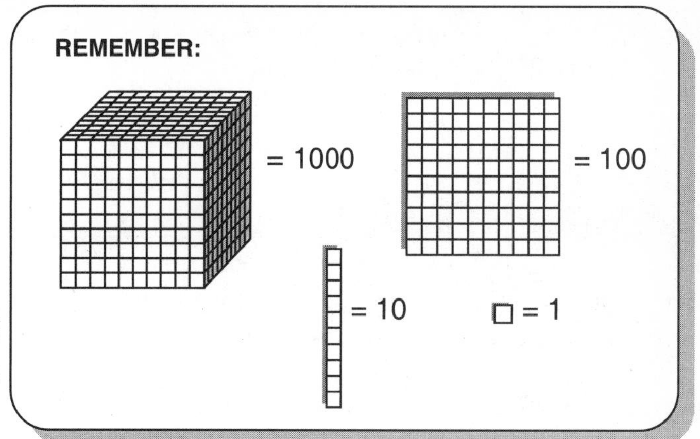

Example:

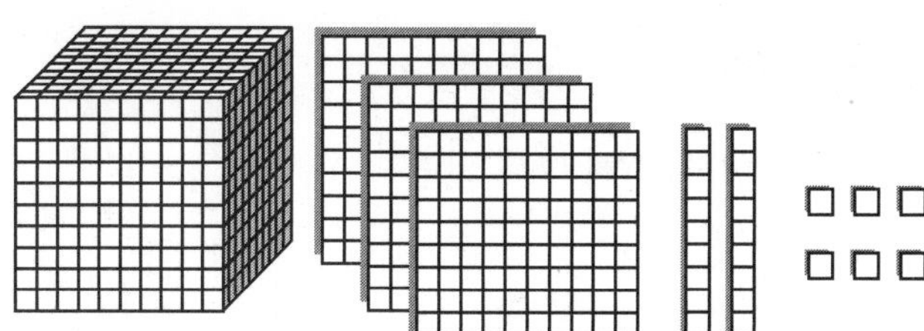

_1_ thousand + _3_ hundreds + _2_ tens + _6_ ones = 1 326

a) 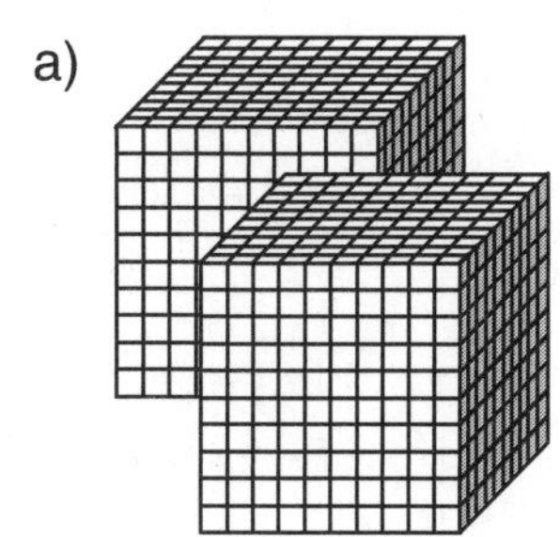 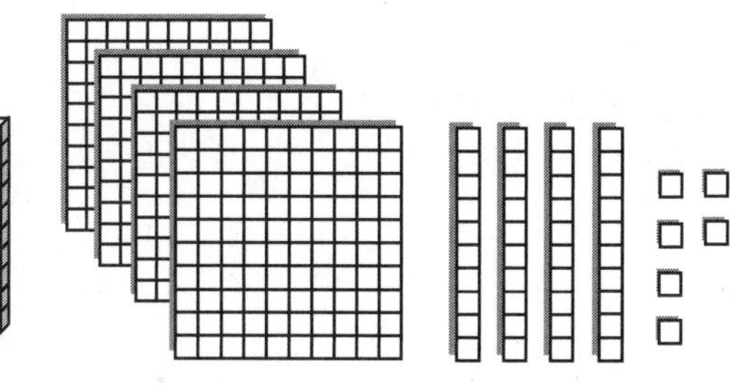

___ thousands + ___ hundreds + ___ tens + ___ ones = ______

b) 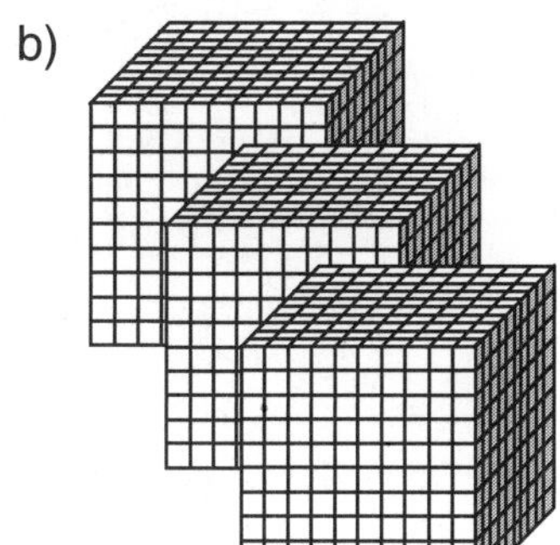 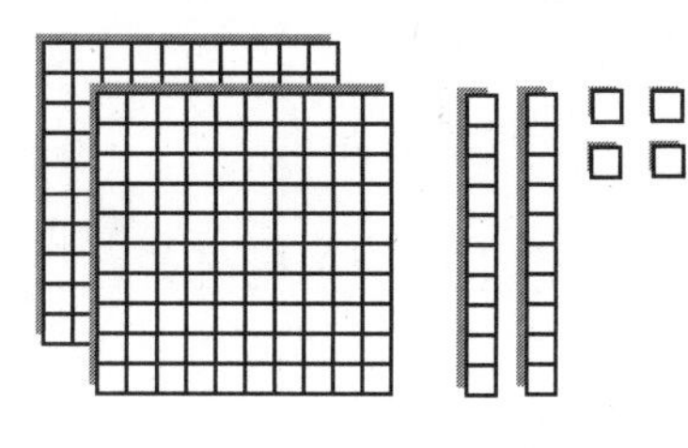

___ thousands + ___ hundreds + ___ tens + ___ ones = ______

c) 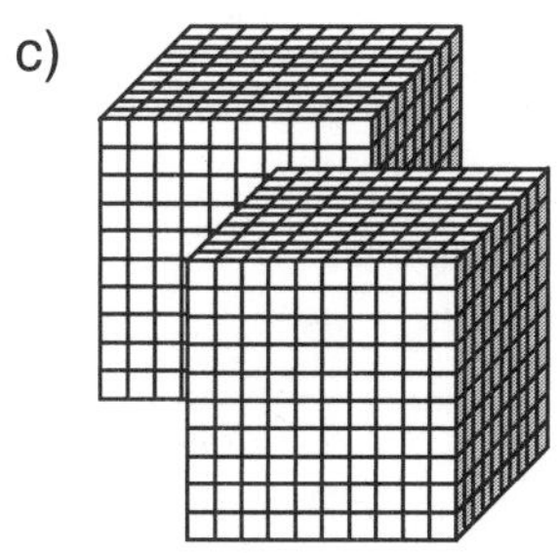 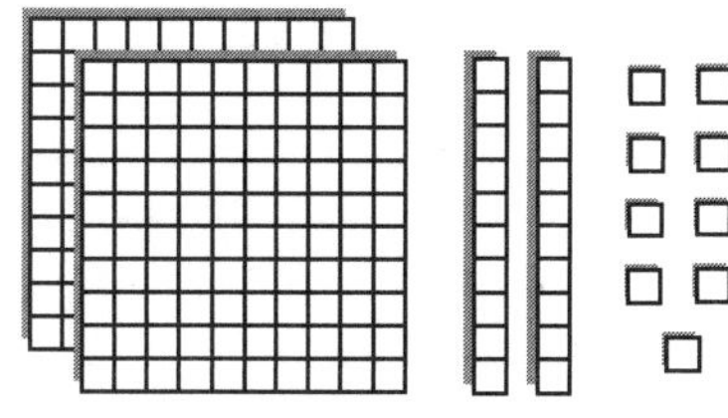

____ = ______

No unauthorized copying

NS5-2: Representation with Base Ten Materials *(continued)*

Steps for drawing a thousands cube:

Step 1: *Draw a square.*

Step 2: *Draw lines from its 3 vertices.*

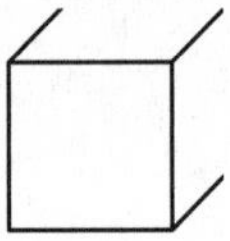

Step 3: *Join the lines.*

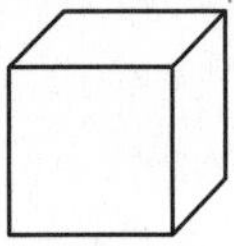

4. Represent the given numbers using base ten blocks in the place value chart. The first one has been started for you.

	Number	Thousands	Hundreds	Tens	Ones
a)	2 435	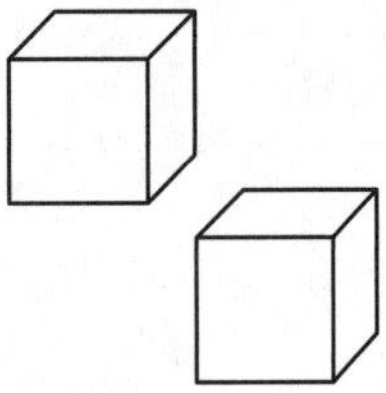	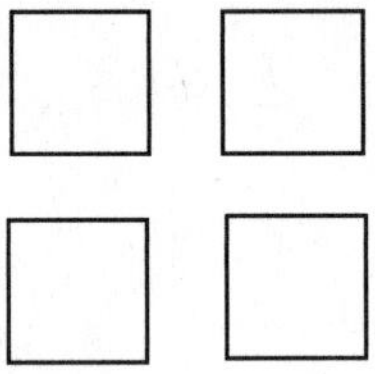		
b)	2 124				
c)	3 302				

5. Write the number for the given base ten blocks.

	Thousands	Hundreds	Tens	Ones	Number
a)	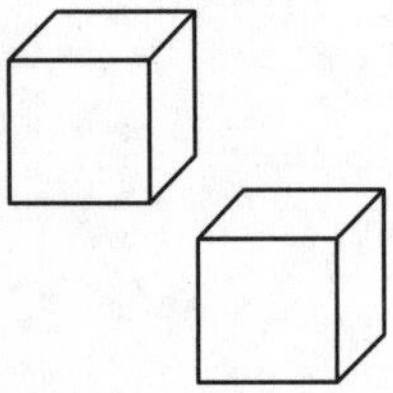	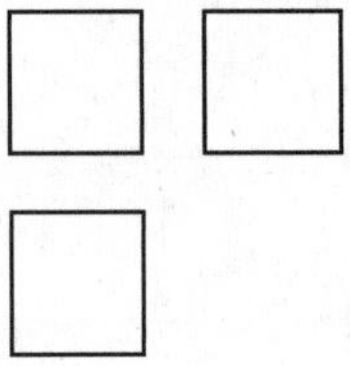	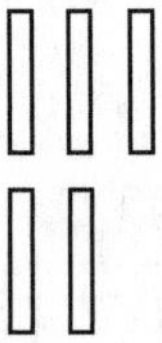		______
b)	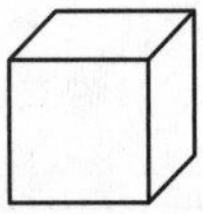	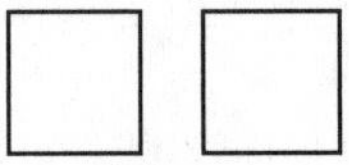	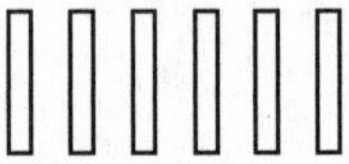		______

No unauthorized copying

NS5-3: Representation in Expanded Form

1. Expand the number using **numerals** and **words**. The first one is done for you.

   a) 43 427 = _4_ ten thousands + _3_ thousands + _4_ hundreds + _2_ tens + _7_ ones

   b) 25 312 = ____ ten thousands + ____ thousands + ____ hundreds + ____ tens + ____ ones

   c) 28 547 = ____

   ____

2. Write the number in expanded form (using **numerals**). The first one is done for you.

   a) 2613 = 2 000 + 600 + 10 + 3

   b) 27 = ____________________

   c) 48 = ____________________

   d) 1 232 = ____________________

   e) 36 273 = ____

   f) 19 384 = ____

   g) 49 805 = ____

3. Write the number for the sum.

   a) 4 000 + 900 + 50 + 3 = ____________________

   b) 2 000 + 30 + 2 = ____________________

   c) 60 000 + 3 000 + 900 + 90 + 7 = ____

   d) 50 000 + 30 + 4 = ____

   BONUS

   e) 500 + 2 000 + 80 + 90 000 + 8 = ____

   f) 40 000 + 500 +1 000 = ____________________

   g) 10 000 + 3 000 + 7 + 600 = ____________________

   h) 300 + 80 000 + 2 = ____________________

   i) 90 + 400 + 70 000 + 6 = ____________________

   j) 90 000 + 5 = ____________________

   k) 80 000 + 8 + 800 = ____________________

   l) 30 000 + 1 + 5 000 = ____________________

   m) 3 000 + 20 000 = ____________________

No unauthorized copying

4. Find the missing numbers.

a) 4 000 + 800 + ______ + 7 = 4 827

b) 3 000 + 200 + ______ + 5 = 3 275

c) 70 000 + 9 000 + ______ + 20 + 5 = 79 825

d) 60 000 + 5 000 + ______ + 60 + 3 = 65 263

e) 10 000 + 7 000 + 200 + 10 + ______ = 17 212

f) 20 000 + 6 000 + 300 + ______ + 8 = 26 328

BONUS

g) ______ + 300 = 7 300

h) 6 000 + ______ = 6 080

i) 30 000 + 9 000 + ______ + ______ = 39 260

j) 60 000 + ______ + ______ = 67 003

5. Write the number in expanded form. Then draw a base ten model for the number.

Example: 2 231 = 2000 + 200 + 30 + 1

a) 5 832 = ______ + ______ + ______ + ______

b) 1 054 = ______ + ______ + ______ + ______

6. Represent the number 1 365 in four different ways:
- by sketching a base ten model
- with number words
- in expanded form (2 ways)

7. How many hundreds blocks would you need to represent the number 100 000? Explain.

NS5-4: Comparing and Ordering Numbers

1. Write the **value** of each digit. Then complete the sentence.

a) 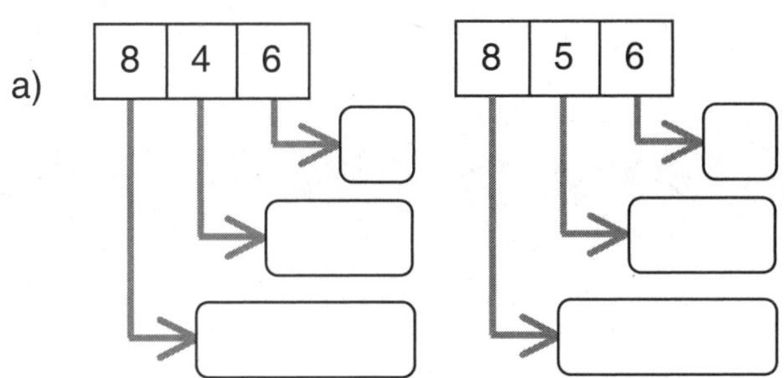

b) 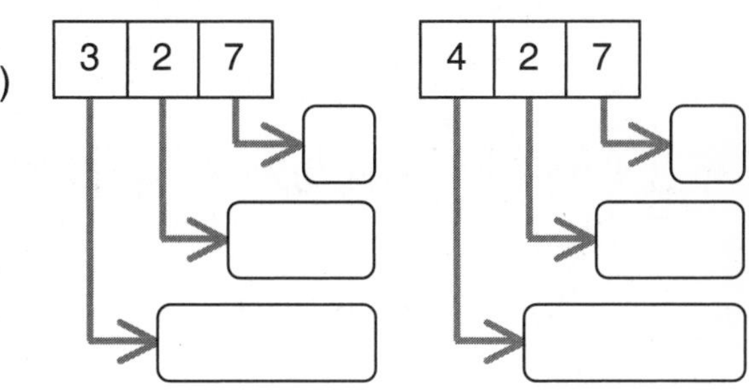

________ is greater than ________ ________ is greater than ________

2. Circle the pair of digits that are different.
Then write the greater number in the box.

a) 6 475
6 465
6475

b) 73 605
72 605

c) 14 852
14 858

d) 3832
4832

3. Read the numbers from left to right.
Circle the first pair of digits you find that are different.
Then write the greater number in the box.

a) 123
134

b) 276
374

c) 875
869

d) 238
221

e) 41 583
41 597

f) 28 293
28 542

g) 57 698
60 347

h) 62 149
62 148

4. Read the numbers from left to right.
Underline the first pair of digits you find that are different.
Then circle the greater number.

a) 32 547 32 562
b) 71 254 81 254
c) 37 123 37 321
d) 61 201 61 275
e) 63 235 63 233
f) 81 234 84 214
g) 32 153 31 278
h) 60 154 66 254
i) 96 567 96 528

 No unauthorized copying

NS5-4: Comparing and Ordering Numbers *(continued)*

5. The inequality sign **>** in **7 > 5** is read "seven is greater than five."
   The sign **<** in **8 < 10** is read "eight is less than ten."
   Write the correct inequality sign in the box.

a) 3 129	☐	4 703	b) 5 332	☐	6 012	c) 16 726	☐	16 591
d) 23 728	☐	23 729	e) 48 175	☐	48 123	f) 59 239	☐	60 009
g) 64 872	☐	64 871	h) 48 025	☐	4 952	i) 91 232	☐	9 327

6. Circle the greater number.

   a) 32 or thirty-five b) three hundred eighty-seven or 392 c) twenty-seven or 81

   d) one thousand one hundred six or 1 232 e) 50 273 or fifty thousand three hundred eighty-five

7. Mark each number on the number line. Then circle the greatest number.

   A 23 800 **B** 23 400 **C** 23 600

   23 000 ——————————————— 24 000

8. Fill in the boxes with any digit that will make the number statement true.

   a) ☐ [5] ☐ ☐ < [4] ☐ ☐ [1]

   b) [3] ☐ ☐ ☐ [1] > ☐ [8] ☐ ☐ [9]

9. Which number must be greater (no matter what digits are placed in the boxes)? Explain.

   ☐ 2 3 5 OR ☐ ☐ 1 2 3

10. How many numbers are greater than 59 990 and less than 60 000?

11. Buenos Aires, Argentina, is 9001 km away from Ottawa.
    Concepcion, Chile, is 9106 km away.
    Which city is farther from Ottawa?
    Explain how you know.

NS5-5: Differences of 10, 100, 1000 or 10 000

1. Write "10 more," "10 less," "100 more," or "100 less" in the blank.

a) 90 is _______________ than 80
b) 400 is _______________ than 500
c) 10 is _______________ than 20
d) 100 is _______________ than 90
e) 400 is _______________ than 300
f) 60 is _______________ than 70

2. Write "100 more," "100 less," "1 000 more," or "1 000 less" in the blank.

a) 6 000 is _______________ than 5 000
b) 12 000 is _______________ than 13 000
c) 4 000 is _______________ than 5 000
d) 800 is _______________ than 900
e) 600 is _______________ than 500
f) 9 000 is _______________ than 8 000

3. Write "1 000 more," "1 000 less," "10 000 more," or "10 000 less" in the blank.

a) 6 000 is _______________ than 5 000
b) 12 000 is _______________ than 13 000
c) 30 000 is _______________ than 40 000
d) 50 000 is _______________ than 40 000
e) 6 000 is _______________ than 7 000
f) 10 000 is _______________ than 20 000
g) 80 000 is _______________ than 70 000
h) 9 000 is _______________ than 10 000

4. Circle the pair of digits that are different. Then fill in the blank.

a) 72 652
72 752

72 652 is ___100 less___ than 72 752

b) 91 385
91 485

91 385 is _______________ than 91 485

c) 43 750
33 750

43 750 is _______________ than 33 750

d) 62 250
63 250

62 250 is _______________ than 63 250

e) 38 405
38 415

38 405 is _______________ than 38 415

f) 85 871
85 872

85 871 is _______________ than 85 872

No unauthorized copying

NS5-5: Differences of 10, 100, 1000 or 10 000 *(continued)*

5. Fill in the blank.

a) _________ is 10 more than 325
b) _________ is 10 less than 1 562
c) _________ is 100 more than 592
d) _________ is 100 less than 4 135
e) _________ is 100 more than 6 821
f) _________ is 100 less than 3 295
g) _________ is 1 000 less than 8 305
h) _________ is 1 000 more than 4 253
i) _________ is 10 000 less than 73 528
j) _________ is 1 000 less than 62 381

6. Fill in the blank.

a) 234 + 10 = _________
b) 2 382 + 10 = _________
c) 19 035 + 10 = _________
d) 21 270 + 100 = _________
e) 3 283 + 100 = _________
f) 7 325 + 1 000 = _________
g) 357 – 10 = _________
h) 683 – 10 = _________
i) 837 – 100 = _________
j) 2 487 – 100 = _________
k) 1 901 – 100 = _________
l) 4 316 – 1 000 = _________
m) 3 301 – 10 = _________
n) 12 507 – 10 000 = _________
o) 39 397 + 10 = _________

7. Fill in the blank.

a) 385 + _________ = 395
b) 608 + _________ = 708
c) 1 483 + _________ = 1 493
d) 2 617 + _________ = 2 717
e) 43 210 + _________ = 44 210
f) 26 287 + _________ = 26 387
g) 1 287 – _________ = 1 187
h) 325 – _________ = 315
i) 14 392 – _________ = 14 292
j) 87 001 – _________ = 86 001
k) 86 043 – _________ = 85 943
l) 61 263 – _________ = 51 263

8. Continue the number pattern.

a) 8 508, 8 518, 8 528, _________, _________
b) 35 730, 36 730, 37 730, _________, _________
c) 41 482, 41 492, _________, 41 512, _________
d) 28 363, _________, _________, 28 393, 28 403

9. Circle the pair of digits that are different. Then fill in the blanks.

a) 45241
45231

45 231 is 10
less than 45 241

b) 82350
92350

_________ is _________
more than _________

c) 68254
69254

_________ is _________
less than _________

NS5-6: Comparing Numbers (Advanced)

1. Write the number represented by the base ten materials in each box. Then circle the greater number.

a) i)

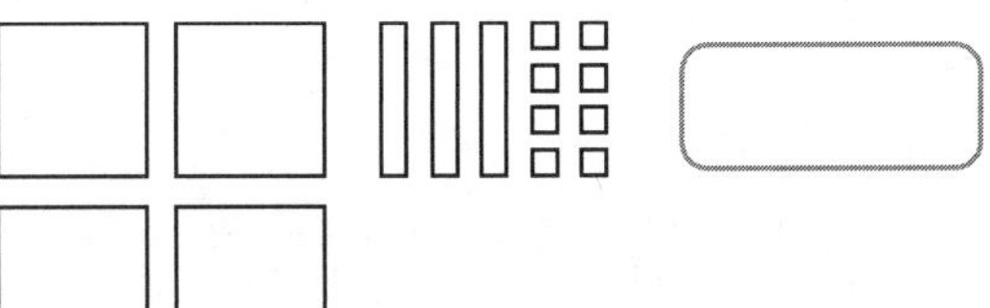

ii)

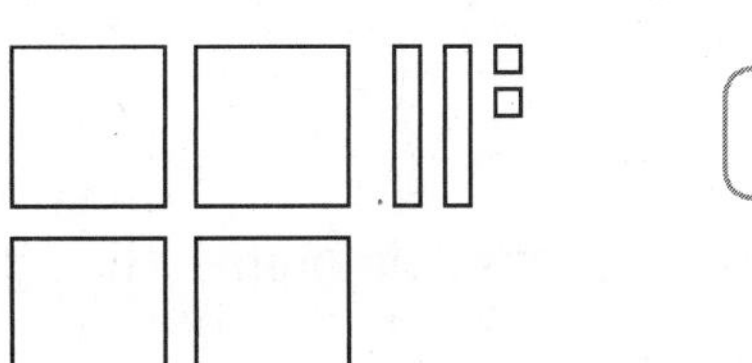

b) i)

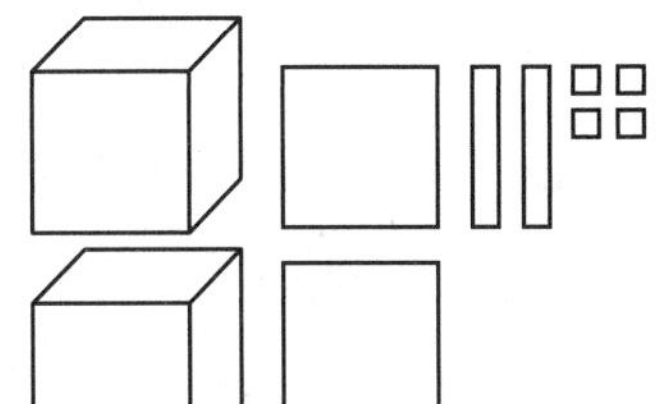

ii)

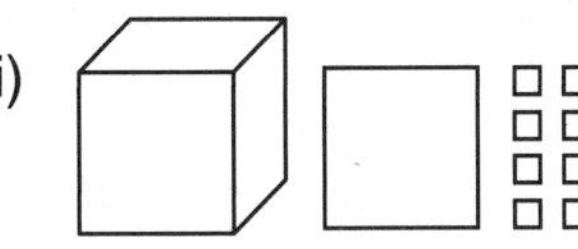

2. List all the two-digit numbers you can make using the digits provided. Then circle the greatest number.

a) 7, 8, and 9

b) 3, 4, and 0

3. What is the greatest number less than 1000 whose digits are all the same? ____________________

4. What is the greatest possible number you can create with:

a) three digits ______________ b) four digits ______________ c) five digits ______________

5. Identify the greater number by writing > or <.

a) 37 432 ☐ 37 512

b) 87 386 ☐ 87 384

c) 17 329 ☐ 8 338

d) 63 923 ☐ 62 857

No unauthorized copying

NS5-6: Comparing Numbers (Advanced) *(continued)*

6. Create the greatest possible **four-digit** number using the digits given.

a) 4, 3, 2, 6 ☐ b) 7, 8, 9, 4 ☐ c) 0, 4, 1, 2 ☐

7. Create the greatest possible number using these digits. Use each digit only once.

a) 3, 4, 1, 2, 8 ______ b) 2, 8, 9, 1, 5 ______ c) 3, 6, 1, 5, 4 ______

8. Use the digits (once) to create the greatest number, the least number, and a number in between.

	Digits	Greatest Number	Number in Between	Least Number
a)	8 5 7 2 1			
b)	2 1 5 3 9			
c)	3 0 1 5 3			

9. Arrange the numbers in order, starting with the **least** number.

a) 3 257, 3 352, 3 183

______ , ______ , ______

b) 17251, 17385, 17256

______ , ______ , ______

c) 87 500, 87 498, 87 499

______ , ______ , ______

d) 36725, 3281, 93859

______ , ______ , ______

e) 60 052, 60 001, 60 021

______ , ______ , ______

f) 273, 5 891, 17

______ , ______ , ______

10. Using the digits 0, 1, 2, 3, and 4, create a number greater than 32 000 and less than 34 000.

____

11. Using the digits 3, 5, 6, 7, and 8, create an even number greater than 85 000 and less than 87 000.

____

12. What digit can be substituted for ☐ to make the statement true?

a) 32 ☐ 56 is between 32 675 and 32 854 b) 68 ☐ 32 is between 68 379 and 68 464

No unauthorized copying

NS5-7: Regrouping

Gwendolyne has 2 hundreds blocks, 16 tens blocks, and 9 ones blocks.
She regroups 10 tens blocks as 1 hundreds block.

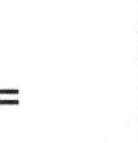
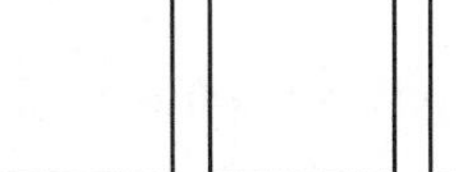

2 hundreds + 16 tens + 9 ones = 3 hundreds + 6 tens + 9 ones

1. Regroup 10 ones blocks as 1 tens block.

a) 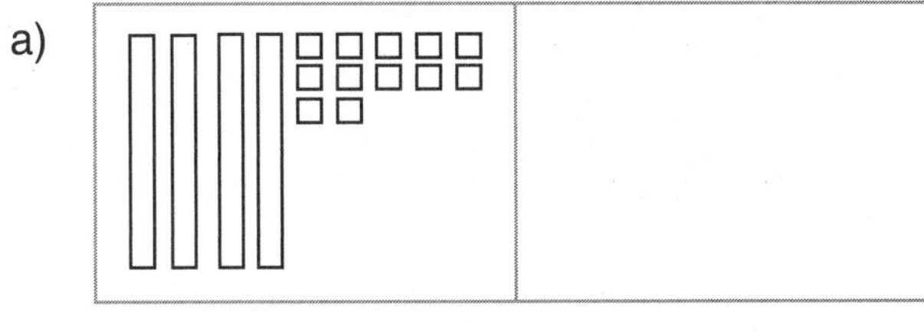

___ tens + ___ ones = ___ tens + ___ ones

b) 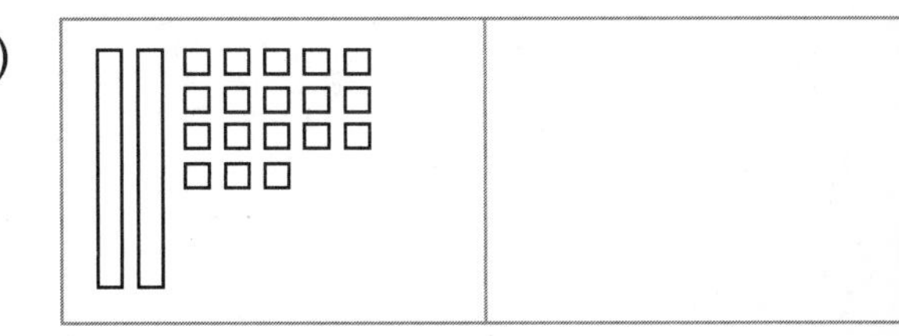

___ tens + ___ ones = ___ tens + ___ ones

2. Regroup ones as tens.

a) 34 ones = 3 tens + 4 ones b) 73 ones = ___ tens + ___ ones c) 26 ones = ___ tens + ___ ones

d) 80 ones = ___ tens + ___ ones e) 78 ones = ___ tens + ___ ones f) 81 ones = ___ tens + ___ ones

g) 19 ones = ___ tens + ___ ones h) 57 ones = ___ tens + ___ ones i) 89 ones = ___ tens + ___ ones

3. Complete the chart by regrouping 10 tens as 1 hundred.

a)

hundreds	tens
6	23
6 +2 = 8	3

b)

hundreds	tens
5	32

c)

hundreds	tens
4	11

d)

hundreds	tens
8	19

e)

hundreds	tens
1	84

f)

hundreds	tens
7	20

4. Regroup tens as hundreds or ones as tens.

a) 5 hundreds + 4 tens + 24 ones = 5 hundreds + 6 tens + 4 ones

b) 7 hundreds + 0 tens + 47 ones = ______________________

c) 3 hundreds + 57 tens + 8 ones = ______________________

 No unauthorized copying

Ara has 1 thousands block, 12 hundreds blocks, 1 tens block, and 2 ones blocks.
She regroups 10 hundreds blocks as 1 thousands block.

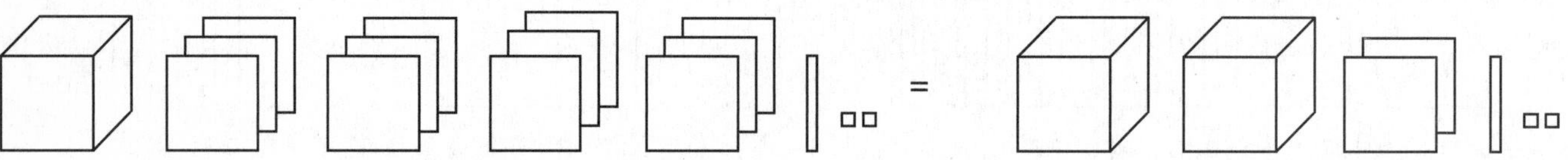

1 thousand + 12 hundreds + 1 ten + 2 ones = 2 thousands + 2 hundreds + 1 ten + 2 ones

5. Complete the chart by regrouping 10 hundreds as 1 thousand.

a)

thousands	hundreds
4	13
4 + 1 = 5	3

b)

thousands	hundreds
2	17

c)

thousands	hundreds
8	10

6. Regroup 10 hundreds as 1 thousand. The first one has been done for you.

a) 6 thousands + 13 hundreds + 4 tens + 8 ones = __7__ thousands + __3__ hundreds + __4__ tens + __8__ ones

b) 2 thousands + 32 hundreds + 1 tens + 4 ones = ____ thousands + ____ hundreds + ____ tens + ____ ones

c) 5 thousands + 10 hundreds + 3 tens + 1 ones = ________________

____

7. Regroup thousands as ten thousands, hundreds as thousands, tens as hundreds, or ones as tens.

a) 2 thousands + 25 hundreds + 4 tens + 2 ones = ____ thousands + ____ hundreds + ____ tens + ____ ones

b) 3 thousands + 7 hundreds + 24 tens + 5 ones = ________________

____

c) 4 ten thousands + 25 thousands + 6 hundreds + 1 ten + 45 ones = ________________

____

8. Karim wants to build a model of four thousand three hundred forty-six.
He has 3 thousands blocks, 13 hundreds blocks, and 50 ones blocks.
Can he build the model? Explain.

No unauthorized copying

NS5-8: Adding with Regrouping

1. Add the numbers by drawing a picture and by adding the digits.

a) **14 + 37**

	with base ten materials		with numerals	
	tens	ones	tens	ones
14			1	4
37			3	7
sum		regroup 10 ones as a ten	4	11
	after regrouping		5	1

b) **35 + 27**

	with base ten materials		with numerals	
	tens	ones	tens	ones

2. Add the ones digits. Show how you would regroup 10 ones as 1 ten.

a) tens go here: 1
$$\begin{array}{r} 14 \\ +\ 19 \\ \hline 3 \end{array}$$
ones go here

b) $\begin{array}{r} 36 \\ +\ 49 \\ \hline \end{array}$ c) $\begin{array}{r} 64 \\ +\ 28 \\ \hline \end{array}$ d) $\begin{array}{r} 35 \\ +\ 45 \\ \hline \end{array}$ e) $\begin{array}{r} 26 \\ +\ 19 \\ \hline \end{array}$

3. Add the numbers by regrouping.

a) $\begin{array}{r} ^{1}\ \ \\ 25 \\ +\ 16 \\ \hline 41 \end{array}$ b) $\begin{array}{r} 19 \\ +\ 32 \\ \hline \end{array}$ c) $\begin{array}{r} 64 \\ +\ 29 \\ \hline \end{array}$ d) $\begin{array}{r} 77 \\ +\ 18 \\ \hline \end{array}$ e) $\begin{array}{r} 36 \\ +\ 36 \\ \hline \end{array}$

f) $\begin{array}{r} 85 \\ +\ 6 \\ \hline \end{array}$ g) $\begin{array}{r} 29 \\ +\ 32 \\ \hline \end{array}$ h) $\begin{array}{r} 43 \\ +\ 18 \\ \hline \end{array}$ i) $\begin{array}{r} 21 \\ +\ 59 \\ \hline \end{array}$ j) $\begin{array}{r} 78 \\ +\ 28 \\ \hline \end{array}$

No unauthorized copying

NS5-9: Adding 3-Digit Numbers

Allen adds 243 + 381 using base ten materials.

243	=	2 hundred	+	4 tens	+	3 ones
+ 381	=	3 hundreds	+	8 tens	+	1 one
	=	5 hundreds	+	12 tens	+	4 ones

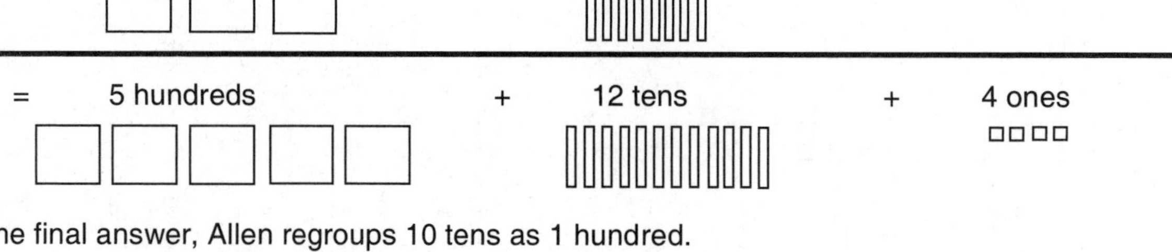

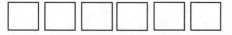

Then, to get the final answer, Allen regroups 10 tens as 1 hundred.

= 6 hundreds + 2 tens + 4 ones

1. Add the numbers using base ten materials or a picture (and record your work).

572	=	_____ hundreds +	_____ tens +	_____ ones
+ 251	=	_____ hundreds +	_____ tens +	_____ ones
	=	_____ hundreds +	_____ tens +	_____ ones
after regrouping	=	_____ hundreds +	_____ tens +	_____ ones

2. Add. You will need to regroup. The first one is started for you.

a) 258 + 371 = (carry 1) 29

b) 361 + 496

c) 823 + 96

d) 950 + 599

e) 643 + 264

3. Add, regrouping where necessary.

a) 282 + 371

b) 156 + 557

c) 642 + 189

d) 390 + 259

e) 856 + 106

f) 289 + 444

4. Add by lining the numbers up correctly in the grid. The first one has been started for you.

a) 643 + 182

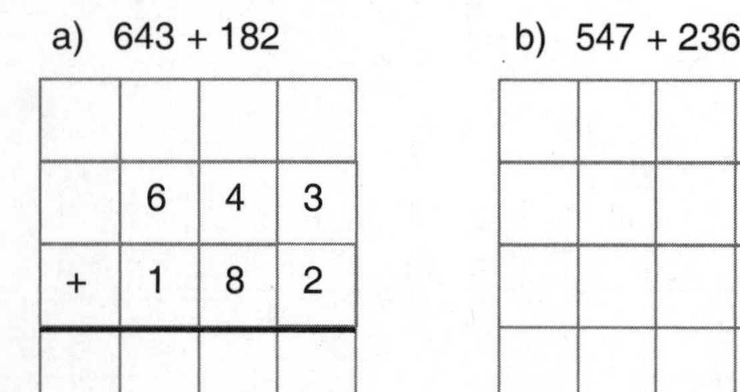

	6	4	3
+	1	8	2

b) 547 + 236

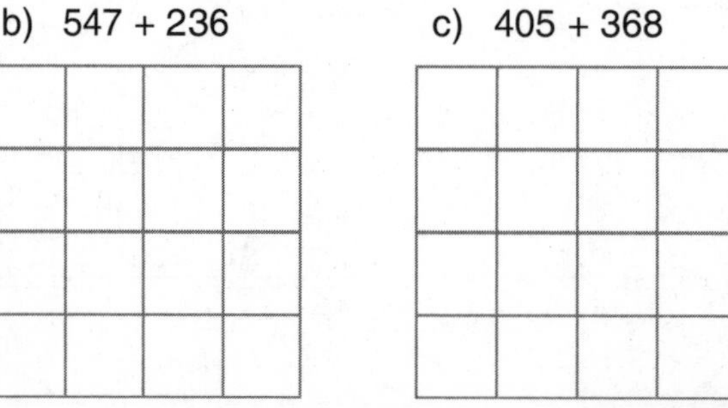

c) 405 + 368

d) 256 + 92

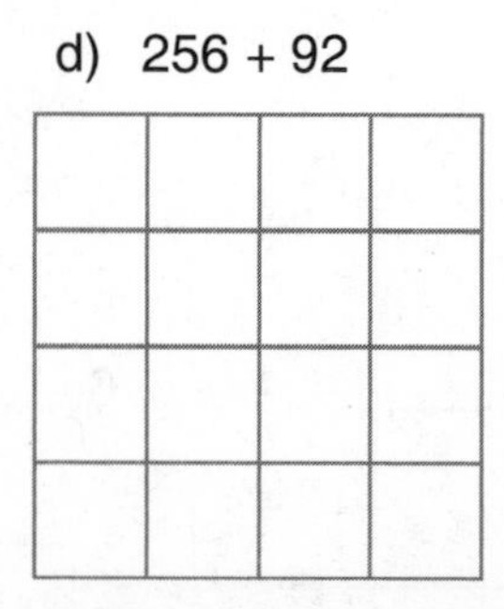

No unauthorized copying

NS5-10: Adding 4 and 5-Digit Numbers

Louisa adds 2 862 + 2 313 using base ten materials.

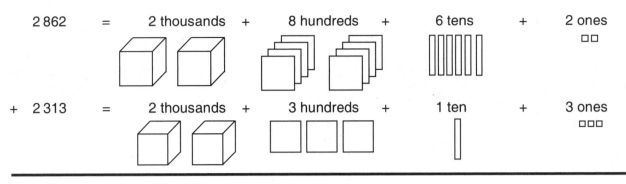

2 862	=	2 thousands	+	8 hundreds	+	6 tens	+	2 ones
+ 2 313	=	2 thousands	+	3 hundreds	+	1 ten	+	3 ones
	=	4 thousands	+	11 hundreds	+	7 tens	+	5 ones

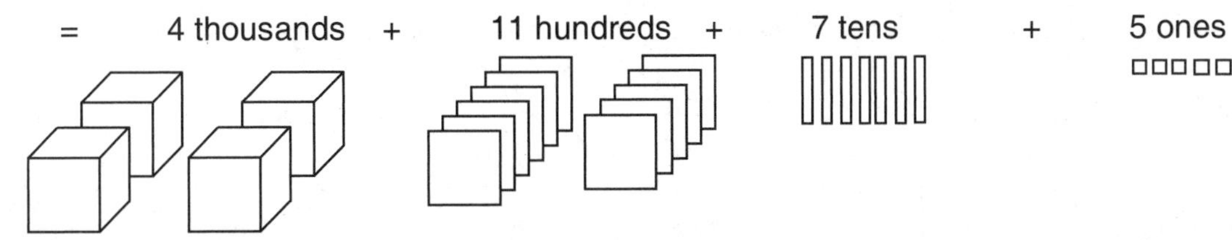

Then, to get the final answer, Louisa regroups 10 hundreds as 1 thousand.

=	5 thousands	+	1 hundred	+	7 tens	+	5 ones

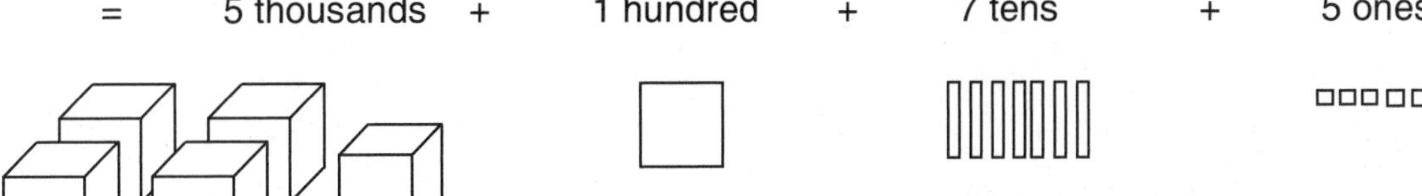

1. Add the numbers using base ten materials or by drawing a picture in a notebook.

6 826	=	_____	thousands	+ _____	hundreds	+ _____	tens	+ _____	ones
+ 2 543	=	_____	thousands	+ _____	hundreds	+ _____	tens	+ _____	ones
	=	_____	thousands	+ _____	hundreds	+ _____	tens	+ _____	ones
after regrouping	=	_____	thousands	+ _____	hundreds	+ _____	tens	+ _____	ones

2. Add. You will need to regroup the hundreds as thousands.

a)
```
   2 3 7 6
 + 3 8 2 3
 ---------
     1 9 9
```

b)
```
   5 8 2 6
 + 2 7 5 2
 ---------
```

c)
```
   7 5 6 9
 + 1 8 3 0
 ---------
```

d)
```
   7 6 5 6
 + 1 5 2 3
 ---------
```

e)
```
   2 9 5 1
 + 4 5 2 6
 ---------
```

3. Add. You will need to regroup the tens as hundreds.

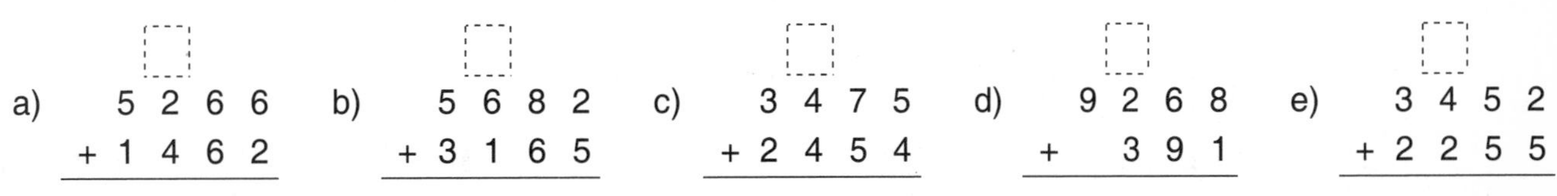

a)
```
   5 2 6 6
 + 1 4 6 2
 ---------
```

b)
```
   5 6 8 2
 + 3 1 6 5
 ---------
```

c)
```
   3 4 7 5
 + 2 4 5 4
 ---------
```

d)
```
   9 2 6 8
 +   3 9 1
 ---------
```

e)
```
   3 4 5 2
 + 2 2 5 5
 ---------
```


No unauthorized copying

4. Add (regrouping when necessary).

a) $\begin{array}{r} 3562 \\ +\ 3624 \\ \hline \end{array}$ b) $\begin{array}{r} 2261 \\ +\ 6925 \\ \hline \end{array}$ c) $\begin{array}{r} 7567 \\ +\ 1382 \\ \hline \end{array}$ d) $\begin{array}{r} 2365 \\ +\ 5492 \\ \hline \end{array}$ e) $\begin{array}{r} 4847 \\ +\ 2005 \\ \hline \end{array}$

f) $\begin{array}{r} 8691 \\ +\ 1222 \\ \hline \end{array}$ g) $\begin{array}{r} 5432 \\ +\ 1834 \\ \hline \end{array}$ h) $\begin{array}{r} 4485 \\ +\ 4814 \\ \hline \end{array}$ i) $\begin{array}{r} 9205 \\ +\ \ \ 758 \\ \hline \end{array}$ j) $\begin{array}{r} 1567 \\ +\ 7291 \\ \hline \end{array}$

5. Add by lining the numbers up correctly in the grid. In some questions you may have to regroup twice.

a) 8 624 + 1 192 b) 2 895 + 2 384 c) 2 469 + 62 d) 5 263 + 3 953

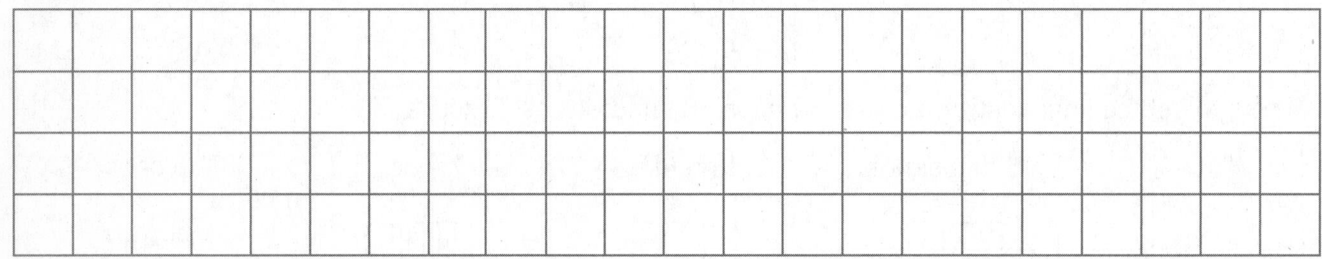

6. Add (regrouping where necessary).

a) $\begin{array}{r} 5263 \\ +\ 1552 \\ \hline \end{array}$ b) $\begin{array}{r} 28547 \\ +\ 34282 \\ \hline \end{array}$ c) $\begin{array}{r} 45489 \\ +\ 26401 \\ \hline \end{array}$ d) $\begin{array}{r} 36179 \\ +\ 33452 \\ \hline \end{array}$

7. A **palindrome** is a number that reads the same forward and backward.

For instance: 363, 51 815, and 2 375 732 are all palindromes.

For each number, follow the steps that are shown for the number 124.

Step 1: *Reverse the digits: 124 —> 421*

Step 2: *Add the two numbers: 124 + 421 = 545*

Step 3: *If the number you create is not a palindrome, repeat steps 1 and 2 with the new number. Most numbers will eventually become palindromes if you keep repeating these steps.*

Create palindromes from the following numbers.

a) 216 b) 154 c) 342 d) 23 153 e) 371 f) 258 g) 1 385

NS5-11: Subtraction

Ken subtracts 34 – 16 using base ten blocks.

Step 1:
Ken represents 34 with base ten materials.

tens	ones
3	4
▯▯▯	▫▫▫▫

Here is how Ken uses numeral to show his work:

$$\begin{array}{r} 34 \\ -\ 16 \\ \hline \end{array}$$

Step 2:
6 (the ones digit of 16) is greater than 4 (the ones digit of 34) so Ken exchanges a tens block for 10 ones.

tens	ones
2	14
▯▯	▫▫▫▫▫ ▫▫▫▫▫ ▫▫▫▫

Here is how Ken shows the regrouping:

$$\begin{array}{r} {\scriptstyle 2\ 14} \\ \not{3}\not{4} \\ -\ 1\ 6 \\ \hline \end{array}$$

Step 3:
Ken subtracts 16 (he takes away 1 tens block and 6 ones).

tens	ones
1	8
▯	▫▫▫▫▫ ▫▫▫

And now Ken can subtract 14 – 6 ones and 2 – 1 tens:

$$\begin{array}{r} {\scriptstyle 2\ 14} \\ \not{3}\not{4} \\ -\ 1\ 6 \\ \hline 1\ 8 \end{array}$$

---

1. Show how Ken can subtract by regrouping a tens block as 10 ones.

a) **66 – 37**

tens	ones
6	6
▯▯▯▯▯▯	▫▫▫▫▫▫

tens	ones
5	16
▯▯▯▯▯	▫▫▫▫▫▫▫▫▫▫▫▫▫▫▫▫

	6	6
–	3	7

	5	16
	~~6~~	~~6~~
–	3	7

b) **75 – 46**

tens	ones
7	5
▯▯▯▯▯▯▯	▫▫▫▫▫

tens	ones

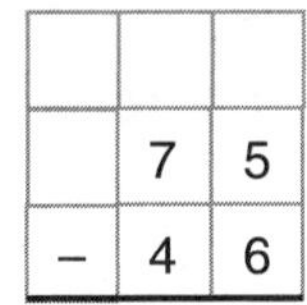

	7	5
–	4	6

	7	5
–	4	6

c) **34 – 16**

tens	ones
3	4
▯▯▯	▫▫▫▫

tens	ones

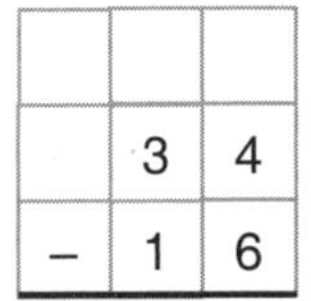

	3	4
–	1	6

	3	4
–	1	6

d) **77 – 29**

tens	ones
7	7
▯▯▯▯▯▯▯	▫▫▫▫▫▫▫

tens	ones

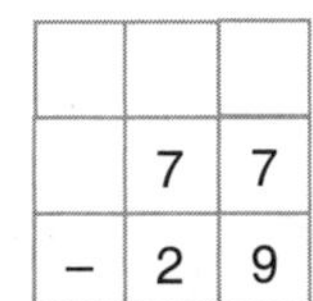

	7	7
–	2	9

	7	7
–	2	9

No unauthorized copying

2. Subtract by regrouping.

a)

	4	16
	~~5~~	~~6~~
−	1	8
	3	8

b)

	7	8
−	3	9

c) 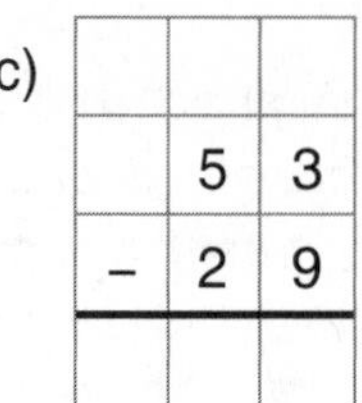

d) 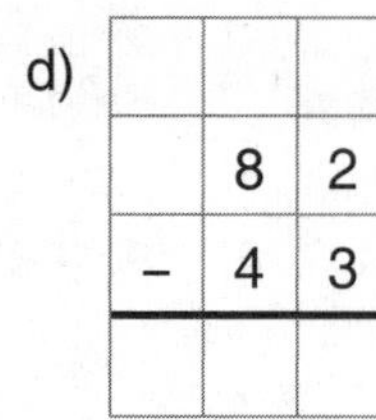

e) 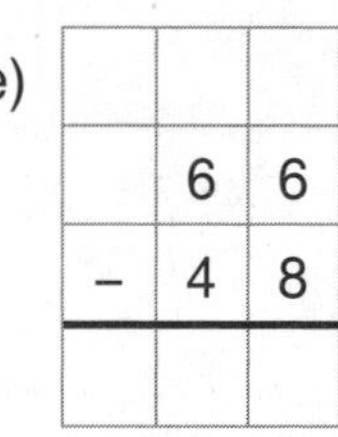

3. For the questions where you need to regroup, write "Help!" in the space provided. How do you know?

a) 46 − 28 Help! 6 is less than 8

b) 52 − 26 ________

c) 73 − 41 ________

d) 32 − 19 ________

e) 56 − 22 ________

f) 95 − 58 ________

g) 66 − 13 ________

h) 24 − 9 ________

i) 84 − 26 ________

j) 79 − 27 ________

k) 52 − 43 ________

l) 41 − 17 ________

4. To subtract 456 − 283, Laura regroups 1 hundreds block as 10 tens blocks.

hundreds	tens	ones
4	5	6

hundreds	tens	ones
3	15	6

hundreds	tens	ones
1	7	3

Subtract by regrouping **hundreds** as tens. The first one has been started for you.

a) 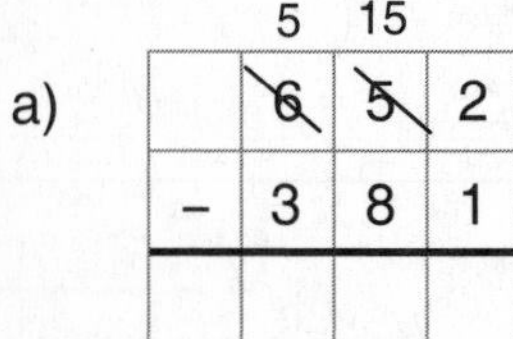

b) 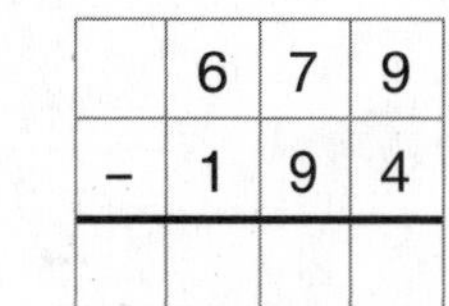

c) 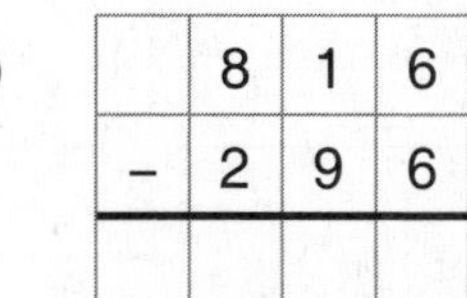

d)

	9	5	8
−	7	6	5

NS5-11: Subtraction *(continued)*

5. Subtract by regrouping the **tens**. The first one has been started for you.

a) 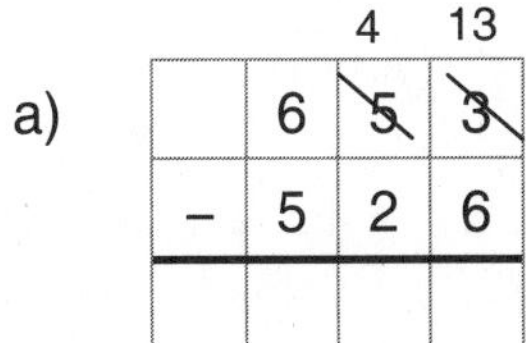

b) 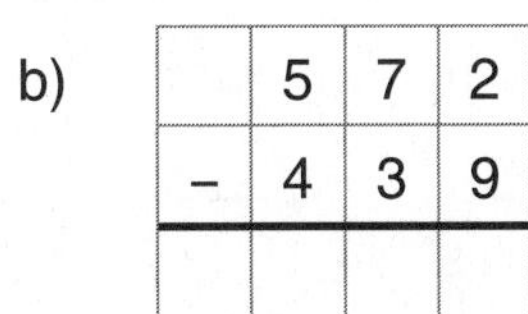

c) 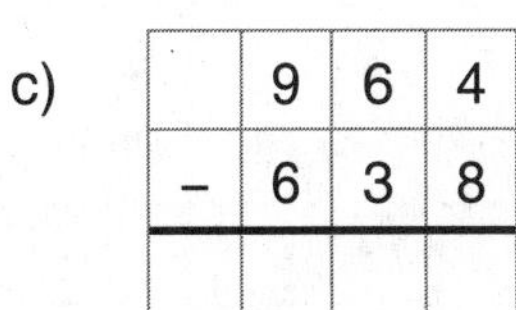

d) 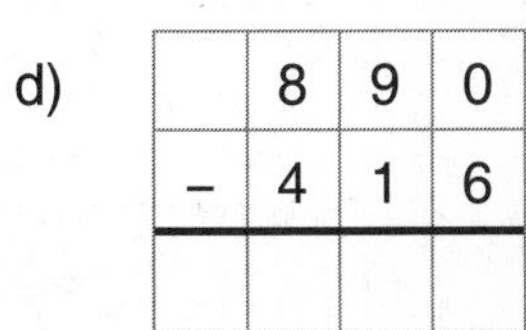

6. For the following questions, you will have to regroup **twice**.

Example:

Step 1:	Step 2:	Step 3:	Step 4:	Step 5:
3 12	3 12	13 6 ~~3~~ 12	13 6 ~~3~~ 12	13 6 ~~3~~ 12
7 ~~4~~ ~~2~~	7 ~~4~~ ~~2~~	~~7~~ ~~4~~ ~~2~~	~~7~~ ~~4~~ ~~2~~	~~7~~ ~~4~~ ~~2~~
– 2 7 4	– 2 7 4	– 2 7 4	– 2 7 4	– 2 7 4
	8	8	6 8	4 6 8

a) 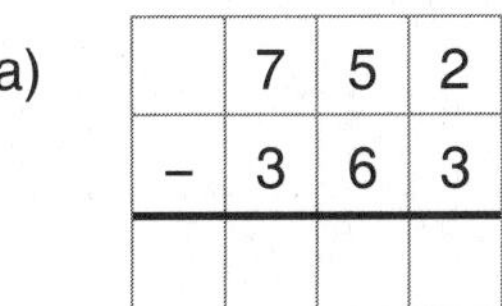

b)

	8	2	3
–	1	7	5

c)

	3	0	4
–		2	7

d)

	9	8	3
–	5	8	4

7. To subtract 4 135 – 2 314, Laura exchanges 1 thousands block for 10 hundreds blocks.

thousands	hundreds	tens	ones
4	1	3	5

thousands	hundreds	tens	ones
3	11	3	5

thousands	hundreds	tens	ones
1	8	2	1

Subtract by regrouping thousands as hundreds. The first one has been done for you.

a) 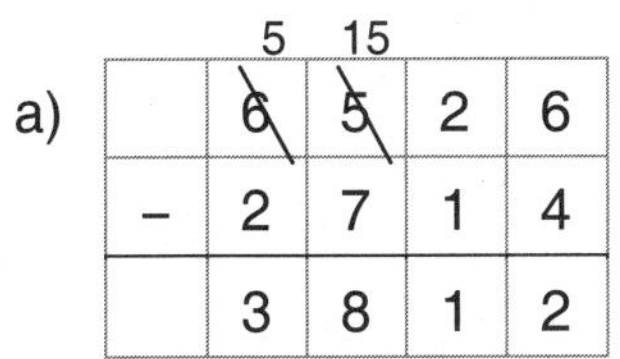

b) 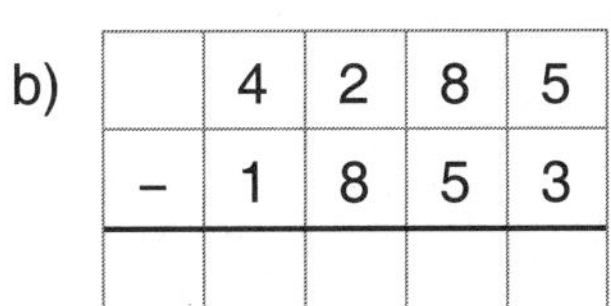

c) 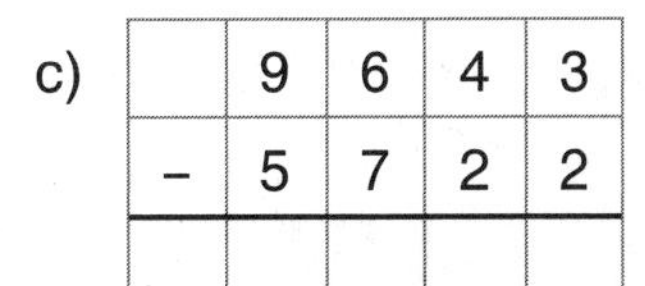

d)

	6	5	7	9
–	3	8	5	7

8. In some of the following questions, you will need to regroup twice.

a)

	2	5	8	7
–	1	2	5	9

b)

	8	5	3	7
–	6	7	2	5

c)

	9	6	2	8
–	5	4	3	4

d)

	3	5	6	0
–	1	9	6	0

e)

	5	6	2	7	3
–	4	2	0	1	6

f)

	8	2	5	2	9
–	3	7	2	5	1

g)

	9	0	5	2	3
–	1	8	2	1	9

9. In the following questions, you will have to regroup three times.

Step 1:

2 16
8 4 ~~3~~ ~~6~~
– 2 5 6 8

Step 2:

2 16
8 4 ~~3~~ ~~6~~
– 2 5 6 8
8

Step 3:

12
3 ~~2~~ 16
8 ~~4~~ ~~3~~ ~~6~~
– 2 5 6 8
6 8

Step 4:

7 13 12
~~3~~ ~~2~~ 16
~~8~~ ~~4~~ ~~3~~ ~~6~~
– 2 5 6 8
8 6 8

Step 5:

7 13 12
~~3~~ ~~2~~ 16
~~8~~ ~~4~~ ~~3~~ ~~6~~
– 2 5 6 8
5 8 6 8

a)

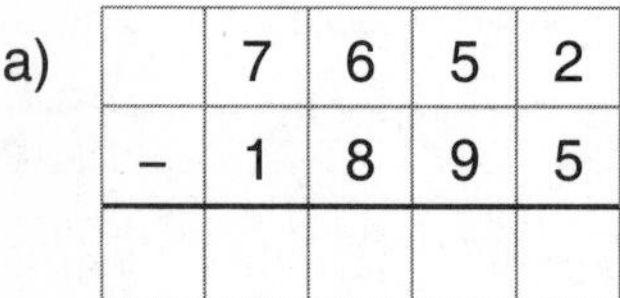

	7	6	5	2
–	1	8	9	5

b)

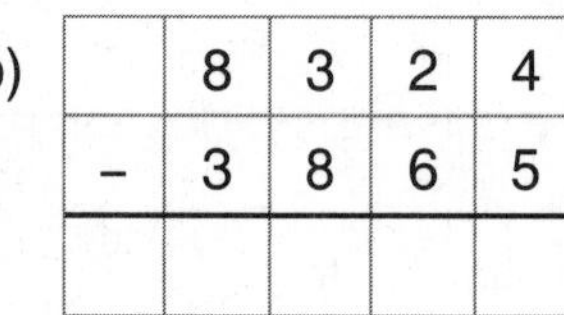

	8	3	2	4
–	3	8	6	5

c)

	4	5	7	1
–	1	8	8	4

d)

	9	0	6	8
–	1	5	7	9

10. In the following questions, you will have to regroup two or three times.

Step 1:

0 10
~~1~~ ~~0~~ 0 0
– 5 3 2

Step 2:

9
0 ~~10~~ 10
~~1~~ ~~0~~ ~~0~~ 0
– 5 3 2

Step 3:

9 9
0 ~~10~~ ~~10~~ 10
~~1~~ ~~0~~ ~~0~~ ~~0~~
– 5 3 2

Step 4:

9 9
0 ~~10~~ ~~10~~ 10
~~1~~ ~~0~~ ~~0~~ ~~0~~
– 5 3 2
4 6 8

a)

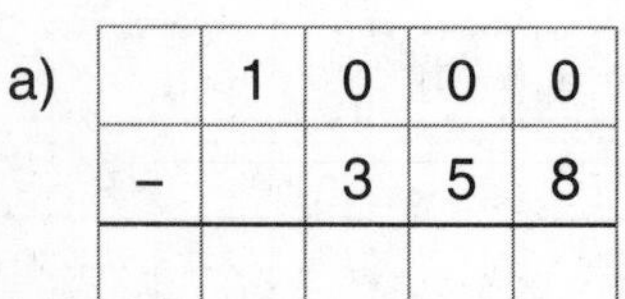

	1	0	0	0
–		3	5	8

b)

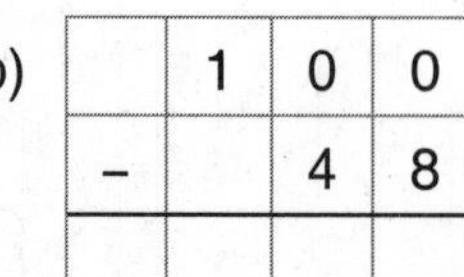

	1	0	0
–		4	8

c)

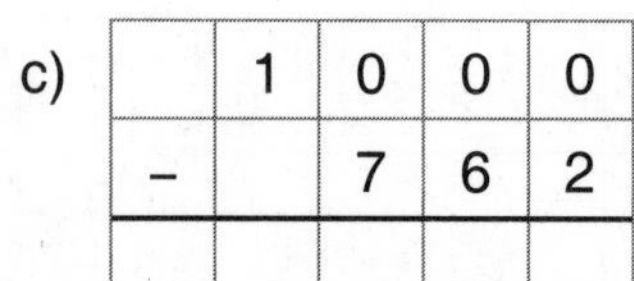

	1	0	0	0
–		7	6	2

d)

	1	0	0	0
–		2	5	9

No unauthorized copying

NS5-12: Larger Numbers

Answer the following questions in a notebook.

1. Alex has \$57 and Borana has \$12.
   How much money do they have altogether?

2. Camile cycled 2 375 km one year and 5 753 the next. How many km did she cycle altogether?

3. The maximum depth of Lake Ontario is 244 m.
   The maximum depth of Lake Superior is 406 m.

   How much deeper is Lake Superior than Lake Ontario?

4. Mount Kilimanjaro in Tanzania is 5 895 m high and Mount Fuji in Japan is 3 776 m high.

   How much higher is Mount Kilimanjaro than Mount Fuji?

5. In space, the Apollo 10 command module travelled 39 666 km per hour.

   How far did it travel in 2 hours?

6. Two nearby towns have populations of 12 475 and 14 832 people.

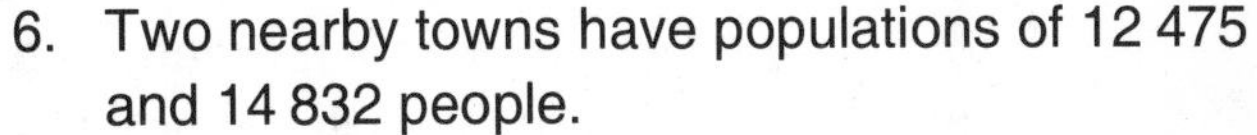

   What is the total population of both towns?

7. Canada was founded in 1867.
   How many years ago was Canada founded?

8. In the number 432:

   The 100s digit is 1 more than the 10s digit.
   The 10s digit is 1 more than the 1s digit.

   Make up your own number with this property.

   _____ _____ _____

   Now write the number backward.

   _____ _____ _____

   Write your two numbers in the grid and subtract (put the greater number on top).

   Try this again with several other numbers.
   You will always get 198!

   BONUS
   Can you explain why this works?

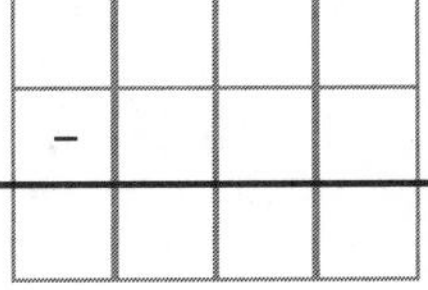

9. Sahar had 20 stickers.
   She put 5 in a book and gave 4 to her friend Nina.
   How many were left over?

10. John has 26 marbles.
    David has 15 fewer marbles than John.
    Claude has 10 more marbles than John.

    How many marbles do David and Claude have altogether?

No unauthorized copying

NS5-13: Concepts in Number Sense

Answer the following questions in a notebook.

1. The chart gives the area of some of the largest lakes in North America.

a) How much more area does Lake Michigan cover than Lake Erie?

b) How much more area does the largest lake cover than the smallest lake?

c) Write the areas of the lakes in order from least to greatest.

d) The largest lake in the world is the Caspian Sea in Asia. Its area is 370 990 km^2.

How much greater than the area of Lake Superior is the area of the Caspian Sea?

Lake	Area (in km^2)
Erie	25 690
Great Slave	28 570
Michigan	58 020
Great Bear	31 340
Superior	82 100

2. A clothing store had 500 shirts. In one week, they sold:

- 20 red shirts
- 50 blue shirts
- 100 green shirts

How many shirts were left?

3. Use the digits 1, 2, 3, 4, 5, 6, 7, and 8 once each to fill in the boxes.

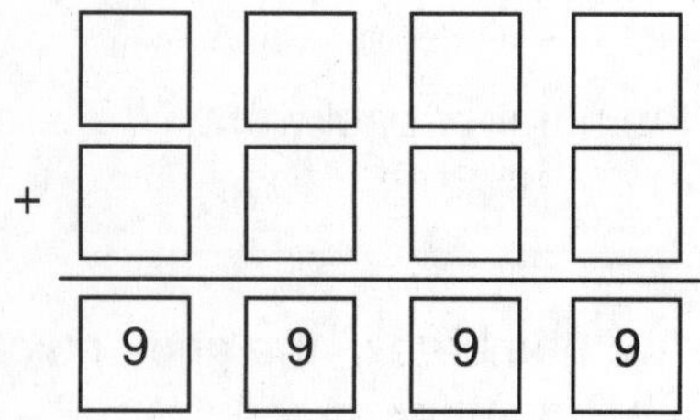

4. Use each of the digits 4, 5, 6, 7, and 8 once to create:

a) The greatest odd number possible.

b) A number between 56 700 and 57 000.

c) An odd number whose tens digit and hundreds digit add to 12.

d) An odd number whose thousands digit is twice its hundreds digit.

5. Design your own problem using the numbers in the chart in Question 1.

6. What is the greatest number you can add to 74 253 without having to regroup?

No unauthorized copying

NS5-14: Arrays

When you multiply a pair of numbers, the result is called the **product** of the numbers.

In the **array** shown, there are 3 **rows** of dots. There are 5 dots **in each row**.

row → • • • • • 5
• • • • • 10
• • • • • 15

Carmelle counts the dots by skip counting by 5s.

Carmelle writes a multiplication statement for the array: **3 × 5 = 15** (3 rows of 5 dots is 15 dots)

The numbers **3** and **5** are called **factors** of 15.

---

1. How many rows? How many dots in each row? Write a multiplication statement.

a)
• • • •
• • • •

__2__ rows

__4__ dots in each row

__2 × 4 = 8__

b)
• • • • •
• • • • •
• • • • •
• • • • •

_____ rows

_____ dots in each row

____

c)
• • • •
• • • •
• • • •
• • • •

____

____

____

2. Write a product for the array.

a) 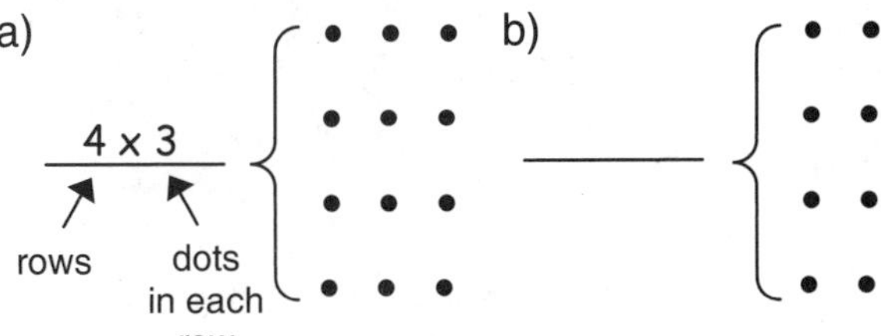

b) 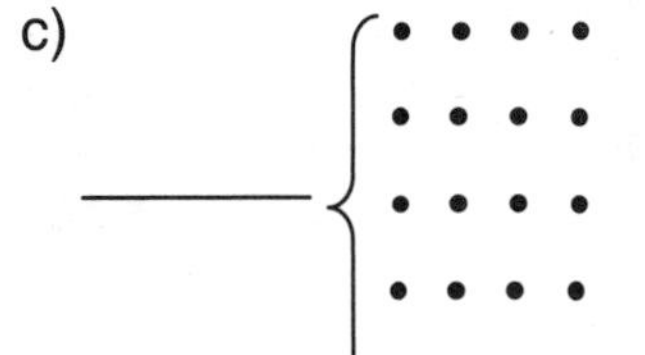

c) 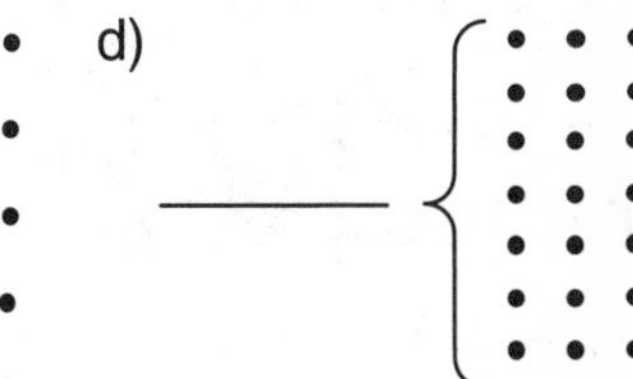

d) _______

3. Draw an array and write a multiplication statement to find the answer.

a) In a garden, there are 6 rows of plants. There are 5 plants in each row. How many plants are there altogether?

b) Paul lines up 7 chairs in each row. There are 3 rows of chairs. How many chairs are there altogether?

4. a) Draw arrays for the products 4 × 3 and 3 × 4. Are the products the same or different?

b) Is 6 × 4 equal to 4 × 6? Explain.

5. Jen finds all the factors of 4 by drawing arrays.

Factors of 4: **1, 2, 4**

• • • •
1 × 4

• •
• •
2 × 2

•
•
•
•
4 × 1

Draw arrays to find all the factors of:

a) 6 b) 10 c) 11 d) 12

No unauthorized copying

NS5-15: Multiplying by Skip Counting and Adding On

Amy finds the product of **3** and **5** by skip counting on a number line. She counts off three 5s. From the picture, Amy can see that the **product** of 3 and 5 is 15.

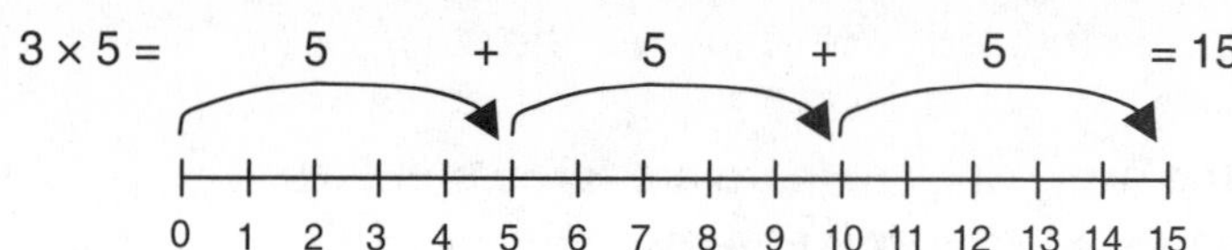

---

1. Draw arrows to find the product by skip counting.

a) **4 x 2 =**

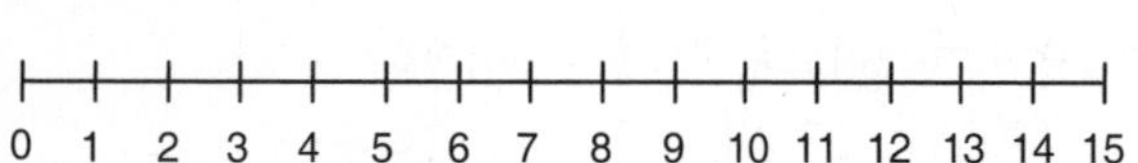

b) **3 x 4 =**

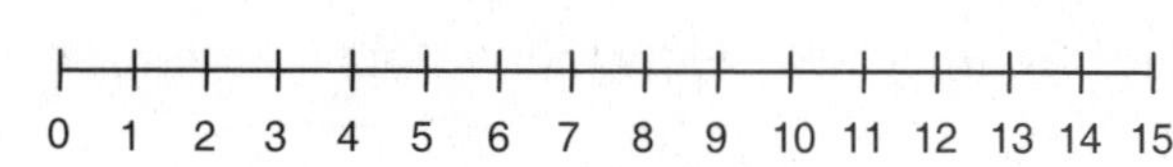

2. Use the number line to skip count by 4s, 6s, and 7s. Fill in the boxes as you count.

0 1 2 3 4 5 6 7 8 9 **10** 11 12 13 14 15 16 17 18 19 **20** 21 22 23 24 25 26 27 28 29 **30** 31 32 33 34 35 36 37 38 39 **40** 41 42

a)

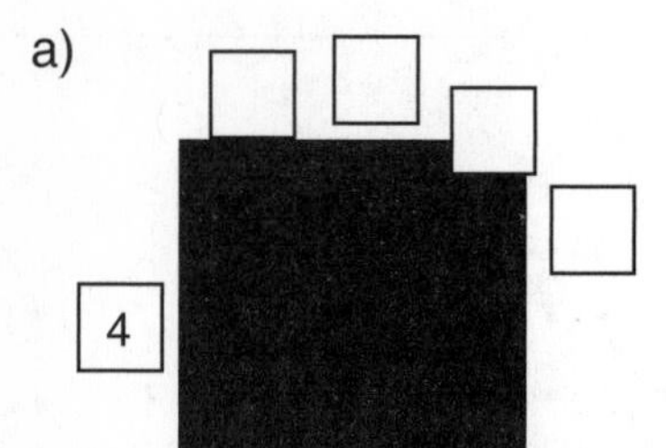

b)

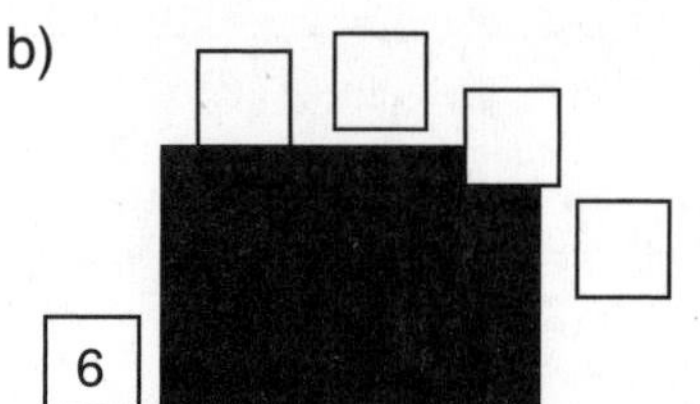

c)

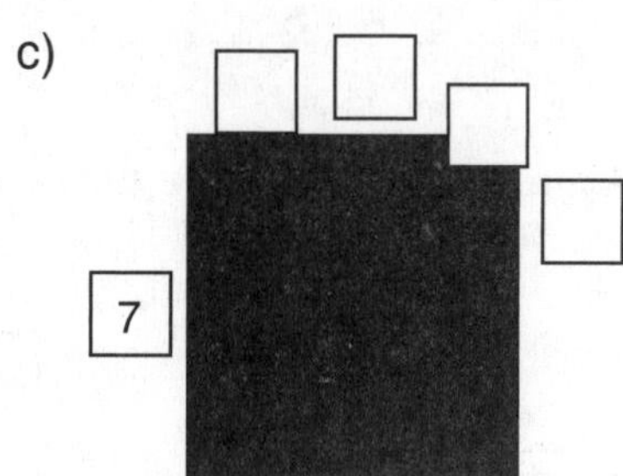

3. Find the product by skip counting on your fingers. Use the hands from Question 2 to help.

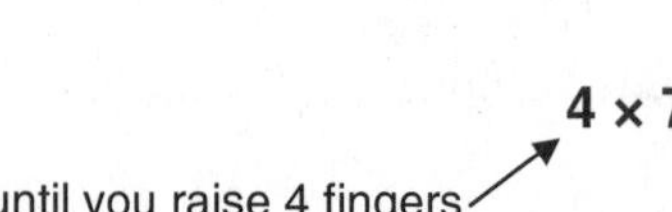

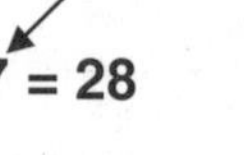

count by 7s

4 × 7 = 28

until you raise 4 fingers

a) 3 × 5 =	b) 5 × 2 =	c) 3 × 4 =	d) 3 × 6 =	e) 1 × 7 =
f) 3 × 7 =	g) 3 × 3 =	h) 6 × 1 =	i) 2 × 7 =	j) 5 × 5 =
k) 2 × 2 =	l) 7 × 1 =	m) 4 × 4 =	n) 4 × 6 =	o) 1 × 6 =

4. Find the number of items in the picture. Write a multiplication statement for the picture.

a)  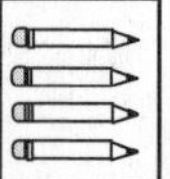 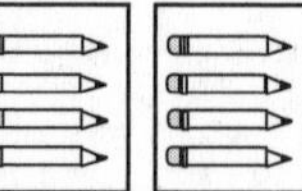 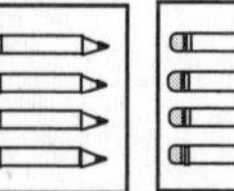 

b) 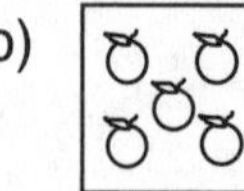  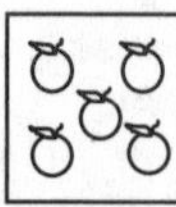 

______________________ ______________________

No unauthorized copying

NS5-16: Multiples of 10

To multiply **4 × 20**, Allen makes 4 groups containing 2 **tens** blocks (20 = 2 tens):

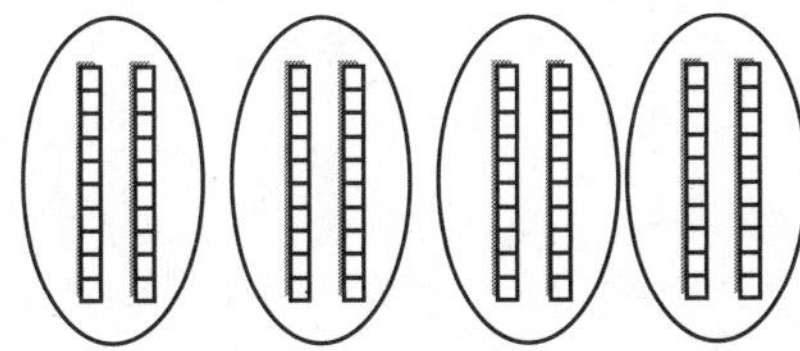

4 × 20 = 4 × 2 tens = 8 tens = 80

To multiply **4 × 200**, Allen makes 4 groups containing 2 **hundreds** blocks (200 = 2 hundreds).

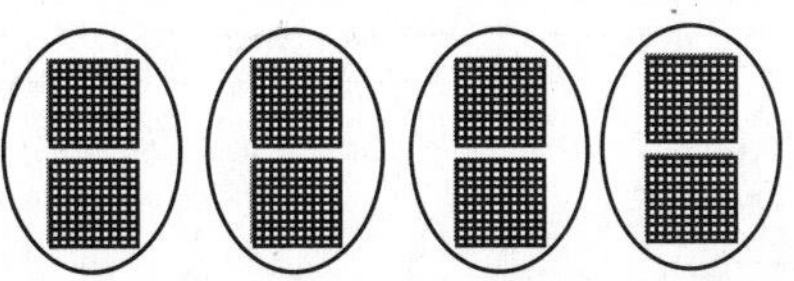

4 × 200 = 4 × 2 hundreds = 8 hundreds = 800

Allen notices a pattern: **4 × 2 = 8** **4 × 20 = 80** **4 × 200 = 800**

---

1. Draw a model for the multiplication statement, then calculate the answer. The first one is started.

   a) 4 × 30

   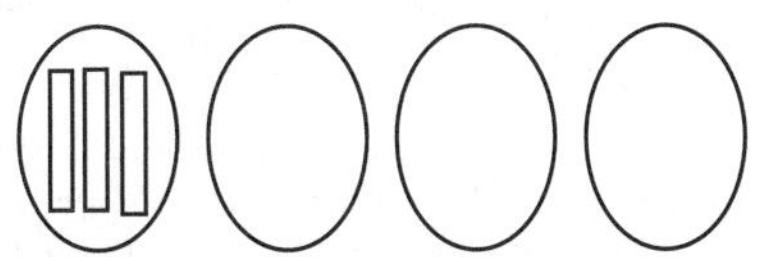

   4 × 30 = 4 × ____ tens = ____ tens = ____

   b) 2 × 20

   2 × 20 = 2 × ____ tens = ____ tens = ____

2. Regroup to find the answer. The first one is done for you.

   a) 3 × 70 = 3 × 7 tens = 21 tens = 210

   b) 4 × 50 = 4 × ________ tens = ________ tens = ________

   c) 3 × 40 = 3 × ________ tens = ________ tens = ________

   d) 6 × 30 = 6 × ________ tens = ________ tens = ________

3. Complete the pattern by multiplying.

a) 2 × 3 = ________	b) 5 × 1 = ________	c) 5 × 4 = ________	d) 4 × 2 = ________
2 × 30 = ________	5 × 10 = ________	5 × 40 = ________	4 × 20 = ________
2 × 300 = ________	5 × 100 = ________	5 × 400 = ________	4 × 200 = ________

4. Multiply.

a) 5 × 30 = ________	b) 30 × 4 = ________	c) 4 × 40 = ________	d) 50 × 3 = ________
e) 3 × 500 = ________	f) 500 × 6 = ________	g) 3 × 80 = ________	h) 500 × 5 = ________
i) 2 × 900 = ________	j) 70 × 6 = ________	k) 8 × 40 = ________	l) 900 × 3 = ________

5. Draw a base ten model (using cubes to represent thousands) to show: 6 × 1 000 = 6000.

6. Knowing that 4 × 2 = 8, how can you use this fact to multiply 4 × 2 000? Explain.

NS5-17: Advanced Arrays

1. Write a multiplication statement for the array.

a) 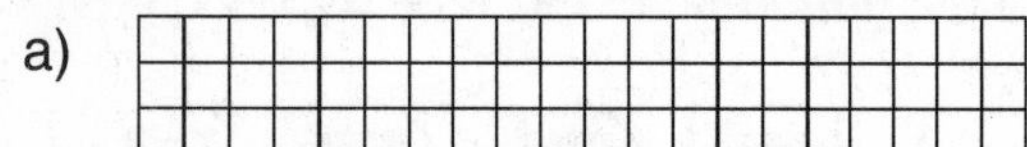

3 × 20

b) 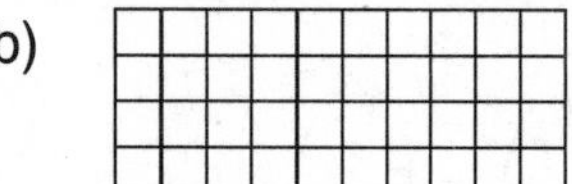

c) 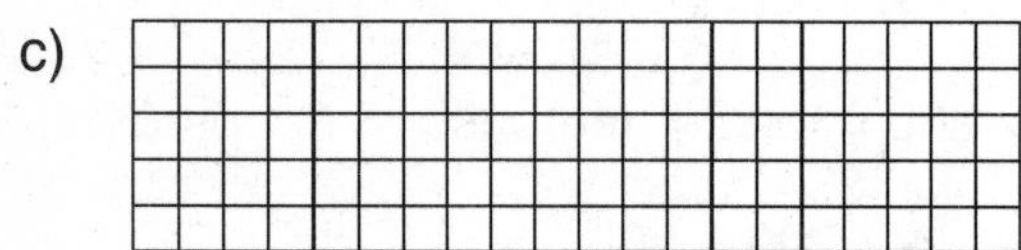

d)

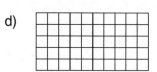

2. Write a multiplication statement for the whole array and each part of the array, as shown in a).

a) 3 × 24

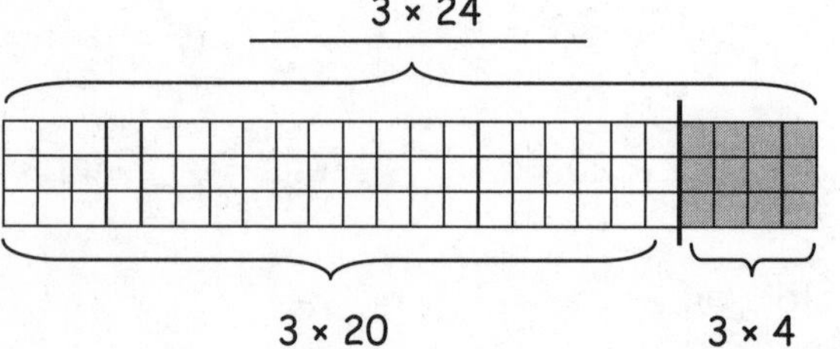

3 × 20 3 × 4

b) 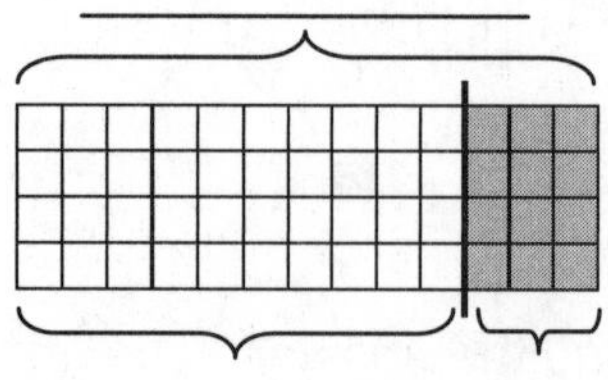

c) 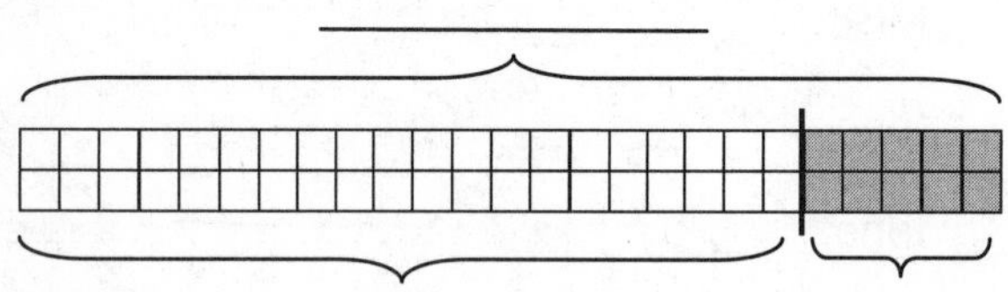

d) 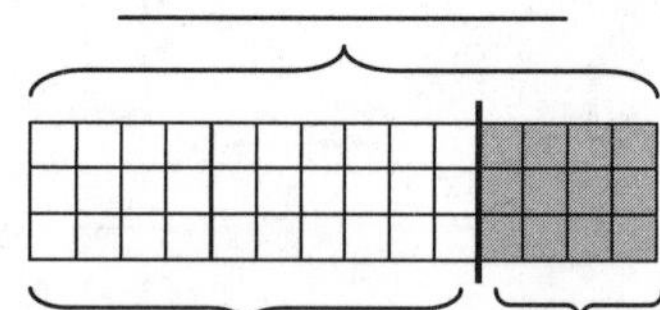

3. Fill in the blanks, as shown in a).

a) 2 × 24

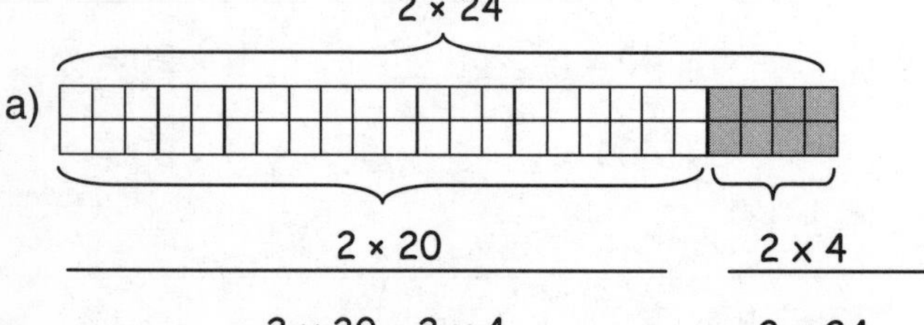

2 × 20 2 × 4

2 x 20 + 2 x 4 = 2 x 24

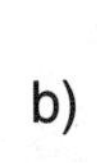

b) 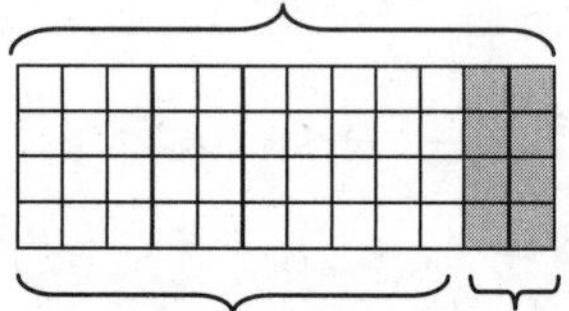

=

c) 4 × 25

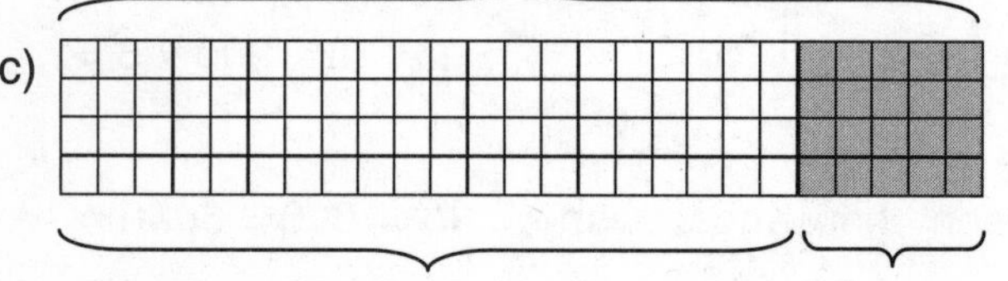

=

d) 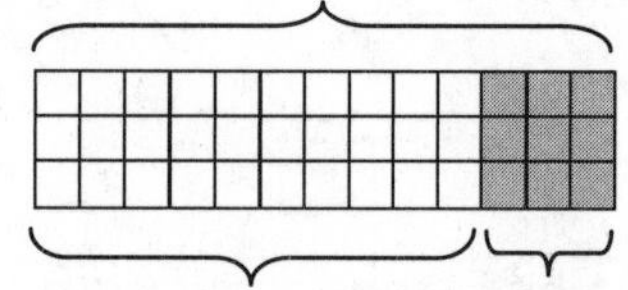

=

No unauthorized copying

NS5-18: Mental Math

To multiply 4 × 23, Anya rewrites 23 as a sum:

23 = 20 + 3

She multiplies 20 by 4: **4 × 20 = 80**

Then she multiplies 4 × 3: **4 × 3 = 12**

Finally she adds the result: **80 + 12 = 92**

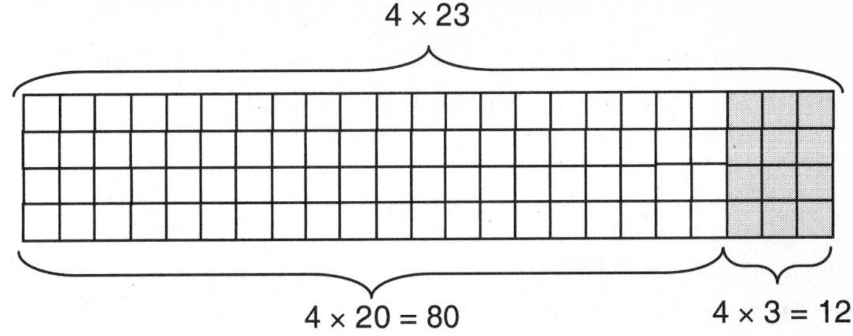

The picture shows why Anya's method works. **4 × 23 = 4 × 20 + 4 × 3 = 80 + 12 = 92**

---

1. Use the picture to write the multiplication statement as a sum. The first one is started for you.

a) 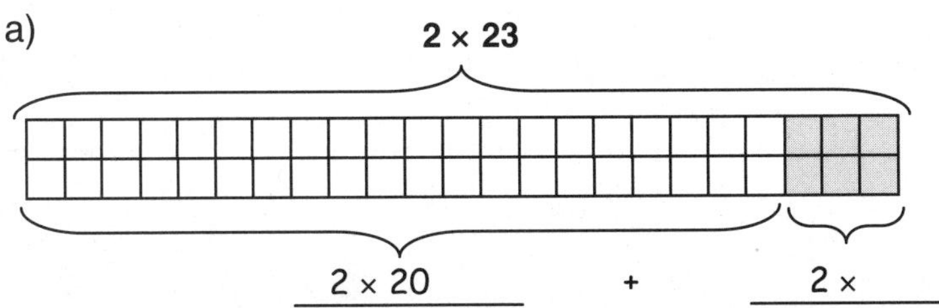

2 × 20 ______ + 2 × ______

b) 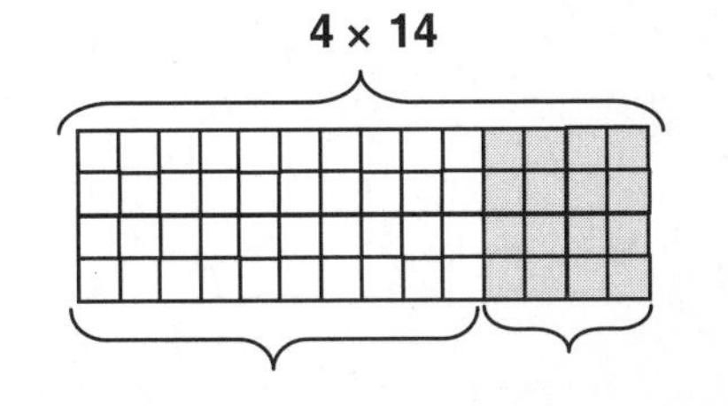

______ ______

2. Multiply using Anya's method. The first one has been done for you.

a) 4 × 12 = 4 × 10 + 4 × 2 = 40 + 8 = 48

b) 3 × 43 = ______ + ______ = ______ = ______

c) 4 × 22 = ______ + ______ = ______ = ______

d) 3 × 231 = 3 × 200 + 3 × 10 + 3 × 3 = 600 + 30 + 9 = 639

e) 2 × 443 = ______ + ______ + ______ = ______ = ______

f) 3 × 313 = ______ + ______ + ______ = ______ = ______

3. Multiply in your head by multiplying the digits separately.

a) 2 × 12 = ______ b) 2 × 42 = ______ c) 3 × 12 = ______ d) 4 × 11 = ______

e) 4 × 21 = ______ f) 3 × 41 = ______ g) 2 × 32 = ______ h) 3 × 23 = ______

i) 3 × 112 = ______ j) 2 × 233 = ______ k) 3 × 232 = ______ l) 4 × 222 = ______

m) 3 × 132 = ______ n) 2 × 442 = ______ o) 4 × 212 = ______ p) 3 × 333 = ______

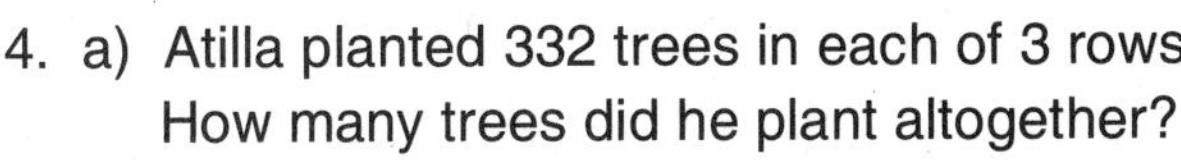

4. a) Atilla planted 332 trees in each of 3 rows. How many trees did he plant altogether?

b) Rema put 320 nails in each of 3 boxes. How many nails did she put in the boxes?

 No unauthorized copying

NS5-19: The Standard Method for Multiplication

Clara uses a chart to multiply 3 × 42.

Step 1:
She multiplies the ones digit of 42 by 3 (3 × 2 = 6).

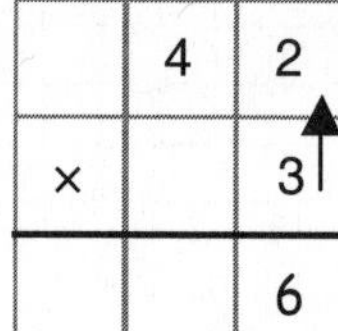

	4	2
×		3
		6

Step 2:
She multiplies the tens digit of 42 by 3 (3 × 4 tens = 12 tens).

She regroups 10 tens as 1 hundred.

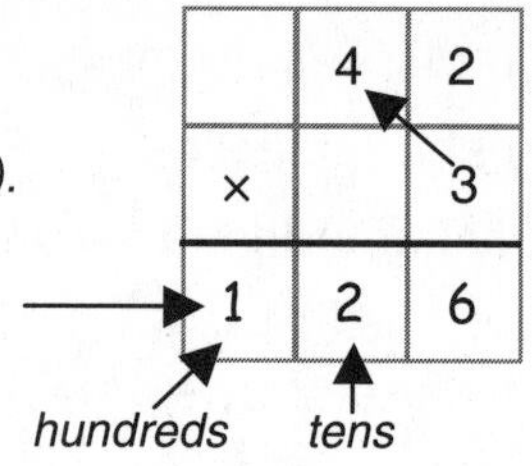

	4	2
×		3
1	2	6

1. Use Clara's method to find the product.

a)

	5	1
×		4

b)

	6	3
×		2

c)

	7	1
×		4

d)

	2	1
×		6

e)

	9	1
×		3

f)

	8	1
×		2

g)

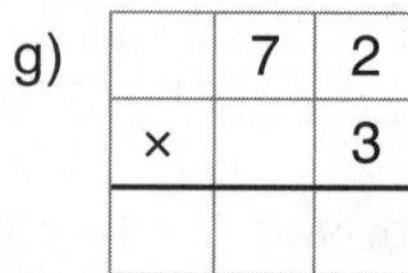

	7	2
×		3

h)

	9	4
×		2

i)

	4	2
×		4

j)

	9	2
×		2

k)

	8	1
×		5

l)

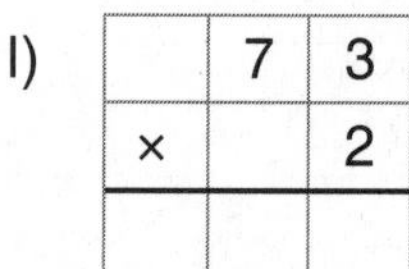

	7	3
×		2

m)

	2	2
×		3

n)

	7	3
×		3

o)

	7	4
×		2

p)

	8	3
×		3

q)

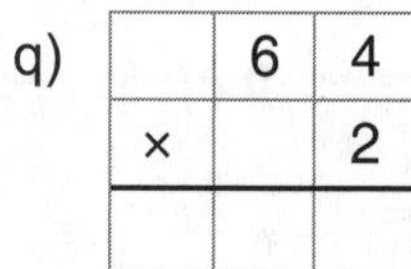

	6	4
×		2

r)

	3	2
×		4

s)

	4	1
×		9

t)

	9	1
×		5

u)

	6	3
×		3

v)

	8	1
×		9

w)

	7	1
×		5

x)

	7	2
×		4

y)

	8	1
×		8

z)

	7	2
×		4

aa)

	9	3
×		3

bb)

	7	1
×		9

cc)

	5	1
×		6

dd)

	6	1
×		8

ee)

	9	2
×		4

ff)

	6	5
×		1

gg)

	5	3
×		3

hh)

	8	1
×		7

ii)

	9	1
×		8

2. Find the product.

a) 2 × 62 b) 2 × 64 c) 5 × 31 d) 4 × 62 e) 6 × 41 f) 7 × 21

No unauthorized copying

NS5-20: Regrouping

Jane uses a chart to multiply 3 × 24.

Step 1:
She multiples 4 ones by 3 (4 × 3 = 12).

She regroups 10 ones as 1 ten.

	1	
	2	4
×		3
		2

Step 2:
She multiples 2 tens by 3 (3 × 2 tens = 6 tens).

She adds 1 ten to the result (6 + 1 = 7 tens).

	1	
	2	4
x		3
	7	2

1. Using Jane's method, complete the first step of the multiplication. The first one has been done.

a)

	2	
	1	4
×		5
		0

b) 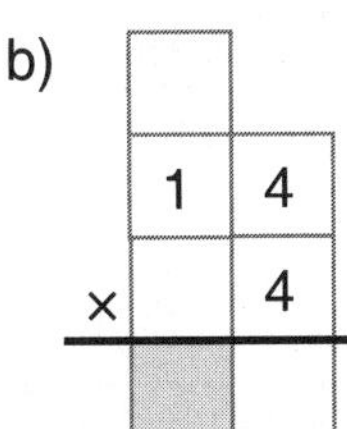

c)

	1	5
×		5

d) 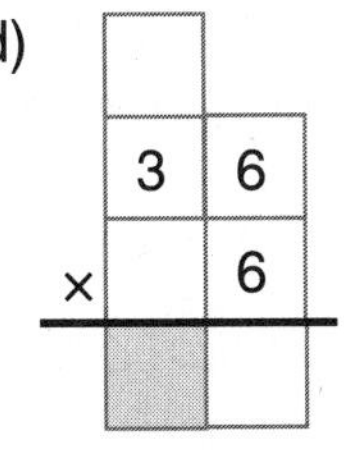

e) 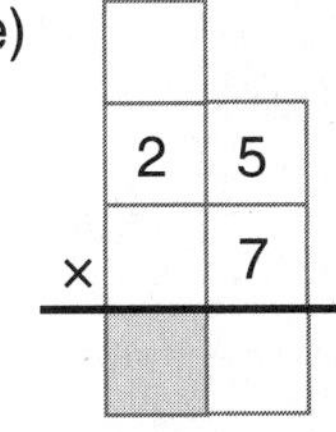

2. Using Jane's method, complete the second step of the multiplication.

a)

	1	
	2	4
×		4
		6

b) 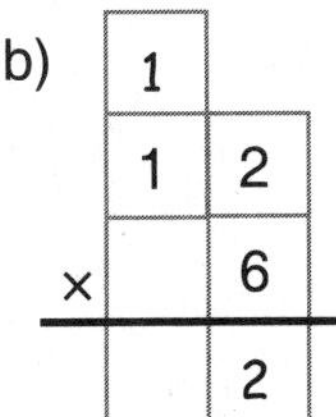

c) 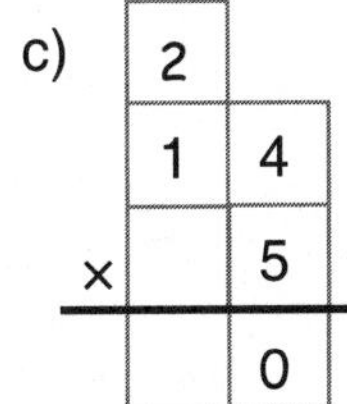

d) 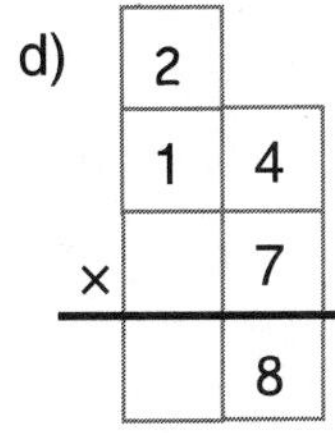

e) 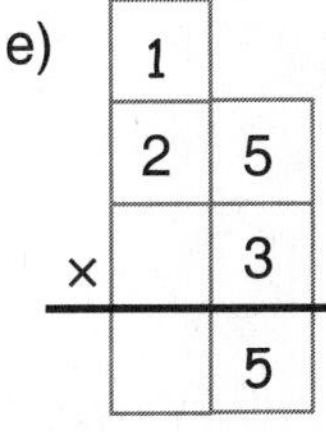

f)

	1	
	4	5
×		2
		0

g) 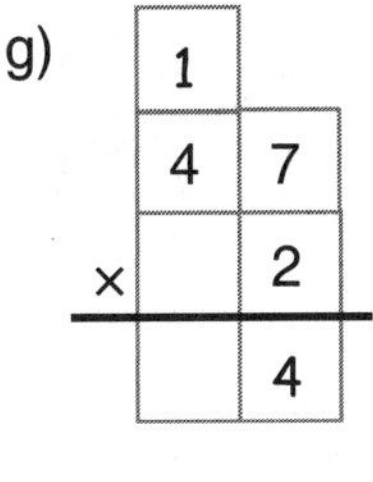

h) 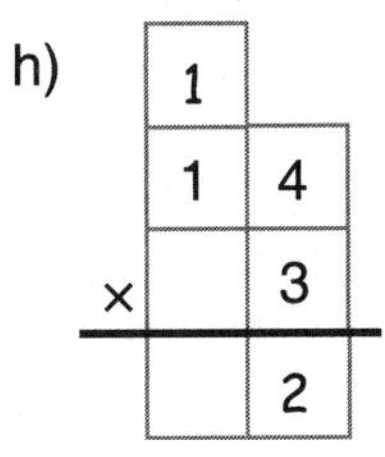

i) 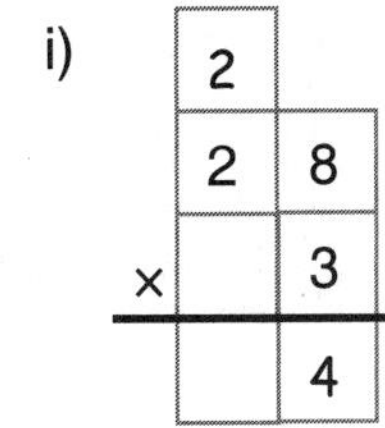

j)

	3	
	1	6
×		6
		6

3. Using Jane's method, complete the first and second steps of the multiplication.

a)

	3	5
×		2

b) 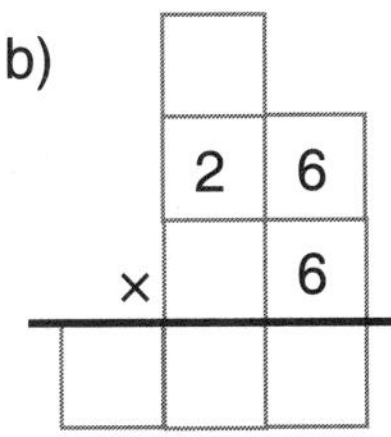

c) 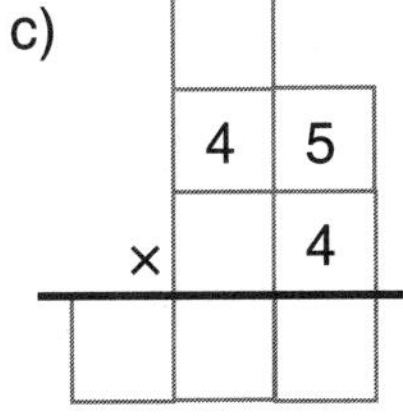

d) 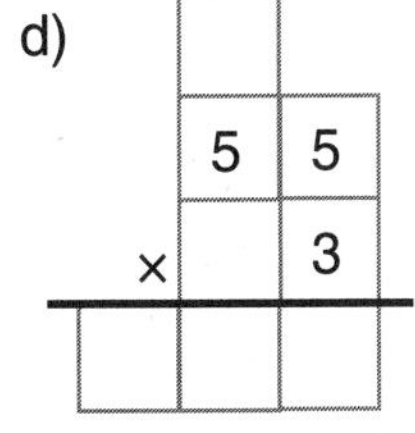

PARENT: Be sure to give your child extra practice at this skill.

e) 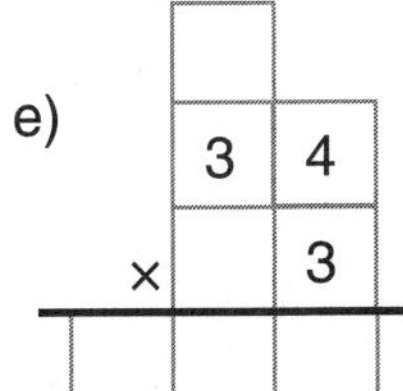

f) 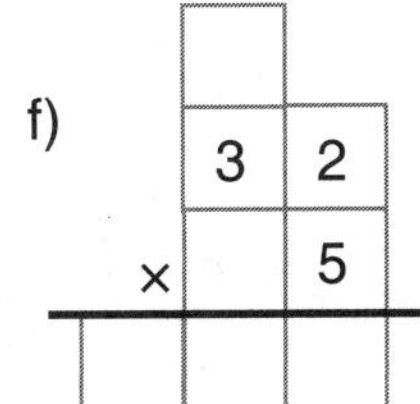

g) 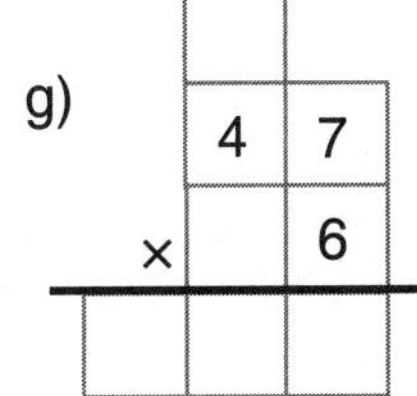

h) 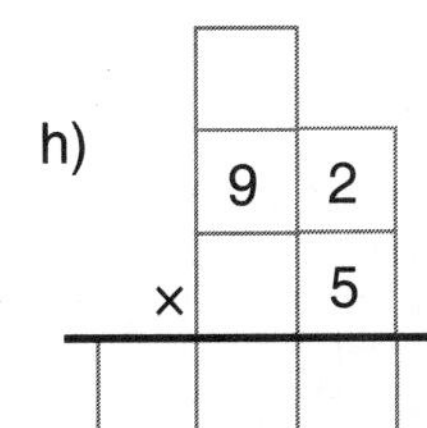

i) 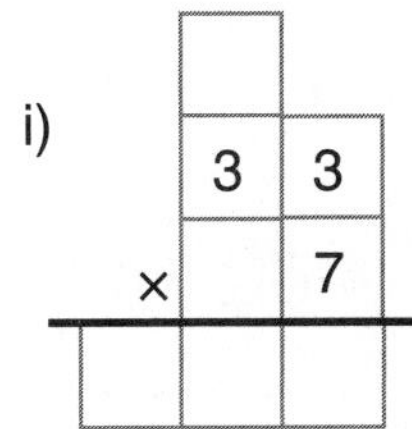

No unauthorized copying

NS5-21: Multiplying – 3-Digit by 1-Digit

Murray multiplies 2 × 321 in 3 different ways.

1. With a chart:

	hundreds	tens	ones
	3	2	1
×			2
	6	4	2

2. In expanded form:

300 + 20 + 1
× 2
= 600 + 40 + 2
= 642

3. With base ten materials:

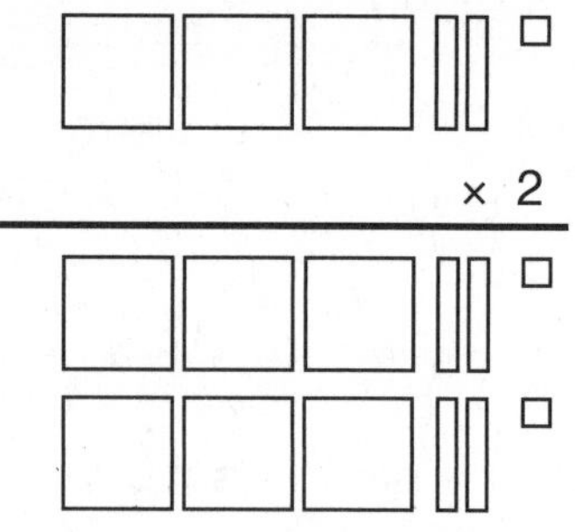

1. Rewrite the multiplication statement in expanded notation. Then perform the multiplication.

a) 412 × 3   ______ + ______ + ______ × 3
= ______ + ______ + ______
= ______

b) 323 × 2   ______ + ______ + ______ × 2
= ______ + ______ + ______
= ______

2. Multiply:

a)
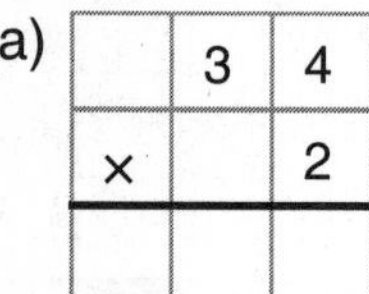

b)

3	1	2
×		3

c)

2	1	2
×		4

d)

3	2	3
×		3

e)

2	1	3
×		3

3. Multiply by regrouping ones as tens.

a)
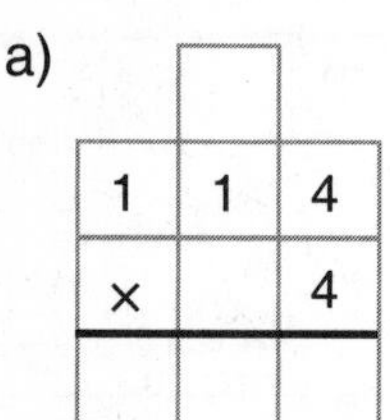

b)

2	2	6
×		3

c)

2	2	4
×		4

d)

2	1	6
×		3

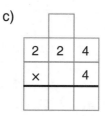

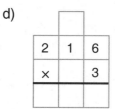

e)
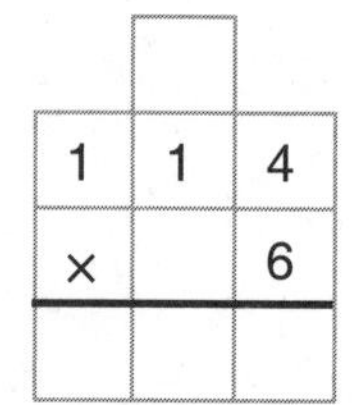

4. Multiply by regrouping tens as hundreds. In the last question, you will also regroup ones as tens.

a)
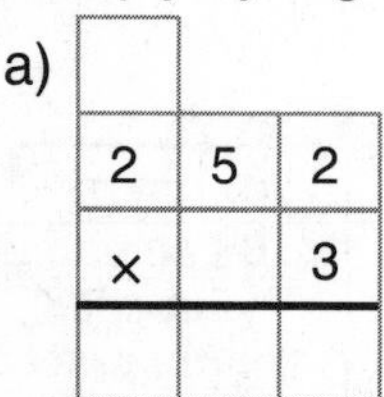

b)
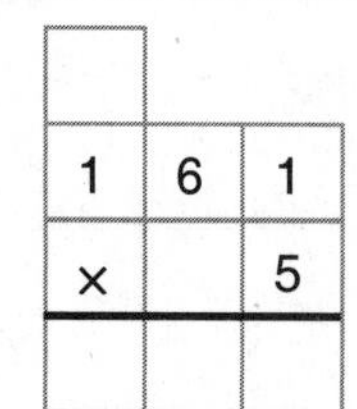

c)
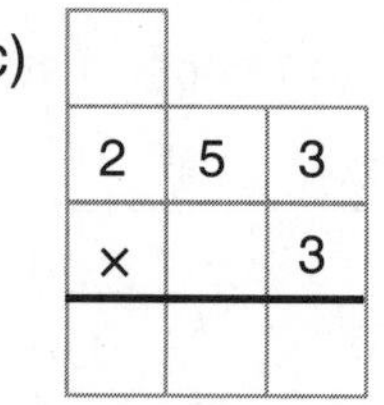

d)
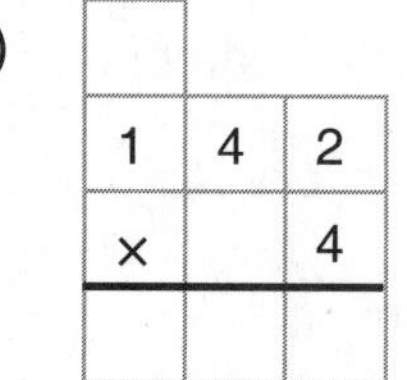

e)
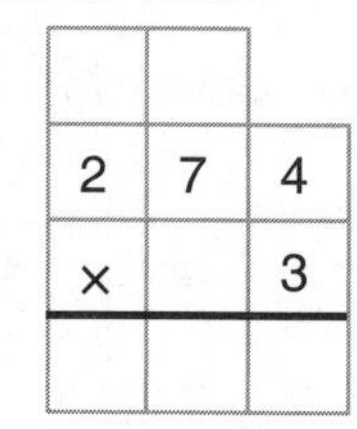

5. Multiply.

a) 4 × 142   b) 6 × 311   c) 7 × 223   d) 8 × 324   e) 9 × 1 432   f) 6 × 2 537

5. Draw a picture to show the result of the multiplication. You might need to regroup.

a)
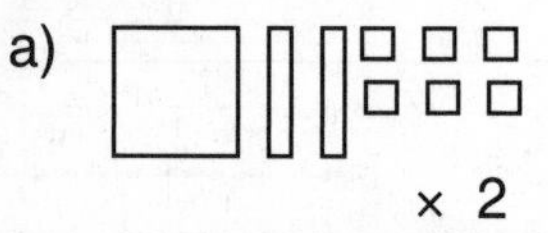

b)
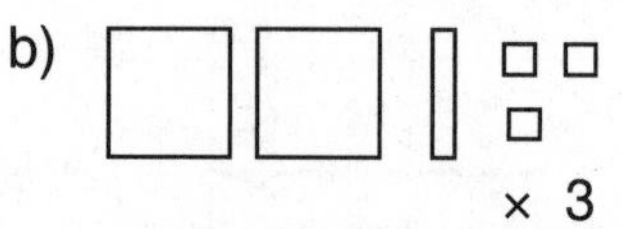

c) × 4

No unauthorized copying

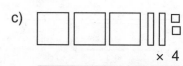

NS5-22: More Mental Math

Erin wants to multiply 20 × 32. She knows how to find 10 × 32. She rewrites 20 x 32 as **double** 10 × 32.

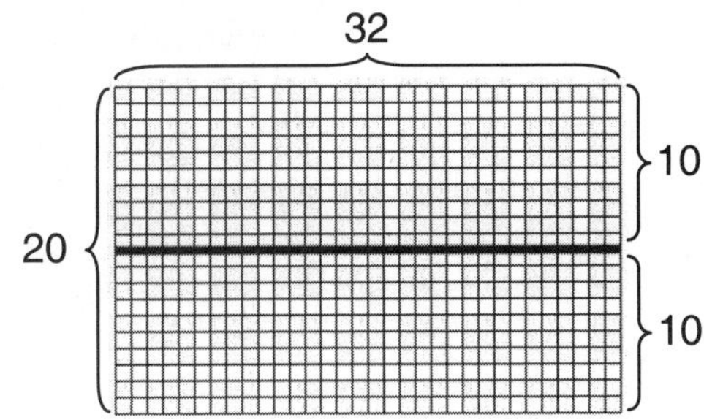

20 × 32 = 2 × **10 × 32**
= 2 × 320
= 640

The picture shows why this works: a 20 by 32 array contains the same number of squares as **two** 10 by 32 arrays.

1. Write the number as a product of 2 factors (where one of the factors is 10).

a) 30 = ____________ b) 40 = ____________ c) 70 = ____________

2. Write 2 equivalent products of the array. The first one is done for you.

a) 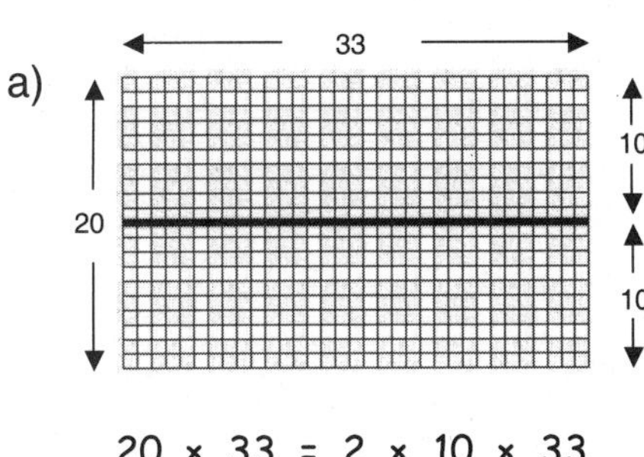

20 × 33 = 2 × 10 × 33

b) 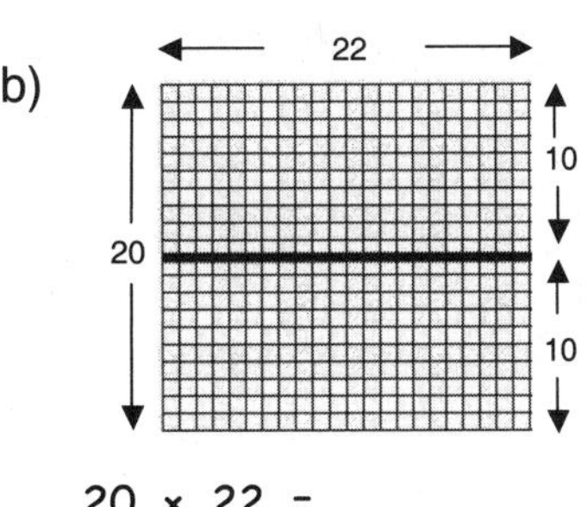

20 × 22 = ____________

c) 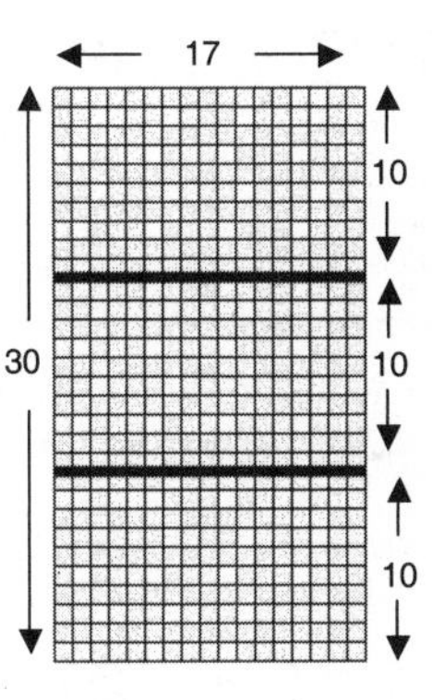

30 × 17 = ____________

3. Find the product in 2 steps:

Step 1: *Multiply the second number by 10.*
Step 2: *Multiply the result by the tens digit of the first number.*

a) 20 × 34 = 2 × 340 b) 30 × 13 = ______ c) 40 × 22 = ______ d) 50 × 31 = ______

= 680 = ______ = ______ = ______

4. Find the product mentally.

a) 30 × 22 = ______ b) 20 × 40 = ______ c) 20 × 60 = ______ d) 40 × 27 = ______

e) 20 × 41 = ______ f) 30 × 92 = ______ g) 51 × 20 = ______ h) 30 × 64 = ______

i) 60 × 41 = ______ j) 61 × 50 = ______ k) 70 x 30 = ______ l) 80 x 20 = ______

5. Estimate the product.

HINT: Round each factor to the leading digit.

a) 27 × 39 ≈ 30 × 40 = 1200 b) 43 × 51 ≈ ____________ c) 22 × 47 ≈ ____________

d) 62 x 41 ≈ ____________ e) 72 x 49 ≈ ____________ f) 38 x 17 ≈ ____________

 No unauthorized copying

NS5-23: Multiplying 2-Digit Numbers by Multiples of Ten

Ed multiplies **20 × 37** by splitting the product into a sum of two smaller products:

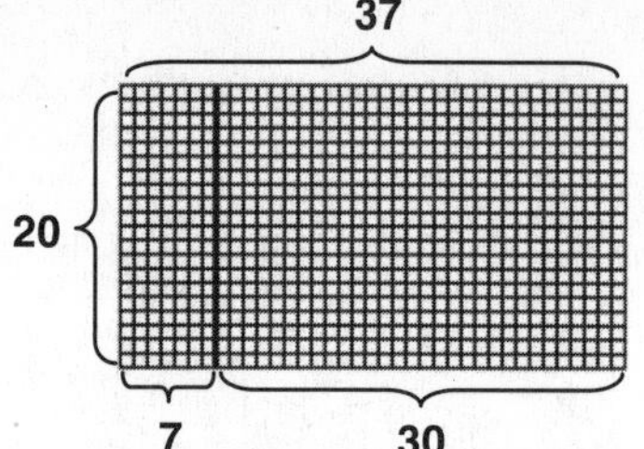

$$20 \times 37 = (20 \times 7) + (20 \times 30)$$
$$= 140 + 600$$
$$= 740$$

He keeps track of the steps of the multiplication in a chart:

		3	7
	×	2	0
			0

Step 1:
*Ed multiplies 2 × 7 = 14. He is really multiplying **20** × 7 so he first writes a zero in the ones place.*

	1		
		3	7
	×	2	0
		4	0

Step 2:
Next, since 2 × 7 = 14, Ed writes the 4 in the tens place and the 1 at the top of the hundreds column.

	1		
		3	7
	×	2	0
	7	4	0

Step 3:
*Ed then multiplies **20** × **30** (= 600). As a short cut, he multiplies 2 × 3 = 6 and then he adds the 1 from the top of the hundreds column: 6 + 1 = 7 (= 700).*

1. Practise the first two steps of the multiplication.
NOTE: In one of the questions, you will not need to regroup the hundreds.

a) 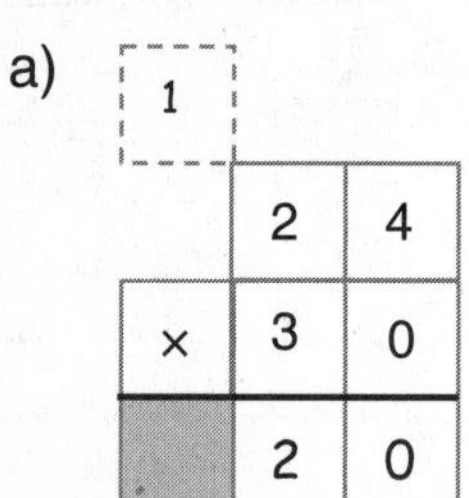

b) 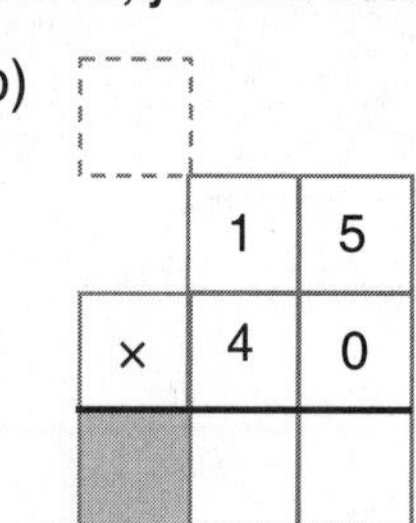

c) 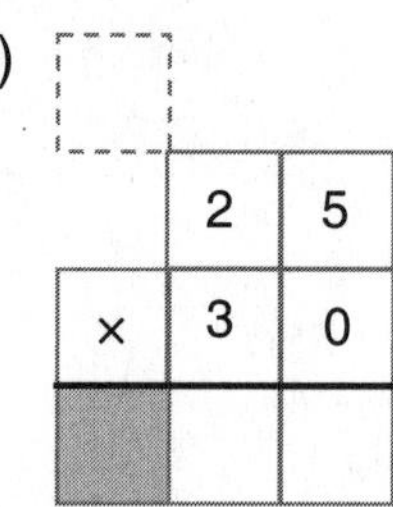

d) 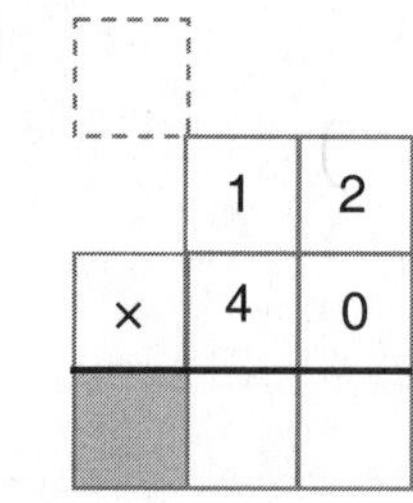

e) 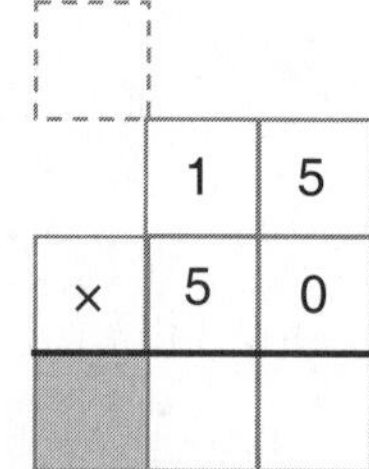

2. Multiply:

a) 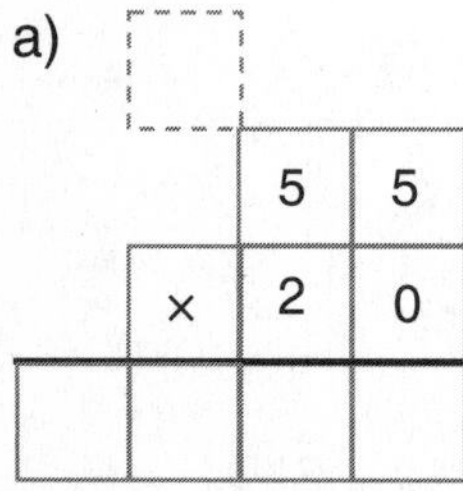

b) 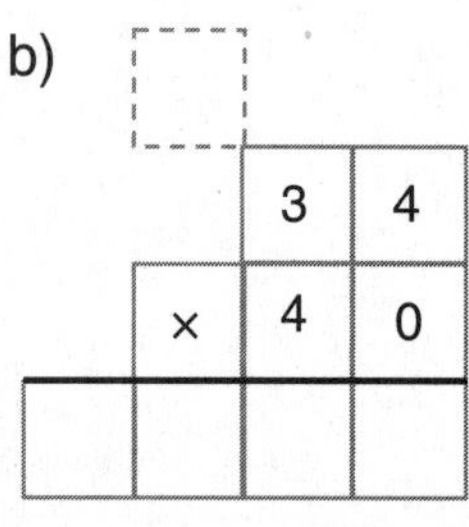

c) 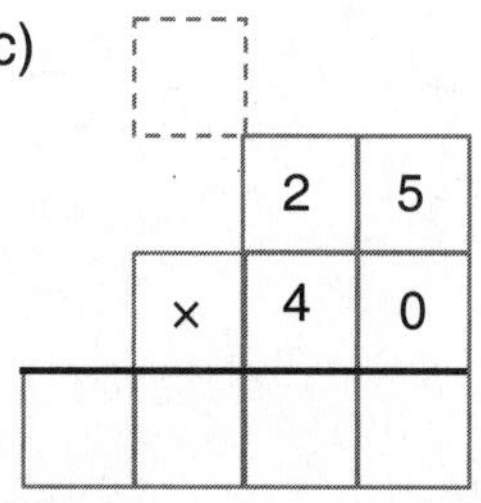

d) 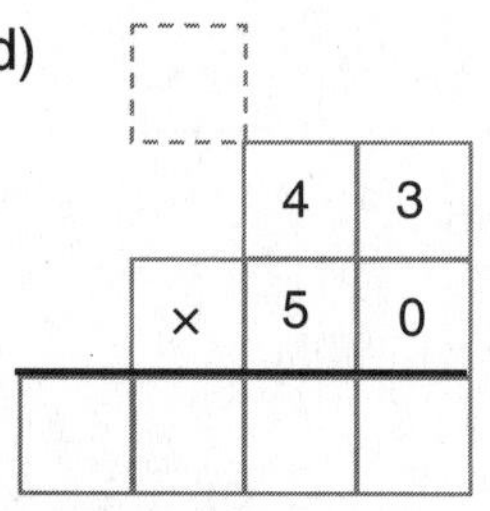

e) 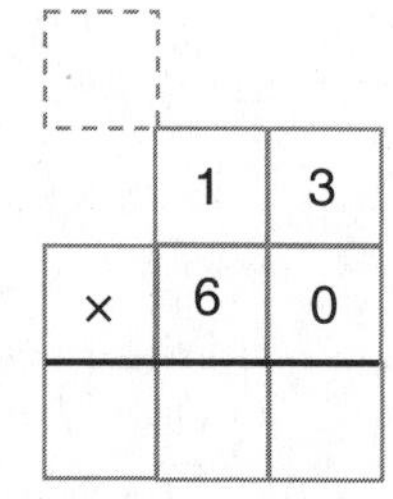

f) 28 × 30 = ____

g) 36 × 20 = ____

h) 27 × 40 = ____

i) 23 × 60 = ____

j) 43 × 70 = ____

3. Rewrite each product as a sum and then find the answer:

a) 20 × 13 = (20 × 10) + (20 × 3) = 200 + 60 = 260

b) 20 × 42 = ____________________

c) 30 × 23 = ____________________

No unauthorized copying

NS5-24: Multiplying 2 Digits by 2 Digits

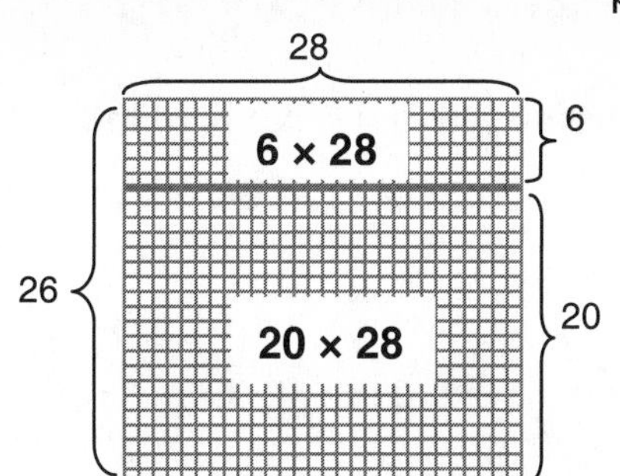

Grace multiplies 26 × 28 by splitting the product into a sum of two smaller products:

26 × 28 = 6 × 28 + 20 × 28
= 168 + 560
= 728

She keeps track of the steps of the multiplication using a chart.

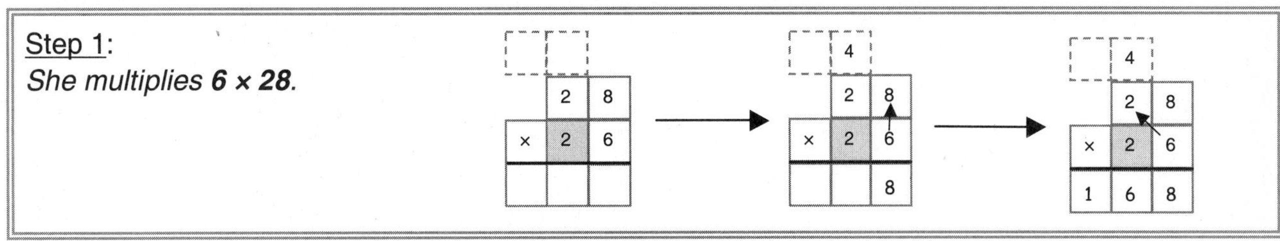

Step 1:
*She multiplies **6 × 28**.*

1. Practice the first step of the multiplication:

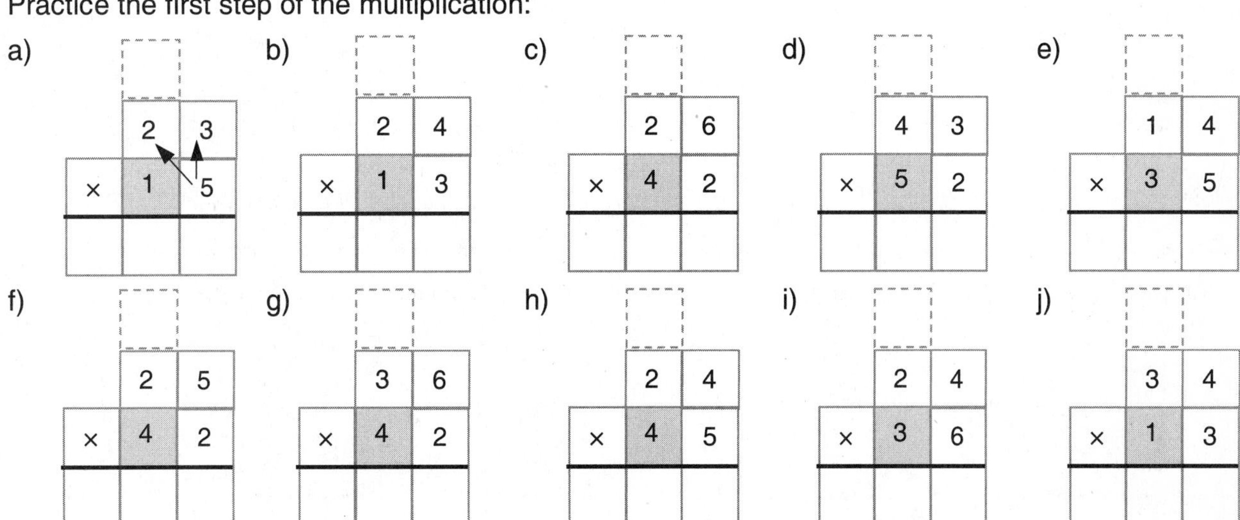

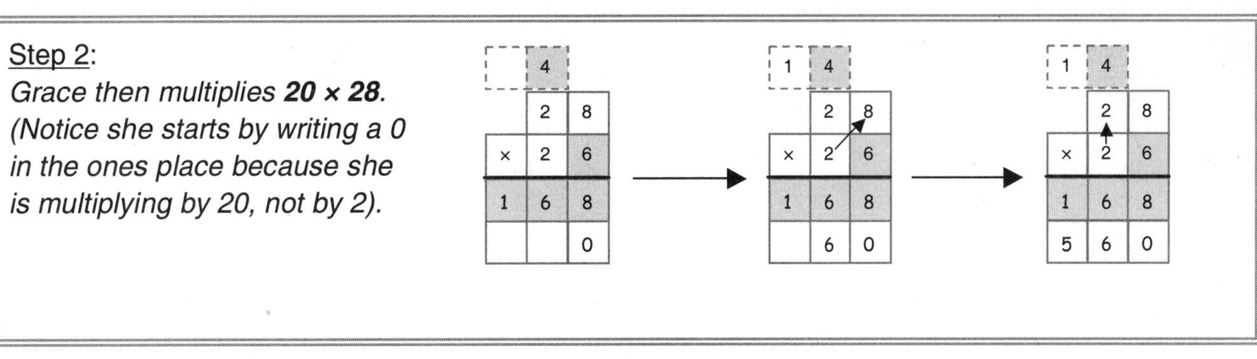

Step 2:
*Grace then multiplies **20 × 28**.*
(Notice she starts by writing a 0 in the ones place because she is multiplying by 20, not by 2).

2. a)

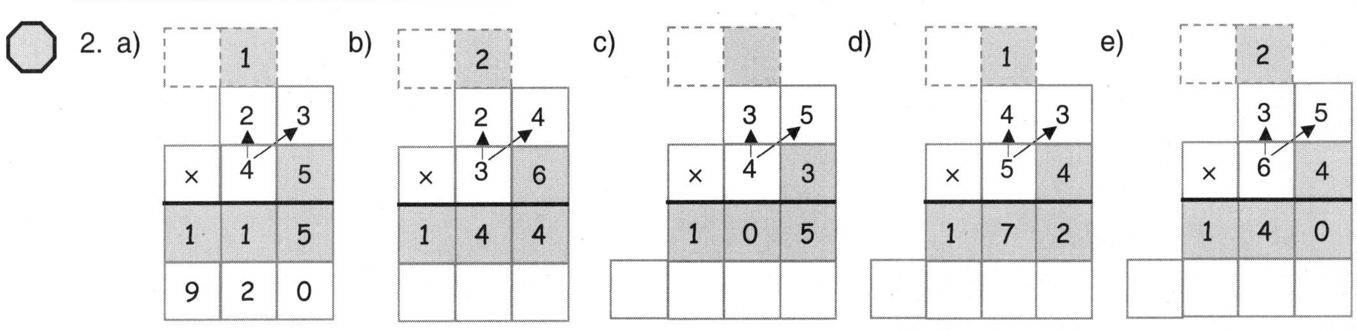

No unauthorized copying

NS5-24: Multiplying 2 Digits by 2 Digits *(continued)*

3. Practise the first 2 steps of the multiplication.

a) 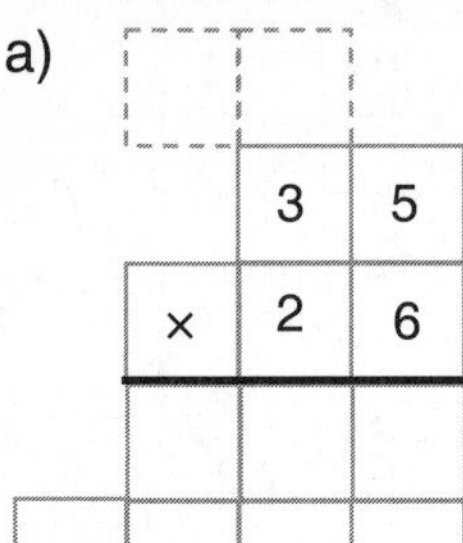

b) 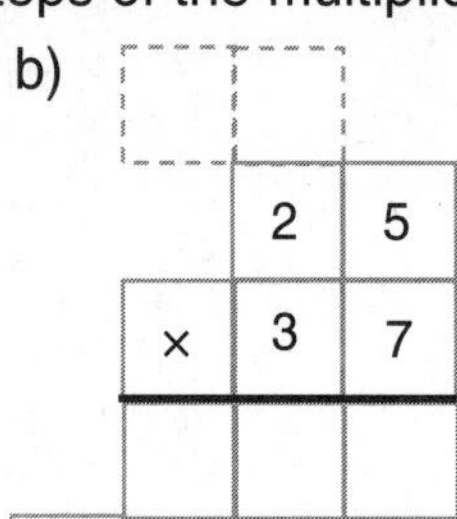

c) 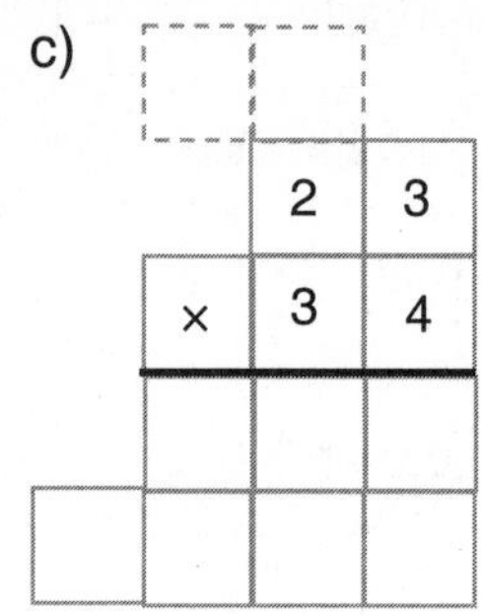

d) 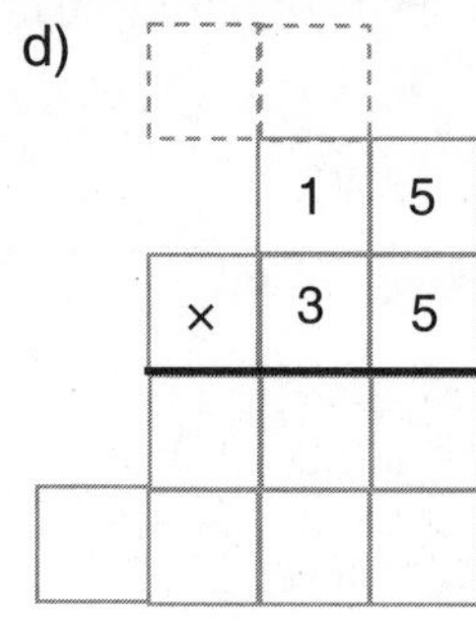

e) 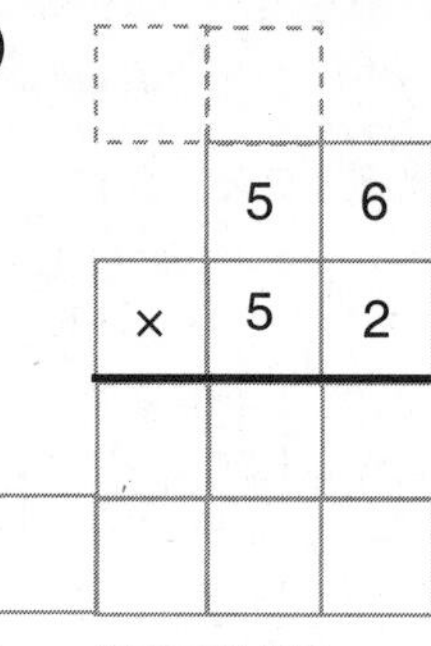

f) 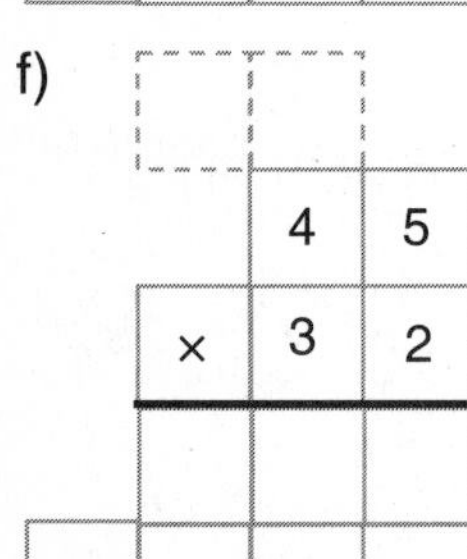

g) 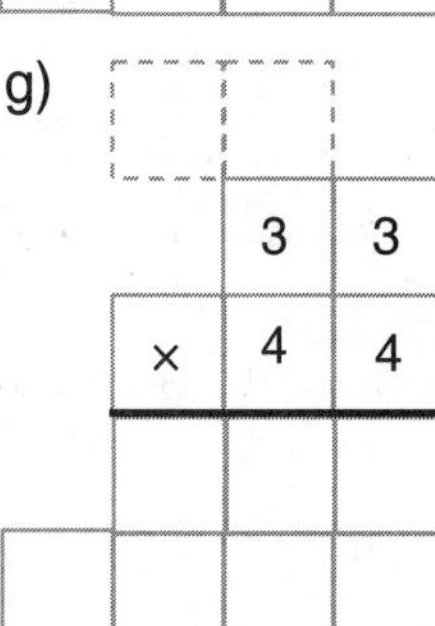

h) 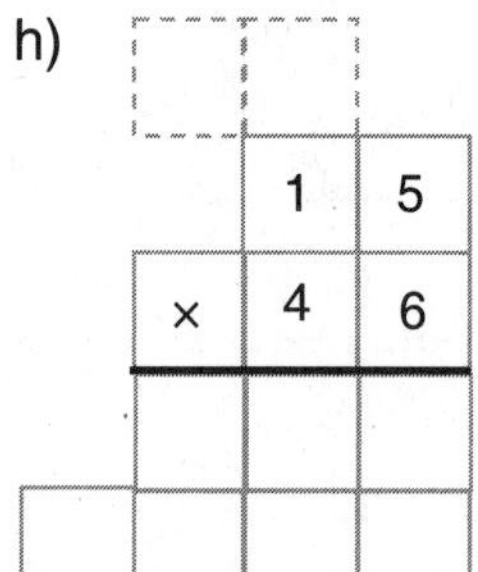

i) 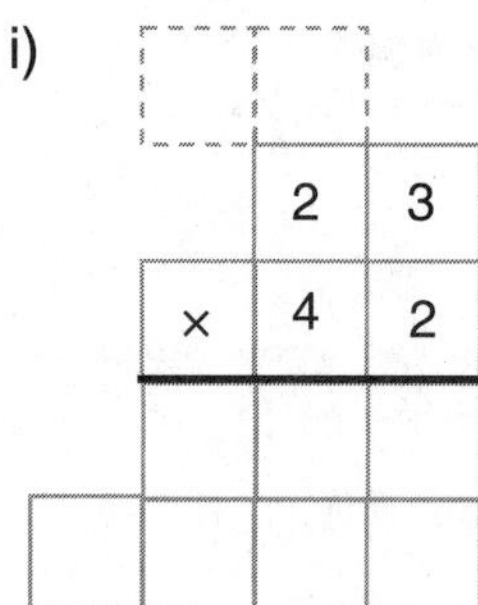

j)

		6	5
	×	4	3

Step 3: *Grace completes the multiplication by adding the products of **6 × 28** and **20 × 28**.*

4. Complete the multiplication by adding the numbers in the last two rows of the chart.

a)

	1	4	
		2	8
	×	2	6
	1	6	8
	5	6	0
	7	2	8

b)

	4	2	
		5	7
	×	6	3
	1	7	1
3	4	2	0

c)

		8	1
	×	3	5
	4	0	5
2	4	3	0

d)

	2	2	
		2	7
	×	4	3
		8	1
1	0	8	0

e)

		1	
		1	2
	×	3	8
		9	6
	3	6	0

5. Multiply:

a) 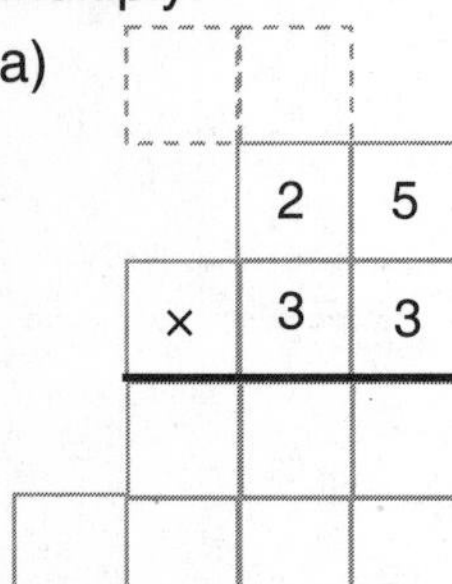

b) 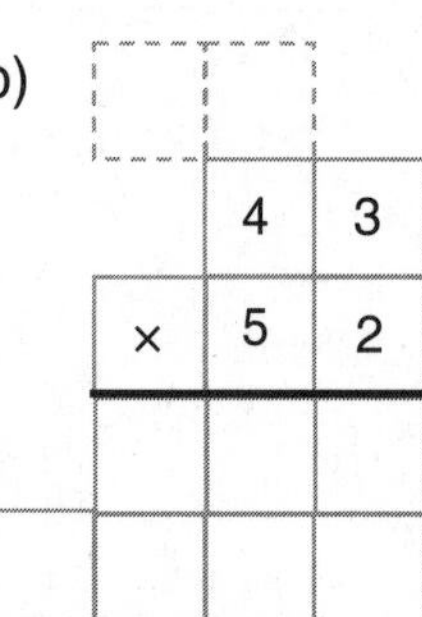

c)

		6	3
	×	2	7

d)

		4	5
	×	2	9

e)

		2	8
	×	3	4

6. Find the product:

a) 27 × 32 b) 56 × 73 c) 85 × 64 d) 19 × 93 e) 74 × 86 f) 64 × 98

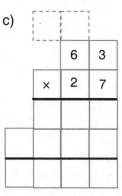

 No unauthorized copying

NS5-25: Mental Math: Rearranging Products

1. Double each number mentally by doubling the ones digit and the tens digit separately.

	23	44	12	31	43	54	83	92	71
Double									

2. Double the ones and tens separately and add the result: $2 \times 36 = 2 \times 30 + 2 \times 6 = 60 + 12 = 72$.

	25	45	16	28	18	17	35	55	39
Double									

3. a) One flower costs 34¢. How much do two flowers cost? ______________

   b) One lizard costs 48¢. How much do two lizards cost? ______________

4. From the arrays you can see:
   3×2 is the same as 2×3.

   Is 4×5 the same as 5×4? Explain.

   • •
   • •
   • •
   3×2
   (3 rows of 2)

   • • •
   • • •
   2×3
   (2 rows of 3)

5. Rearrange the products so you can find the answer mentally.

   Example: $2 \times 8 \times 35$
   $= 2 \times 35 \times 8$
   $= 70 \times 8$
   $= 560$

   Example: $4 \times 18 \times 25$
   $= 4 \times 25 \times 18$
   $= 100 \times 18$
   $= 1800$

   a) $2 \times 4 \times 25$ b) $2 \times 3 \times 45$ c) $2 \times 6 \times 35$

   d) $2 \times 27 \times 50$ e) $4 \times 75 \times 250$ f) $2 \times 97 \times 500$

   g) $372 \times 4 \times 25$ h) $2 \times 2 \times 15 \times 250$ i) $25 \times 2 \times 50 \times 4$

6. Double the number in the box and halve the number in the circle.

   Example:
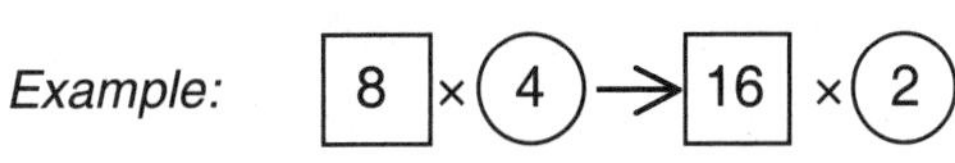

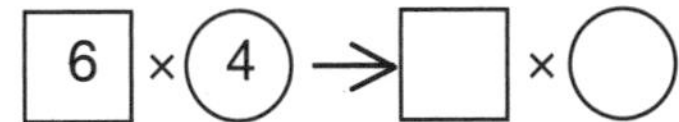

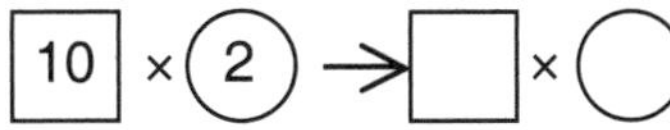

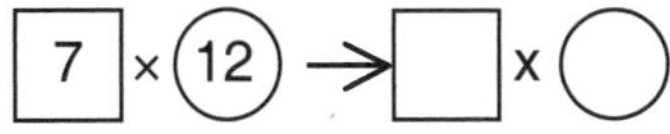

   Does the product change or stay the same? Explain

6. Use halving and doubling to find each product mentally.

   Example: 32×5
   $= 16 \times 10$
   $= 160$

   a) 42×5 b) 64×5 c) 86×5

No unauthorized copying

NS5-26: Topics in Multiplication (Advanced)

1. Fill in the blanks.

a) 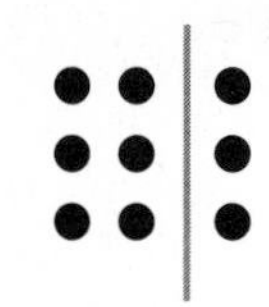

$3 \times \underline{2} + 3 \times \underline{1}$
$= 3 \times (\underline{2} + \underline{1})$
$= 3 \times \underline{3}$

b) 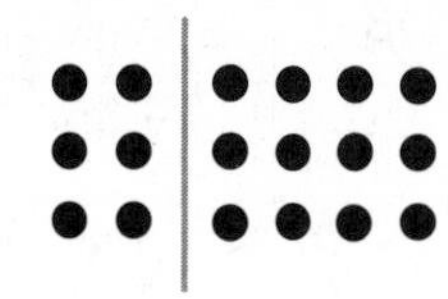

3 × ___ + 3 × ___
= 3 × (___ + ___)
= 3 × ___

c) 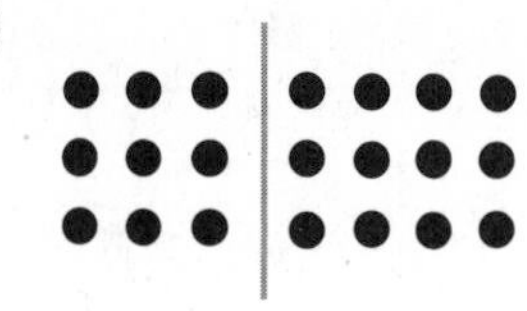

3 × ___ + 3 × ___
= 3 × (___ + ___)
= 3 × ___

d) 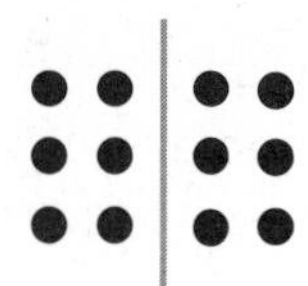

3 × ___ + 3 × ___
= 3 × (___ + ___)
= 3 × ___

e) $3 \times 5 + 3 \times 4$
$= 3 \times (\underline{5} + \underline{4})$
$= 3 \times \underline{9}$

f) $3 \times 2 + 3 \times 6$
= 3 × (___ + ___)
= 3 × ___

g) $7 \times 4 + 7 \times 3$
= 7 × (___ + ___)
= 7 × ___

h) $9 \times 3 + 9 \times 2$
= 9 × (___ + ___)
= 9 × ___

2. Write each number in expanded form.

a) 32 753 = $3 \times 10000 + 2 \times 1000 + 7 \times 100 + 5 \times 10 + 3$

b) 45 326 = ______________________

c) 72 023 = ______________________

3. 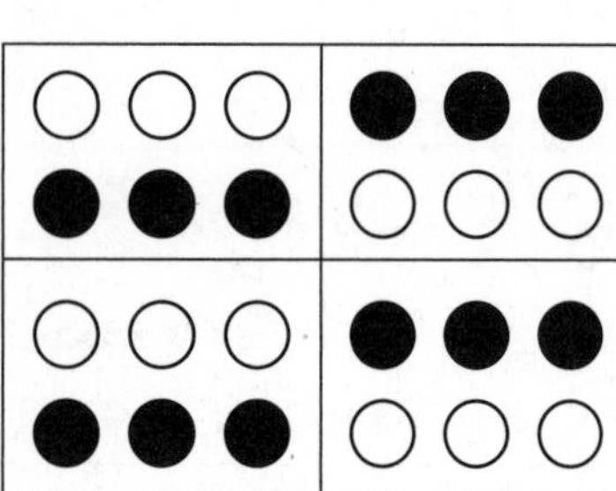

Write as many statements as you can for the array using multiplication, addition, or both.

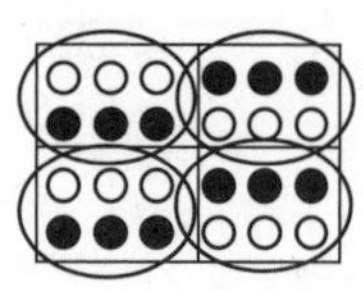

Example: $(2 \times 3) + (2 \times 3) + (2 \times 3) + (2 \times 3) = 24$

4. Is the given statement always, sometimes, or never true? Explain.

a) 3 × ☐ is even

b) 5 × ☐ is a multiple of 5

c) 7 × ☐ is 0

d) 2 × ☐ is even

e) 6 × ☐ is a multiple of 2

f) A factor of a number is greater than the number

5. Explain why the product of two 2-digit numbers must be at least 100.

6. Using the digits 1, 2, 3, and 4, create:

a) the greatest product

☐ × ☐☐☐

b) the least product

☐ × ☐☐☐

No unauthorized copying

NS5-27: Concepts in Multiplication

Answer the following questions in a notebook.

1. A bee has 6 legs. How many legs do 325 bees have?

2. How many hours are there in the month of January?

3. A 12-sided field has sides 87 metres long. What is the perimeter of the field?

4. Sapin's heart beats 98 times a minute. How many times would it beat in an hour?

5. A harp has 47 strings. How many strings do 12 harps have?

6. Find the first four products. (Show your work on a separate piece of paper.) Use the pattern in the products to find the products in e) and f) without multiplying:

a) 3 7 × 9

b) 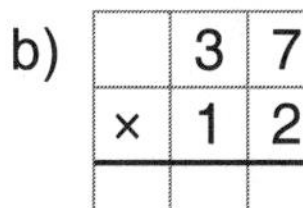

c) 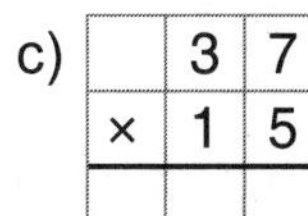

d) 3 7 × 1 8

e) 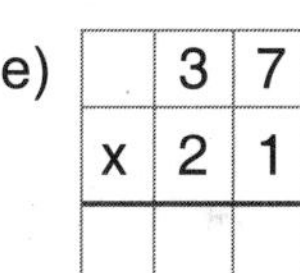

f) 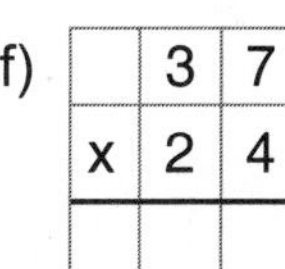

7. A hummingbird flaps its wings 15 times a second.

How many times does it flap its wings in a minute?

8.

Planets	Width (in km)
Mercury	4 850
Mars	6 790
Pluto	3 400

The circumference of a planet is the distance around the planet.

The circumference is always about 3 times the width of the planet.

Use the numbers in the chart to find the approximate circumferences of the planets.

9. Tickets to a play cost $14.

How much will it cost for a class of 26 students to attend the play?

How much change will they receive from a $500 payment?

10. Recall that **factors** of a number are whole numbers that multiply to give the number. Two **factors** of 15 are 3 and 5. 15 is called the **product** of 3 and 5.

Say whether each statement is true or false. Explain your answer.

a) The factors of a number are never greater than the number.

b) The least factor of a number is always 1.

c) A number is always a factor of itself.

d) The sum of a pair of factors of a number is always less than the number (e.g., 3 and 2 are factors of 6 and 3 + 2 < 6).

No unauthorized copying

NS5-28: Sets

Rita has 12 sandwiches. A tray holds 4 sandwiches:

There are 3 trays:   

What has been shared or divided into **sets** or **groups**? *(Sandwiches)*

How many sets are there? *(There are 3 sets of sandwiches.)*

How many of the things being divided are in each set? *(There are 4 sandwiches in each set.)*

---

1. a) 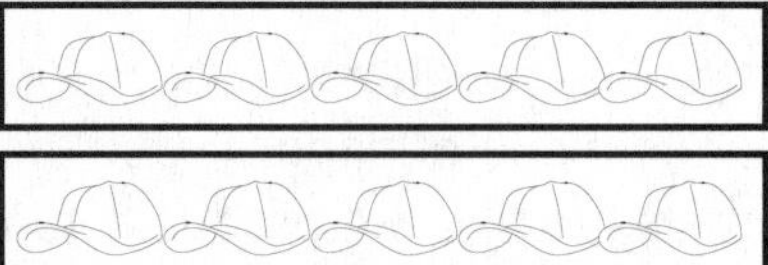

   What has been shared or divided into sets?

   ____

   How many sets? _______

   How many in each set? _______

   b) 

   What has been shared or divided into sets?

   ____

   How many sets? _______

   How many in each set? _______

2. Using circles for **sets** and dots for **things**, draw a picture to show…

   a) 5 sets
   4 things in each set

   b) 6 groups
   3 things in each group

   c) 7 sets
   3 things in each set

   d) 3 sets
   4 things in each set

 No unauthorized copying

NS5-28: Sets *(continued)*

3.

	What has been shared or divided into sets?	How many sets?	How many in each set?
a) 24 toys 4 toys for each girl/boy 6 girls/boys	24 toys	6	4
b) 8 children 32 crackers 4 cookies for each child			
c) 18 flowers 3 bouquets 6 flowers in each bouquet			
d) 9 trees 45 oranges 5 oranges in each tree			
e) 8 apples in each pack 80 apples 10 packs			
f) 6 taxis 24 passengers 4 passengers in each taxi			
g) 35 cows 7 cows in each herd 5 herds			
h) 7 litters 42 puppies 6 puppies in each litter			

4. Draw a picture for Questions 3 a), b), and c) using **circles** for sets and **dots** for the things being divided.

 No unauthorized copying

NS5-29: Two Ways of Sharing

Tory has 18 cookies. There are two ways she can share or divide her cookies equally:

I ☐ She can decide how many sets (or groups) of cookies she wants to make:

For example:
Tory wants to make 3 sets of cookies. She draws 3 circles:

She then puts one cookie at a time into the circles until she has placed 18 cookies.

II ☐ She can decide how many cookies she wants to put in each set:

For example:
Tory wants to put 6 cookies in each set. She counts out 6 cookies:

She counts out sets of 6 cookies until she has placed 18 cookies in sets.

---

1. Share **12** dots equally. How many dots are in each set? **HINT: Place one dot at a time.**

   a) 4 sets:

   There are _____ dots in each set.

   b) 3 sets:

   There are _____ dots in each set.

2. Share the triangles equally among the sets. **HINT: Count the triangles first. Divide by the number of circles.**

   △△△△
   △△△△
   △△△△
   △△△△

   a)

   b)

3. Share the squares equally among the sets:

   □□□□□□
   □□□□□□

4. Group the lines so that there are 4 lines in each set. Say how many sets there are:

   a) | | | | | | | |

   There are _____ sets.

   b) | | | | | | | | | | | | | | | |

   There are _____ sets

   c) | | | | | | | | | | | |

   There are _____ sets.

5. Group **16** flowers so that:

   a) there are 8 flowers in each set.

   b) there are 4 flowers in each set.

No unauthorized copying

6. In each question, fill in what you know. Write a question mark for what you don't know:

	What has been shared or divided into sets?	How many sets?	How many in each set?
a) Kathy has 30 stickers. She put 6 stickers in each box.	30 stickers	?	6
b) 24 children are in 6 vans.	24 children	6	?
c) Andy has 14 apples. He gives them to 7 friends.			
d) Manju has 24 comic books. She puts 3 in each bin.			
e) 35 children sit at 7 tables.			
f) 24 people are in 2 boats.			
g) 12 books are shared among 4 children.			
h) 10 flowers are in 2 rows.			
i) 8 hamsters are in 4 cages.			

 No unauthorized copying

NS5-29: Two Ways of Sharing *(continued)*

7. Draw a picture using dots and circles to solve each question.

a) 10 dots; 5 sets

_____ dots in each set

b) 12 dots; 4 dots in each set

_____ sets

c) 15 dots; 5 dots in each set

_____ sets

d) 8 dots; 4 sets

_____ dots in each set

e) 3 friends share 12 tickets.

How many tickets does each friend get? _____

f) 10 students go canoeing in 5 boats.

How many kids are in each boat? _____

g) Pria has 14 stickers.
She gives 7 to each friend.

How many friends receive stickers? _____

h) Each basket holds 5 plums.
There are 15 plums altogether.

How many baskets are there? _____

i) 16 flowers are planted in 2 pots.

How many flowers are in each pot? _____

j) Keith has 15 stamps.
He puts 3 on each page.

How many pages does he use? _____

No unauthorized copying

NS5-30: Dividing by Skip Counting

Every **division** statement implies an **addition** statement.

For example, the statement "20 divided into sets of size 4 gives 5 sets" can be represented as:

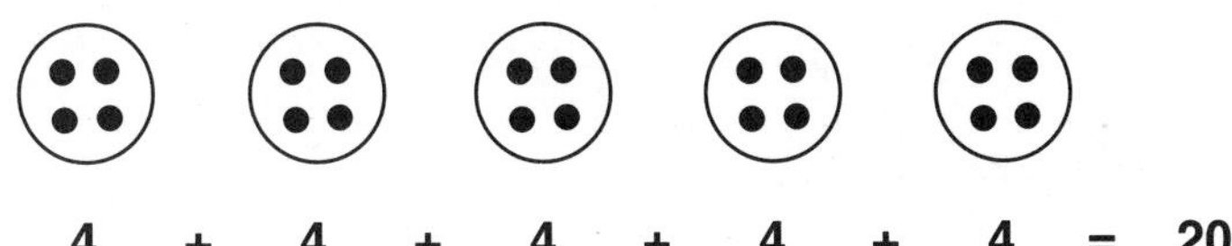

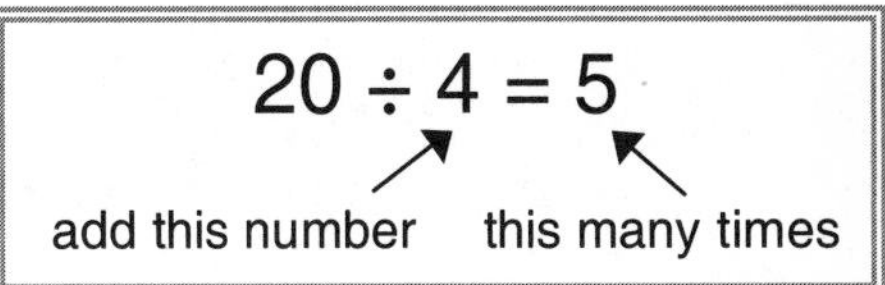

Hence the division statement 20 ÷ 4 = 5 can be read as "add four five times."
The number 4 is called the **divisor** and the number 5 is called the **quotient** of the division statement.

---

1. Draw a picture and write an addition statement for each division statement.

a) 12 ÷ 3 = 4

3 + 3 + 3 + 3 = 12

b) 8 ÷ 2 = 4

c) 20 ÷ 5 = 4

2. Draw a picture and write a division statement for each addition statement.

a) 6 + 6 + 6 + 6 = 24

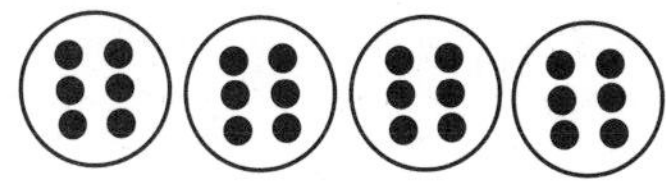

b) 4 + 4 + 4 + 4 + 4 + 4 = 24

c) 7 + 7 + 7 = 21

d) 3 + 3 + 3 + 3 + 3 = 15

e) 4 + 4 + 4 + 4 = 16

f) 8 + 8 + 8 = 24

No unauthorized copying

NS5-30: Dividing by Skip Counting *(continued)*

You can solve the division problem **12 ÷ 4 = ?** by skip counting on the number line:

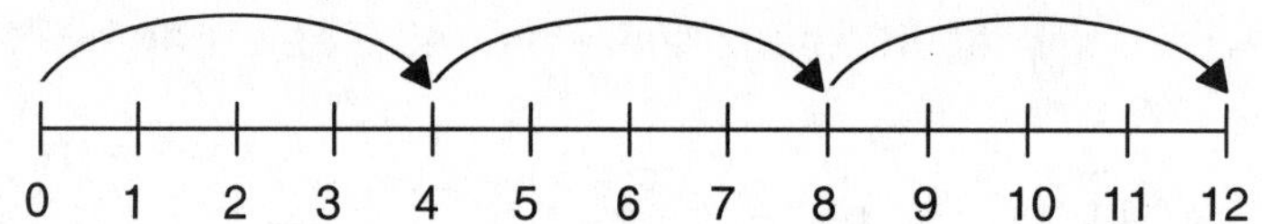

The number line shows that it takes 3 skips of size 4 to get 12:

4 + 4 + 4 = 12 so ... **12 ÷ 4 = 3**

3. Draw arrows to show how you can divide by skip counting:

a)

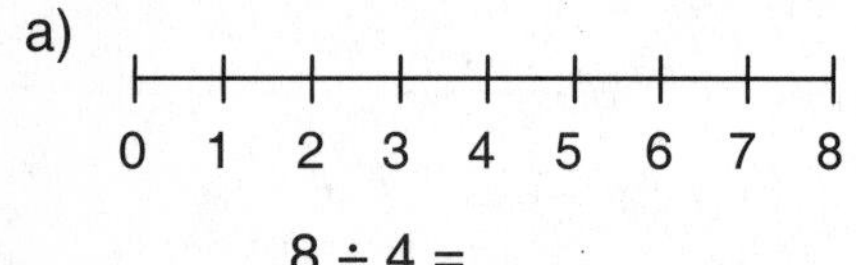

8 ÷ 4 = ____

b)

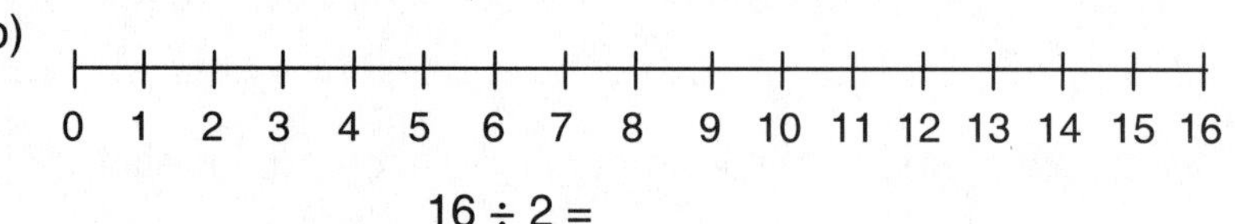

16 ÷ 2 = ____

4. What division statement does the picture represent?

a)

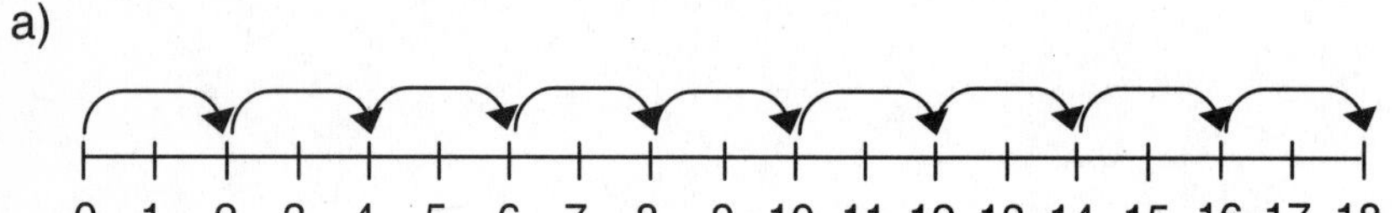

____

b)

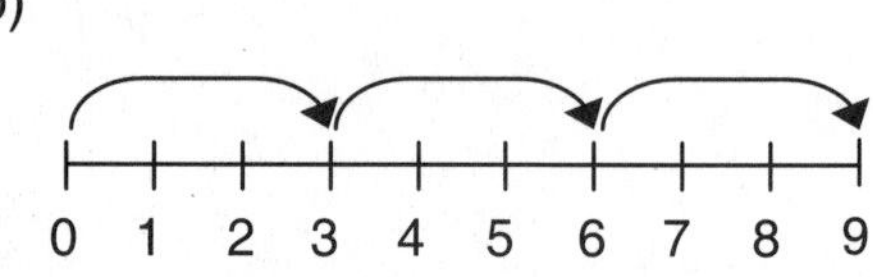

____

5. You can also find the answer to a division question by skip counting on your fingers.

For instance, to find **40 ÷ 8**, count by 8s until you reach 40.

The number of fingers you have up when you say "40" is the answer:

8

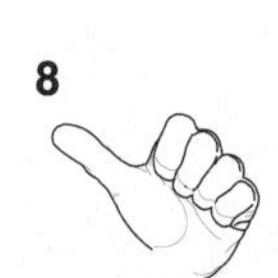

16

24

32

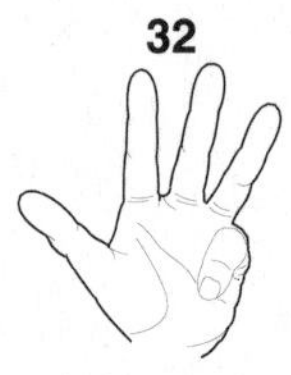

40

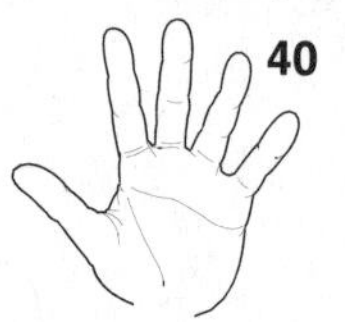

So 40 ÷ 8 = 5

Find the answer by skip counting on your fingers:

a) 18 ÷ 6 = ____ b) 12 ÷ 6 = ____ c) 32 ÷ 8 = ____ d) 21 ÷ 7 = ____ e) 45 ÷ 5 = ____

f) 25 ÷ 5 = ____ g) 36 ÷ 4 = ____ h) 35 ÷ 5 = ____ i) 27 ÷ 3 = ____ j) 16 ÷ 2 = ____

k) 36 ÷ 9 = ____ l) 35 ÷ 7 = ____ m) 12 ÷ 3 = ____ n) 18 ÷ 3 = ____ o) 24 ÷ 6 = ____

6. 8 friends split the cafeteria bill of $32.
How much does each friend have to pay?

____

7. 35 candles are in 5 rows.
How many candles are in each row?

____

 No unauthorized copying

NS5-31: Division and Multiplication

Every division statement implies a multiplication statement. The statement:

"14 divided into sets of size 2 gives 7 sets" (or **14 ÷ 2 = 7**)

can be rewritten as: "7 sets of size 2 equals 14" (**7 × 2 = 14** or **2 × 7 = 14**)

---

1. Write two multiplication statements and two division statements for each picture:

a)    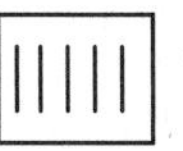 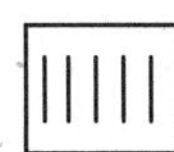

5 × 4 = 20   4 × 5 = 20

20 ÷ 4 = 5   20 ÷ 5 = 4

b)   

____

____

c) 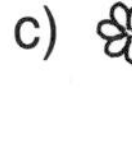    

____

____

How many flowers? _____

How many sets? _____

How many flowers in each set? _____

d)   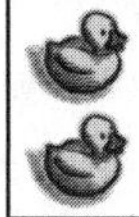 

____

____

How many ducks? _____

How many sets? _____

How many ducks in each set? _____

2. Find the answer to the division problem by first finding the answer to the multiplication statement.

a) 6 × [5] = 30	b) 8 × [ ] = 24	c) 5 × [ ] = 40	d) 9 × [ ] = 27	e) 7 × [ ] = 35
30 ÷ 6 = [5]	24 ÷ 8 = [ ]	40 ÷ 5 = [ ]	27 ÷ 9 = [ ]	35 ÷ 7 = [ ]

3. The picture shows that 2 sets of size 5 contain the same number of dots as 5 sets of size 2 (that is, 2 × 5 = 5 × 2):

a) In a notebook, draw a picture and explain how your picture shows that:

i) 7 × 4 = 4 × 7   ii) 9 × 2 = 2 × 9

b) Draw an array and explain how your picture shows that:

6 + 6 + 6 + 6 = 4 + 4 + 4 + 4 + 4 + 4

No unauthorized copying

NS5-32: Knowing When to Multiply or Divide

TEACHER:

To solve word problems involving multiplication or division, your child should ask:

- **How many things are there altogether?**
- **How many sets or groups are there?**
- **How many things are in each set?**

Your child should also know (and be able to explain using pictures or concrete materials):

- **When you know the number of sets and the number of things in each set, you multiply to find the total number of things.**
- **When you know the total number of things and the number of sets, you divide to find the number of things in each set.**
- **When you know the total number of things and the number of things in each set, you divide to find the number of sets.**

---

1. For each picture, fill in the blanks:

a) |||| |||| |||| ||||

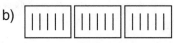

_____ lines in total

_____ lines in each set

_____ sets

b) ||||| ||||| |||||

_____ lines in total

_____ sets

_____ lines in each set

c) |||||| |||||| |||||| ||||||

_____ lines in each set

_____ sets

_____ lines altogether

d) 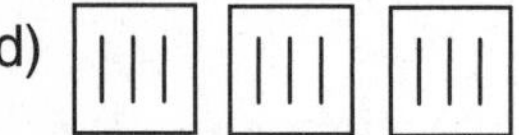

_____ lines in each set

_____ sets

_____ lines altogether

e) |||| |||| ||||

_____ lines

_____ lines in each set

_____ sets

f) 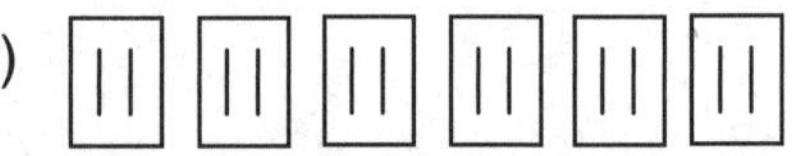

_____ lines in total

_____ sets

_____ lines in each set

2. Draw a picture of:

a) 10 lines altogether; 2 lines in each set; 5 sets

b) 15 lines; 3 lines in each set; 5 sets

c) 4 sets; 7 lines in each set; 28 lines in total

d) 18 lines; 3 sets; 6 lines in each set

3. Draw a picture of <u>and</u> write two division statements and a multiplication statement for:

a) 21 lines altogether; 3 lines in each set; 7 sets

b) 14 lines; 7 lines in each set; 2 sets

No unauthorized copying

NS5-32: Knowing When to Multiply or Divide *(continued)*

4. In each question, some information is missing (indicated by a question mark).

   Write a multiplication or division statement to find the missing information.

	Total number of things	Number of sets	Number of things in each set	Multiplication or division statement
a)	?	6	3	6 × 3 = 18
b)	20	4	?	20 ÷ 4 = 5
c)	15	?	5	
d)	10	2	?	
e)	?	4	6	
f)	21	7	?	

5. For each question, write a multiplication or a division statement to solve the problem:

a) 15 things in total
5 things in each set

____

How many sets?

____

b) 6 sets
4 things in each set

____

How many things in total?

____

c) 25 things in total
5 sets

____

How many things in each set?

____

d) 9 groups
4 things in each group

____

How many things in total?

____

e) 9 things in each set
18 things in total

____

How many sets?

____

f) 3 groups
18 things altogether

____

How many in each group?

____

g) 16 things in each set
3 sets

____

How many things in total?

____

h) 8 things in each set
24 things in total

____

How many sets?

____

i) 20 things in total
5 sets

____

How many things in each set?

____

No unauthorized copying

NS5-32: Knowing When to Multiply or Divide *(continued)*

6. Fill in the chart. Use a question mark to show what you don't know.
   Then write a multiplication or division statement in the right hand column.

	Total Number of things	Number of sets	Number in each set	Multiplication or division statement
a) 8 chairs at each table 3 tables	?	3	8	3 x 8 = 24 How many chairs? 8
b) 9 marbles in each jar 5 jars				How many marbles? _____
c) 35 flowers 7 pots				How many flowers in each pot? _____
d) 32 people 4 boats				How many people in each boat? _____
e) 24 flowers 6 plants				How many flowers on each plant? _____
f) 36 candles 6 candles in each packet				How many packets? _____

7. The fact family for the multiplication statement **3 × 5 = 15** is: **5 × 3 = 15**; **15 ÷ 3 = 5** and **15 ÷ 5 = 3**.
   Write the fact family of equations for the multiplication statements:

a) 4 × 2 = 8

____
____
____

b) 6 × 3 = 18

____
____
____

c) 7 × 8 = 56

____
____
____

d) 9 × 4 = 36

____
____
____

No unauthorized copying

NS5-33: Remainders

Guy wants to share 9 apples with 3 friends.
He sets out 4 plates, one for himself and one for each of his friends.
He puts one apple at a time on a plate:

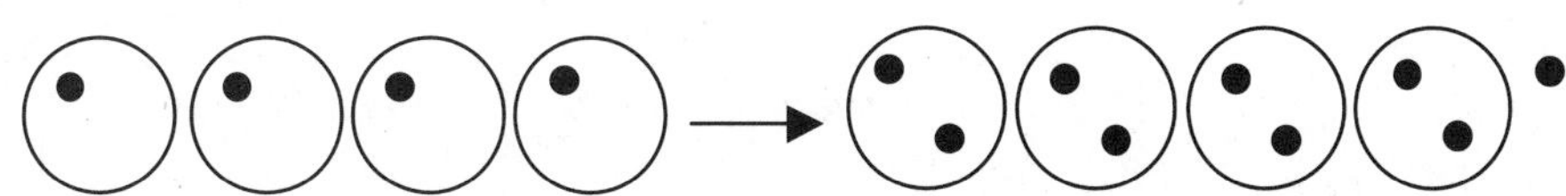

← ***There is one apple left over.***

9 apples cannot be shared equally into 4 sets. Each person gets 2 apples, but one is left over.

9 ÷ 4 = 2 Remainder 1 OR 9 ÷ 4 = 2 R 1

---

1. Can you share 7 apples equally onto 2 plates? Show your work using dots and circles:

2. Share the dots as equally as possible among the circles.

   a) 8 dots in 3 circles

   ____ dots in each circle; ____ dots remaining

   b) 13 dots in 4 circles

   ____ dots in each circle; ____ dot remaining

3. Share the dots as equally as possible. Draw a picture and write a division statement.

   Example: 9 dots in 2 circles

   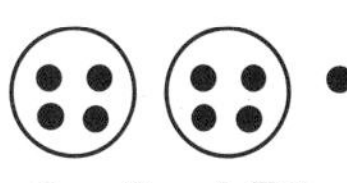

   9 ÷ 2 = 4 R1

   a) 14 dots in 4 circles b) 18 dots in 6 circles c) 17 dots in 4 circles d) 22 dots in 3 circles

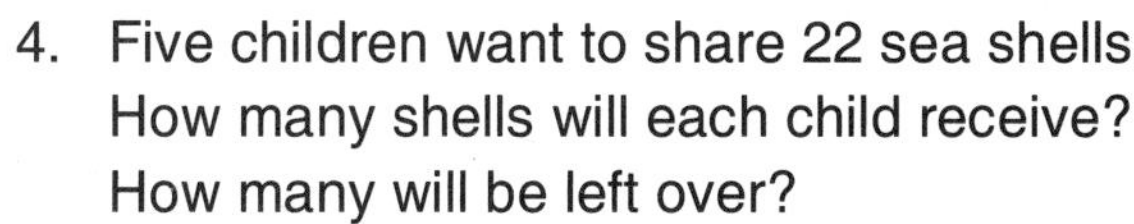

4. Five children want to share 22 sea shells. How many shells will each child receive? How many will be left over?

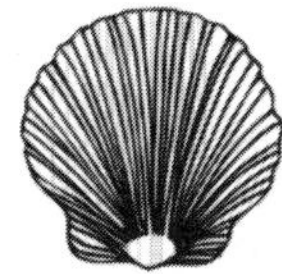

5. Find two different ways to share 29 pens into equal groups so that one is left over.

6. Four friends have more than 7 stickers and less than 13 stickers. They share the stickers evenly. How many stickers do they have? (Is there more than one answer?)

No unauthorized copying

NS5-34: Long Division — 2-Digit by 1-Digit

Manuel is preparing snacks for 4 classes.
He needs to divide 97 oranges into 4 groups.
He will use long division and a model to solve the problem:

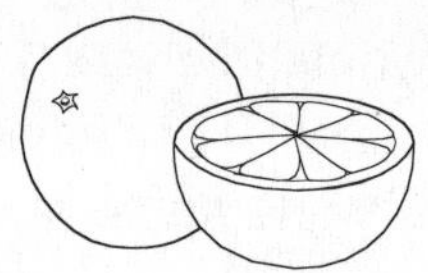

Step 1:

4) 97 ← He writes the number of oranges here.

He writes the number of groups he needs to make here.

He puts 2 tens blocks in each group. → 2

4) 9 7 ← There are 7 ones.

There are 9 tens blocks in the model.

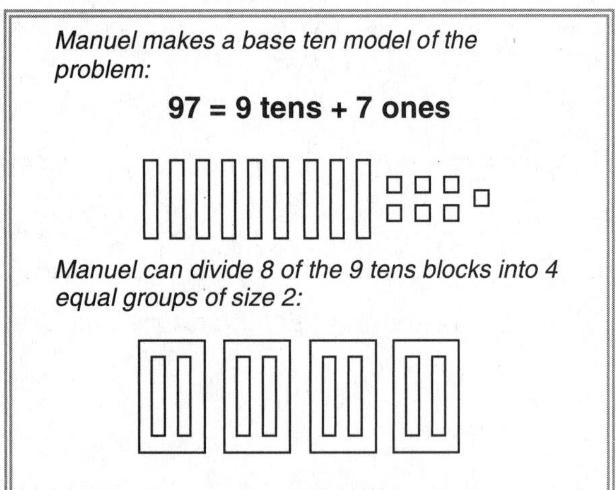

Manuel makes a base ten model of the problem:
97 = 9 tens + 7 ones
Manuel can divide 8 of the 9 tens blocks into 4 equal groups of size 2:

1. Manuel has written a division statement to solve a problem.
How many groups does he want to make?
How many tens and how many ones would he need to model the problem?

a) 3) 76
groups ______
tens blocks ______
ones ______

b) 4) 95
groups ______
tens blocks ______
ones ______

c) 4) 92
groups ______
tens blocks ______
ones ______

d) 5) 86
groups ______
tens blocks ______
ones ______

2. How many tens blocks can be put in each group?

a) 3) 4 5 — 1
b) 5) 9 3
c) 4) 6 2
d) 3) 8 9
e) 4) 8 2
f) 3) 3 8
g) 5) 9 7
h) 4) 8 1
i) 6) 8 5
j) 7) 9 6

3. For each division statement, how many groups have been made?
How many tens are in each group?

a) 3) 8 5 — 2
groups __3__
number of tens in each group __2__

b) 4) 9 4
groups ______
number of tens in each group _____

c) 5) 7 5
groups ______
number of tens in each group _____

d) 2) 8 9
groups ______
number of tens in each group _____

NS5-34: Long Division — 2-Digit by 1-Digit *(continued)*

Step 2:

There are 2 tens blocks in each group. → 2 over $4\overline{)97}$ → 2 over $4\overline{)97}$ with 8 below

There are 4 groups.

2 × 4 = 8 tens blocks have been placed.

In the model:

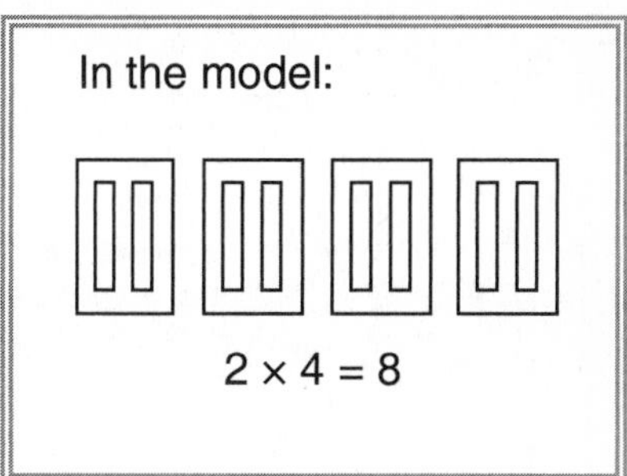

2 × 4 = 8

4. Find how many tens have been placed by multiplying:

a) 4 over $2\overline{)97}$

How many groups? ______

How many tens to be placed? ______

How many tens in each group? ______

How many tens placed altogether? ______

b) 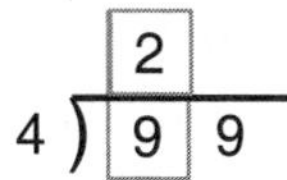

2 over $4\overline{)99}$

How many groups? ______

How many tens to be placed? ______

How many tens in each group? ______

How many tens placed altogether? ______

5. Use skip counting to find out how many tens can be placed in each group.
Then use multiplication to find out how many tens have been placed:

a) 2 over $3\overline{)83}$, 6 below

b) 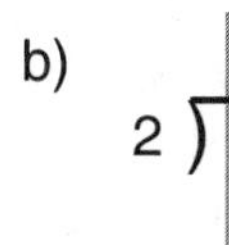 $2\overline{)72}$

c) 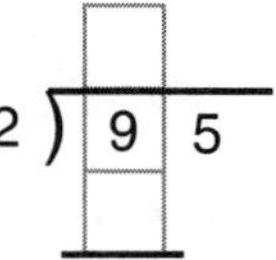 $2\overline{)95}$

d) 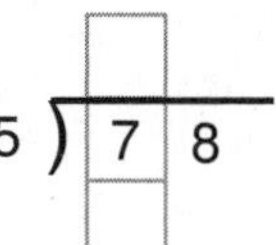 $5\overline{)78}$

e) 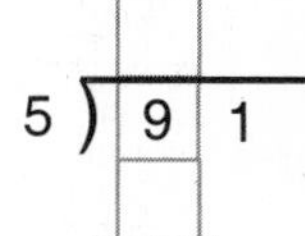 $5\overline{)91}$

f) $5\overline{)53}$

g) $4\overline{)93}$

h) $3\overline{)84}$

i) $6\overline{)93}$

j) $7\overline{)95}$

k) $9\overline{)93}$

l) $8\overline{)91}$

m) $7\overline{)82}$

n) $3\overline{)90}$

o) $3\overline{)87}$

p) $4\overline{)85}$

q) $9\overline{)92}$

r) $7\overline{)85}$

s) $3\overline{)81}$

t) $2\overline{)94}$

No unauthorized copying

Step 3:

There are 9 tens blocks. Manuel has placed 8.

He subtracts to find out how many are left over (9 – 8 = 1).

$$\begin{array}{r|l} & 2 \\ 4\,) & 9\ 7 \\ - & 8 \\ \hline & 1 \end{array}$$

In the model:

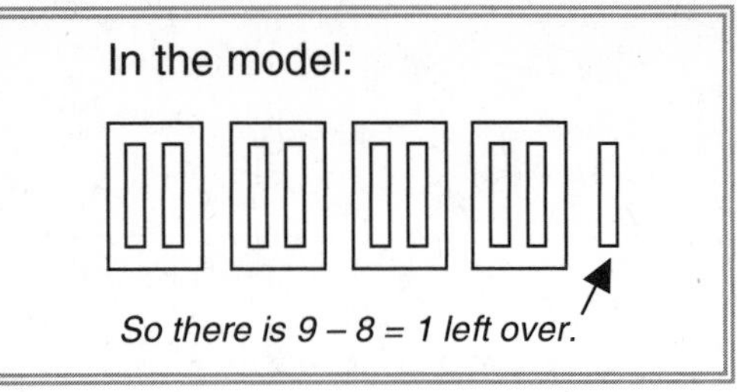

So there is 9 – 8 = 1 left over.

6. Carry out the first three steps of the long division:

a) 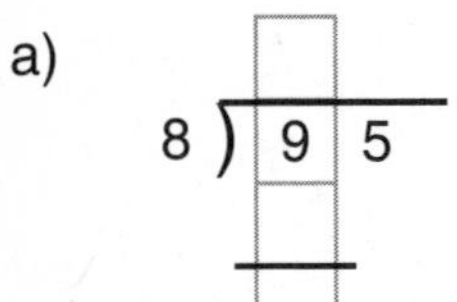

b) 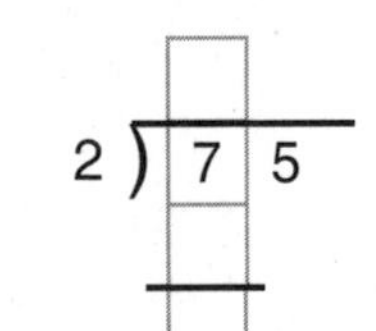

c) 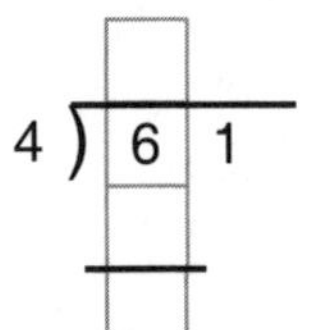

d) 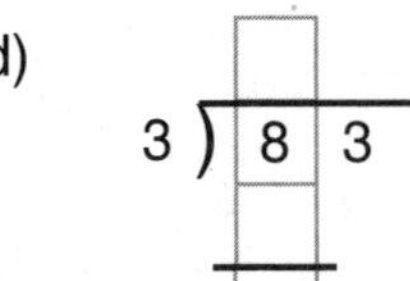

e) 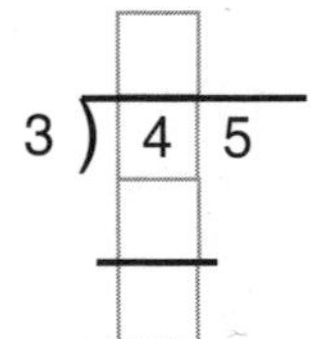

f) 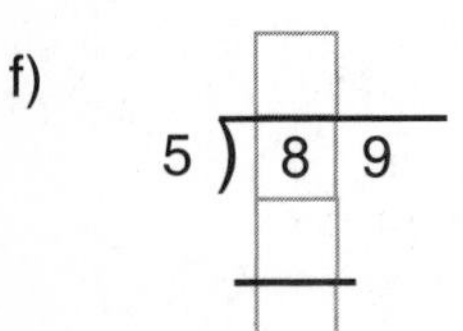

g) 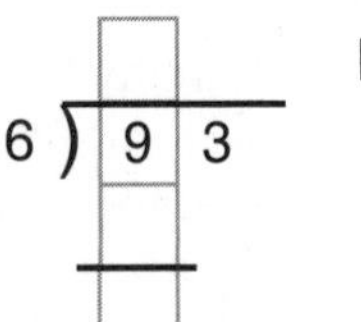

h) 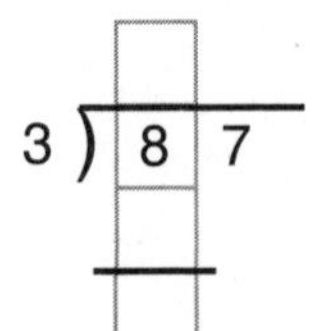

i) 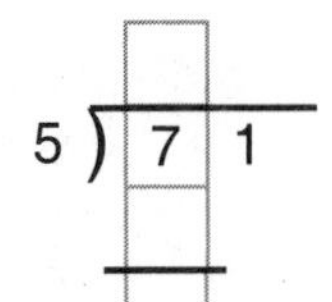

j) 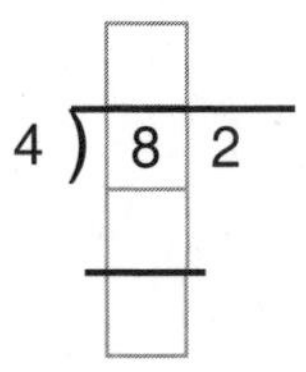

Step 4:

There is one tens block left over and 7 ones. So there are 17 ones left over. Manuel writes the 7 beside the 1 to show this.

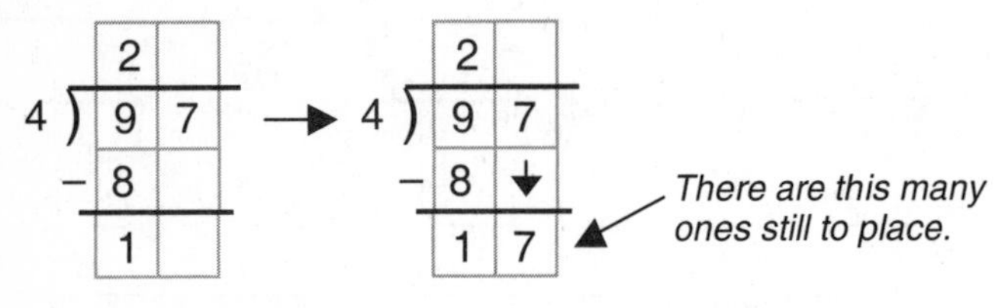

In the model:

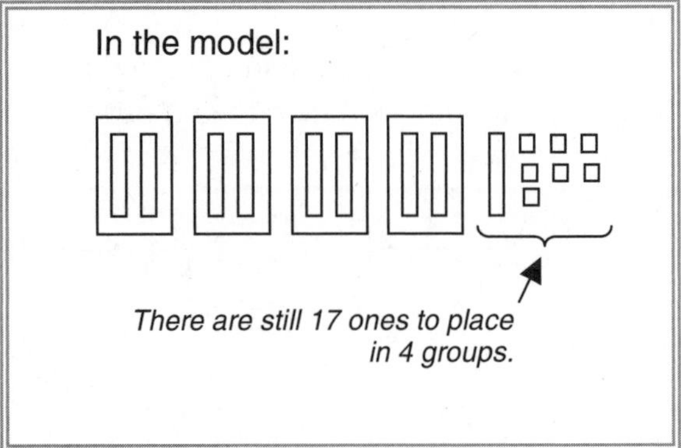

There are still 17 ones to place in 4 groups.

7. Carry out the first four steps of the division:

a) 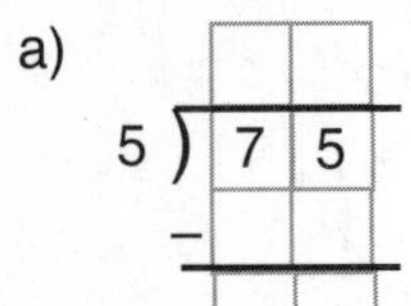

b) 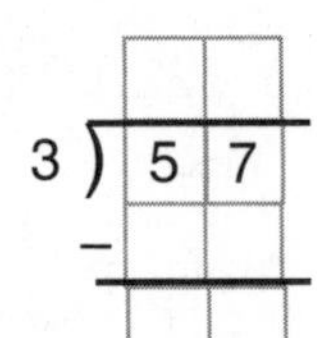

c) 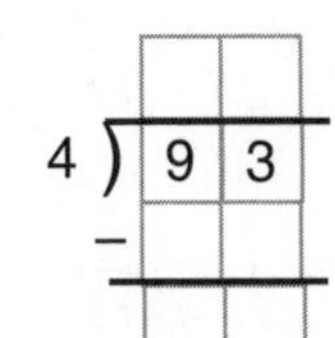

d) 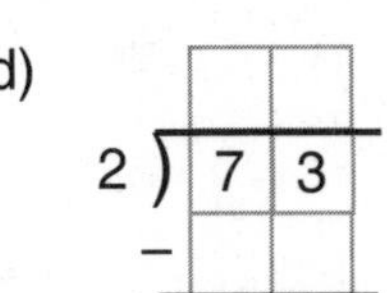

e) 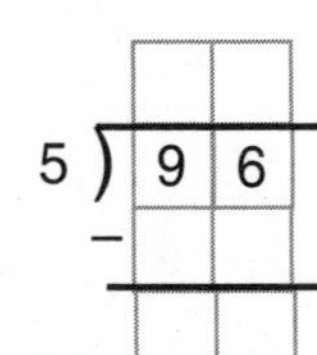

f) 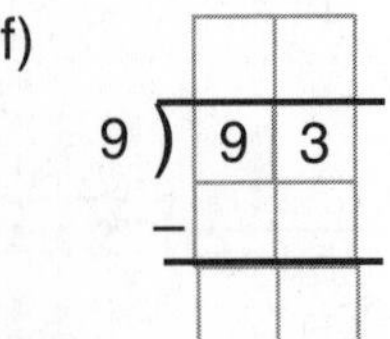

g) 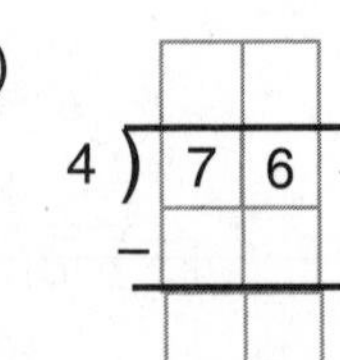

h) 8) 9 8

i) 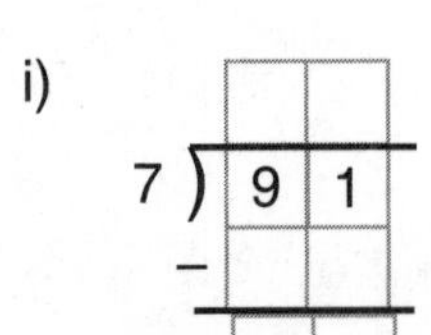

j) 8) 9 6

Step 5:

Manuel finds the number of ones he can put in each group by dividing 17 by 4.

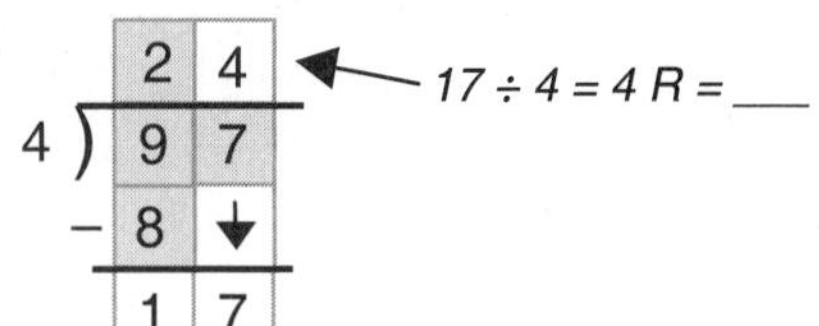

In the model:

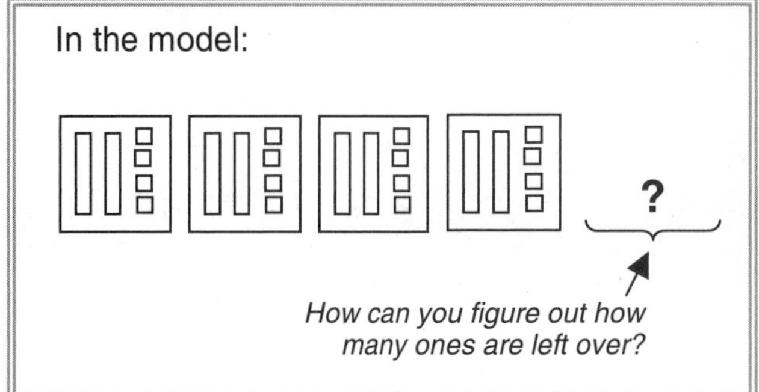

?
How can you figure out how many ones are left over?

8. Carry out the first five steps of the division:

a) 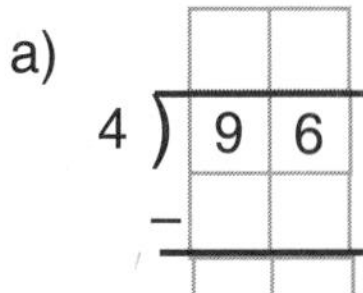

b) 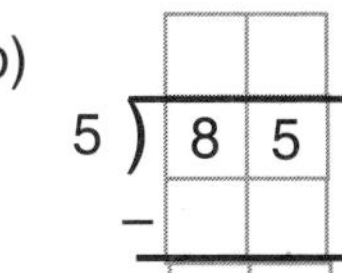

c) 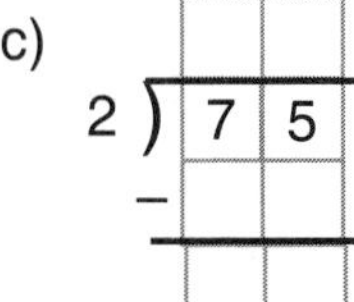

d) 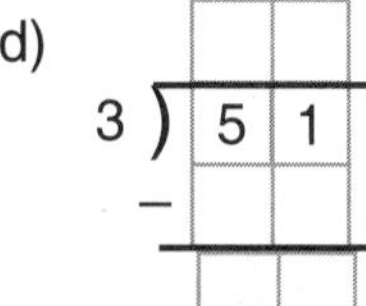

e) 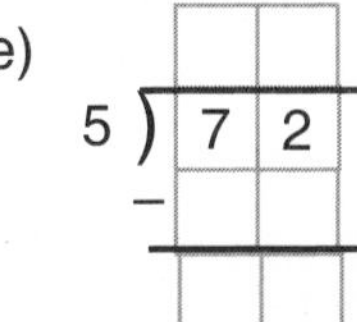

f) 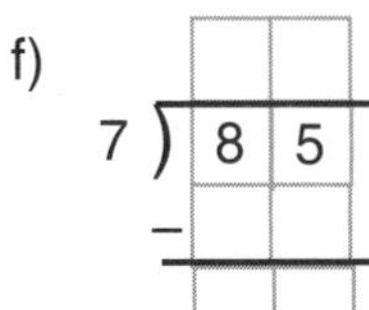

g) 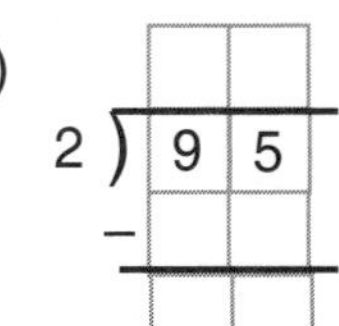

h) 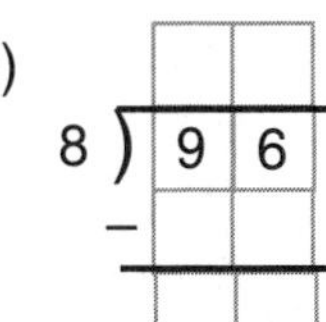

i) 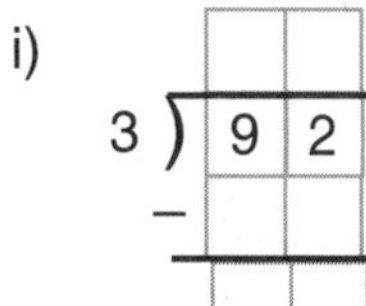

j) 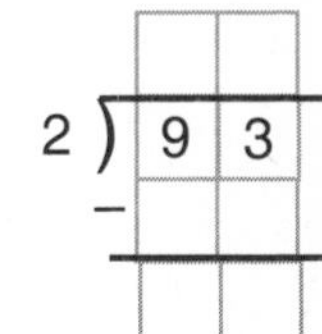

Steps 6 and 7:

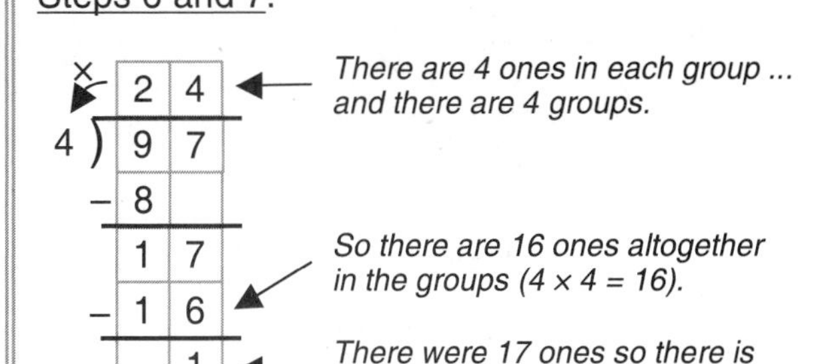

There are 4 ones in each group ... and there are 4 groups.
So there are 16 ones altogether in the groups (4 × 4 = 16).
There were 17 ones so there is 1 one left over (17 – 16 = 1).

In the model:

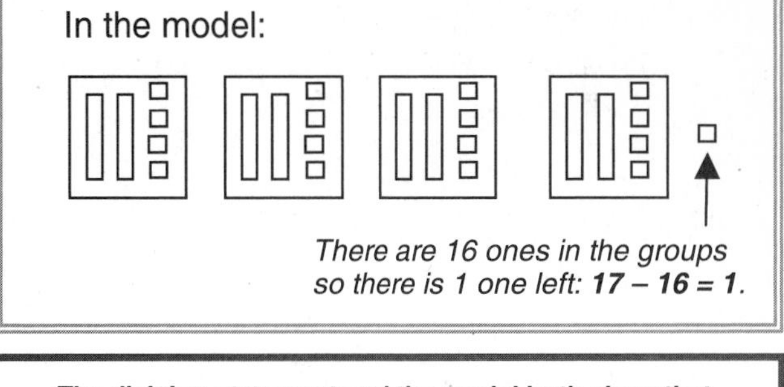

*There are 16 ones in the groups so there is 1 one left: **17 – 16 = 1**.*

The division statement and the model both show that he can give each class 24 oranges with one left over.

9. Carry out all seven steps of the division:

a) 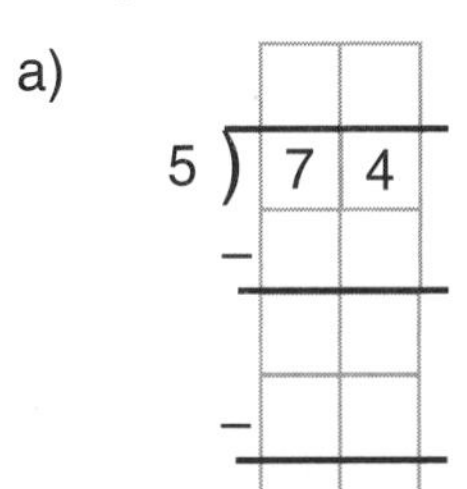

b) 3) 7 7

c) 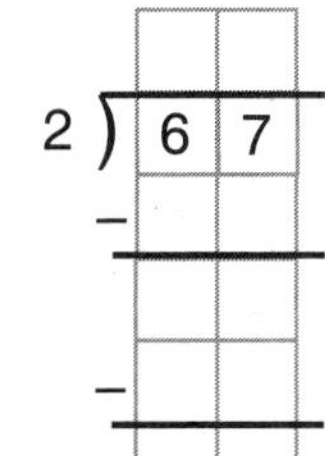

d) 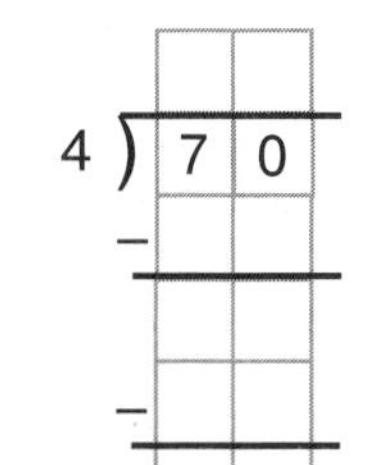

e) 4) 9 0

No unauthorized copying

f) 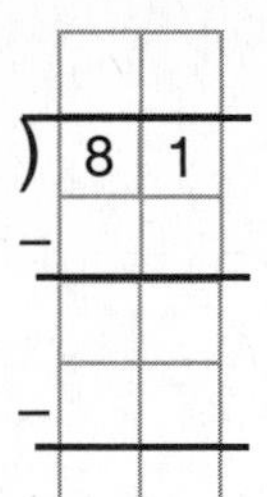

g) 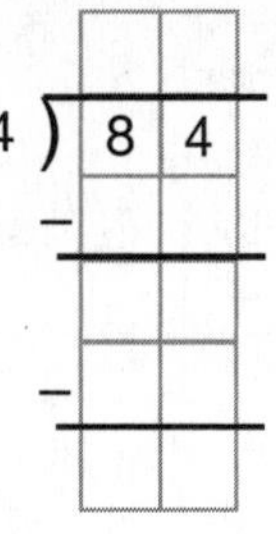

h) 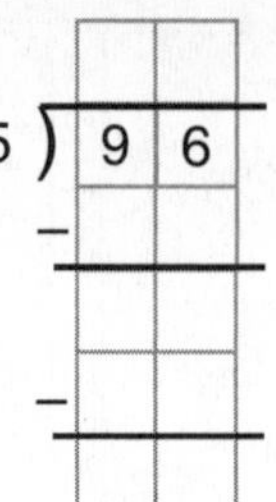

i) 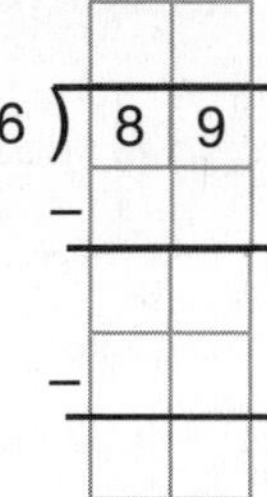

j) 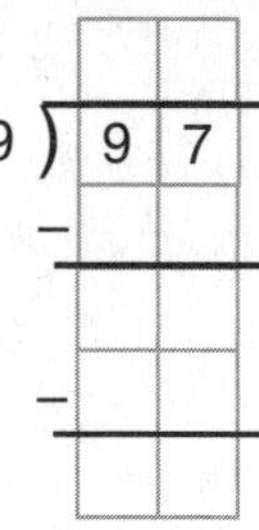

k) 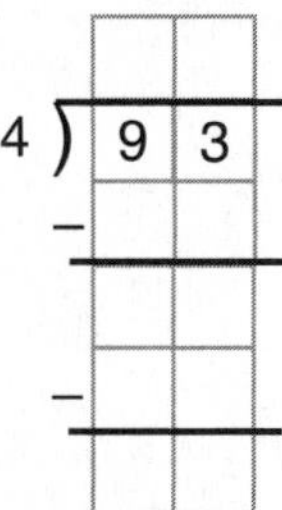

l) 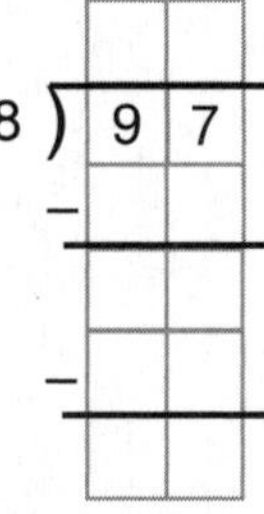

m) 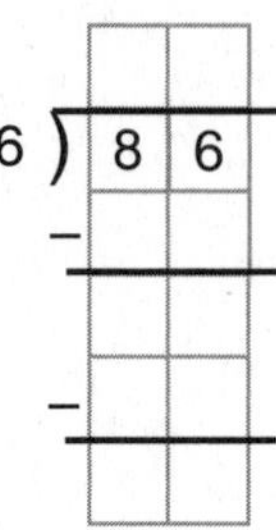

n) 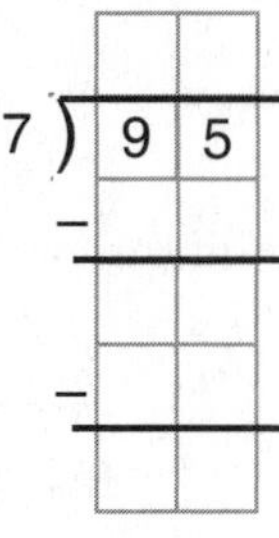

o) 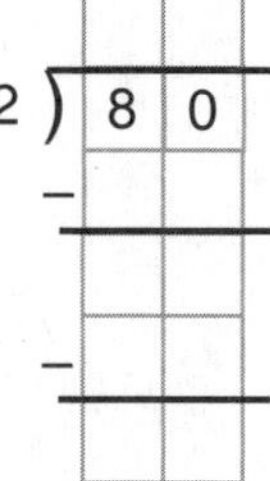

10. Avi put 98 flowers in bouquets of 8. How many flowers are left over?

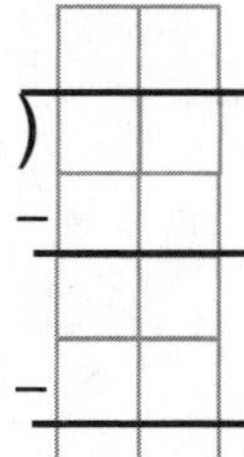

11. How many weeks are in 93 days?

12. Michelle jogs for 3 km every day. How many days will she take to run 45 km?

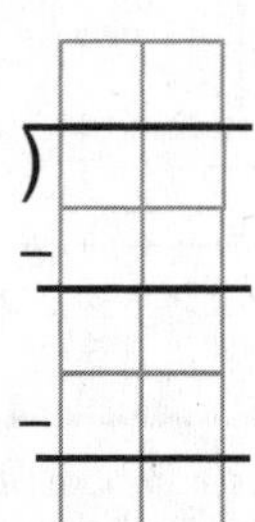

13. A six sided pool has perimeter 72 m. How long is each side?

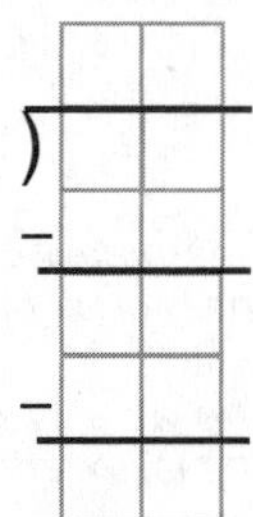

14. Guerdy packs 85 books into boxes of 6, and Tyree packs 67 books into boxes of 4. Who uses more boxes?

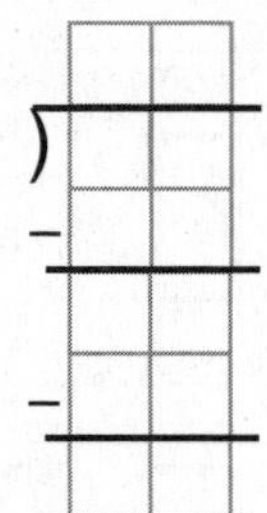

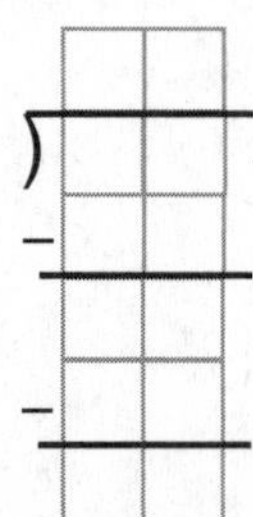

No unauthorized copying

NS5-35: Long Division — 3- and 4-Digit by 1-Digit

1. Find 335 ÷ 2 by drawing a base ten model and by long division:

Step 1: *Draw a base ten model of 335.*

Step 2: *Divide the hundreds squares into 2 equal groups.*

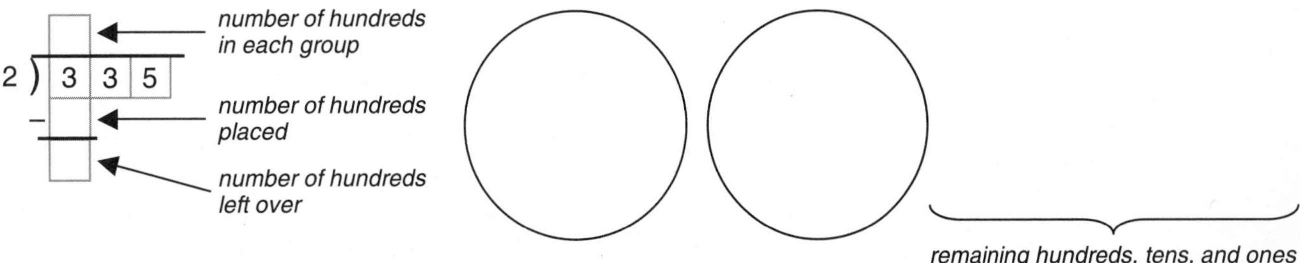

Step 3: *Exchange the leftover hundreds square for 10 tens.*

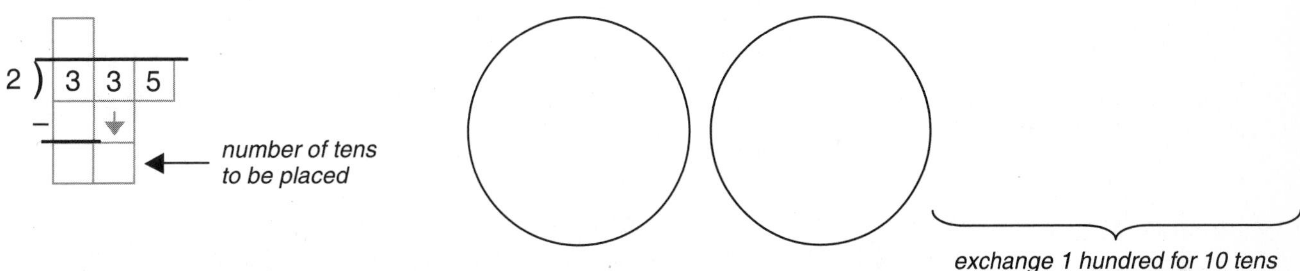

Step 4: *Divide the tens blocks into 2 equal groups.*

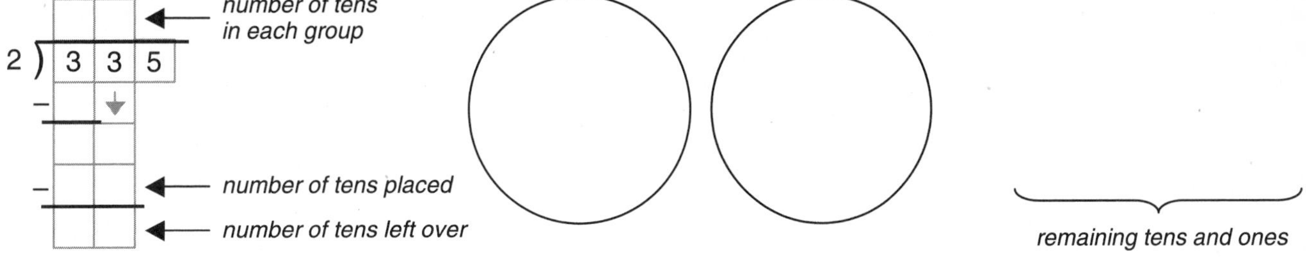

Step 5: *Exchange the leftover tens blocks for 10 ones.*

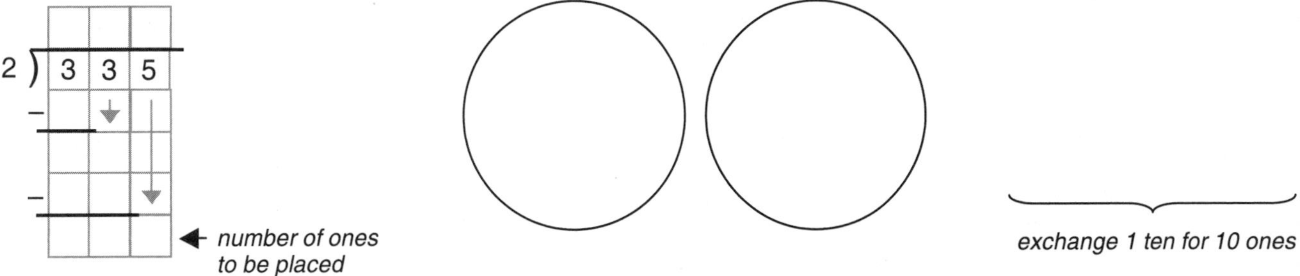

 No unauthorized copying

Steps 6 and 7: *Divide the ones into 2 equal groups.*

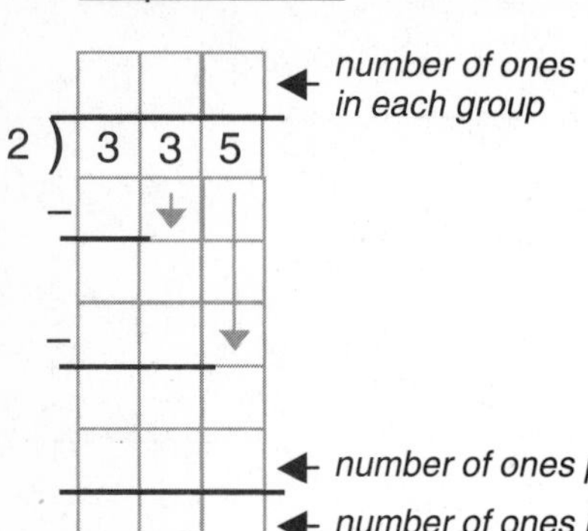

number of ones in each group

number of ones placed

number of ones left over

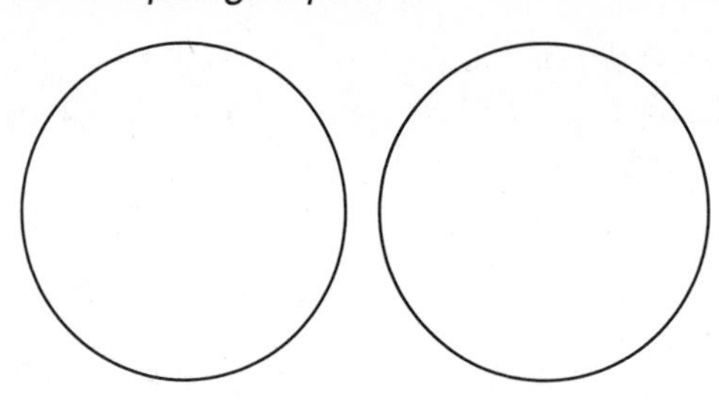

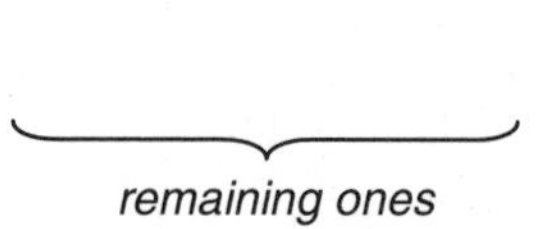

2. Divide:

a)
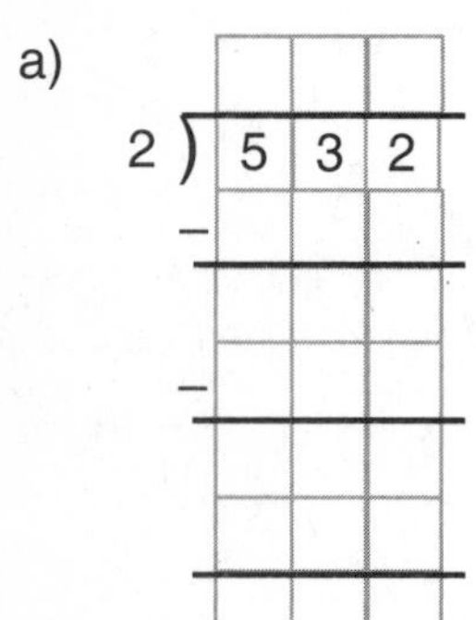

b)
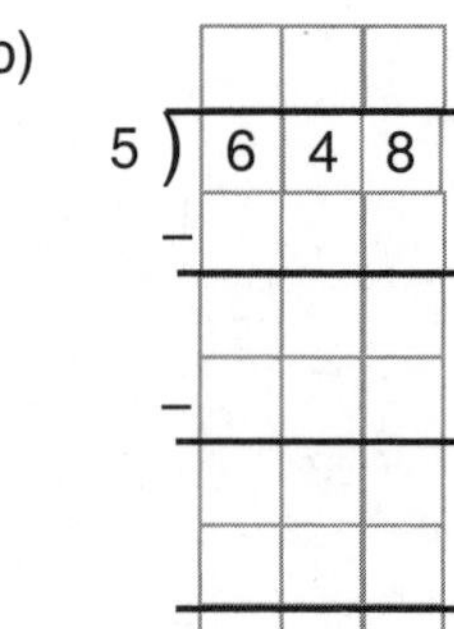

c)
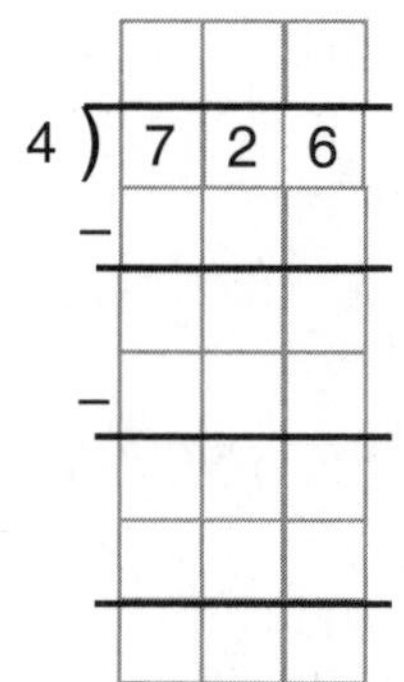

d)
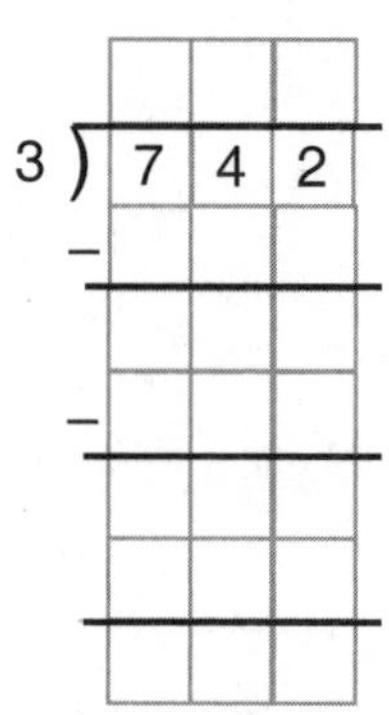

e)
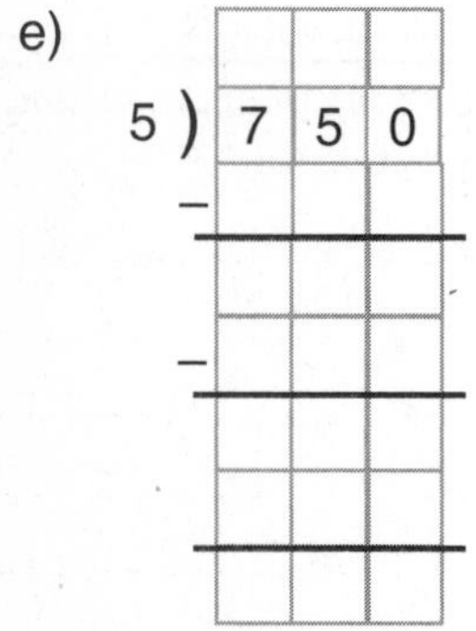

f)
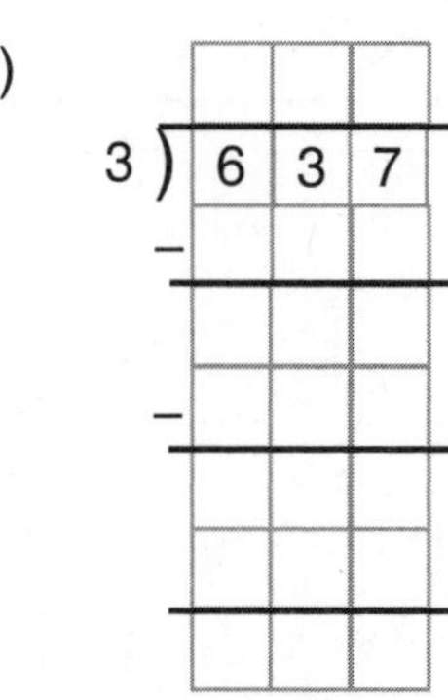

g)
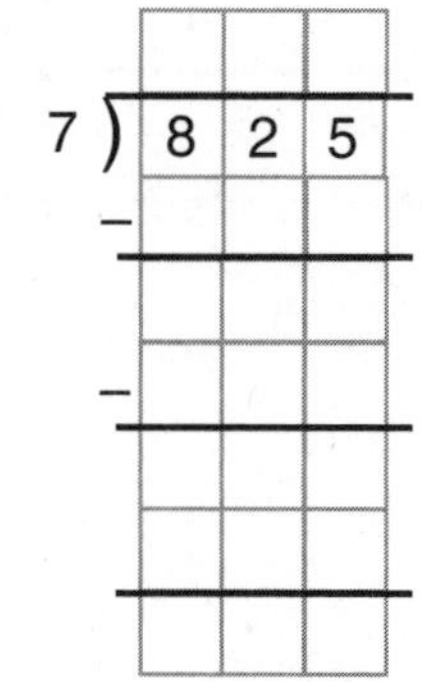

h)
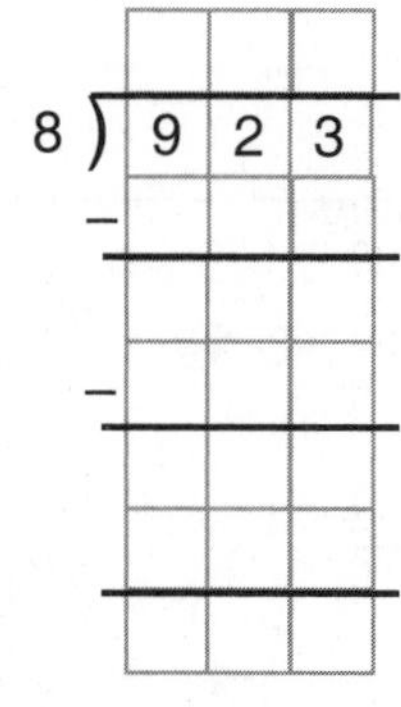

i)
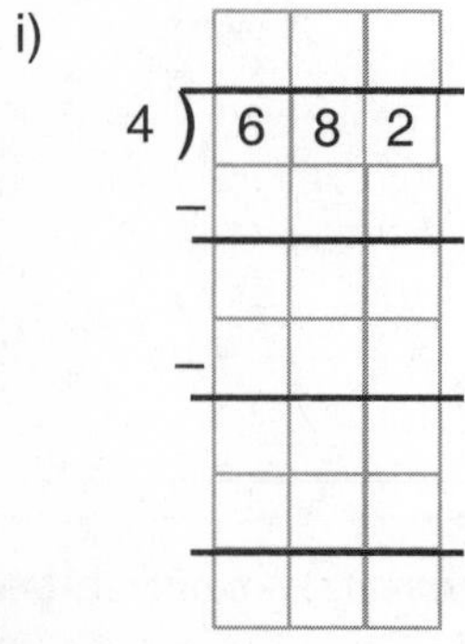

j)
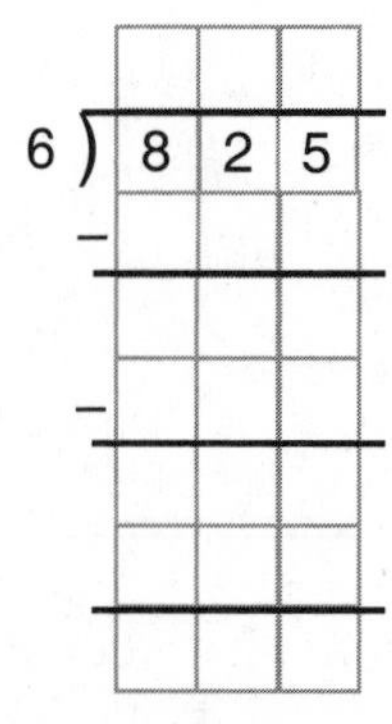

k)
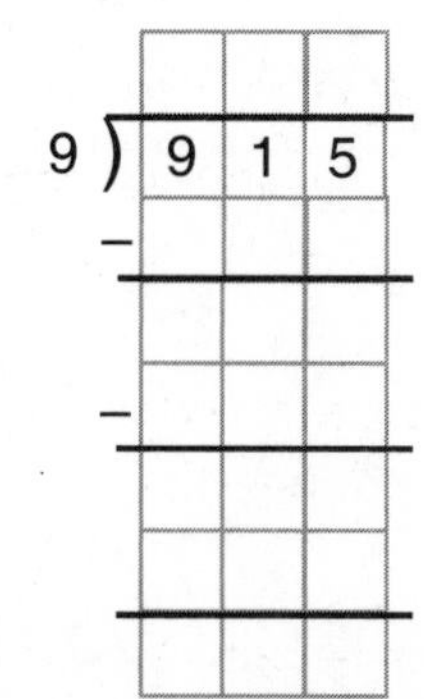

l) 8) 8 3 2

 No unauthorized copying

NS5-35: Long Division – 3- and 4-Digit by 1-Digit *(continued)*

3. In each question, there are fewer hundreds than the number of groups.
   Write a '0' in the hundreds position to show that no hundreds can be placed in equal groups.
   Then perform the division as if the hundreds had automatically been exchanged for tens.

   Divide. The first one has been done for you:

a) 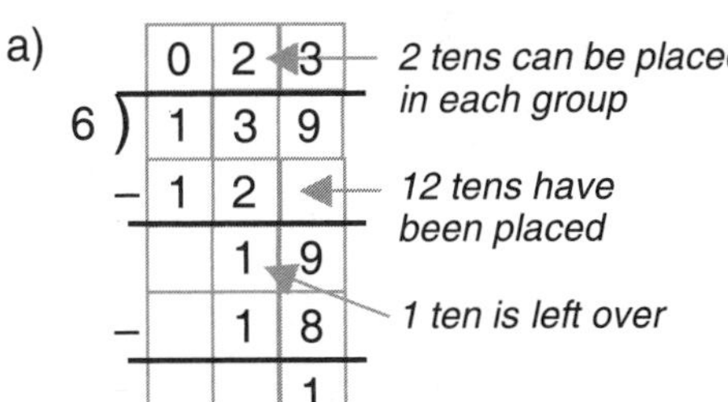

b) 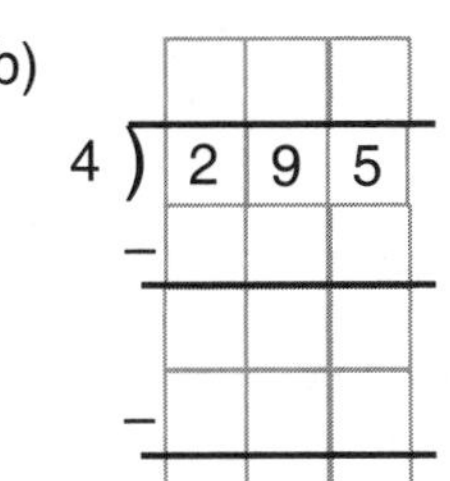

c) 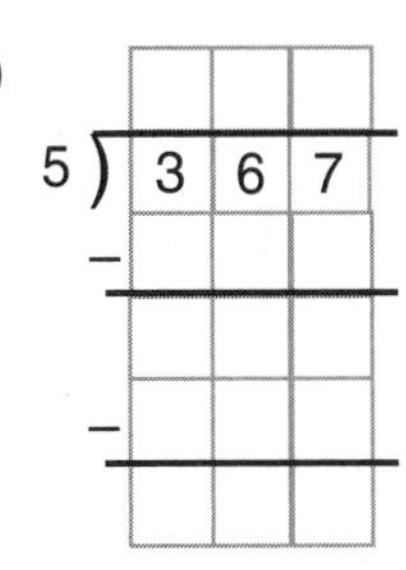

d) 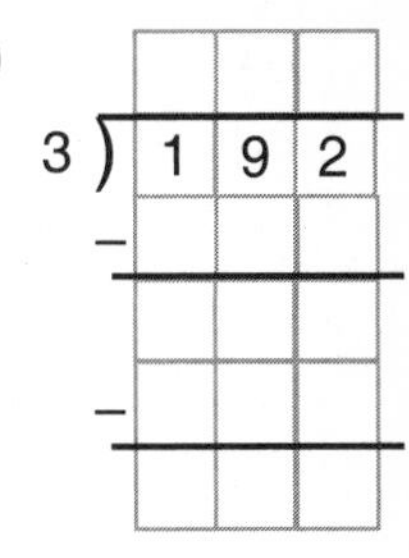

e) 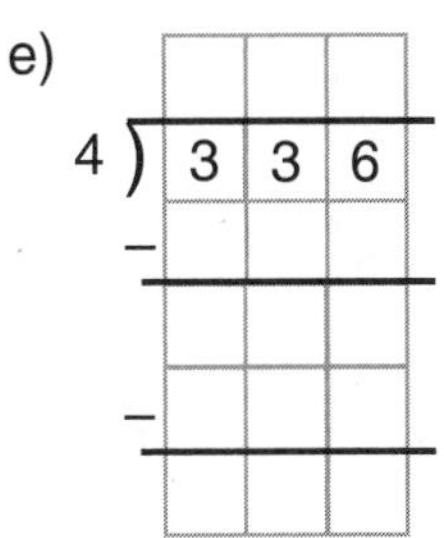

f) 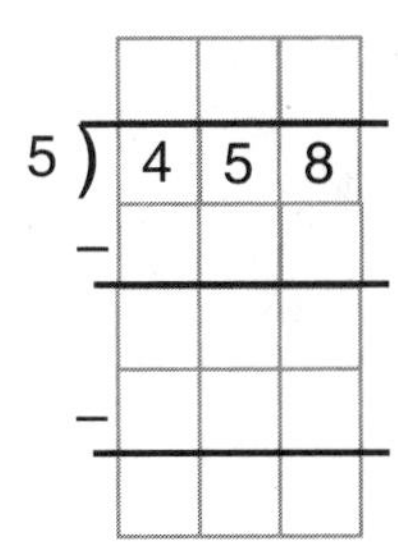

g) 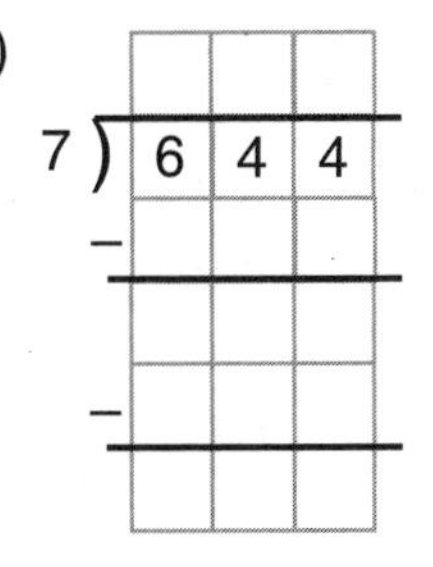

h) 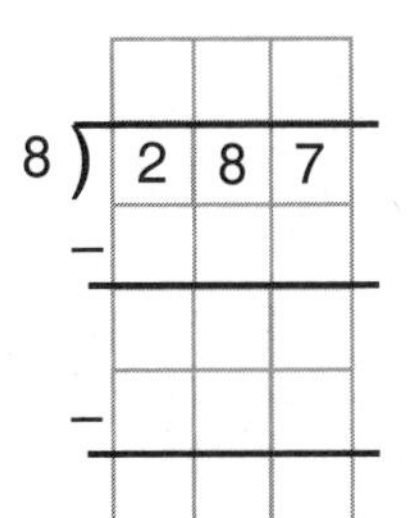

i) 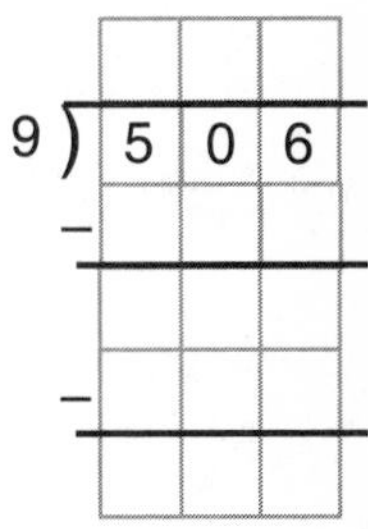

4. Divide.

a) 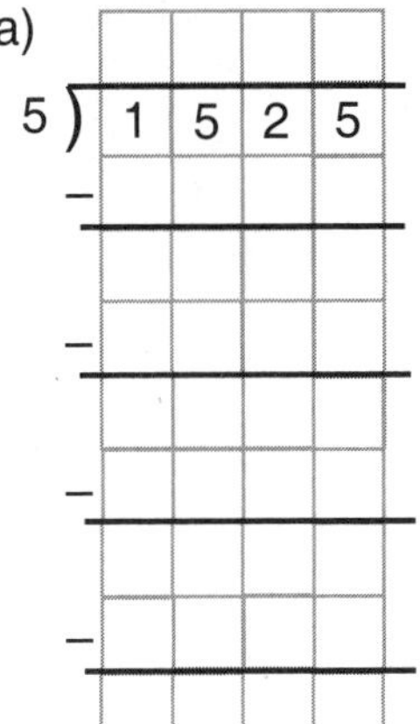

b) 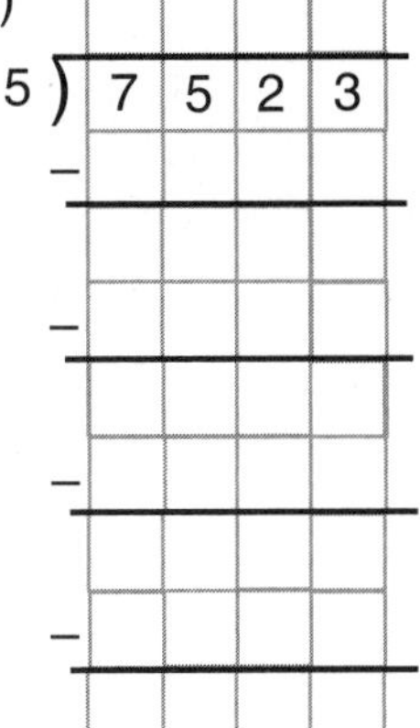

c) 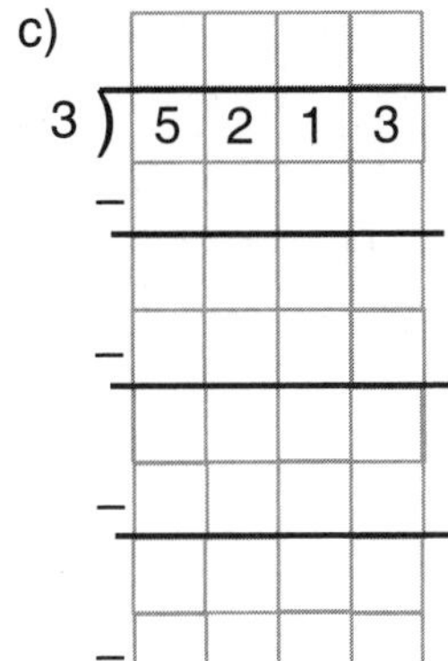

d) 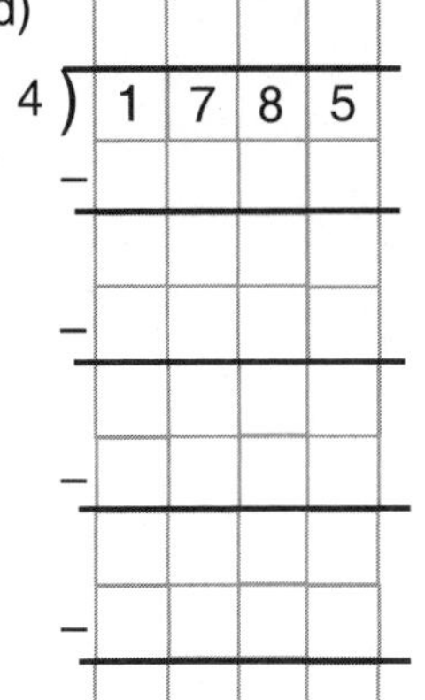

e) 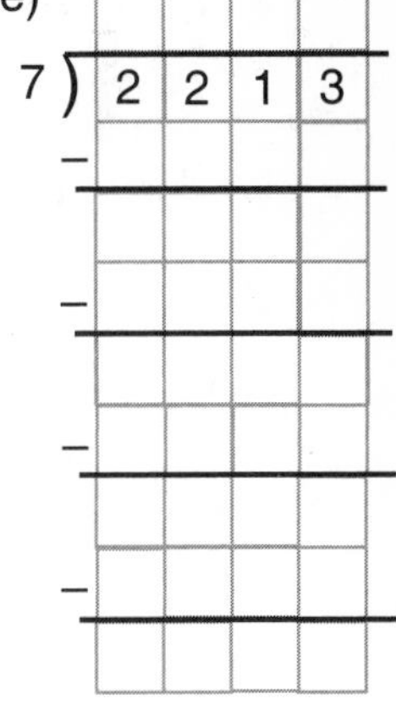

5. Ken swims 4 laps of a pool. Altogether he swims 144 metres.
   How long is the pool?

6. The perimeter of a hexagonal park is 852 km.
   How long is each side of the park?

7. Seven friends collect 2 744 books for charity. Each friend collects the same number of books.
   How many books did each friend collect?

No unauthorized copying

NS5-36: Topics in Division (Advanced)

Answer the following questions in a notebook.

1. A class paid $20 for a cake and $4 per child for a slice of pizza.

   They paid $140.

   How many children are in the class?

2. Make as many 3-digit numbers as you can using the digits 5, 1, and 0. (Use each digit once.)

   Which of your numbers are divisible by:

   a) 2 b) 5

   c) 10 d) 3

3. A number has:

   - remainder 2 when divided by 3
   - remainder 4 when divided by 5

   What is the number?

4. Raj wants to divide 24 apricots, 64 raisins, and 56 peanuts evenly into packets (with no food left over).

   What is the greatest number of packets he can make? Explain.

In the questions below, you will have to interpret what the remainder means.

Example: Cindy wants to put 64 cookies onto trays. Each tray holds 5 cookies.

How many trays will she need?

64 ÷ 5 = 12 remainder 4

She will need 13 trays (because she needs a tray for the four leftover cookies).

5. A car can hold 5 passengers.

   How many cars will 29 passengers need?

6. Manu colours 4 pictures in her picture book every day.

   How many days will she take to colour 50 pictures?

7. Jay shares 76 plums as evenly as possible among 9 friends.

   How many plums does each friend get?

8. Siru wants to place her stamps in an album.

   Each page holds 9 stamps.

   How many pages will she need for 95 stamps?

 No unauthorized copying

NS5-37: Concepts in Multiplication and Division

Answer the following questions in a notebook.

1. 

A bus carries 36 students.

How many students can 25 buses carry?

2. A racer snake lays at least 3 eggs and no more than 40 eggs.

What is the least number of eggs 6 snakes would lay?

What is the greatest number?

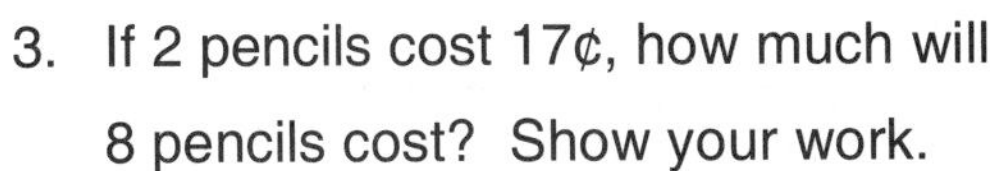

3. If 2 pencils cost 17¢, how much will 8 pencils cost? Show your work.

4. How much do 7 books cost at $19 per book?

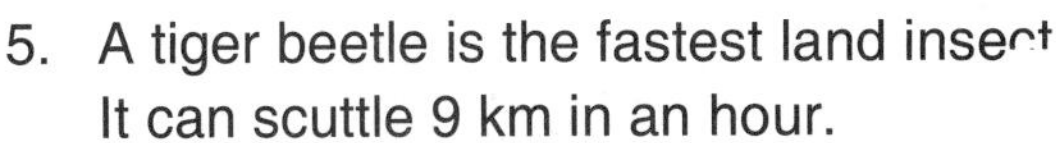

5. A tiger beetle is the fastest land insect. It can scuttle 9 km in an hour.

How many metres could it crawl in half an hour?

6. Create a division problem to go with the expression below.

$$72 \div 8$$

7. What is the least number of whole apples that can be shared equally among 2, 3, or 4 people?

8. a) Alice is between 20 and 40 years old. Last year, her age was a multiple of 4. This year, her age is a multiple of 5. How old is Alice?

   b) George is between 30 and 50 years old. Last year, his age was a multiple of 6. This year it is a multiple of 7. How old is George?

9. Nandita ran 24 laps of her school track. The track is 75 metres long.

   a) How far has she run?

   b) How much farther must she run if she wants to run 2000 metres?

   c) About how many extra laps must she run?

10. 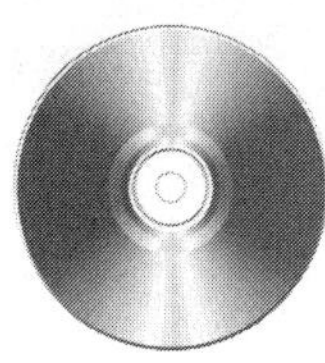

If 3 CDs cost $23, how would you calculate the cost of 12 CDs?

11. What digit could be in the box? Explain.

☐ **569 ÷ 6** is about 400.

12. Three letter carriers delivered a different number of letters in 1 week:

- Carl: 2 624 letters
- Sally: 1 759 letters
- Selma: 3 284 letters

Did any one letter carrier deliver more than half of all the letters?

No unauthorized copying

NS5-38: Rounding on a Number Line

1. Draw an arrow to the 0 or 10 to show whether the circled number is closer to **0 or 10**:

a) 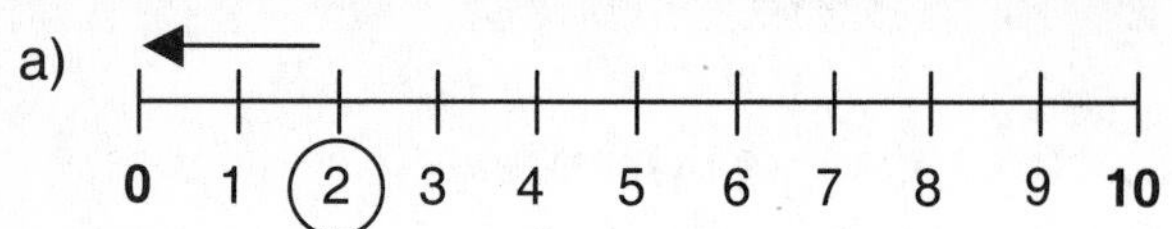

b) 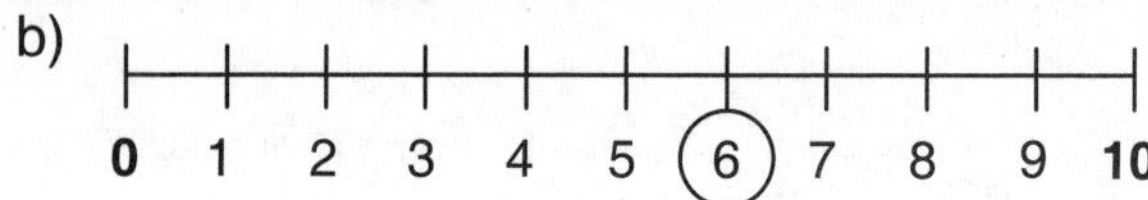

c) 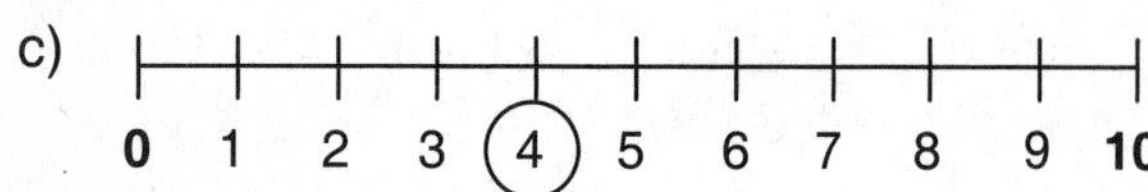

d) 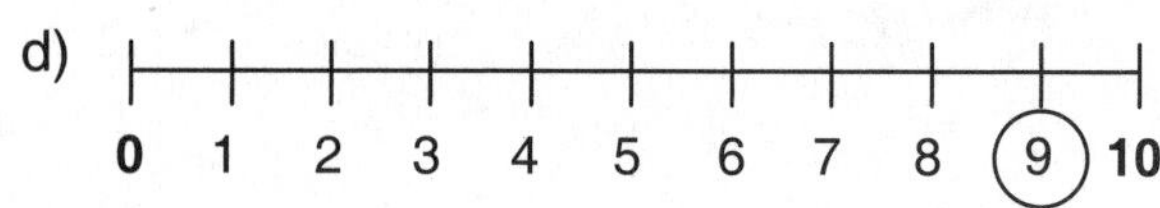

2. a) Which one-digit numbers are closer to i) 0? ______________ ii) 10? ______________

b) Why is 5 a special case? ____

3. Draw an arrow to show which multiple of ten you would round to.
Then round each number to the nearest tens.

a) 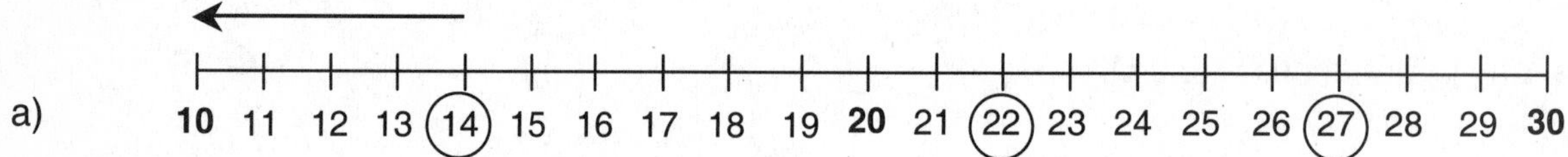

Round to 10 _____ _____

b) 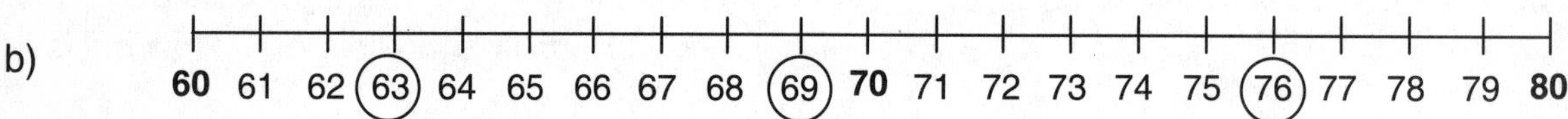

Round to _____ _____ _____

c) 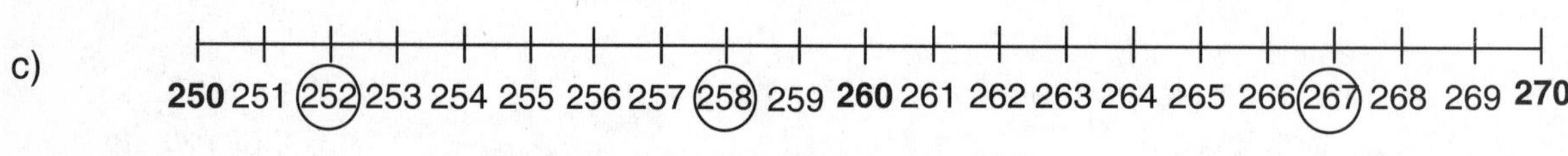

Round to _____ _____ _____

4. Circle the correct answer.

a) 29 is closer to 20 or 30

b) 14 is closer to 10 or 20

c) 36 is closer to 30 or 40

d) 72 is closer to 70 or 80

e) 254 is closer to 250 or 260

f) 488 is closer to 480 or 490

5. Draw an arrow to show whether the circled number is closer to 0 or 100:

a) 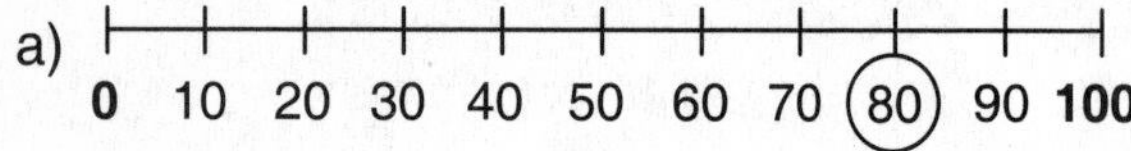

b) 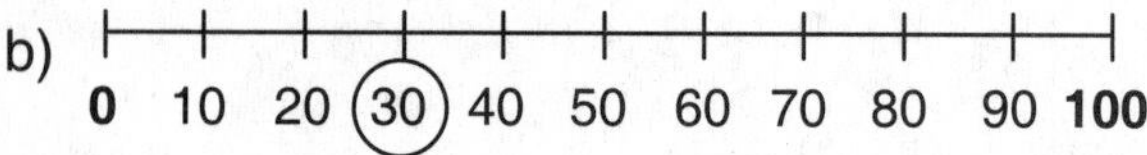

6. Is 50 closer to 0 or to 100? Why is 50 a special case?

____

No unauthorized copying

NS5-38: Rounding on a Number Line *(continued)*

7. Circle the correct answer:

a) 80 is closer to: 0 or 100

b) 20 is closer to: 0 or 100

c) 40 is closer to: 0 or 100

d) 60 is closer to: 0 or 100

8. Show the approximate position of each number on the line. What multiple of 100 would you round to?

a) 627 b) 683 c) 795 d) 706

Round to ______

9. Circle the correct answer.

a) 165 is closer to: 100 or 200

b) 635 is closer to: 600 or 700

c) 870 is closer to: 800 or 900

d) 532 is closer to: 500 or 600

10. Draw an arrow to show whether the circled number is closer to 0 or 1 000.

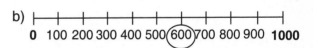

a) 0 100 200 (300) 400 500 600 700 800 900 **1000**

b) 0 100 200 300 400 500 (600) 700 800 900 **1000**

11. Circle the correct answer.

a) 100 is closer to 0 or 1 000 b) 900 is closer to 0 or 1 000 c) 600 is closer to 0 or 1 000

12. Draw an arrow to show which multiple of 1000 you would round to.

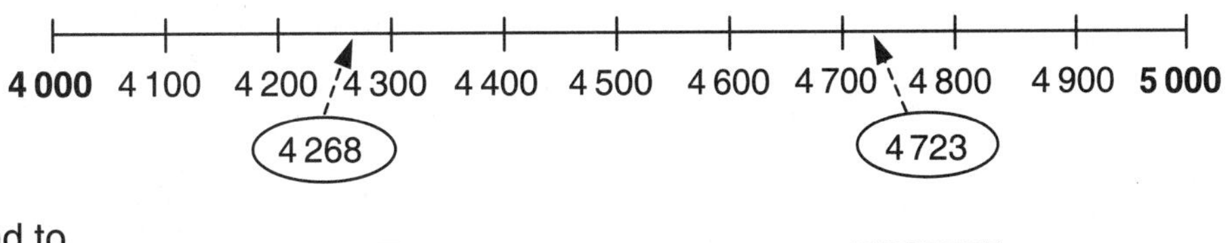

Round to ______ ______

13. Circle the correct answer:

a) 2 953 is closer to: 2 000 or 3 000

b) 7 293 is closer to: 7 000 or 8 000

c) 5 521 is closer to: 5 000 or 6 000

d) 8 232 is closer to: 8 000 or 9 000

14. Write a rule for rounding a four-digit number to the nearest thousands.

 No unauthorized copying

NS5-39: Rounding

1. Round to the nearest **tens** place:

REMEMBER:
If the number in the ones digit is:
0, 1, 2, 3 or 4 – you round down
5, 6, 7, 8 or 9 – you round up

a) 22 ☐   b) 26 ☐
c) 73 ☐   d) 58 ☐
e) 94 ☐   f) 83 ☐
g) 15 ☐   h) 49 ☐
i) 27 ☐   j) 37 ☐   k) 91 ☐

2. Round to the nearest **tens** place. Underline the tens digit first. Then put your pencil on the digit to the right (the ones digit). This digit tells you whether to round up or down:

a) 1<u>4</u>5 ↓ 150   b) 183 ☐   c) 361 ☐
d) 342 ☐   e) 554 ☐   f) 667 ☐
g) 656 ☐   h) 847 ☐   i) 938 ☐

3. Round to the nearest **hundreds** place. Underline the hundreds digit first. Then put your pencil on the digit to the right (the tens digit):

a) <u>7</u>30 ↓ 700   b) 490 ☐   c) 540 ☐
d) 270 ☐   e) 167 ☐   f) 317 ☐
g) 160 ☐   h) 873 ☐   i) 791 ☐
j) 6 <u>2</u>37 6 200   k) 1 286 ☐   l) 8 218 ☐
m) 4 905 ☐   n) 6 321 ☐   o) 9 583 ☐

4. Round to the nearest thousands place. Underline the thousands digit first. Then put your pencil on the digit to the right (the hundreds digit).

a) <u>7</u> 872 ↓ 8 000   b) 8 952 ☐   c) 5 231 ☐
d) 3 092 ☐   e) 3 871 ☐   f) 1680 ☐

No unauthorized copying

NS5-40: Rounding to Any Decimal Place

1. Underline the digit you wish to round to. Then say whether you would round up or down.

a) *hundreds*

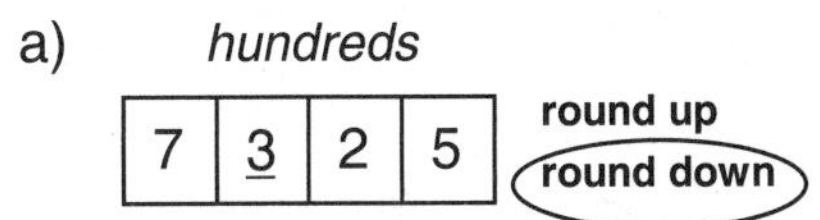

7	<u>3</u>	2	5

round up
round down (circled)

b) *hundreds*

6	5	6	3

round up
round down

c) *tens*

3	8	5	2

round up
round down

d) *thousands*

7	2	8	5	3

round up
round down

e) *ten thousands*

5	7	6	3	4

round up
round down

f) *ten thousands*

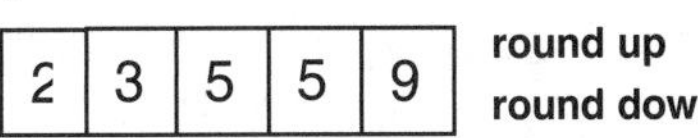

2	3	5	5	9

round up
round down

2. Complete the steps of rounding from Question 1. Then follow these steps:

Round the digit underlined up or down.

- To round up, add 1 to the digit.
- To round down, keep the digit the same.

2	<u>3</u>	4	5
	3		

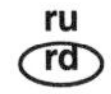

ru
rd

The digits to the right of the rounded digit become zeros.

The digits to the left remain the same.

2	<u>3</u>	4	5
2	3	0	0

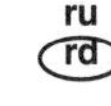

ru
rd

a) *thousands*

7	3	2	0	1

ru
rd

b) *ten thousands*

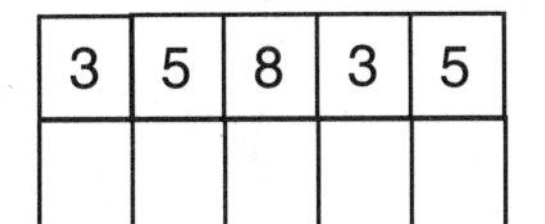

3	5	8	3	5

ru
rd

c) *hundreds*

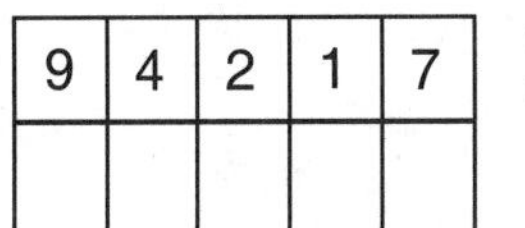

9	4	2	1	7

ru
rd

d) *hundreds*

2	8	6	8	1

ru
rd

e) *tens*

5	2	3	7	2

ru
rd

f) *tens thousands*

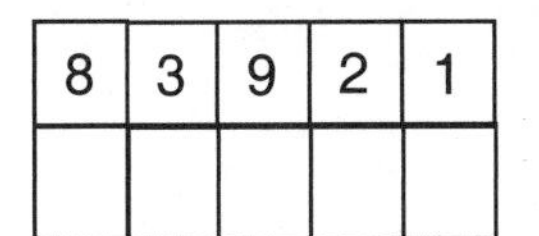

8	3	9	2	1

ru
rd

3. Sometimes when rounding, you have to regroup:

Example:
Round 3985 to the nearest hundred.

3	9	<u>8</u>	5
	10		

985 rounds to 1000.

3	<u>9</u>	8	5
4	0		

Regroup the 10 hundreds as 1 (thousand) and add it to the 3 (thousand).

3	<u>9</u>	8	5
4	0	0	0

Complete the rounding.

Round to the digit given (regroup if necessary):

a) 2195 *tens* b) 3942 *hundreds* c) 9851 *thousands* d) 13291 *tens*

e) 4921 *hundreds* f) 6973 *hundreds* g) 1239 *tens* h) 7896 *tens*

 No unauthorized copying

NS5-41: Estimating Sums and Differences

1. Estimate by rounding to the nearest tens.

≈ ← *Mathematicians use this symbol to mean* ***"approximately equal to."***

a) 42 → 40
+ 23 → + 20
60

b) 28 → ☐
+ 54 → + ☐

c) 62 → ☐
− 19 → − ☐

d) 87 → ☐
− 57 → − ☐

e) 73 + 17 ≈ 70 + 20 = 90

f) 89 − 46 ≈ ____________

g) 16 + 34 ≈ ____________

h) 63 + 26 ≈ ____________

i) 82 + 47 ≈ ____________

j) 46 − 17 ≈ ____________

k) 48 + 27 ≈ ____________

l) 76 + 14 ≈ ____________

m) 62 − 47 ≈ ____________

2. Estimate by rounding to the nearest hundreds.

a) 290 → 300
+ 360 → + 400
700

b) 390 ☐
+ 460 + ☐

c) 620 ☐
− 180 − ☐

d) 840 ☐
− 550 − ☐

e) 680 + 160 ≈ ____________________

f) 470 − 220 ≈ ____________________

g) 610 + 240 ≈ ____________________

h) 840 + 180 ≈ ____________________

i) 670 + 340 ≈ ____________________

j) 941 − 463 ≈ ____________________

k) 126 + 567 ≈ ____________________

l) 523 + 285 ≈ ____________________

3. Estimate by rounding to the nearest thousands or ten thousands.

a) 1 275 → 1 000
+ 3 940 → + 4 000
5 000

b) 6 231 → ☐
− 4 123 → − ☐

c) 7 537 → ☐
+ 6 425 → + ☐

d) 29 753 → ☐
− 23 123 → − ☐

4. Round to the nearest hundreds and then find the sum or difference:

a) 9 232 + 1 503 ≈ __________

b) 4 692 − 1 931 ≈ __________

c) 64 857 − 42 345 ≈ __________

No unauthorized copying

NS5-42: Estimation

Answer the following questions in a notebook.

1. Newfoundland joined Canada in 1949.

   The Yukon joined in 1889.

   About how many years after the Yukon did Newfoundland join Canada?

Yukon Territory **Newfoundland**

2. The area of Prince Edward Island is 5660 km^2 and the area of Nova Scotia is 55 284 km^2.

   Estimate the difference in the areas.

Prince Edward Island **Nova Scotia**

3. The population of the Northwest Territories is 42 000.

   The population of Nunavut is 29 400.

   Estimate the difference in the two populations.

Northwest Territories **Nunavut**

4. Manitoba joined Canada in 1870.

   Is this an exact date or an estimate?

Manitoba

5. The populations of New Brunswick and Nova Scotia are listed in an almanac as 750 000 and 936 900.

   What digits do you think these numbers have been rounded to? Explain.

New Brunswick **Nova Scotia**

6. To estimate the difference 1675 – 1432, should you round the numbers to the nearest thousands or the nearest hundreds?

   Justify your answer.

7. A sporting goods store has the following items for sale:

A. Bike $472 | **B.** Golf Set $227 | **C.** Tennis Racquet $189 | **D.** Skis $382 | **E.** Rollerblades $112

a) What could you buy if you had $800 to spend? Estimate to find out. Then add the actual prices.

b) List a different set of items you could buy.

No unauthorized copying

NS5-43: Multiplying by 10, 100, 1 000, and 10 000

1. a) Skip count by 10 twelve times. What number did you reach? __________

   b) Find the product: 10 × 12 = __________

   c) Skip count by 100 twelve times. What number did you reach? __________

   d) Find the product: 100 × 12 = __________

2. How many zeroes do you add to a number when you multiply the number by:

   a) 10: You add _____ zero. b) 100: You add _____ zeroes. c) 1000: You add _____ zeroes.

3. Continue the pattern.

a)	b)	c)
10 × 8 = __________	10 × 25 = __________	10 × 62 = __________
100 × 8 = __________	100 × 25 = __________	100 × 62 = __________
1 000 × 8 = __________	1 000 × 25 = __________	1 000 × 62 = __________
10 000 × 8 = __________	10 000 × 25 = __________	10 000 × 62 = __________

4. Find the products.

a) 17 × 10 = __________	b) 10 × 50 = __________	c) 10 × 97 = __________
d) 69 × 100 = __________	e) 20 × 100 = __________	f) 19 × 100 = __________
g) 100 × 89 = __________	h) 37 × 100 = __________	i) 46 × 10 000 = __________

5. Round each number to the leading digit.
   Then find the product of the rounded numbers:

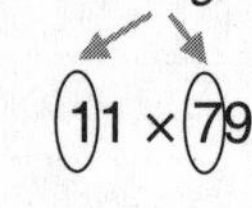

a) 11 × 79	b) 12 × 22	c) 13 × 79	d) 11 × 64	e) 59 × 110	f) 91 × 120
10 × 80	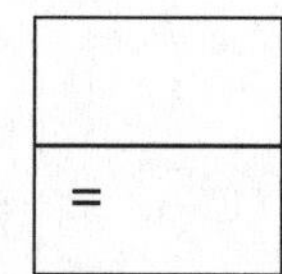				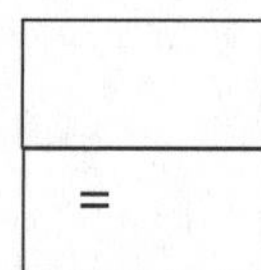
= 800	=	=	=	=	=

6. How many digits will the answer have? Write your answer in the box provided.

   a) (2 + 5) × 100: ☐ digits b) (7 + 5) × 100: 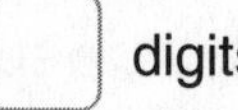 digits c) (5 + 69) × 1000:  digits

NS5-44: Counting Coins

1. Count by the first number given, then by the second number after the vertical line.

a) 5, ___, ___, ___, ___ | ___, ___, ___
Count by 5s | Continue counting by 1s

b) 5, ___, ___, ___ | ___, ___, ___
Count by 5s | Continue counting by 1s

2. Complete each pattern.

(10¢) (10¢) (10¢) (5¢) (5¢) (5¢) (5¢) (5¢)

a) 10, ___, ___ | ___, ___, ___, ___, ___
Count by 10s | Continue counting by 5s

(10¢) (10¢) (10¢) (5¢) (5¢) (5¢) (5¢)

b) ___, ___, ___ | ___, ___, ___, ___
Count by 10s | Continue counting by 5s

(25¢) (25¢) (25¢) | (5¢) (5¢)

c) ___, ___, ___ | ___, ___
Count by 25s | Count by 5s

(25¢) (25¢) (25¢) | (10¢) (10¢)

d) ___, ___, ___ | ___, ___
Count by 25s | Count by 10s

3. Complete each pattern.

a) 25, 50, 75 | 80, 85 | 86
Count by 25s | Count by 5s | Count by 1s

b) ___, ___ | ___, ___ | ___, ___, ___
Count by 25s | Count by 10s | Count by 1s

c) ___, ___ | ___, ___ | ___, ___
Count by 25s | Count by 10s | Count by 5s

d) ___, ___, ___ | ___, ___ | ___, ___
Count by 25s | Count by 10s | Count by 1s

BONUS

___, ___ | ___, ___, ___ | ___, ___ | ___, ___, ___, ___
Count by 25s | Count by 10s | Count by 5s | Count by 1s

4. Complete each pattern by counting by the first number given, then by the numbers after the coin type changes.

(10¢) (10¢) (5¢) (5¢) (1¢) (1¢)

a) 10, 20, 25, 30, 31, 32

(25¢) (25¢) (10¢) (10¢) (10¢) (1¢)

b) ___, ___, ___, ___, ___, ___

BONUS
Complete the pattern.

(25¢) (25¢) (25¢) (25¢) (25¢) (10¢) (10¢) (5¢) (5¢) (5¢) (1¢) (1¢) (1¢)

___, ___, ___, ___, ___, ___, ___, ___, ___, ___, ___, ___, ___

No unauthorized copying

NS5-44: Counting Coins *(continued)*

5. Complete the pattern by counting each number given:

a) 10 , 20 , 30 (*Count by 10s*) | 35 , 40 (*Count by 5s*) | 41 (*Count by 1s*)

b) ___ , ___ (*Count by 25s*) | ___ , ___ (*Count by 5s*) | ___ , ___ , ___ (*Count by 1s*)

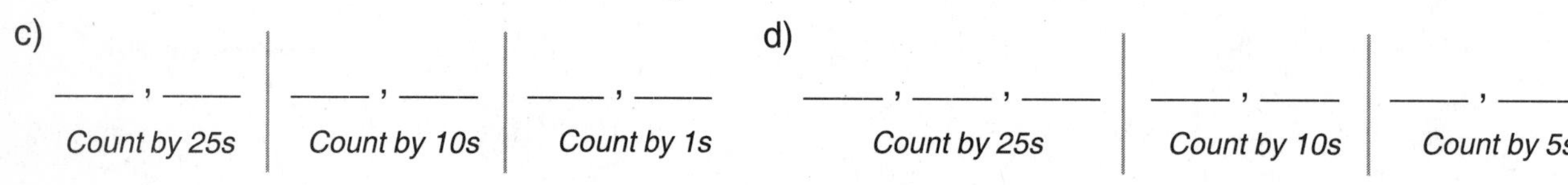

c) ___ , ___ (*Count by 25s*) | ___ , ___ (*Count by 10s*) | ___ , ___ (*Count by 1s*)

d) ___ , ___ , ___ (*Count by 25s*) | ___ , ___ (*Count by 10s*) | ___ , ___ (*Count by 5s*)

BONUS

e) ___ , ___ (*Count by 25s*) | ___ , ___ , ___ (*Count by 10s*) | ___ , ___ (*Count by 5s*) | ___ , ___ , ___ , ___ (*Count by 1s*)

6. Write the total amount of money in cents for the number of coins given in the charts below.
HINT: Count by the greatest amount first.

a)

Nickels	Pennies
6	7

Total amount = ________

b)

Quarters	Dimes
3	2

Total amount = ________

c)

Quarters	Nickels
5	5

Total amount = ________

d)

Quarters	Nickels	Pennies
4	2	4

Total amount = ________________

e)

Quarters	Dimes	Nickels
6	3	7

Total amount = ________________

f)

Quarters	Dimes	Nickels	Pennies
2	3	1	5

Total amount = ________________

g)

Quarters	Dimes	Nickels	Pennies
5	2	2	2

Total amount = ________________

7. Count the given coins and write the total amount:
HINT: Count by the greatest amount first.

a) Total amount = ________________

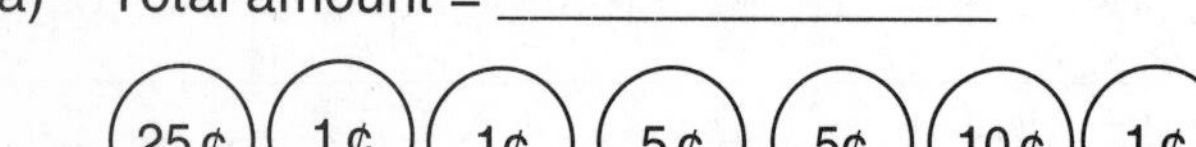

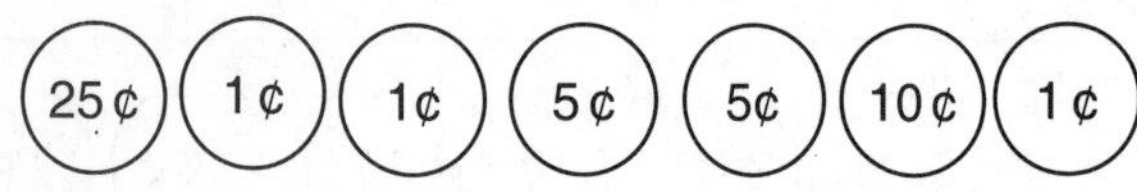

b) Total amount = ________________

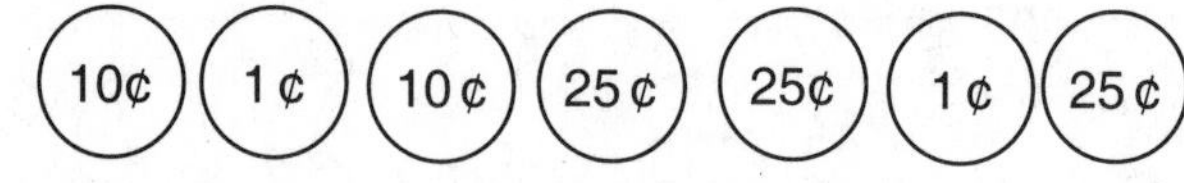

c) Total amount = ________________

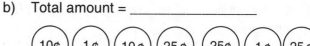

10¢ 1¢ 25¢ 5¢ 10¢ 25¢ 10¢

d) Total amount = ________________

5¢ 10¢ 25¢ 5¢ 1¢ 5¢ 25¢

BONUS

e) Total amount = ________________

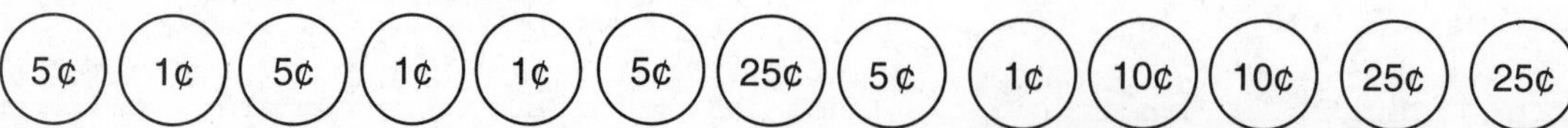

 No unauthorized copying

NS5-45: Counting by Different Denominations

1. Draw the additional coins needed to make each total:

a) (10¢) (10¢) (10¢) + = 50¢ *How many dimes?*	b) (25¢) (5¢) + = 80¢ *How many quarters?*
c) (25¢) (25¢) + = 70¢ *How many dimes?*	d) (25¢) (10¢) + = 85¢ *How many quarters?*

2. Draw the additional coins needed to make each total.
You can only draw **two** coins for each question:

a) 26¢ (10¢) (10¢)	b) 50¢ (25¢) (10¢)
c) 50¢ (25¢) (10¢)	d) 85¢ (25¢) (25¢)
e) 31¢ (10¢) (1¢)	f) 65¢ (25¢) (25¢)
g) 105¢ (25¢) (25¢) (25¢)	h) 95¢ (25¢) (25¢) (25¢)
i) $5 ($2)	j) $7 ($2) ($2)
k) $3 ($1)	l) $10 ($2) ($2) ($2) ($1)
m) 131¢ ($1) (5¢)	n) 340¢ ($2) ($1) (25¢)

3. Draw a picture to show the fewest extra coins the child will need to pay for the item:
   a) Ron has 25¢. He wants to buy an eraser for 55¢.
   b) Alan has 3 quarters, a dime, and a nickel. He wants to buy a notebook for 97¢.
   c) Jane has 2 toonies and 2 loonies. She wants to buy a plant for ten dollars.
   d) Raiz has 3 toonies and a loonie. He wants to buy a book for nine dollars and forty-five cents.

4. Show how to make 80¢ using only:
   a) dimes and quarters b) nickels and quarters

5. Make up a problem like one of the problems in Question 3 and exchange it with a parent to solve.

No unauthorized copying

NS5-46: Least Number of Coins

1. What is the greatest amount you could pay in quarters without exceeding the amount? Draw the quarters to show your answer:

Amount	Greatest amount you could pay in quarters	Amount	Greatest amount you could pay in quarters
a) 45¢		b) 52¢	
c) 79¢		d) 83¢	
e) 63¢		f) 64¢	
g) 49¢		h) 31¢	
i) 82¢		j) 96¢	

2. Find the greatest amount you could pay in quarters. Represent the amount remaining using the least number of coins:

Amount	Amount paid in quarters	Amount remaining	Amount remaining in coins
a) 82¢	75¢	82¢ - 75¢ = 7¢	(5¢) (1¢) (1¢)
b) 57¢			
c) 85¢			
d) 95¢			

3. Trade coins to make each amount with the least number of coins. Draw a picture in a notebook to show your final answer:

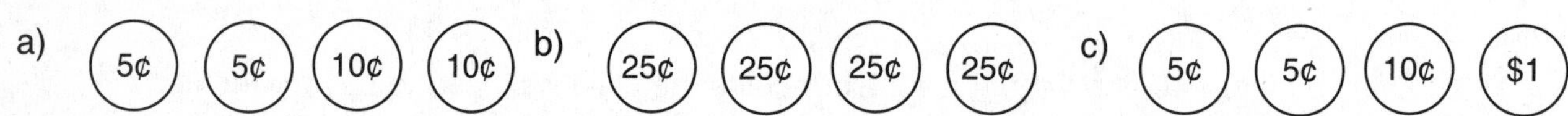

d) 10¢ 10¢ 5¢ $1

e) 25¢ 5¢ 10¢ 10¢ 25¢ $2 25¢ 25¢

f) 10¢ 10¢ 5¢ $1 10¢ $1 $1 10¢ 1¢ 1¢ 1¢ 5¢

4. Show how you could trade the amounts for the least number of coins:

a) 6 quarters

b) 6 dimes and 2 nickels

c) 8 loonies

d) 9 loonies and 5 dimes

e) 10 loonies, 6 dimes, 2 nickels, and 5 pennies

No unauthorized copying

NS5-47: Dollar and Cent Notation

1. Write the given amount in dollars, dimes, and pennies, then in dollar notation.

	Dollars	Dimes	Pennies	Amount in $
a) 173¢	1	7	3	$ 1.73
c) 62¢				

	Dollars	Dimes	Pennies	Amount in $
b) 465¢				
d) 2¢				

2. Change the amount to cent notation, then dollar notation.

a) 7 pennies = 7¢ = $ .07
b) 4 nickels = _____ = _____
c) 6 dimes = _____ = _____
d) 4 pennies = _____ = _____
e) 13 pennies = _____ = _____
f) 1 quarter = _____ = _____
g) 5 nickels = _____ = _____
h) 3 quarters = _____ = _____
i) 8 dimes = _____ = _____
j) 6 toonies = _____ = _____
k) 4 loonies = _____ = _____
l) 7 loonies = _____ = _____

3. Count the dollar amount and the cent amount. Write the total amount in dollar (decimal) notation.

	Dollar Amount	Cent Amount	Total
a)	$2 $2 $1 = _____	25¢ 25¢ 5¢ = _____	_____
b)	10 5 = _____	25¢ 10¢ 1¢ = _____	_____
c)	10 10 = _____	25¢ 25¢ 1¢ = _____	_____

4. Count the given coins. Write the total amount in cents and in dollars (decimals).

	Coins	Cent Notation	Dollar Notation
a)	25¢ 25¢ 25¢ 25¢ 5¢	105¢	$1.05
b)	25¢ 25¢ 25¢ 10¢ 10¢ 10¢ 5¢	_____	_____

5. Write each number of cents in dollar notation.

a) 325¢ = _____ b) 20¢ = _____ c) 6¢ = _____ d) 283¢ = _____ e) 205¢ = _____

No unauthorized copying

NS5-47: Dollar and Cent Notation *(continued)*

6. Write each amount of money in cents notation.

   a) \$2.99 = ______   b) \$3.43 = ______   c) \$1.41 = ______   d) \$0.08 = ______

7. Circle the greater amount of money in each pair:

   a) 193¢ or \$1.96   b) \$1.01 or 103¢   c) 840¢ or \$8.04

8. Circle the larger amount of money in each pair:

   a) seven dollars and sixty-five cents or seven dollars and seventy cents

   b) nine dollars and eighty-three cents or 978¢

   c) fifteen dollars and eighty cents or \$15.08

9. Tally the amount of each type of denomination and then find the total.

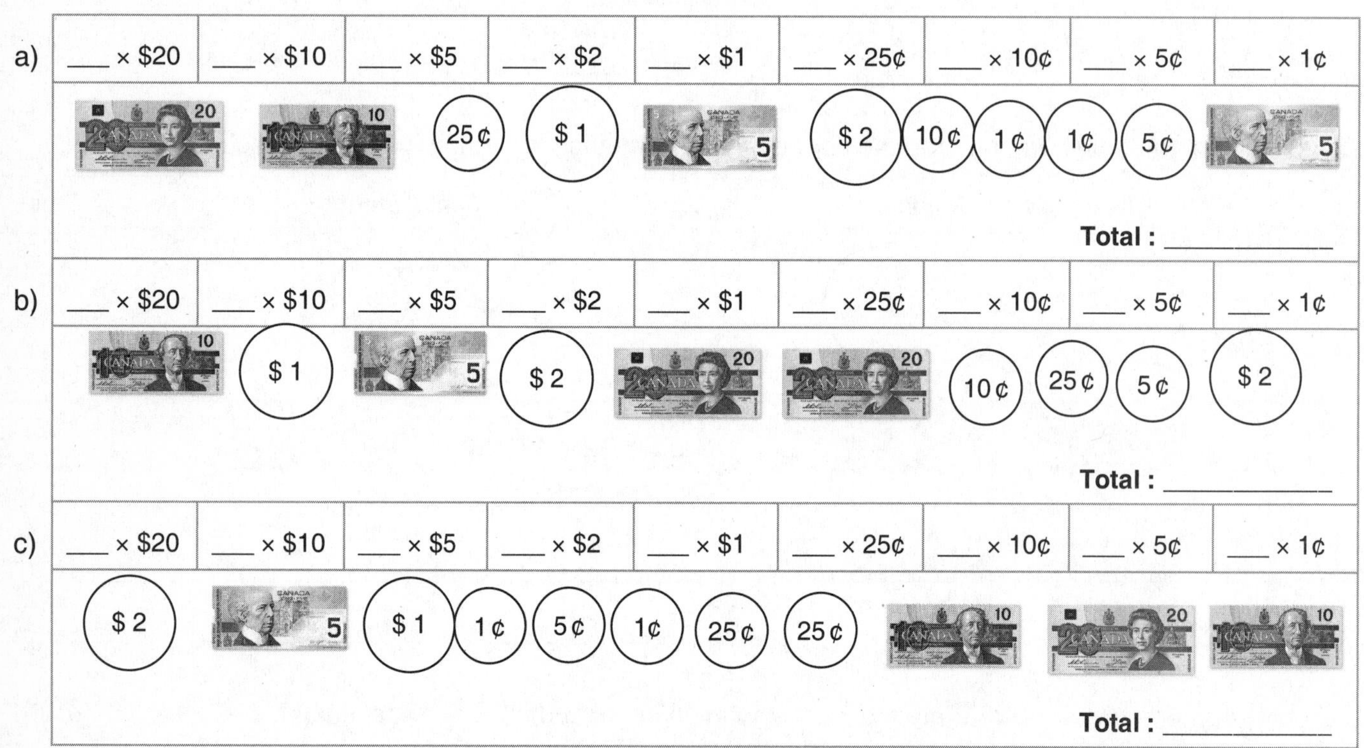

a)	___ × \$20	___ × \$10	___ × \$5	___ × \$2	___ × \$1	___ × 25¢	___ × 10¢	___ × 5¢	___ × 1¢
									Total : __________
b)	___ × \$20	___ × \$10	___ × \$5	___ × \$2	___ × \$1	___ × 25¢	___ × 10¢	___ × 5¢	___ × 1¢
									Total : __________
c)	___ × \$20	___ × \$10	___ × \$5	___ × \$2	___ × \$1	___ × 25¢	___ × 10¢	___ × 5¢	___ × 1¢
									Total : __________

10. Which is a greater amount of money: 256¢ or \$2.62? Explain how you know.

11. Alan bought a pack of markers for \$3.50. He paid for it with 4 coins. Which coins did he use?

12. Tanya's weekly allowance is \$5.25. Her mom gave her 6 coins. Which coins did she use? Can you find more than one answer?

13. Write words for the following amounts:

    a) \$3.57   b) \$12.23   c) \$604.80   d) \$327.25   e) \$26.93   f) \$766.03

No unauthorized copying

NS5-48: Least Number of Coins and Bills

1. Find the number of coins you need to make the amount in the right hand column of the chart.
HINT: Count up by quarters until you are as close to the amount as possible. Then count on by dimes, and so on.

	Number of Quarters	Subtotal	Number of Dimes	Subtotal	Number of Nickels	Subtotal	Number of Pennies	Total Amount
a)	3	75¢	0	75¢	1	80¢	3	83¢
b)								52¢
c)								97¢
d)								23¢
e)								42¢
f)								94¢

2. Write the greatest amount you could pay in $20 bills without exceeding the amount.

a) **$45** = ______ b) **$32** = ______ c) **$27** = ______ d) **$48** = ______ e) **$37** = ______

3. Write the number of each type of bill (or coin) that you would need to get the amounts in **bold**:

		#	Type	#	Type	#	Type	#	Type	#	Type	#	Type
a)	**$21.00**	0	$50.00	1	$20.00	0	$10.00	0	$5.00	0	$2.00	1	$1.00
b)	**$30.00**		$50.00		$20.00		$10.00		$5.00		$2.00		$1.00
c)	**$54.00**		$50.00		$20.00		$10.00		$5.00		$2.00		$1.00
d)	**$85.00**		$50.00		$20.00		$10.00		$5.00		$2.00		$1.00
e)	**$64.00**		$50.00		$20.00		$10.00		$5.00		$2.00		$1.00

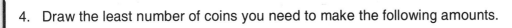

4. Draw the least number of coins you need to make the following amounts.

a) 72¢ b) 93¢ c) 82¢ d) 52¢

5. Draw the least number of coins and bills you need to make the following amounts.

a) $55.00 b) $67.00 c) $64.00 d) $123.00
e) $62.35 f) $42.12 g) $57.61 h) $78.18
i) $73.08 j) $157.50 k) $92.82 l) $85.23

No unauthorized copying

NS5-49: Making Change Using Mental Math

1. Calculate the change owing for each purchase.

a) Price of a pencil = 44¢
Amount paid = 50¢

Change = ________

b) Price of an eraser = 41¢
Amount paid = 50¢

Change = ________

c) Price of a sharpener = 84¢
Amount paid = 90¢

Change = ________

d) Price of a ruler = 53¢
Amount paid = 60¢

Change = ________

e) Price of a marker = 76¢
Amount paid = 80¢

Change = ________

f) Price of a notebook = 65¢
Amount paid = 70¢

Change = ________

g) Price of a folder = 68¢
Amount paid = 70¢

Change = ________

h) Price of a juice box = 49¢
Amount paid = 50¢

Change = ________

i) Price of a freezie = 28¢
Amount paid = 30¢

Change = ________

2. Count up by 10s to find the change owing from a dollar (100¢):

Price Paid	Change	Price Paid	Change	Price Paid	Change
a) 90¢		b) 40¢		c) 20¢	
d) 70¢		e) 10¢		f) 60¢	
g) 50¢		h) 30¢		i) 80¢	

3. Find the change owing for each purchase:

a) Price of a binder = 80¢
Amount paid = $1.00

Change = ________

b) Price of an eraser = 70¢
Amount paid = $1.00

Change = ________

c) Price of an apple = 20¢
Amount paid = $1.00

Change = ________

d) Price of a marker = 60¢
Amount paid = $1.00

Change = ________

e) Price of a patty = 50¢
Amount paid = $1.00

Change = ________

f) Price of a pencil = 30¢
Amount paid = $1.00

Change = ________

g) Price of a sharpener = 10¢
Amount paid = $1.00

Change = ________

h) Price of juice = 40¢
Amount paid = $1.00

Change = ________

i) Price of a popsicle = 60¢
Amount paid = $1.00

Change = ________

4. Find the smallest two-digit number ending in zero (i.e., 10, 20, 30, …) greater than the number given.

a) 74 __80__ b) 56 _____ c) 43 _____ d) 28 _____ e) 57 _____ f) 4 _____

 No unauthorized copying

NS5-49: Making Change Using Mental Math *(continued)*

5. Make change for the number written below. Follow steps that are shown for 16¢:

Step 1: *Find the smallest multiple of 10 greater than 16¢:*

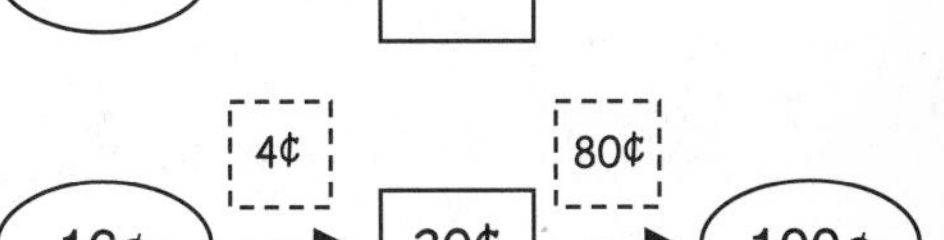

Step 2: *Find the differences:* 20 – 16 *and* 100 – 20

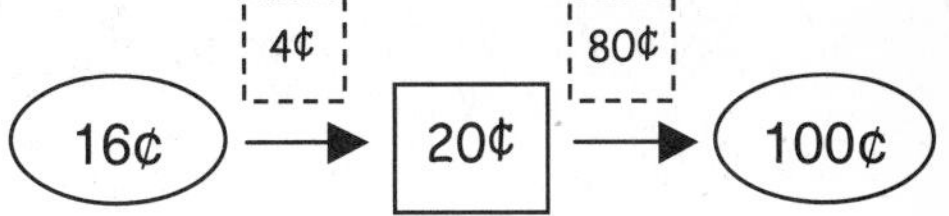

Step 3: *Add the differences:* 4¢ + 80¢ **Change = 84¢**

a)

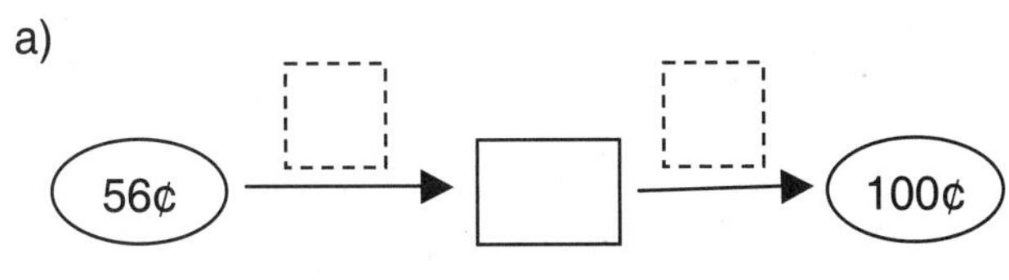

Change = ___________

b)

83¢ → → 100¢

Change = ___________

c)

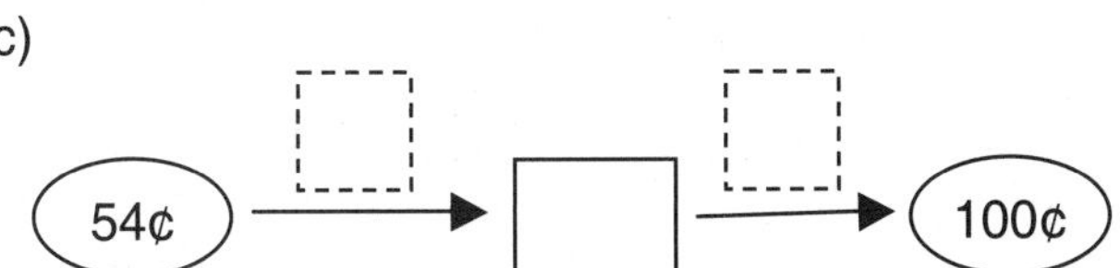

Change = ___________

d)

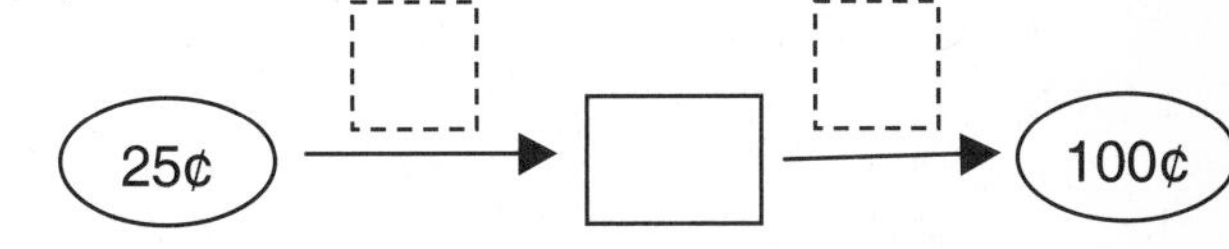

Change = ___________

e)

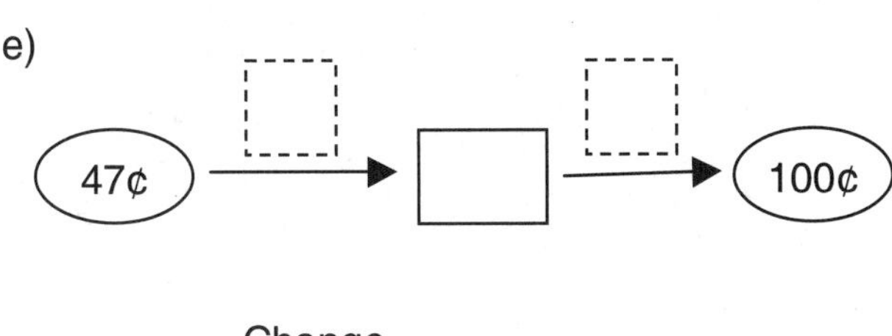

Change = ___________

f)

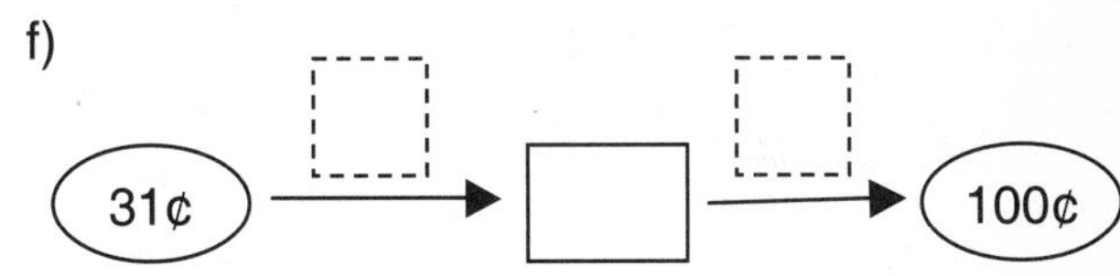

Change = ___________

6. Find the change from 100¢. Try to do the work in your head:

a) 74¢ _______ b) 67¢ _______ c) 36¢ _______ d) 53¢ _______ e) 72¢ _______

f) 35¢ _______ g) 97¢ _______ h) 59¢ _______ i) 89¢ _______ j) 92¢ _______

7. Find the change doing the work in your head:

a) Price: 37¢ Amount Paid: 50¢
Change Required: _________

b) Price: 58¢ Amount Paid: 75¢
Change Required: _________

8. Paul paid for a 42¢ stamp with $1.00.
Draw the change he receives using the least number of coins:

 No unauthorized copying

NS5-49: Making Change Using Mental Math *(continued)*

9. Find the change:

Amount Paid	Price	Change	Amount Paid	Price	Change
a) $30.00	$22.00		b) $70.00	$64.00	
c) $40.00	$34.00		d) $90.00	$87.00	
e) $50.00	$46.00		f) $20.00	$13.00	

10. Follow the steps shown below for finding the change from $50.00 on a payment of $22.00:

Step 1: *Find the smallest multiple of 10 greater than $22.00*: $22 → $30

Step 2: *Find the differences:* 30 – 22 *and* 50 – 30 — $22 → ($8) → $30 → ($20) → $50

Step 3: *Add the differences:* $8 + $20 **Change = $28.00**

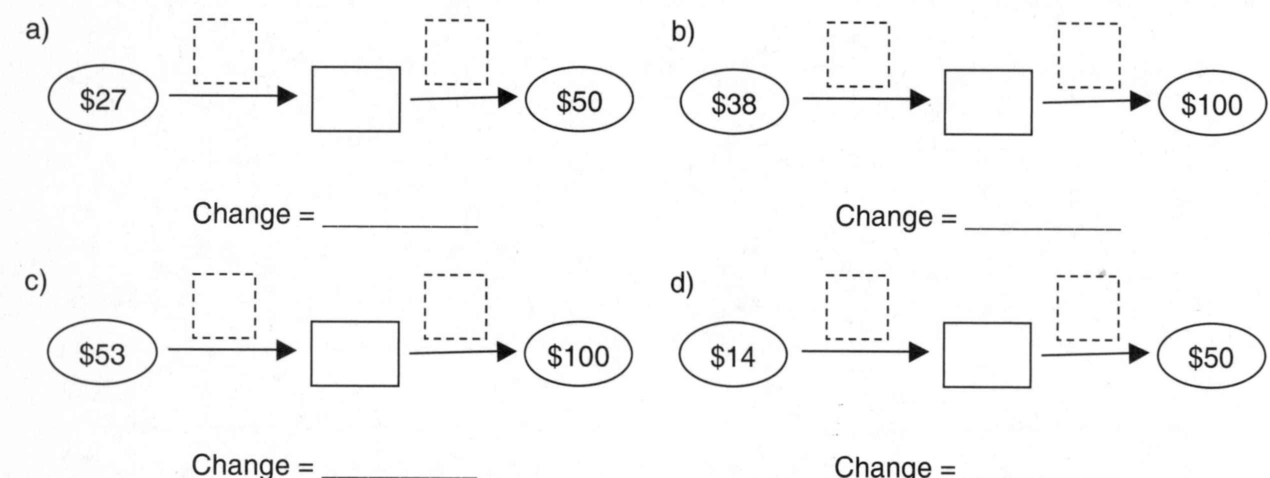

11. Find the change from $100. Try to do the work in your head:

a) $84 = ______ b) $25 = ______ c) $46 = ______ d) $88 = ______ e) $52 ______

BONUS

12. Find the change by first finding the change from the nearest dollar amount and then the change from the nearest multiple of 10:

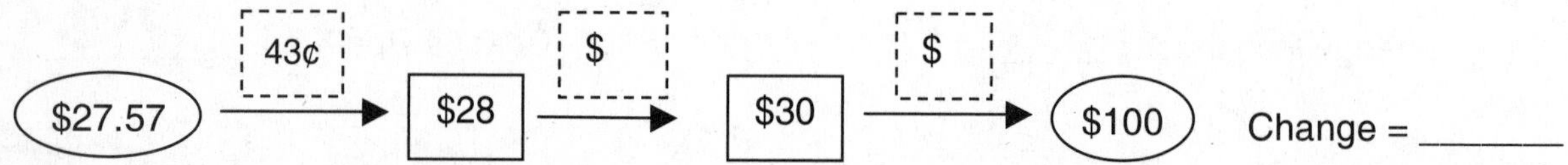

13. Using the method of Question 12, find the change from $100 for the following amounts.

a) $32.85 b) $86.27 c) $52.19 d) $66.43

NS5-50: Adding Money

1. Sara spent $14.42 on a plant and $3.53 on a vase.
   To find out how much she spent, she added the amounts using the following steps:

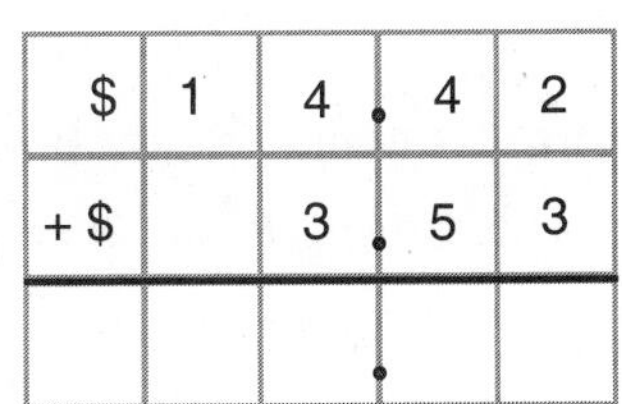

$	1	4 .	4	2
+ $		3 .	5	3
		.		

Step 1:
She lined up the numerals: she put dollars above dollars, dimes above dimes and pennies above pennies.

$	1	4 .	4	2
+ $		.	5	
				5

Step 2:
She added the numerals, starting with the ones digits (the pennies).

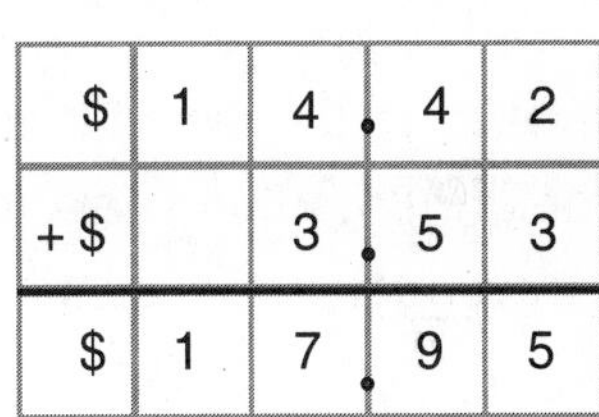

$	1	4 .	4	2
+ $		3 .	5	3
$	1	7 .	9	5

Step 3:
She added a decimal to show the amount in dollars.

Add:

a) $5.45 + $3.23

$	5 .	4	5
+ $	3 .	2	3
	.		

b) $26.15 + $32.23

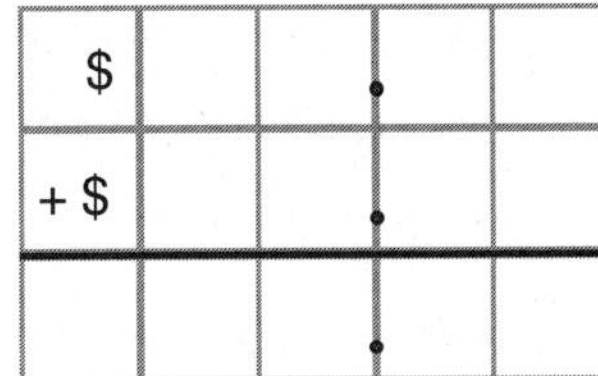

c) $19.57 + $30.32

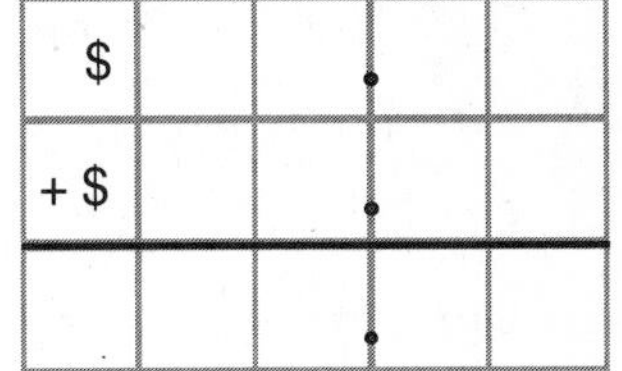

2. In order to add the amounts below, you will have to regroup:

a)

$	1	6 .	6	0
+ $	2	3 .	7	5
		.		

b)

$	2	7 .	4	5
+ $	4	5 .	1	2

c)

$	8	7 .	4	3
+ $		6 .	5	2
$		.		

d)

$	3	4 .	6	0
+ $	2	6 .	0	0
		.		

e)

$	3	8 .	4	0
+ $	4	4 .	2	5

f)

$	1	6 .	5	2
+ $	4	8 .	2	5
$		.		

3. Jasmine bought a pack of socks for $7.25 and a cap for $23.53.
   How much money does she need to pay the bill?

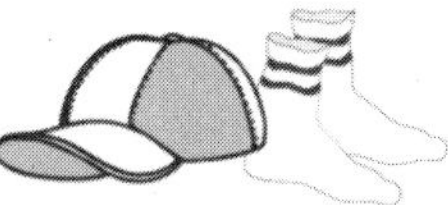

4. A library spent $270.25 on novels and $389.82 on non-fiction books.
   How much did the library spend in total?

5. Eli bought three CDs that cost $12.30 each.
   How much did he pay in total?

No unauthorized copying

NS5-50: Adding Money *(continued)*

Answer the following questions in a notebook.

6. Sakku has $25.

   If he buys a chess game for $9.50 and a book for $10.35, will he have enough money left to buy a book which costs $5.10?

7. Find the amounts each child earned shovelling snow:

   a) Karen earned 3 twenty dollar bills, 1 toonie, 2 loonies, 2 quarters, and 1 nickel.

   b) Jill earned 4 ten dollar bills, 6 toonies, and 3 quarters.

   c) Sandor earned 2 twenty and 3 ten dollar bills, 2 loonies, and 5 quarters.

   d) Tory earned 5 ten dollar bills, 6 toonies, 2 loonies, and 6 dimes.

8. a) If you bought a watch and a soccer ball, how much would you pay?

   b) Which costs more: a watch and a cap or a pair of pants and a soccer ball?

   c) Could you buy a soccer ball, a pair of tennis rackets, and a pair of pants for $100?

   d) What is the total cost of the three most expensive things in the picture?

   e) Make up your own problem using the items.

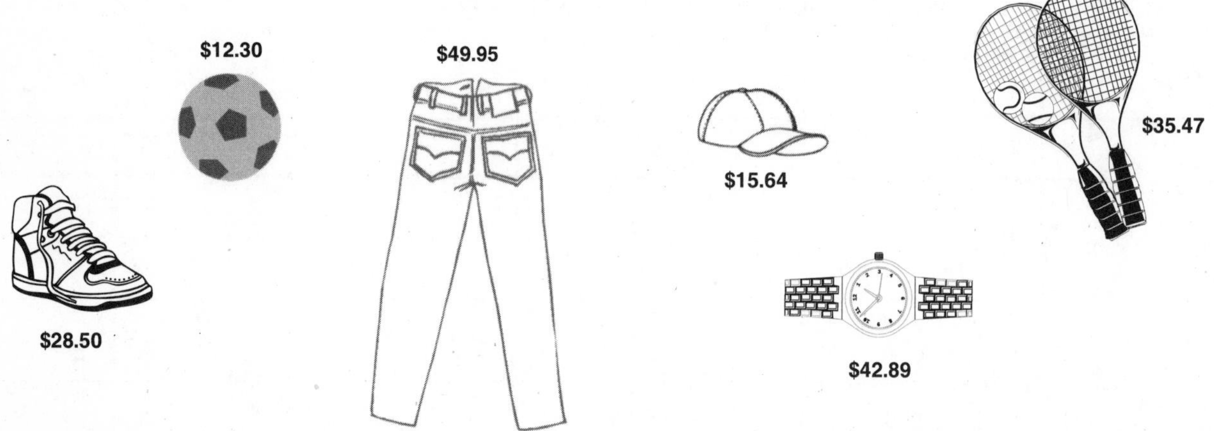

9. Try to find the answer mentally.

   a) How much do 4 loaves of bread cost at $2.30 each?

   b) How many apples, costing 40¢, could you buy with $3.00?

   c) Permanent markers cost $3.10.

      How many could you buy if you had $25.00?

   d) Is $10.00 enough to pay for a book costing $4.75 and a pen costing $5.34?

   e) Which costs more, 4 apples at 32¢ an apple, or 3 oranges at 45¢ an orange?

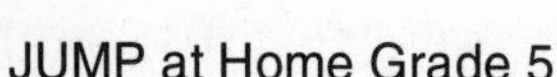

 No unauthorized copying

NS5-51: Subtracting Money

1. Find the remaining amount by subtracting:

a)
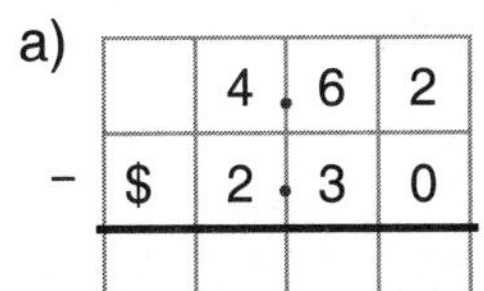

	4	. 6	2
−	$	2 .	3	0
		.	

b)
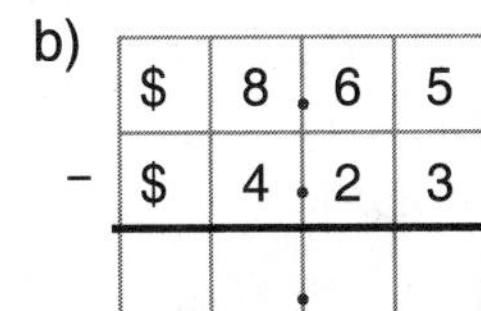

$	8 .	6	5
− $	4 .	2	3
	.		

c)
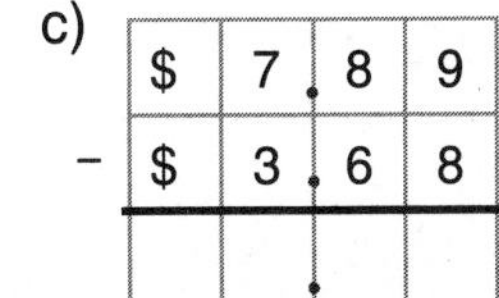

$	7 .	8	9
− $	3 .	6	8
	.		

d)
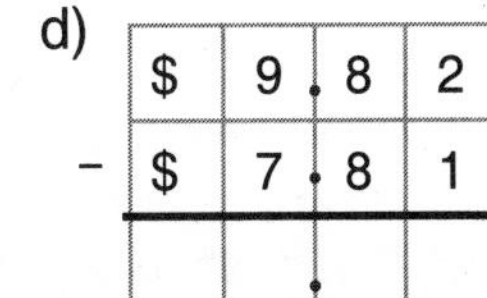

$	9 .	8	2
− $	7 .	8	1
	.		

e)
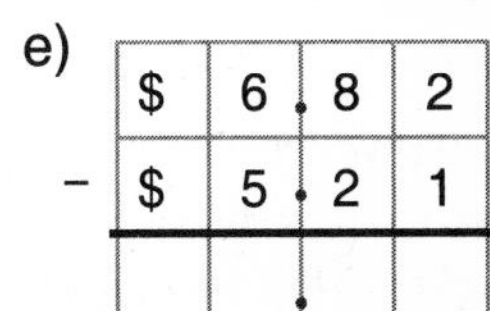

$	6 .	8	2
− $	5 .	2	1
	.		

2. Subtract the given money amounts by regrouping once or twice:

Example:

Step 1:
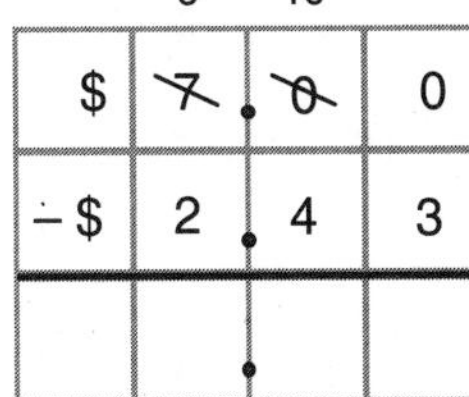

	6	10	
$	~~7~~ .	~~0~~	0
− $	2 .	4	3
	.		

Step 2:
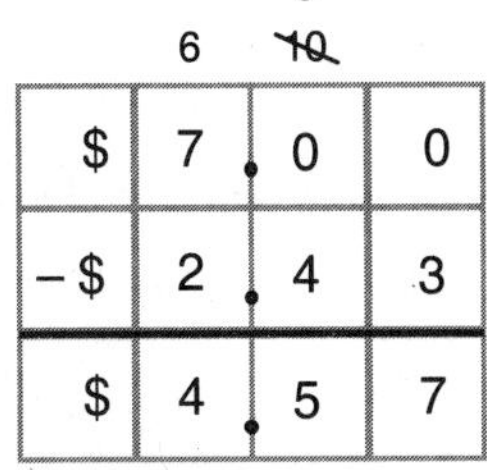

		9	
	6	~~10~~	
$	7 .	0	0
− $	2 .	4	3
$	4 .	5	7

a)

$	4 .	0	0
− $	2 .	2	9
	.		

b)

$	9 .	0	0
− $	6 .	2	4
	.		

c)
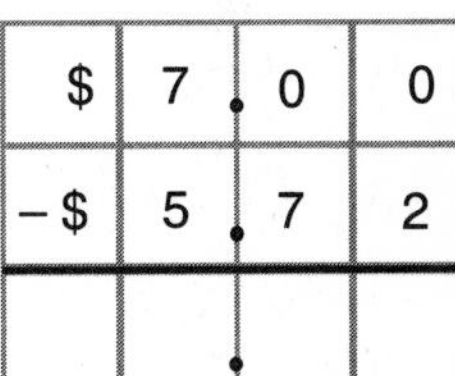

$	7 .	0	0
− $	5 .	7	2
	.		

d)

$	4	6 .	0	0
− $	2	3 .	4	5
		.		

e)

$	5	8 .	4	5
− $	2	7 .	7	8
		.		

f)

$	6	7 .	2	3
− $	3	4 .	6	4
		.		

3. Andrew spent $3.67 on his breakfast.

He paid for it with a five dollar bill.

Calculate his change.

4. Mera has $12.16 and Wendy has $13.47.

How much more money does Wendy have than Mera?

5. Rita has $20.00. She wants to buy vegetables for $7.70, juice for $3.45, and dairy products for $9.75.

Does she have enough money to buy all these items?

If not, by how much is she short?

6. Mark has $30.00.

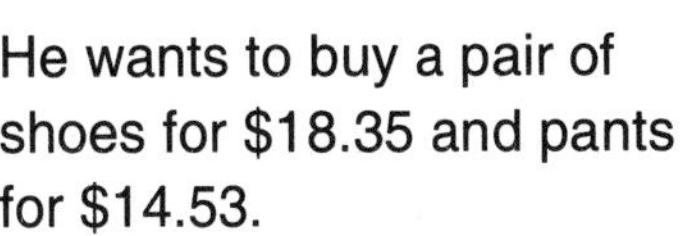

He wants to buy a pair of shoes for $18.35 and pants for $14.53.

How much more money does he need?

No unauthorized copying

LSS-1: Organized Lists

Many problems in mathematics and science have more than one solution.

If a problem involves two quantities, list the values of one quantity in increasing order. Then you won't miss any solutions.

For instance, to find all the ways you can make 35¢ with dimes and nickels, start by assuming you have no dimes, then 1 dime, and so on up to 3 dimes (4 would be too many).

In each case, count on by 5s to 35 to find out how many nickels you need to make 35¢.

Step 1:

dimes	nickels
0	
1	
2	
3	

Step 2:

dimes	nickels
0	7
1	5
2	3
3	1

---

1. Fill in the amount of pennies, nickels, or dimes you need to:

a) make 17¢.

nickels	pennies
0	
1	
2	
3	

b) make 45¢.

dimes	nickels
0	
1	
2	
3	
4	

c) make 23¢.

nickels	pennies
0	
1	
2	
3	
4	

d) make 32¢.

dimes	pennies
0	
1	
2	
3	

e) make 65¢.

quarters	nickels
0	
1	
2	

f) make 85¢.

quarters	nickels
0	
1	
2	
3	

2.

quarters	nickels
0	
1	
2	

Ben wants to find all the ways he can make 60¢ using quarters and nickels. He lists the number of quarters in increasing order. Why did he stop at 2 quarters?

____

____

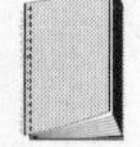

3. Make a chart to show all the ways you can make the given amount.

a) Make 27¢ using nickels and pennies.

b) Make 70¢ using quarters and nickels.

c) Make 65¢ using dimes and nickels.

d) Make $13 using loonies and toonies.

 No unauthorized copying

LSS-1: Organized Lists *(continued)*

Alana wants to find all pairs of numbers that multiply to give 15.

There are no numbers that will multiply by 2 or 4 to give 15, so Alana leaves those rows in her chart blank.

The numbers in the last row of the chart are the same as those in the 3rd row so Alana knows she has found all possible pairs of numbers that multiply to give 15: $1 \times 15 = 15$ and $3 \times 5 = 15$.

1st Number	2nd Number
1	15
2	---
3	5
4	---
5	3

---

4. Find all pairs of numbers that multiply to give the number provided.

a) **6**

First Number	Second Number

b) **8**

First Number	Second Number

5.

quarters	dimes
0	
1	
2	

Alicia wants to find all the ways she can make 70¢ using quarters and dimes.

One of the entries on her chart won't work. Which one is it?

6. Find all the ways to make the amounts using quarters and dimes. (Some entries on your chart may not work.)

a) 80¢

quarters	dimes
0	
1	
2	
3	

b) 105¢

quarters	dimes

7.

Width	1	2	3	4
Length				

Find all rectangles with side lengths that are whole numbers that have area 16 square units.

8. Make a chart to find all the pairs of numbers that multiply to give:

a) 12 b) 14 c) 20 d) 24

9. Find all the rectangles with side lengths that are whole numbers and with a perimeter of 14 units.

10. Find all the rectangles with side lengths that are whole numbers and with an area of 10 square units

 No unauthorized copying

PA5-20: Patterns with Increasing & Decreasing Steps

1. In the sequences below, the step or gap between the numbers increases or decreases. Can you see a pattern in the way the gap changes? Use the pattern to extend the sequence.

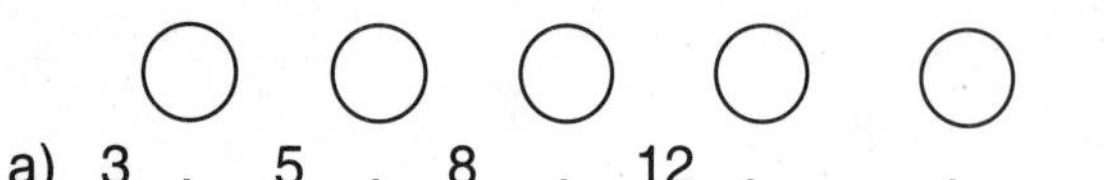

a) 3 , 5 , 8 , 12 , ____ , ____

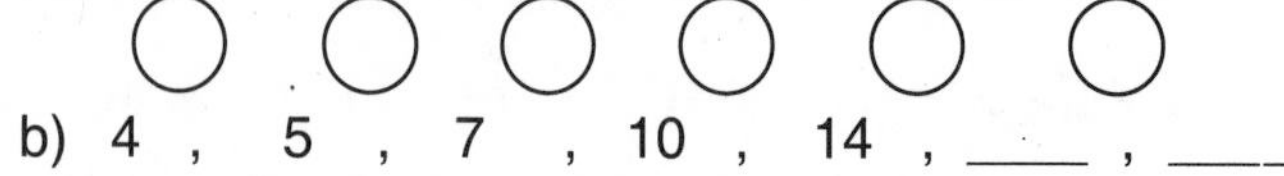

b) 4 , 5 , 7 , 10 , 14 , ____ , ____

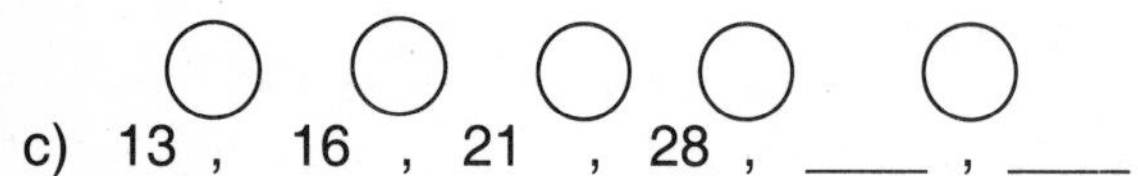

c) 13 , 16 , 21 , 28 , ____ , ____

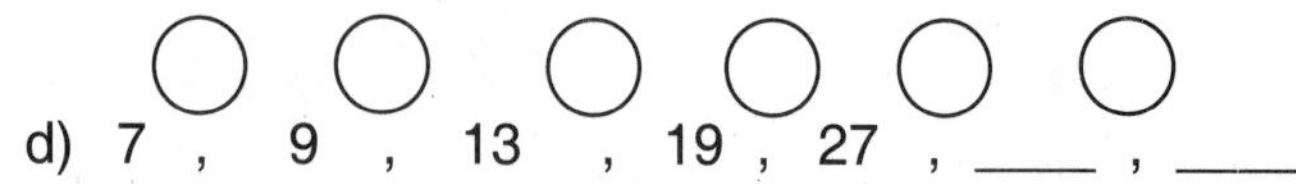

d) 7 , 9 , 13 , 19 , 27 , ____ , ____

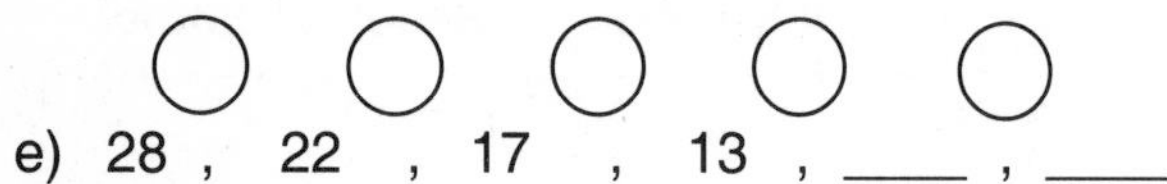

e) 28 , 22 , 17 , 13 , ____ , ____

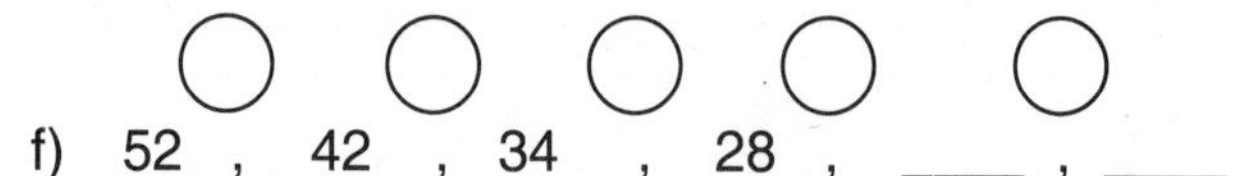

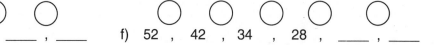

f) 52 , 42 , 34 , 28 , ____ , ____

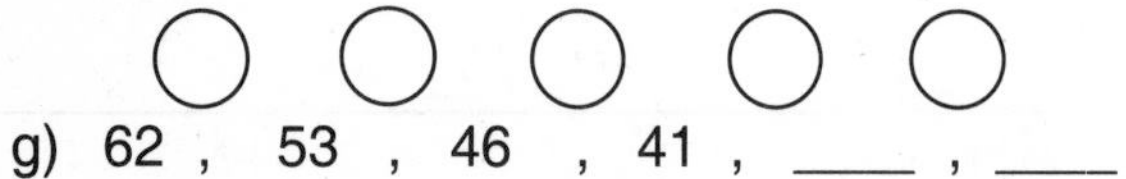

g) 62 , 53 , 46 , 41 , ____ , ____

h) 310 , 280 , 255 , 235 , 220 , ____ , ____

2. Complete the T-table for Figure 3 and Figure 4. Then use the pattern in the gap to predict the number of squares needed for Figures 5 and 6.

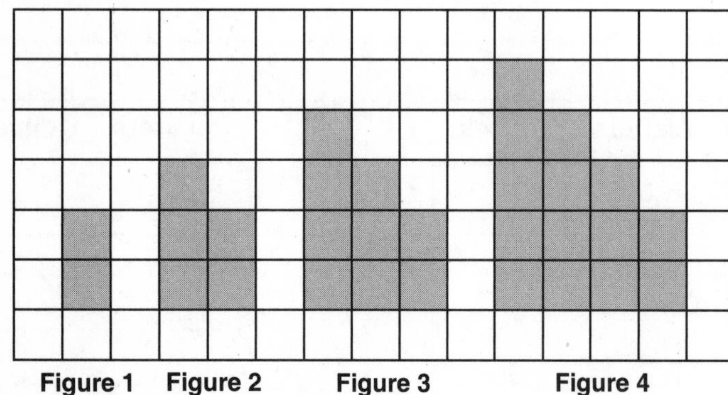

Figure	Number of Squares
1	2
2	5
3	
4	
5	
6	

Write the number of squares added each time here

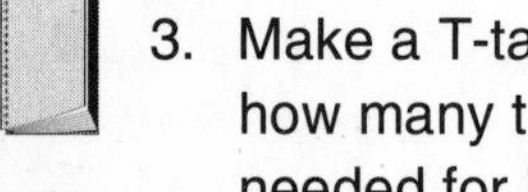

3. Make a T-table to predict how many triangles will be needed for Figure 6.

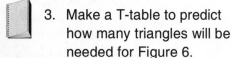

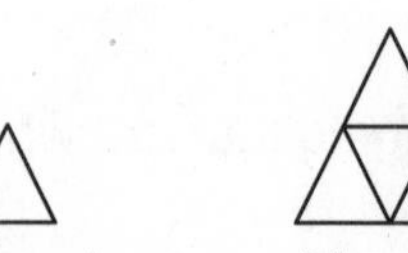

Figure 1

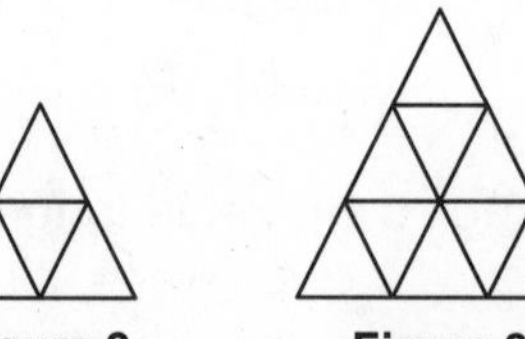

Figure 2

Figure 3

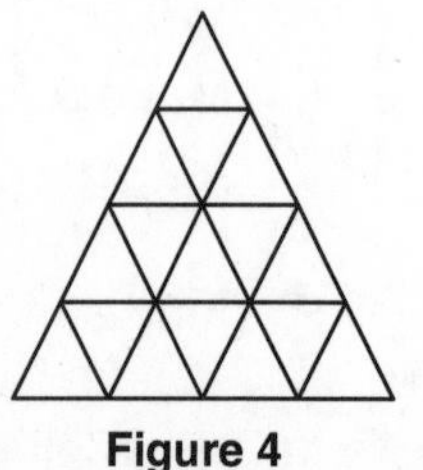

Figure 4

No unauthorized copying

PA5-20: Patterns with Increasing & Decreasing Steps
(continued)

4. In each sequence below, the gap changes in a regular way. Write a rule for each pattern.

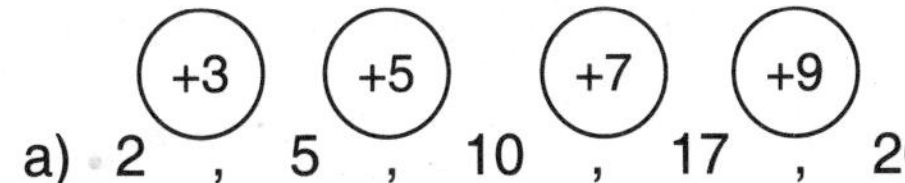

a) 2 , 5 , 10 , 17 , 26

Rule: Start at 2. Add 3, 5, 7 ... (The gap increases by 2.)

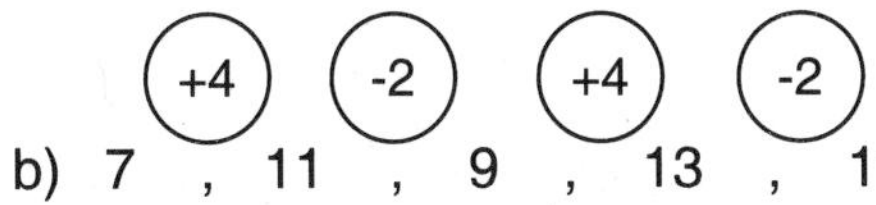

b) 7 , 11 , 9 , 13 , 11

Rule : Start at 7. Add 4, then subtract 2. Repeat.

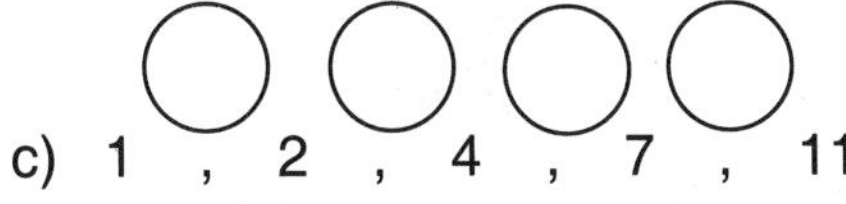

c) 1 , 2 , 4 , 7 , 11

Rule: ______________________________

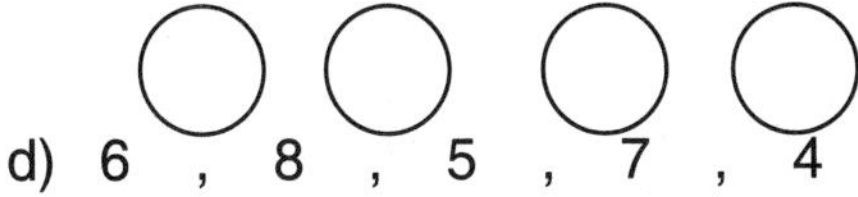

d) 6 , 8 , 5 , 7 , 4

Rule: ______________________________

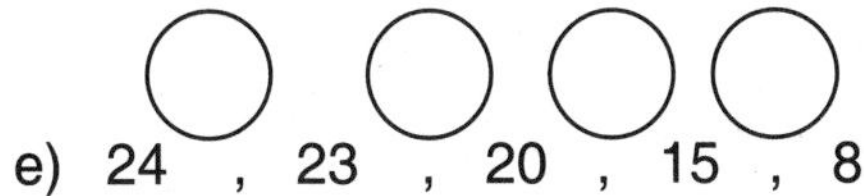

e) 24 , 23 , 20 , 15 , 8

Rule: ______________________________

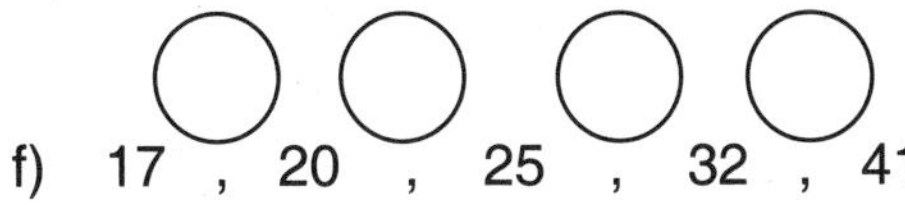

f) 17 , 20 , 25 , 32 , 41

Rule: ______________________________

5. Write a rule for each pattern. Then give the value of the 5th term.

a) 0 , 3 , 8 , 15

b) 1 , 3 , 9 , 27

6. Write a rule for the number of shaded squares or triangles in each figure.
Use your rule to predict the number of shaded parts in the 5th figure.
HINT: To count the number of triangles in the last figure in b), try skip counting by 3s.

a)

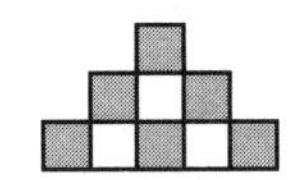

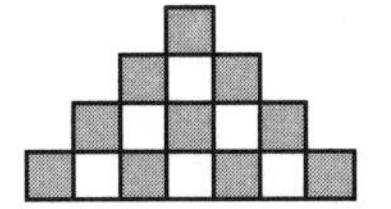

Figure 1 **Figure 2** **Figure 3** **Figure 4**

b)

Figure 1 **Figure 2** **Figure 3** **Figure 4**

No unauthorized copying

PA5-21: Patterns with Larger Numbers

1. Use addition or multiplication to complete the following charts.

a)

Days	Hours
1	24
2	
3	
4	
5	

b)

Years	Days
1	365
2	
3	

c)

Tonnes	Kilograms
1	1000
2	
3	
4	

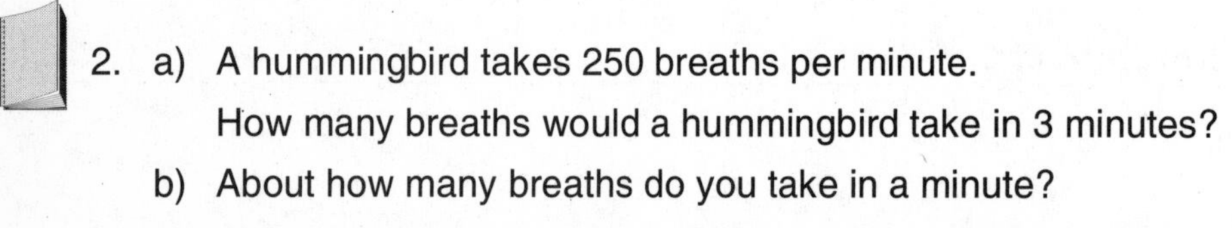

2. a) A hummingbird takes 250 breaths per minute.
   How many breaths would a hummingbird take in 3 minutes?
   b) About how many breaths do you take in a minute?
   c) About how many breaths would you take in 3 minutes?
   d) How many more breaths would a hummingbird take in 3 minutes than you would take?

3. Can you find the answer quickly by grouping the terms in a clever way?

   a) 52 – 52 + 52 – 52 + 52 – 52 + 52   b) 375 + 375 + 375 – 75 – 75 – 75

4. 

In a leap year, February has 29 days.
There is a leap year every 4 years.
The year 2008 is a leap year.
Is the year 2032 a leap year?

5. Use multiplication or a calculator to find the first few products. Look for a pattern. Use the pattern you've discovered to fill in the rest of the numbers.

a) 37 x 3 = ________

37 x 6 = ________

37 x 9 = ________

________ = ________

________ = ________

b) 1 x 1 = ________

11 x 11 = ________

111 x 111 = ________

________ = ________

________ = ________

BONUS

6. Using a calculator, can you discover any patterns like the ones in Question 5?

No unauthorized copying

PA5-22: Introduction to Algebra

1. Some apples are inside a box and some are outside. The total number of apples is shown. Draw the missing apples in the box provided.

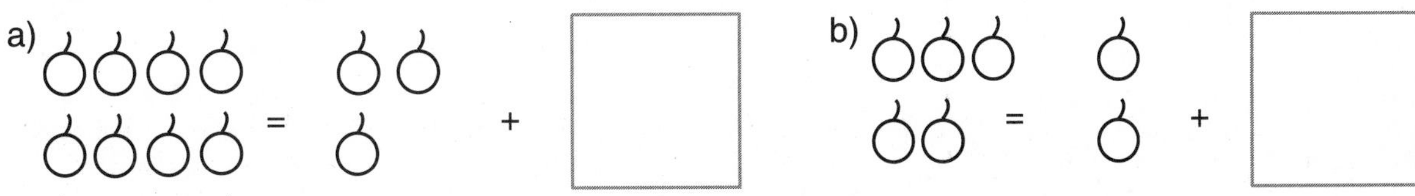

total number of apples

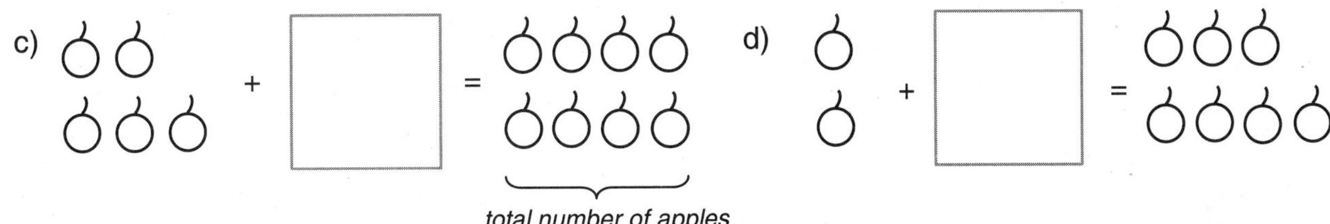

total number of apples

2. Draw the missing apples in the box given. Then write an equation (with numbers) to represent the picture.

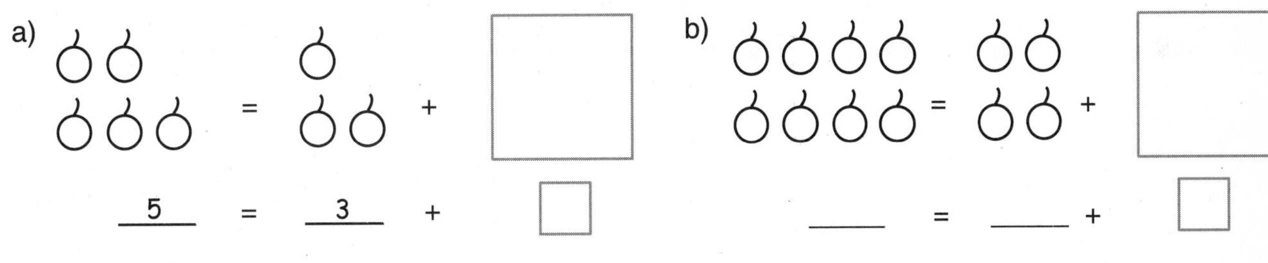

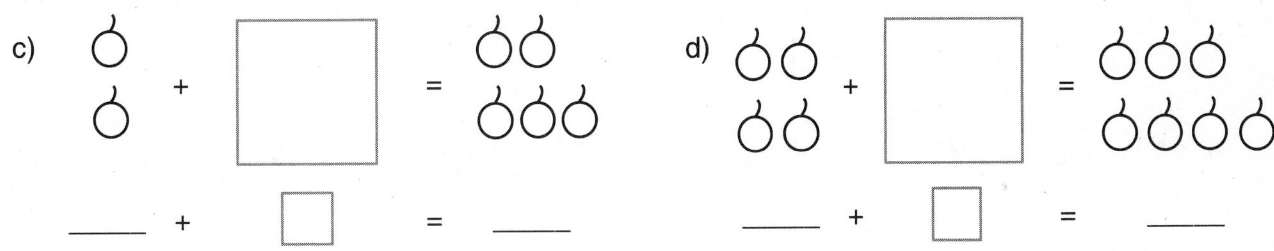

3. Write an equation for each situation. (Use a box to stand for the unknown quantity.)

a) There are 9 apples altogether.
5 are outside of a box.
How many are inside?

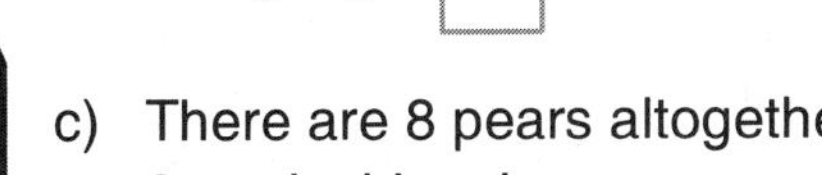

b) There are 7 apples altogether.
3 are outside of a box.
How many are inside?

c) There are 8 pears altogether.
3 are inside a bag.
How many are outside?

d) 10 students are in a library.
2 are inside the computer room.
How many are outside?

e) 7 children are in a gym.
2 are in the pool.
How many are out of the pool?

f) Rena has 13 stamps.
5 are Canadian.
How many are from other countries?

g) 15 children are in a camp.
9 are girls.
How many are boys?

h) 9 dogs are in a pet store.
5 are puppies.
How many are adults?

No unauthorized copying

PA5-23: Algebra

1. Tim took some apples from a box. Show how many apples were in the box originally.

a)  − (3 apples) = (5 apples)

Tim took away this many. *This is how many were left.*

b) □ − (2 apples) = (4 apples)

c) 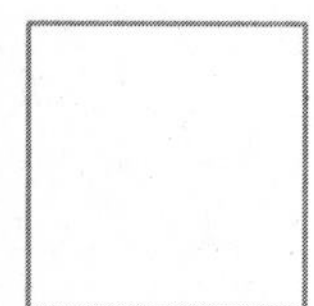 − (2 apples) = (3 apples)

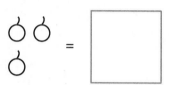

d) (3 apples) = □ − (5 apples)

2. Show how many apples were in the box originally. Then write an equation to represent the picture.

a) 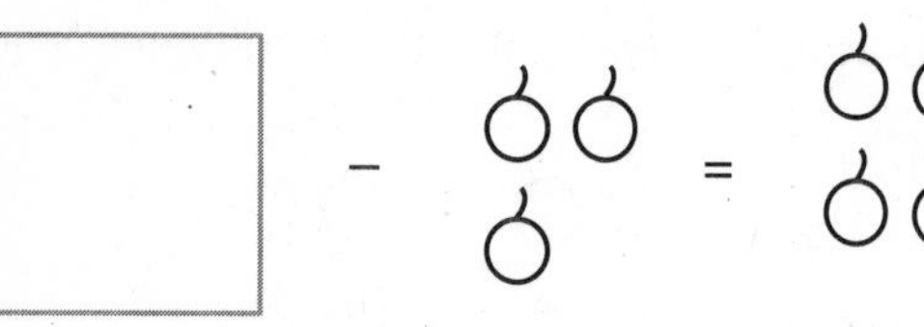 − (3 apples) = (4 apples)

□ − 3 = 4

b)  − (2 apples) = (5 apples)

3. In the equations below, 2 × □ is a short form for two identical boxes. Show how many apples are in each box.

a) 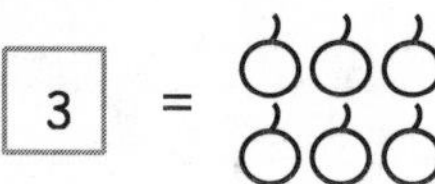 2 × 3 = (6 apples)

b) 2 × □ = (4 apples)

c) 3 × □ = (9 apples)

d) 3 × □ = (6 apples)

e) 4 × □ = 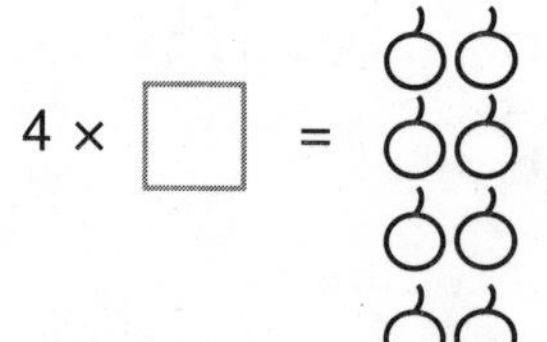 (8 apples)

f) 2 × □ = 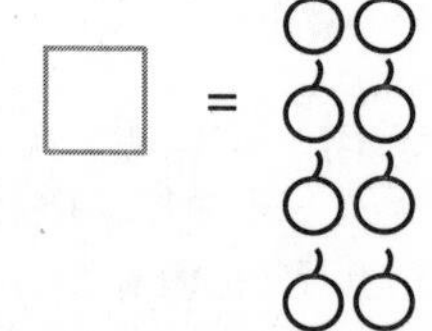 (8 apples)

4. Write an equation for each situation.

a) Tom took 3 apples from a box. 2 apples were left.
How many apples were in the box?

b) Sarah took 3 eggs from a carton. 5 eggs were left.
How many eggs were in the carton?

c) Ed has 15 apples in 3 boxes.
Each box contains the same number of apples.
How many apples are in each box?

5. Write a problem to match each equation.

a) 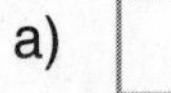 □ + 2 = 5

b) □ − 4 = 6

c) 3 × □ = 12

PA5-24: Variables

A **variable** is a letter or symbol (such as **x**, **n**, or **h**) that represents a number.

In the product of a number and a variable, the multiplication sign is usually dropped.

For example: 3 × T is written 3T and 5 × z is written 5z.

1. Write a numerical expression for the cost of renting skates for:

Rent a pair of skates
$3 for each hour

a) 2 hours: 3 x 2 b) 5 hours: ________ c) 6 hours: ________

2. Write an expression for the distance a car would travel at:

a) Speed: 60 km per hour
Time: 2 hours
Distance: ________ km

b) Speed: 80 km per hour
Time: 3 hours
Distance: __________ km

c) Speed: 70 km per hour
Time: h hours
Distance: ___________ km

3. Write an algebraic expression for the cost of renting skis for:

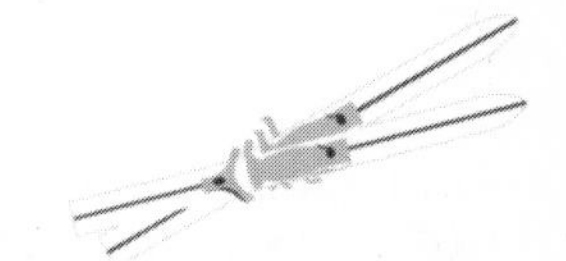

Rent a pair of skis
$ 5 per hour

a) h hours: ______ or ______ b) t hours: ______ or ______

c) x hours: ______ or ______ d) n hours: ______ or ______

4. Write an equation that tells you the relationship between the numbers in column A and column B.

a)

A	B
1	4
2	5
3	6

A + 3 = B

b)

A	B
1	2
2	4
3	6

2 × A = B

c)

A	B
1	3
2	4
3	5

____

d)

A	B
1	3
2	6
3	9

____

e)

A	B
1	5
2	10
3	15

____

5. Use the variable x to write an expression for the number of apples outside of a box.

a) There are 10 apples altogether.
4 are outside of a box.
How many are in the box?

b) There are 12 apples altogether.
7 are outside of a box.
How many are in the box?

 No unauthorized copying

PA5-25: Equations

1. Find the number that makes each equation true (by guessing and checking) and write it in the box.

a) □ + 3 = 9 b) □ + 2 = 5 c) □ + 4 = 10

d) 8 – □ = 6 e) 18 – □ = 14 f) 10 – □ = 7

g) 2 × □ = 8 h) 5 × □ = 20 i) 3 × □ = 12

j) □ ÷ 3 = 2 k) □ ÷ 5 = 3 l) □ ÷ 2 = 5

BONUS

m) 7 + 3 = 6 + □ n) 10 – 3 = □ + 2 o) □ + □ + 3 = 7

p) 9 = 1 + 2+ □ q) 7 + 8 = □ + 2 r) □ + 12 = 20 – 7

s) 5 x □ = 9 + 11 t) □ ÷ 2 = 7 – 4 u) 2 x 3 = □ ÷ 5

2. Find a set of numbers that makes each equation true. (Some questions have more than one answer.)
NOTE: In a given question, congruent shapes represent the <u>same</u> number.

a) □ + □ + ○ = 10 b) □ + □ + ○ = 8

c) ◇ + ◇ + ○ + ○ = 8 d) □ + △ + ○ = 9

3. Find two answers for the equation.

□ + □ + ○ = 7 □ + □ + ○ = 7

4. Find a single number that makes both equations true. 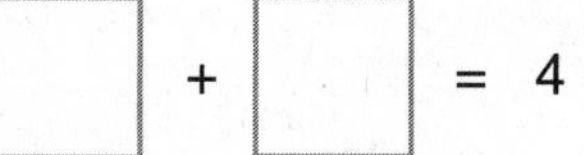 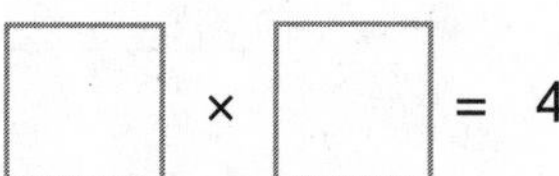

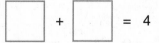

5. Find three different numbers that make both equations true.

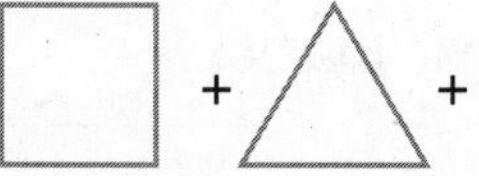 + ○ = 6 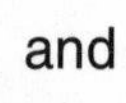 and 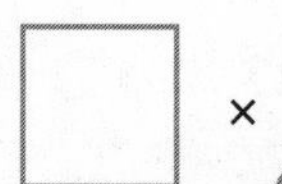 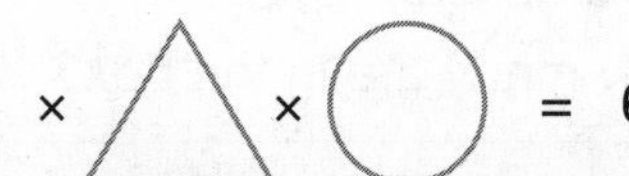 = 6

PA5-25: Equations *(continued)*

6. Find a combination of numbers that make the equation true. (You cannot use the number 1.)

a)  □ × △ = 6

b) □ × △ = 8

c) □ × ○ = 10

d) 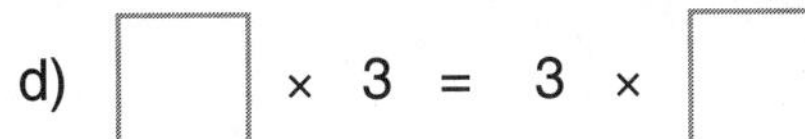 □ × 3 = 3 × □

e) □ × □ × ○ = 12

f)  □ × □ × ○ = 18

g) 3 × 10 = 2 × □ × △

7. Complete the patterns.

a)	b)	c)
10 + [1] = ○	10 − [1] = ○	10 × [1] = ○
10 + [2] = ○	10 − [2] = ○	10 × [2] = ○
10 + [3] = ○	10 − □ = ○	10 × □ = ○
10 + □ = ○	10 − □ = ○	10 × □ = ○

8. For each pattern in Question 7, say how the number in the circle changes as the number in the box increases by one.

9. When the number in each box below <u>doubles</u>, what happens to the product? (Use the pattern to fill in the numbers in the last question.)

5 × □ = 10   5 × □ = 20   5 × □ = 40   5 × □ = ______

10. Knowing that 6 is double 3, and that 7 × 3 = 21, how can you find 7 × 6 = 42 without multiplying 7 × 6?

11. Fran threw 3 darts and scored 10 points.
The dart in the centre ring is worth more than the others.
Each dart in the outer ring is worth more than two points.
How much is each dart worth?
HINT: How can an equation like the one in 2 a) help you solve the problem?

No unauthorized copying

PA5-26: Problems and Puzzles

Answer the following questions in your notebook.

1. The picture shows how many chairs can be placed at each arrangement of tables.

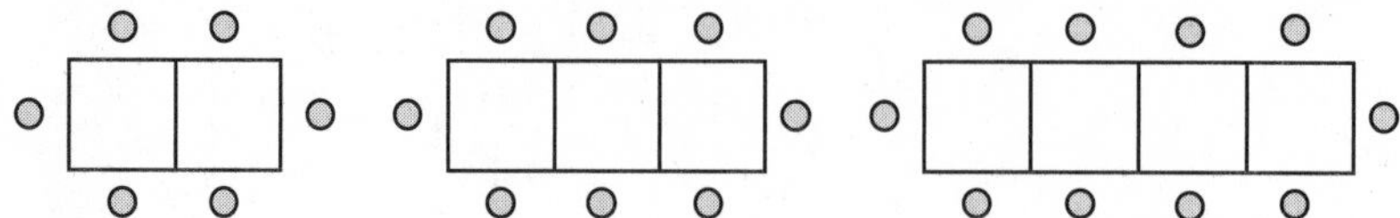

a) Make a T-table and state a rule that tells the relationship between the number of tables and the number of chairs.

b) How many chairs can be placed at 15 tables?

2. Julia makes an ornament using triangles and squares. She has 16 squares.

How many triangles will she need to make ornaments with all 16 squares?

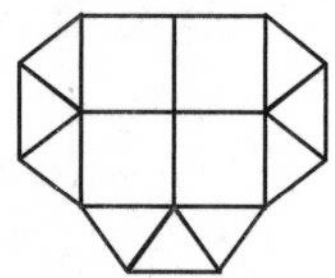

3. Raymond is 400 km from home Wednesday morning.

He cycles 65 km toward home each day.

How far away from home is he by Saturday evening?

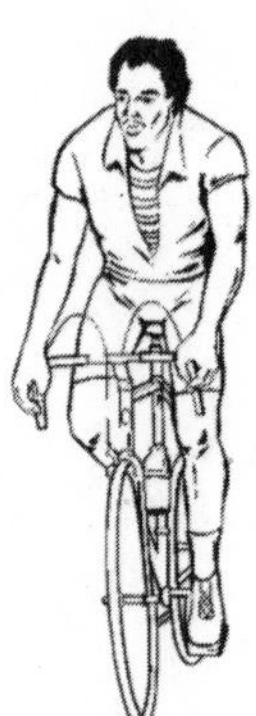

4. Explain why the underlined term is or is not the next step in the pattern.

a) 127, 124, 121, <u>118</u>

b) 27, 31, 35, <u>40</u>

c) 7, 5, 8, 6, <u>9</u>

5. A recipe calls for 3 cups of flour for every 4 cups of water.

How many cups of water will be needed for 18 cups of flour?

6. Find the mystery numbers.

a) I am a 2 digit number. I am a multiple of 4 and 6. My tens digit is 2.

b) I am between 20 and 40. I am a multiple of 3. My ones digit is 6.

7. Every 6th person who arrives at a book sale receives a free calendar. Every 8th person receives a free book.

Which of the first 50 people receive a book and a calendar?

No unauthorized copying

PA5-26: Problems and Puzzles *(continued)*

8. Describe how each picture was made from the one before.

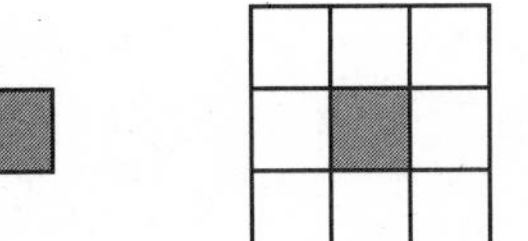
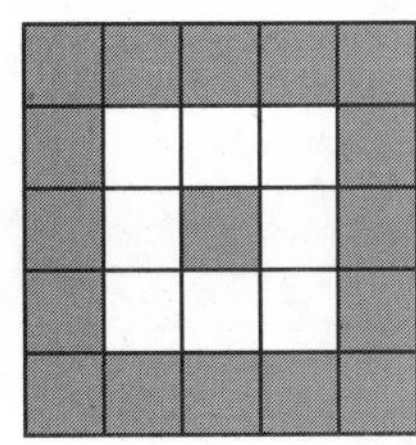

9. What strategy would you use to find the 63rd shape in the pattern below?

What is the shape?

10. Paul shovelled 26 sidewalks in 4 days.

Each day, he shovelled 3 more sidewalks than the day before.

How many sidewalks did he shovel each day?
Guess and check!

11. A camp offers 2 ways to rent a sailboat.

You can pay \$8.50 for the first hour and \$4.50 for every hour after that.

Or, you can pay \$6.00 for every hour.

If you wanted to rent the canoe for 5 hours, which way would you choose to pay?

12. The picture shows how the temperature inside a cloud changes at different heights.

a) Does the temperature increase or decrease at greater heights?

b) What distance does the arrow represent in real life?

c) Measure the length of the arrow.

d) What is the scale of the picture?

__________ cm = ____________ m

9° 10 000 m
12°
15°
18°
21°
earth

e) Do temperatures change by the same amount each time?

f) If the pattern continued, what would the temperature be at:

i) 12 000 m?
ii) 14 000 m?

13. Marlene says she will need 27 blocks to make Figure 7.

Is she right? Explain.

Figure 1

Figure 2

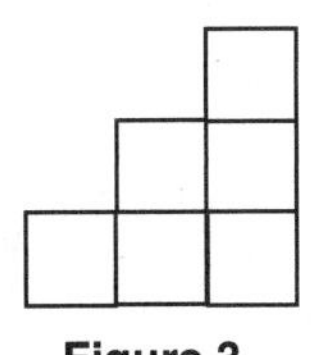
Figure 3

No unauthorized copying

NS5-52: Equal Parts and Models of Fractions

Fractions name equal parts of a whole.

The pie is cut into 4 equal parts.

3 parts out of 4 are shaded.

$\frac{3}{4}$ of a pie is shaded.

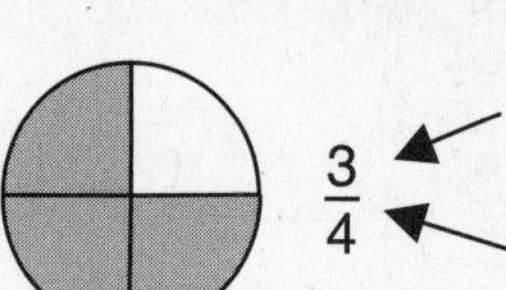

$\frac{3}{4}$

The **numerator** (3) tells you how many parts are counted.

The **denominator** (4) tells you how many parts are in a whole.

1. Name the fraction shown by the shaded part of each image.

a) 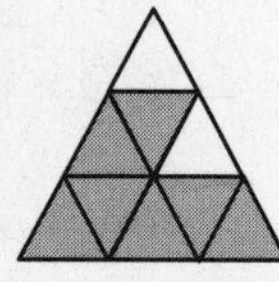 b) 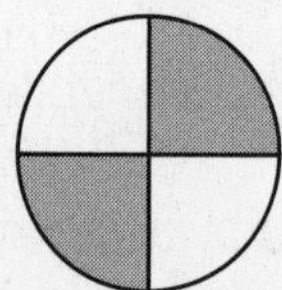 c)  d) 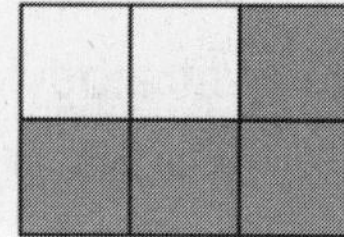

2. You have $\frac{5}{8}$ of a pie.

a) What does the bottom (denominator) of the fraction tell you?

____

b) What does the top (numerator) of the fraction tell you?

____

3. Use a **ruler** to divide each box into equal parts.

a) 4 equal parts 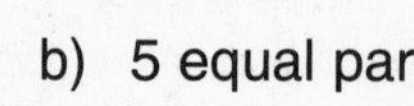

b) 5 equal parts 

4. Using a **ruler**, find what fraction of the box is shaded.

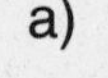

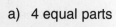

a)  _____ is shaded

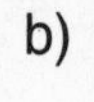

b)  _____ is shaded

5. Using a **ruler**, complete the following figures to make a whole.

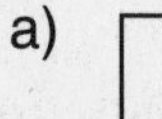

a) 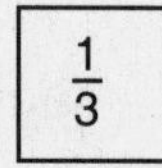

b) 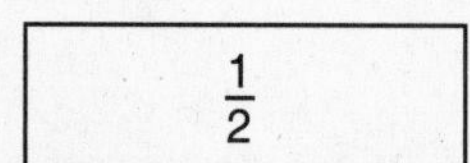

c) 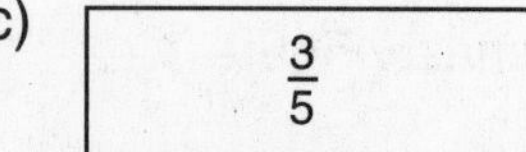

6. Each of the lines below is $\frac{1}{3}$ of a line. Using a **ruler**, fill in the rest to make a whole line.

a) 

b) __________

7. Explain why each picture does (or does not) show $\frac{1}{3}$.

a) 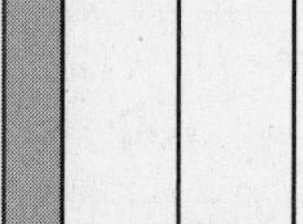 b) 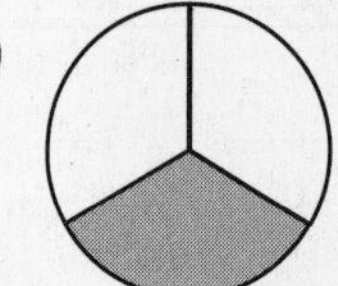 c)  d) 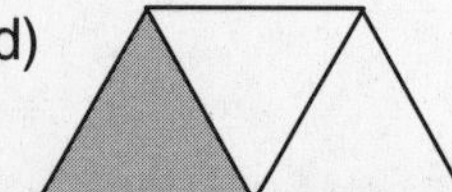

No unauthorized copying

NS5-53: Equal Parts of a Set

Fractions can name parts of a set: $\frac{3}{5}$ of the figures are triangles, $\frac{1}{5}$ are squares and $\frac{1}{5}$ are circles.

1. Fill in the blanks.

a)

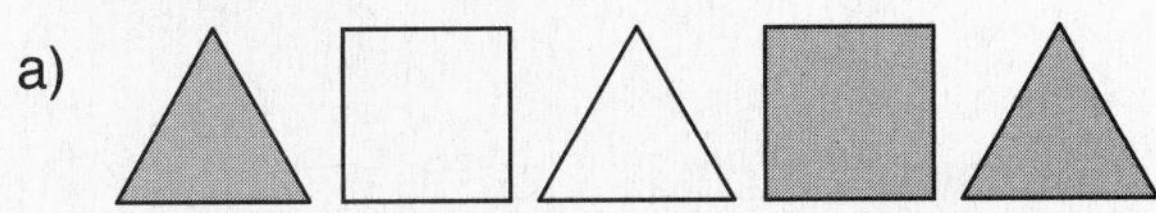

______ of the figures are triangles.

______ of the figures are shaded.

b)

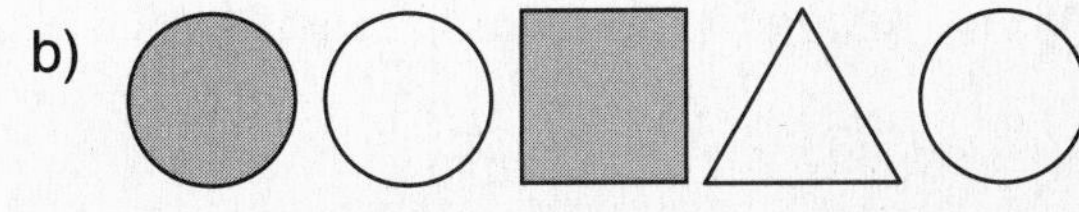

______ of the figures are squares.

______ of the figures are shaded.

2. Fill in the blanks.

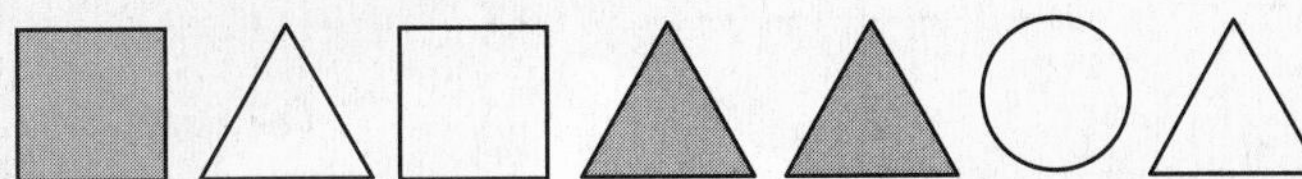

a) $\frac{4}{7}$ of the figures are ____________________

b) $\frac{2}{7}$ of the figures are ____________________

c) $\frac{1}{7}$ of the figures are ____________________

d) $\frac{3}{7}$ of the figures are ____________________

3. Describe this picture in two different ways using the fraction $\frac{3}{5}$.

4. A football team wins 7 games and loses 5 games.

a) How many games did the team play? _______________

b) What <u>fraction</u> of the games did the team win? _______________

c) Did the team win more than half its games? _______________

No unauthorized copying

NS5-53: Equal Parts of a Set *(continued)*

5.

	Number of boys	Number of girls
The Smith Family	2	3
The Sinha Family	1	2

a) What fraction of the children in each family are boys?

Smiths _______ Sinhas _______

b) What fraction of all the children are boys? _______

6. What fraction of the letters in the word "Canada" are:

a) vowels? _________ b) consonants? _________

7. Express 7 months as a fraction of one year: ___________

8. Write a fraction for each statement.

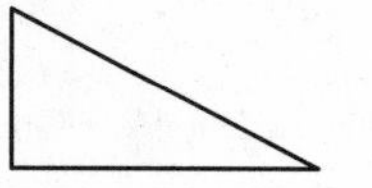 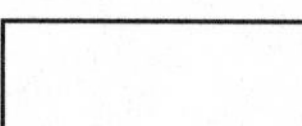 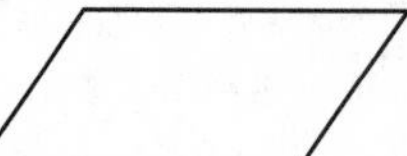 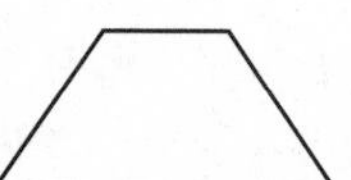 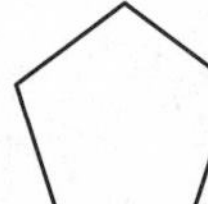 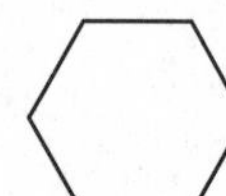

a) ☐ of the figures have 4 vertices

b) ☐ of the figures have more than 4 sides

c) ☐ of the figures have exactly one right angle

d) ☐ of the figures have exactly 2 pairs of parallel sides

9. Write two fraction statements for the figures in Question 8 above.

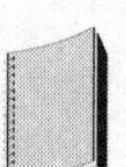

10. Draw a picture to solve the puzzle.

a) There are 7 circles and squares.

$\frac{2}{7}$ of the figures are squares.

$\frac{5}{7}$ of the figures are shaded.

Three circles are shaded.

b) There are 8 triangles and squares.

$\frac{6}{8}$ of the figures are shaded.

$\frac{2}{8}$ of the figures are triangles.

One triangle is shaded.

 No unauthorized copying

NS5-54: Parts and Wholes

1. 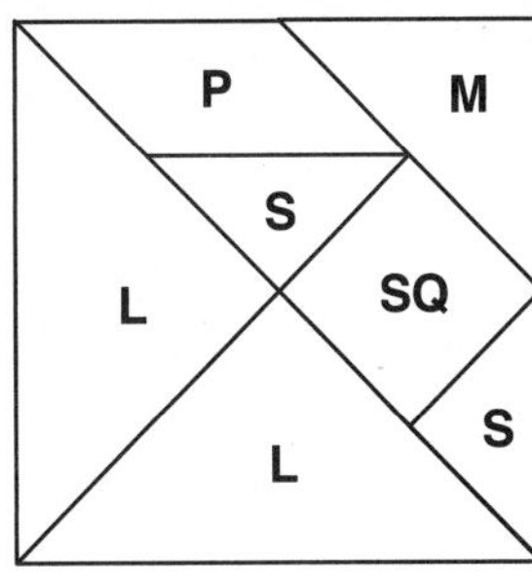

In a tangram:

- 2 small triangles (**S**) cover a medium triangle (**M**)
- 2 small triangles (**S**) cover a square (**SQ**)
- 2 small triangles (**S**) cover a parallelogram (**P**)
- 4 small triangles (**S**) cover a large triangle (**L**)

What fraction of each shape is covered by a single small triangle?

a) 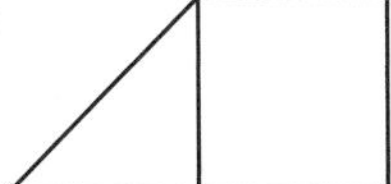

b) 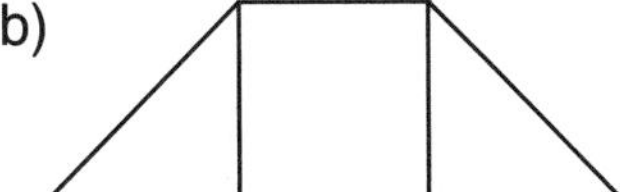

c) 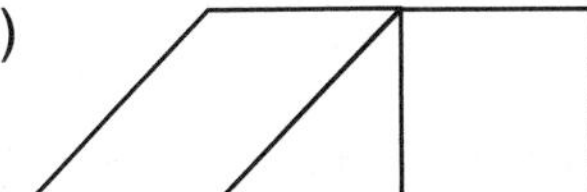

d) 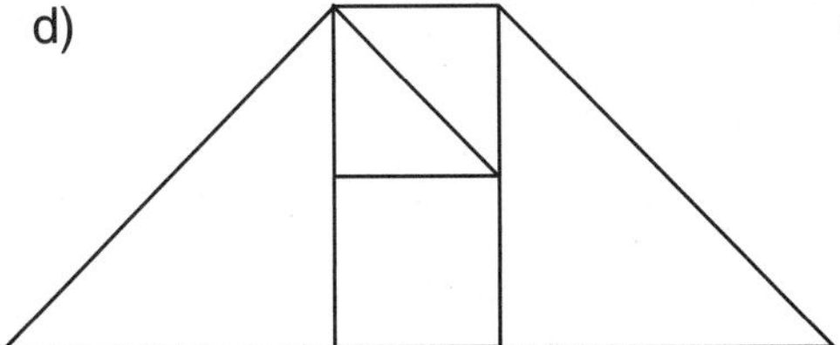

e) 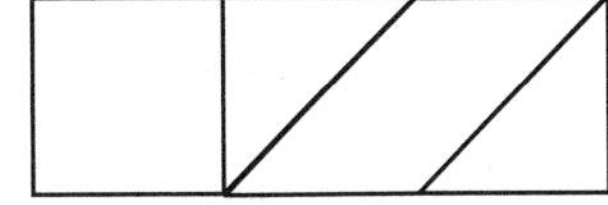

f) 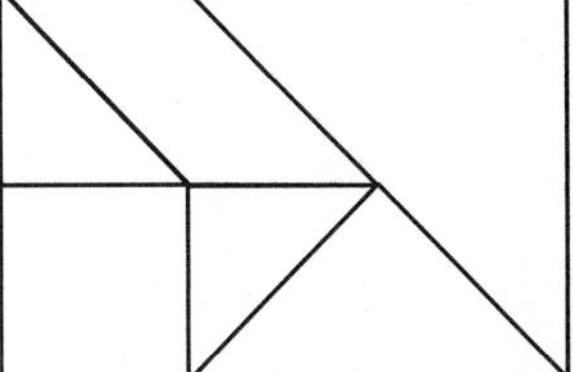

2. What fraction of each shape is shaded? Explain how you know.

a) 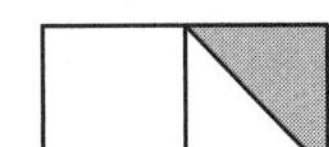

b) 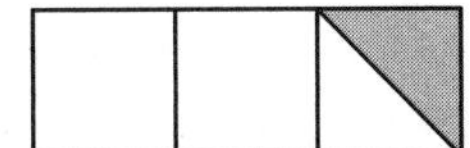

c) 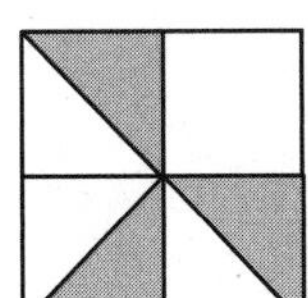

d) 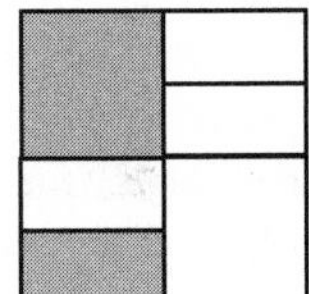

3. What fraction of the trapezoid is covered by a single small triangle?

Show your work.

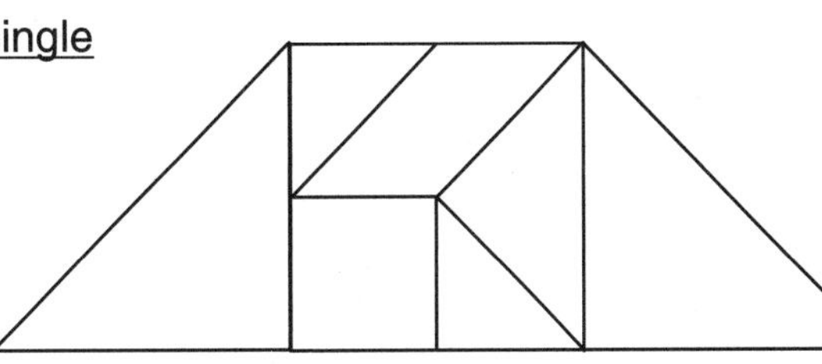

4. If [red square] = red and [dotted square] = blue, approximately what fraction of each flag is shaded red? Explain.

a) 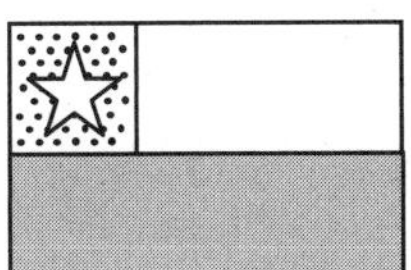

b) 

c) 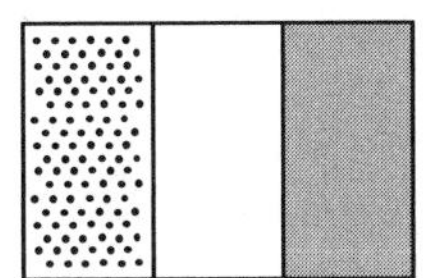

d) 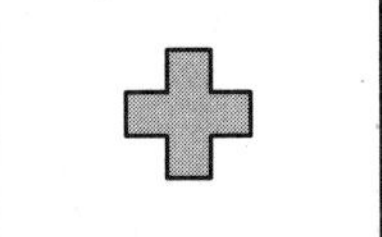

No unauthorized copying

NS5-55: Ordering and Comparing Fractions

1. 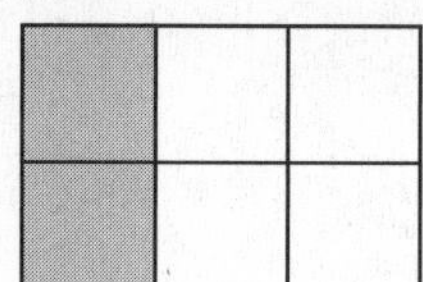 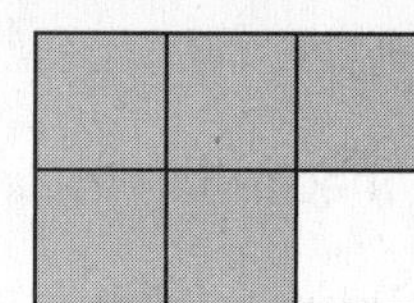

What fraction has a greater numerator, $\frac{2}{6}$ or $\frac{5}{6}$? _______

Which fraction is greater? _______

Explain your thinking. ____

____

2. Circle the greater fraction in each pair.

a) $\frac{6}{16}$ or $\frac{9}{16}$ b) $\frac{5}{8}$ or $\frac{3}{8}$ c) $\frac{24}{25}$ or $\frac{22}{25}$ d) $\frac{37}{53}$ or $\frac{27}{53}$

3. Two fractions have the same denominators (bottoms) but different numerators (tops).
How can you tell which fraction is greater?

____

4. Circle the greater fraction in each pair.

a) $\frac{1}{8}$ or $\frac{1}{9}$ b) $\frac{12}{12}$ or $\frac{12}{13}$ c) $\frac{5}{225}$ or $\frac{5}{125}$

5. Fraction A and Fraction B have the same numerators but different denominators. How can you tell which fraction is greater?

____

6. Write the fractions in order from least to greatest.

a) $\frac{2}{3}$, $\frac{1}{3}$, $\frac{3}{3}$ b) $\frac{9}{10}$, $\frac{2}{10}$, $\frac{1}{10}$, $\frac{5}{10}$

c) $\frac{1}{7}$, $\frac{1}{3}$, $\frac{1}{13}$ d) $\frac{2}{11}$, $\frac{2}{5}$, $\frac{2}{7}$, $\frac{2}{16}$

7. Circle the greater fraction in each pair.

a) $\frac{2}{3}$ or $\frac{2}{9}$ b) $\frac{7}{17}$ or $\frac{11}{17}$ c) $\frac{6}{288}$ or $\frac{6}{18}$

8. Which fraction is greater, $\frac{1}{2}$ or $\frac{45}{100}$? Explain your thinking.

9. Is it possible for $\frac{2}{3}$ of a pie to be bigger than $\frac{3}{4}$ of another pie? Show your thinking with a picture.

No unauthorized copying

NS5-56: Mixed Fractions

Mattias and his friends ate the amount of pie shown.

They ate three and three quarter pies altogether (or $3\frac{3}{4}$ pies).

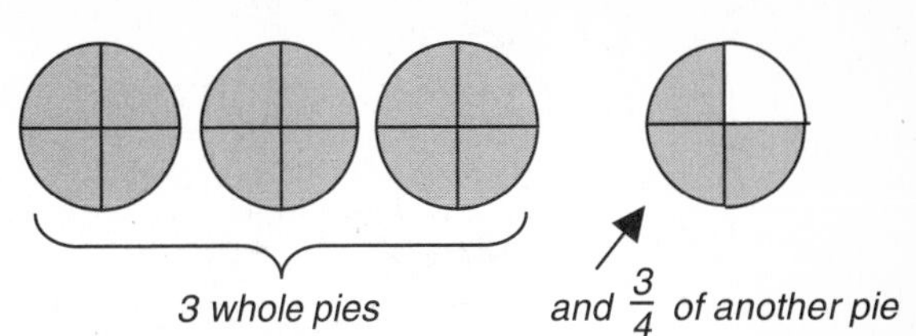

NOTE: $3\frac{3}{4}$ is called a <u>mixed fraction</u> because it is a mixture of a whole number and a fraction.

---

1. Write how many <u>whole</u> pies are shaded.

a) 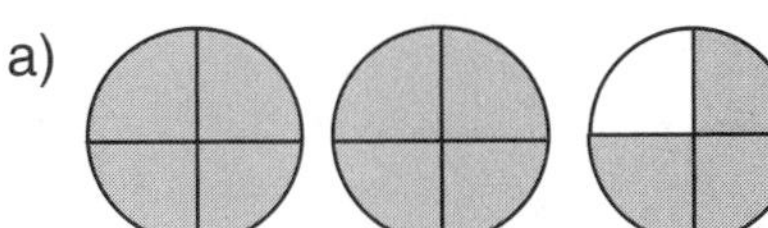

b) 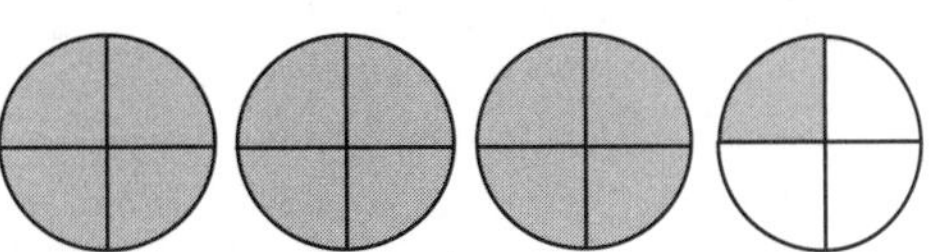

c) 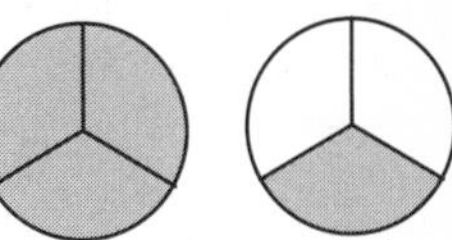

__2__ whole pies ______ whole pies ______ whole pie

2. Write the fractions as <u>mixed fractions</u>.

a) 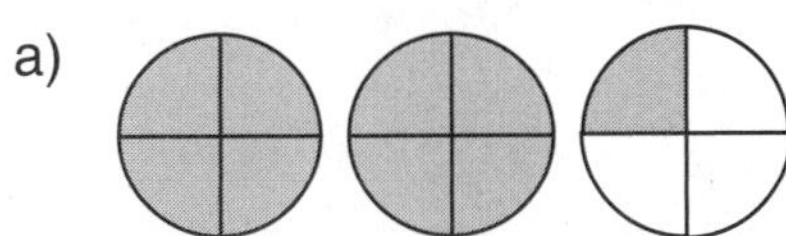 ______

b) 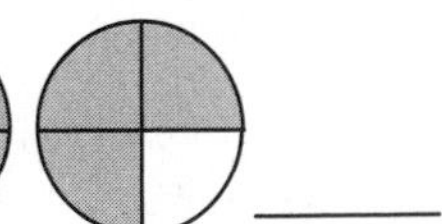 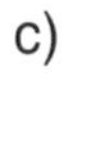 ______

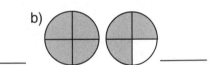

c) 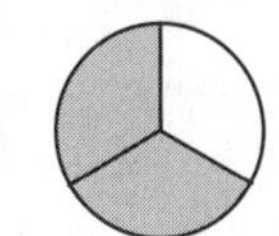 ______

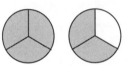

d) 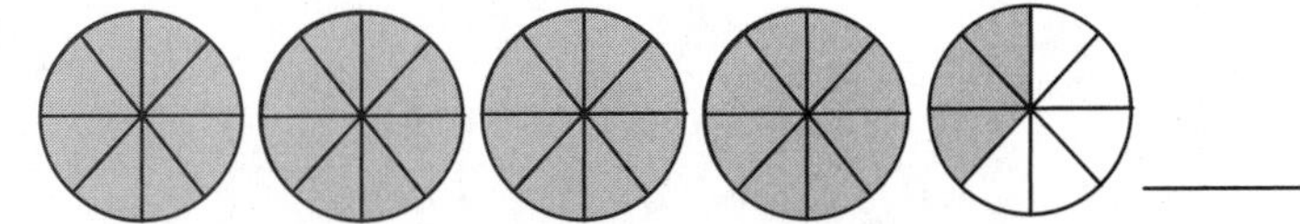 ______

e) 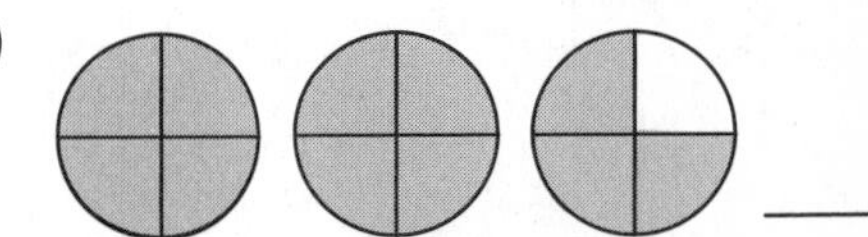 ______

f) 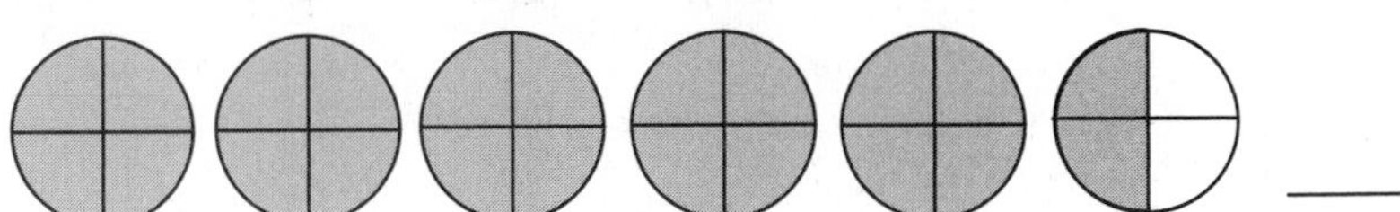 ______

g) 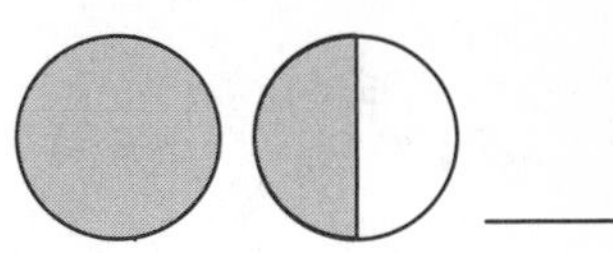 ______

3. Shade the amount of pie given in bold.
NOTE: There may be more pies than you need.

a) **$3\frac{1}{2}$**  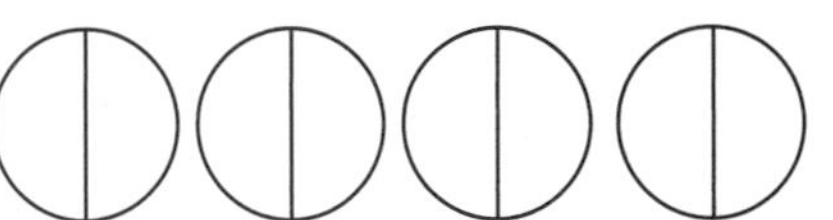

b) **$1\frac{1}{4}$** 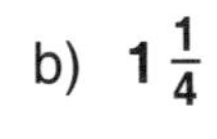 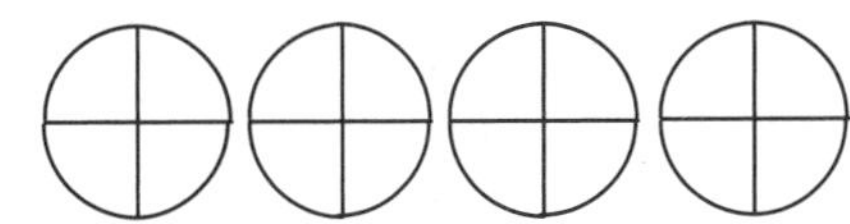

c) **$2\frac{3}{4}$** 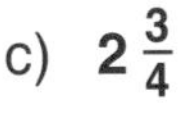 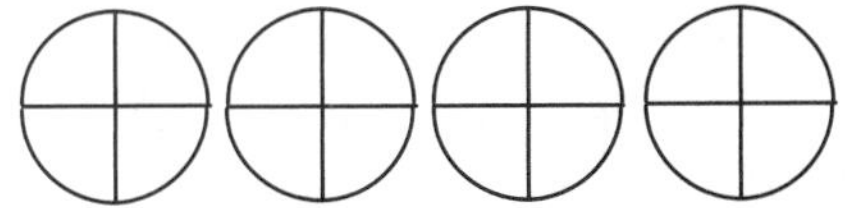

d) **$3\frac{2}{3}$** 

e) **$1\frac{2}{5}$** 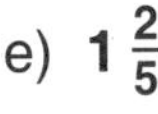 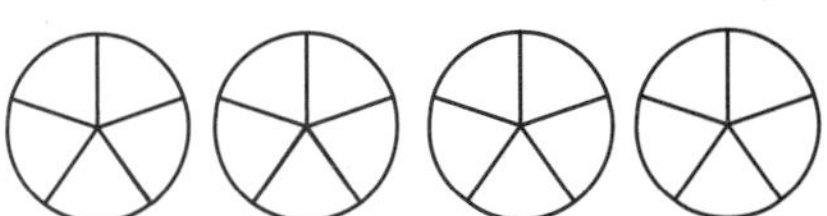

f) **$2\frac{5}{6}$** 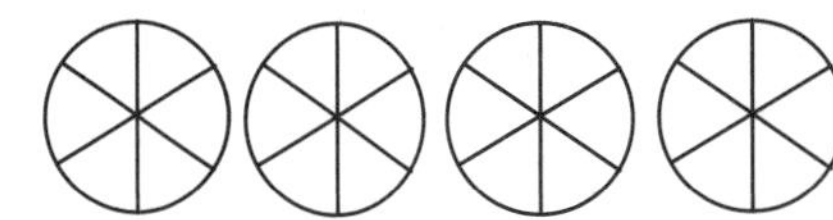

4. Sketch. a) $2\frac{1}{3}$ pies b) $3\frac{3}{4}$ pies c) $2\frac{3}{5}$ pies d) $3\frac{1}{2}$ pies

 No unauthorized copying

NS5-57: Improper Fractions

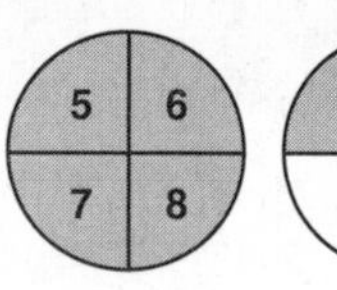

Improper Fraction: $\frac{9}{4}$ = *Mixed Fraction:* $2\frac{1}{4}$

Huan-Yue and her friends ate **9** quarter-sized pieces of pizza. Altogether they ate $\frac{9}{4}$ pizzas.

NOTE: When the numerator of a fraction is larger than the denominator, the fraction represents *more than* a whole. Such fractions are called improper fractions.

---

1. Write these fractions as improper fractions.

a) 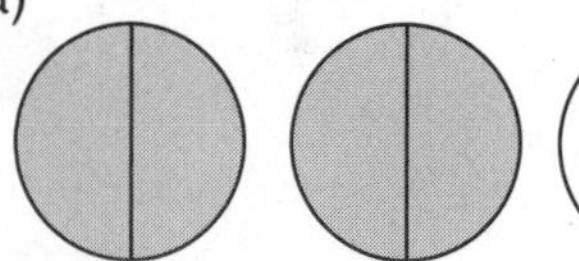 ______

b) 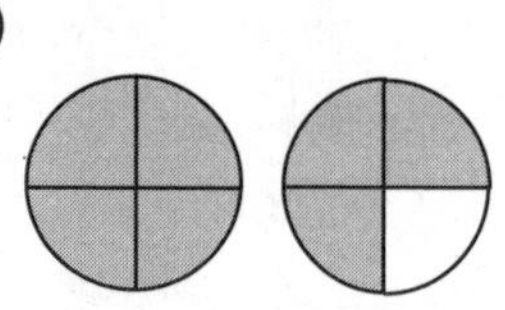 ______

c) 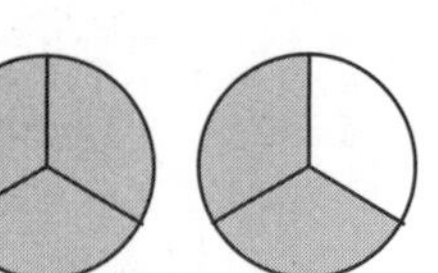 ______

d) 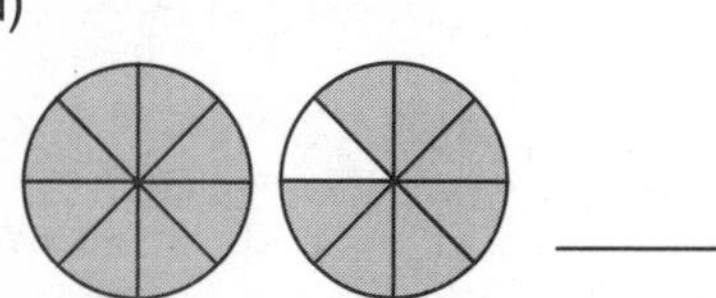 ______

e) 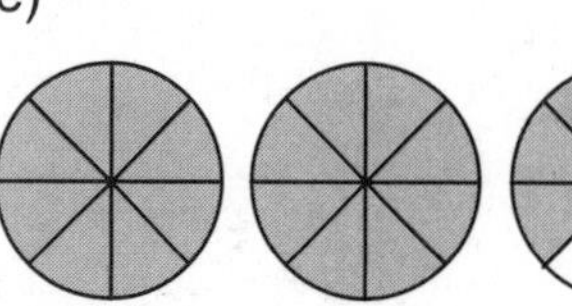 ______

f) 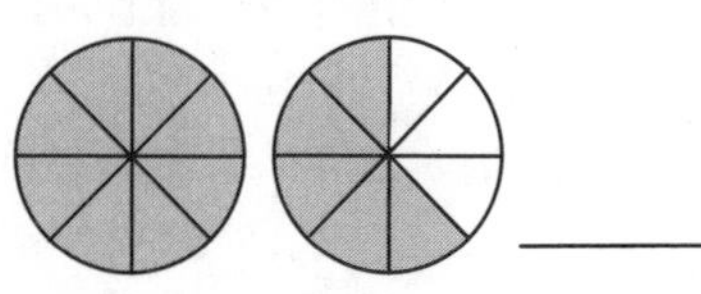 ______

g) 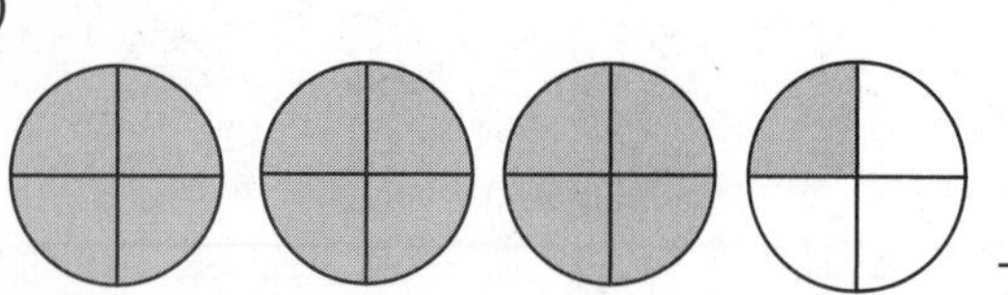 ______

h) 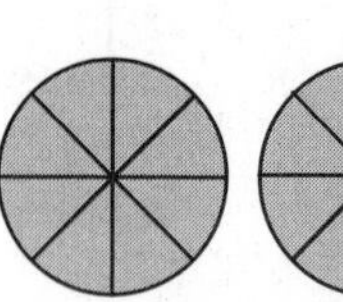 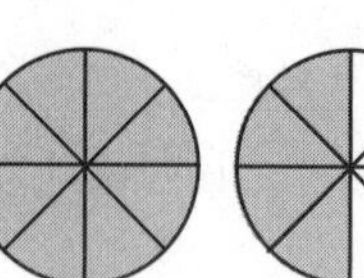 ______

2. Shade one piece at a time until you have shaded the amount of pie given.

a) $\frac{7}{2}$ 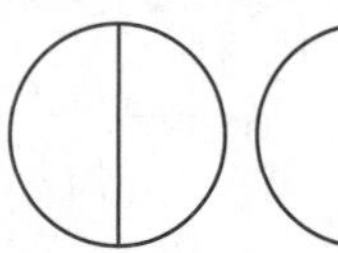  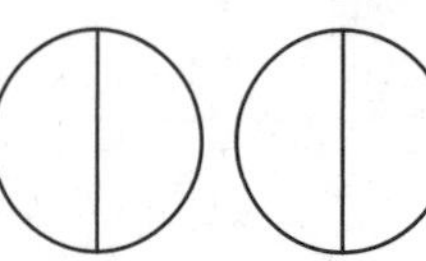

b) $\frac{7}{4}$ 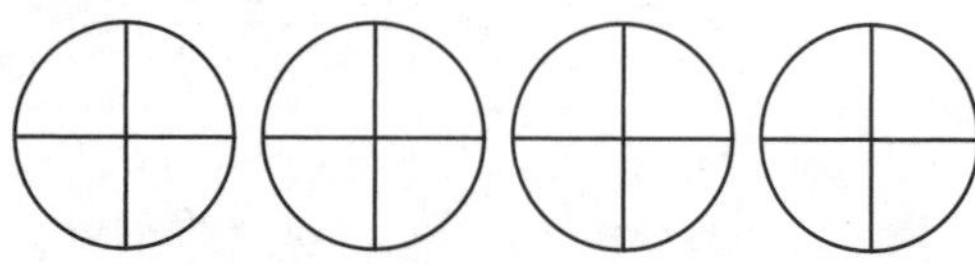

c) $\frac{11}{3}$ 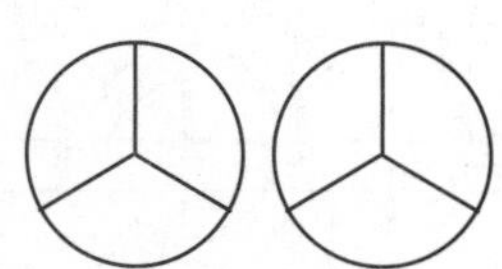 

d) $\frac{12}{4}$ 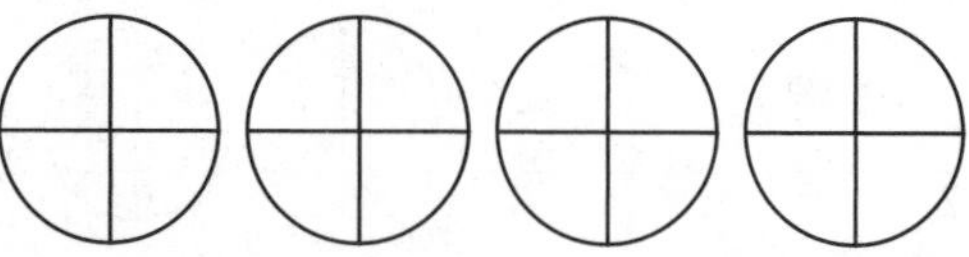

e) $\frac{17}{5}$ 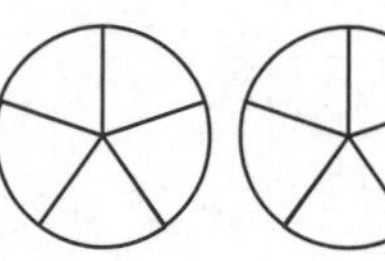 

f) $\frac{19}{8}$ 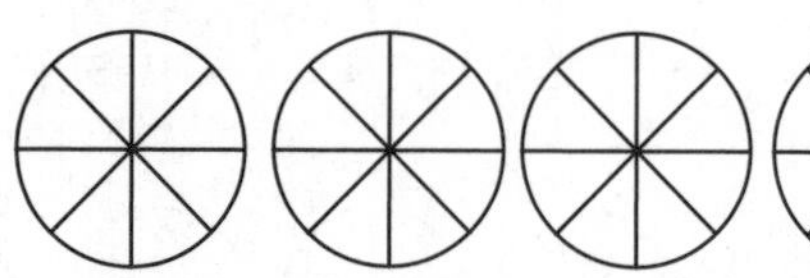

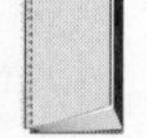

3. Sketch. a) $\frac{6}{4}$ pies b) $\frac{7}{2}$ pies c) $\frac{11}{4}$ pies d) $\frac{13}{3}$ pies

4. Which fractions are more than a whole? How do you know? a) $\frac{9}{10}$ b) $\frac{15}{7}$ c) $\frac{12}{8}$

 No unauthorized copying

NS5-58: Mixed and Improper Fractions

1. Write these fractions as mixed fractions and as improper fractions.

a) 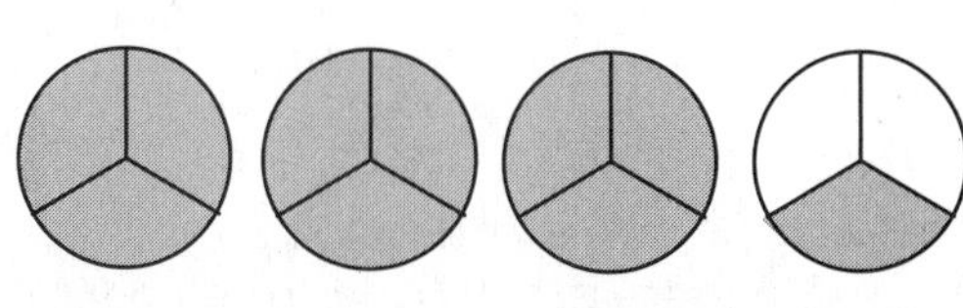 ______

b) 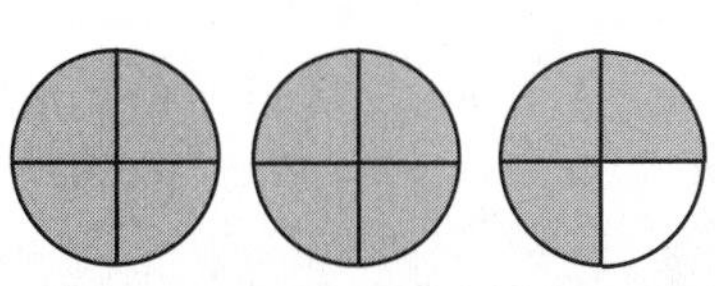 ______

c) 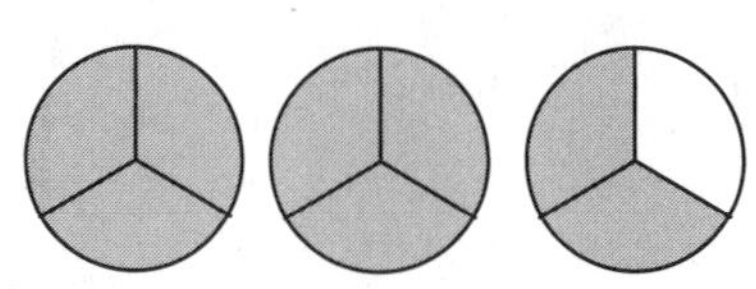 ______

d) 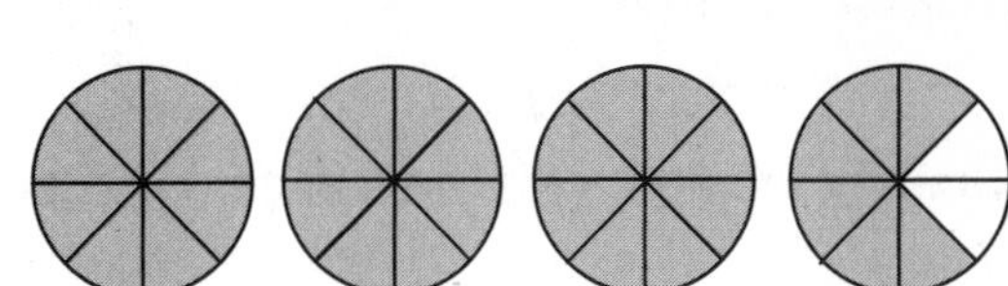 ______

e) 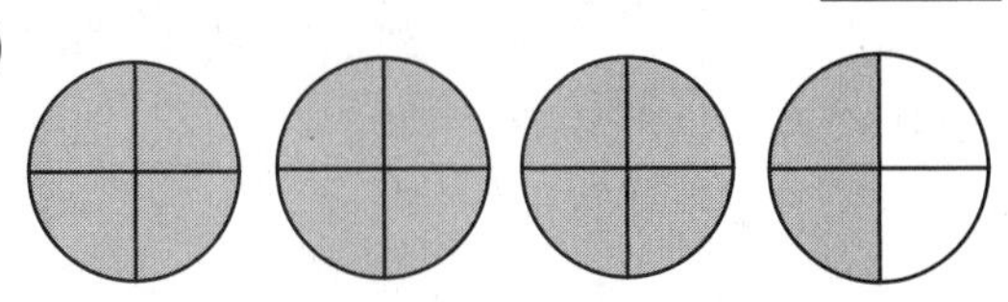 ______

f) 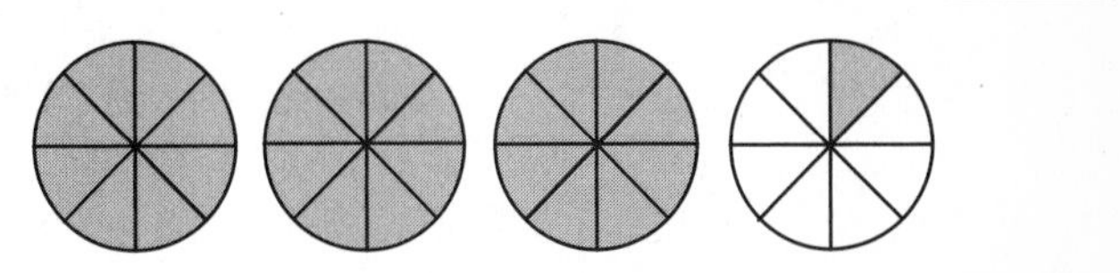 ______

2. Shade the amount of pie given in bold. Then write an improper fraction for the amount of pie.

a) $\mathbf{4\frac{1}{2}}$ 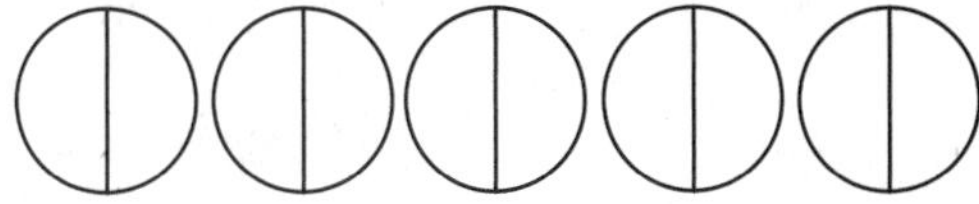

Improper Fraction: ________

b) $\mathbf{2\frac{3}{4}}$ 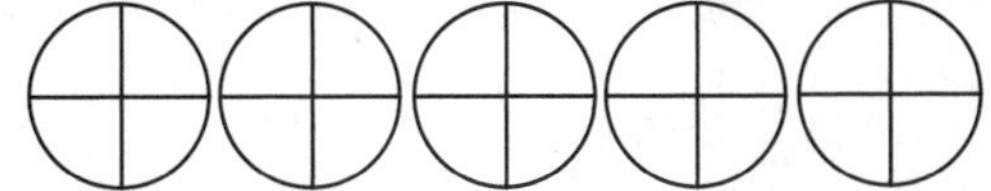

Improper Fraction: ________

c) $\mathbf{2\frac{2}{5}}$ 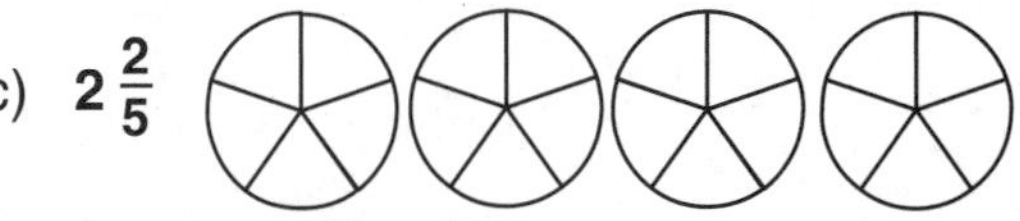

Improper Fraction: ________

d) $\mathbf{3\frac{3}{8}}$ 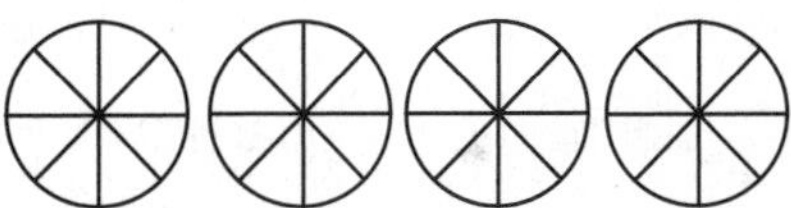

Improper Fraction: ________

3. Shade one piece at a time until you have shaded the amount of pie given in bold. Then write a mixed fraction for the amount of pie.

a) $\mathbf{\frac{10}{3}}$ 

Mixed Fraction: ________

b) $\mathbf{\frac{22}{6}}$ 

Mixed Fraction: ________

c) $\mathbf{\frac{9}{4}}$ 

Mixed Fraction: ________

d) $\mathbf{\frac{17}{5}}$ 

Mixed Fraction: ________

4. Draw a picture to find out which fraction is greater.

a) $3\frac{1}{2}$ or $\frac{5}{2}$

b) $2\frac{4}{5}$ or $\frac{12}{5}$

c) $4\frac{1}{3}$ or $\frac{14}{3}$

No unauthorized copying

NS5-59: Mixed Fractions (Advanced)

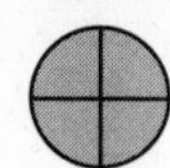

There are 4 quarter pieces in 1 pie.

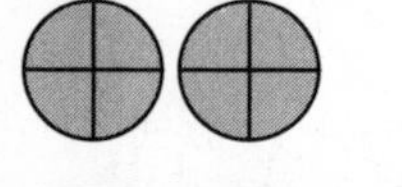

There are 8 (2 × 4) quarters in 2 pies.

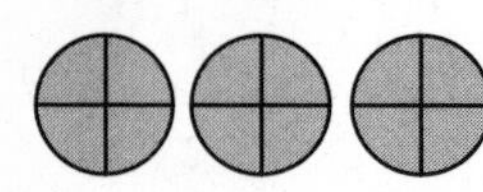

There are 12 (3 × 4) quarters in 3 pies.

How many quarter pieces are in $3\frac{3}{4}$ pies?

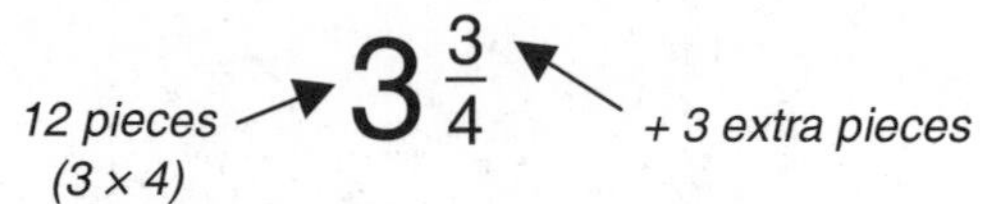

So there are 15 quarter pieces altogether.

---

1. Find the number of **halves** in each amount.

a) 1 pie = ______ halves b) 2 pies = ______ halves c) 3 pies = ______ halves

d) $2\frac{1}{2}$ pies = ______ halves e) $3\frac{1}{2}$ pies = ______ halves f) $4\frac{1}{2}$ pies = ____________

2. Find the number of **thirds** or **quarters** in each amount.

a) 1 pie = ______ thirds b) 2 pies = ______ thirds c) 3 pies = ______ thirds

d) $1\frac{2}{3}$ pies = ______ thirds e) $2\frac{1}{3}$ pies = ____________ f) $4\frac{2}{3}$ pies = ____________

g) 1 pie = ______ quarters h) 2 pies = ______ quarters i) 5 pies = ______ quarters

j) $2\frac{3}{4}$ pies = ______ quarters k) $5\frac{1}{4}$ pies = ____________ l) $5\frac{3}{4}$ pies = ____________

3. A box holds 4 cans.

a) 2 boxes hold ______ cans b) 3 boxes hold ______ cans c) 4 boxes hold ______ cans

d) 2 boxes hold ______ cans e) $3\frac{1}{4}$ boxes hold ______ cans f) $4\frac{3}{4}$ boxes hold ______ cans

4. A box holds 6 cans.

a) $2\frac{1}{6}$ boxes hold ______ cans b) $2\frac{5}{6}$ boxes hold ______ cans c) $3\frac{1}{6}$ boxes hold ______ cans

5. Pens come in packs of 6. Peter used $1\frac{5}{6}$ packs. How many pens did he use? ________

6. A: $\frac{1}{3}$ cup
B: $\frac{1}{4}$ cup

Jerome needs $4\frac{2}{3}$ cups of flour.

a) Which scoop should he use? ______________

b) How many scoops will he need? ______________

 No unauthorized copying

NS5-60: Mixed and Improper Fractions (Advanced)

How many whole pies are there in $\frac{13}{4}$ pies?

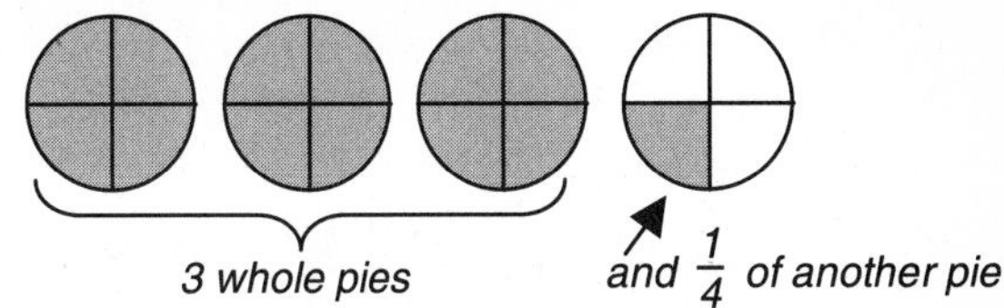

There are 13 pieces altogether, and each pie has 4 pieces.
So you can find the number of whole pies by dividing 13 by 4: **13 ÷ 4 = 3 remainder 1**

There are 3 whole pies and 1 quarter left over, so: $\mathbf{\frac{13}{4} = 3\frac{1}{4}}$

---

1. Find the number of whole pies in each amount by dividing.

a) $\frac{6}{2}$ pies = ______ whole pies b) $\frac{8}{2}$ pies = ______ whole pies c) $\frac{12}{2}$ pies = ______ whole pies

d) $\frac{9}{3}$ pies = ______ whole pies e) $\frac{15}{3}$ pies = ______ whole pies f) $\frac{16}{4}$ pies = ______ whole pies

2. Find the number of whole pies and the number of pieces remaining by dividing.

a) $\frac{7}{2}$ pies = __3__ whole pies and __1__ half pie = __$3\frac{1}{2}$__ pies

b) $\frac{13}{3}$ pies = ______ whole pies and ______ third = ______ pies

c) $\frac{11}{3}$ pies = ______ whole pies and ______ thirds = ______ pies

d) $\frac{15}{4}$ pies = ______ whole pies and ______ quarter pies = ______ pies

3. Write the following improper fractions as mixed fractions.

a) $\frac{5}{2}$ = b) $\frac{9}{2}$ = c) $\frac{10}{3}$ = d) $\frac{11}{4}$ = e) $\frac{13}{5}$ =

4. a) Write a mixed and improper fraction for the number of litres.

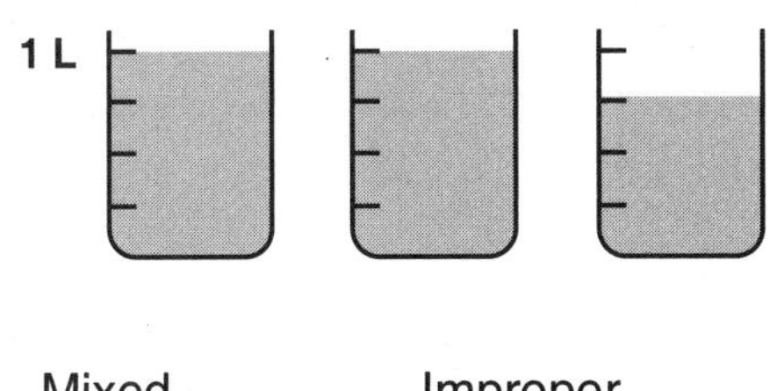

Mixed _______ Improper _______

b) Write a mixed and improper fraction for the length of the rope.

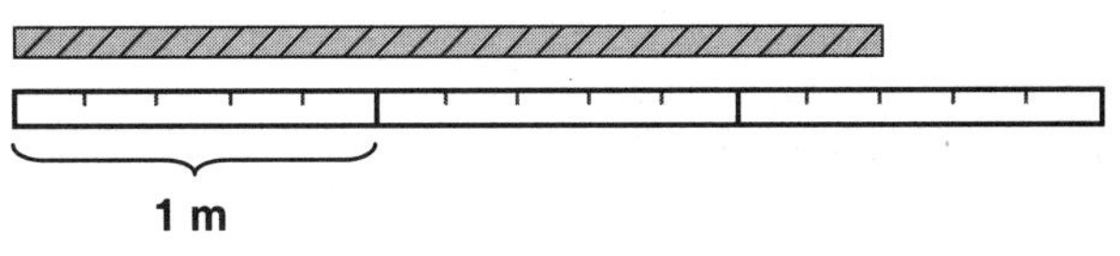

Mixed _______ Improper _______

5. How much greater than a whole is: a) $\frac{10}{7}$? b) $\frac{6}{5}$? c) $\frac{4}{3}$?

 No unauthorized copying

NS5-61: Equivalent Fractions

Aidan shades $\frac{2}{6}$ of the squares in an array: 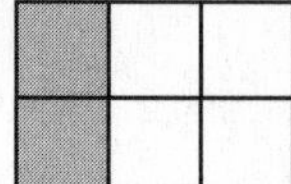

He then draws heavy lines around the squares to group them into 3 equal groups: 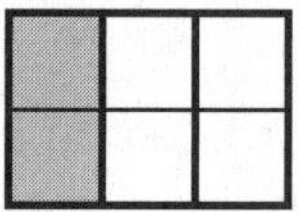

He sees that $\frac{1}{3}$ of the squares are shaded.

The pictures show that two sixths are equal to one third: $\frac{2}{6} = \frac{1}{3}$

Two sixths and one third are **equivalent fractions**.

---

1. Group squares to show an equivalent fraction.

a) 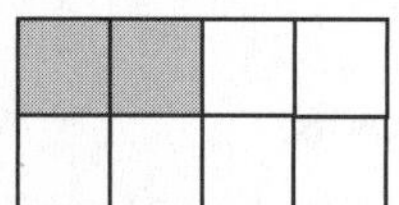

$\frac{2}{8} = \frac{\quad}{4}$

b) 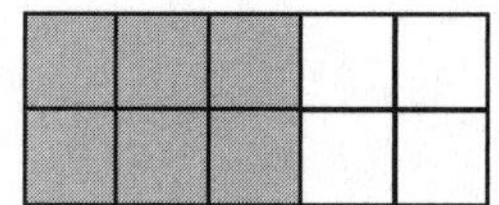

$\frac{6}{10} = \frac{\quad}{5}$

c) 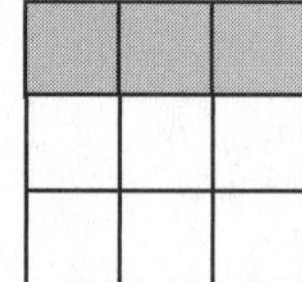

$\frac{3}{9} = \frac{\quad}{3}$

2. Group the squares to show:

a) Six twelfths equals one half ($\frac{6}{12} = \frac{1}{2}$)

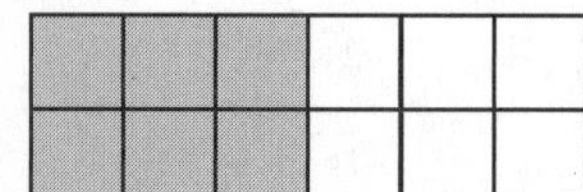

b) Six twelfths equals three sixths ($\frac{6}{12} = \frac{3}{6}$)

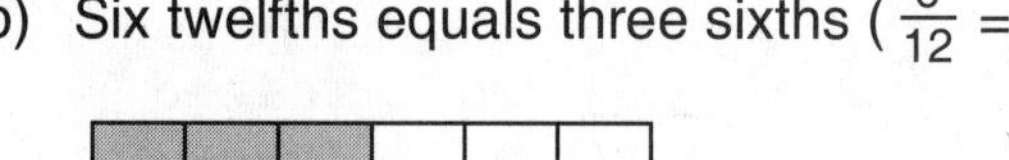

3. Group the squares to make an equivalent fraction.

a) 

$\frac{8}{10} = \frac{\quad}{5}$

b) 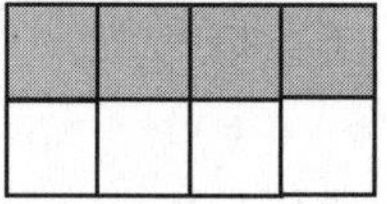

$\frac{4}{8} = \frac{\quad}{2}$

c) 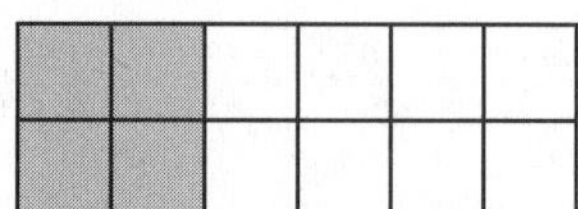

$\frac{4}{12} = \frac{\quad}{3}$

d) 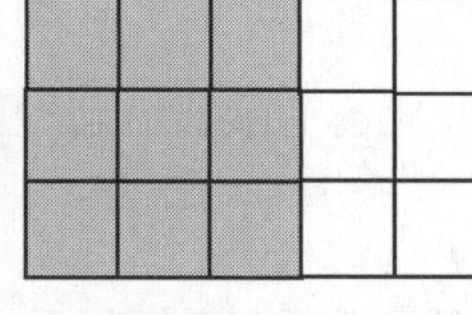

$\frac{9}{15} = \frac{\quad}{\quad}$

e) 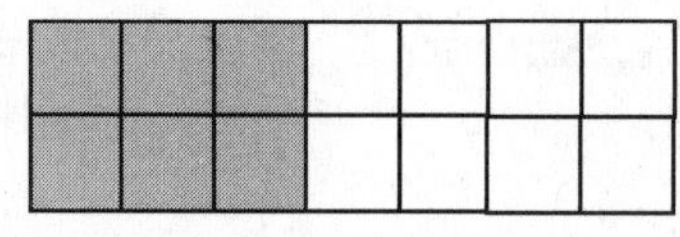

$\frac{6}{14} = \frac{\quad}{\quad}$

f) 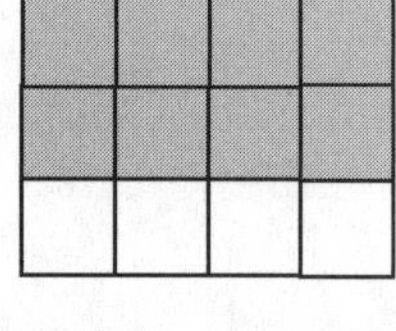

$\frac{8}{12} = \frac{\quad}{\quad}$

4. Write four equivalent fractions for the amount shaded here.

________ ________ ________ ________

No unauthorized copying

NS5-61: Equivalent Fractions *(continued)*

Candice has a set of grey and white buttons.
Four of the six buttons are grey.

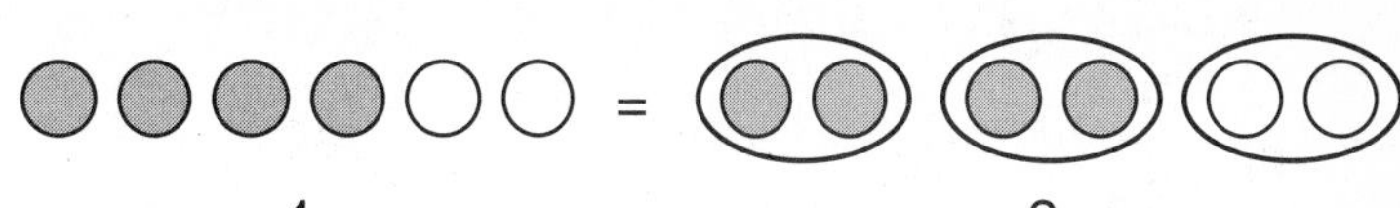

Candice groups buttons to show
that two thirds of the buttons are grey:

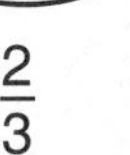

$\frac{4}{6} = \frac{2}{3}$

---

5. Group the buttons to make an equivalent fraction.

a) 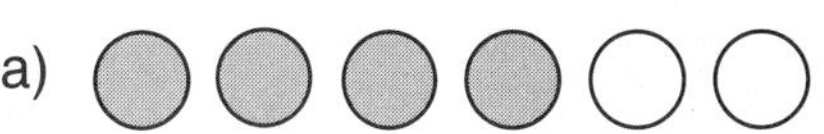

$\frac{4}{6} = \frac{\ }{\ }$

b) 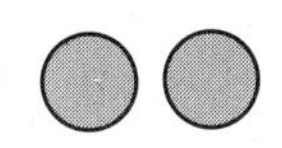 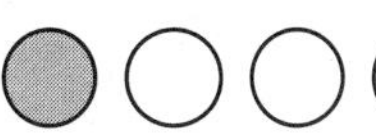

$\frac{3}{6} = \frac{\ }{\ }$

c) 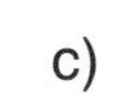 

$\frac{2}{6} = \frac{\ }{\ }$

d) 

$\frac{6}{9} = \frac{\ }{\ }$

e) 

$\frac{8}{10} = \frac{\ }{\ }$

6. Group the pie pieces to make an equivalent fraction.
The grouping in the first question has already been done for you.

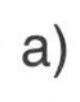

a)  $\frac{2}{8} = \frac{\ }{4}$

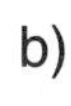

b) 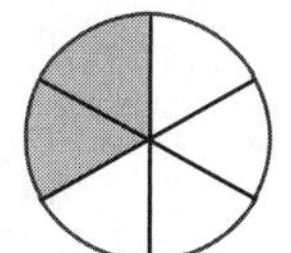 $\frac{2}{6} = \frac{\ }{3}$

c) 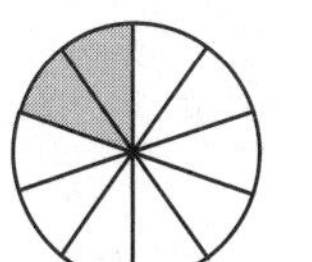 $\frac{2}{10} = \frac{\ }{5}$

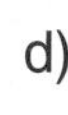

d) 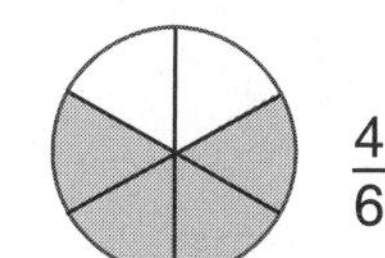 $\frac{4}{6} = \frac{\ }{\ }$

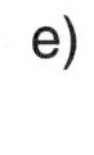

e) 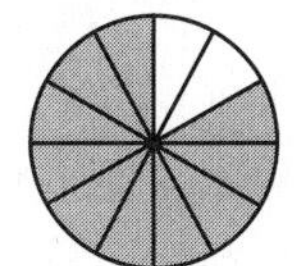 $\frac{8}{10} = \frac{\ }{\ }$

f) 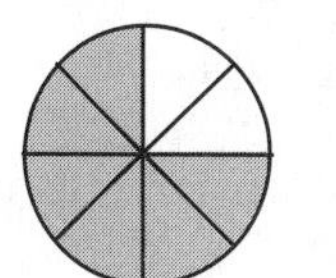 $\frac{6}{8} = \frac{\ }{\ }$

7. Cut each pie into smaller pieces to make an equivalent fraction.

a) 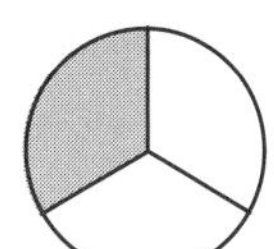 $\frac{1}{3} = \frac{\ }{6}$

b) 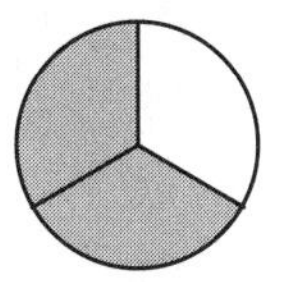 $\frac{2}{3} = \frac{\ }{9}$

c) 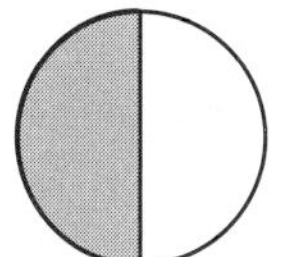 $\frac{1}{2} = \frac{\ }{4}$

8. Write as many equivalent fractions as you can for each picture.

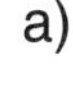

a) 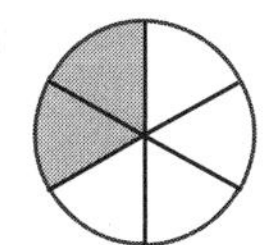

b) 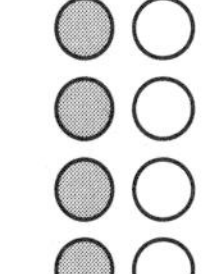

c) 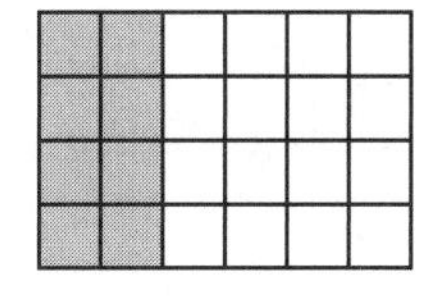

9. A pizza is cut into 8 pieces. Each piece is covered with olives, mushrooms or both.
$\frac{1}{4}$ of the pizza is covered in olives.
$\frac{7}{8}$ of the pizza is covered in mushrooms.
Draw a picture to show how many pieces have both olives and mushrooms on them.

No unauthorized copying

NS5-62: Models of Equivalent Fractions

1. Draw lines to cut the pies into more pieces. Then fill in the numerators of the equivalent fractions:

a) 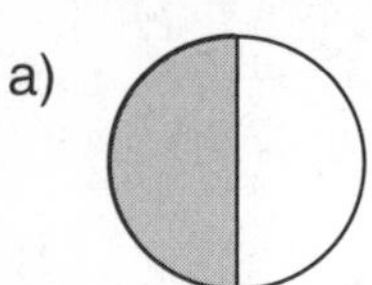 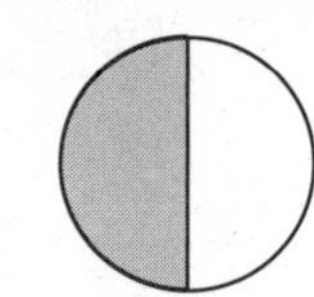 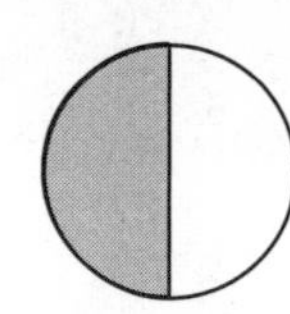

4 pieces 6 pieces 8 pieces

$\frac{1}{2} = \frac{}{4} = \frac{}{6} = \frac{}{8}$

b) 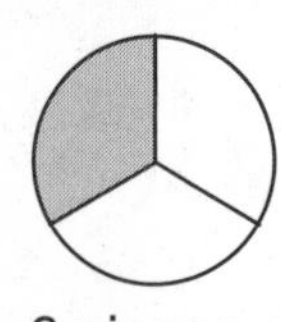 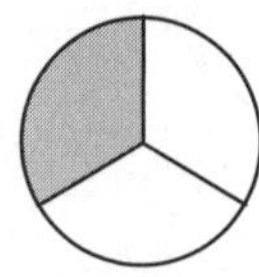 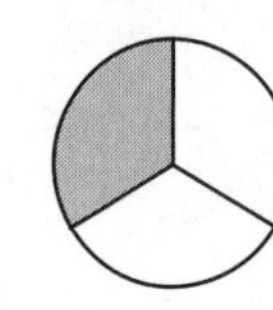

6 pieces 9 pieces 12 pieces

$\frac{1}{3} = \frac{}{6} = \frac{}{9} = \frac{}{12}$

2. Cut each pie into more pieces. Then fill in the missing numbers.

a) 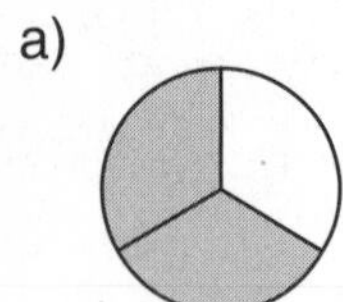 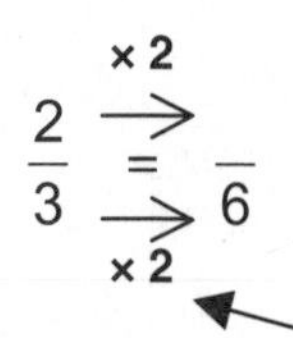

$\frac{2}{3} \overset{\times 2}{\rightarrow} = \frac{}{6}$ (× 2)

This number tells you how many pieces to cut the pie into.

b) 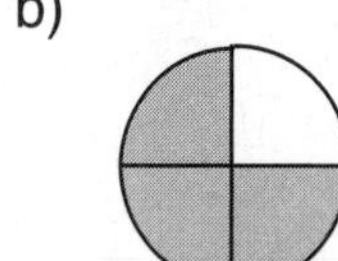 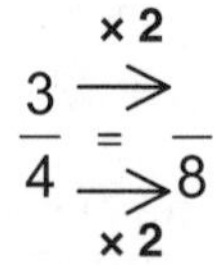

$\frac{3}{4} \overset{\times 2}{\rightarrow} = \frac{}{8}$ (× 2)

c) 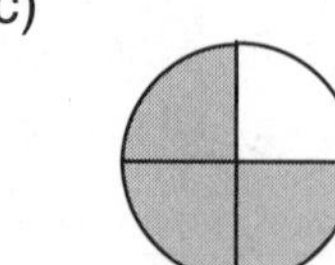

$\frac{2}{3} \overset{\times}{\rightarrow} = \frac{}{9}$ (×)

3. Use multiplication to find the equivalent fractions below.

a) $\frac{1}{3} \overset{\times 2}{\rightarrow} = \frac{}{6}$ (× 2) b) $\frac{1}{2} = \frac{}{10}$ c) $\frac{2}{5} = \frac{}{10}$ d) $\frac{3}{4} = \frac{}{8}$ e) $\frac{1}{4} = \frac{}{12}$

4. Use the patterns in the numerators and denominators to find 6 equivalent fractions.

a) $\frac{1}{2} = \frac{2}{4} = \frac{3}{} = \frac{}{8} = \frac{}{10} = \frac{}{}$ b) $\frac{3}{5} = \frac{6}{} = \frac{9}{15} = \frac{12}{20} = \frac{}{} = \frac{}{}$

5. To show that $\frac{3}{4}$ is equivalent to $\frac{9}{12}$, Brian makes a model of $\frac{9}{12}$ using blocks.

Step 1:  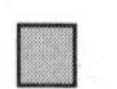

Brian makes a model of the original fraction $\frac{3}{4}$.
(He leaves a space between the blocks.)

Step 2:   

Step 3:

He adds blocks until he has placed 12 blocks.

From Step 3, Brian can see $\frac{3}{4}$ is equivalent to $\frac{9}{12}$: 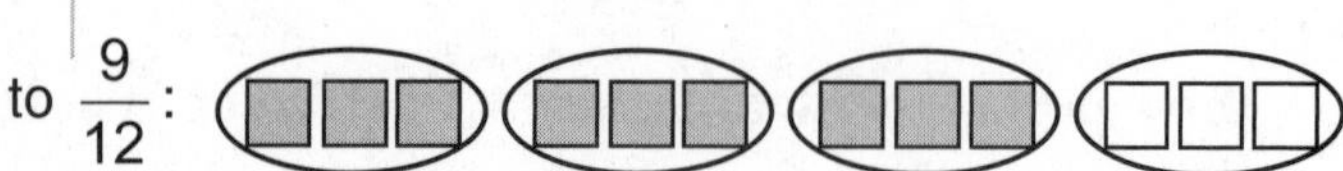

Use Brian's method to show that the fractions are equivalent.

a) $\frac{3}{5}$ and $\frac{9}{15}$ b) $\frac{2}{3}$ and $\frac{8}{12}$ c) $\frac{3}{4}$ and $\frac{12}{16}$

No unauthorized copying

NS5-63: Fractions of Whole Numbers

Dan has 6 cookies. He wants to give $\frac{2}{3}$ of his cookies to his friends. To do so, he shares the cookies equally onto 3 plates:

There are 3 equal groups, so each group is $\frac{1}{3}$ of 6.

There are 2 cookies in each group, so $\frac{1}{3}$ of 6 is 2.

There are 4 cookies in two groups, so $\frac{2}{3}$ of 6 is 4.

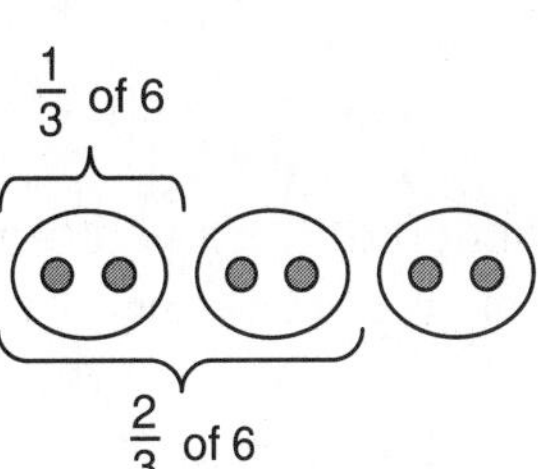

---

1. Write a fraction for the amount of dots shown. The first one has been done for you.

a) 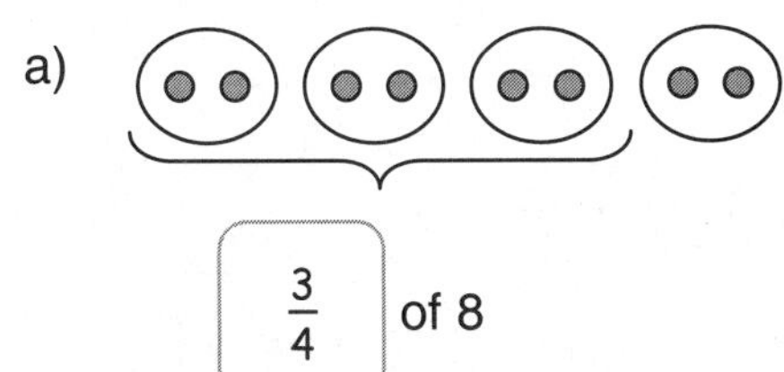

b) 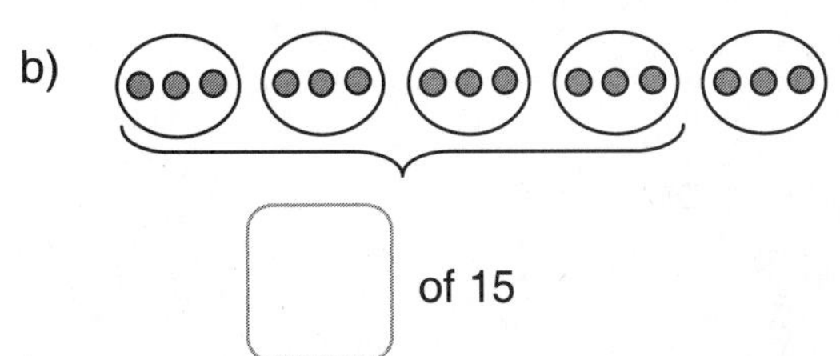

2. Fill in the missing numbers.

a) 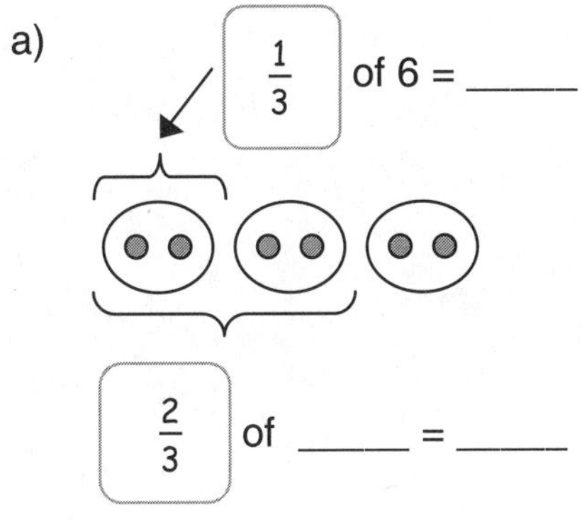

b) 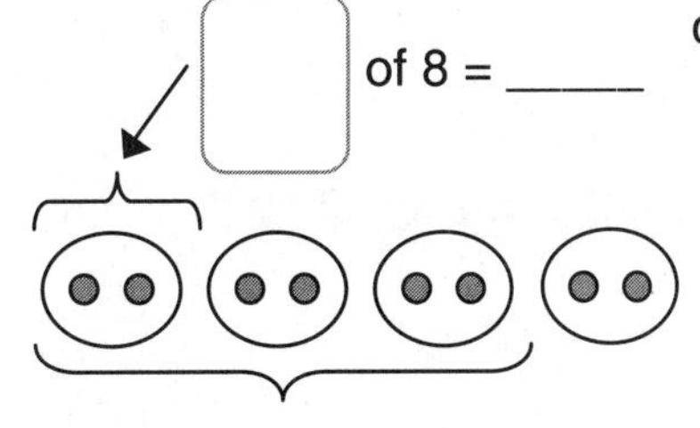

of ______ = ______

c) 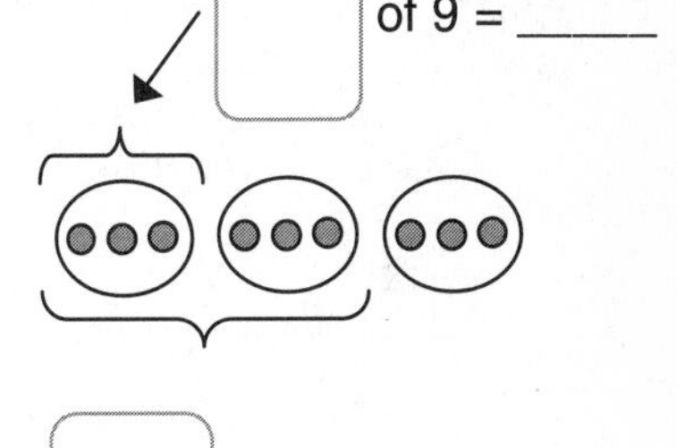

of ______ = ______

d) 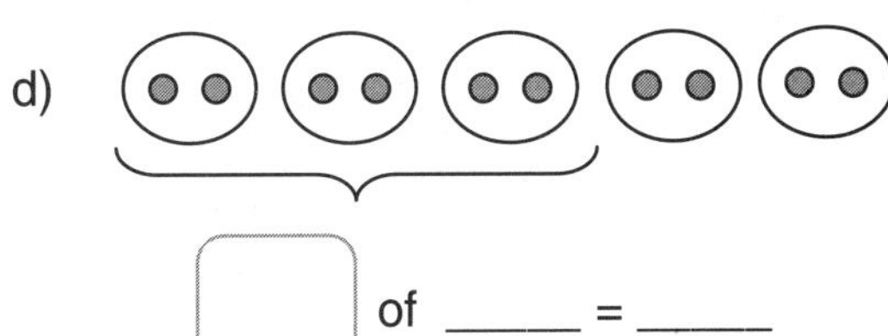

of ______ = ______

e) 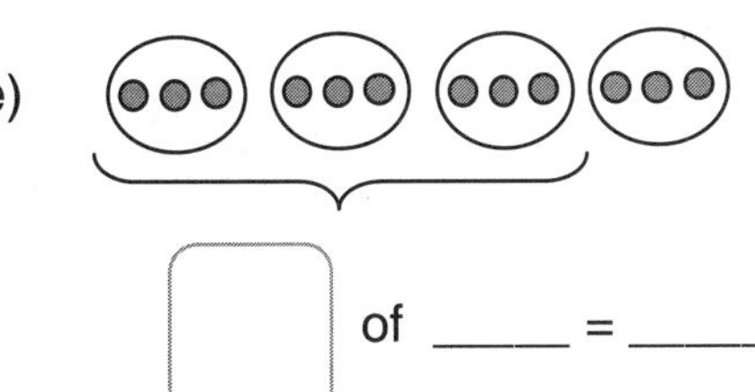

of ______ = ______

3. Draw a circle to show the given amount. The first one has been done for you.

a) $\frac{2}{3}$ of 6 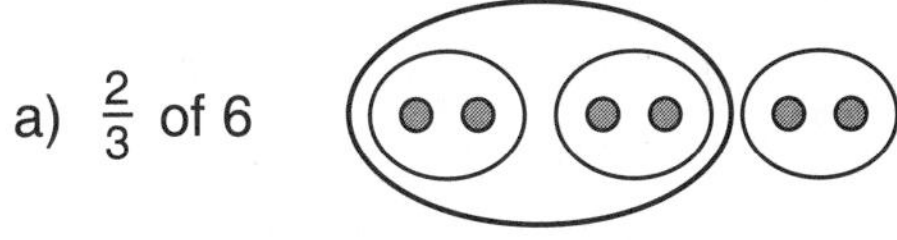

b) $\frac{3}{4}$ of 8 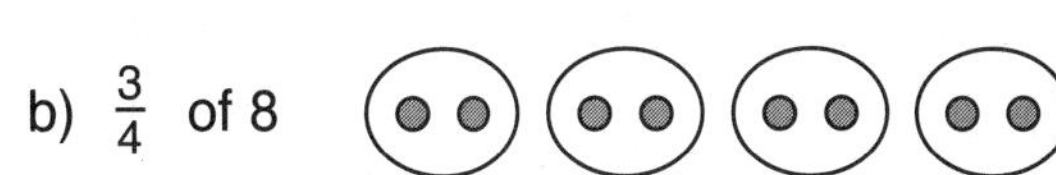

c) $\frac{3}{5}$ of 10

d) $\frac{3}{4}$ of 12

No unauthorized copying

4. Fill in the correct number of dots in each circle, then draw a larger circle to show the given amount.

a) $\frac{2}{3}$ of 12 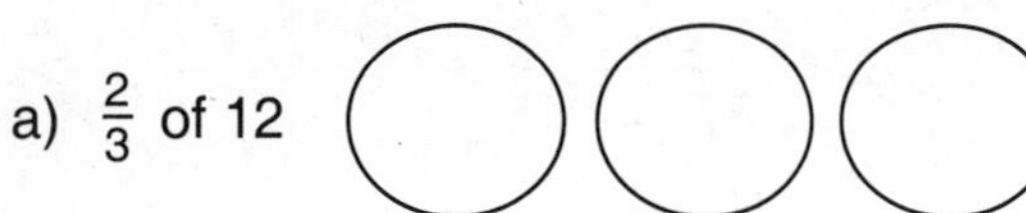

b) $\frac{2}{3}$ of 9

5. Find the fraction of the whole amount by sharing the cookies equally.
HINT: Draw the correct number of plates, then place the cookies one at a time. Then circle the correct amount.

a) Find $\frac{1}{4}$ of 8 cookies.

$\frac{1}{4}$ of 8 is _______

b) Find $\frac{1}{2}$ of 10 cookies.

$\frac{1}{2}$ of 10 is _______

c) Find $\frac{2}{3}$ of 6 cookies.

$\frac{2}{3}$ of 6 is _______

d) Find $\frac{3}{4}$ of 12 cookies.

$\frac{3}{4}$ of 12 is _______

6. Andy finds $\frac{2}{3}$ of 12 as follows:

Step 1: *He finds $\frac{1}{3}$ of 12 by dividing 12 by 3.*

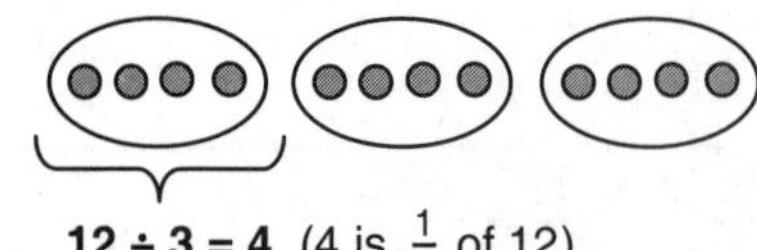

Step 2: *Then he multiplies the result by 2.*

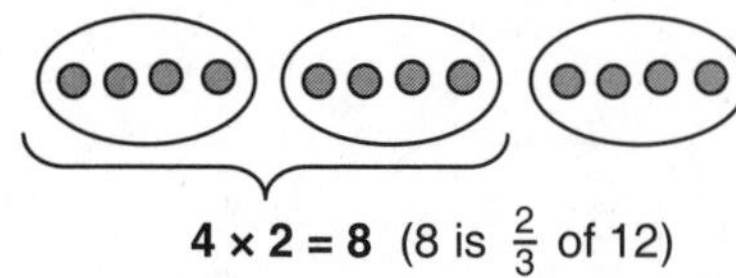

Find the following amounts using Andy's method.

a) $\frac{2}{3}$ of 9 _______

b) $\frac{3}{4}$ of 8 _______

c) $\frac{2}{3}$ of 15 _______

d) $\frac{2}{5}$ of 10 _______

e) $\frac{3}{5}$ of 25 _______

f) $\frac{2}{7}$ of 14 _______

g) $\frac{1}{6}$ of 18 _______

h) $\frac{1}{2}$ of 12 _______

i) $\frac{3}{4}$ of 12 _______

j) $\frac{2}{3}$ of 21 _______

k) $\frac{3}{8}$ of 16 _______

l) $\frac{3}{7}$ of 21 _______

No unauthorized copying

NS5-63: Fractions of Whole Numbers *(continued)*

7. a) Shade $\frac{2}{5}$ of the boxes.

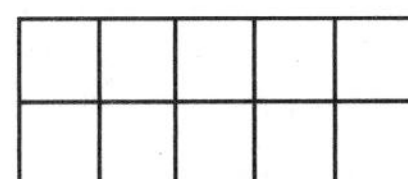

b) Shade $\frac{2}{3}$ of the boxes.

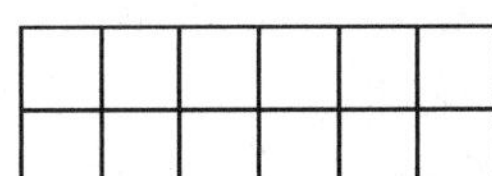

c) Shade $\frac{3}{4}$ of the boxes.

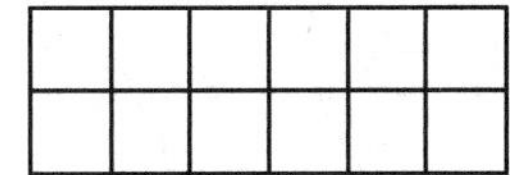

d) Shade $\frac{5}{6}$ of the boxes.

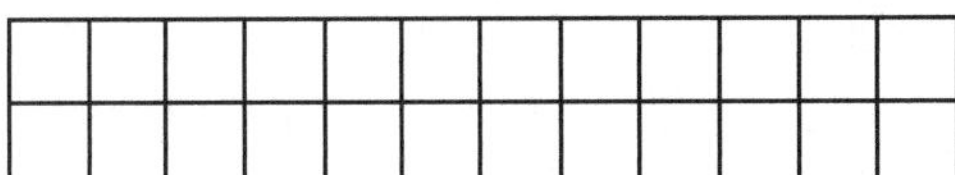

e) Shade $\frac{2}{7}$ of the boxes.

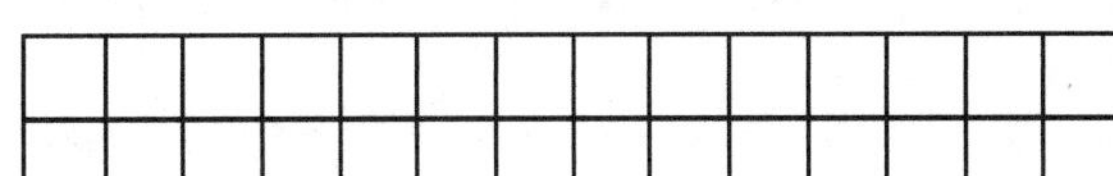

8. a) Shade $\frac{1}{4}$ of the boxes.

Draw stripes in $\frac{1}{6}$ of the boxes.

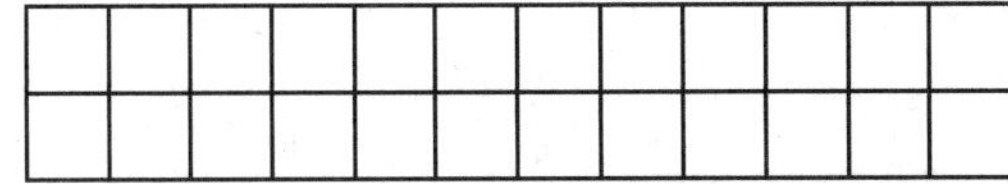

b) Shade $\frac{1}{3}$ of the boxes.

Draw stripes in $\frac{1}{6}$ of the boxes.

Put dots in $\frac{1}{8}$ of the boxes.

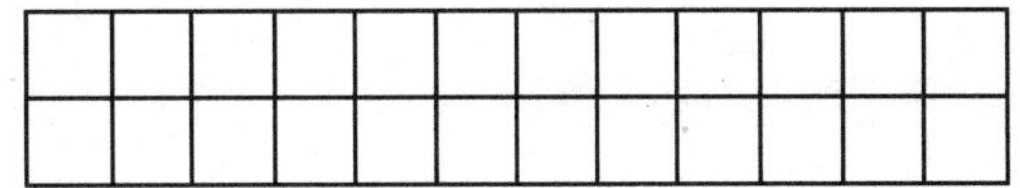

9. In the problems below, each circle represents a child. Solve the problem by writing **J** for "juice" and **W** for "water" on the correct number of circles. The first one is done for you.

a) 8 children had drinks at lunch.
$\frac{1}{2}$ drank juice and $\frac{1}{4}$ drank water.

How many didn't drink juice or water? 2 didn't drink juice or water

b) 6 children had drinks at lunch.
$\frac{1}{2}$ drank juice and $\frac{1}{3}$ drank water.

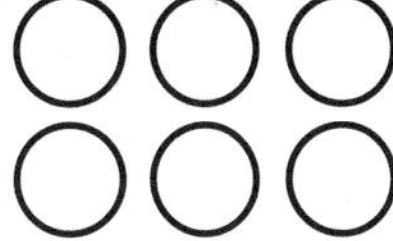

How many didn't drink juice or water? ______

10. 12 children had drinks.
$\frac{1}{4}$ drank juice and $\frac{2}{3}$ drank water.
How many didn't drink juice or water?

11. Carol has a collection of 12 shells. $\frac{1}{3}$ of the shells are scallop shells.
$\frac{1}{4}$ of the shells are conch shells. The rest of the shells are cone shells.
How many of Carol's shells are cone shells?

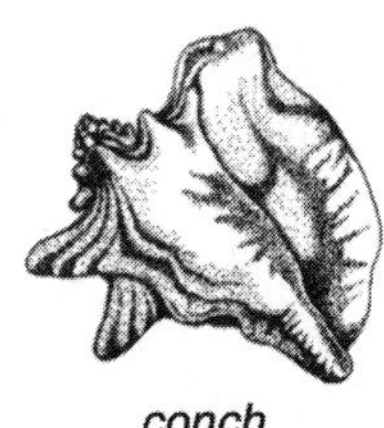
conch

 No unauthorized copying

NS5-64: Fractions of Whole Numbers (Advanced)

1. A kilogram of nuts costs $8.

How much would $\frac{3}{4}$ of a kilogram cost? _______________

2. 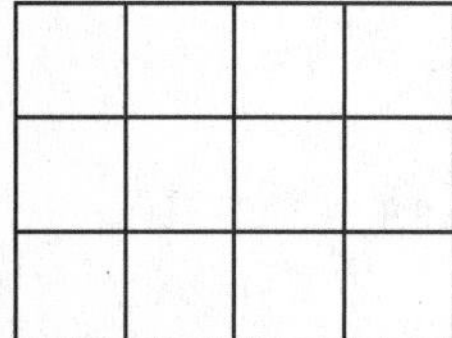

Gerald has 10 oranges.

He gives away $\frac{3}{5}$ of the oranges.

a) How many oranges did he give away? _______ b) How many did he keep? ______

3.

Shade $\frac{1}{3}$ of the squares.

Draw stripes in $\frac{1}{6}$ of the squares.

How many squares are blank? ______

4. Sapin has 20 marbles.

$\frac{2}{5}$ are blue. $\frac{1}{4}$ are yellow.

The rest are green.

How many are green?

5. Which is longer:

17 months or $1\frac{3}{4}$ years?

6. How many months are in $\frac{3}{4}$ of a year?

7. How many minutes are in $\frac{2}{3}$ of an hour?

8. Fong had 28 stickers.

She kept $\frac{1}{7}$ herself and divided the rest evenly among 6 friends.

How many stickers did each friend get?

9. Nancy put 4 of her 10 shells on a shelf.

Explain how you know she put $\frac{2}{5}$ of her shells on the shelf.

10. Karl started studying at 7:15.

He studied for $\frac{3}{5}$ of an hour.

At what time did he stop studying?

11. Linda had 12 apples.

She gave $\frac{1}{4}$ to Nandita and she gave 2 to Amy.

She says that she has half left.

Is she correct?

CHALLENGING:

12. Draw a picture or make a model to solve this problem.

♣ $\frac{2}{5}$ of Kim's marbles are yellow ♣ $\frac{3}{5}$ are blue ♣ 8 are yellow

How many of Kim's marbles are blue?

 No unauthorized copying

NS5-65: Comparing and Ordering Fractions

Use the fraction strips below to answer Questions 1 to 3.

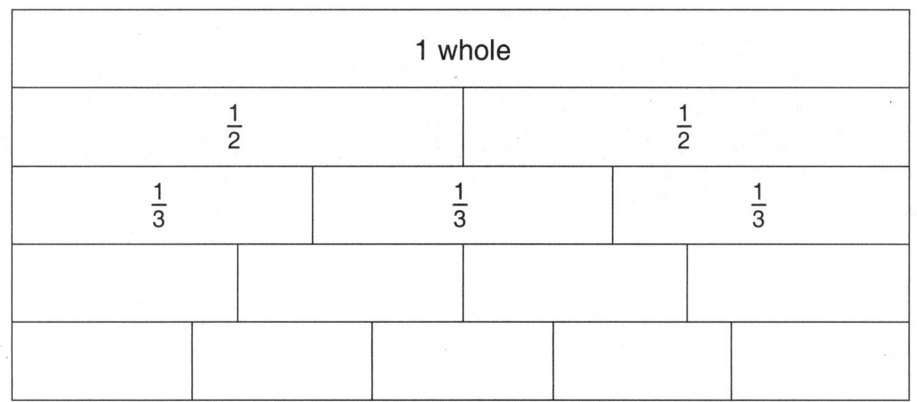

1. Fill in the missing numbers on the fraction strips above. Then write > (greater than) or < (less than) between each pair of numbers below.

   a) $\frac{1}{2}$ ☐ $\frac{2}{3}$ b) $\frac{3}{4}$ ☐ $\frac{2}{3}$ c) $\frac{2}{5}$ ☐ $\frac{3}{4}$ d) $\frac{4}{5}$ ☐ $\frac{3}{4}$

2. Circle the fractions that are greater than $\frac{1}{3}$.

   $\frac{1}{5}$ $\frac{2}{5}$ $\frac{1}{2}$

3. Circle the fractions that are greater than $\frac{1}{2}$.

   $\frac{3}{5}$ $\frac{2}{5}$ $\frac{3}{4}$

4. Draw lines to cut the left-hand pie into the same number of pieces as the right-hand pie. Then circle the greater fraction.

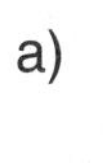

a) 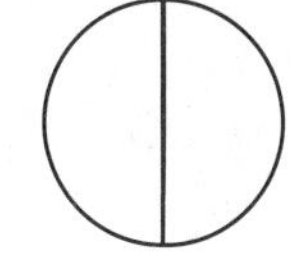 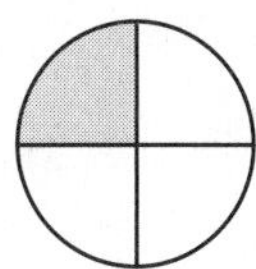

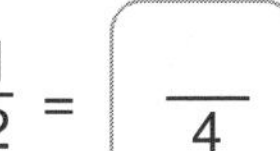

$\frac{1}{2} = \frac{}{4}$ $\frac{1}{4}$

b)  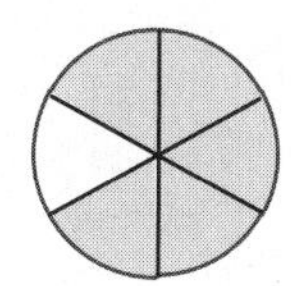

$\frac{2}{3} = \frac{}{6}$ $\frac{5}{6}$

5. Turn each fraction on the left into an equivalent fraction with the same denominator as the fraction on the right. Then write > or < to show which fraction is greater.

   a) $\frac{1 \times 3}{2 \times 3} = \frac{3}{6}$ [<] $\frac{4}{6}$ b) $\frac{1 \times}{2 \times} = \frac{}{8}$ ☐ $\frac{5}{8}$ c) $\frac{1}{2} = \frac{}{}$ ☐ $\frac{3}{4}$

   d) $\frac{1}{2} = \frac{}{}$ ☐ $\frac{4}{10}$ e) $\frac{1}{2} = \frac{}{}$ ☐ $\frac{3}{12}$ f) $\frac{1}{3} = \frac{}{}$ ☐ $\frac{4}{9}$

   g) $\frac{1}{5} = \frac{}{}$ ☐ $\frac{7}{10}$ h) $\frac{1}{5} = \frac{}{}$ ☐ $\frac{4}{10}$ i) $\frac{1}{4} = \frac{}{}$ ☐ $\frac{7}{16}$

No unauthorized copying

NS5-66: Lowest Common Denominator

1. Cut each pie evenly into the given number of pieces. Then write a fraction for the result.

a) $\frac{2}{4}$ — 4 pieces

b) 6 pieces

c) 6 pieces

d) 9 pieces

e) 12 pieces

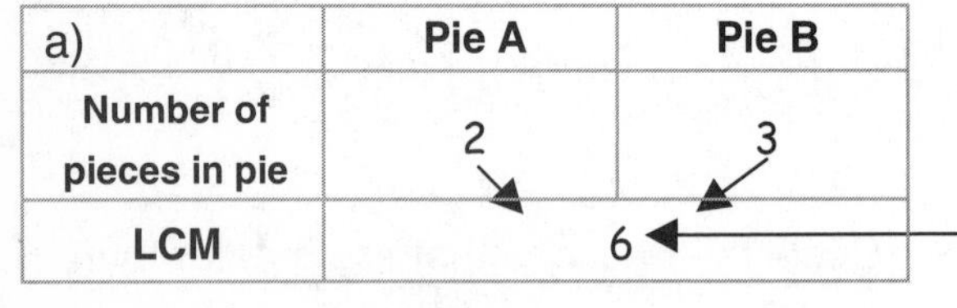

2. Recall that to find the **lowest common multiple** (LCM) of a pair of numbers, you first write out the multiples of the number.

Example:

4: 4 8 12

6: 6 12 18

Stop when the same number appears on both lists.

***12** is the LCM of 4 and 6.*

Follow the steps in chart a) below to cut each pair of pies into the same number of pieces.

a)	Pie A	Pie B
Number of pieces in pie	2	3
LCM	6	

Cut each pie into this many pieces

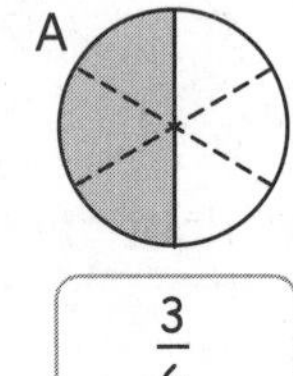

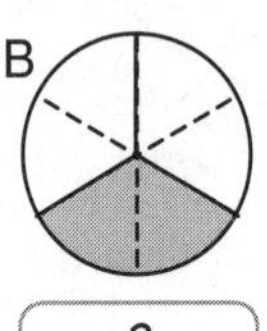

A: $\frac{3}{6}$ B: $\frac{2}{6}$

b)	Pie A	Pie B
Number of pieces in pie		
LCM		

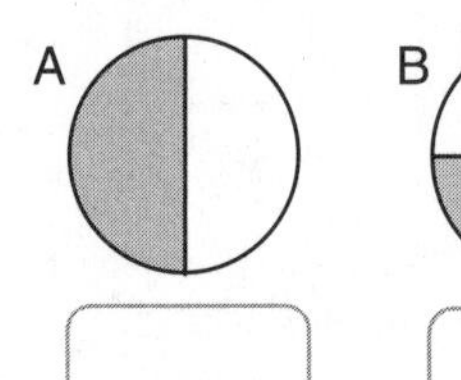

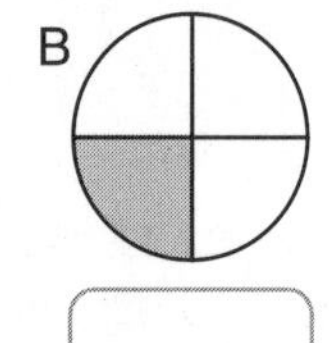

c)	Pie A	Pie B
Number of pieces in pie		
LCM		

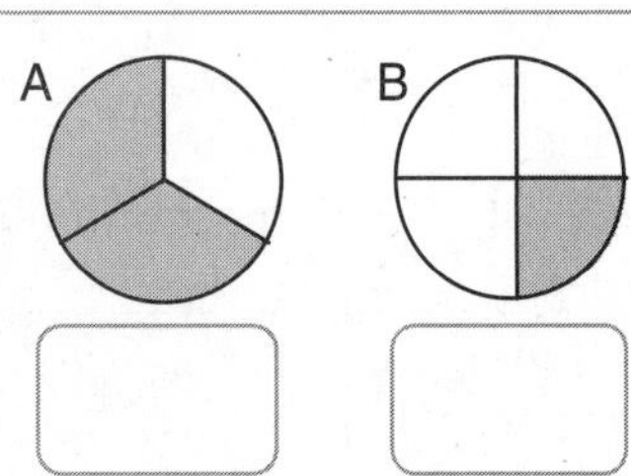

d)	Pie A	Pie B
Number of pieces in pie		
LCM		

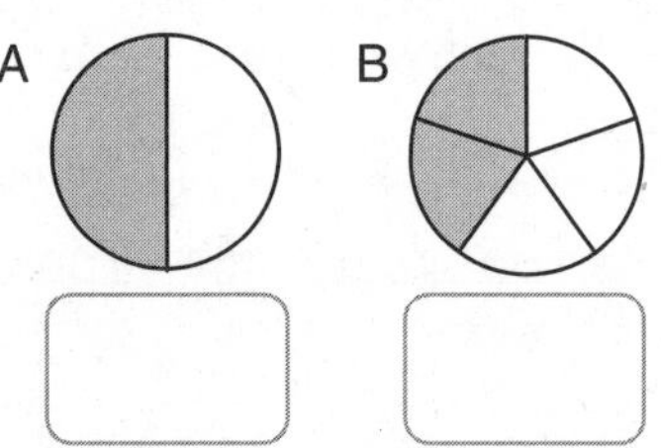

3. Create a pair of fractions with the same denominator. Circle the greater fraction.

a) $\frac{3 \times 1}{3 \times 2}$ $\frac{1 \times 2}{3 \times 2}$ → $\frac{3}{6}$ (circled) $\frac{2}{6}$

The LCM of 2 and 3 is 6

Multiply 2 by 3 to make 6

Multiply 3 by 2 to make 6

b) $\frac{1}{3}$ $\frac{1}{4}$

c) $\frac{1}{2}$ $\frac{1}{5}$

No unauthorized copying

NS5-67: Adding and Subtracting Fractions

1. Imagine moving the shaded pieces from pies A and B onto pie plate C. Show how much of pie C would be filled and then write a fraction for pie C.

A 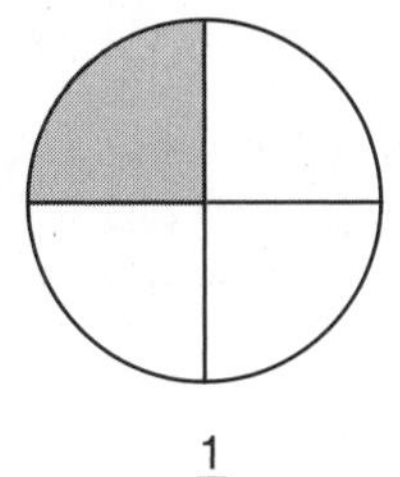 B 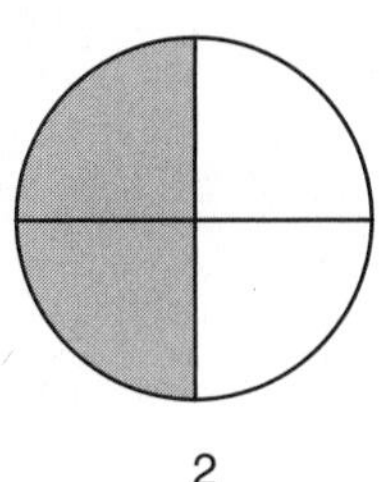 C 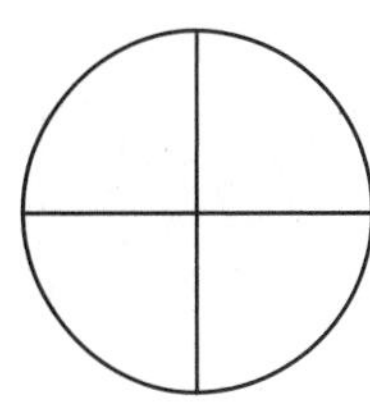

$\frac{1}{4} + \frac{2}{4} = \_\_\_$

2. Imagine pouring the liquid from cups A and B into cup C.
Shade the amount of liquid that would be in C.
Then complete the addition statements.

a) 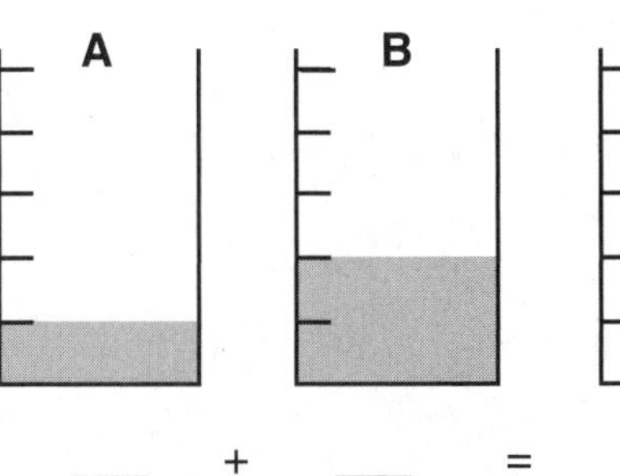 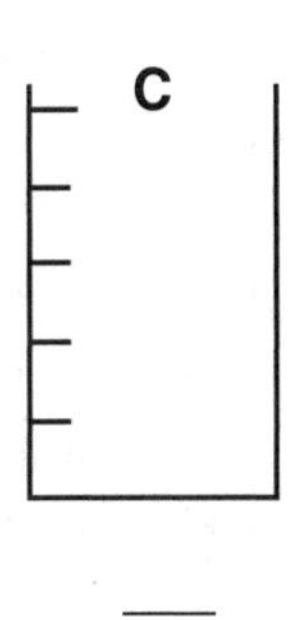

$\frac{\_\_\_}{5} + \frac{\_\_\_}{5} = \_\_\_$

b) 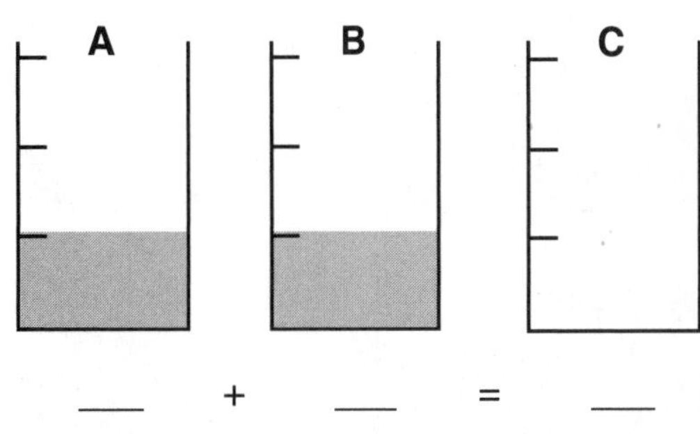

$\frac{\_\_\_}{3} + \frac{\_\_\_}{3} = \_\_\_$

3. Add.

a) $\frac{3}{5} + \frac{1}{5} =$ b) $\frac{2}{4} + \frac{1}{4} =$ c) $\frac{3}{7} + \frac{2}{7} =$ d) $\frac{5}{8} + \frac{2}{8} =$

e) $\frac{3}{11} + \frac{7}{11} =$ f) $\frac{5}{17} + \frac{9}{17} =$ g) $\frac{11}{24} + \frac{10}{24} =$ h) $\frac{18}{57} + \frac{13}{57} =$

4. Show how much pie would be left if you took away the amount shown.
Then complete the fraction statement.

a) 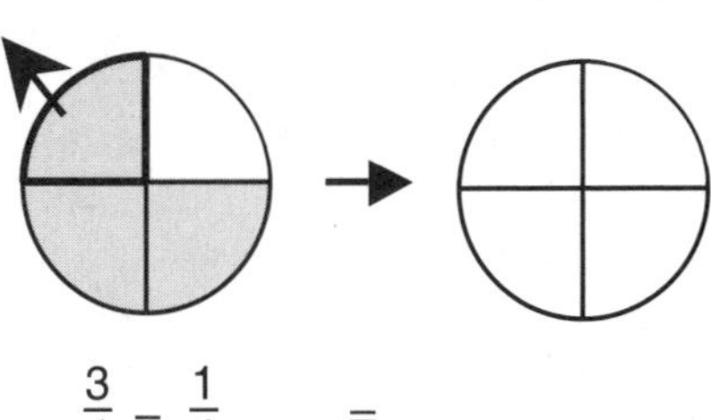

$\frac{3}{4} - \frac{1}{4} = \_\_\_$

b) 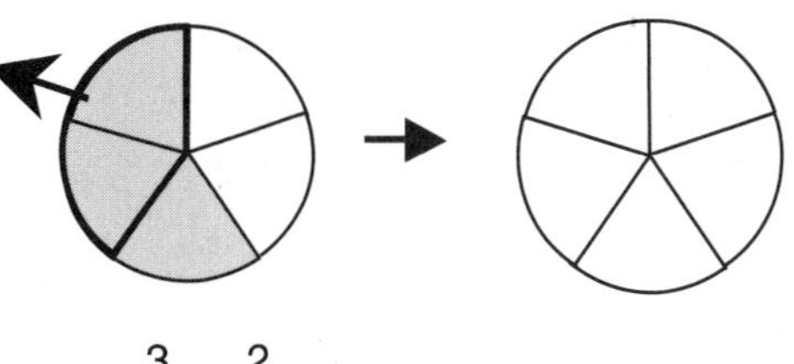

$\frac{3}{5} - \frac{2}{5} = \_\_\_$

5. Subtract.

a) $\frac{2}{3} - \frac{1}{3} =$ b) $\frac{3}{5} - \frac{1}{5} =$ c) $\frac{6}{7} - \frac{3}{7} =$ d) $\frac{5}{8} - \frac{2}{8} =$

e) $\frac{9}{12} - \frac{2}{12} =$ f) $\frac{6}{19} - \frac{4}{19} =$ g) $\frac{9}{28} - \frac{3}{28} =$ h) $\frac{17}{57} - \frac{12}{57} =$

 No unauthorized copying

NS5-68: Fractions Review

1. Fill in the missing mixed fractions on the number line.

a)

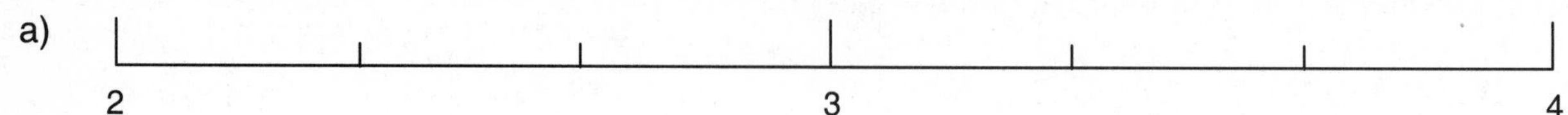

2   3   4

b)

3   4   5

c)

7   8   9

2. Continue the patterns.

a) $2\frac{1}{4}$, $2\frac{2}{4}$, $2\frac{3}{4}$, ______ , ______

b) $7\frac{1}{5}$, $7\frac{2}{5}$, $7\frac{3}{5}$, ______ , ______

3. Fill in the blanks.

a) $2\frac{3}{4}$ pies = ___11___ quarters

$2\frac{3}{4} = \frac{11}{4}$

b) $3\frac{2}{5}$ = ______ fifths

$3\frac{2}{5}$ =

c) $4\frac{1}{3}$ = ______ thirds

$4\frac{1}{3}$ =

4. Write the fractions in order from least to greatest.
HINT: First write each fraction with the same denominator.

a) $\frac{1}{2}$ $\frac{2}{5}$ $\frac{3}{10}$

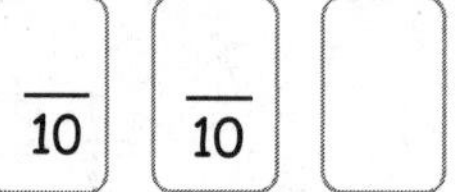

$\frac{}{10}$ $\frac{}{10}$

____

b) $\frac{1}{3}$ $\frac{5}{6}$ $\frac{1}{2}$

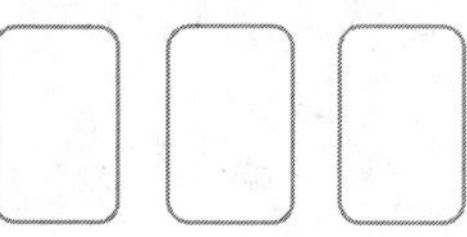

____

c) $\frac{5}{8}$ $\frac{1}{2}$ $\frac{3}{4}$

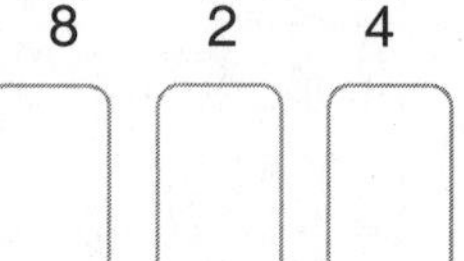

____

5. Use <u>two</u> of 2, 3, 4, and 5 to create:

a)

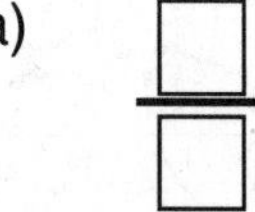

the least possible fraction

b)

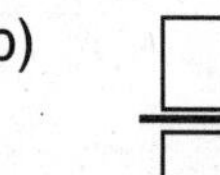

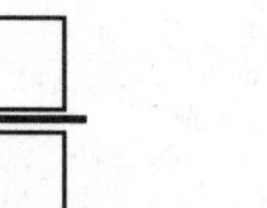

a fraction greater than 2

c)

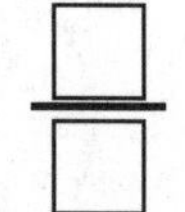

a fraction equivalent to $\frac{1}{2}$

d)

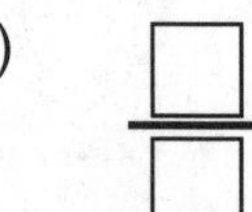

a fraction equivalent to $1\frac{1}{2}$

6. Which fraction is greater than 2 but less than 3?   a) $\frac{11}{3}$ b) $\frac{5}{4}$ c) $\frac{10}{4}$
How do you know?

7. How could you use division to find out how many <u>whole</u> pies are in $\frac{13}{4}$ of a pie? Explain.

No unauthorized copying

NS5-69: Place Value: Decimals

Fractions with denominators that are multiples of ten (tenths, hundredths) commonly appear in units of measurement.

- A millimetre is a tenth of a centimetre (10 mm = 1 cm)
- A centimetre is a tenth of a decimetre (10 cm = 1 dm)
- A decimeter is a tenth of a metre (10 dm = 1 m)
- A centimetre is a hundredth of a metre (100 cm = 1 m)

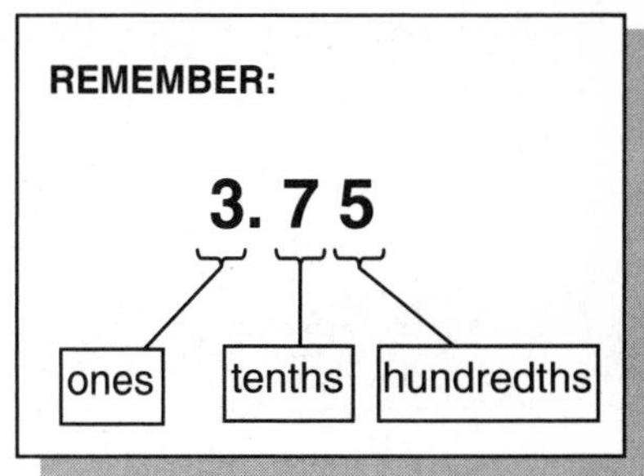

Decimals are short forms for fractions. The chart shows the value of the decimal digits.

---

1. Write the place value of the underlined digit.

a) 3.7<u>2</u> hundredths b) 3.<u>2</u>1 ______ c) <u>7</u>.52 ______

d) 5.<u>2</u>9 ______ e) 9.9<u>8</u> ______ f) <u>1</u>.05 ______

g) <u>0</u>.32 ______ h) 5.5<u>5</u> ______ i) 6.<u>4</u>2 ______

2. Give the place value of the number 6 in each of the numbers below.

a) 3.65 ______ b) 2.36 ______ c) 0.63 ______

d) 9.06 ______ e) 0.06 ______ f) 3.61 ______

g) 1.60 ______ h) 6.48 ______ i) 7.26 ______

3. Write the following numbers into the place value chart.

	Ones	Tenths	Hundredths
a) 5.03	5	0	3
b) 9.47			
c) 0.36			
d) 2.30			
e) 0.05			

No unauthorized copying

NS5-70: Decimal Hundredths

1. Count the number of shaded squares. Write a fraction for the shaded part of the hundreds square. Then write the fraction as a decimal.
   HINT: Count by 10s for each column or row that is shaded.

a) 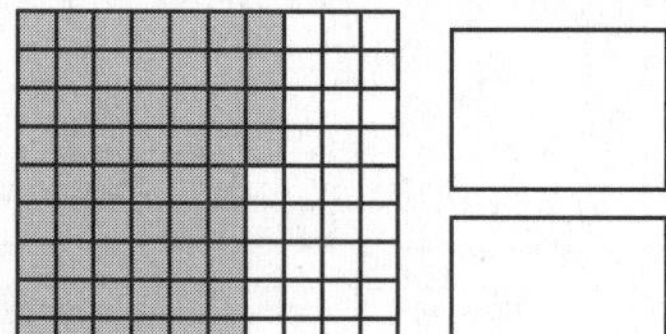

b) 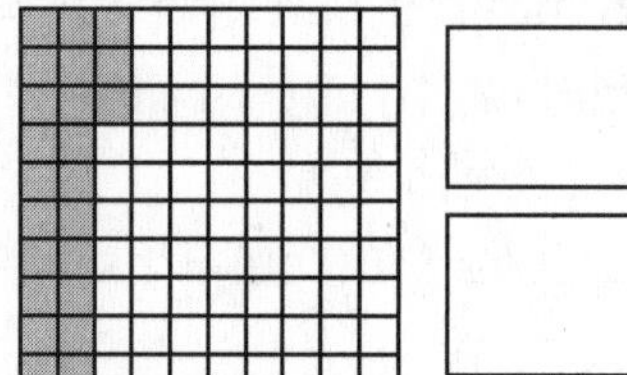

c) 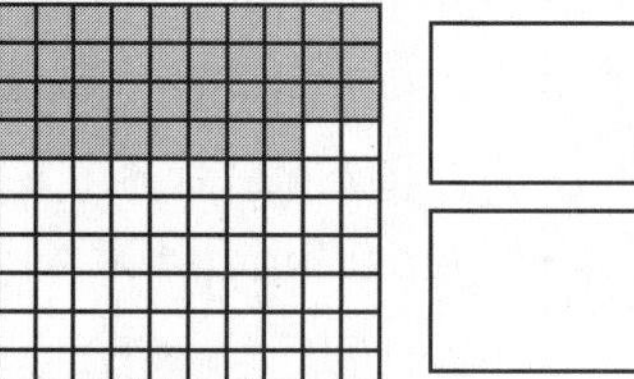

d) 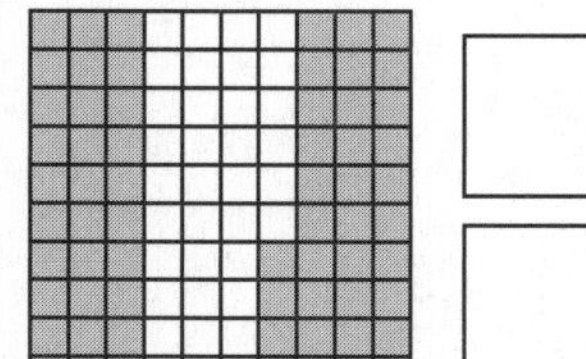

e) 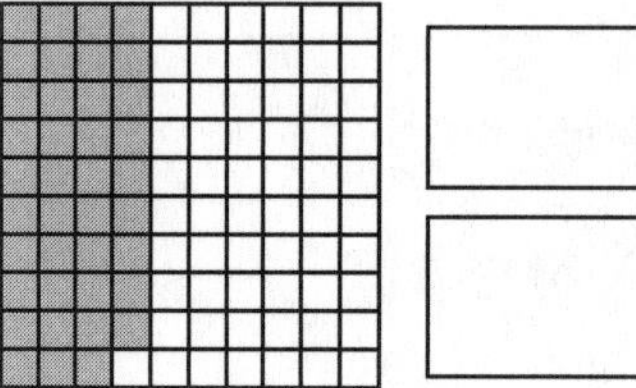

f) 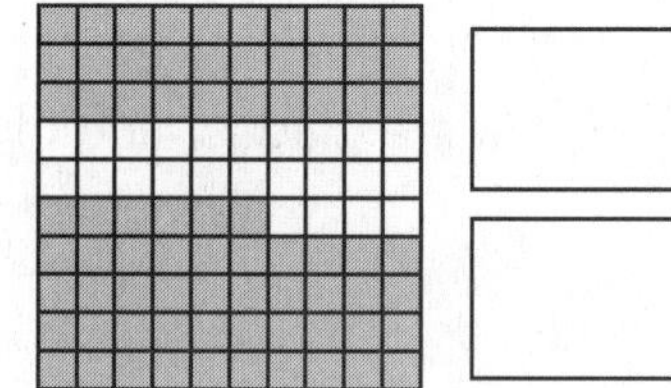

2. Convert the fraction to a decimal. Then shade.

a) $\frac{38}{100}$ = ☐

b) $\frac{45}{100}$ = ☐

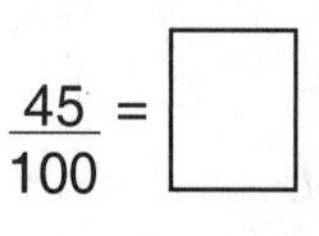

c) $\frac{5}{100}$ = ☐

3. The picture shows a floor plan of a museum. Write a fraction and a decimal for each shaded part.

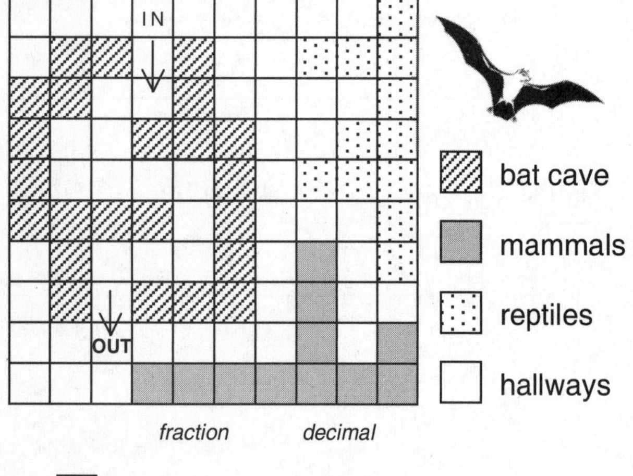

	fraction	decimal
bat cave	______	______
mammals	______	______
reptiles	______	______
hallways	______	______

4. Make your own floor plan for a museum. Write a fraction and a decimal for each shaded part.

	fraction	decimal
☐	______	______
☐	______	______
☐	______	______
☐	______	______

No unauthorized copying

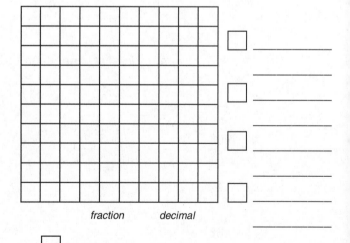

NS5-71: Tenths and Hundredths

1. Draw lines around the columns to show tenths, as shown in a). Then write a fraction and a decimal to represent the number of shaded squares.

a) 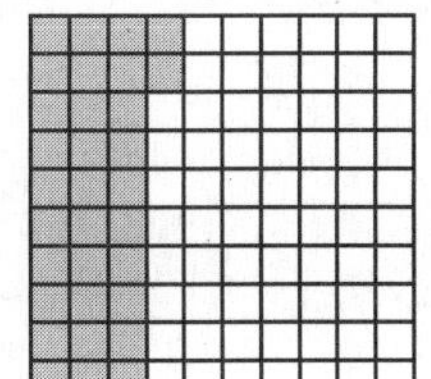 = 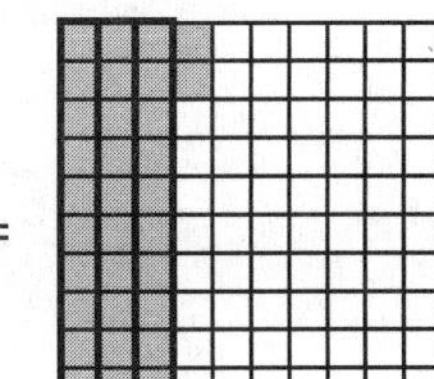

32 hundredths = 3 tenths ___ hundredths

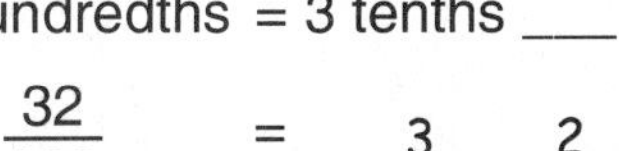

$\frac{32}{100}$ = . 3 2

b) 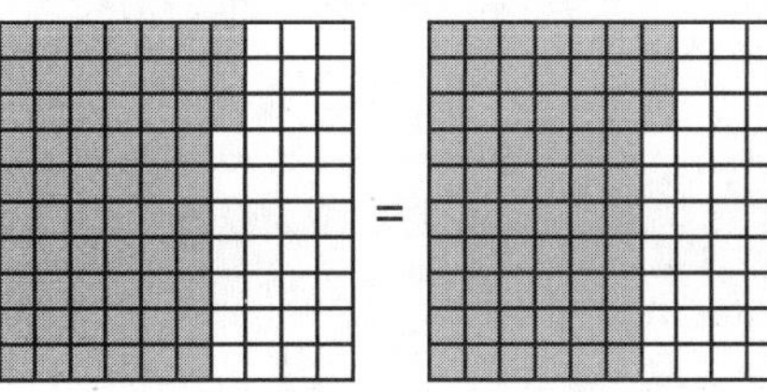

___ hundredths = ___ tenths ___ hundredths

$\frac{\_\_\_}{100}$ = . ___ ___

c) 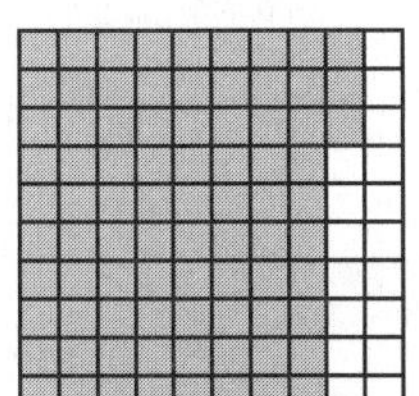 = 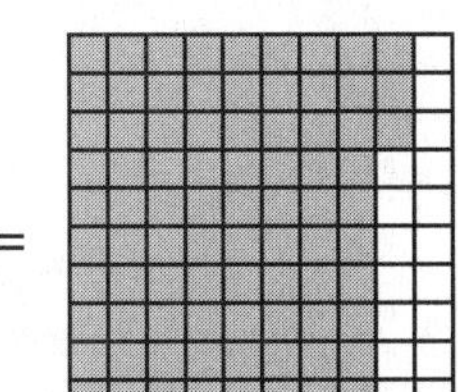

___ hundredths = ___ tenths ___ hundredths

$\frac{\_\_\_}{100}$ = . ___ ___

d) 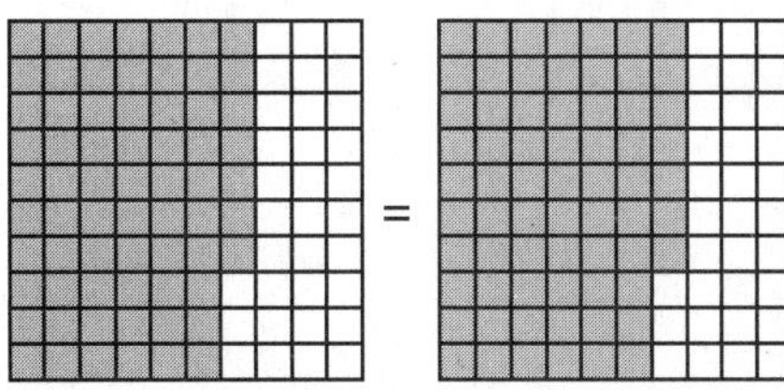

___ hundredths = ___ tenths ___ hundredths

$\frac{\_\_\_}{100}$ = . ___ ___

2. Fill in the blanks.

a) 53 hundredths = ___ tenths ___ hundredths

$\frac{53}{100}$ = . 5 3

b) 27 hundredths = ___ tenths ___ hundredths

$\frac{\_\_\_}{100}$ = . ___ ___

c) 65 hundredths = ___ tenths ___ hundredths

$\frac{\_\_\_}{100}$ = . ___ ___

d) 90 hundredths = ___ tenths ___ hundredths

$\frac{\_\_\_}{100}$ = . ___ ___

e) 6 hundredths = ___ tenths ___ hundredths

$\frac{\_\_\_}{100}$ = . ___ ___

f) 3 hundredths = ___ tenths ___ hundredths

$\frac{\_\_\_}{100}$ = . ___ ___

3. Describe each decimal in two ways.

a) .52 = 5 tenths 2 hundredths

= 52 hundredths

b) .44 = ___ tenths ___ hundredths

= ______________________

c) .30 = ___ tenths ___ hundredths

= ______________________

d) .23 = ___ tenths ___ hundredths

= ______________________

e) .05 = ___ tenths ___ hundredths

= ______________________

f) .08 = ___ tenths ___ hundredths

= ______________________

No unauthorized copying

NS5-72: Changing Tenths to Hundredths

1. Fill in the chart below. The first one has been done for you.

Drawing	Fraction	Decimal	Equivalent Decimal	Equivalent Fraction	Drawing
	$\frac{4}{10}$	0.4	0.40	$\frac{40}{100}$	

2. Write a fraction for the number of <u>hundredths</u>. Then count the shaded columns and write a fraction for the number of <u>tenths</u>.

a)
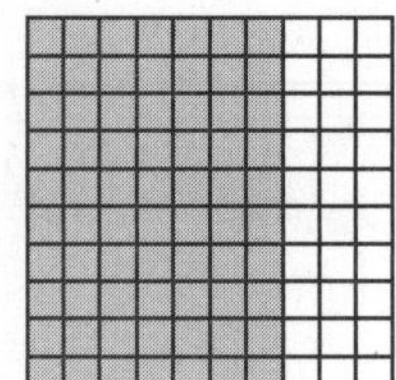

$\frac{\quad}{100} = \frac{\quad}{10}$

b)
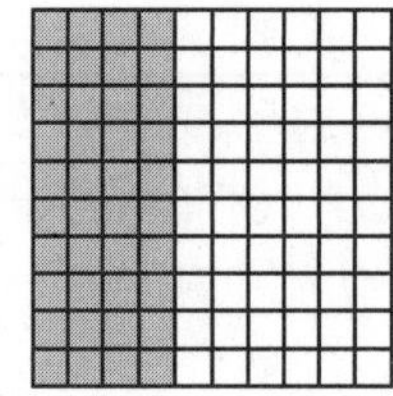

$\frac{\quad}{100} = \frac{\quad}{10}$

c)
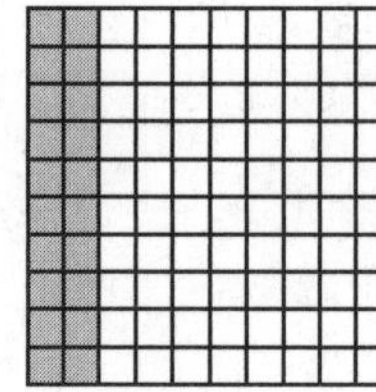

$\frac{\quad}{100} = \frac{\quad}{10}$

d)
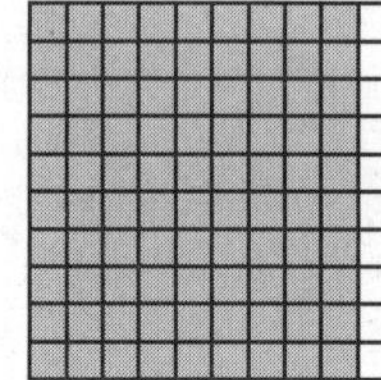

$\frac{\quad}{100} = \frac{\quad}{10}$

3. Fill in the missing numbers.

REMEMBER: $\frac{10}{100} = \frac{1}{10}$

a) $.8 = \frac{8}{10} = \frac{\quad}{100} = .\_\_\,\_\_$

b) $.\_\_ = \frac{2}{10} = \frac{\quad}{100} = .20$

c) $.\_\_ = \frac{6}{10} = \frac{\quad}{100} = .60$

d) $.\_\_ = \frac{7}{10} = \frac{\quad}{100} = .\_\_\,\_\_$

e) $.\_\_ = \frac{\quad}{10} = \frac{40}{100} = .\_\_\,\_\_$

f) $.\_\_ = \frac{\quad}{10} = \frac{30}{100} = .\_\_\,\_\_$

g) $.\_\_ = \frac{4}{10} = \frac{\quad}{100} = .\_\_\,\_\_$

h) $.\_\_ = \frac{9}{10} = \frac{\quad}{100} = .\_\_\,\_\_$

i) $.3 = \frac{\quad}{10} = \frac{\quad}{100} = .\_\_\,\_\_$

No unauthorized copying

NS5-73: Decimals and Money

A **dime** is **one tenth** of a dollar. A **penny** is **one hundredth** of a dollar.

1. Express the value of each decimal in four different ways.

a) .64

6 dimes 4 pennies

6 tenths 4 hundredths

64 pennies

64 hundredths

b) .62

____

____

____

____

c) .57

____

____

____

____

d) .05

____

____

____

____

e) .08

____

____

____

____

f) .13

____

____

____

____

2. Express the value of each decimal in 4 different ways.
HINT: First add a zero in the hundredths place.

a) .4 ____ dimes ____ pennies

____ tenths ____ hundredths

____ pennies

____ hundredths

b) .9 ____ dimes ____ pennies

____ tenths ____ hundredths

____ pennies

____ hundredths

3. Express the value of each decimal in four different ways. Then circle the greater number.

.17 ____ dimes ____ pennies

____ tenths ____ hundredths

____ pennies

____ hundredths

.2 ____ dimes ____ pennies

____ tenths ____ hundredths

____ pennies

____ hundredths

4. Tanya says .53 is greater than .7 because 53 is greater than 7. Can you explain her mistake?

No unauthorized copying

NS5-74: Changing Notation: Fractions and Decimals

1. Fill in the missing numbers.

a) 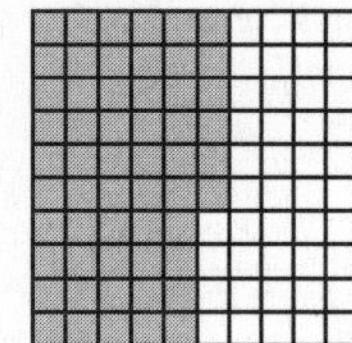

b) 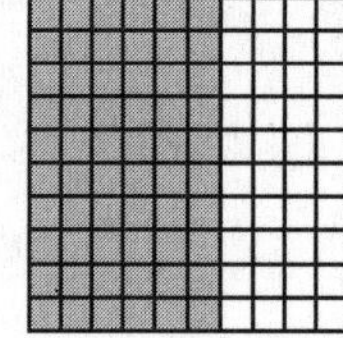

c) 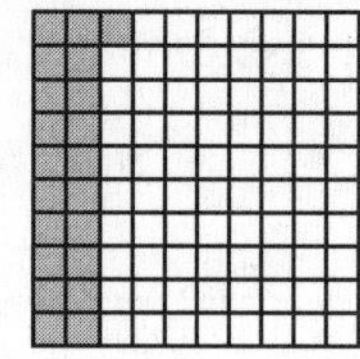

d) 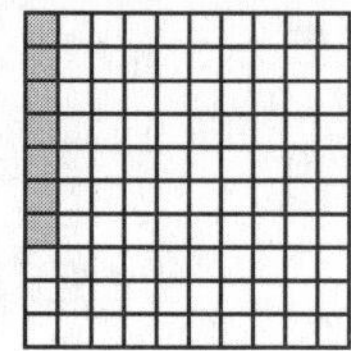

tenths	hundredths

tenths	hundredths

tenths	hundredths

tenths	hundredths

$\frac{\ \ }{100}$ = . ___ ___ (tenths, hundredths) $\frac{\ \ }{100}$ = . ___ ___ $\frac{\ \ }{100}$ = . ___ ___ $\frac{\ \ }{100}$ = . ___ ___

2. Write the following decimals as fractions.

a) .5 = $\frac{\ \ }{10}$ b) .3 = $\frac{\ \ }{10}$ c) .6 = $\frac{\ \ }{10}$ d) .2 = $\frac{\ \ }{10}$ e) .1 = $\frac{\ \ }{10}$

f) .34 = $\frac{\ \ }{100}$ g) .59 = $\frac{\ \ }{100}$ h) .77 = $\frac{\ \ }{100}$ i) .84 = $\frac{\ \ }{100}$ j) .31 = $\frac{\ \ }{100}$

k) .08 = $\frac{\ \ }{100}$ l) .03 = $\frac{\ \ }{100}$ m) .09 = $\frac{\ \ }{100}$ n) .05 = $\frac{\ \ }{100}$ o) .01 = $\frac{\ \ }{100}$

p) .7 = q) .3 = r) .06 = s) .8 = t) .08 =

u) .6 = v) .46 = w) .05 = x) .9 = y) .6 =

3. Change the following fractions to decimals.

a) $\frac{5}{10}$ = . ___ b) $\frac{4}{10}$ = . ___ c) $\frac{6}{10}$ = . ___ d) $\frac{9}{10}$ = . ___

e) $\frac{93}{100}$ = . ___ ___ f) $\frac{8}{100}$ = . ___ ___ g) $\frac{88}{100}$ = . ___ ___ h) $\frac{4}{100}$ = . ___ ___

4. Circle the equalities that are incorrect.

a) .63 = $\frac{63}{100}$ b) .9 = $\frac{9}{10}$ c) .6 = $\frac{6}{100}$ d) $\frac{27}{100}$ = .27 e) $\frac{4}{100}$ = .04

f) .7 = $\frac{7}{100}$ g) .64 = $\frac{64}{10}$ h) .75 = $\frac{75}{100}$ i) .06 = $\frac{6}{100}$ j) .03 = $\frac{3}{10}$

5. Explain how you know .7 is equal to .70.

No unauthorized copying

NS5-75: Decimals and Fractions Greater Than One

A hundreds block may be used to represent a whole. 10 is a tenth of 100, so a tens block represents a tenth of the whole. 1 is a hundredth of 100, so a ones block represents a hundredth of the whole.

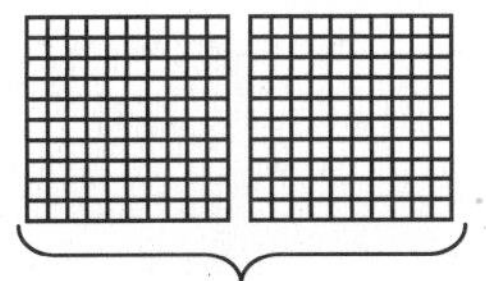
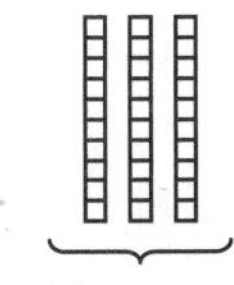

2 wholes   3 tenths   4 hundredths

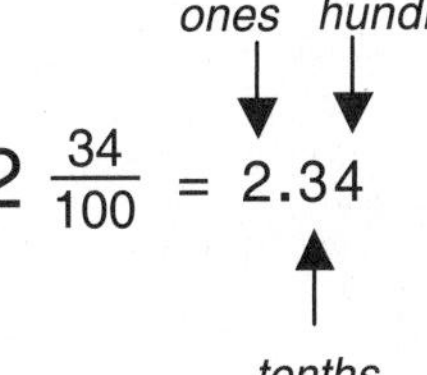

$2\frac{34}{100} = 2.34$

NOTE: A mixed fraction can be written as a decimal.

1. Write a mixed fraction and a decimal for the base ten models below.

a)   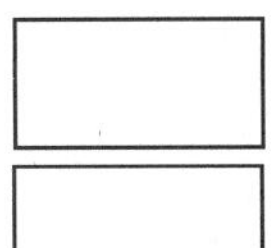

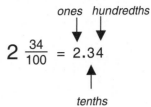

b) 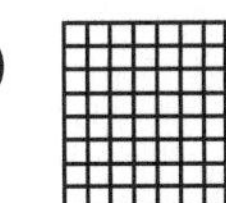 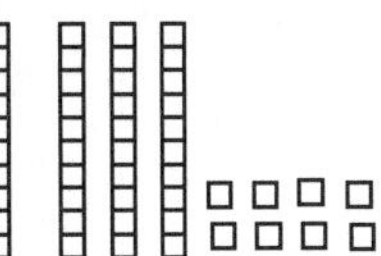 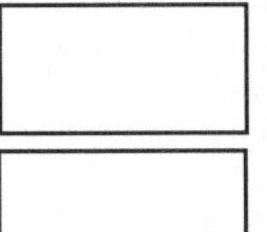

c) 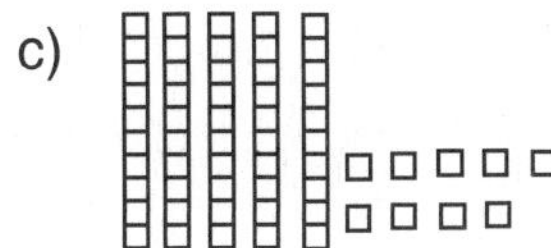 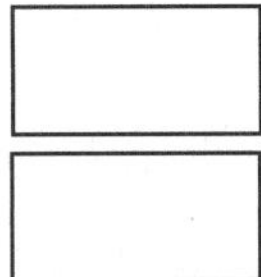

d) 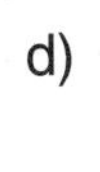 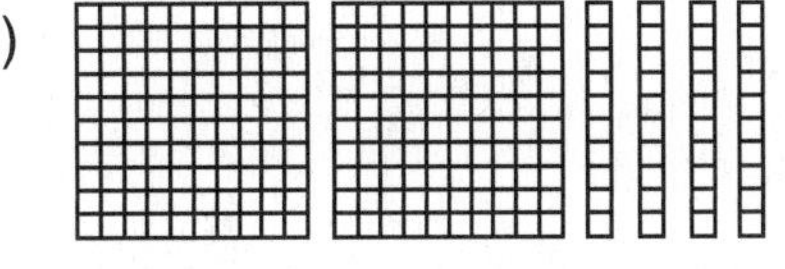 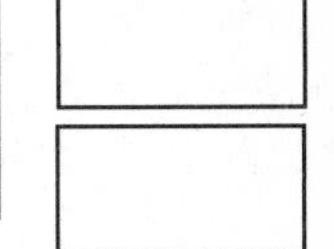

e) 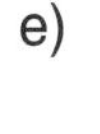 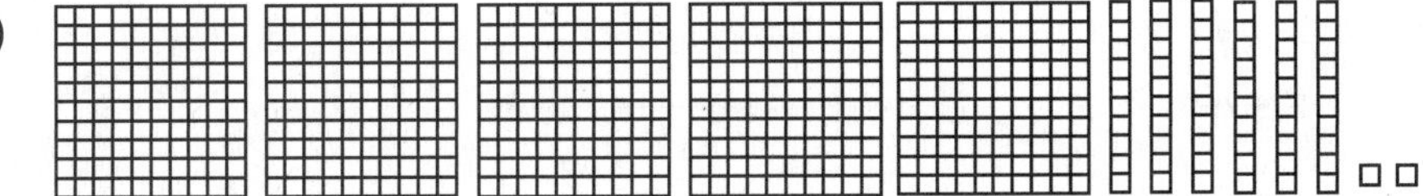 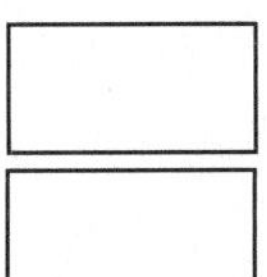

2. Draw a base ten model for the following decimals.

a) 2.52   b) 1.04

3. Write a decimal and a mixed fraction for each of the pictures below.

a) 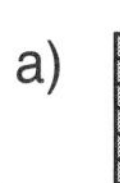 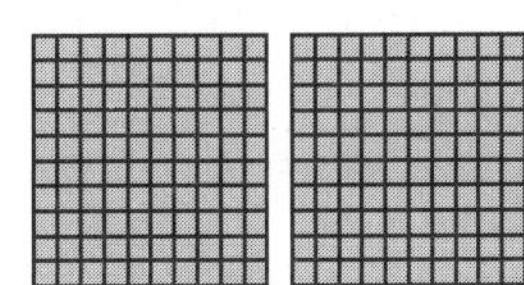 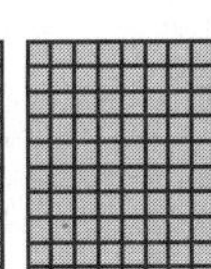 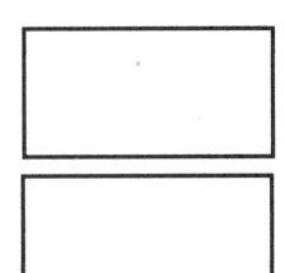

b)  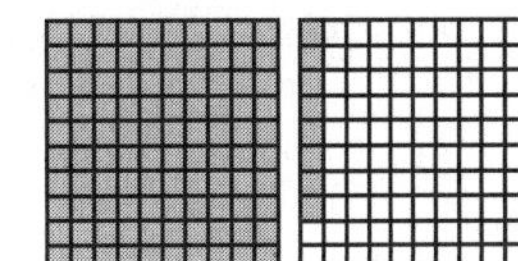 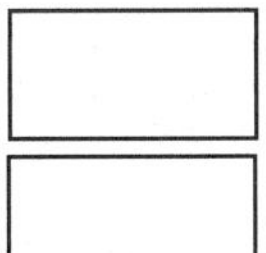

4. Write a decimal for each of the mixed fractions below.

a) $2\frac{57}{100} =$ b) $3\frac{17}{100} =$ c) $5\frac{3}{10} =$ d) $1\frac{3}{100} =$

e) $2\frac{7}{100} =$ f) $19\frac{9}{10} =$ g) $35\frac{1}{100} =$ h) $87\frac{6}{100} =$

5. Which decimal represents a greater number? Explain your answer with a picture.

a) 3 tenths or 3 hundredths?   b) .7 or .07?   c) 1.08 or 1.80?

No unauthorized copying

NS5-76: Decimals and Fractions on Number Lines

This number line is divided into tenths. The number represented by Point A is $2\frac{3}{10}$ or 2.3:

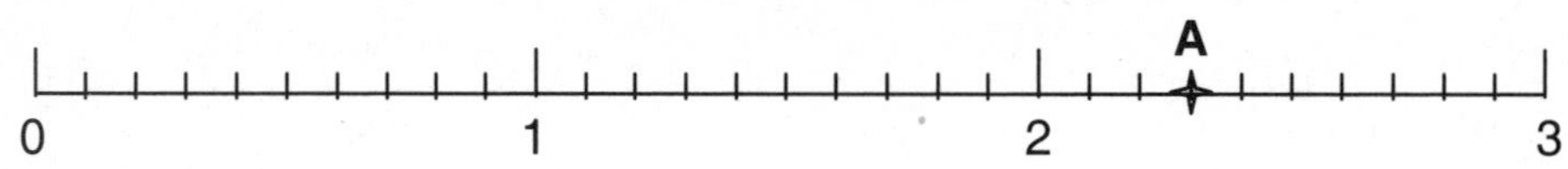

1. Write a decimal and a fraction (or mixed fraction) for each point.

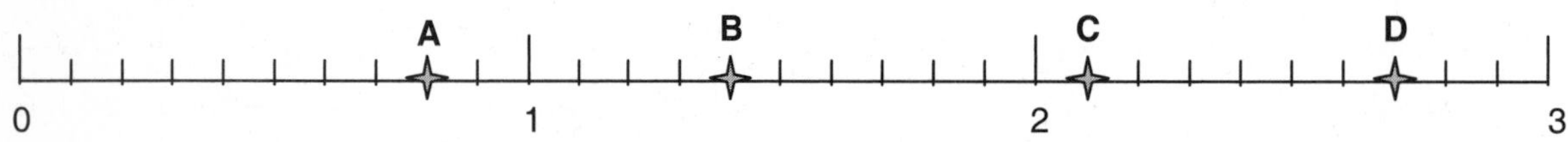

A: $\frac{8}{10} = .8$ **B:** **C:** **D:**

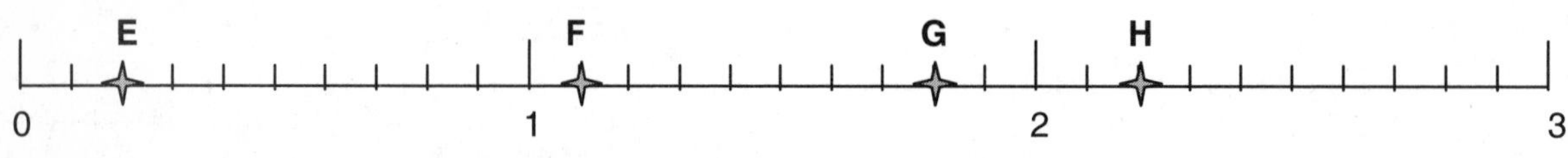

E: **F:** **G:** **H:**

2. Mark each point with an 'X' and label the point with the correct letter.

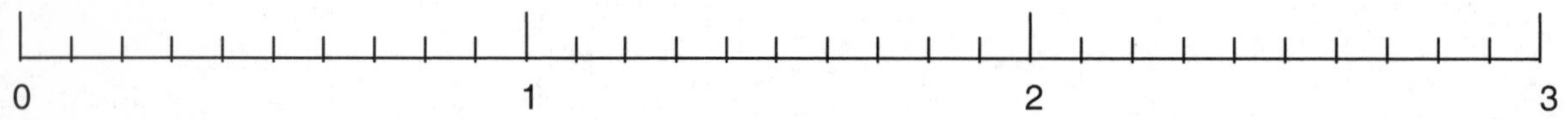

A: 1.3 **B:** 2.7 **C:** .70 **D:** 1.1

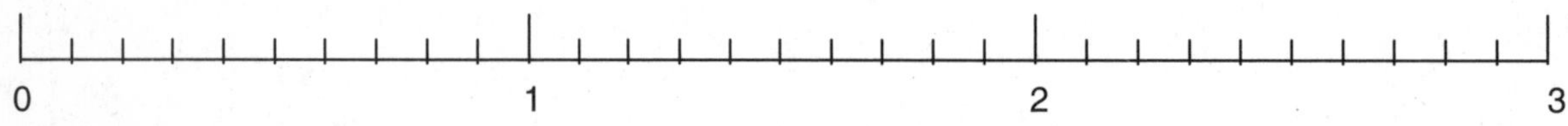

E: $1\frac{2}{10}$ **F:** $2\frac{9}{10}$ **G:** $\frac{27}{10}$ **H:** $1\frac{3}{10}$

3. Write the name of each point as a decimal in words.

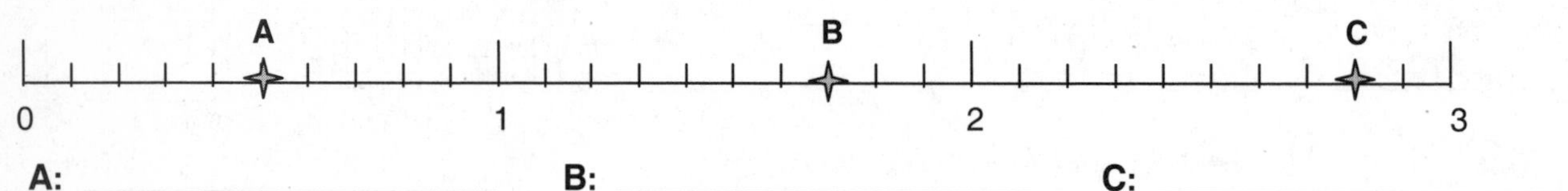

A: ____________________ **B:** ____________________ **C:** ____________________

BONUS

4. Mark the following fractions and decimals on the number line.

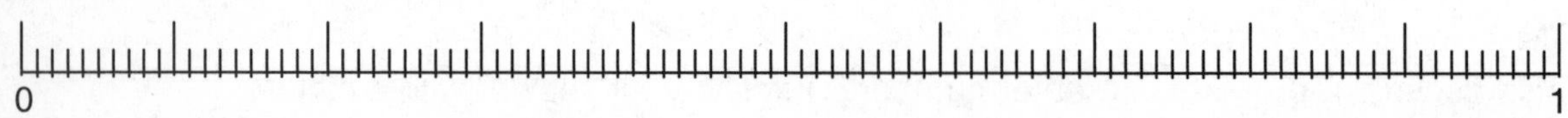

A. .72 **B.** $\frac{34}{100}$ **C.** .05 **D.** $\frac{51}{100}$

 No unauthorized copying

NS5-77: Comparing and Ordering Fractions and Decimals

1.

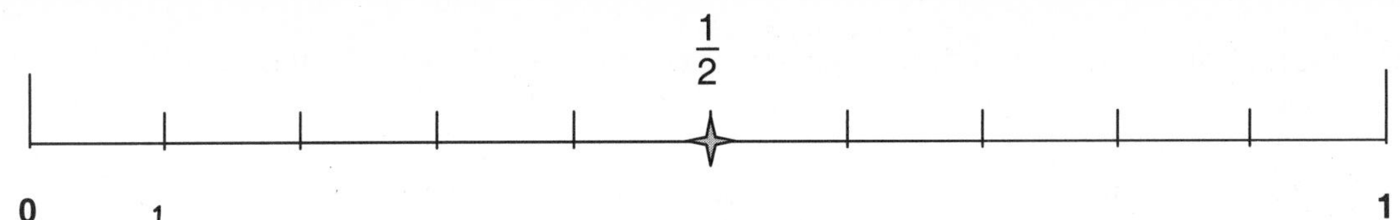

a) Write a decimal for each point marked on the number line. (The first decimal is written for you.)

b) Which decimal is equal to one half? $\frac{1}{2}$ =

2. Use the number line in Question 1 to say whether each decimal is closer to "zero," "a half," or "one."

a) .2 is closer to ___________ b) .6 is closer to ___________ c) .9 is closer to ___________

d) .4 is closer to ___________ e) .8 is closer to ___________ f) .1 is closer to ___________

3. Use the number lines below to compare the numbers given. Write < (less than) or > (greater than) between each pair of numbers.

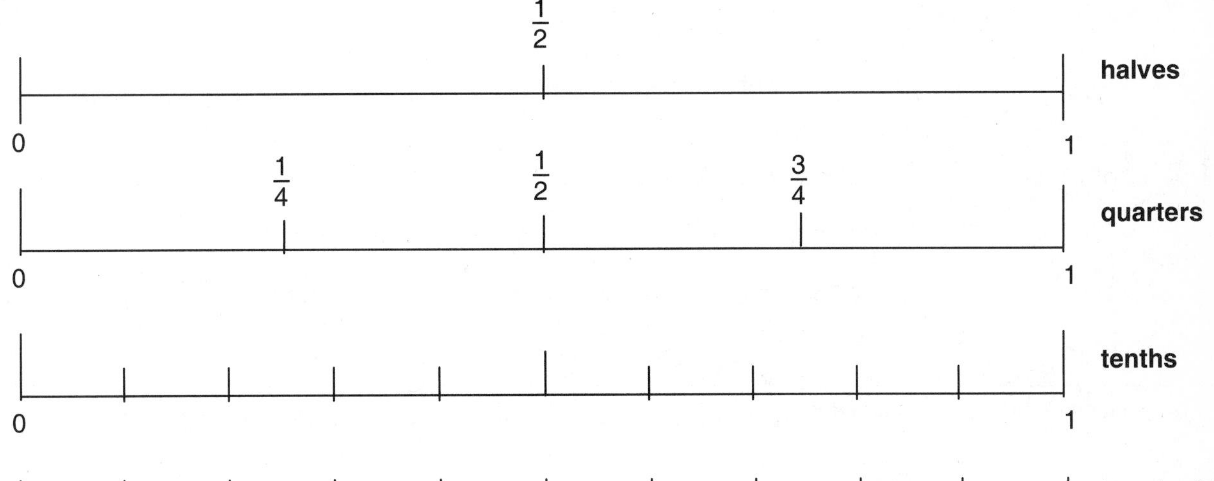

a) 0.4 ☐ $\frac{1}{2}$ b) 0.9 ☐ $\frac{3}{4}$ c) 0.7 ☐ $\frac{1}{4}$ d) 0.6 ☐ $\frac{1}{4}$

e) 0.3 ☐ $\frac{1}{2}$ f) 0.25 ☐ $\frac{1}{2}$ g) 0.85 ☐ $\frac{3}{4}$ h) $\frac{1}{3}$ ☐ .45

4. Which whole number is each decimal or mixed fraction closest to: "zero," "one," "two," or "three"?

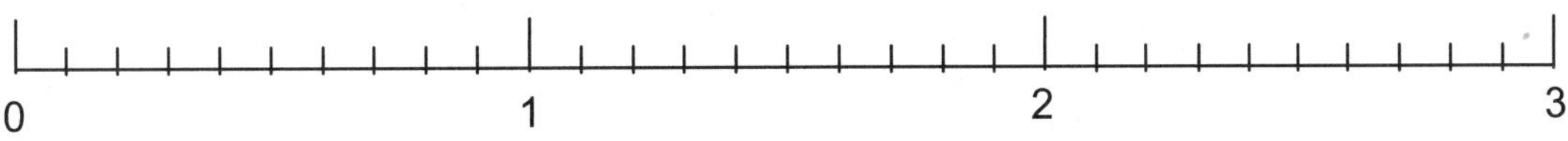

a) 1.3 is closest to ________ b) 1.9 is closest to ________ c) $2\frac{2}{10}$ is closest to ________

No unauthorized copying

NS5-78: Ordering Fractions and Decimals

1. Write the numbers in order by first changing each decimal to a fraction with a denominator of 10.
NOTE: Show your work below each number.

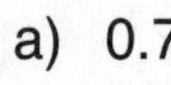

a) 0.7   0.3   0.5

$\frac{7}{10}$

b) $\frac{1}{10}$ 0.3   0.9

c) 0.2   0.6 $\frac{3}{10}$

d) 1.2   3.5   3.1

$1\frac{2}{10}$

e) 1.5   1.2   1.7

f) $1\frac{1}{10}$ .7   3.5

g) $1\frac{3}{10}$ 1.2   1.1

h) 4.5   3.2 $1\frac{7}{10}$

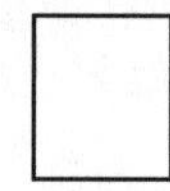

i) 2.3   2.9 $2\frac{1}{2}$

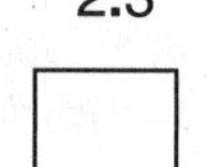
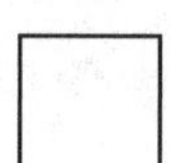

2. Karen says: "To compare .6 and .42, I add a zero to .6:

.6 = 6 tenths = 60 hundredths = .60

60 (hundredths) is greater than 42 (hundredths).

So .6 is greater than .42."

Add a zero to the decimal expressed in tenths. Then circle the greater number in each pair.

a) .7   .52   b) .34   .6   c) .82   .5

3. Write each decimal as a fraction with denominator 100 by first adding a zero to the decimal.

a) .7 = .70 = $\frac{70}{100}$ b) .6 =   =   c) .5 =   =

4. Write the numbers in order from least to greatest by first changing all of the decimals to fractions with denominator 100.

a) .2   .8   .35

b) $\frac{27}{100}$ .9   .25

c) 1.3 $1\frac{22}{100}$ $1\frac{39}{100}$

No unauthorized copying

5. 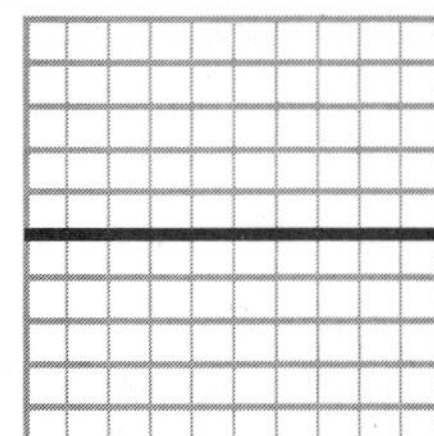

Shade $\frac{1}{2}$ of the squares. Write 2 fractions and 2 decimals for $\frac{1}{2}$.

Fractions: $\frac{1}{2} = \frac{\quad}{10} = \frac{\quad}{100}$

Decimals: $\frac{1}{2}$ = .____ = .____

6. 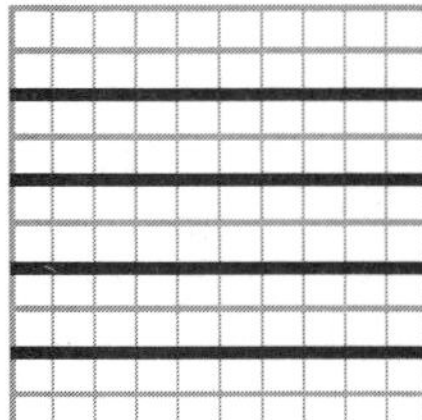

Shade $\frac{1}{5}$ of the boxes. Write 2 fractions and 2 decimals for $\frac{1}{5}$.

Fractions: $\frac{1}{5} = \frac{\quad}{10} = \frac{\quad}{100}$

Decimals: $\frac{1}{5}$ = .____ = .____

7. Write equivalent fractions.

a) $\frac{2}{5} = \frac{\quad}{10} = \frac{\quad}{100}$ b) $\frac{3}{5} = \frac{\quad}{10} = \frac{\quad}{100}$ c) $\frac{4}{5} = \frac{\quad}{10} = \frac{\quad}{100}$

8. 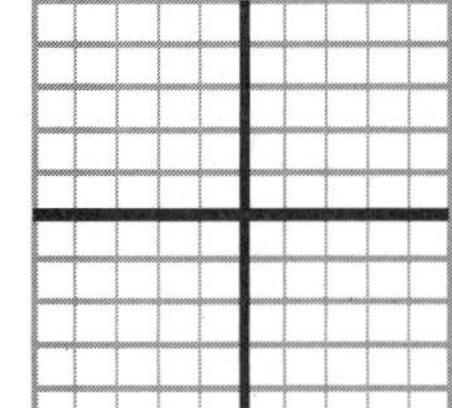

Shade $\frac{1}{4}$ of the squares. Write a fraction and a decimal for $\frac{1}{4}$.

Fraction: $\frac{1}{4} = \frac{\quad}{100}$ *Decimal:* $\frac{1}{4}$ = .____

Fraction: $\frac{3}{4} = \frac{\quad}{100}$ *Decimal:* $\frac{3}{4}$ = .____

9. Circle the greater number.
HINT: First change all fractions and decimals to fractions with denominator 100.

a) $\frac{1}{2}$ .37 b) $\frac{1}{4}$ .52 c) $\frac{2}{5}$ .42

d) .7 $\frac{3}{5}$ e) .23 $\frac{1}{5}$ f) .52 $\frac{1}{2}$

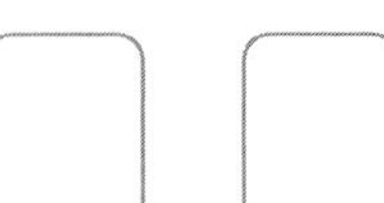

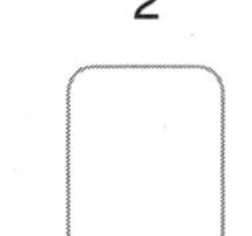

10. Write the numbers in order from least to greatest. Explain how you found your answers.

a) .7 .32 $\frac{1}{2}$ b) $\frac{1}{4}$ $\frac{3}{5}$ .63 c) $\frac{2}{5}$ .35 $\frac{1}{2}$

NS5-79: Adding and Subtracting Tenths

1. 1.3 is one whole and 3 tenths. How many tenths is that altogether? ________________

2. a) 4.7 = _____ tenths   b) 7. 1 = _____ tenths   c) 3. 0 = _____ tenths

   d) ______ = 38 tenths   e) ______ = 42 tenths   f) ______ = 7 tenths

3. Add or subtract the decimals by first writing them as whole numbers of tenths.

a)

2.1	21 tenths
+ 1.0	10 tenths
3.1	← 31 tenths

b)

1.3	___ tenths
+ 1.1	___ tenths
	← ___ tenths

c)

1.4	___ tenths
+ 7.3	___ tenths
	← ___ tenths

d)

2.5	___ tenths
− 1.0	___ tenths
	← ___ tenths

e)

7.6	___ tenths
− 4.2	___ tenths
	← ___ tenths

f)

8.9	___ tenths
− 1.4	___ tenths
	← ___ tenths

4. Find the sum or difference.

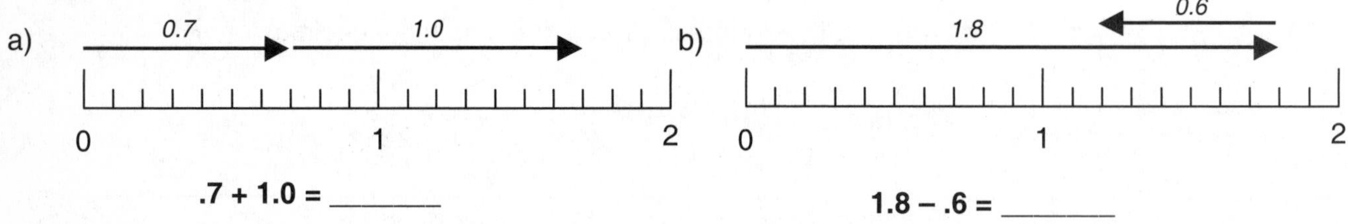

.7 + 1.0 = _______   **1.8 – .6 =** _______

Now draw your own arrows.

c)

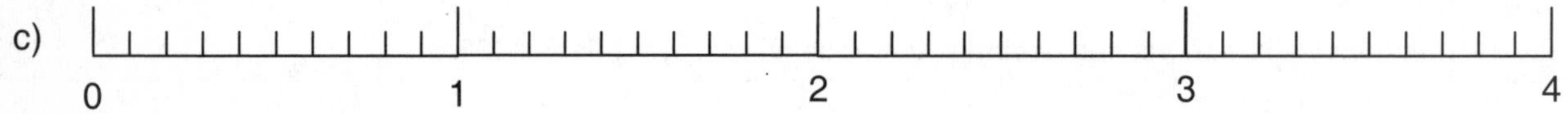

2.5 + 1.2 = _______

d)

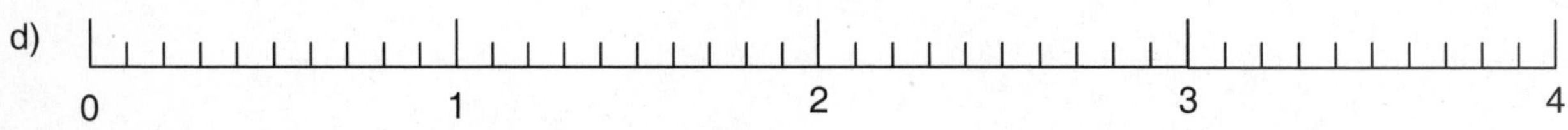

2.7 – 1.9 = _______

5. Add or subtract.

a)	b)	c)	d)	e)	f)
3.5	4.6	5.4	9.2	3.7	2.8
− 1.2	+ 3.2	+ 1.7	− 4.9	+ 4.9	− 1.9

No unauthorized copying

NS5-80: Adding Hundredths

1. Write a fraction for each shaded part. Then add the fractions, and shade your answer. The first one has been done for you.

a) 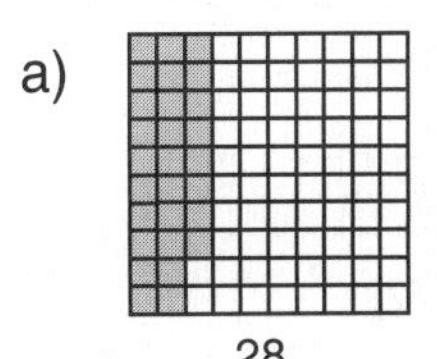 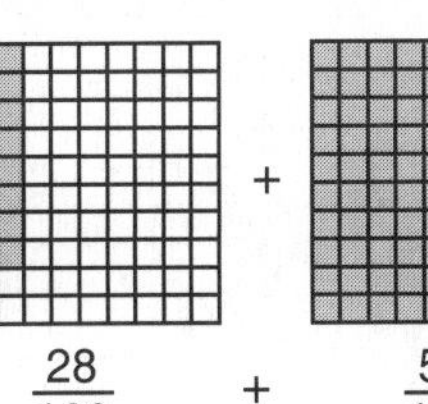 + 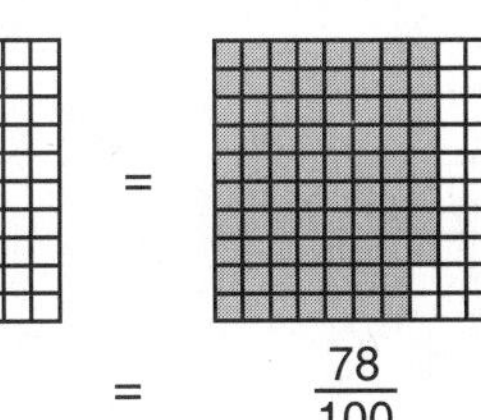 =

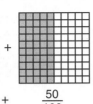

$\frac{28}{100} + \frac{50}{100} = \frac{78}{100}$

b) 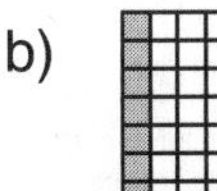 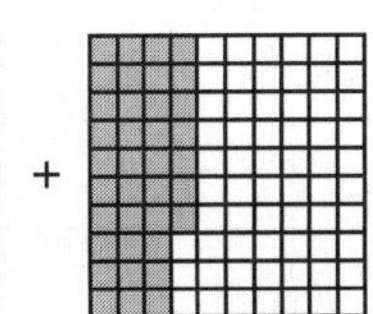 + 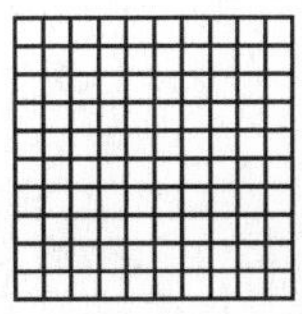 =

c) 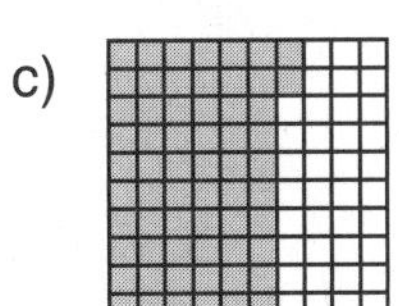 + 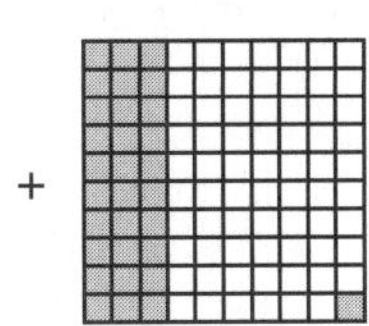 = 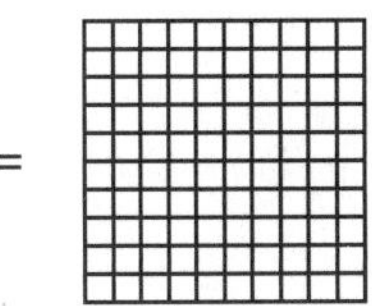

d) 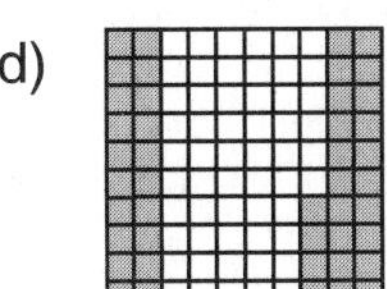 + 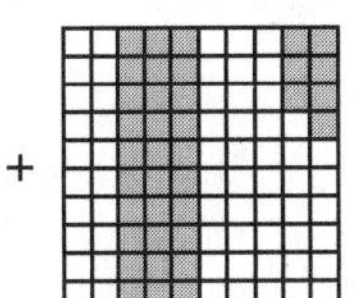 = 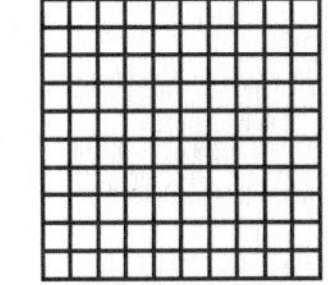

2. Write the decimals that correspond to the fractions in Question 1.

a) .28 + .50 = .78	b)
c)	d)

3. Add the decimals by lining up the digits. Be sure that your final answer is expressed as a decimal.

a) 0.42 + 0.36 b) 0.91 + 0.04 c) 0.42 + 0.72 d) 0.22 + 0.57

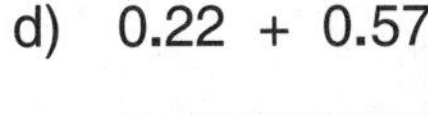

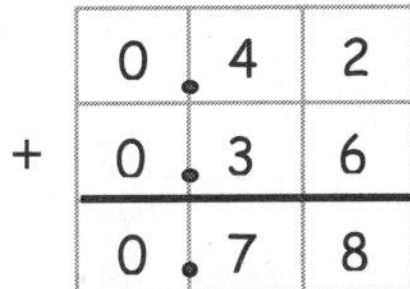

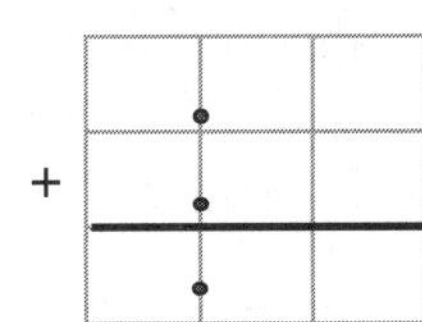
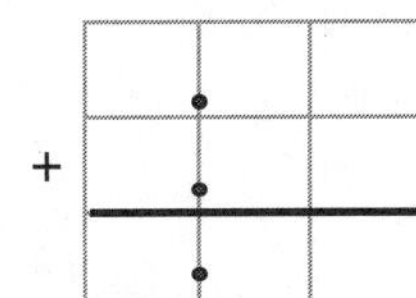
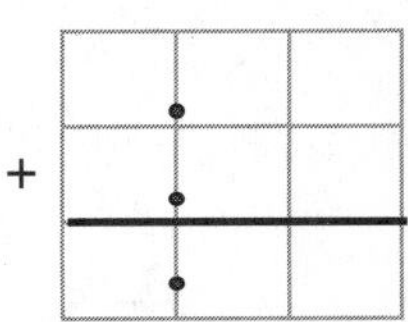

e) 0.3 + 0 .36 f) 0.5 + 0.48 g) 0.81 + 0.58 h) 0.46 + 0.22

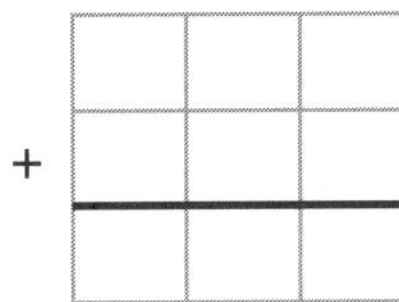
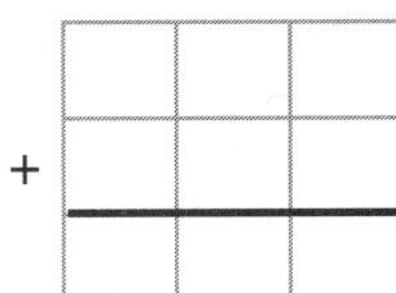
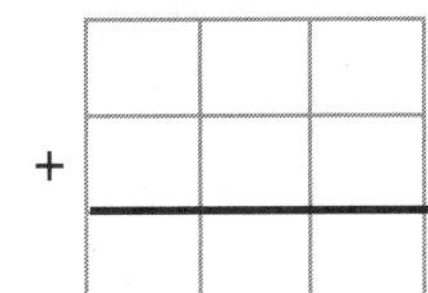
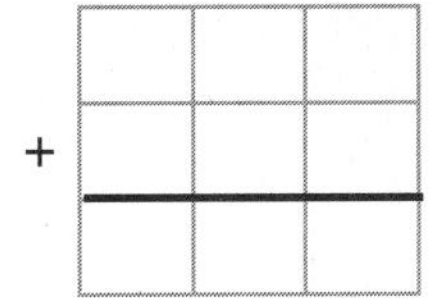

4. Line up the decimals and add the following numbers.

a) 0.32 + 0.17 b) 0.64 + 0.23 c) 0.46 + 0.12 d) 0.87 + 0.02 e) 0.48 + 0.31

5. Anne mixed .63 litres of juice with .36 litres of ginger ale.
How many litres of punch did she make?

6. A snake is .56 metres long.
What fraction of a metre is this?

If two snakes of the same length lay end to end, would they be more or less than a metre long?

No unauthorized copying

NS5-81: Subtracting Hundredths

1. Subtract by crossing out the correct number of boxes.

a) 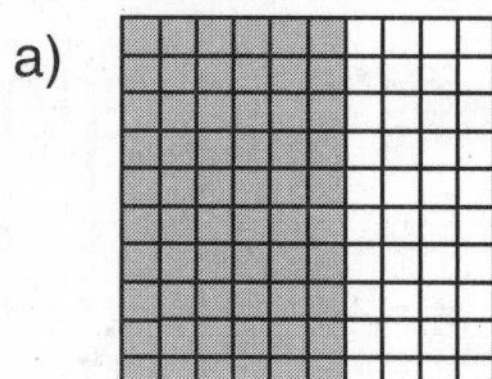

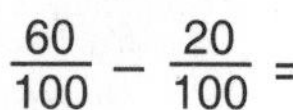

$\frac{60}{100} - \frac{20}{100} =$

b) 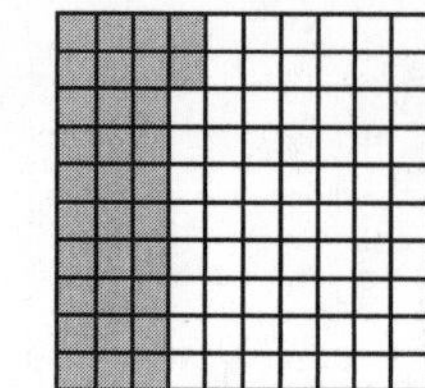

$\frac{32}{100} - \frac{22}{100} =$

c) 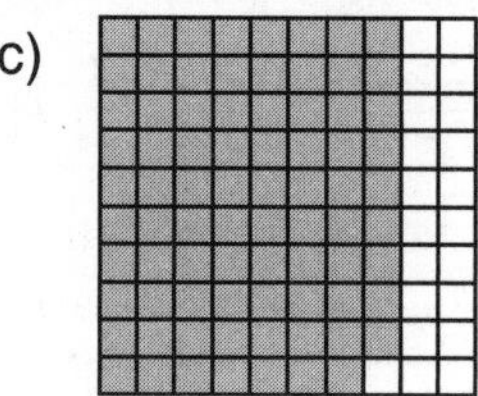

$\frac{79}{100} - \frac{53}{100} =$

2. Write the decimals that correspond to the fractions in Question 1.

a) .60 - .20 = .40 b) c)

3. Subtract the decimals by lining up the digits.

a) 0.74 – 0.31

	0.	7	4
–	0.	3	1
	0.	4	3

b) 0.88 – 0.34

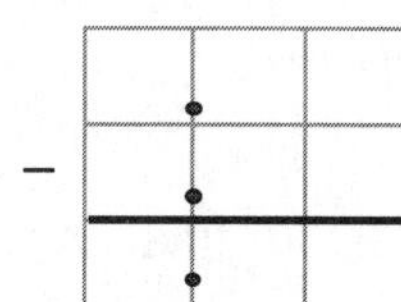

c) 0.46 – 0.23

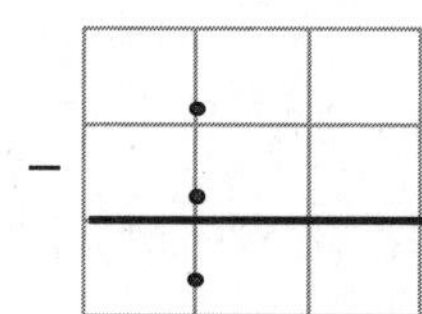

d) 0.75 – 0.21

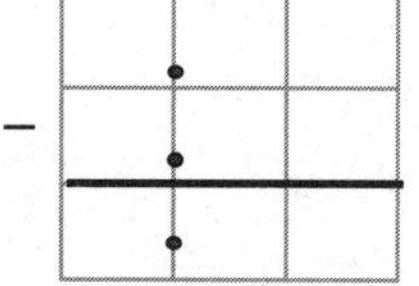

e) 0.33 – .17

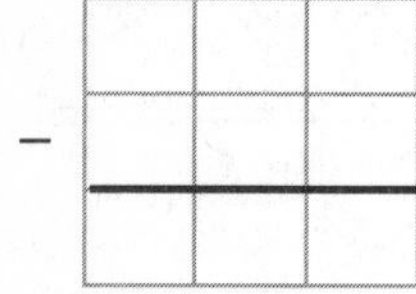

f) 0.64 – 0.38

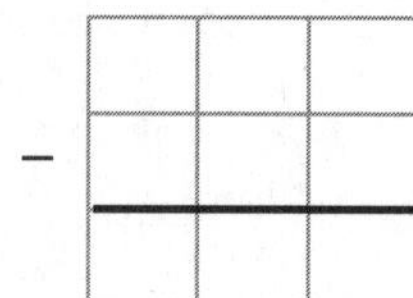

g) 0.92 – 0.59

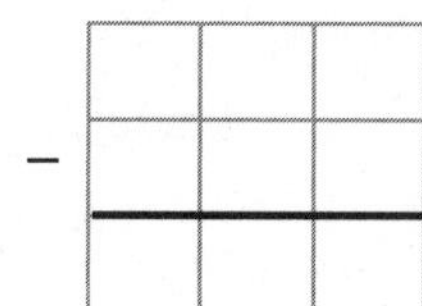

h) 0.53 – 0.26

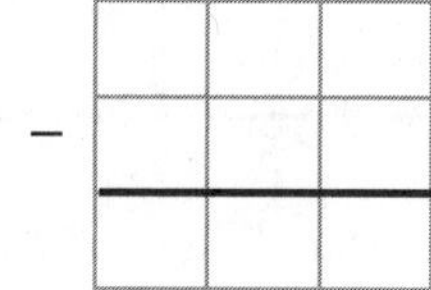

i) 1.00 – .82

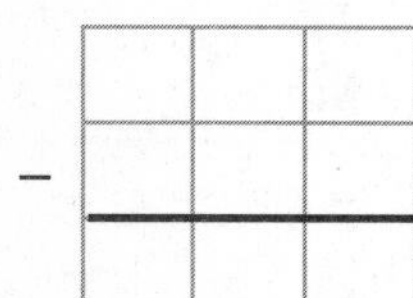

j) 1.00 – 0.36

k) 1.00 – 0.44

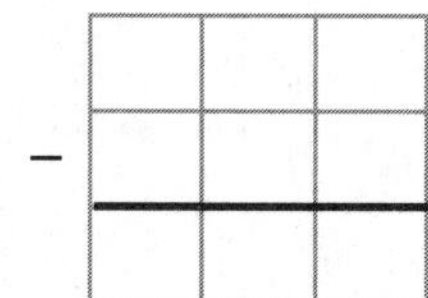

l) 1.00 – 0.29

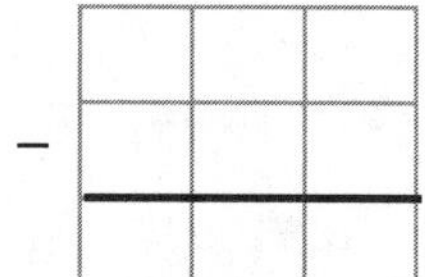

4. Subtract the following decimals.

a) .82 – .45 b) .97 – .38 c) .72 – .64 d) .31 – .17

e) .58 – .3 f) .62 – .6 g) .98 – .03 h) .53 – .09

5. Find the missing decimal in each of the following.

a) 1 = .35 + ☐ b) 1 = .72 + ☐ c) 1 = .41 + ☐

No unauthorized copying

NS5-82: Adding and Subtracting Decimals (Review)

1. Add by drawing a base ten model. Then, using the chart provided, line up the decimal points and add.
NOTE: Use a hundreds block for a whole and a tens block for one tenth.

a) 1.32 + 1.15

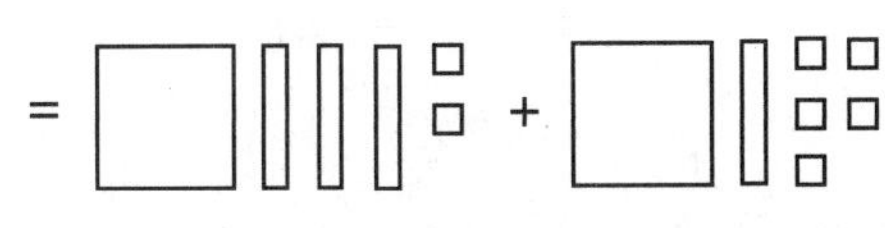

b) 1.46 + 1.33

	ones	tenths	hundredths
	.		
+	.		
	.		

	ones	tenths	hundredths
	.		
+	.		
	.		

2. Subtract by drawing a base ten model of the greater number and then crossing out as many ones, tenths and hundredths as are in the lesser number, as shown in part a).

a) 2.15 – 1.13

b) 2.33 – 1.12

3. Add or subtract.

a) 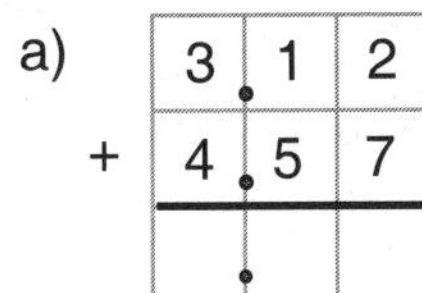

b)

	5.	8	9
+	1.	3	4
	.		

c) 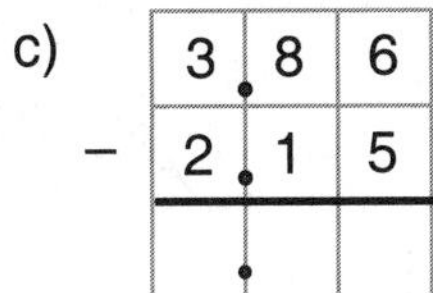

d)

	4.	2	3
–	2.	1	9
	.		

e) 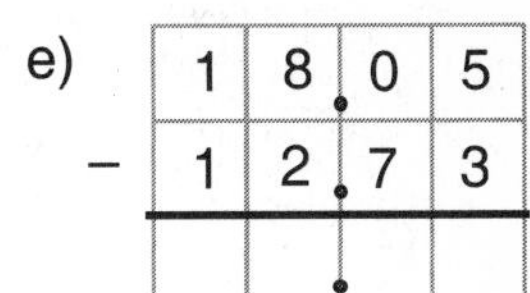

f)

	7.	8	7
+	4.	0	3
	.		

g)

	9.	7	4
+	6.	3	5
	.		

h)

	2.	7	5
–	.	2	8
	.		

i)

	8.	7	1
–	.	1	4
	.		

j) 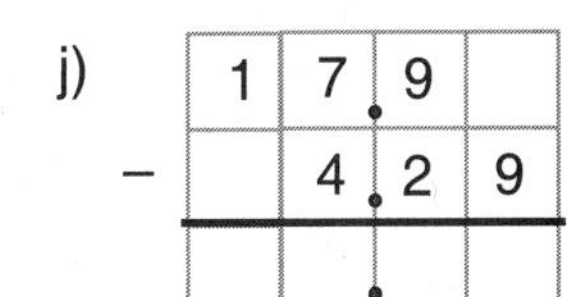

4. Bamboo can grow up to 0.3 m in a single day in ideal conditions.
How high could it grow in 3 days?

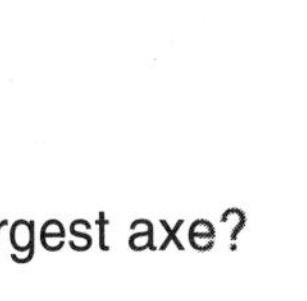

5. The largest axe in the world is 18.28 m long.
If a regular axe is 1.5 metres long, how much longer is the world's largest axe?

6. Continue the patterns. a) .2 , .4 , .6 , ____ , ____ , ____ b) .3 , .6 , .9 , ____ , ____ , ____

No unauthorized copying

NS5-83: Multiplying Decimals by 10

= 1.0 = 0.1 *and* → 10 × =

If a hundreds block represents 1 whole, then a tens block represents 1 tenth (or 0.1).

10 tenths make 1 whole: 10 × 0.1 = 1.0

---

1. Multiply the number of tens blocks by 10. Then show how many hundreds blocks you would have. The first one is done for you.

a) 10 × =

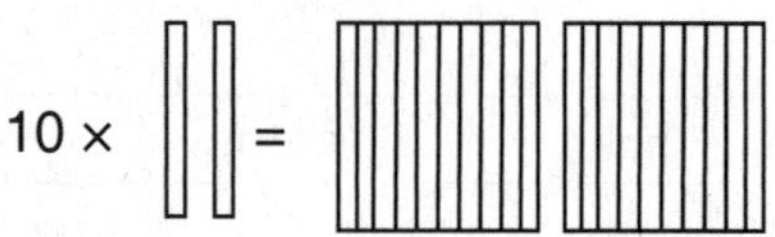

10 × 0.2 = 2

b) 10 × =

10 × 0.3 = ______

c) 10 × =

10 × 0.6 = ______

2. Multiply.

a) 10 × .5 = ____ b) 10 × .7 = ____ c) 10 × 1.4 = ____ d) 10 × .9 = ____

e) 10 × 1.7 = ____ f) 1.6 × 10 = ____ g) 18.2 × 10 = ____ h) 17.3 × 10 = ____

i) 10 × 23.5 = ____ j) 10 × 1.72 = ____ k) 10 × 42.6 = ____ l) 5.36 × 10 = ____

3. To change from dm to cm, you multiply by 10 (because there are 10 cm in 1 dm).

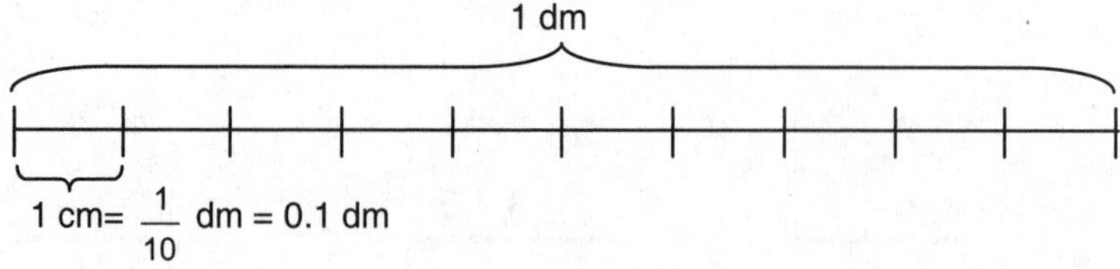

Find the answers.

a) .6 dm = __________ cm b) .8 dm = __________ cm c) 1.6 dm = __________ cm

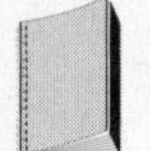

4. 10 × 3 can be written as a sum: 3 + 3 + 3 + 3 + 3 + 3 + 3 + 3 + 3 + 3.
Write 10 × .3 as a sum and skip count by .3 to find the answer.

5. A dime is a tenth of a dollar (10¢ = $0.10).
Draw a picture or use play money to show that 10 × $0.20 = $2.00.

 No unauthorized copying

NS5-84: Multiplying Decimals by 100

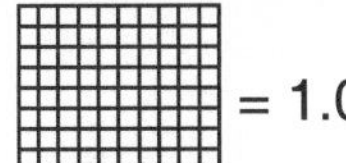 = 1.0 □ = 0.01 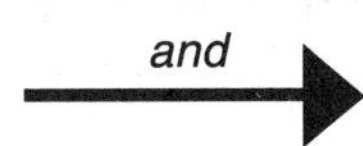 100 × □ = 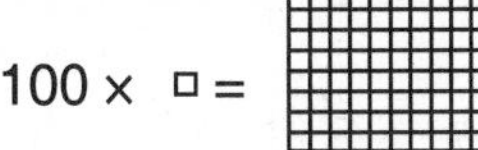

If a hundreds block represents 1 whole, then a ones block represents 1 hundredth (or .01).

100 hundredths makes 1 whole: 100 × .01 = 1.00

---

1. Write a multiplication statement for each picture.

   a) 100 × □□ = ▦ ▦

   100 × .02 = ________

   b) 100 × □□□ = ▦ ▦ ▦

   ________ = ________

2. The picture below shows why the decimal shifts two places to the right when multiplying by 100.

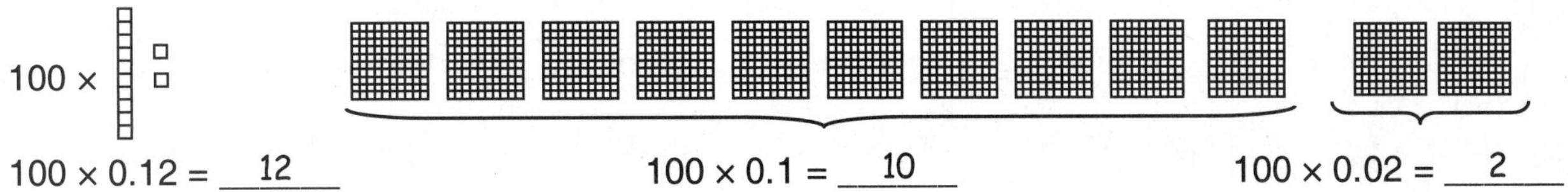

100 × 0.12 = 12 100 × 0.1 = 10 100 × 0.02 = 2

In each case, shift the decimal one or two places to the right. Draw arrows as shown in part a).

a) 100 × .7 = 70 b) 100 × 1.8 = ______ c) 100 × 4.6 = ______

d) 100 × .03 = ______ e) 100 × 6.25 = ______ f) 100 × 3.07 = ______

g) 100 × .07 = ______ h) 100 × .06 = ______ i) 10 × .67 = ______

j) .95 × 100 = ______ k) 100 × 1.82 = ______ l) 100 × 4.07 = ______

m) 100 × .50 = ______ n) 100 × .7 = ______ o) 10 × 1.8 = ______

p) 1.9 × 100 = ______ q) 100 × .6 = ______ r) 100 × 1.7 = ______

3. There are 10 centimetres in a decimetre and 100 millimetres in a decimetre.

a) 1.52 dm = ______ cm b) 3.75 dm = ______ mm c) .05 dm = ______ mm

d) .08 dm = ______ cm e) .6 dm = ______ mm f) 1.23 dm = ______ cm

4. Explain why: a) 100 × \$0.02 = \$2.00 b) 100 × \$0.10 = \$10.00

5. Explain why the decimal moves 2 places to the right when you multiply by 100.

No unauthorized copying

NS5-85: Multiplying Decimals by Whole Numbers

The picture shows how to multiply a decimal by a whole number.

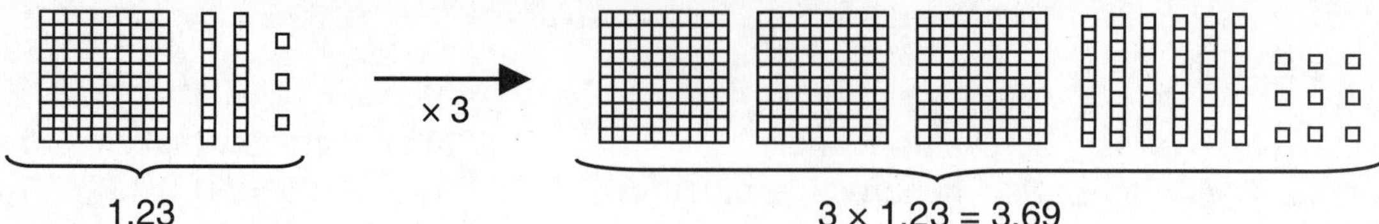

HINT: Simply multiply each digit separately.

---

1. Multiply mentally.

a) 2 × 1.43 = ______ b) 3 × 1.2 = ______ c) 5 × 1.01 = ______ d) 4 × 2.1 = ______

e) 2 × 5.34 = ______ f) 4 × 2.1 = ______ g) 3 × 3.12 = ______ h) 3 × 4.32 = ______

2. Multiply by regrouping tenths as ones (the first one is done for you).

a) 6 × 1.4 = __6__ ones + __24__ tenths = __8__ ones + __4__ tenths = __8.4__

b) 3 × 2.5 = ______ ones + ______ tenths = ______ ones + ______ tenths = ______

c) 3 × 2.7 = ______ ones + ______ tenths = ______ ones + ______ tenths = ______

d) 4 × 2.6 = ____

3. Multiply by regrouping tenths as ones or hundredths as tenths.

a) 3 × 2.51 = ______ ones + ______ tenths + ______ hundredths

= ______ ones + ______ tenths + ______ hundredths = ______

b) 4 × 2.14 = ______ ones + ______ tenths + ______ hundredths

= ______ ones + ______ tenths + ______ hundredths = ______

c) 5 × 1.41 = ______ ones + ______ tenths + ______ hundredths

= ______ ones + ______ tenths + ______ hundredths = ______

4. Multiply. In some questions you will have to regroup twice.

a) 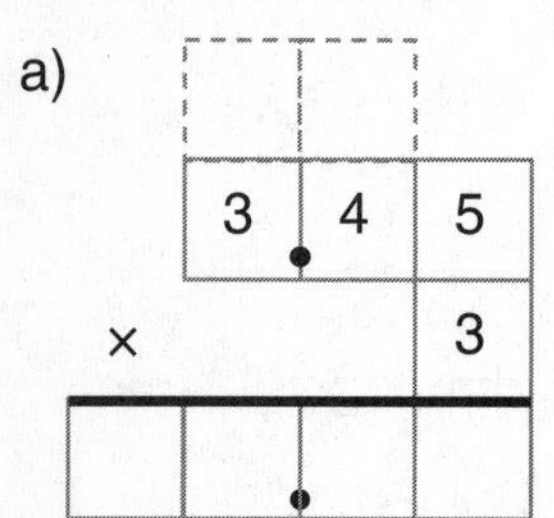

b) 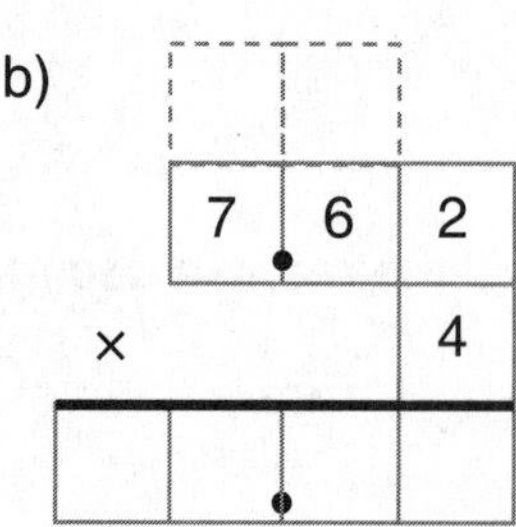

c) 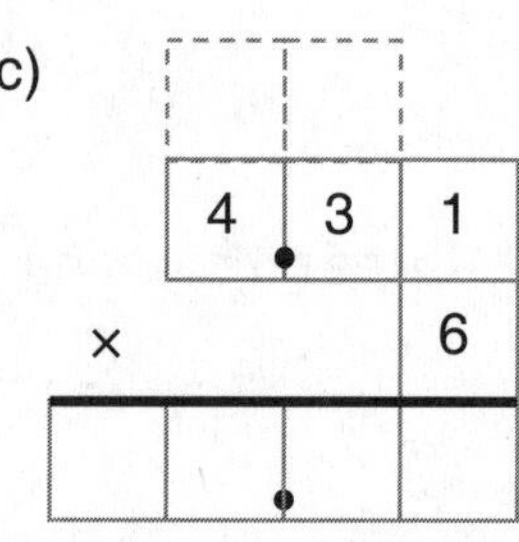

d) 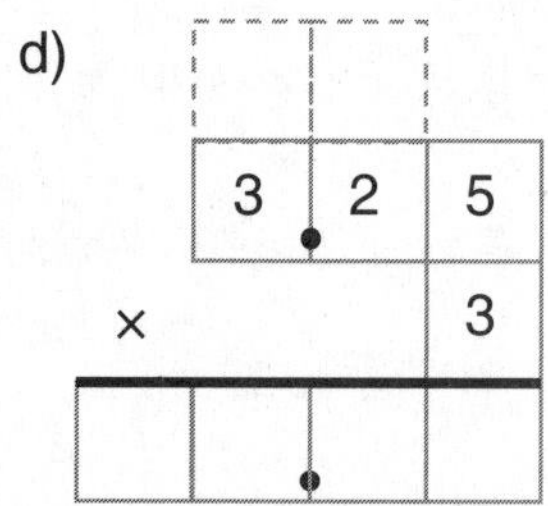

5. Find the products.

a) 5 × 2.1 b) 3 × 8.3 c) 5 × 7.5 d) 9 × 2.81 e) 7 × 3.6 f) 6 × 3.4

g) 4 × 3.2 h) 5 × 6.35 i) 6 × 3.95 j) 8 × 2.63 k) 3 × 31.21 l) 4 × 12.32

 No unauthorized copying

NS5-86: Dividing Decimals by 10

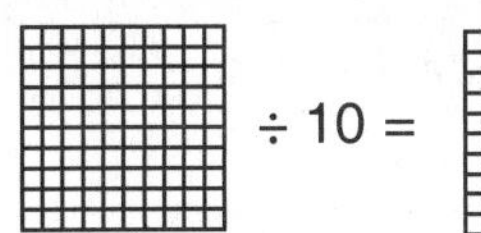

÷ 10 =

Divide 1 whole into 10 equal parts.

Each part is 1 tenth:
1.0 ÷ 10 = 0.1

÷ 10 =

Divide 1 tenth into 10 equal parts.

Each part is 1 hundredth:
0.1 ÷ 10 = 0.01.

When you divide a decimal by 10, the decimal shifts <u>one place to the left</u>:

0 . 7 ÷ 10 = .07

7 . 0 ÷ 10 = .7

---

1. Complete the picture and write a division statement for each picture.

a) 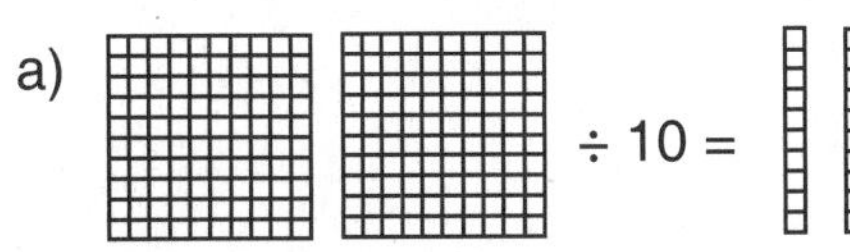 ÷ 10 =

2.0 ÷ 10 = .2

b) 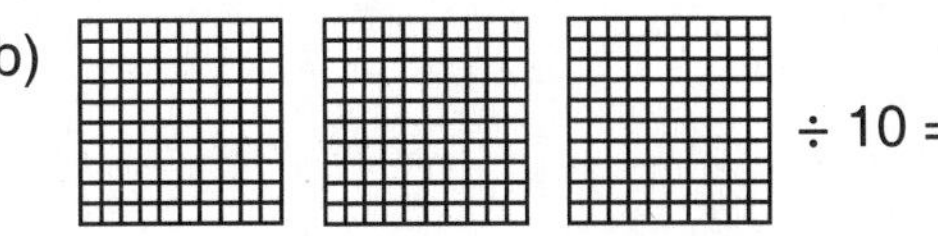 ÷ 10 =

__________ = ______

c) 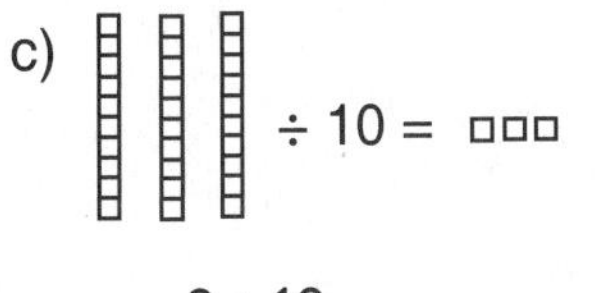 ÷ 10 =

.3 ÷ 10 = ______

d)  ÷ 10 =

__________ = ______

e)  ÷ 10 =

__________ = ______

2. Complete the picture and write a division statement (the first one is done for you).

a) 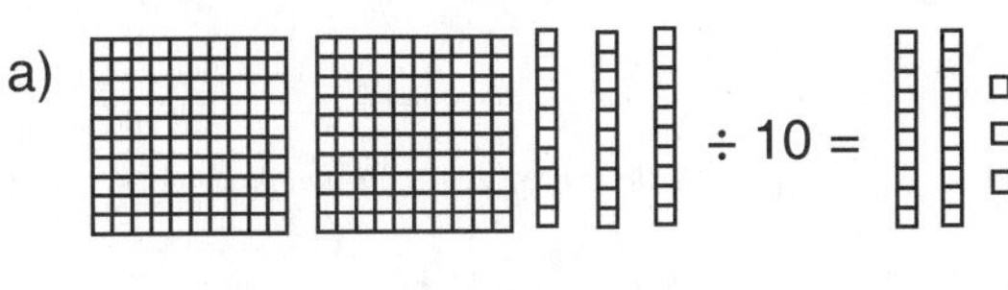 ÷ 10 =

2.3 ÷ 10 = .23

b) 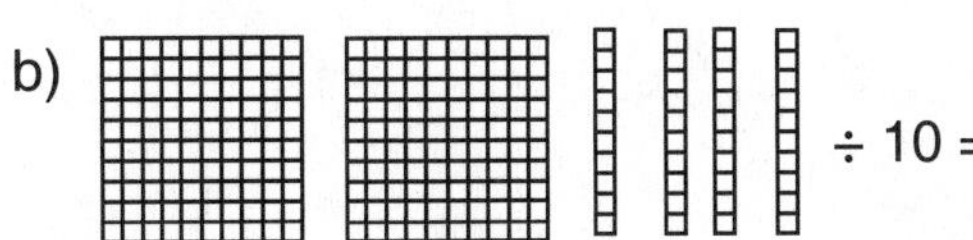 ÷ 10 =

__________ = ______

3. Shift the decimal one place to the left by drawing an arrow. (If there is no decimal, add one.)

a) 0.3 ÷ 10 = .03 b) 0.5 ÷ 10 = ______ c) 0.7 ÷ 10 = ______ d) 1.3 ÷ 10 = ______

e) 7.6 ÷ 10 = ______ f) 12.0 ÷ 10 = ______ g) 9 ÷ 10 = ______ h) 6 ÷ 10 = ______

i) 42 ÷ 10 = ______ j) 17 ÷ 10 = ______ k) .9 ÷ 10 = ______ l) 27.3 ÷ 10 = ______

4. Change the following measurements by dividing by 10.

a) 5 cm = _____ dm b) 1.7 cm = _____ dm c) 3.5 mm = _____ cm d) 2mm = _____ cm

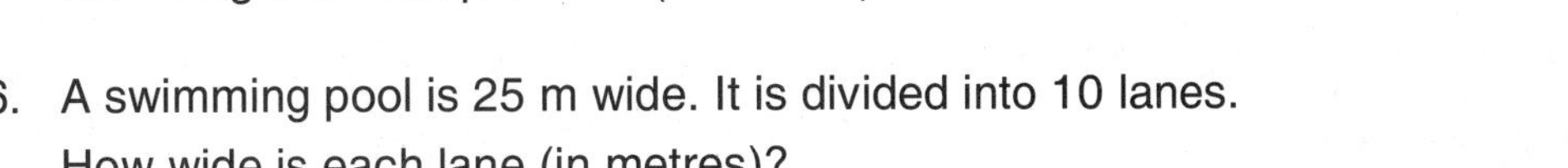

5. Sarah has 2.7 m of ribbon. She wants to cut the ribbon into 10 equal lengths. How long will each piece be (in metres)?

6. A swimming pool is 25 m wide. It is divided into 10 lanes. How wide is each lane (in metres)?

No unauthorized copying

NS5-87: Dividing Decimals by Whole Numbers

You can divide a decimal by a whole number using base ten blocks. Keep track of your work using long division. Use the hundreds block to represent 1 whole, the tens block to represent 1 tenth, and the ones block to represent 1 hundredth.

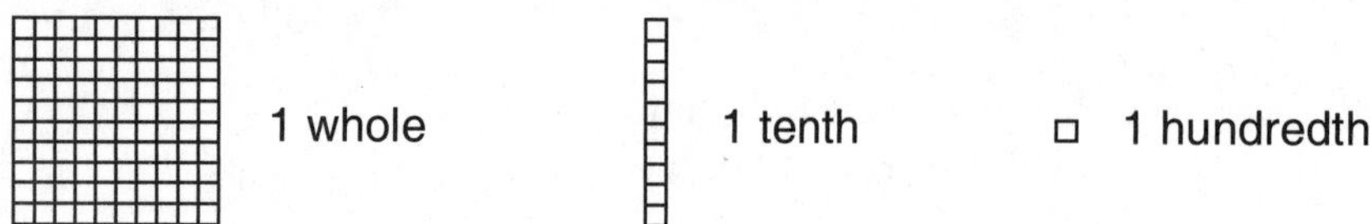

1. Find **5.12 ÷ 2** by drawing a base ten model and by long division.

Step 1: Draw a base ten model of 5.12.

Step 2: Divide the ones (hundreds blocks) into 2 equal groups.

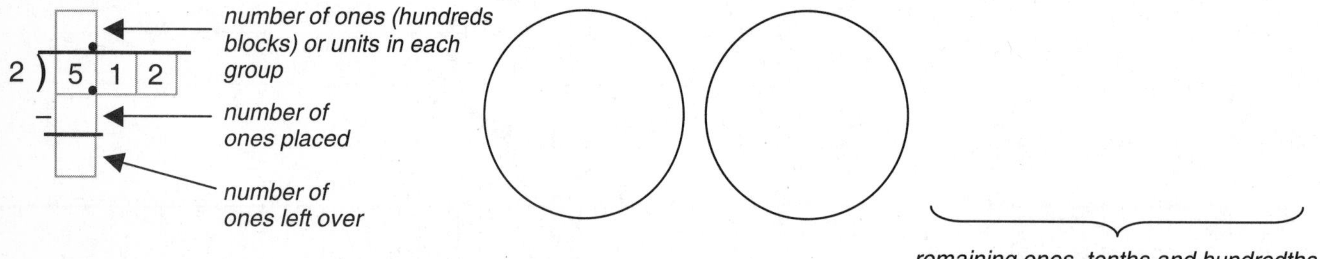

Step 3: Exchange the leftover one (hundreds blocks) for 10 tenths (tens blocks).

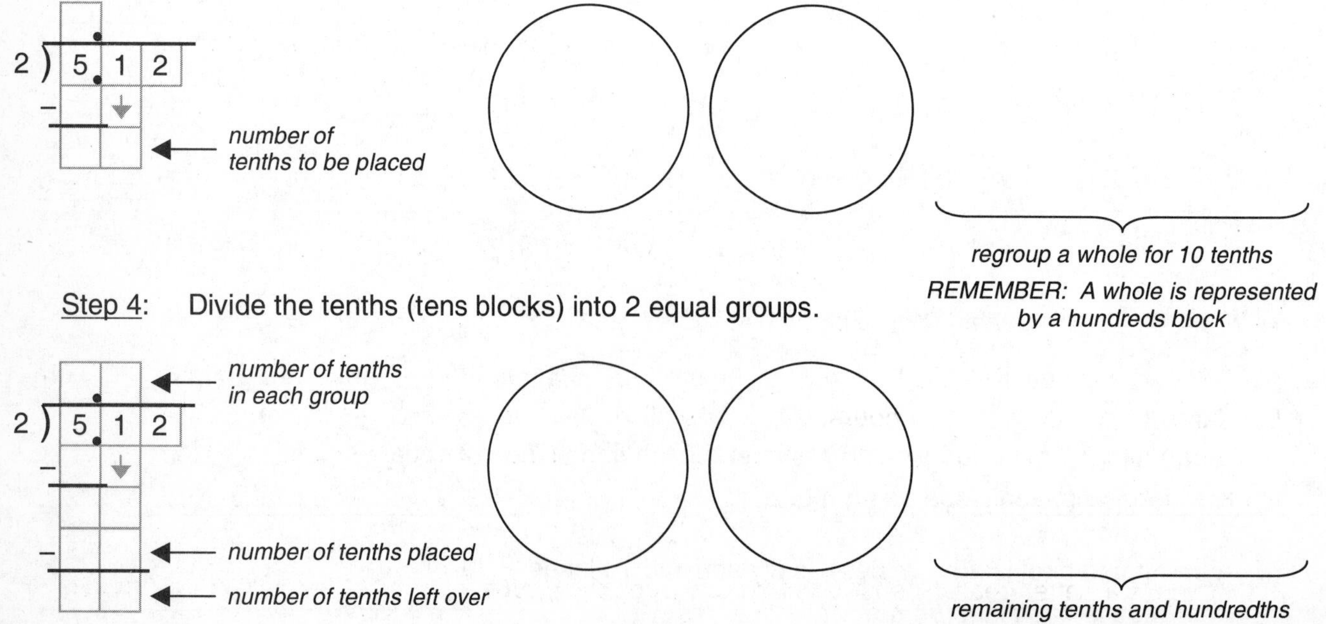

Step 4: Divide the tenths (tens blocks) into 2 equal groups.

 No unauthorized copying

Step 5: Regroup the leftover tenths (tens blocks) as 10 hundredths (ones blocks).

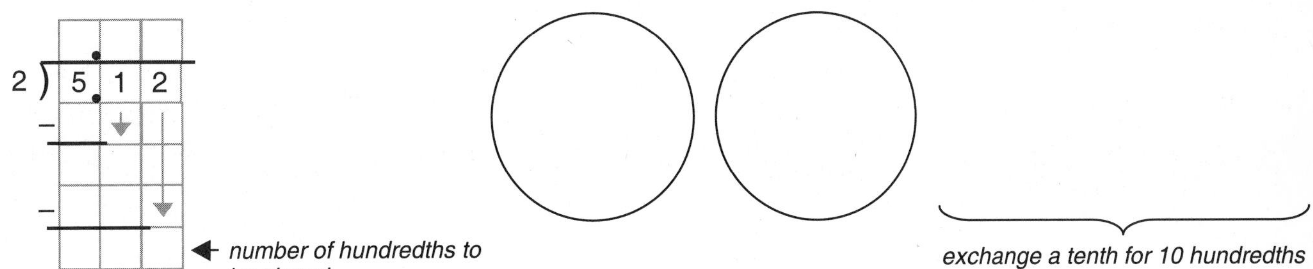

Steps 6 and 7: Divide the hundredths (ones blocks) into 2 equal groups.

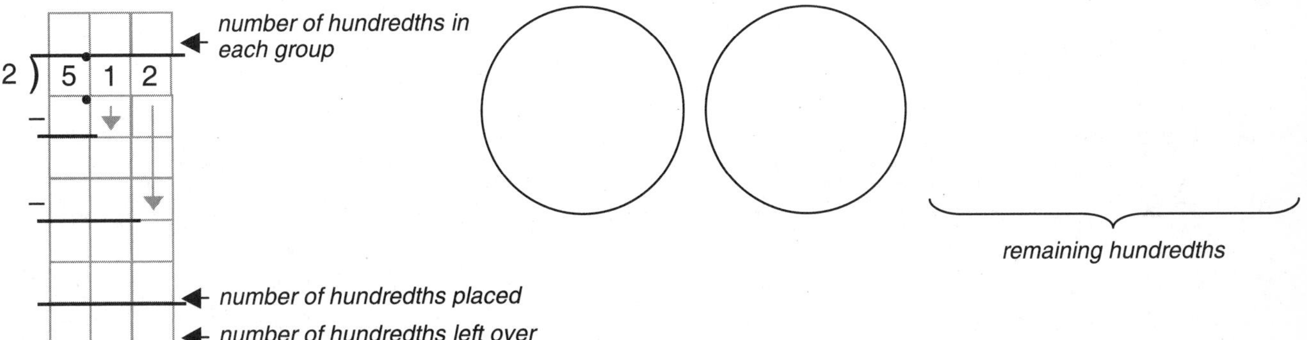

2. Divide.

a) 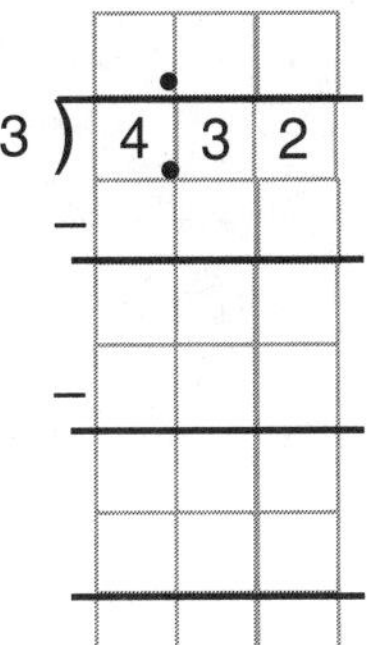

b) 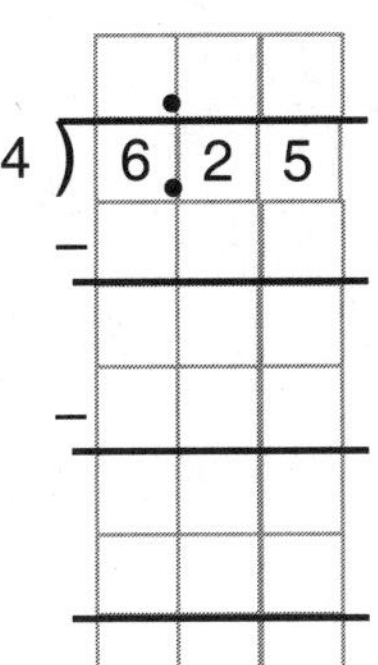

c) 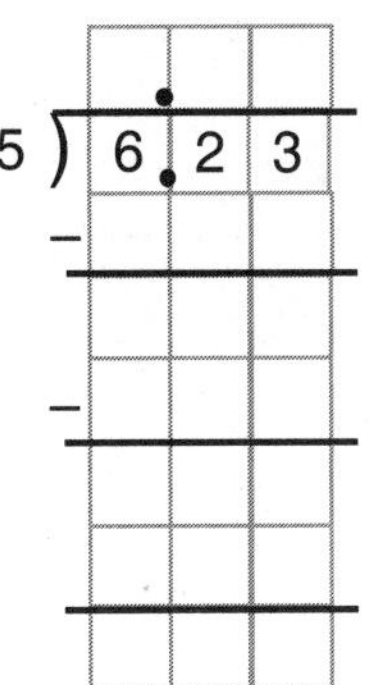

d) 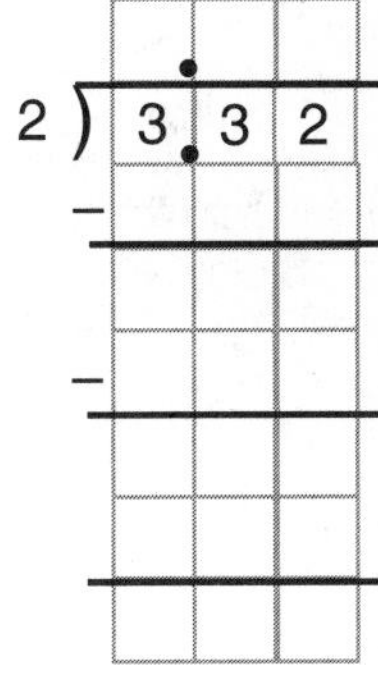

3. Divide. a) 8) 1.44 b) 7) 9.4 c) 8) 2.72 d) 9) 6.13 e) 5) 20.5

4. Five apples cost \$2.75. How much does each apple cost?

5. Karen cycled 62.4 km in 4 hours. How many kilometres did she cycle in an hour?

6. Four friends earn a total of \$29.16 shovelling snow. How much does each friend earn?

7. Which is a better deal: 6 pens for \$4.98 or 8 pens for \$6.96?

 No unauthorized copying

NS5-88: Differences of 0.1 and 0.01

1. Fill in the blanks.

a) .64 + .1 = _______ b) .35 + .1 = _______ c) .06 + .1 = _______

d) .89 + .1 = _______ e) .73 + .01 = _______ f) .40 + .01 = _______

g) 4.23 + .01 = _______ h) 2.87 + .1 = _______ i) 11.95 + .01 = _______

2. Fill in the blanks.

a) _______ is .1 more than .7

b) _______ is .1 more than 2.6

c) _______ is .1 more than 1.32

d) _______ is .1 more than .63

e) _______ is .01 more than .35

f) _______ is .01 more than .2

3. Fill in the blanks.

a) 1.35 + ______ = 1.36 b) 2.3 + ______ = 2.4 c) 3.06 – ______ = 3.05

d) 4.95 – ______ = 4.94 e) 3.7 + ______ = 4.7 f) 7.85 + ______ = 7.95

4. Fill in the missing numbers on the number lines.

a) 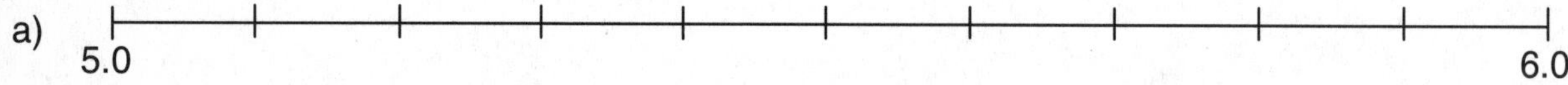

b) 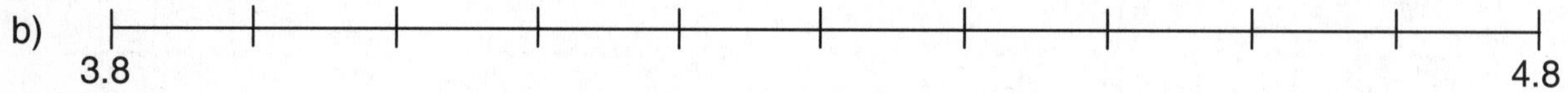

c) 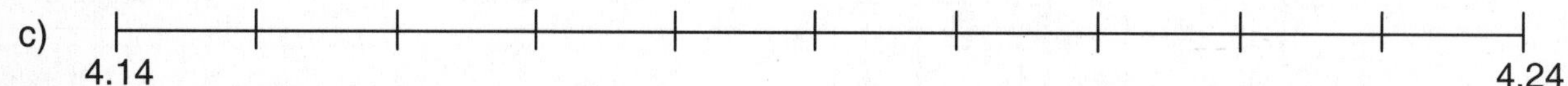

5. Continue the patterns.

a) .2, .3, .4, ______, ______, ______

b) 6.6, 6.7, 6.8, ______, ______, ______

c) 3.5, 3.6, 3.7, ______, ______, ______

d) 9.6, 9.7, 9.8, ______, ______, ______

e) 4.71, 4.72, 4.73, ______, ______, ______

f) 5.96, 5.97, 5.98, ______, ______, ______

6. Fill in the blanks.

a) 3.9 + .1 = _______ b) 4.9 + .1 = _______ c) 8.93 + .1 = _______

d) 3.79 + .01 = _______ e) 6.09 + .01 = _______ f) 7.99 + .01 = _______

No unauthorized copying

NS5-89: Decimals (Review)

The size of a unit of measurement depends on which unit has been selected as the **whole**.

A millimetre is a **tenth** of a centimetre, but it is only a **hundredth** of a decimetre.

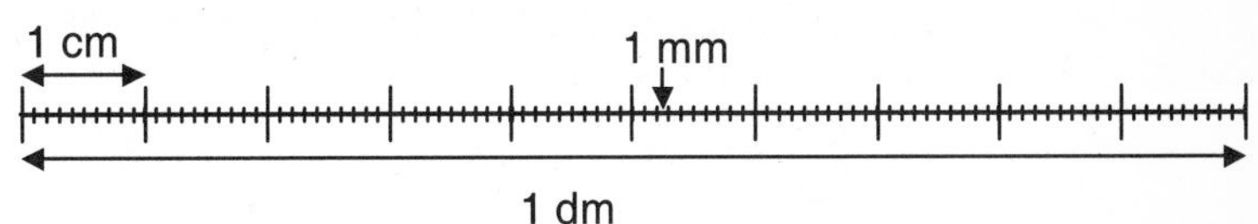

1. Draw a picture in the space provided to show 1 tenth of each whole.

a) 

1 whole 1 tenth

b) 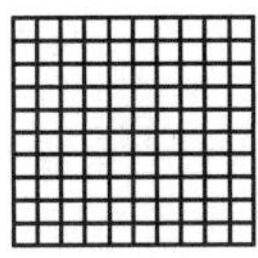

1 whole 1 tenth

c) 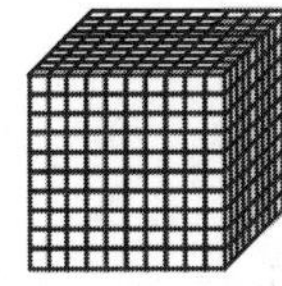

1 whole 1 tenth

2. Write each measurement as a fraction then as a decimal.

a) 1 cm = $\frac{1}{10}$ dm = .1 dm

b) 100 cm = ☐ dm = ______ dm

c) 1 mm = ☐ cm = ______ cm

d) 16 mm = ☐ cm = ______ cm

e) 77 mm = ☐ dm = ______ dm

f) 83 cm = ☐ m = ______ m

3. Add by first changing the <u>smaller unit</u> into a decimal in the <u>larger unit</u>.

a) 4 cm + 9.2 dm = 0.4 dm + 9.2 dm = 9.6 dm

b) 6 cm + 2.9 dm = ______________________

c) 9 mm + 8.4 cm = ______________________

d) 33 cm + 1.64 m = ______________________

4. What amount is represented by the tenths digits?

a) 7.52 m 5 dm

b) $6.29 ______________

c) 2.32 m ______________

d) 3.7 million ______________

e) 2.8 thousand ______________

f) 5.35 dm ______________

5. Round each decimal to the nearest tenth.
HINT: Underline the hundredths digit first. It will tell you whether you round up or down.

a) .2<u>5</u> ______

b) .32 ______

c) .68 ______

d) 1.35 ______

6. Round each decimal to the nearest whole number. **HINT: Underline the tenths digit first.**

a) 3.<u>2</u>5 ______

b) 4.13 ______

c) 2.95 ______

d) 8.3 ______

No unauthorized copying

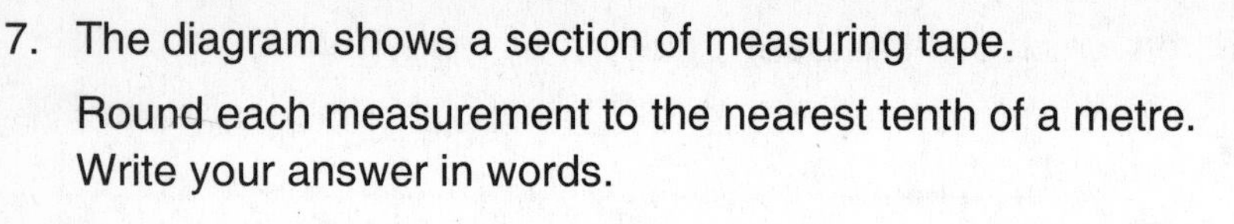

7. The diagram shows a section of measuring tape.
   Round each measurement to the nearest tenth of a metre.
   Write your answer in words.

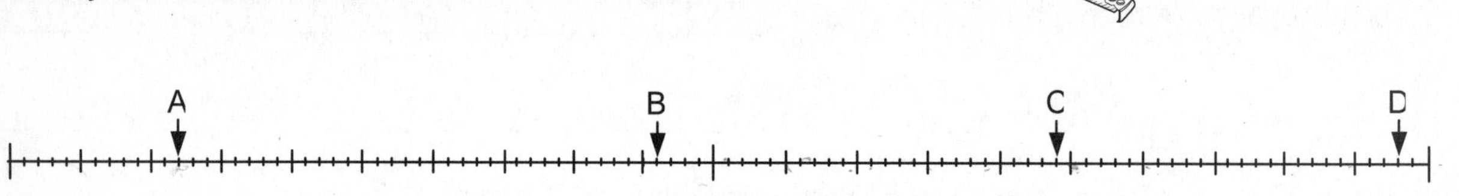

A: Five and two tenths **B:** ______

C: ______ **D:** ______

8. Write a decimal for each description.

   a) Between 3.52 and 3.57: __ . __ __ b) Between 1.70 and 1.80: __ . __ __

   c) Between 12.65 and 12.7: __ __ . __ __ d) Between 2.6 and 2.7: __ . __ __

9. Add.

   a) 3000 + 200 + 7 + 0.02 = ______ b) 10 000 + 500 + 20 + 0.1 + 0.05 = ______

   c) 6000 + 300 + 8 + 0.1 = ______ d) 400 + 7 + .02 = ______

10. Write < or > to show which decimal is greater.

   a) 3.7 ☐ 3.5 b) 2.32 ☐ 2.37 c) 1.7 ☐ 1.69 d) 0.5 ☐ 0.55

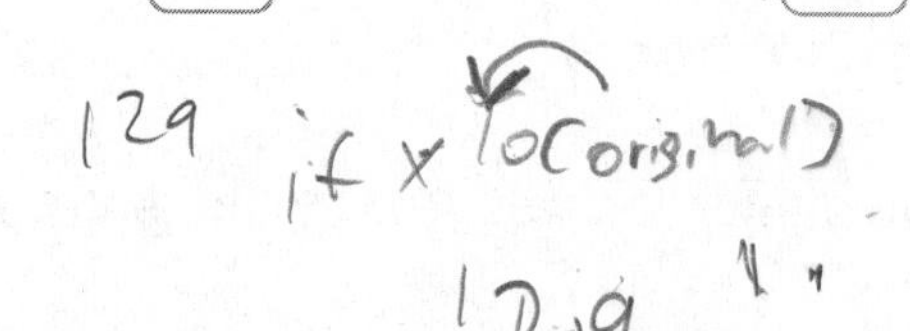

11. If you divide a number by 10, the result is 12.9.
    What was the original number? Explain.

12. The Olympic gold medal throw for the shot put in 2004 was 21.16 m.
    The bronze throw was 21.07 m.

    a) Was the difference in the throws more or less than 0.1 m?

    b) Round both throws to the nearest tenth.
       What is the difference in the rounded amounts?

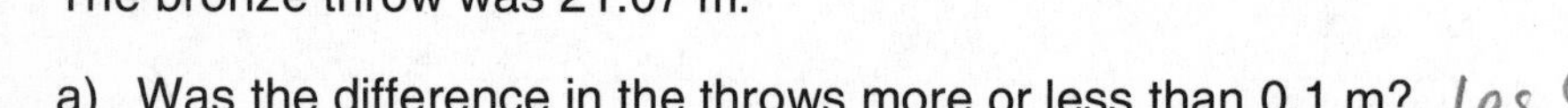

    c) Make up two throws which would round to the same number (when rounded to the tenths).

    d) Why are Olympic shot put throws measured so precisely?

NS5-90: Word Problems with Decimals

Answer the following questions in your notebook.

1. Giant Kelp is the fastest growing ocean plant. It can grow 0.67 m in a day. How much could it grow in a week?

2. Lichen grows slowly at a rate of 3.4 mm a year. Could it grow 1 cm in 3 years?

3. How much do 7 books cost at $8.99 per book?

4. Under which deal do you pay less for 1 pen: 4 pens for $2.96 or 6 pens for $4.99?

5. On a map, 1 cm represents 15 km. Two towns are 2.3 cm apart on the map. How far apart are the towns?

6.
$$\begin{array}{r} 6 : 4\ 2 \\ +\ 7 . 1\ 9 \\ \hline 7\ 8 . 3\ 2 \end{array}$$

Tim added the numbers on his calculator.

What mistake do you think Tim made pressing the buttons on the calculator?

7. $0.45 means 4 dimes and 5 pennies.
Why do we use decimal notation for money?
What is a dime a tenth of?
What is a penny a hundredth of?

8. Here are the greatest lengths of some sea creatures.
   a) How much longer than the great white shark is the blue whale?
   b) About how many times longer than the turtle is the great white shark?
   c) About how long would 3 ocean sunfish be if they swam in a row?

Animal	Length (m)
Blue Whale	34
Great White Shark	7.9
Pacific Leather Back Turtle	2.1
Ocean Sunfish	2.9

No unauthorized copying

NS5-91: Unit Rates

A **rate** is a comparison of two quantities in different units.

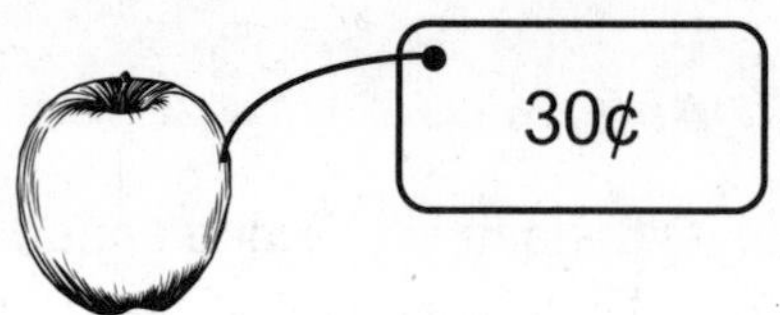

In a **unit rate**, one of the quantities is equal to one.
For instance, "1 apple costs 30¢" is a unit rate.

---

1. Fill in the missing information.

a) 1 book costs $5

2 books cost _____

3 books cost _____

4 books cost _____

b) 1 ticket costs 6¢

2 tickets cost _____

3 tickets cost _____

4 tickets cost _____

c) 1 apple costs 20¢

2 apples cost _____

3 apples cost _____

4 apples cost _____

d) 30 km in 1 hour

____ km in 3 hours

e) $15 allowance in 1 week

____ allowance in 4 weeks

f) 1 teacher for 24 students

3 teachers for ____

g) 1 kg of rice for 12 cups of water

5 kg of rice for ______ cups of water

2. In the pictures below, 1 centimetre represents 60 metres.
Use a ruler to find the actual height of each tower.

a) Height in cm ______

Height in m _______

b) Height in cm ______

Height in m _______

c) Height in cm ______

Height in m _______

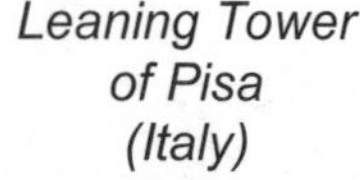

Leaning Tower of Pisa (Italy)

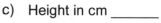

Eiffel Tower (France)

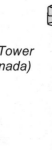

CN Tower (Canada)

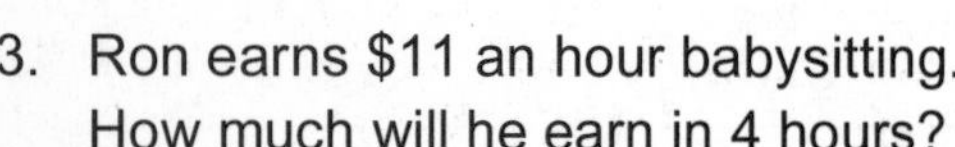

3. Ron earns $11 an hour babysitting.
How much will he earn in 4 hours?

____

4. Tina earns $15 an hour cutting lawns.
How much will she earn in 8 hours?

____

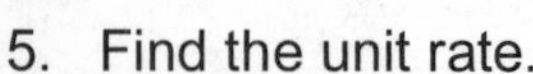

5. Find the unit rate.

a) 2 books cost $10
1 book costs ________

b) 4 mangoes cost $12
1 mango costs ______

c) 6 cans of juice cost $12
1 can costs ______

 No unauthorized copying

NS5-92: Scale Diagrams

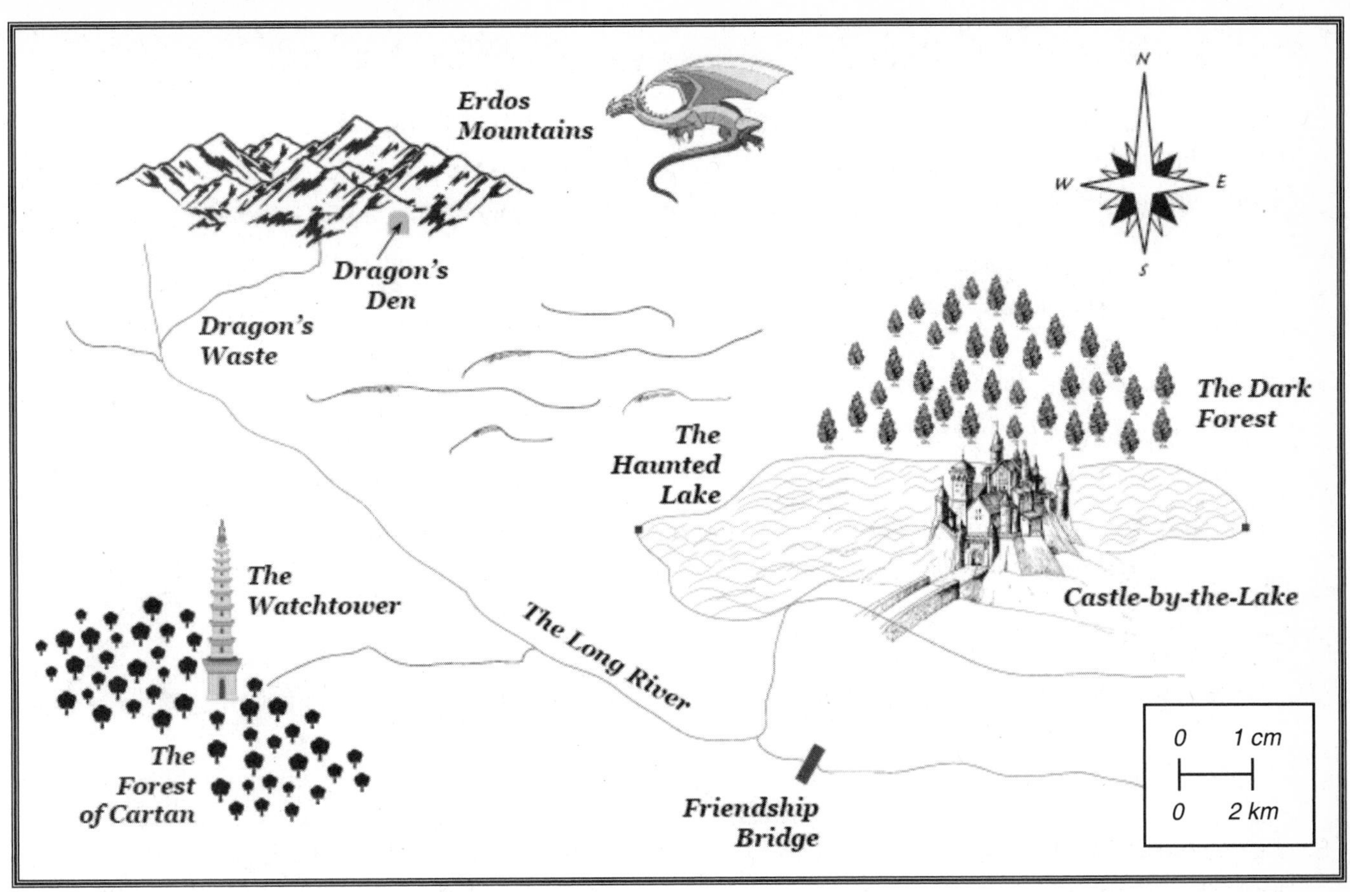

1. Sharon has drawn a map of a fantasy world. Use the scale to answer the questions below.

   a) How many kilometres must the dragon fly from its den to reach Castle-by-the-Lake's entrance?

   ____

   b) How long is the Haunted Lake (from East to West)?

   ____

   c) How wide is the Dark Forest (from North to South)?

   ____

   d) How far must a knight ride to get from the Watchtower to the entrance of Castle-by-the-Lake? (Assume the only way across the river is by Friendship Bridge.)

   ____

2. On a map that Jacob drew, 2 cm = 50 km.
   How many kilometres would each of the following distances on the map represent?

   a) 8 cm: _____ b) 10 cm: _____ c) 1 cm: _____ d) 5 cm: _____ e) 9 cm: _____

 No unauthorized copying

NS5-93: Word Problems

Answer the following questions in your notebook.

1. On a 3-day canoe trip, Pamela canoed 25.5 km on the first day, 32.6 km on the second, and 17.25 km on the third.

   a) How far did she canoe in total?

   b) What was the average distance she paddled each day?

   c) If she canoes for 6 hours each day, about how many kilometres does she travel each hour?

   d) Pamela's canoe can hold 100 kg. Pamela weighs 45 kg, her tent weighs 10 kg and her supplies weigh 15 kg. How much more weight can the canoe carry?

2. Jessica has 78 beads.
   She gave her 3 friends 23 beads each.
   How many did she have left over?

3. James bought a slice of pizza for $3.21, a video game for $15.87, a bottle of pop for $1.56, and a bag of chips for $1.37.
   How much change did he get from $25.00?

4. Six classes went skating.
   There are 24 students in each class.
   Each bus holds 30 students.
   The teachers ordered 4 buses.
   Will there be enough room?
   Explain.

5. Janice earned $28.35 on Monday. On Thursday, she spent $17.52 for a shirt.
   She now has $32.23.
   How much money did she have before she started work Monday?
   HINT: Work backwards. How much money did she have before she bought the shirt?

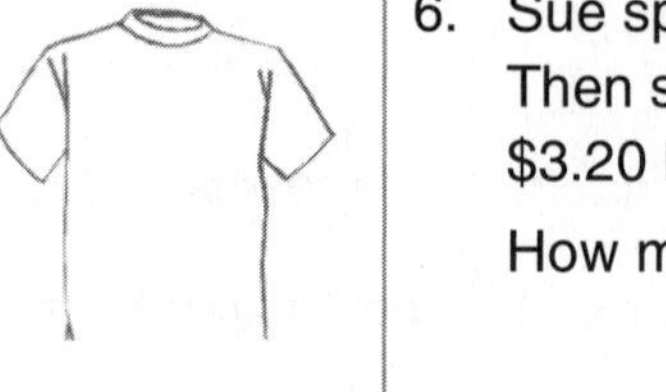

6. Sue spent half of her money on a book. Then she spent $1.25 on a pen. She has $3.20 left.
   How much did she start with?

   $4.45

7. Anne travelled 12.5 m in 10 steps.
   How many metres was each step?

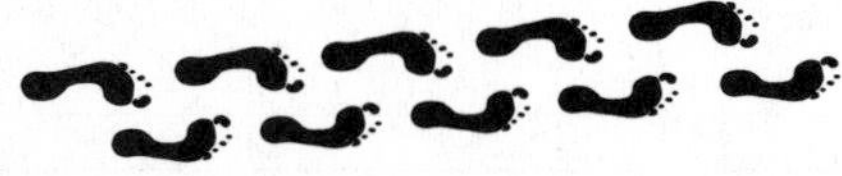

8. Gravity on Jupiter is 2.3 times as strong as gravity on Earth.
   How much more would a 7 kg dog weigh on Jupiter than on Earth?

9. Ruby lives 2.4 km from the park. She walks to the park and back each day.
   How many kilometres does she walk to and from the park in a week?

10. Encke's Comet appears in our sky every 3.3 years. It was first seen in 1786.
    When was the last time the comet was seen in the 1700s (i.e. before 1800)?
    Show your work.

No unauthorized copying

ME5-1: Centimetres

A **centimetre** is a unit of measurement for length (or height, or thickness).

1. Measure the length of each line using your ruler.

   a)  _____ cm

   b) _____ cm

   c) _____ cm

2. Measure the length of each object using your ruler.

   a) _____ cm

   b) _____ cm

3. Measure all the sides of each shape.

   a)

   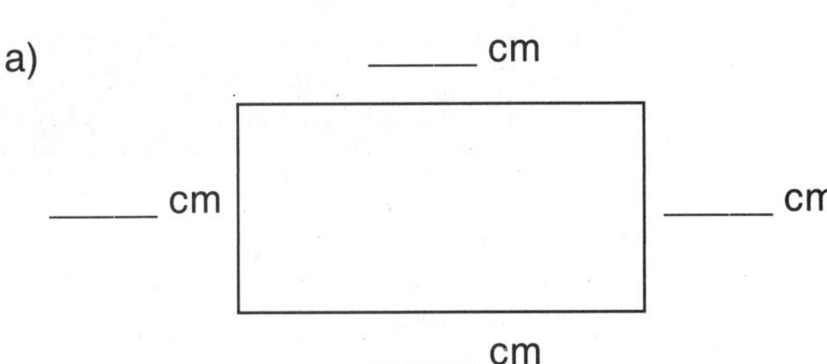

   _____ cm

   _____ cm   _____ cm

   _____ cm

   b)

   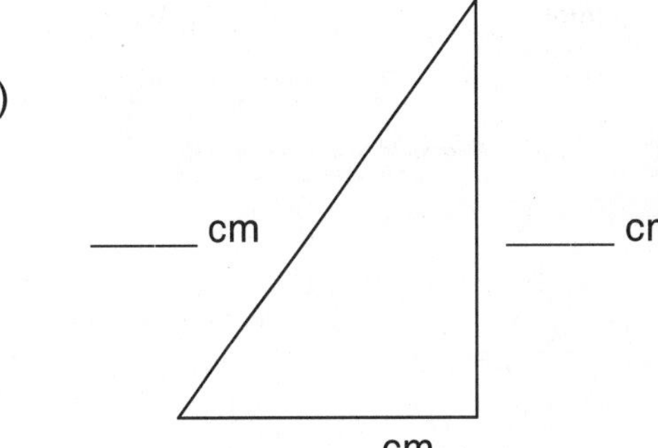

   _____ cm   _____ cm

   _____ cm

4. Draw two arrows on each ruler that are the given distance apart.

   a) Two arrows 4 cm apart.

   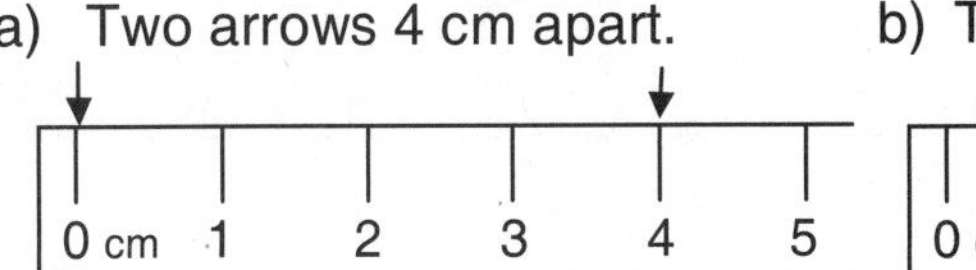

   b) Two arrows 3 cm apart.

   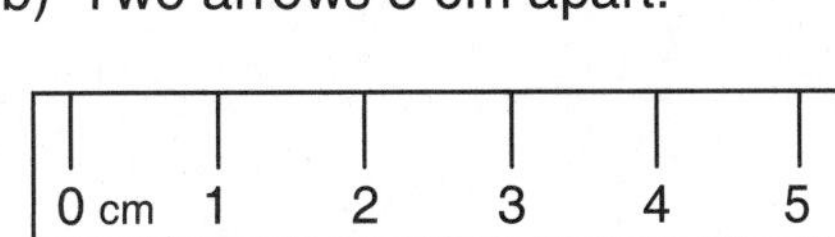

   c) Two arrows 5 cm apart.

   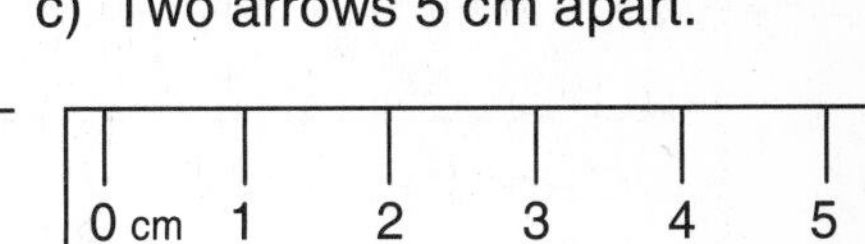

5. Draw the following objects.

   a) a line 3 cm long

   b) a line 5 cm long

   c) a ladybug 1 cm long

   d) a shoe 4 cm long

6. Your index finger is about 1 cm wide. Measure an object on your desk with your index finger:

   My ______________________________ is approx. ________ cm long.

7. How far do you need to spread your fingers to make 10 cm?
   Use your hand to find the approximate length of your desk in cm.
   Then measure the exact length of your desk in cm:

   Approximate length: _______________ Exact length: _______________

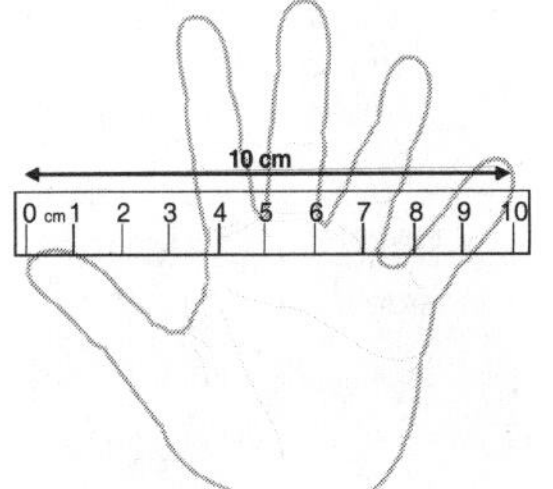

No unauthorized copying

ME5-2: Millimetres and Centimetres

If you look at a ruler with **millimetre** markings, you can see that 1 cm is equal to 10 mm.

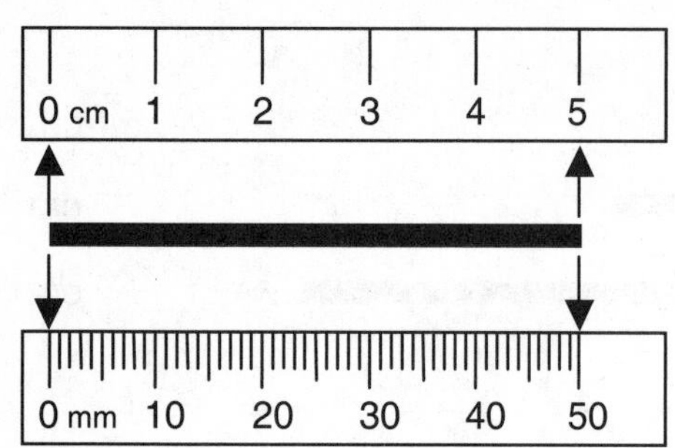

How long is the line in cm? How long is it in mm?

The line is _____ cm long, or _____ mm long.

To convert a measurement from cm to mm, we have to multiply the measurement by _____.

---

1. Your index finger is about 1 cm or 10 mm wide. Measure the objects below using your index finger. Then convert your measurement to mm.

a) 

The paper clip measures about _____ index fingers.

So, the paper clip is approximately _____ mm long.

b) 

The rectangle measures about _____ index fingers.

So, the rectangle is approximately _____ mm long.

2. Measure the distance between the two arrows on each ruler.

a) 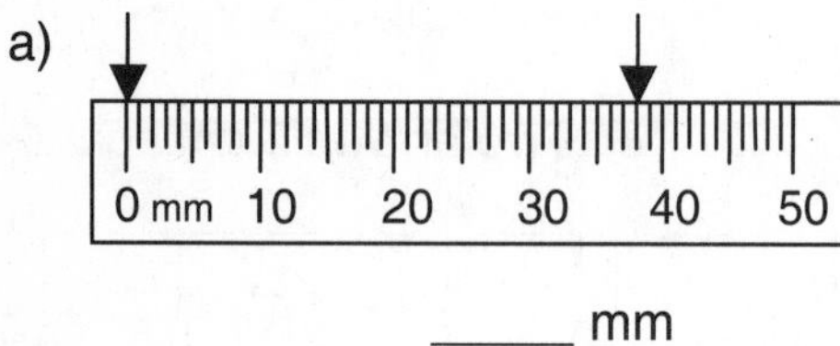

_____ mm

b) 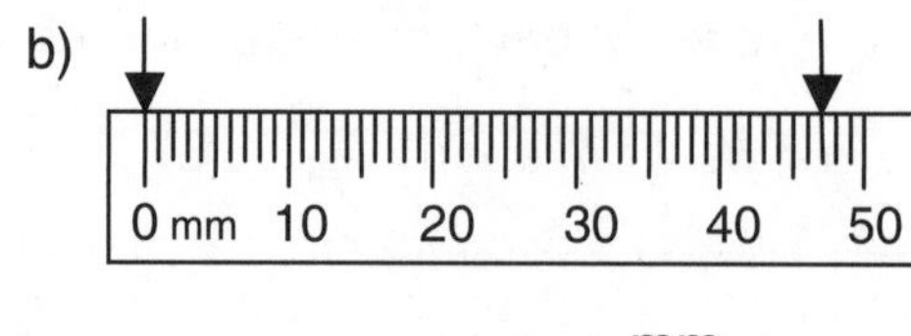

_____ mm

3. Measure the sides of the rectangle in cm.
Then measure the distance between the two diagonal corners in cm and mm.
NOTE: Your answer in cm will be a decimal.

_____ cm

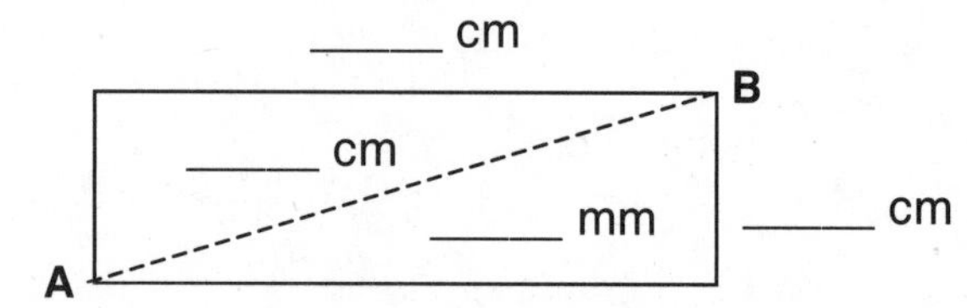

_____ cm

4. Use a ruler to draw the following objects to the exact millimetre.

a) A line 20 mm long.

b) A line 52 mm long.

c) A beetle 35 mm long.

d) A pencil 70 mm long.

 No unauthorized copying

ME5-2: Millimetres and Centimetres *(continued)*

5. Estimate whether each line is <u>less</u> than 40 mm or <u>more</u> than 40 mm.
   Place a checkmark in the appropriate column.
   Then measure the actual length.

	Less than 40 mm	More than 40 mm
a) ▬▬▬▬▬		
b) ▬▬		
c) ▬▬▬▬▬▬▬▬		

a) _____ mm b) _____ mm c) _____ mm

6. To change a measurement from centimetres (cm) into millimetres (mm), what should you <u>multiply</u> the measurement by?

____

7. Fill in the numbers missing from the following charts.

mm	cm
	13
	32

mm	cm
	8
	18

mm	cm
	213
	170

mm	cm
	9
	567

8. To change a measurement from mm to cm, what should you <u>divide</u> by? _______

9. Change the measurements.

a) 460 mm = ____ cm b) 60 mm = ____ cm c) 580 mm = ____ cm

10. Circle the greater measurement in each pair.
HINT: Convert one of the measurements so that both units are the same. Show your work.

a) 5 cm 70 mm

b) 83 cm 910 mm

c) 45 cm 53 mm

d) 2 cm 12 mm

e) 60 cm 6200 mm

11. Draw a rectangle 2 cm high and 50 mm long.

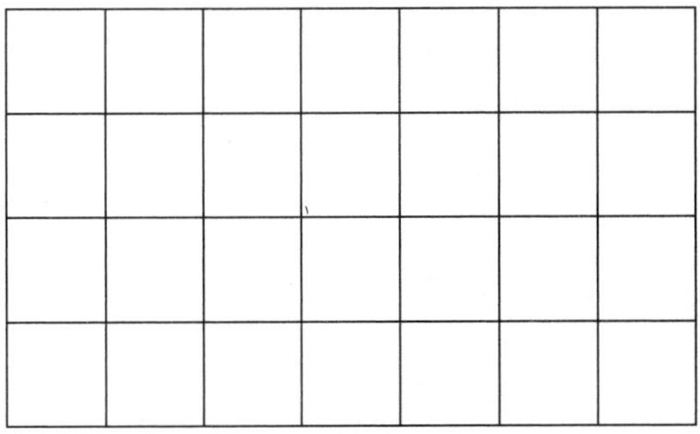

 No unauthorized copying

ME5-2: Millimetres and Centimetres *(continued)*

12. Using your ruler, draw a second line so that the pair of lines are the given distance apart. Complete the chart.

	Distance apart	
	in cm	in mm
| |	4	40
|	3	
|		80

13. In the space provided, draw a line that is between:

a) 4 and 5 cm.

How long is your line in mm? _______

b) 6 and 7 cm.

How long is your line in mm? _______

14. Write a measurement in mm that is between:

a) 7 and 8 cm: __________ mm   b) 27 and 28 cm: __________ mm

15. Write a measurement in a whole number of cm that is between:

a) 67 mm and 75 mm: _____ cm   b) 27 mm and 39 mm: _______   c) 52 mm and 7 cm: _______

16. Draw a line that is a whole number of centimetres long and is between:

a) 35 and 45 mm   b) 55 and 65 mm   c) 27 and 33 mm

17. Carl has a set of sticks: some are 5 cm long and some are 3 cm long.
The picture (not drawn to scale) shows how he could line up the sticks to measure 14 cm:

5 cm   3 cm   3 cm   3 cm

Draw a sketch to show how Carl could measure each length by lining the sticks up end to end.

a) 8 cm   b) 11 cm   c) 13 cm   d) 26 cm   e) 19 cm   f) 17 cm

BONUS

g) Use two 5 cm sticks and one 3 cm stick to draw a line 7 cm long.

 No unauthorized copying

ME5-3: Decimetres

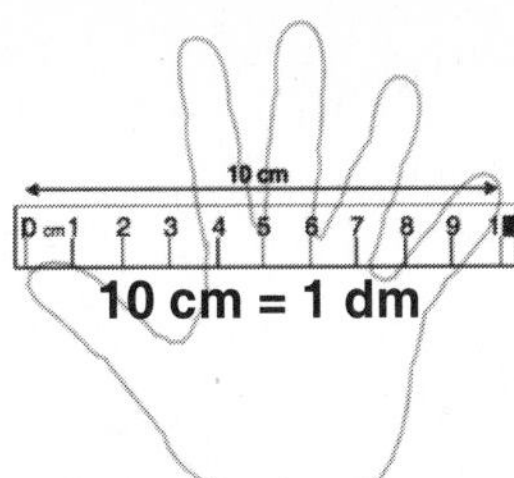

If you spread your fingers wide, your hand is about 10 cm wide:
10 centimetres are equal to 1 **decimetre** (dm).

So there are 10 **cm** in 1 **dm**.

(Similarly, 10 **mm** is equal to 1 **cm**.)

---

1. Place a checkmark in the correct column.
HINT: Remember that 1 dm = 10 cm.

	Less than 1 dm	More than 1 dm
My arm		
A paperclip		
My pencil		
The height of the classroom door		

2. To change a measurement from decimetres (dm) to centimetres (cm), what should you multiply by?

____

3. To change a measurement from cm to dm, what should you divide by?

____

4. Find the numbers missing from the following charts.

a)

cm	dm
150	15
	23
	32

b)

cm	dm
90	
	510
400	

c)

cm	dm
610	
	1
780	

5. Draw a line that is between 1 and 2 decimetres long.

a) How long is your line in cm? ___________ b) How long is your line in mm? ___________

6. Write a measurement in cm that is between:

a) 4 and 5 dm ___________ b) 3 and 4 dm ___________ c) 7 and 8 dm ___________

7. Write a measurement in dm that is between:

a) 72 and 82 cm ___________ b) 27 and 35 cm ___________ c) 68 and 74 cm ___________

There are 10 mm in 1 cm. There are 10 cm in 1 dm. How many mm are in 1 dm? Explain.

No unauthorized copying

ME5-4: Metres and Kilometres

A **metre** is a unit of measurement for **length** (or **height** or **thickness**) equal to 100 cm.

A metre stick is 100 cm long. 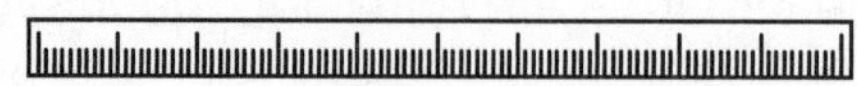

A **kilometre** is a unit of measurement for length equal to 1000 metres.

Here are some measurements you can use for estimating in metres.

about 2 metres

The height of a (tall) adult

about 2 metres

The length of an adult's bicycle

about 10 metres

The length of a school bus

about 100 metres

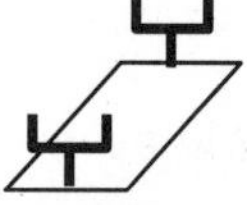

The length of a football field

1. How many adults do you think could lie head to foot across your classroom? ________________

2. a) About how many school buses high is your school? ____________________

   b) About how high is your school? ____________________

3. A small city block is about 100 m long.

   Name a place you can walk to from your home. ____

   Approximately how many metres away from your home is the place you named? ________________

4. Change these measurements into metres.

   a) 3 km = _________ b) 6 km = _________ c) 7 km = _________ d) 12 km = _________

5. A football field is about 100 m long. About how many football fields long is a kilometre?

   ____

6. You can travel 1 km if you walk for 15 minutes at a regular speed.
   Name a place that is about 1 km from your school.

   ____

7. The CN Tower is 531 metres tall.
   About how many CN Towers, laid end to end, would make a kilometre?
   Explain.

No unauthorized copying

ME5-5: Changing Units

1. Finish the table by following the pattern.

m	1	2	3	4	5	6
dm	10	20				
cm	100	200				
mm	1000	2000				

2. What would you multiply by to change each measurement?

a) m to cm ________ b) m to mm ________ c) cm to mm ________

3. Convert the following measurements.

m	cm
8	
70	

M	Mm
5	
17	

cm	mm
4	
121	

dm	cm
32	
5	

4. Kathy measured her bedroom door with both a metre stick and a measuring tape.

- When she measured with the metre stick, the height of the door was 2 m with 25 cm.
- When she measured with the measuring tape, she got a measurement of 225 cm.

Was there a difference in the two measurements? Explain.

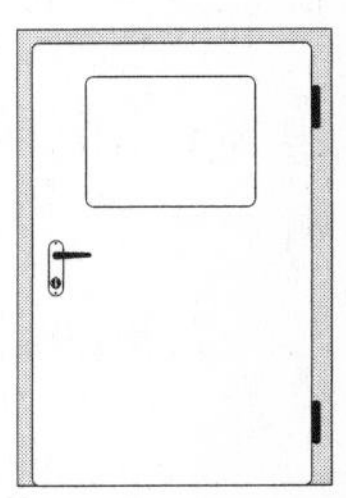

____

____

____

5. Convert the measurement given in cm to a measurement using multiple units.

a) 423 cm = 4 m 23 cm b) 514 cm = ___ m ____ cm c) 627 cm = ___ m ____ cm

d) 673 cm = ___ m _____ cm e) 381 cm = ___ m ____ cm f) 203 cm = ___ m ____ cm

6. Convert the following multiple units of measurements to a single unit.

a) 2 m 83 cm = 283 cm b) 3 m 65 cm = _____ cm c) 4 m 85 cm = _____ cm

d) 9 m 47 cm = _____ cm e) 7 m 4 cm = _____ cm f) 6 m 40 cm = _____ cm

7. Change the following measurements to multiple units then to decimal notation.

a) 546 cm = 5 m 46 cm = 5.46 m b) 217 cm = ______ m ______ cm = ______ m

c) 783 cm = ______ m ______ cm = ______ m d) 648 cm = ______ m ______ cm = ______ m

8. Why do we use the same decimal notation for dollars and cents and for metres and centimetres?

No unauthorized copying

ME5-6: Changing Units (Advanced)

1. Measure the line below in mm, cm, and dm.

_______ mm _______ cm _______ dm

a) Which of the units (mm, cm, or dm) is largest? __________ smallest? __________

b) Which unit did you need more of to measure the line, the larger unit or the smaller unit?

____

c) To change a measurement from a **larger** to a **smaller** unit, do you need:

more of the smaller units or **fewer** of the smaller units?

____

2. Fill in the missing numbers.

a) 1 cm = ______ mm b) 1 dm = ______ cm

c) 1 dm = ______ mm d) 1 m = ______ dm

e) 1 m = ______ cm f) 1 m = ______ mm

Units **decrease** in size going **down** the stairway:

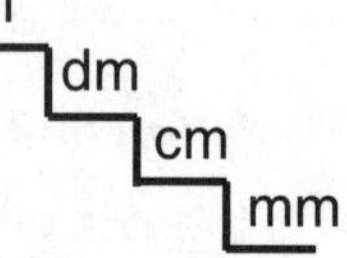

- 1 step down = 10 × smaller
- 2 steps down = 100 × smaller
- 3 steps down = 1 000 × smaller

3. Change the measurements below by following the steps. The first one has been done for you.

a) Change 3.5 cm to mm

i) The new units are 10 times smaller

ii) So I need 10 times more units

iii) So I multiply by 10

3.5 cm = 35 mm

b) Change 2.7 cm to mm

i) The new units are _______ times _______

ii) So I need _______ times _______ units

iii) So I _______ by _______

2.7 cm = _______ mm

c) Change 6.3 dm to cm

i) The new units are _______ times _______

ii) So I need _______ times _______ units

iii) So I multiply by ______

6.3 dm = _______ cm

d) Change 3 m to cm

i) The new units are _______ times _______

ii) So I need ______ times ______ units

iii) So I ______ by ______

3 m = _______ cm

 No unauthorized copying

e) Change 4 m to dm

i) The new units are _______ times _______

ii) So I need _______ times _______ units

iii) So I _______ by _______

4 m = _______ dm

f) Change 17.3 cm to mm

i) The new units are _______ times _______

ii) So I need _______ times _______ units

iii) So I _______ by _______

17.3 cm = _______ mm

g) Change 5.2 cm to mm

i) The new units are _______ times _______

ii) So I need _______ times _______ units

iii) So I _______ by _______

5.2 cm = _______ mm

h) Change 2.14 dm to mm

i) The new units are _______ times _______

ii) So I need _______ times _______ units

iii) So I _______ by _______

2.14 dm = _______ mm

4. Change the units by following the steps in Question 3 mentally.

a) 4 m = _________ dm b) 1.3 dm = _________ mm c) 20 cm = _________ mm

5. Order the fern leaves from longest to shortest.
(Express each measurement in the smallest unit first.)

Fern	Length of leaf	In smallest units
Oak Fern	18 cm	
Ostrich Fern	1.5 m	
Bracken Fern	90 cm	
Royal Fern	1.30 m	

1. ______________________________
2. ______________________________
3. ______________________________
4. ______________________________

6. Is 362 mm longer or shorter than 20 cm?
How do you know?

7. A fence is made of 4 parts each 32 cm long.
Is the fence longer or shorter than a metre?

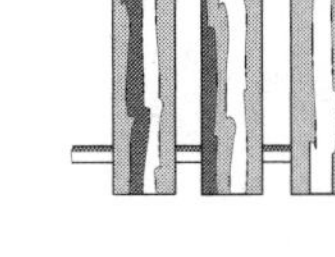

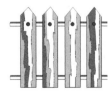

8. A decimetre of ribbon costs 5¢.
How much will 90 cm cost?

9. Michelle says that to change 6 m 80 cm to metres, you multiply the 6 by 100 and then add 80.
Is Michelle correct? Why does Michelle multiply by 100?

 No unauthorized copying

ME5-7: Ordering & Assigning Appropriate Units

1. Match the word with the symbol. Then match the object with the appropriate unit of measurement.

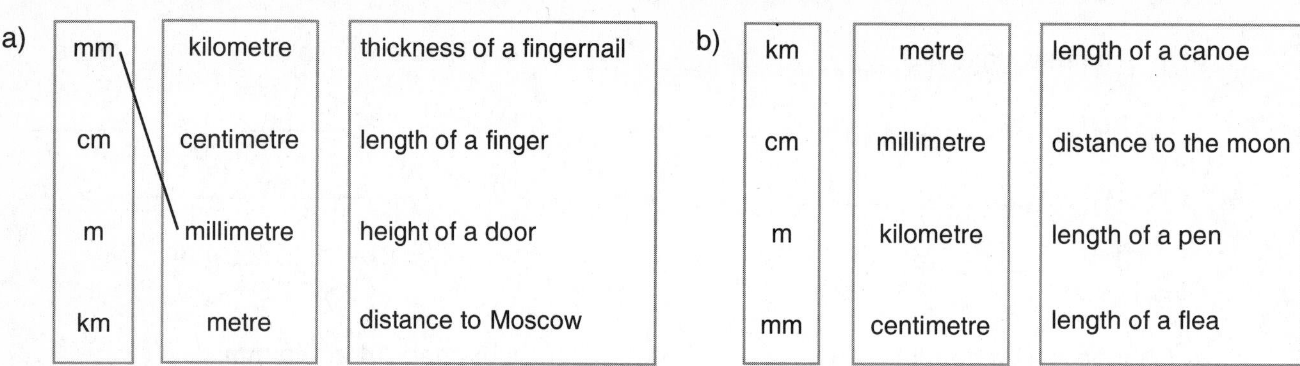

a)

mm	kilometre	thickness of a fingernail
cm	centimetre	length of a finger
m	millimetre	height of a door
km	metre	distance to Moscow

b)

km	metre	length of a canoe
cm	millimetre	distance to the moon
m	kilometre	length of a pen
mm	centimetre	length of a flea

2. Circle the unit of measurement that makes the statement correct:

   a) A very tall adult is about 2 **dm** / **m** tall.

   b) The width of your hand is close to 1 **dm** / **cm**.

   c) The Calgary Tower is 191 **cm** / **m** tall.

3. Julie measured some objects, but she forgot to include the units. Add the appropriate unit.

   a) bed: 180 ______ b) car: 2 ______ c) hat: 25 ______

   d) toothbrush: 16 ______ e) driveway: 11 ______

4. Which unit of measurement (mm, cm, m or km) would make the statement correct?

   a) A fast walker can walk 1 ______ in 10 minutes.

   b) The length of your leg is about 70 ______ .

   c) A great white shark can grow up to 4 ______ long.

   d) A postcard is about 150 ______ long.

   e) The Trans-Canada Highway from Newfoundland to British Columbia is 7604 ______ long.

   f) Niagara Falls is 48 ______ high.

   g) A porcupine can grow up to 80 ______ long.

5. Name an object in your classroom that has:

   a) a thickness of about 20 mm: ______________________

   b) a height of about 2 m: ______________________

No unauthorized copying

ME5-7: Ordering & Assigning Appropriate Units *(continued)*

6. Order the lengths of the tails from longest to shortest.

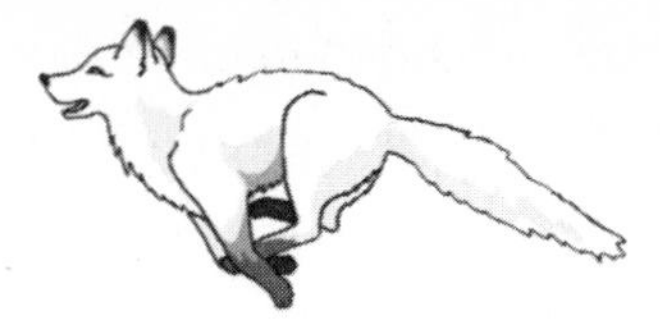

Animal	Length of tail	In smallest units
Red Fox	5.5 dm	
Beaver	40 cm	
Black Bear	12 cm	
Grey Squirrel	2.3 dm	

1. ______________________
2. ______________________
3. ______________________
4. ______________________

7. The number line is a decimetre long. Mark each measurement on the number line with an arrow as shown.

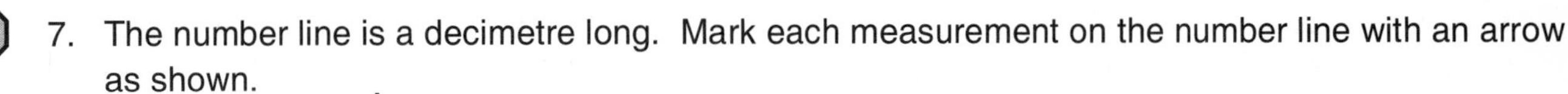

A 12 mm **B** 35 mm **C** 2.0 cm **D** 49 mm **E** 9.9 cm **F** 5.7 cm **G** 6.3 cm

8. Mark the approximate location of each measurement with an X.

0 dm |—|—|—|—|—|—|—|—|—|—| 1 dm

A 3 cm **B** 5 cm **C** 25 mm **D** 9 cm **E** 4.5 cm **F** 8.2 cm **G** .7 cm

0 km |—|—|—|—|—|—|—|—|—|—| 1 km

H 200 m **I** 500 m **J** 700 m **K** 350 m **L** 850 m **M** 630 m **N** 90 m

9. Fill in the numbers in the box in the correct places.

a) The CN Tower is ________ **m** high.

It is located about _______ **km** from the nearest subway stop.

It was built more than ______ **years** ago.

20	553	2

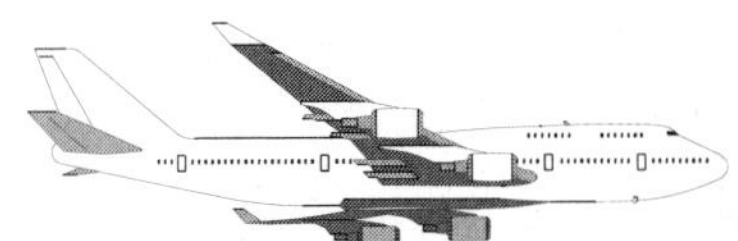

b) Toronto is about ________ **km** from Vancouver.

It takes _______ **hours** to fly between the cities.

Planes flying between the cities can

cruise as high as ________ **km**.

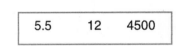

5.5	12	4500

ME5-8: Mathematics and Architecture

Mathematics has been used to design many beautiful buildings, including the pyramids of Egypt.
Each pyramid is drawn to a scale: 1 millimetre on the diagram represents 5 metres on the actual pyramid.

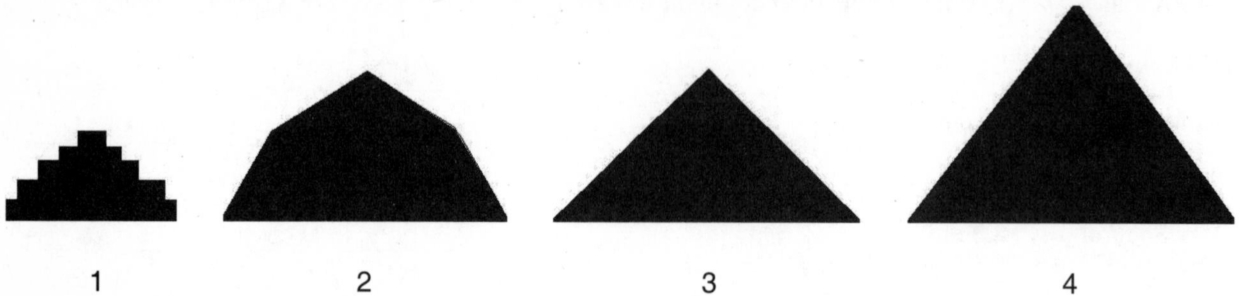

1. Measure the diagrams above in mm, then calculate the actual measurements of the pyramids.
NOTE: 1 mm = 5 m.

No.	Name	Height of diagram in mm	Actual height of pyramid in m	Length of base of diagram in mm	Actual length of base in m
1.	Step Pyramid of Djoser				
2.	Bent Pyramid at Dashur				
3.	Red Pyramid of Snefru				
4.	Great Pyramid at Giza				

2. The bricks used to build the Pyramid of Giza measure 0.66 m high and 1.00 m long.

   a) How high are the bricks in: i) centimetres ______________ ii) decimetres ______________

   b) How long are the bricks in: i) centimetres ______________ ii) decimetres ______________

   c) If a pyramid was 100 bricks high, how high would it be in metres? ______________

   d) How many bricks are along the bottom of one side of the Pyramid of Giza? ______________ bricks.

3. Fill in the chart. Then, in your notebook, draw a scale diagram of each pyramid below using the scale **1 mm = 5 m**. (Each pyramid looks like a triangle from the side).

No.	Name	Height in mm	Approx. height in m	Base length in mm	Approx. base Length in m
1.	Black Pyramid		80 m		105 m
2.	Pyramid at Meidum		90 m		145 m
3.	Pyramid of Kharfe		145 m		230 m

 No unauthorized copying

ME5-9: Problem Solving with Measurement

The Confederation Bridge, which links New Brunswick and Prince Edward Island, was finished in 1997.

On the diagram, 1 cm represents approximately 860 m.

1. a) Measure the length of the diagram to the nearest cm: ____________________

   b) Estimate the length of the bridge: ____________________

   HINT: Round the scale to 1 cm = 1000 m.

2. The actual length of the bridge is 12.9 km.
   How many metres long is the bridge?

3. A school bus is about 10 m long.
   About how many school buses would span the bridge if they were parked end to end?

4. The bridge is made of three segments:
   - the East Approach Bridge, which is 600 m long
   - the West Approach Bridge, which is 1300 m long
   - and the Main Bridge (which connects the two).

   How long is the Main Bridge in metres?

5. The distance between the bridge piers is 250 m.
   A boat 20 m wide passes between the two piers in the middle of the channel.
   How far is the pier from the side of the boat?

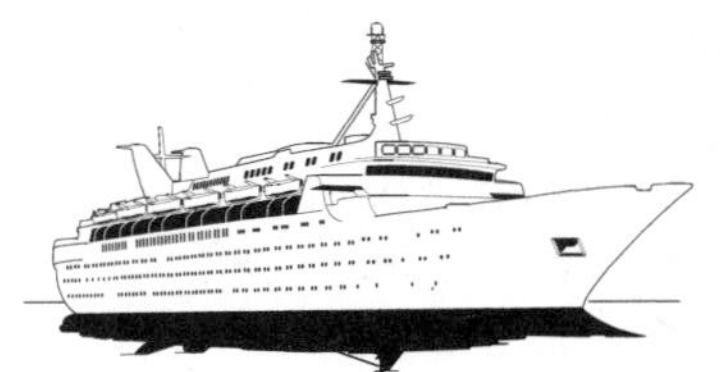

6. Emergency telephones are placed every 750 m along the bridge.
   About how many telephones are on the bridge?

No unauthorized copying

ME5-10: Perimeter

1. Each edge is 1 cm long. Write the total length of each side in cm as shown in figure a). Then write an addition statement and find the perimeter.

a) 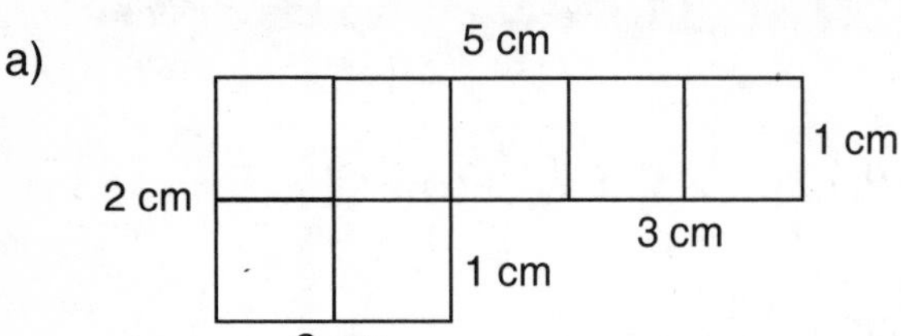

Perimeter: ___________________

b) 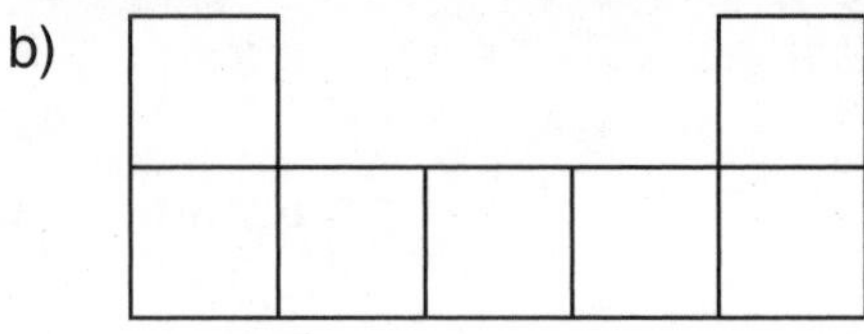

Perimeter: ___________________

c) 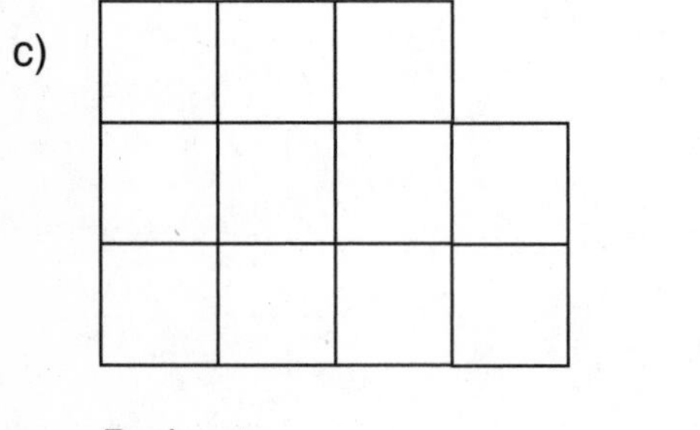

Perimeter: ___________________

d) 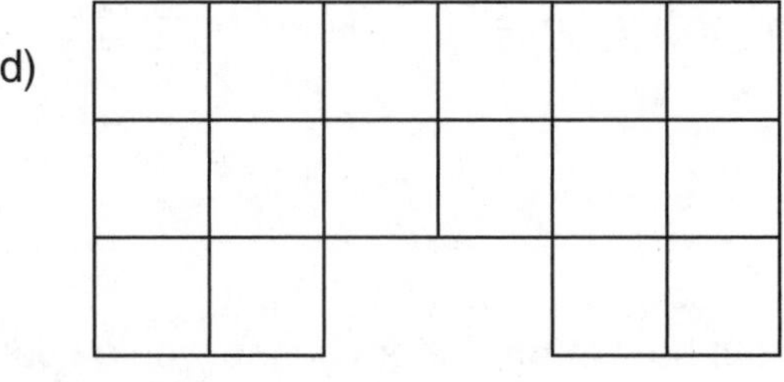

Perimeter: ___________________

1. Each edge is 1 unit long. Write the length of each side beside the figure (don't miss any edges!). Then use the side lengths to find the perimeter.

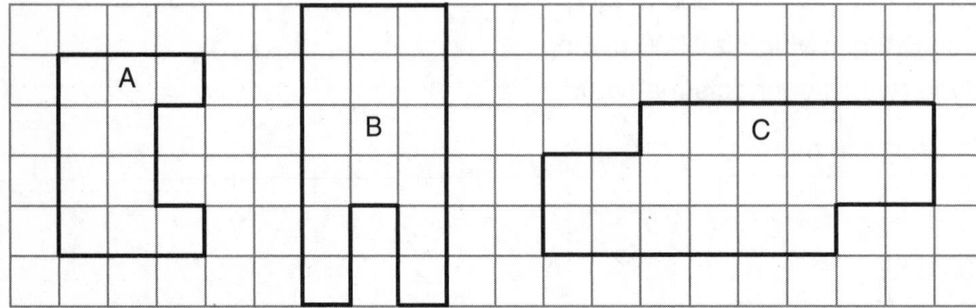

3. Draw your own figure and find the perimeter.

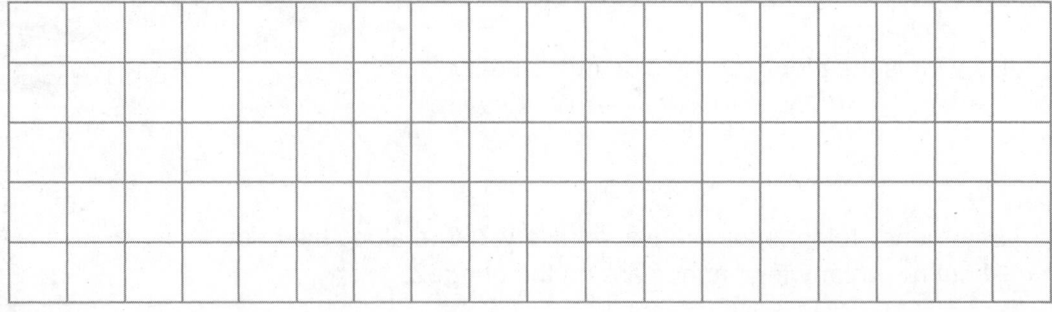

4. On grid paper, draw your own figures and find their perimeters. Try making letters or other shapes.

ME5-11: Problem Solving with Perimeter

1. Measure the perimeter of each figure in cm using a ruler.

a) 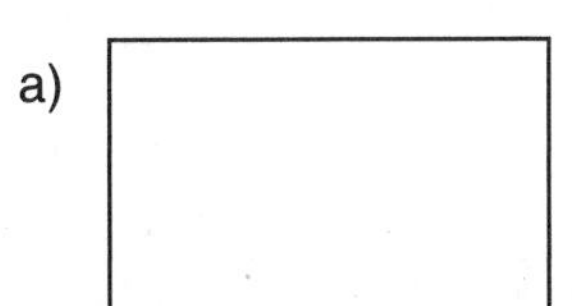 ______

b) 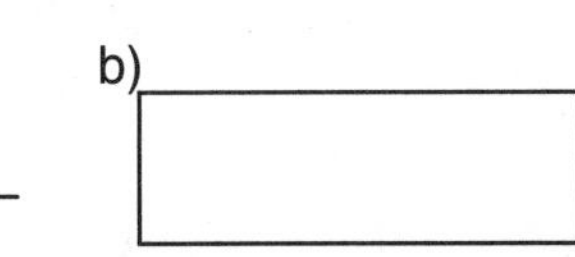 ______

c) 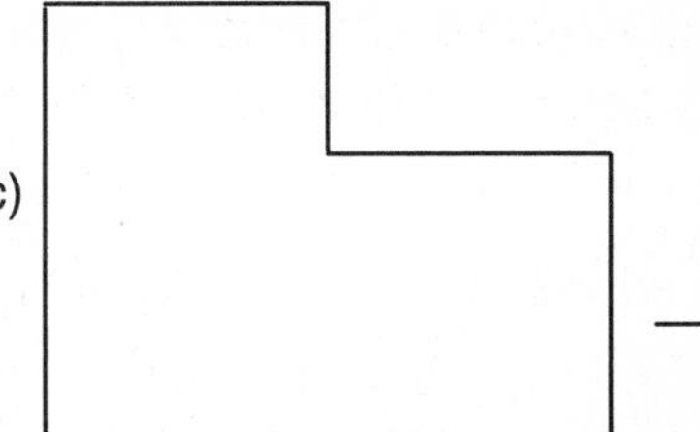 ______

2. Find the perimeter of each shape. (Include the units in your answer.)

a) 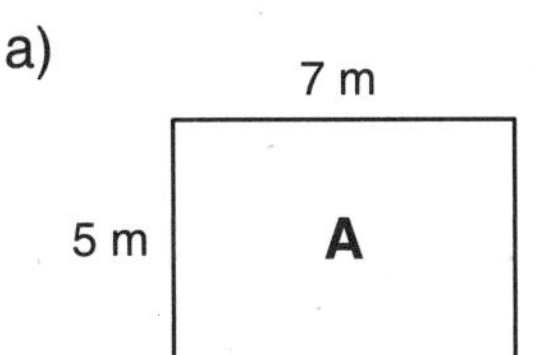

b) 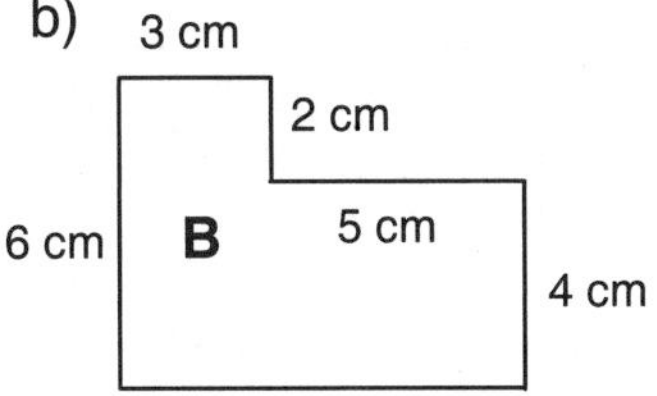

c) 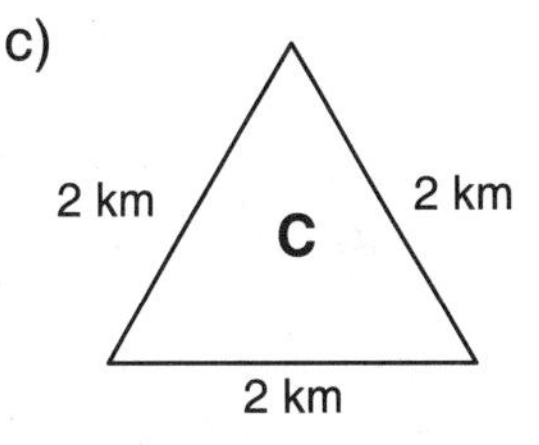

d) 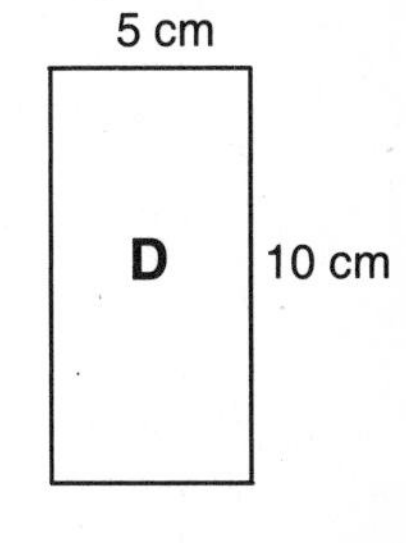

Perimeter ________ Perimeter ________ Perimeter ________ Perimeter ________

e) Write the letters of the shapes in order from greatest to least perimeter. (Watch the units!)

____

3. Your index finger is about 1 cm wide. Estimate, then measure, the perimeter of each shape in cm.

a) 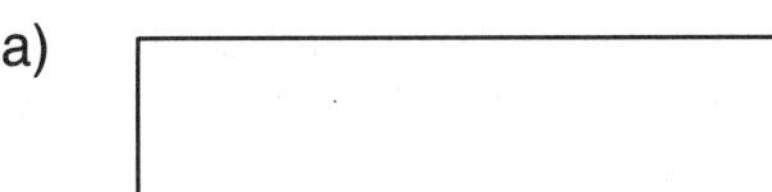 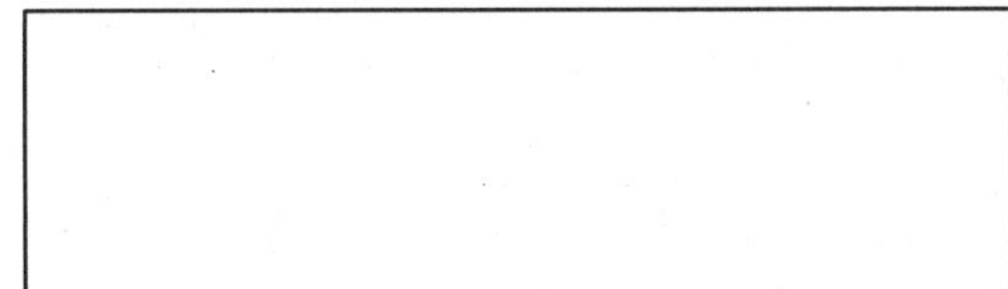

b) 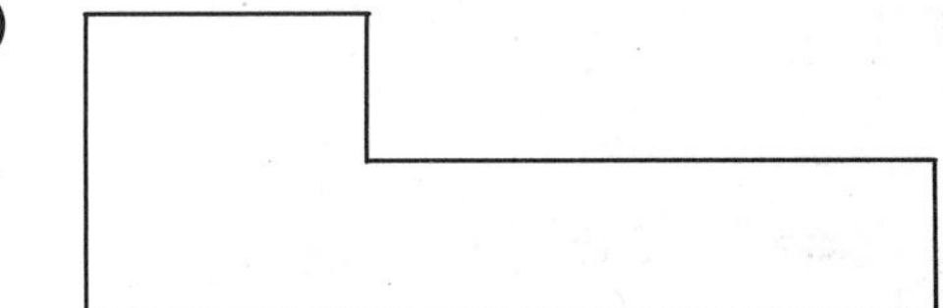

Estimated Perimeter ____________ Estimated Perimeter ____________

Actual Perimeter ______________ Actual Perimeter ______________

4. On grid paper, show all the ways you can make a rectangle using:

a) 10 squares b) 12 squares c) 7 squares

d) Which of the rectangles in b) above has the greatest perimeter?

5. a) Ribbon costs 35¢ for each metre.
How much will a ribbon border for the poster cost?

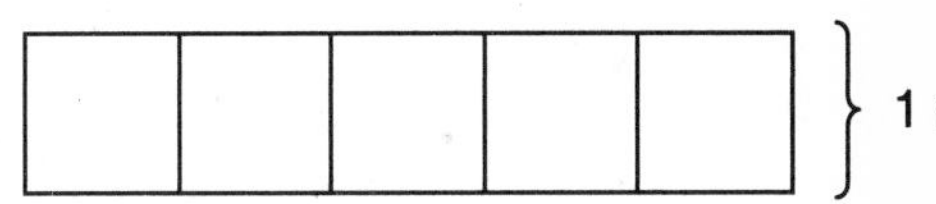

b) How many different rectangles can you make using 8 squares of cardboard with sides 1 metre long?
For which arrangement would the border be least expensive?

ME5-12: Exploring Perimeters

Serge buys 12 metres of fence to make a rectangular garden.
Each section of fence is 1 m long.
What dimensions can Serge's garden have?

Serge tries widths 1 m, 2 m, and 3 m.

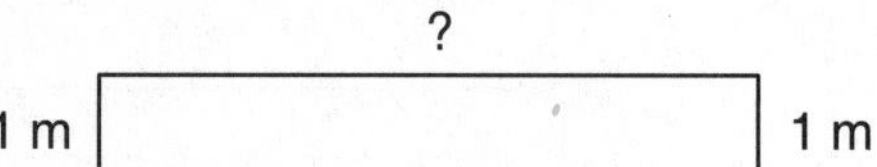

The widths add to 2 m.
The missing lengths are 12 – 2 = 10 m altogether.
Each length is 10 ÷ 2 = 5 m.

?
2 m
2 m

The widths add to 4 m.
The missing lengths are 12 – 4 = 8 m altogether.
Each length is 8 ÷ 2 = 4 m.

---

1. 3 cm 3 cm

Perimeter = 12 m

Complete Serge's calculations:

a) The widths add to __________ m.

b) The missing lengths are ____________________ altogether.

c) Each missing length is ________________________________.

2. Find the missing lengths or widths in each figure. (Note that the pictures are not drawn to scale.)

a) perimeter = 12 m

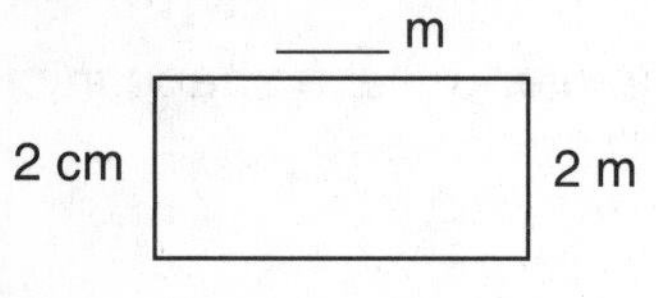

b) perimeter = 14 cm

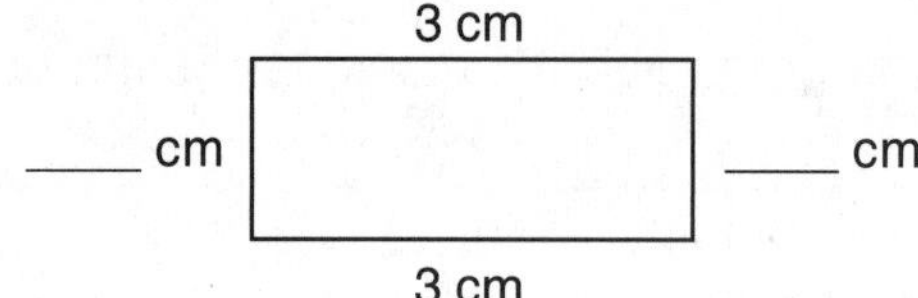

c) perimeter = 10 cm

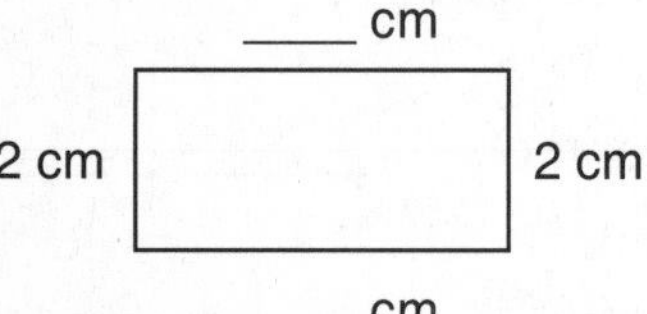

d) perimeter = 14 m

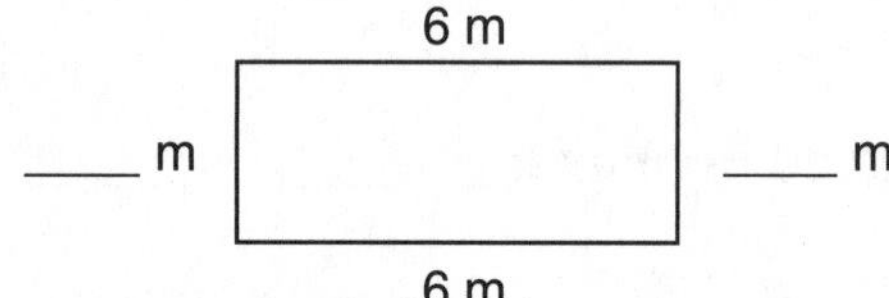

3. Find all rectangles with the given perimeter (with lengths and widths that are whole numbers).

Width	Length
Perimeter = 6 units	

Width	Length
Perimeter = 12 units	

Width	Length
Perimeter = 16 units	

Width	Length
Perimeter = 18 units	

4. Write a rule for finding the perimeter of a rectangle from its width and length. ________________

____

No unauthorized copying

ME5-12: Exploring Perimeters *(continued)*

5. Mark makes a sequence of figures with toothpicks.

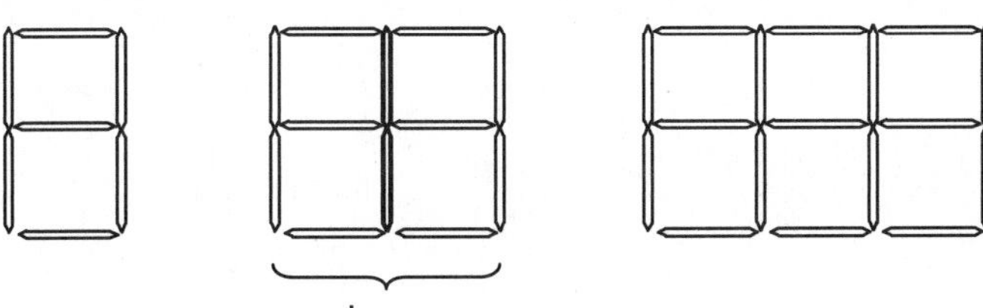

INPUT *Number of toothpicks in base*	**OUTPUT** *Perimeter*
1	6

a) Complete the chart.

b) Complete the rule that tells how to make the OUTPUT numbers from the INPUT numbers:

Multiply the INPUT by _______ and add ___________.

c) Use the rule to predict the perimeter of a figure with a base of 10 toothpicks. ________________

6. Add one square to the figure so that the perimeter of the new figure is 10 units.

NOTE: Assume all edges are 1 unit.

a) 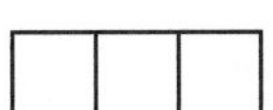

Original Perimeter = _____ units

New Perimeter = 10 units

b) 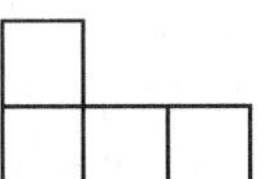

Original Perimeter = _____ units

New Perimeter = 10 units

c) 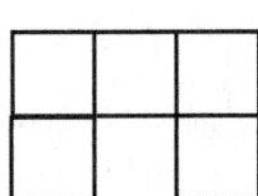

Original Perimeter = _____ units

New Perimeter = 10 units

7. Add one triangle to the figure so that the perimeter of the new figure is 6 units.

a) 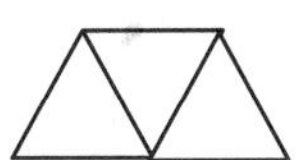

Original Perimeter = _____ units

New Perimeter = 6 units

b) 

Original Perimeter = _____ units

New Perimeter = 6 units

8. Repeat steps a) to c) of question 5 for the following patterns.

a) 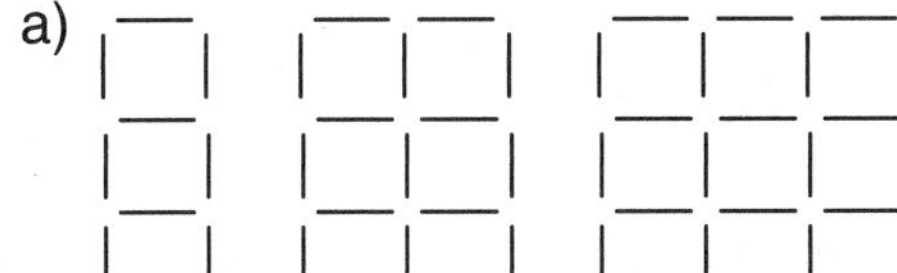

b) 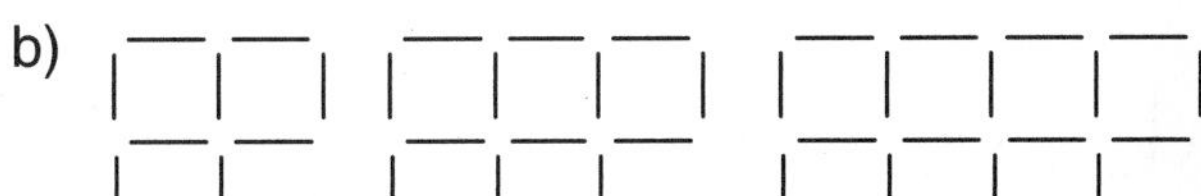

9. Emma says the formula 2 x (length + width) gives the perimeter of a rectangle. Is she correct?

No unauthorized copying

ME5-13: Area in Square Centimetres

Shapes that are flat are called **two-dimensional** (2-D) shapes.
The area of a 2-dimensional shape is the amount of space it takes up.

A square centimetre is a unit for measuring area.
A square with sides of 1 cm has an area of one square centimetre.
The short form for a square centimetre is 1 cm^2.

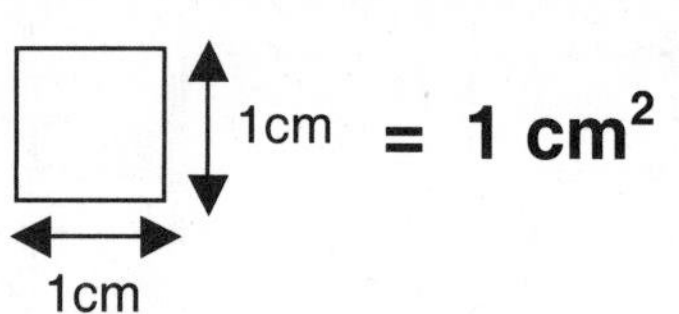

1. Find the area of these figures in square centimetres.

a) 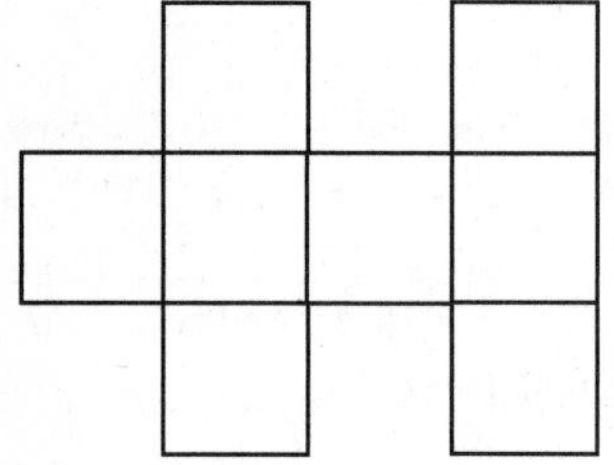

Area = _______ cm^2

b) 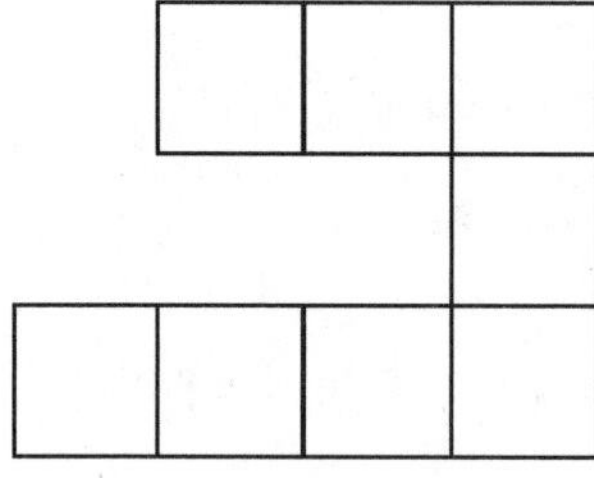

Area = _______ cm^2

c)

Area = _______ cm^2

2. Using a ruler, draw lines to divide each rectangle into square centimetres.

a) 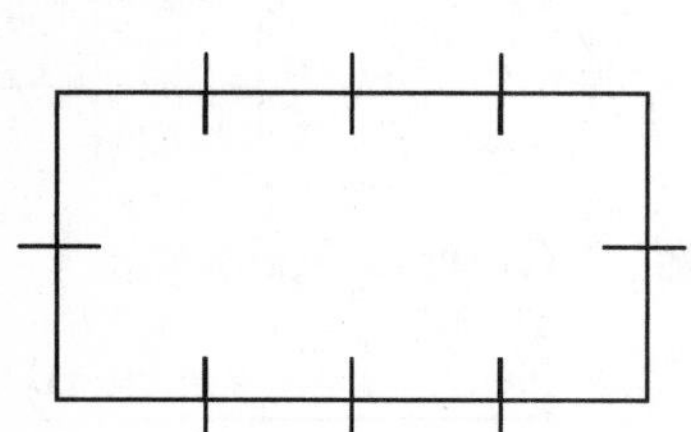

Area = _______ cm^2

b) 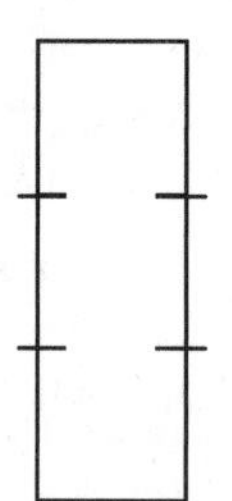

Area = _______ cm^2

c) 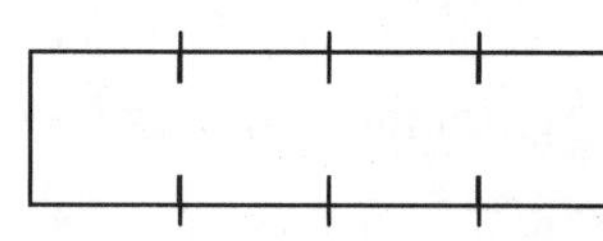

Area = _______ cm^2

3. How can you find the area (in square units) of each of the given shapes?

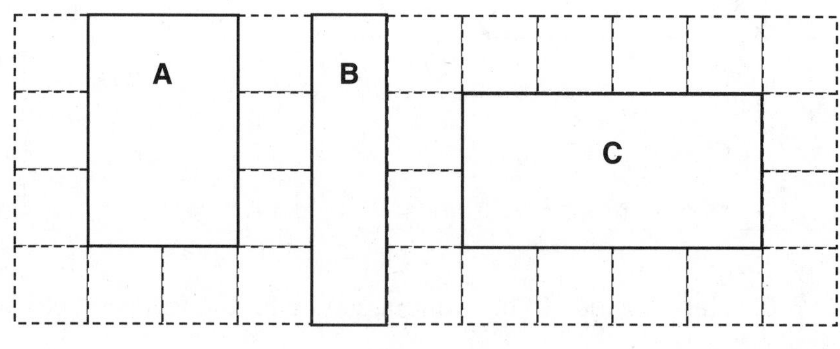

Area of A = ______ Area of B = ______ Area of C = ______

On grid paper:

4. Draw 3 different shapes that have an area of 10 cm^2 (the shapes don't have to be rectangles).

5. Draw several shapes and find their area and perimeter.

6. Draw a rectangle with an area of 12 cm^2 and perimeter of 14 cm.

No unauthorized copying

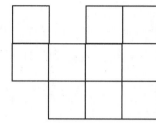

ME5-14: Area of Rectangles

1. Write a multiplication statement for each array.

a) 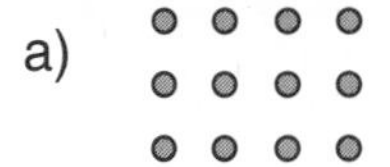
____

b) _______________

c) _______________

d) _______________

2. Draw a dot in each box.
Then write a multiplication statement that tells you the number of boxes in the rectangle.

a) 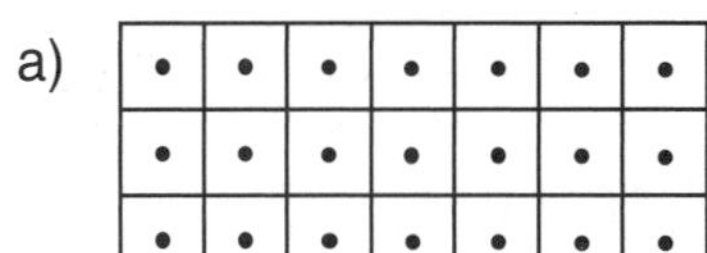
3 × 7 = 21

b) 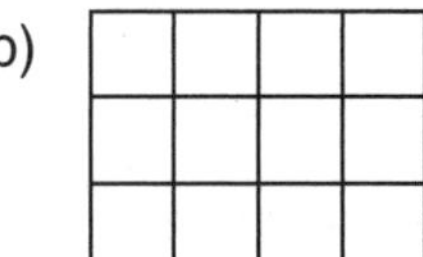
____

c) 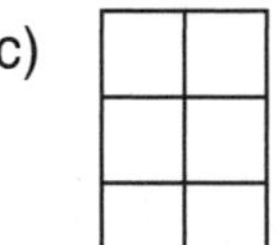
____

d) 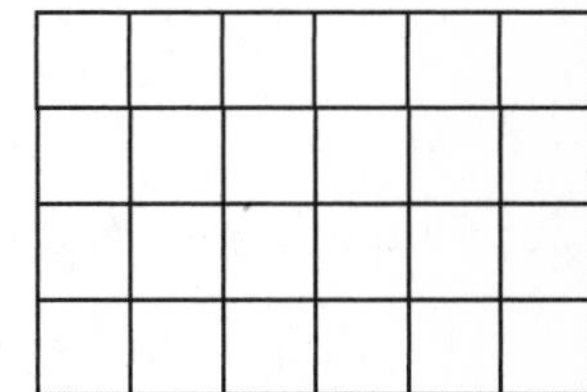
____

3. Write the number of boxes along the width and length of each rectangle.
Then write a multiplication statement for the area of the rectangle (in square units).

a) 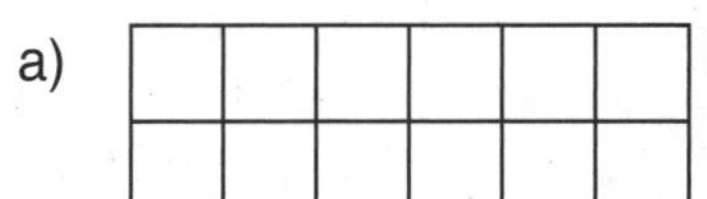
Width = 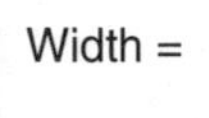
Length = ____
____

b) 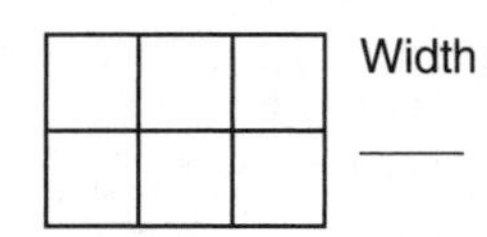
Width = ____
Length = ____
____

c) 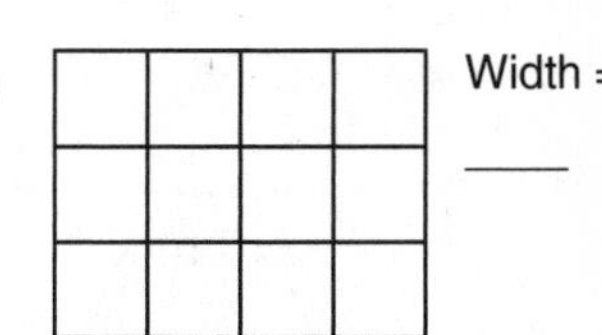
Width = ____
Length = ____
____

4. The sides of the rectangles have been marked in centimetres. Using a ruler, draw lines to divide each rectangle into squares. Write a multiplication statement for the area of the boxes in cm^2.
NOTE: You will have to mark the last row of boxes yourself using a ruler.

a) 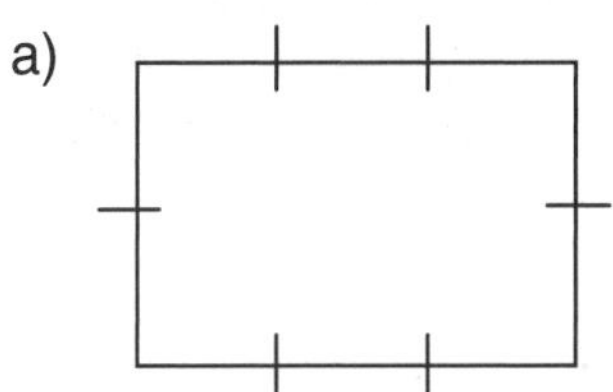

b) 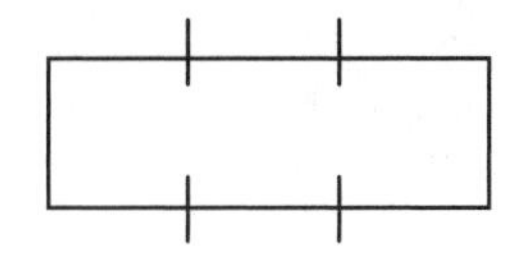

c) 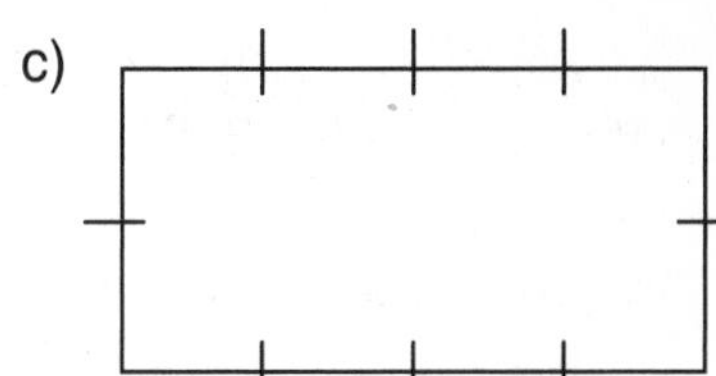

d) 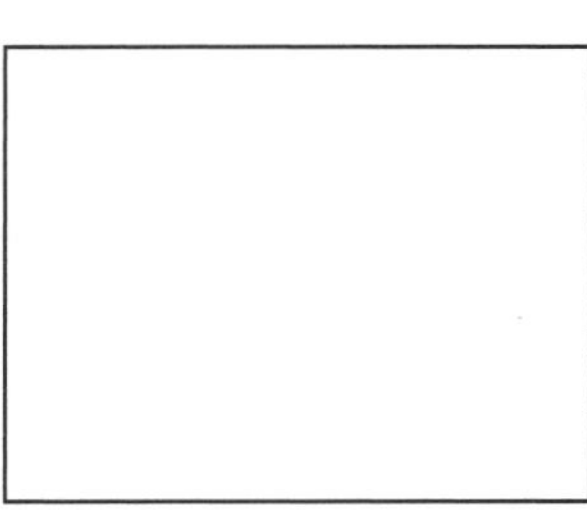

e) 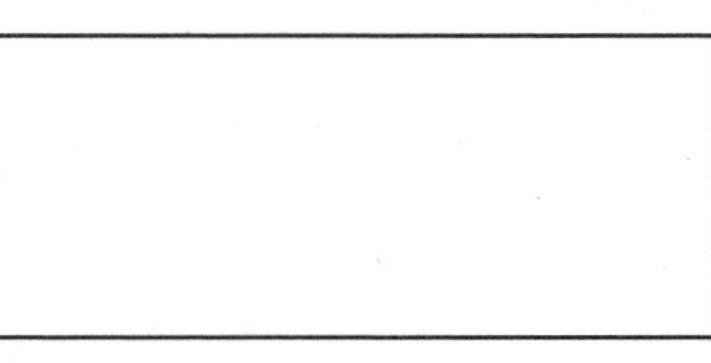

5. If you know the length and width of a rectangle, how can you find its area?

____

No unauthorized copying

ME5-15: Exploring Area

1. Measure the length and width of the figures, then find the area.

a) 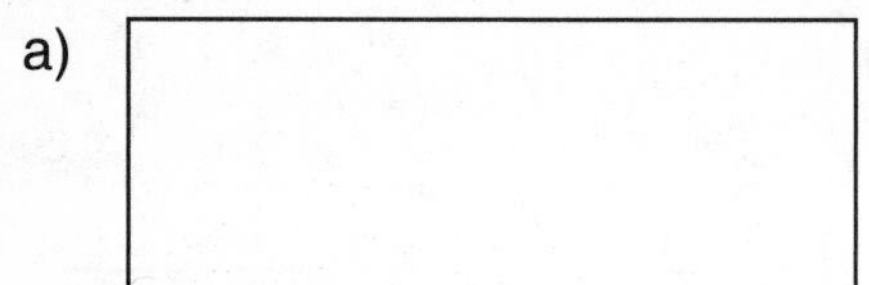

b) 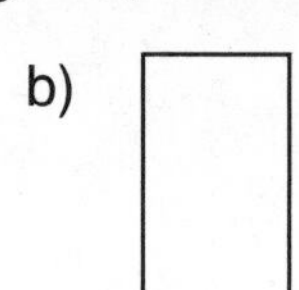

c) 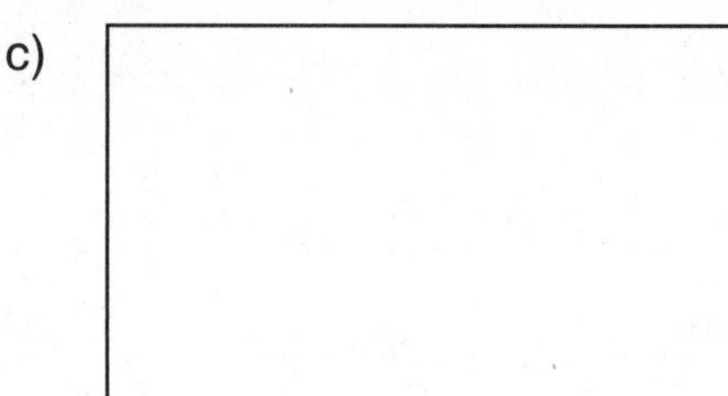

______________ ______________ ______________

2. Find the area of a rectangle with the following dimensions:

a) width: 6 m length: 7 m

b) width: 3 m length: 7 m

c) width: 4 cm length: 8 cm

______________ ______________ ______________

3. a) Calculate the area of each rectangle (be sure to include the units).

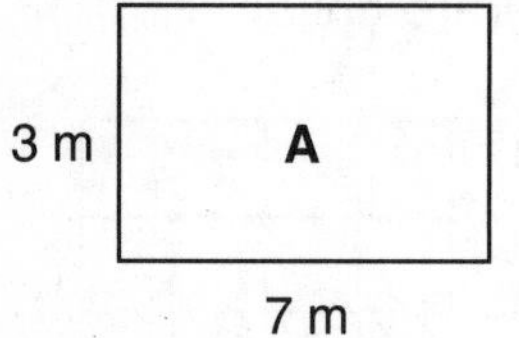

Area: ________

4 cm B 5 cm

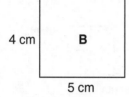

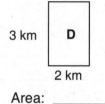

Area: ________

11 m C 6 m

Area: ________

3 km D 2 km

Area: ________

b) By letter, list in order the rectangles from greatest to least area: ______________________

4. A rectangle has an area of 18 cm^2 and a length of 6 cm. How can you find its width?

____

5. A rectangle has an area of 24 cm^2 and a width of 8 cm. What is its length? ______________

6. A square has an area of 25 cm^2. What is its width? ______________________

7. Write the lengths of each side on the figure.

Divide the figure into two boxes.

Calculate the area by finding the area of the two boxes.

Area of box 1:__________

Area of box 2:__________

Total Area:

____

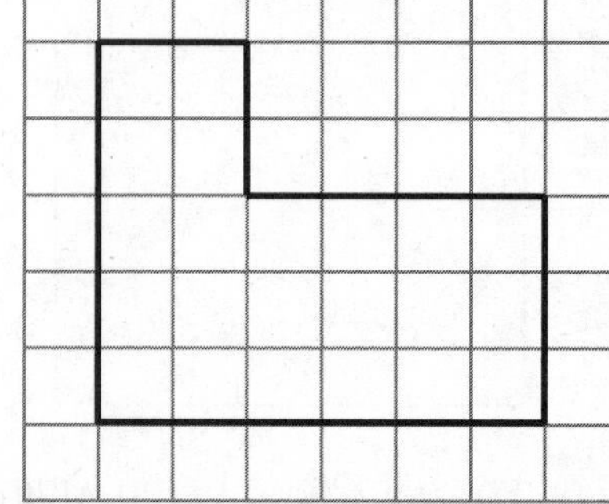

8. On grid paper, draw as many rectangles as you can with an area of 20 square units.

 No unauthorized copying

ME5-16: Area of Polygons

1. Two half squares cover the same area as a whole square.

Count each pair of half squares as a whole square to find the area shaded.

a) = ______ whole squares

b) = ______ whole squares

c) = ______ whole squares

d)

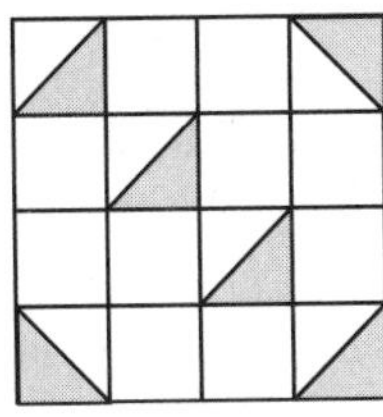

= ______ whole squares

e)

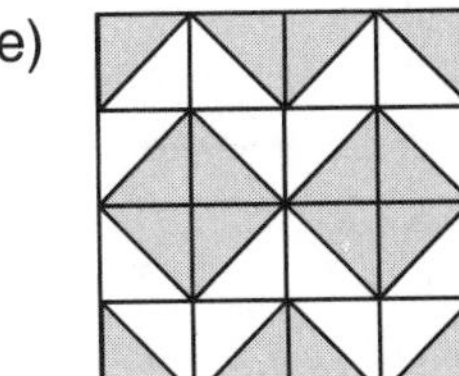

= ______ whole squares

f)

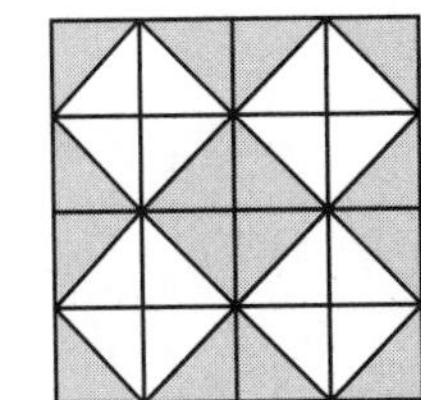

= ______ whole squares

g)

= ______ whole squares

h)

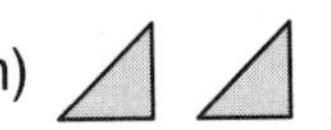

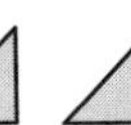

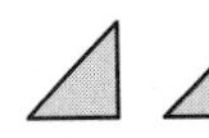

= ______ whole squares

i)

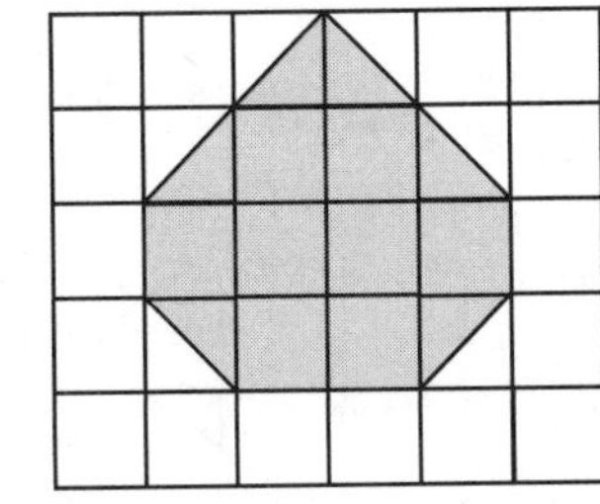

= ______ whole squares

j)

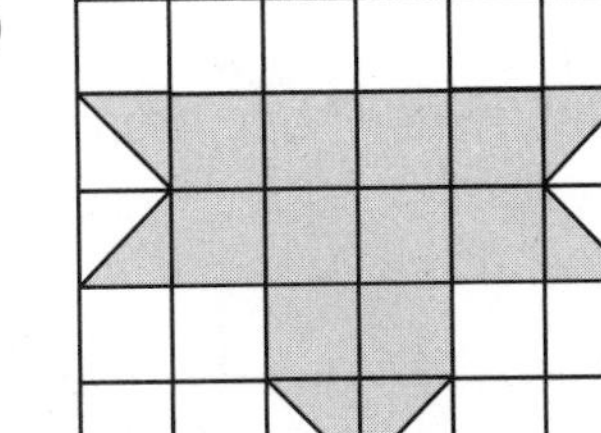

= ______ whole squares

k)

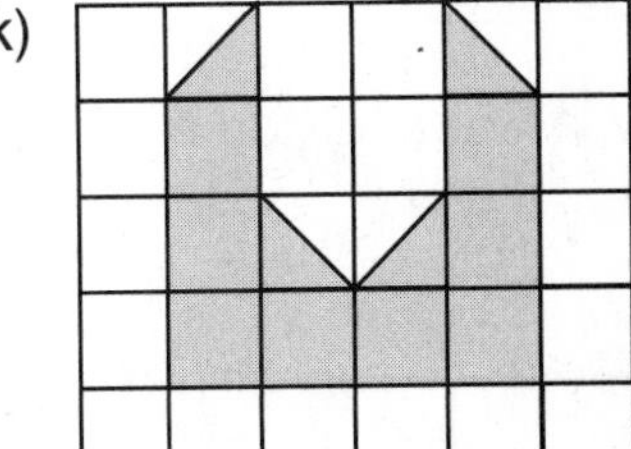

= ______ whole squares

2. Estimate and then find the area of each figure in square units.
HINT: Draw lines to show all the half squares.

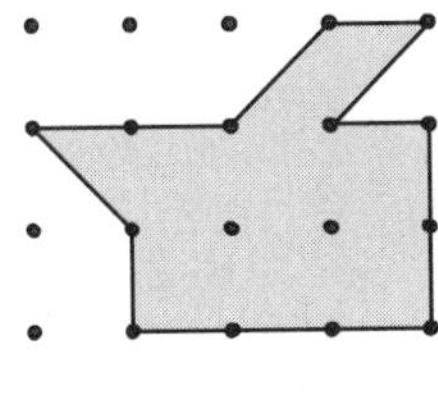

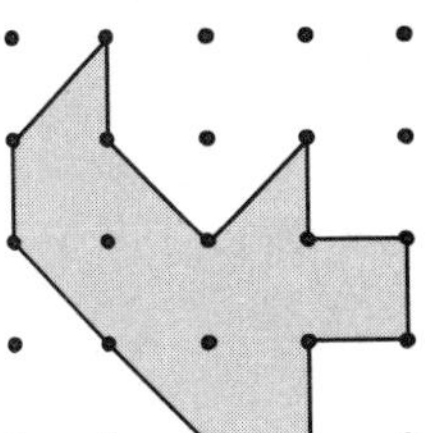

3. For each picture say whether the shaded area is more than, less than, or equal to the unshaded area. Explain how you know in your notebook.

a)

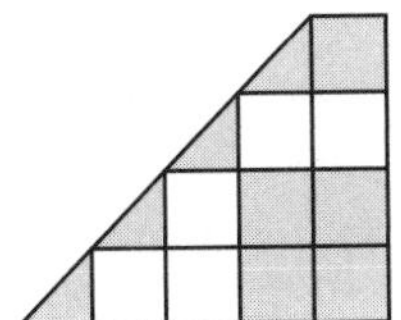

b)

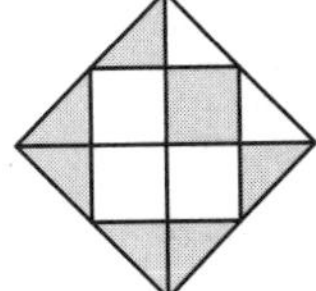

c)

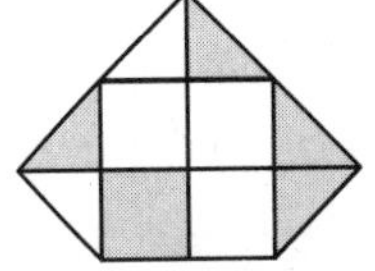

No unauthorized copying

4. a) What fraction of the rectangle is the shaded part?__________

   b) What is the area of the rectangle in square units?__________

   c) What is the area of the shaded part?__________

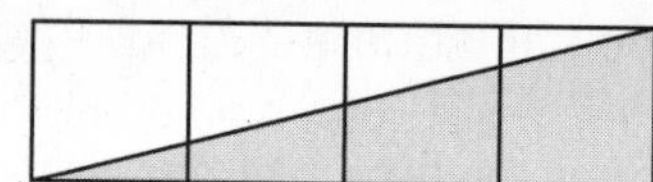

5. Find the shaded area in square units.

a) 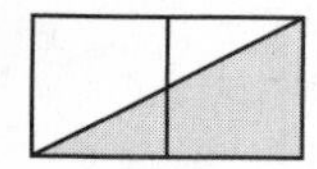 __________

b) 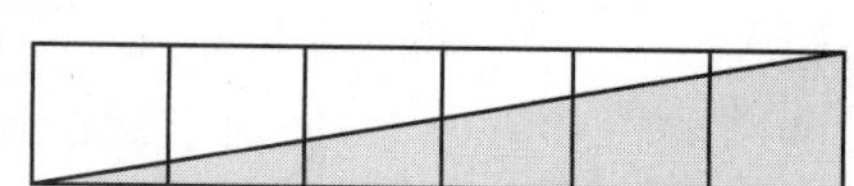 __________

c) 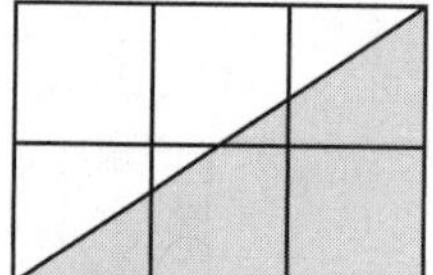 __________

d) 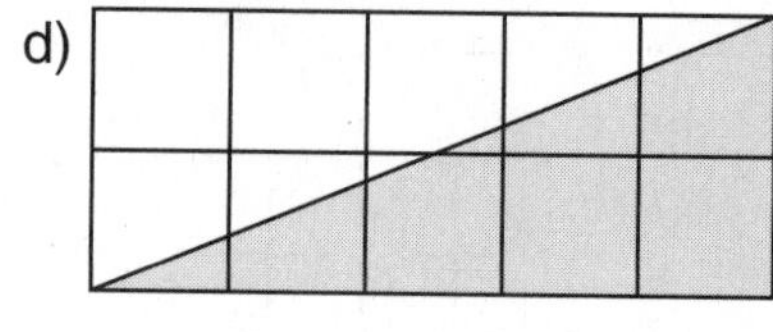 __________

6. Draw a line to divide each shape into a triangle and a rectangle.
   Then calculate the area of each shape.

a) 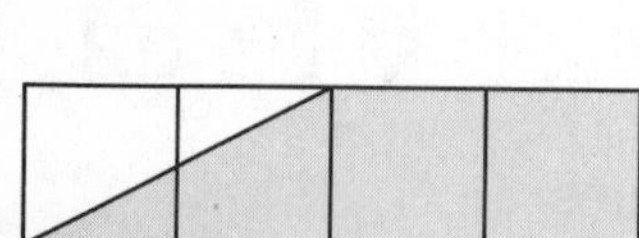 __________

b) 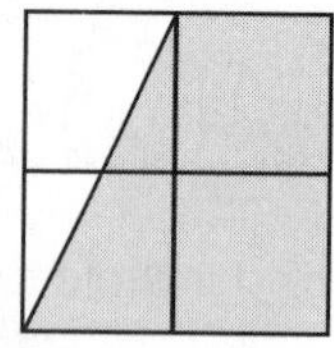 __________

c) 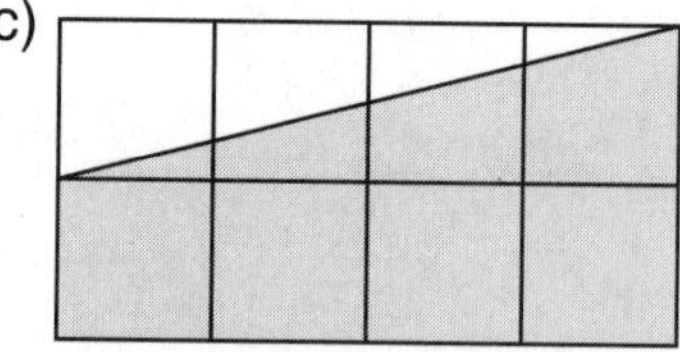 __________

d) 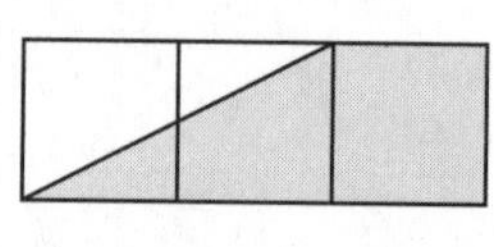 __________

7. Draw a line to divide each shape into 2 shapes whose area you can easily calculate.

a) 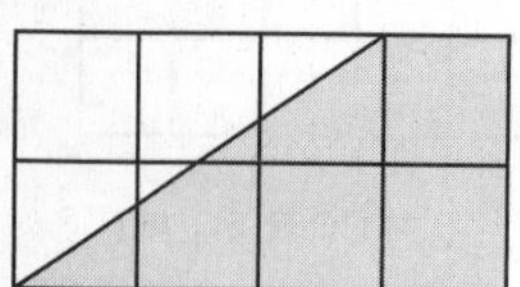 __________

b)  __________

c) __________

d) 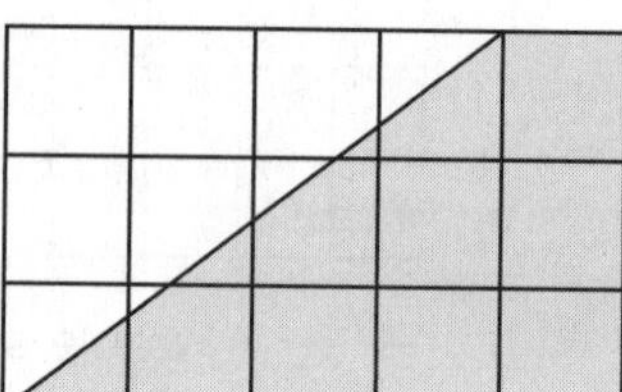 __________

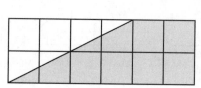

8. Calculate the area of each shape.

a) 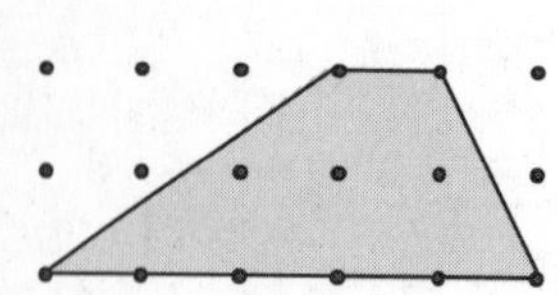

b) 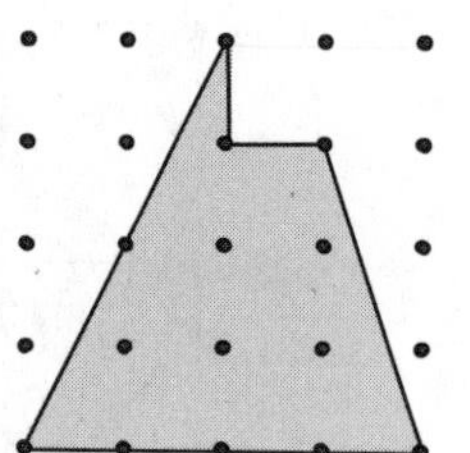

c) 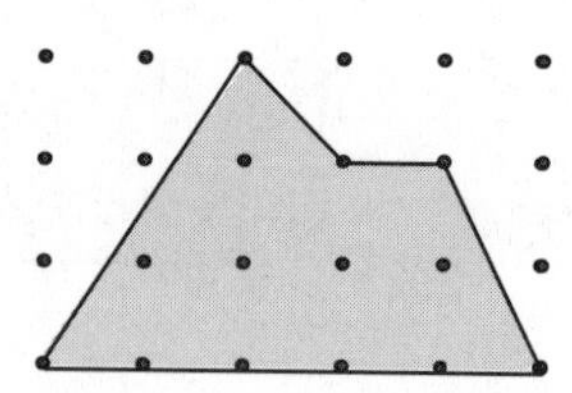

9. Find the area of the shaded part. Then, say what fraction of the grid is shaded.
HINT: How can you use the area of the unshaded part and the area of the grid?

a) 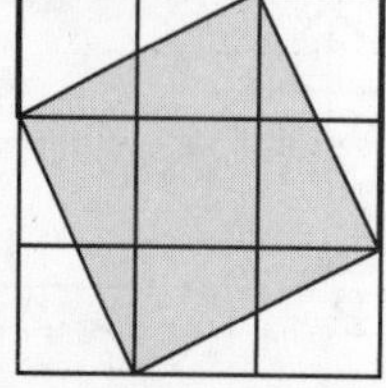
Area: __________
Fraction: __________

b) 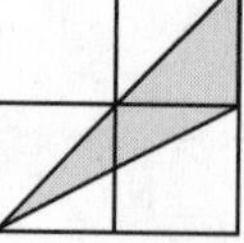
Area: __________
Fraction: __________

c) 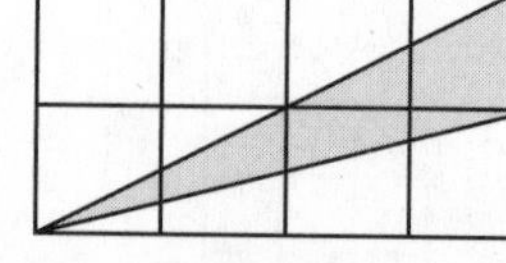
Area: __________
Fraction: __________

ME5-17: More Area and Perimeter

1. Estimate the area (in square units) and perimeter of the shapes below.

HINT (For Estimating Perimeter):

- **Count line segments that are almost horizontal and vertical as 1 unit long.**
- **Count line segments that are almost diagonal as $1\frac{1}{2}$ (or 1.5).**
- **Count line segments that are close to half as $\frac{1}{2}$.**

Approximate Area: __________	Approximate Area: __________	Approximate Area: __________
Approximate Perimeter: ________	Approximate Perimeter: ________	Approximate Perimeter: ________

2.

A B C D

a) Draw a copy of the shape but make the base and height 2 times as long as the original.

b) Find the perimeter and area of each original shape. (Count each diagonal line as 1.4 units long.) Then find the perimeter and area of the new shapes.

	A	B	C	D
Old Shape	Area: ______	Area: ______	Area: ______	Area: ______
	Perimeter: ____	Perimeter: ____	Perimeter: ____	Perimeter: ____
New Shape	Area: ______	Area: ______	Area: ______	Area: ______
	Perimeter: ____	Perimeter: ____	Perimeter: ____	Perimeter: ____

c) When the base and the height of a shape are doubled, what happens to the area of the shape?

____

d) When the base and the height of a shape are doubled, what happens to the perimeter?

____

No unauthorized copying

ME5-18: Comparing Area and Perimeter

1. For each shape below, calculate the perimeter and area of each shape, and write your answers in the chart below. The first one has been done for you. **NOTE: Each square represents a centimetre.**

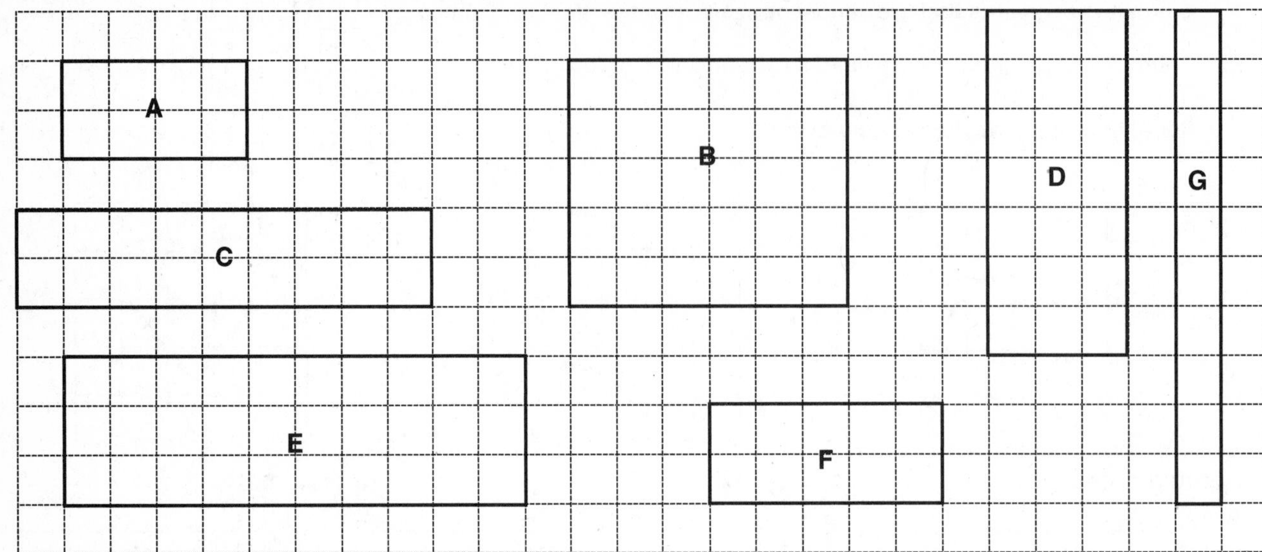

Shape	Perimeter	Area
A	2 + 4 + 4 + 2 = 12 cm	2 x 4 = 8 cm^2
B		
C		
D		
E		
F		
G		

2. Shape C has a greater perimeter than shape D. Does it also have greater area? ______________

3. Name two other shapes where one has a greater perimeter and the other has a greater area.

____

4. Write the shapes in order from greatest to least perimeter: ______________________________

5. Write the shapes in order from greatest to least area: ________________________________

6. Are the orders in Questions 4 and 5 the same? ______________________

7. What is the difference between PERIMETER and AREA? ______________________________

____

____

 No unauthorized copying

ME5-19: Area and Perimeter

1. Measure the length and width of each rectangle, and then record your answers in the chart below.

5 cm

2 cm

A

B

C

D

F

G

E

Rectangle	Estimated Perimeter	Estimated Area	Length	Width	Actual Perimeter	Actual Area
A	cm	cm^2	cm	cm	cm	cm^2
B						
C						
D						
E						
F						
G						

2. Find the area of the rectangle using the clues.

   a) Width = 2 cm Perimeter = 10 cm
   Area = ?

   b) Width = 4 cm Perimeter = 18 cm
   Area = ?

3. Draw a square on grid paper with the given perimeter. Then find the area of the square.

   a) Perimeter = 12 cm Area = ?

   b) Perimeter = 20 cm Area = ?

4. On grid paper or a geoboard, create a rectangle with:

   a) an area of 10 square units and a perimeter of 14 units.

   b) an area of 8 square units and a perimeter of 12 units.

5. The length of a rectangle is increased by 1 and its width is decreased by 1. What happens to the perimeter?

No unauthorized copying

ME5-20: Problems and Puzzles

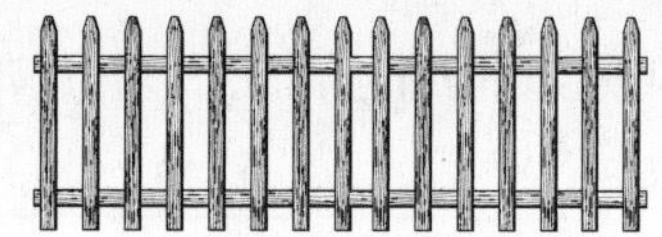

1. George wants to build a rectangular flower bed in his garden.
The width of the flower bed will be 3 m and the perimeter will be 14 m.

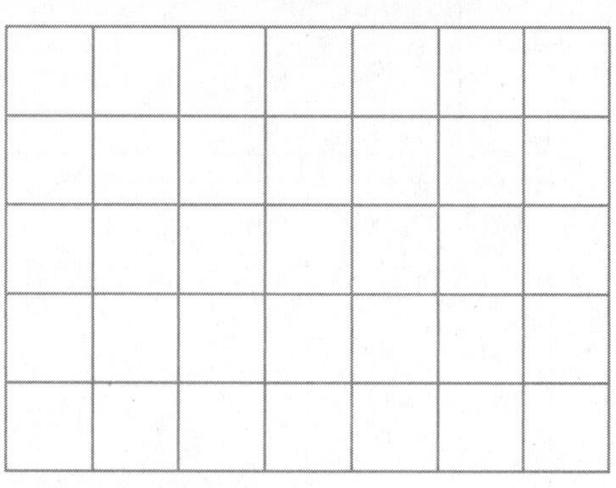

Each edge on the grid represents 1 metre.

a) What is the length of the bed? ____________________

b) Show the shape of the flower bed in the grid.

c) If fencing is $12 a metre, how much will a fence cost?

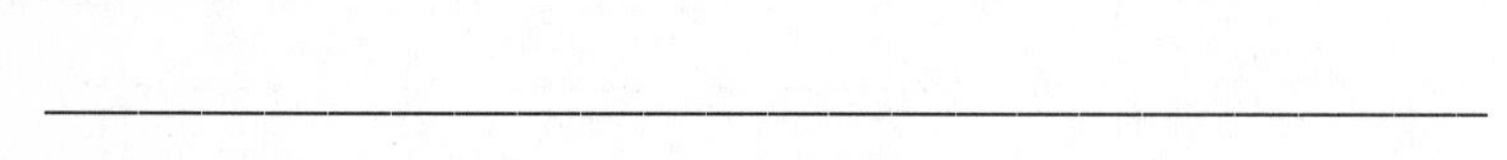

d) George will plant 16 flowers on each square metre of land.
Each flower is 5¢. How much will the flowers cost?

____

e) If George pays for the flowers with a twenty dollar bill, how much change will he get back?

____

2. A rectangle has sides whose lengths are whole numbers.
Find all the possible lengths and widths for the given area.

Area = 8 cm^2	
Width	Length

Area = 14 cm^2	
Width	Length

Area = 18 cm^2	
Width	Length

3. Name something you would measure in:

a) square metres ____________________ b) square kilometres ____________________

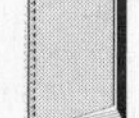

4. Crystal wants to make a rectangular garden with 12 m of fencing.
What width and length will give the greatest area?

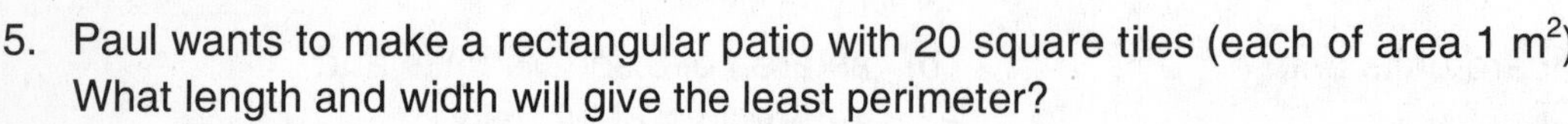

5. Paul wants to make a rectangular patio with 20 square tiles (each of area 1 m^2)
What length and width will give the least perimeter?

6. The length of a rabbit hut is twice its width.
How could you calculate the perimeter without adding the lengths of the sides?

 No unauthorized copying

ME5-21: More Area and Perimeter

Answer the following questions in your notebook.

1. What is the perimeter of these signs?

a) 

Stop

b) 35 cm, 30 cm, 45 cm

School Crossing

c) 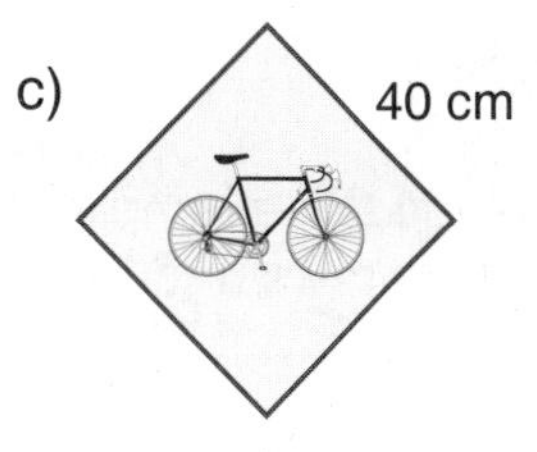

Bicycle Crossing

d) 

Wheelchair Accessible

2. The figures shown are all regular (all sides are the same length). Find the perimeter of each figure without adding the sides.

a) 

b) 

c) 

3. 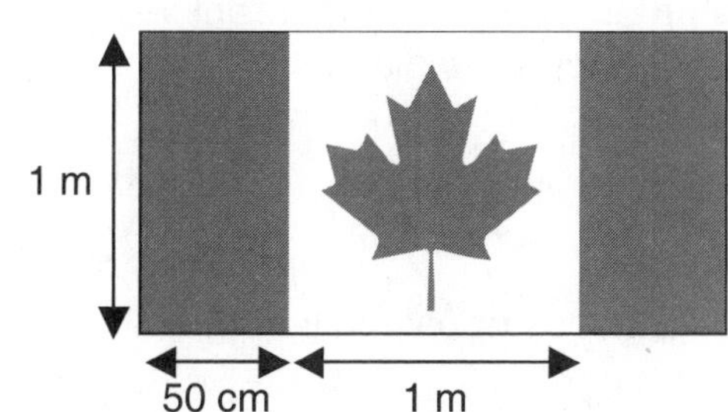

a) What is the area of each red rectangle on the flag?
HINT: Change the measurements to the same unit.

b) What is the area of the flag?

c) What is the perimeter of the flag?

d) About how many flags would cover the floor in your room?

4. *Example:*

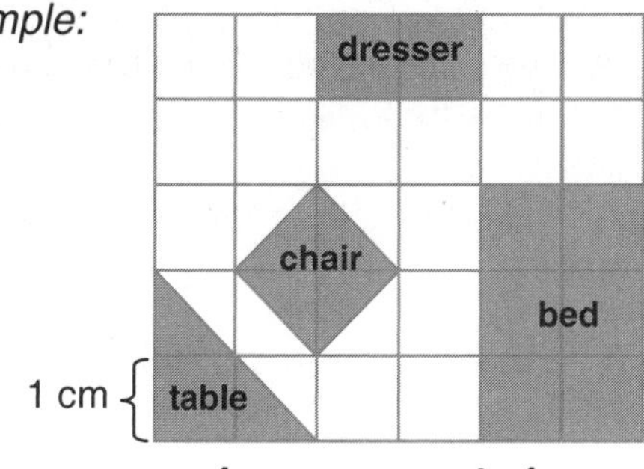

1 cm represents 1 m

The diagram shows a floor plan for a bedroom. Find:

a) The perimeter and area of the room.

b) The area of the room covered by furniture.

c) Draw your own floor plan for a room and answer parts a) and b).

5. A square garden has sides of length 6 m.
Fence posts are placed every 2 metres along the sides of the garden.
How many fence posts are in the garden?

6. Your thumbnail has an area of about 1 cm^2.
Find something in your home that has an area of about 1 cm^2.
Justify your answer.

7. Your arm span has a length of about 1 m.
Find something in your home with an area of about 1 m^2

No unauthorized copying

add to find the total when combining two or more numbers together

area the amount of space occupied by the face or surface of an object

array an arrangement of things (for example, objects, symbols, or numbers) in rows and columns

base-10 materials materials used to represent ones (ones squares or cubes), tens (tens strips or rods), hundreds (hundreds squares or flats), and thousands (thousands cubes)

centimetre (cm) a unit of measurement used to describe length, height, or thickness

cent notation a way to express an amount of money (for example, 40¢)

column things (for example, objects, symbols, numbers) that run up and down

consecutive numbers numbers that occur one after the other on a number line

coordinate system a grid with labelled rows and columns, used to describe the location of a dot or object, for example the dot is at (A,3)

core the part of a pattern that repeats

decimal a short form for tenths (for example, 0.2) or hundredths (for example, 0.02), and so on

decimetre (dm) a unit of measurement used to describe length, height, or thickness; equal to 10 cm

decreasing sequence a sequence where each number is less than the one before it

denominator the number on the bottom portion of a fraction; tells you how many parts are in a whole

diagonal things (for example, objects, symbols, or numbers) that are in a line from one corner to another corner

difference the "gap" between two numbers; the remainder left after subtraction

divide to find how many times one number contains another number

dividend in a division problem, the number that is being divided or shared

divisible by containing a number a specific number of times without having a remainder (for example, 15 is divisible by 5 and 3)

divisor in a division problem, the number that is divided into another number

dollar notation a way to express an amount of money (for example, $4.50)

equivalent fractions fractions that represent the same amount, but have different denominators (for example, $\frac{2}{3} = \frac{4}{6}$)

estimate a guess or calculation of an approximate number

expanded form a way to write a number that shows the place value of each digit (for example, 27 in expanded form can be written as 2 tens + 7 ones, or 20 + 7)

factors whole numbers that are multiplied to give a number

fraction a number used to name a part of a set or a region

greater than a term used to describe a number that is higher in value than another number

growing pattern a pattern in which each term is greater than the previous term

improper fraction a fraction that has a numerator that is larger than the denominator; this represents more than a whole

No unauthorized copying

increasing sequence a sequence where each number is greater than the one before it

kilometre (km) a unit of measurement for length; equal to 1000 cm

less than a term used to describe a number that is lower in value than another number

litre (L) a unit of measurement used to describe capacity; equal to 1000 mL

lowest common multiple (LCM) the least nonzero number that two numbers can divide into evenly (for example, 6 is the LCM of 2 and 3)

metre (m) a unit of measurement used to describe length, height, or thickness; equal to 100 cm

millilitre (mL) a unit of measurement used to describe capacity

millimetre (mm) a unit of measurement used to describe length, height, or thickness; equal to 0.1 cm

mixed fraction a mixture of a whole number and a fraction

model a physical representation (for example, using base-10 materials to represent a number)

multiple of a number that is the result of multiplying one number by another specific number (for example, the multiples of 5 are 0, 5, 10, 15, and so on)

multiply to find the total of a number times another number

number line a line with numbers marked at intervals, used to help with skip counting

numerator the number on the top portion of a fraction; tells you how many parts are counted

pattern (repeating pattern) the same repeating group of objects, numbers, or attributes

perimeter the distance around the outside of a shape

period the part of a pattern that repeats; the core of the pattern

product the result from multiplying two or more numbers together

quotient the result from dividing one number by another number

regroup to exchange one place value for another place value (for example, 10 ones squares for 1 tens strip)

remainder the number left over after dividing or subtracting (for example, 10 ÷ 3 = 3 R1)

row things (for example, objects, symbols, or numbers) that run left to right

set a group of like objects

skip counting counting by a number (for example, 2s, 3s, 4s) by "skipping" over the numbers in between

square centimetre (cm2) a unit of measurement used to describe area

subtract to take away one or more numbers from another number

sum the result from adding two or more numbers together

T-table a chart used to compare two sequences of numbers

 No unauthorized copying

Patterns & Algebra 1

Worksheet PA5-1

1. a) 5
   b) 3
   c) 6
   d) 4
2. a) 8
   b) 12
   c) 12
   d) 19
3. a) 11
   b) 33
   c) 25
   d) 34

Worksheet PA5-2

1. a) Gap = 3: 10, 13, 16
   b) Gap = 4: 13, 17, 21
   c) Gap = 5: 18, 23, 28
   d) Gap = 3: 12, 15, 18

Worksheet PA5-3

1. a) – 3
   b) – 5
   c) – 5
   d) – 7
2. b) – 2
   c) – 5
   d) – 7
3. a) – 5
   b) – 9
   c) – 2
   d) – 2

Worksheet PA5-4

1. a) 4
   b) 10
   c) 5
   d) 16
2. a) 12
   b) 16
   c) 16
   d) 20
3. a) Gap = – 2: 7, 5, 3
   b) Gap = – 5: 18, 13, 8
   c) Gap = – 3: 55, 52, 49
   d) Gap = – 9: 28, 19, 10

Worksheet PA5-5

1. a) 17, 23, 29
   b) 9, 13, 17
   c) 11, 15, 19
   d) 12, 15, 18
2. a) Gap = + 4: 16, 20
   b) Gap = + 7: 24, 31
   c) Gap = + 3: 10, 13
   d) Gap = + 4: 33, 37
3. 28 stamps are left.
4. She will save $66.

Worksheet PA5-6

1. a) 47, 50, 53
   b) 70, 75, 80
   c) 78, 80, 82
   d) 40, 50, 60
2. a) 20, 18, 16
   b) 19, 16, 13
   c) 75, 70, 65
   d) 50, 40, 30
4. b)
5. Hyun is correct.

Worksheet PA5-7

1. a) 4
   b) 3
   c) 6
   d) 7
2. a) 2
   b) 5
   c) 1
   d) 3
3. a) subtract 7
   b) add 8
   c) add 4
   d) subtract 12
4. a) 37, 42, 47; add 5
   b) 59, 66, 73; add 7
   c) 160, 172, 184; add 12
5. a) Genevieve's rule is correct.
   b) Jonah said to subtract (instead of add) 4.
   Pria said to add 5 (instead of 4).

Worksheet PA5-8

1. a) Start at 2 and add 5.
   b) Start at 2 and add 7.
   c) Start at 1 and add 3.
   d) Start at 1 and add 6.
2.

	Fig.	Sq.
a)	4	23
	5	30
	6	37
b)	4	14
	5	18
	6	22
c)	4	21
	5	26
	6	31

3. a) Fig. 4 – 19 sq; NO
   b) Fig. 4 – 17 sq; NO
   c) Fig. 4 – 15 sq; YES
4. a) Need 11 squares
   b) Need 12 triangles

Worksheet PA5-9

1. a) 7
   b) 10
   c) 8
   d) 9
2.

Figure	Line Seg.
1	3
2	6
3	9
4	12
5	**15**

3.

Figure	Line Seg.
1	4
2	7
3	10
4	13
7	**22**

4. a) 13
   b) 6
   c) 15
5. a) 17
   b) 8
   c) 19
6. a) Start at 6 and add 2.
   b) Start at 2 and add 2.
   c) 10 squares
   d) No, she would need 16 triangles.
7. a) 18 triangles
   b) 20 trapezoids
   c) 12 triangles & 24 trapezoids
   d) 28 trapezoids

Worksheet PA5-10

1. a) 3 L
   b) 9 L
   c) 7 hours (at 1am there will be 0 L)
2. $49
3. $21
4. 105 cm
5. 27 cm

Worksheet PA5-11

1.

Term #	Term
1	3
2	5
3	7
4	9
5	11

2. a) 17
   b) 51
3. No, it's 15.
5. $31
6. Adrian
7. a) 7 kg
   b) 77 L

No unauthorized copying

c) 77 days

Worksheet PA5-12

2. a) 3 squares
   b) Square, triangle, square
   c) A B C
   d) 2 8 9 6

Worksheet PA5-13

1. a) BBYBBY
   b) BYBYBYB
   c) BBYBBBYB
   d) YBBYBBYBB
2. a) Yes
   b) Yes
   c) No
   d) Yes
3. a) Yes
   b) Yes
   c) No – RYRR
   d) No – YRRR
4. a) YRR
   b) RY
   c) YYRR
   d) YRRY
5. Yellow
6. Yellow
7. Red
8. YRY; red
9. Red
10. Daisy
11. Every 5th block is the end of the core. By skip counting, then, the 45th box is the end of a core. So the 48th box is the 3rd box in a new core: it is yellow.
13. a) Dime (10¢)
    b) $2.75

Worksheet PA5-14

1. 1 km
2. 100 km
3. 8 blocks
4. 3 blocks

Worksheet PA5-15

1. 25 km (from the finish line)
2. 250 m
3. 250 m
4. 17 m
5. 2 m

Worksheet PA5-16

1. a) 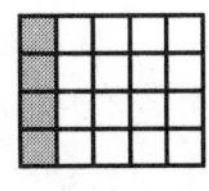
   b) 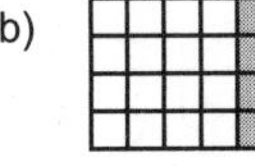
   c) 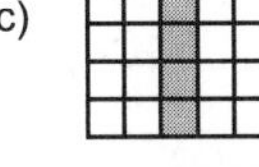
   d) 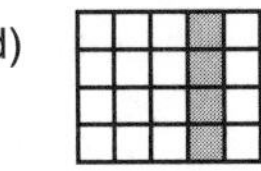
2. a) 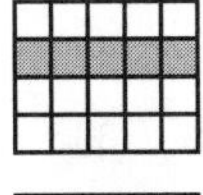
   b)
   c) 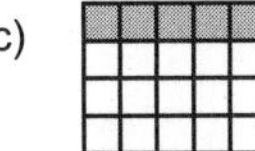
   d) 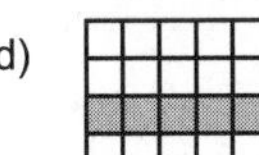
3. a)

2	4	6
8	10	12
14	16	18

   b)

2	4	6
8	10	12
14	16	18

   c)

2	4	6
8	10	12
14	16	18

   d)

2	4	6
8	10	12
14	16	18

4. a) Across rows: add 2
   Down columns: add 2
   Diagonal (l to r): add 4
   Diagonal (r to l): stay the same
   b) Across rows: add 5
   Down columns: add 5
   Diagonal (l to r): add 10
   Diagonal (r to l): stay the same
   c) Across rows: add 3
   Down columns: subtract 3
   Diagonal (l to r): stay the same
   Diagonal (r to l): subtract 6
6. a) Both R3 and R5
   b) C5
   c) C1 – Start at 0 and add 6.
   C2 – Start at 5 and add 2.
   d) C3 = 2 × C4
7. Answers will vary but one option would be:

A	B	A	B
B	A	B	A
A	B	A	B
B	A	B	A

8.

2	7	6
9	5	1
4	3	8

Worksheet PA5-17

1. a) Ones digit is any of the following: 0, 2, 4, 6, 8
   b) Circle: 418, 132, 64, 76, 234, 94, 506
2. a) 5, 10, 15, 20, 25, 30, 35, 40, 45, 50, 55, 60
   b) Ends on 0 or 5
   c) Circle: 45, 150, 190, 65, 235, 1645
3. The sum of the ones and tens digits in each number in a given diagonal is either 3, 6, 9, 12, etc: all multiples of 3!
4. Divisible by 3: 42, 63, 87, 93, 123.

Worksheet PA5-18

2.

08	48
16	56
24	64
32	72
40	80

Pattern: 8, 6, 4, 2, 0

3. Gap: 1, 1, 1, 1, 0 (repeats)
   Pattern: 0, 1, 2, 3, 4, 4, 5, 6, 7, 8
4.

88	128
96	136
104	144
112	152
120	160

Worksheet PA5-19

1. a) Multiples of 2 (only): 4, 6, 34, 66, 74
   Multiples of 5 (only): 5, 15, 75
   Multiples of both 2 & 5: 10, 20, 50, 60, 70
   Multiples of neither 2 nor 5: 19, 27, 27, 39, 63
2. Multiples of 3 (only): 6, 21, 30, 60, 75
   Multiples of 8 (only): 16, 40, 56, 80
   Multiples of both 3 & 8: 24, 48, 72
   Multiples of neither 3 nor 8: 10, 11, 13, 26, 35, 47

Number Sense 1

Worksheet NS5-1

1. a) tens
   b) thousands
   c) thousands
   d) thousands
2. a) thousands

No unauthorized copying

b) tens
c) thousands
d) ones

3. b) 4, 5, 0, 0, 1
c) 0, 3, 6, 9, 9
d) 1, 9, 0 5, 3

4. a) 2, 60, 300, 4 000, 50 000
b) 7, 30, 500, 8 000, 20 000
c) 5, 70, 200, 3 000, 10 000

5. b) 40
c) 400
d) 40 000

6. a) 500
b) 30
c) 60 000
d) 8 000

Worksheet NS5-2

1. a) 3, 4, 5; 345
b) 2, 5, 3, 253
c) 1, 7, 8; 178
d) 5, 0, 6; 506

4. a) 2, 4, 4, 6; 2 446
b) 3, 2, 2, 4; 3 224
c) 2 thousands + 2 hundreds + 2 tens + 9 ones; 2 229

5. a) 2 354
b) 1 266

Worksheet NS5-3

1. a) 4, 3, 4, 2, 7
b) 2, 5, 3, 1, 2
c) 2 ten thousands + 8 thousands + 5 hundreds + 4 tens + 7 ones

2. b) 20 + 7
c) 40 + 8
d) 1 000 + 200 + 30 + 2

3. a) 4 953
b) 2 032
c) 63 997
d) 50 034

4. a) 20
b) 70
c) 800
d) 200

5. a) (i) 5 000 + 800 + 30 + 2
b) (i) 1 000 + 0 + 50 + 4

6. b) one thousand, three hundred sixty-five
c) 1 365 = 1 thousands + 3 hundreds + 6 tens + 5 ones
d) 1 365 = 1 000 + 300 + 60 + 5

7. 1 000

Worksheet NS5-4

1. a) 6, 40, 800; 6, 50, 800; 856 > 846
b) 7, 20, 300; 7, 20, 400: 427 > 327

2. b) 3, 2; 73 605
c) 2, 8; 14 858
d) 3, 4; 4 832

3. a) 2, 3: 134
b) 2, 3; 374
c) 7, 6; 875
d) 3, 2; 238

4. a) 32 562
b) 81 254
c) 37 321
d) 61 275

5. b) <
c) >
d) <

6. a) Thirty-five
b) 392
c) 81
d) 1 232

7. Circle A

9. A 5-digit number will always be bigger than a 4-digit number, if the fist digit is not 0.

10. Nine

11. Conceptíon

Worksheet NS5-5

1. a) 10 more
b) 100 less
c) 10 less
d) 10 more

2. a) 1 000 more
b) 1 000 less
c) 1 000 less
d) 100 less

3. a) 1 000 more
b) 1 000 less
c) 10 000 less
d) 10 000 more

4. b) 3, 4; 100 less
c) 4, 3; 10 000 more
d) 2, 3; 1 000 less

5. a) 335
b) 1 552
c) 692
d) 4 035

6. a) 244
b) 2 392
c) 19 045
d) 21 370

7. a) 10
b) 100
c) 10
d) 100

8. a) 8 538, 8 548
b) 38 730, 39 730
c) 41 502, 41 522
d) 28 373, 28 383

9. b) 8, 9; 92 350 is 10 000 greater than 82 350
c) 8, 9; 68 254 is 1 000 less than 69 254

Worksheet NS5-6

1. a) (i) 438
(ii) 422
(iii) 438 is greater
b) (i) 2 224
(ii) 1 108
(iii) 2 224 is greater

2. a) 78, 79, 87, 89, 97, 98; 98 is greatest.
b) 30, 34, 40, 43; 43 is greatest. NOTE: 03 and 04 are equal to 3 and 4, which are one-digit numbers (so not allowed in list).

3. 999

4. a) 999
b) 9 999
c) 99 999

5. a) <
b) >
c) >
d) >

6. a) 6 432
b) 9 874
c) 4 210

7. a) 84 321
b) 98 521
c) 65 431

8. a) 87 521, answers may vary, 12 578
b) 95 321, answers may vary, 12 359
c) 53 310, answers may vary, 10 335

9. a) 3 183, 3 257, 3 352
b) 17 251, 17 256, 17 385
c) 87 498, 87 499, 87 500
d) 3 281, 36 725, 93 859

12. a) 7
b) 4

Worksheet NS5-7

1. a) 4, 12, 5, 2
b) 2, 18, 3, 8

2. a) 3, 4
b) 7, 3
c) 2, 6
d) 8, 0

3. a) 6 + 2 = 8; 3
b) 5 + 3 = 8; 2
c) 4 + 1 = 5; 1
d) 8 + 1 = 9; 9

4. a) 5 hundreds + 6 tens + 4 ones
b) 7 hundreds + 4 tens + 7 ones

No unauthorized copying

c) 8 hundreds + 7 tens + 8 ones

5. a) 4 + 1 = 5; 3
b) 2 + 1 = 3; 7
c) 8 + 1 = 9; 0

6. a) 7, 3, 4, 8
b) 5, 2, 1, 4
c) 6 thousands + 0 hundreds + 3 tens + 1 ones

7. a) 4, 5, 4, 2
b) 3 thousands + 9 hundreds + 4 tens + 5 ones
c) 6 ten thousands + 5 thousands + 6 hundreds + 5 tens + 5 ones

8. Yes; by regrouping, he has 4 thousands, 3 hundreds, 4 tens and 10 ones – which is 4 more ones than he needs.

Worksheet NS5-8

1. b)

tens	ones
3	5
2	7
5	12
6	2

2. a) 3 ones, 1 ten; sum = 33
b) 5 ones, 1 ten; sum = 85
c) 2 ones, 1 ten; sum = 92
d) 0 ones, 1 ten; sum = 80

3. a) 41
b) 51
c) 93
d) 95

Worksheet NS5-9

1. = 5, 7, 2
= 2, 5, 1
= 7, 12, 3
= 8, 2, 3

2. a) 629
b) 857
c) 919
d) 1 549

3. a) 653
b) 713
c) 831
d) 649

4. a) 825
b) 783
c) 773
d) 348

Worksheet NS5-10

1. = 6, 8, 2, 6
= 2, 5, 4, 3
= 8, 13, 6, 9
= 9, 3, 6, 9

2. a) 6 199
b) 8 578
c) 9 399
d) 9 179

3. a) 6 728
b) 8 847
c) 5 929
d) 9 659

4. a) 7 186
b) 9 186
c) 8 949
d) 7 857

5. a) 9 816
b) 5 279
c) 2 531
d) 9 216

6. a) 6 815
b) 62 829
c) 71 890
d) 69 631

7. a) 216 + 628 = 828
b) 154 + 451 = 605
605 + 506 = 1111
c) 342 + 243 = 585
d) 23 153 + 35 132 = 58 285

Worksheet NS5-11

1. a) 29
b) 6, 15; 29
c) 2, 14: 18
d) 6, 17; 48

2. b) 6, 18; 39
c) 4, 13; 24
d) 7, 12; 39

3. b) Help! 2 is less than 6
c) 32
d) Help! 2 is less than 9

4. a) 271
b) 5, 17; 485
c) 7, 11; 520
d) 8, 15; 193

5. a) 127
b) 6, 12; 133
c) 5, 14; 326
d) 8, 10; 474

6. a) 6, 14, 12; 389
b) 7, 11, 13; 648
c) 2, 9, 14; 277
d) 8, 13, 13; 359

7. b) 3,12; 2 432
c) 8, 16; 3 921
d) 5, 15; 2 722

8. a) 7, 17; 1 328
b) 7, 15; 1 812
c) 5, 12; 4 194
d) 2, 15; 1 600

9. a) 5 757
b) 4 459
c) 2 687
d) 7 489

10. a) 642
b) 52
c) 238
d) 741

Worksheet NS5-12

1. $57 + $12 = $69

2. 2 375 + 5 753 = 8 128 km

3. 406 – 244 = 162 m

4. 5 895 – 3 776 = 2 119 m

5. 39 666 + 39 666 = 79 332 km

6. 12 475 + 14 832 = 27 307

7. Answers will vary.
2008 – 1867 = 141

8. Answers will vary. The difference is always 198 because, in a number with this property, the digit in the hundreds place is always 2 greater than the digit in the ones place.

9. 20 – 5 – 4 = 11

10. David:
26 – 15 = 11
Claude:
26 + 10 = 36
David and Claude:
11 + 36 = 47

Worksheet NS5-13

1. a) 58 020 – 25 690 = 32 330
b) 82 100 – 25 690 = 56 410
c) 25 690, 28 570, 31 340, 58 020, 82 100
d) 370 990 – 82 100 = 288 890

2. 330

3. Order of numbers may vary but additions are:
8 + 1, 7 + 2, 6 + 3, 5 + 4

4. a) 87 645
b) 56 748 or 56 784 or 56 847 or 56 874
c) Exact answers will vary but possible combinations include:
7+ 5 with 4, 6, or 8 as the ones digit and 4 + 8 with 6 as the ones digit.
d) Exact answers will vary but the thousands digit will be 8 and the hundreds digit

No unauthorized copying

will be 4.

6. 25 746

Worksheet NS5-14

1. a) 2; 4; 2 × 4 = 8
   b) 4; 5; 4 × 5 = 20
   c) 4 rows
   4 dots in each row
   4 × 4 = 16
2. a) 4 × 3
   b) 4 × 2
   c) 5 × 4
   d) 7 × 3
3. a) 6 × 5 = 30
   b) 3 × 7 = 21
4. a) Same
   b) Yes

Worksheet NS5-15

1. a) 0 → 4 → 8 ;
   4 + 4 = 8
   OR
   0 → 2 → 4 → 6 → 8;
   2 + 2 + 2 + 2 = 8
   b) 0 → 3 → 6 → 9 → 12;
   3 + 3 + 3 + 3 = 12
   OR
   0 → 4 → 8 → 12;
   4+ 4 + 4 = 12
2. a) 8, 12, 16, 20
   b) 12, 18, 24, 30
   c) 14, 21, 28, 35
3. a) 15
   b) 10
   c) 12
   d) 18
4. a) 4 × 6 = 24
   b) 5 × 4 = 20

Worksheet NS5-16

1. a) 3, 12, 120
   b) (ii) 2, 4, 40
2. b) 5, 20, 200
   c) 4, 12, 120
   d) 3, 18, 180
3. a) 6, 60, 600
   b) 5, 50, 500
   c) 20, 200, 2 000
   d) 8, 80 800

4. a) 150
   b) 120
   c) 160
   d) 150
6. 4 × 2 thousands
   = 8 thousands
   = 8 000

Worksheet NS4-17

1. a) 3 × 20
   b) 4 × 10
   c) 5 × 20
   d) 5 × 10
2. Answers are top to bottom, left to right
   a) 3 × 24, 3 ×20, 3 × 4
   b) 4 × 13, 4 ×10, 4 × 3
   c) 2 × 25, 2 ×20, 2 × 5
   d) 3 × 14, 3 ×10, 3 × 4
3. a) 2×24 =2×20+2×4
   b) 4×12 =4×10+4×2
   c) 4×25 =4×20+4×5
   d) 3×13 =3×10+3×3

Worksheet NS5-18

1. a) 3, 20, 3
   b) 4 × 10; 4 × 4;
   4 × 10 + 4 × 4
2. a) 4 × 40 + 4 × 2
   = 40 + 8
   = 48
   b) 3 × 40 + 3 × 3
   = 120 + 9
   = 129
   c) 4 × 20 + 4 × 2
   = 80 + 8
   = 88
   d) 3 × 200 + 3 × 10 + 3 × 3
   = 600 + 30 + 9
   = 639
3. a) 24
   b) 84
   c) 36
   d) 44
4. a) Atilla planted 996 trees altogether.
   b) 960

Worksheet NS5-19

1. a) 204
   b) 126
   c) 284
   d) 126
2. a) 124
   b) 128
   c) 155
   d) 248

Worksheet NS5-20

1. a) 2; 0
   b) 1; 6
   c) 2; 5
   d) 3; 6
2. a) 9
   b) 7
   c) 7
   d) 9
3. a) 1; 70
   b) 3; 156
   c) 2; 180
   d) 1; 165

Worksheet NS5-21

1. a) 400, 10, 2; 1 200, 30, 6; 1 236
   b) 300, 20, 3; 600, 40, 6; 646
2. a) 68
   b) 936
   c) 848
   d) 646
3. a) 1, 456
   b) 1, 678
   c) 1, 896
   d) 1, 648
4. a) 1, 756
   b) 3, 805
   c) 1, 759
   d) 1, 568
5. a) 568
   b) 1 866
   c) 1 561
   d) 2 592

Worksheet NS5-22

1. a) 3 × 10
   b) 4 × 10
   c) 7 × 10
2. a) 2 × 10 × 33
   b) 2 × 10 × 21
   c) 3 × 10 × 17
3. a) 2 × 340 = 680
   b) 3 × 130 = 390
   c) 4 × 220 = 880
   d) 5 × 310 = 1 550
4. a) 660
   b) 800
   c) 1 200
   d) 1 080
5. b) 40 × 50 = 2 000
   c) 20 × 50 = 1 000
   d) 60 × 40 = 2 400

Worksheet NS5-23

1. a) 1; 20
   b) 2, 00
   c) 1, 50
   d) 80
2. a) 1, 1 100
   b) 1, 1 360
   c) 2, 1 000
   d) 1, 2 150
3. a) 20 × 10 + 20 × 3
   = 200 + 60
   = 260
   b) 20 × 40 + 20 × 2
   = 800 + 40
   = 840
   c) 30 × 20 + 30 × 3
   = 600 + 90
   = 690

Worksheet NS5-24

1. a) 1, 115
   b) 1, 72
   c) 1, 52
   d) 86
2. a) 1, 920
   b) 1, 720
   c) 2, 1400
   d) 1, 2150
3. a) 1, 3, 210, 700
   b) 1, 3, 175, 750
   c) 1, 92, 690
   d) 1, 2, 75, 450
4. b) 3 591
   c) 2 835
   d) 1 161
5. a) 1, 1, 75, 750, 825
   b) 1, 86, 2 150, 2 236

No unauthorized copying

c) 1, 2, 441, 1 260, 1 701

d) 1, 4, 405, 900, 1 305

6. a) 864

b) 4 088

c) 5 440

d) 1 767

Worksheet NS5-25

1. 46, 88, 24, 62, 86, 108, 166, 184, 142

2. 50, 90, 32, 56, 36, 34, 70, 110, 78

3. a) 64

b) 96

4. Yes.

5. a) 200

b) 270

c) 420

d) 2 700

6. Stay the same

7. a) 210

b) 320

c) 430

d) 440

Worksheet NS5-26

1. a) 2, 1; = 3 × 3

b) 2, 4; = 3 × 6

c) 3, 4; = 3 × 7

d) 2, 2; = 3 × 4

2. a) 3 × 10 000 + 2 × 1 000 + 7 × 100 + 5 × 10 + 3

b) 4 × 10 000 + 5 × 1 000 + 3 × 100 + 2 × 10 + 6

c) 7 × 10 000 + 2 × 1 000 + 2 × 10 + 3

4. a) Sometimes

b) Always

c) Sometimes

d) Always

5. The smalles two digit number is 10. Thus the product of 10 × 10 = 100. Everything that is greater than 10 will produce a greater product.

6. a) 4 × 321 = 1284

b) 1 × 234

Worksheet NS5-27

1. 1 950 legs

2. 744 hours

3. 1 044 m

4. 5 880 times

5. 564 strings

6. a) 333

b) 444

c) 555

d) 666

7. 900 times

8. Mercury: 14 550 km
Mars: 20 370 km
Pluto: 10 200 km

9. $364; $136

10. a) True

b) True

c) True

d) False

Worksheet NS5-28

1. a) caps, 2, 5

b) Birds, 4, 3

3. a) toys, 6, 4

b) cookies, 8, 4

c) flowers, 3, 6

d) Oranges, 9, 5

Worksheet NS5-29

1. a) 3

b) 4

2. a) 5 Δ per set

b) 3 Δ per set

3. 2 □ per set

4. a) 2

b) 4

c) 3

5. a) 2 sets

b) 4 sets

6. a) 5 boxes

b) 4 children per car

c) (i) Apples

(ii) There are 2 apples for each friend.

d) (i) comic books

(ii) There are 8 bins.

7. a) 2

b) 3

c) 3

d) 2

Worksheet NS5-30

1. b) 2 + 2 + 2 + 2 = 8

c) 5 + 5 + 5 + 5 = 20

2. a) 24 ÷ 6 = 4

b) 24 ÷ 4 = 6

c) 21 ÷ 7 = 3

d) 15 ÷ 3 = 5

3. a) 0 → 4 → 8; 2

b) 0 → 2 → 4 → 6 → 8 → 10 → 12 → 14 → 16; 8

4. a) 18 ÷ 2 = 9

b) 9 ÷ 3 = 3

5. a) 3

b) 2

c) 4

d) 3

6. $4

7. 7 candles

Worksheet NS5-31

1. a) 5 × 4 = 20;
4 × 5 = 20;
20 ÷ 4 = 5

b) 6 × 4 = 24;
4 × 6 = 24;
24 ÷ 4 = 6

c) 3 × 4 = 12;
4 × 3 = 12;
12 ÷ 3 = 4;
12 ÷ 4= 3;
12, 4, 3

d) 2 × 4 = 8;
4 × 2 = 8;
8 ÷ 2 = 4;
8 ÷ 4= 2;
8, 4, 2

2. a) 5, 5

b) 3, 3

c) 8, 8

d) 3, 3

Worksheet NS5-32

1. a) 16, 4, 4

b) 15, 3, 5

c) 6, 4, 24

d) 3, 3, 9

3. a) 21 ÷ 3 = 7

b) 14 ÷ 7 = 2

4. a) 6 × 3 = 18

b) 20 ÷ 4 = 5

c) 15 ÷ 5 = 3

d) 10 ÷ 2 = 5

5. a) 15 ÷ 5 = 3; 3

b) 6 × 4 = 24; 24

c) 25 ÷ 5 = 5; 5

d) 9 × 4 = 36; 36

6. a) 3 × 8 = 24 chairs

b) 5 × 9 = 45 marbles

c) 35 ÷ 7 = 5 flowers

d) 32 ÷ 4 = 8 people

7. a) 4 × 2 = 8
2 × 4 = 8
8 ÷ 4 = 2
8 ÷ 2 = 4

b) 6 × 3 = 18
3 × 6 = 18
18 ÷ 6 = 3
18 ÷ 3 = 6

c) 7 × 8 = 56
8 × 7 = 56
56 ÷ 7 = 8
56 ÷ 8 = 7

d) 9 × 4 = 36
4 × 9 = 36
36 ÷ 9 = 4
36 ÷ 4 = 9

Worksheet NS5-33

1. No; since 7 ÷ 2 = 3 R1

2. a) 2, 2

b) 3, 1

3. b) 14 ÷ 4 = 3 R2

c) 18 ÷ 6 = 3

d) 17 ÷ 4 = 4 R1

No unauthorized copying

4. Each child will receive 4 sea shells, and 2 will be left over.
5. 7 groups of 4 pens, R1
OR
4 groups of 7 pen, R1
6. There are two answers: 8 or 12 stickers

Worksheet NS5-34

1. a) 3, 7, 6
b) 4, 9, 5
c) 4, 9, 2
d) 5, 8, 6
2. a) 1
b) 1
c) 1
d) 2
3. b) 2, 4, 2
c) 1, 5, 1
d) 4, 2, 4
4. a) 2, 9, 4, 8
b) 4, 9, 2, 8
5. b) 3, 6
c) 4, 8
d) 1, 5
6. a) 1, 8, 1
b) 3, 6, 1
c) 1, 4, 2
d) 2, 6, 2
7. a) 1, 5, 25
b) 1, 3, 27
c) 2, 8, 13
d) 3, 6, 13
8. a) 24, 8, 16
b) 17, 5, 35
c) 37, 6, 15
d) 17, 3, 21
9. a) 14, 5, 24, 20, 4
b) 25, 6, 17, 15, 2
c) 33, 6, 7, 6, 1
d) 17, 4, 30, 28, 2
10. 2 are left over (since 98 ÷ 8 = 12 R2)
11. There are 13 full weeks in 93 days (since 93 ÷ 7 = 13 R2)
12. 15 days
13. 12 m
14. Tyree

Worksheet NS5-35

1. 335 ÷ 2 = 167 R1
2. a) 266
b) 129 R3
c) 181 R2
d) 247 R1
3. a) 23 R 1
b) 73 R3
c) 73 R2
d) 64
4. a) 305
b) 1 504 R3
c) 1 737 R2
d) 446 R1
5. 36 m
6. 142 km
7. 39 books

Worksheet NS5-36

1. 30 children
2. a) 150, 510
b) 105, 150, 510
c) 150, 510
d) 150, 510
3. 50
4. 8 packets
5. 6 cars
6. 13 days
7. 9 plums
8. 11 pages

Worksheet NS5-37

1. 900 students
2. 18 eggs; 240 eggs
3. 2 pencils in a set;
4 sets in total;
cost is 17¢ per set and 68¢ in total
4. $133
5. 4 500 m
7. 12 apples
8. a) 25
b) 49
9. a) 1 800 m
b) 200 m
c) 3 laps
10. 12 ÷ 3 = 4
So there are 4 groups of 3 in 12 CDs:
4 × $23 = $92
11. 2
12. Total # of letters
= 2 624 + 1 759 + 3 284
= 7 667
Half of all the letters
= 7 667 ÷ 2
= 3 833 R1
So none of the letter carriers delivered more than half the letters.

Worksheet NS5-38

1. a) 0
b) 10
c) 0
d) 10
2. a) 1 2 3 4
b) 6 7 8 9
c) It's in the middle
3. a) 10 20 30
b) 60 70 80
c) 250 260 270
4. a) 30
b) 10
c) 40
d) 70
5. a) 100
b) 0
6. 50 is exactly halfway between 0 and 100
7. a) 100
b) 0
c) 0
d) 100
8. a) 600
b) 700
c) 800
d) 700
9. a) 200
b) 600
c) 900
d) 500
10. a) 0
b) 1000
11. a) 0
b) 1 000
c) 1 000
12. 4 000, 5 000
13. a) 3 000
b) 7 000
c) 6 000
d) 8 000

Worksheet NS5-39

1. a) 20
b) 30
c) 70
d) 60
2. a) 150
b) 180
c) 360
d) 350
3. a) 700
b) 500
c) 500
d) 300
4. a) 8 000
b) 8 000
c) 5 000
d) 3 000

Worksheet NS5-40

1. a) 3 round down
b) 5 round up
c) 5 round down
d) 2 round up
2. a) 73 000 rd
b) 36 000 ru
c) 94200 rd
d) 28700 ru
3. a) 2 200
b) 3 900
c) 10 000
d) 13 290

Worksheet NS5-41

1. a) 40 + 20 = 60
b) 30 + 50 = 80
c) 60 – 20 = 40
d) 90 – 60 = 30
2. a) 300 + 400 = 700
b) 400 + 500 = 900
c) 600 – 200 = 500
d) 800 – 600 = 200
3. a) 1 000 + 4 000
= 5 000

No unauthorized copying

b) 6 000 + 4 000
= 2 000
c) 8 000 + 6 000
= 14 000
d) 30 000 – 20 000
= 10 000

4. a) 9 200 + 1 500
= 8700
b) 4 700 – 1 900
= 14 000
c) 64 900 – 42 300
= 22 600

Worksheet NS5-42

1. 60 years
2. 49 000 square km
3. 12 000 people
4. Exact date
5. Hundreds

Worksheet NS5-43

1. a) 120
b) 120
c) 1200
d) 1200

2. a) 1 zero
b) 2 zeroes
c) 3 zeroes

3. a) 80
800
8 000
80 000
b) 250
2 500
25 000
250 000
c) 620
6 200
62 000
620 000

4. a) 170
b) 500
c) 970
d) 6 900

5. a) 10 × 80 = 800
b) 10 × 20 = 200
c) 10 × 80 = 800
d) 10 × 60 = 600

6. a) 3
b) 4
c) 5

Worksheet NS5-44

1. a) 5, 10, 15, 20, 25, 26, 27, 28
b) 5, 10, 15, 20, 21, 22, 23

2. a) 10, 20, 30, 35, 40, 45, 50, 55
b) 10, 20, 30, 35, 40, 45, 50
c) 25, 50, 75, 80, 85
d) 25, 50, 75, 85, 95

3. b) 25. 50, 60, 70, 71, 72, 73
c) 25, 50, 60, 70, 75, 80
d) 25, 50, 75, 85, 95, 96, 97

BONUS:
25, 50, 60, 70, 80, 85, 90, 91, 92, 93, 94

4. b) 5, 10, 20, 30, 40, 41

BONUS:
25, 50, 75, 100, 125, 135, 145, 150, 155, 160,161, 162, 163

5. b) 25, 50, 55, 60, 61, 62, 63
c) 25, 50, 60, 70, 71, 72
d) 25, 50, 75, 85, 95, 100, 105

BONUS:

6. a) 37¢
b) 95¢
c) 150¢
d) 114¢

7. a) 48¢
b) 97¢
c) 86¢
d) 76¢

BONUS:

Worksheet NS5-45

1. a) + 10¢ + 10¢
b) + 25¢ + 25¢
c) + 10¢ + 10¢
d) + 25¢ + 25¢

2. a) + 5¢ + 1¢
b) + 10¢ + 5¢
c) + 10¢ + 5¢
d) + 25¢ + 10¢

3. a) + 25¢ + 5¢
b) + 5¢ + 1¢ + 1¢
c) + $2 + $2
d) + $2 + 25¢ +10¢ + 10¢

4. a) Yes,
25¢ + 25¢ + 10¢ + 10¢ + 10¢
b) Yes,
25¢ + 25¢ + 25¢ + 5¢

Worksheet NS5-46

1. a) 25¢
b) 25¢, 25¢
c) 25¢, 25¢, 25¢
d) 25¢, 25¢, 25¢

2. b) 50¢;
57¢ – 50¢ = 7¢;
coins: 5¢, 1¢, 1¢
c) 75¢;
85¢ - 75¢ = 10¢;
coins: 10¢
d) 75¢;
96¢ - 75¢ = 21¢;
coins: 10¢, 10¢, 1¢

3. a) 25¢ + 5¢
b) $1
c) 10¢ + $10 + $1
d) 25¢ + $1

4. a) $1 + 25¢ + 25¢
b) 25¢ + 25¢ + 10¢ + 10¢
c) $2 + $2 + $2 + $2
d) $2 + $2 + $2 + $2 + $1 + 25¢ + 25¢

Worksheet NS5-47

1. a) 1, 7, 3, $1.73
b) 0, 6, 2, $0.62
c) 4, 6, 5, $4.65
d) 0, 0, 2, $0.02

2. a) 7¢, $0.70
b) 20¢, $0.20
c) 60¢, $0.60
d) 4¢, $0.04

3. a) $5.00, 55¢, $5.55
b) $15.00, 36¢, $15.36
c) $20.00, 51¢, $20.51

4. b) 110¢, $1.10

5. a) $3.25
b) $0.20
c) $0.06
d) $2.83

6. a) 299¢
b) 343¢
c) 141¢ – 10
d) 8¢

7. a) $1.96
b) 103¢
c) 840¢

8. a) Seven dollars and seventy cents
b) Nine dollars and eighty-three cents
c) Fifteen dollars and eighty cents

9. a) 1, 1, 2, 1, 1, 1, 1, 1, 2;
$43.42
b) 2, 1, 1, 2, 1, 1, 1, 1, 0;
$60.40
c) 1, 2, 1, 1, 1, 2, 0, 1, 2;
$48.57

10. $2.62;
200¢ = $2.00 and $.62 > 56¢

11. 1 toonie, 1 loonie, 2 quarters

12. 2 toonies, 1 loonie, 2 dimes, 1 nickel
OR
5 loonies, 1 quarter

13. a) Three dollars and fifty-seven cents
b) Twelve dollars and twenty-three cents
c) Six hundred and four dollars and eighty cents

No unauthorized copying

d) Three hundred twenty-seven dollars and twenty-five cents

Worksheet NS5-48

1. a) 3, 75¢, 0, 75¢, 1, 80¢, 3
   b) 2, 50¢, 0, 50¢, 0, 50¢, 2
   c) 3, 75¢, 2, 95¢, 0, 95¢, 2
   d) 0, 0¢, 2, 20¢, 0, 20¢, 3
2. a) $40
   b) $20
   c) $20
   d) $40
3. a) 0, 1, 0, 0, 0, 1
   b) 0, 1, 1, 0, 0, 0
   c) 1, 0, 0, 0, 2, 0
   d) 1, 1, 1, 1, 0, 0
4. a) 25¢ + 25¢ + 10¢ + 10¢ + 1¢ + 1¢
   b) 25¢ + 25¢ + 25¢ + 10¢ + 5¢ + 1¢ + 1¢
   c) 25¢ + 25¢ + 25¢ + 5¢ + 1¢ + 1¢
   d) 25¢ + 25¢ + 1¢ + 1¢
5. a) $50 + $5
   b) $50 + $10 + $5 + $2
   c) $50 + $10 + $2 + $2
   d) $100 + $20 + $2 + $1

Worksheet NS5-49

1. a) 6¢
   b) 9¢
   c) 6¢
   d) 7¢
2. a) 10¢
   b) 30¢
   c) 50¢
   d) 60¢
3. a) 20¢
   b) 30¢
   c) 80¢
   d) 40¢
4. b) 60
   c) 50
   d) 30
5. a) 4, 60, 40, 44¢
   b) 7, 90, 10, 17¢
   c) 6, 60, 40, 46¢
   d) 5, 30, 70, 75¢
6. a) 26¢
   b) 53¢
   c) 64¢
   d) 47¢
7. a) 13¢
   b) 17¢
8. 58¢;
   25¢ + 25¢ + 5¢ + 1¢ + 1¢ + 1¢
9. a) $8.00
   b) $6.00
   c) $6.00
   d) $6.00
10. a) 3, 30, 20, $23.00
    b) 2, 40, 60, $62.00
    c) 7, 60, 40, $47.00
    d) 6, 20, 30, $36.00
11. a) $16
    b) $75
    c) $54
    d) $12
12 $2, $70, $72.43
13. a) 15¢, $7, $60, $67.15
    b) 73¢, $3, $10, $13.73
    c) 81¢, $7, $40, $47.81
    d) 57¢, $3, $30, $33.57

Worksheet NS5-50

1. a) $8.68
   b) $58.38
   c) $49.89
2. a) $40.35
   b) $72.57
   c) $93.95
   d) $60.60
3. $30.78
4. $660.07
5. $36.90
6. Yes
7. a) $64.55
   b) $52.75
   c) $73.25
   d) $64.60
8. a) $55.19
   b) Pants & soccer ball
   c) Yes
   d) $128.31
9. a) $9.20
   b) 7
   c) 8
   d) No

Worksheet NS-51

1. a) $1.32
   b) $4.42
   c) $4.21
   d) $2.01
2. a) $1.71
   b) $2.76
   c) $1.28
   d) $22.55
3. $1.33
4. $1.31
5. No, she is short by 90¢.
6. $2.88

Logic and Systematic Search

Worksheet LSS5-1

1. a)

nickels	pennies
0	17
1	12
2	7
3	2

b)

dimes	nickels
0	9
1	7
2	5
3	3
4	1

c)

nickels	pennies
0	23
1	18
2	13
3	8
4	3

d)

dimes	pennies
0	32
1	22
2	12
3	2

2.

quarters	nickels
0	12
1	7
2	2

He stops at 2 quarters because 3 quarters is 75¢ (and larger than 60¢).

3. a)

nickels	pennies
0	27
1	22
2	17
3	12
4	7
5	2

b)

quarters	dimes
0	7
2	2

c)

dimes	nickels
0	13
1	11
2	9
3	7
4	5
5	3
6	1

d)

loonies	toonies
1	6
3	5
5	4
7	3
9	2

No unauthorized copying

11	1
13	0

4\. a)

1st number	2nd number
1	6
2	3
3	2
4	-

b)

1st number	2nd number
1	8
2	4
3	-
4	2

5\.

quarters	dimes
0	7
1	-
2	2

6\. a)

quarters	dimes
0	8
1	-
2	3
3	-

b)

quarters	dimes
0	-
1	8
2	-
3	3

7\.

S 1	S 2	S 3
1	1	10
2	2	8
3	3	6
5	5	2

8\. a)

1st number	2nd number
1	12
2	6
3	4
4	3
6	2
12	1

b)

1st number	2nd number
1	14
2	7
7	2
14	1

c)

1st number	2nd number
1	20
2	10
4	5
5	4
10	2
20	1

d)

1st number	2nd number
1	24
2	12
3	8
4	6
6	4
8	3
12	2
24	1

9\. Side lengths:
1, 1, 6, 6
2, 2, 5, 5
3, 3, 4, 4,

10\. Side lengths:
1, 1, 10, 10
2, 2, 5, 5

Patterns & Algebra 2

Worksheet PA5-20

1\. a) Gaps:
+ 2, + 3, + 4, + 5, + 6
Rest of Pattern:
17, 23

b) Gaps:
+ 1, + 2, + 3, + 4, + 5,
+ 6
Rest of Pattern:
19, 25

c) Gaps:
+ 3, + 5, + 7, + 9, + 11
Rest of Pattern:
37, 48

d) Gaps:
+ 2, + 4, + 6, + 8, + 10, + 12
Rest of Pattern:
37, 49

2\.

Figure	# of Sq
1	2
2	5
3	9
4	14
5	20
6	27

3\.

Figure	# of Tri
1	1
2	4
3	9
4	16
5	25
6	36

So Figure 6 will need 36 triangles.

4\. c) Start at 1. Add 1, 2, 3… (The step increases by 1)

d) Start at 6. Add 2, then subtract 3. Repeat.

5\. a) Start at 0. Add 3, 5, 7… (The step increases by 2)
5th term = 24

b) Start at 1. Multiply by 3. Repeat.
5th term = 81

6\. a) Start at 1. Add 2, 3, 4…(The step increases by 1)
The 5th figure will have 15 shaded parts.

b) Start at 1. Multiply by 3. Repeat.
The 5th figure will have 81 shaded parts.

Worksheet PA5-21

1\. a)

Days	Hours
1	24
2	48
3	72
4	96
5	120

b)

Years	Days
1	365
2	730
3	1095

c)

Tonnes	Kg
1	1000
2	2000
3	3000
4	4000

2\. a) 750 breaths
b) 24 breaths / minute
c) 72 breaths
d) 678 breaths more

3\. a) 52
b) 900

4\. Yes

5\. a) 37 × 3 = 111
37 × 6 = 222
37 × 9 = 333
37 × 12 = 444
37 × 15 = 555

b) 1 × 1 = 1
11 × 11 = 121
111 × 111 = 12 321
1111 × 1111
= 1 234 321
11111 × 11111
= 123 454 321

Worksheet PA5-22

2\. a) 5 = 3 + 2
b) 8 = 4 + 4
c) 2 + 3 = 5
d) 4 + 3 = 7

3\. a) 9 = 5 + 4
b) 7 = 3 + 4
c) 8 = 3 + 5
d) 10 – 2 = 8

Worksheet PA5-23

2\. a) 7 – 3 = 4
b) 7 – 2 = 5

No unauthorized copying

3. a) 3
 b) 2
 c) 3
 d) 2
4. a) 3 + 2 = 5
 b) 3 + 5 = 8
 c) 15 ÷ 3 = 5
5. a) 3 + 2 = 5
 b) 10 – 4 = 6
 c) 3 × 4 = 12

Worksheet PA5-24

1. a) 3 × 2
 b) 5 × 3
 c) 6 × 3
2. a) 60 × 2
 b) 80 × 3
 c) 70 ×h
3. a) 5h or 5 × h
 b) 5t or 5 × t
 c) 5x or 5 × x
 d) 5n or 5 × n
4. a) A + 3 = B
 b) 2 × A = B
 c) A + 2 = B
 d) A × 3 = B
5. a) 10 – 4 = x
 b) 12 – 7 = x

Worksheet PA5-25

1. a) 6
 b) 3
 c) 6
 d) 2
2. a) 0 + 0 + 10 = 10;
 1 + 1 + 8 = 10;
 2 + 2 + 6 = 10;
 3 + 3 + 4 = 10;
 4 + 4 + 2 = 10;
 5 + 5 + 0 = 10
 b) 0 + 0 + 8 = 8;
 1 + 1 + 6 = 8;
 2 + 2 + 4 = 8;
 3 + 3 + 2 = 8;
 4 + 4 + 0 = 8
 c) 1 + 1 + 3 + 3 = 8;
 4 + 4 + 0 + 0 = 8
 d) 1 + 2 + 6 = 9;
 1 + 3 + 5 = 9;
 1 + 8 + 0 = 9;
 2 + 3 + 4 = 9;
 2 + 7 + 0 = 9;
 3 + 6 + 0 = 9;
 4 + 5 + 0 = 9
3. Answers will vary – must be two of the following:
 0 + 0 + 7 = 7;
 1 + 1 + 5 = 7;
 3 + 3 + 1 = 7;
 2 + 2 + 3 = 7
4. 2
5. 1; 2 ; 3
6. a) 2; 3
 b) 2; 4
 c) 2; 5
 d) Any number would work here.
7. a) 10 + 1 = 11
 10 + 2 = 12
 10 + 3 = 13
 10 + 4 = 14
 b) 10 - 1 = 9
 10 - 2 = 8
 10 - 3 = 7
 10 - 4 = 6
 c) 10 × 1 = 10
 10 × 2 = 20
 10 × 3 = 30
 10 × 4 = 40
8. a) The number in a circle increases by 1 as the number in a square increases by 1.
 b) Decreases by 1
 c) Increases by 10
9. The product doubles.
 2, 4, 8, 16
 5 × 16 = 80
10 7 × 3 × 2 =
 = 7 × 6 = 21
11. Outer darts = 3 points each
 Inner dart = 4 points

Worksheet PA5-26

1. a)

# of Tables	# of Chairs
2	6
3	8
4	10

 RULE:
 Multiply # of tables by 2 and add 2
 b) 32 chairs
2. 36 triangles
3. 140 km
4. a) Yes (118 is 121 – 3)
 b) No (40 is not 35 + 4)
 c) Yes (9 is 6 + 3)
5. 24 cups of water
6. a) 24
 b) 32
7. 24th and 48th
9. The patter repeats every five figures, so #63 will be 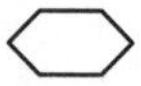
10. Day 1: 2
 Day 2: 5
 Day 3: 8
 Day 4: 11
 Total: 26
11. 8.50 + 4.5 × 4 =26.5
 6 × 5 = 30
 Way #1
12. a) Decrease
 b) 2000 m
 d) 0.5 cm = 2000 m
13. Pattern: start at 1; add 2, 3, etc. Figure 7 needs 28 blocks. Marlene is wrong.

Number Sense 2

Worksheet NS5-52

1. a) $\frac{7}{9}$
 b) $\frac{2}{4}$
 c) $\frac{3}{4}$
 d) $\frac{4}{6}$
2. a) The total number of pieces in the pie
 b) The number of pieces in the pie that you have

3. a) 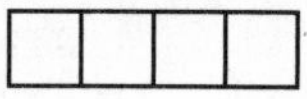
 b) 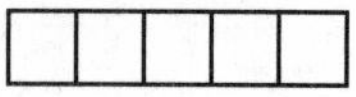
4. a) $\frac{2}{3}$
 b) $\frac{1}{5}$
5. a) 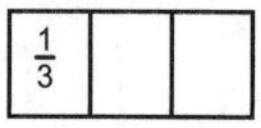

 b) 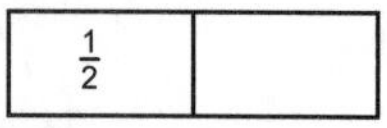

 c) 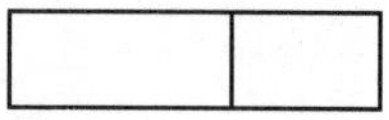
6. a) final line should be 3 cm long.
 b) final line should be 6 cm long.
7. a) <u>Doesn't</u> show $\frac{1}{3}$: there are three pieces but they're not the same size.
 b) <u>Does</u> show $\frac{1}{3}$: the circle is cut into three equal pieces and one piece is shaded.
 c) <u>Doesn't</u> show $\frac{1}{3}$: there are four pieces in the pie.
 d) <u>Does</u> show $\frac{1}{3}$: the circle is cut into three equal pieces and one piece is shaded.

Worksheet NS5-53

1. a) $\frac{3}{5}$, $\frac{3}{5}$
 b) $\frac{1}{5}$, $\frac{2}{5}$
2. a) Triangles
 b) Squares
 Or
 Shadeed triangles
 Or
 Not shaded triangles
 c) circles
 d) Shaded
 Or
 Not triangles

3. $\frac{3}{5}$ are shaded;

   $\frac{3}{5}$ are triangles

4. a) 12

   b) $\frac{7}{12}$

   c) Yes: $\frac{7}{12} > \frac{6}{12} = \frac{1}{2}$

5. a) Smiths: $\frac{2}{5}$

   Sinhas: $\frac{1}{3}$

   b) $\frac{3}{8}$

6. a) $\frac{3}{6} = \frac{1}{2}$

   b) $\frac{3}{6} = \frac{1}{2}$

7. $\frac{7}{12}$

8. a) $\frac{3}{6} = \frac{1}{2}$

   b) $\frac{2}{6} = \frac{1}{3}$

   c) $\frac{1}{6}$

   d) $\frac{3}{6} = \frac{1}{2}$

10. NOTE: In these two answers, the order of shapes doesn't matter.

    a)

    b)

Worksheet NS5-54

1. a) $\frac{1}{3}$

   b) $\frac{1}{4}$

   c) $\frac{1}{5}$

   d) $\frac{1}{12}$

2. a) $\frac{1}{4}$

   since 2 triangles = 1 square

   b) $\frac{1}{6}$

   since 2 triangles = 1 square

   c) $\frac{3}{8}$

   since 2 triangles = 1 square

   d) $\frac{3}{8}$

   since 2 rectangles = 1 square

3. First, divide the trapezoid into equal-sized triangles:

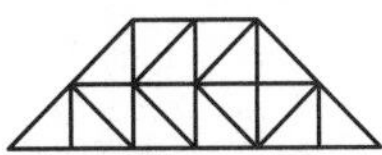

A single small triangle = $\frac{1}{16}$ of the figure.

4. a) $\frac{1}{2}$

   b) $\frac{2}{3}$ but may vary

   c) $\frac{1}{3}$

   d) $\frac{1}{9}$ but may vary

Worksheet NS5-55

1. $\frac{5}{6}$ has the greater numerator and is also the greater fraction.

   Sample Explanation: The denominators are the same (6) and, from the diagram, the pieces are the same size. So we can simply look at the numerator to tell which fraction is greater.

2. a) $\frac{9}{16}$

   b) $\frac{5}{8}$

   c) $\frac{24}{25}$

   d) $\frac{37}{53}$

3. The fraction with the *larger* numerator is greater.

4. a) $\frac{1}{8}$

   b) $\frac{12}{12}$

   c) $\frac{5}{125}$

5. The fraction with the *smaller* denominator is greater.

6. a) $\frac{1}{3}, \frac{2}{3}, \frac{3}{3}$

   b) $\frac{1}{10}, \frac{2}{10}, \frac{5}{10}, \frac{9}{10}$

   c) $\frac{1}{13}, \frac{1}{7}, \frac{1}{3}$

   d) $\frac{2}{16}, \frac{2}{11}, \frac{5}{7}, \frac{2}{5}$

7. a) $\frac{2}{3}$

   b) $\frac{11}{17}$

   c) $\frac{6}{18}$

8. $\frac{1}{2} = \frac{50}{100} > \frac{45}{100}$

9. Yes, since the pies can be very different sizes:

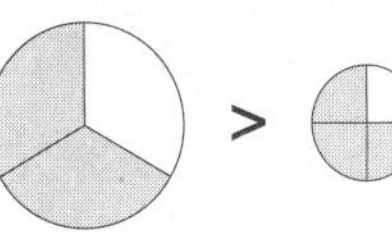

Worksheet NS5-56

1. a) 2

   b) 3

   c) 1

2. a) $2\frac{1}{4}$

   b) $1\frac{3}{4}$

   c) $1\frac{2}{3}$

   d) $4\frac{3}{8}$

3. a)

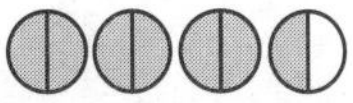

   b)

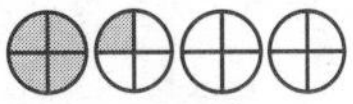

   c)

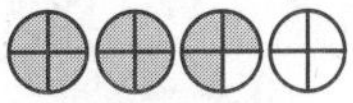

   d)

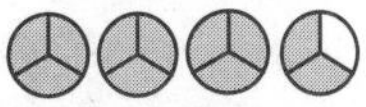

4. a)

   b)

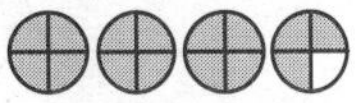

   c)

   d)

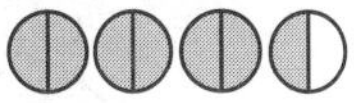

Worksheet NS5-57

1. a) $\frac{5}{2}$

   b) $\frac{7}{4}$

   c) $\frac{5}{3}$

   d) $\frac{15}{8}$

2. a)

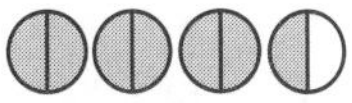

   b)

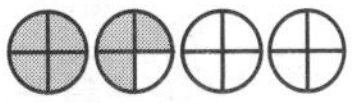

   c)

   d)

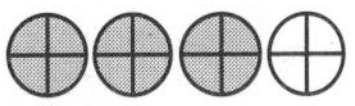

3. a)

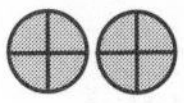

   b)

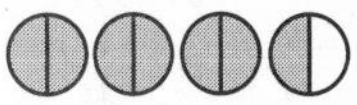

   c)

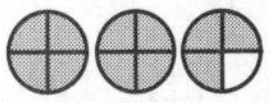

   d)

4. Fractions (b) and (c) are more than a whole – you can tell this since their numerators are greater than their denominators.

Worksheet NS5-58

1. a) $3\frac{1}{3}, \frac{10}{3}$

   b) $2\frac{3}{4}, \frac{11}{4}$

   c) $2\frac{2}{3}, \frac{8}{3}$

   d) $3\frac{6}{8}, \frac{30}{8}$

2. a) 9/2

   b) 11/4

   c) $\frac{12}{5}$

   d) $\frac{27}{8}$

3. a) $3\frac{1}{3}$

   b) 3 4/6

   c) $2\frac{1}{4}$

   d) 3 2/5

4. a) $3\frac{1}{2}$ is greater

   b) $\frac{14}{5}$ is greater

   c) $\frac{14}{3}$ is greater

Worksheet NS5-59

1. a) 2 halves

   b) 4 halves

   c) 6 halves

   d) 5 halves

2. a) 3 thirds

   b) 6 thirds

   c) 9 thirds

   d) 5 thirds

3. a) 8 cans

   b) 12 cans

   c) 16 cans

4. a) 13 cans

   b) 17 cans

   c) 19 cans

 No unauthorized copying

5. 11

6. a) A

b) 14

Worksheet NS5-60

1. a) 3 whole pies

b) 4 whole pies

c) 6 whole pies

d) 3 whole pies

2. a) 3; 1; $3\frac{1}{2}$

b) 4; 1; $4\frac{1}{3}$

c) 3; 1; $3\frac{1}{3}$

d) 3; 3; $3\frac{2}{4}$

3. a) $2\frac{1}{2}$

b) $4\frac{1}{2}$

c) $3\frac{1}{3}$

d) $3\frac{2}{3}$

4. a) $2\frac{3}{4}$ L, $\frac{11}{4}$ L

b) $2\frac{2}{5}$ m, $\frac{12}{5}$ m

5. a) $\frac{3}{7}$

b) $\frac{1}{5}$

c) $\frac{1}{3}$

Worksheet NS5-61

1. a) $\frac{1}{4}$

b) $\frac{3}{5}$

c) $\frac{1}{3}$

2. a)

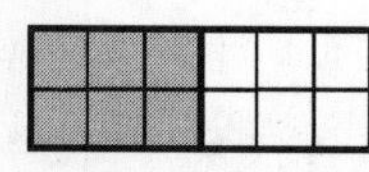

b)

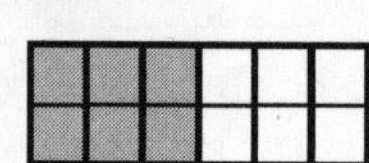

3. a) $\frac{4}{5}$

b) $\frac{1}{2}$

c) $\frac{1}{3}$

d) $\frac{3}{5}$

4. Answers may vary.

Sample Answer:
$\frac{6}{12}, \frac{3}{6}, \frac{2}{4}, \frac{1}{2}$

5. a) $\frac{4}{6} = \frac{2}{3}$

b) $\frac{4}{6} = \frac{2}{3}$

c) $\frac{2}{6} = \frac{1}{3}$

d) $\frac{6}{9} = \frac{2}{3}$

6. a) $\frac{2}{8} = \frac{1}{4}$

b) $\frac{2}{6} = \frac{1}{3}$

c) $\frac{2}{10} = \frac{1}{5}$

d) $\frac{4}{6} = \frac{2}{3}$

7. a) 1/3 = 2/6

b) $\frac{2}{3} = \frac{6}{9}$

c) $\frac{1}{2} = \frac{2}{4}$

8. a) *Sample Answer:*
$\frac{2}{6}, \frac{1}{3}$

b) *Sample Answer:*
$\frac{4}{8}, \frac{2}{4}, \frac{1}{2}$

c) *Sample Answer:*
$\frac{8}{24}, \frac{4}{12}, \frac{2}{6}, \frac{1}{3}$

9 One (1) piece has both olives and mushrooms:

Worksheet NS5-62

1. a) $\frac{1}{2} = \frac{2}{4} = \frac{3}{6} = \frac{4}{8}$.

b) $\frac{1}{3} = \frac{2}{6} = \frac{3}{9} = \frac{4}{12}$

2. a) $\frac{4}{6}$

b) $\frac{6}{8}$

c) $\frac{6}{9}$

3. a) $\frac{2}{6}$

b) $\frac{5}{10}$

c) $\frac{4}{10}$

d) 6/8

4. a) $\frac{1}{2} = \frac{2}{4} = \frac{3}{6} = \frac{4}{8} =$
$\frac{5}{10} = \frac{6}{12}$

b) $\frac{3}{5} = \frac{6}{10} = \frac{9}{15} =$
$\frac{12}{20} = \frac{15}{25} = \frac{18}{30}$

Worksheet NS5-63

1. a) $\frac{3}{4}$

b) $\frac{4}{5}$

2. a) 2; 6, 4

b) $\frac{1}{4}$, 2;
$\frac{3}{4}$, 8, 6

c) $\frac{1}{3}$, 3;
$\frac{2}{3}$, 9, 6

d) $\frac{3}{5}$, 10, 6

3. b)

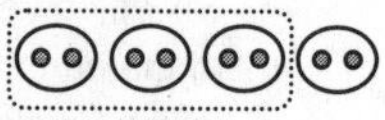

c)

d)

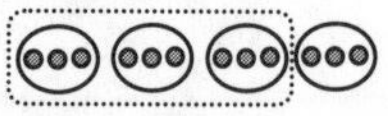

4. a)

b)

5. a) 2

b) 5

c) 4

d) 9

6. a) 6

b) 6

c) 10

d) 4

9. a) 4 – juice
2 – water

b) 3 – juice
2 – water

10. 3 Did not drink juice or water

11. 5 cone shaped

Worksheet NS5-64

1. $6

2. a) 6 oranges

b) 4 oranges

3. 6 squares are blank.

4. 7 are green.

5. $1\frac{3}{4}$ years, or a year and 9 months = 21 months, is longer

6. 9 months

7. 40 minutes

8. 4 stickers

10. 7:51

11. No, she has 7 left, which is more than half

12. 12 marbles

Worksheet NS5-65

1. a) <

b) >

c) <

d) >

2. $\frac{2}{5}, \frac{1}{2}$

3. $\frac{3}{5}, \frac{3}{4}$

4. a) $\frac{2}{4}$

b) $\frac{5}{6}$

5. a) <

b) <

c) <

d) >

Worksheet NS5-66

1. a) $\frac{2}{4}$

b) $\frac{3}{6}$

c) $\frac{2}{6}$

d) $\frac{3}{9}$

2. a) $\frac{3}{6}, \frac{2}{6}$

b) 2/4, 1/4

c) 8/12, $\frac{3}{12}$

d) $\frac{5}{10}, \frac{4}{10}$

3. a) $\frac{3}{6} > \frac{2}{6}$

b) $4/12 > \frac{3}{12}$

c) $\frac{5}{10} > \frac{2}{10}$

Worksheet NS5-67

1. $\frac{3}{4}$

2. a) $\frac{3}{5}$
   b) $\frac{2}{3}$

3. a) $\frac{4}{5}$
   b) $\frac{3}{4}$
   c) $\frac{5}{7}$
   d) $\frac{7}{8}$

4. a) $\frac{2}{4}$
   b) $\frac{1}{5}$

5. a) $\frac{1}{3}$
   b) $\frac{1}{5}$
   c) $\frac{3}{7}$
   d) $\frac{3}{8}$

Worksheet NS5-68

1. a) 2, 2 1/3, 2 2/3, 3, 3 1/3, 3 2/3, 4
   b) 3, 3 1/4, 3 2/4, 3 3/4, 4, 4 1/4, 4 2/4, 4 3/4, 5
   c) 7, 7 1/5, 7 2/5, 7 3/5, 7 4/5, 8, 8 1/5, 8 2/5, 8 3/5, 8 4/5, 9

2. a) $3, 3\frac{1}{4}$
   b) $7\frac{4}{5}, 8$

3. a) 11 quarters
   b) 17 fifths
   c) 13 thirds

4. a) $\frac{3}{10}, \frac{2}{5}, \frac{1}{2}$
   b) $\frac{1}{3}, \frac{1}{2}$, 5/6
   c) $\frac{1}{2}, \frac{5}{8}, \frac{3}{4}$

5. a) $\frac{2}{5}$
   b) $\frac{5}{2}$
   c) $\frac{2}{4}$

d) $\frac{3}{2}$

6. (c)

Worksheet NS5-69

1. a) hundredths
   b) tenths
   c) ones
   d) tenths

2. a) tenths
   b) hundredths
   c) tenths
   d) hundredths

3.

a)	5	0	3
b)	9	4	7
c)	0	3	6
d)	2	3	0

Worksheet NS5-70

1. a) 0.64
   b) 0.23
   c) 0.38
   d) 0.64

3. 0.23
   0.11
   0.12
   0.54

Worksheet NS5-71

1. a) 32 hundredths = 3 tenths 2 hundredths
   $\frac{32}{100} = 0.32$
   b) 63 hundredths = 6 tenths 3 hundredths
   63/100 = .63
   c) 83 hundredths = 8 tenths 3 hundredths
   83/100 = .83

2. a) 53 hundredths = 5 tenths 3 hundredths
   $\frac{53}{100} = 0.53$
   b) 27 hundredths = 2 tenths 7 hundredths
   27/100 = .27
   c) 65 hundredths = 6 tenths 5 hundredths
   65/100 = .65

3. a) 0.52 = 5 tenths 2 hundredths
   = 52 hundredths
   b) .44 = 4 tenths 4 hundredths
   = 44 hundredths
   c) .30 = 3 tenths 0 hundredths
   = 30 hundredths

Worksheet NS5-72

2. a) $\frac{70}{100} = \frac{7}{10}$
   b) $\frac{40}{100} = \frac{4}{10}$
   c) $\frac{20}{100} = \frac{2}{10}$
   d) $\frac{90}{100} = \frac{9}{10}$

3. a) $\frac{80}{100}$, .80
   b) .2, $\frac{20}{100}$
   c) .6, $\frac{60}{100}$

Worksheet NS5-73

1. b) 6 dimes 2 pennies
   6 tenths 2 hundredths
   62 pennies
   62 hundredths
   c) 5 dimes 7 pennies
   5 tenths 7 hundredths
   57 pennies
   57 hundredths

2. a) 4 dimes 0 pennies
   4 tenths 0 hundredths
   40 pennies
   40 hundredths
   b) 9 dimes 0 pennies
   9 tenths 0 hundredths
   90 pennies
   90 hundredths

3. 1 dime 7 pennies
   1 tenth 7 hundredths
   17 pennies
   17 hundredths
   2 dimes 0 pennies
   2 tenths 0 hundredths
   20 pennies
   20 hundredths
   .2 is greater than .17

4. .53 is less than .7 because 53 is less than 70.

Worksheet NS5-74

1.

	Tenths	Hund.
a)	5	6
b)	6	0
c)	2	1
d)	0	7

$\frac{56}{100} = 0.56$

$\frac{60}{100} = 0.60$

$\frac{21}{100} = 0.21$

$\frac{7}{100} = 0.07$

2. a) 5/10
   b) 3/10
   c) 6/10

3. a) 0.5
   b) 0.4
   c) 0.6
   d) 0.9

4. Circle as incorrect: (c), (f), (g), (j)

5. .7 = 7 tenths = 70 hundredths = .70

Worksheet NS5-75

1. a) $1\frac{21}{100} = 1.21$
   b) $1\frac{38}{100} = 1.38$
   c) $\frac{59}{100} = 0.59$
   d) $2\frac{40}{100} = 2.40$

3. a) $2.98 = 2\frac{98}{100}$
   b) $1.08 = 1\frac{8}{100}$

4. a) 2.57
   b) 3.17
   c) 5.30
   d) 1.03

5. a) 0.3
   b) 0.7
   c) 1.80

No unauthorized copying

Worksheet NS5-76

1. A: $\frac{8}{10}$ = .8
   B: $1\frac{4}{10}$ = 1.4
   C: $2\frac{1}{10}$ = 2.1
   D: $2\frac{7}{10}$ = 2.7
   E: $\frac{2}{10}$ = 0.2
   F: $1\frac{1}{10}$ = 1.1
   G: $1\frac{8}{10}$ = 1.8
   H: $2\frac{2}{10}$ = 2.2
3. A: five tenths
   B: one and five tenths
   C: two and eight tenths

Worksheet NS6-77

1. b) 0.5
2. a) Zero
   b) Half
   c) One
   d) Half
3. a) <
   b) >
   c) >
   d) >
4. a) 1
   b) 2
   c) 2

Worksheet NS5-78

1. a) 0.3 0.5 0.7
   b) $\frac{1}{10}$ 0.3 0.9
   c) 0.2 $\frac{3}{10}$ 0.6
   d) 1.2 3.1 3.5
2. a) 0.7
   b) 0.6
   c) 0.82
3. a) 0.7 = 0.70 = $\frac{70}{100}$
   b) 0.6 = 0.60 = $\frac{60}{100}$
   c) 0.5 = 0.50 = $\frac{50}{100}$
4. a) 0.2 0.35 0.8
   b) 0.9 0.25 $\frac{27}{100}$
   c) $1\frac{22}{100}$ $1\frac{39}{100}$ 1.3
5. a) $\frac{1}{2} = \frac{5}{10} = \frac{50}{100}$
   $\frac{1}{2}$ = .5 = .50
   b) $\frac{1}{5} = \frac{2}{10} = \frac{20}{100}$
   $\frac{1}{5}$ = .2 = .20
7. a) $\frac{2}{5} = \frac{4}{10} = \frac{40}{100}$
   b) $\frac{3}{5} = \frac{6}{10} = \frac{60}{100}$
   c) $\frac{4}{5} = \frac{8}{10} = \frac{80}{100}$
8. $\frac{1}{4} = \frac{25}{100}$
   $\frac{1}{4}$ = 0.25
   3/4 = 75/100
   3/4 = 0.75
9. a) $\frac{1}{2}$
   b) .52
   c) .42
   d) .7
10. a) .32 $\frac{1}{2}$ .7
   b) $\frac{1}{4}$ $\frac{3}{5}$ .63
   c) .35 $\frac{2}{5}$ $\frac{1}{2}$

Worksheet NS5-79

1. 13
2. a) 47
   b) 71
   c) 30
   d) 3.8
3. a) 3.1
   b) 2.4
   c) 8.7
   d) 1.5
4. a) 1.7
   b) 1.2
   c) 3.7
   d) 0.8
5. a) 2.3
   b) 7.8
   c) 7.1
   d) 4.3

Worksheet NS5-80

1. a) $\frac{28}{100} + \frac{50}{100} = \frac{78}{100}$
   b) $\frac{30}{100} + \frac{37}{100} = \frac{67}{100}$
   c) $\frac{62}{100} + \frac{31}{100} = \frac{93}{100}$
   d) $\frac{44}{100} + \frac{37}{100} = \frac{81}{100}$
2. a) .28 + .50 = .78
   b) .3 + .37 = .67
   c) .62 + .31 = .93
   d) .44 + .37 = .81
3. a) 0.78
   b) 0.95
   c) 1.14
   d) 0.79
4. a) 0.49
   b) 0.87
   c) 0.58
   d) 0.89
5. 0.99 L
6. 56/100 m
   More than 1 m

Worksheet NS5-81

1. a) $\frac{40}{100}$
   b) $\frac{10}{100}$
   c) $\frac{26}{100}$
2. a) .60 – .20 = .40
   b) .32 – .22 = .10
   c) .79 – .55 = .26
3. a) 0.43
   b) 0.54
   c) 0.23
   d) 0.54
4. a) .37
   b) .59
   c) .08
   d) .14
5. a) 0.65
   b) 0.28
   c) 0.59

Worksheet NS5-82

1. a) 2.47
   b) 2.79
2. a) 1.02
   b) 1.21
3. a) 7.69
   b) 7.23
   c) 1.71
   d) 2.04
4. 0.9 m
5. 16.78 m
6. a) .2, .4, .6, .8, 1.0, 1.2
   b) .3, .6, .9, 1.2, 1.5, 1.8

Worksheet NS5-83

1. a) 10 × 0.2 = 2
   b) 10 × 0.3 = 3
   c) 10 × 0.6 = 6
2. a) 5
   b) 7
   c) 14
   d) 9
3. a) .6 dm = 6 cm
   b) .8 dm = 8 cm
   c) 1.6 dm = 16 cm
4. 3.0

Worksheet NS5-84

1. a) 100 × 0.02 = 2
   b) 100 × 0.03 = 3
2. a) 70
   b) 180
   c) 460
   d) 3
3. a) 15.2 cm
   b) 375 mm
   c) 5 mm
   d) 0.8 cm

Worksheet NS5-85

1. a) 2.86
   b) 3.6
   c) 5.05
   d) 8.4
2. a) 6, 24, 8, 4, 8.4
   b) 6, 15, 7, 5, 7.5
   c) 6, 21, 8, 1, 8.1
   d) 8 ones + 24 tenths = 10 ones + 4 tenths = 10.4
3. a) 6, 15, 3, 7, 5, 3, 7.53
   b) 8, 4, 16, 8, 5, 6, 8.56
   c) 5, 20, 5, 7, 0, 5, 7.05
4. a) 10.35
   b) 30.48
   c) 25.86

d) 9.75

5. a) 10.5
   b) 24.9
   c) 37.5
   d) 25.29

Worksheet NS5-86

1. a) 2.0 ÷ 10 = .2
   b) 3.0 ÷ 10 = .3
   c) .3 ÷ 10 = .03
   d) .4 ÷ 10 = .04
2. a) 2.3 ÷ 10 = .23
   b) 2.4 ÷ 10 = .24
3. a) 0.03
   b) 0.05
   c) 0.07
   d) 0.13
4. a) 5 cm = .5 dm
   b) 1.7 cm = 0.17 dm
   c) 3.5 mm = .35 cm
   d) 2 mm = .2 cm
5. 0.27 m
6. 2.5 m

Worksheet NS5-87

1. 2.56
2. a) 1.44
   b) 1.5625
   c) 1.246
   d) 1.66
3. a) 0.18
   b) 1.34
   c) 0.34
   d) 0.68
4. 55 cents
5. 15.6 km
6. $7.29
7. 6 for 4.98
   = .83 per one
   8 for 6.96
   = .87 per one
   The first choice is better.

Worksheet NS5-88

1. a) 0.74
   b) 0.45
   c) 0.16
   d) 0.99
2. a) 0.8
   b) 2.7
   c) 1.42
   d) 0.73
3. a) 0.01
   b) 0.1
   c) 0.01
   d) 0.01
4. a) 5.1, 5.2, 5.3, 5.4, 5.5, 5.6, 5.7, 5.8, 5.9
   b) 3.9, 4.0, 4.1, 4.2, 4.3, 4.4, 4.5, 4.6, 4.7
   c) 4.15, 4.16,. 4.17, 4.18, 4.19, 4.20, 4.21, 4.22, 4.23
5. a) .5, .6, .7
   b) 6.9, 7.0, 7.1
   c) 3.8, 3.9, 4.0
   d) 9.9, 10.0, 10.1
6. a) 4.0
   b) 5.0
   c) 9.03
   d) 3.80

Worksheet NS5-89

2. a) 1 cm = $\frac{1}{10}$ dm
   = .1 dm
   b) 100 cm = $\frac{100}{10}$ dm
   = 10 dm
   c) 1 mm = $\frac{1}{10}$ cm
   = .1 cm
   d) 16 mm = $\frac{16}{10}$ cm
   = 1.6 cm
3. a) 9.6 dm
   b) 3.5 dm
   c) 9.3 cm
   d) 1.97 m
4. a) 5 dm = 50 cm = 500 mm
   b) 20 cents
   c) 30 cm = 3 dm
   d) 700 000
5. a) .3
   b) .3
   c) .7
   d) 1.4
6. a) 3.0
   b) 4
   c) 3
   d) 8
7. A Five and two tenths
   B Five and nine tenths
   C Six and five tenths
   D Seven
9. a) 3207.02
   b) 10520.15
   c) 6308.01
   d) 407.02
10. a) >
    b) <
    c) >
    d) <
11. 129
12. a) 0.09 < 0.1; less
    b) 21.2 – 21.1 = 0.1

Worksheet NS5-90

1. 7 × 0.67 = 4.69 m
2. Yes
3. $62.93
4. 4 pens for $2.96
5. 34.5 km
7. A dollar
8. a) 26.1 m
   b) About 4
   c) About 24 m

Worksheet NS5-91

1. a) $5, $10, $15, $20
   b) 6¢, 12¢, 18¢, 24¢
   c) 20¢, 40¢, 60¢, 80¢
   d) 90
2. a) 1 cm
   60 m
   b) About 5.7 mm
   About 330 m
   c) 9 cm
   540 m
3. $44
4. $120
5. a) $5
   b) $3
   c) $2

Worksheet NS5-92

1. a) about 9 cm
   = 18 km
   b) 8.3 cm = 16.6 km
   c) About 2 cm
   = 4 km
   d) About 10 cm
   = 20 km
2. a) 200 km
   b) 250 km
   c) 25 km
   d) 125 km

Worksheet NS5-93

1. a) 75.35 km
   b) 25.11 km
   c) 4.19 km
   d) 30 kg
2. 9 beads
3. $2.99
4. 144 students but only 120 seats
   There is not enough room.
5. $21.40
6. $8.90
7. 1.25 m
8. 13.8 kg
9. 33.6 km
10. 1799

Measurement

Worksheet ME5-1

1. a) 9 cm
   b) 10 cm
   c) 13 cm
2. a) 5 cm
   b) 3 cm
3. a) Top and bottom: 4 cm
   Sides: 2 cm
   b) Base: 3 cm
   Height: 4 cm
   Hypotenuse: 5 cm
4. a) Arrows at 0 and 4.
   b) Arrows at: 0 and 3 or
   1 and 4 or 2 and 5.

No unauthorized copying

c) Arrows at 0 and 5.

Worksheet ME5-2

1. a) About 4 index fingers = About 40 mm
   b) About 6 index fingers = About 60 mm
2. a) 38 mm
   b) 47 mm
3. Top and bottom: 5 cm
   Sides: 1.5 cm
   Diagonal: 5.2 cm = 52 mm
6. 10
7.

mm	cm
130	13
320	32
80	8
180	18
2 130	213
1 700	170
90	9
5 670	567

8. 10
9. a) 46 cm
   b) 6 cm
   c) 58 cm
10. a) 70 mm
    b) 910 mm
    c) 45 cm
    d) 2 cm
12.

in cm	in mm
4	40
3	30
8	80

15. a) 6 cm
    b) 3 cm
    c) 6 cm
16. a) 4-cm line
    b) 6-cm line
    c) 3-cm line
17. a) 5 + 3
    b) 5 + 3 + 3
    c) 5 + 5 + 3
    d) 5 + 5 + 5 + 5 + 3 + 3
    OR
    5 + 3 + 3 + 3 + 3 + 3 + 3 + 3
    e) 5 + 3 + 3 + 3 + 3

Worksheet ME5-3

1. arm – more;
   paper clip – less;
   Pencil – more (or less, depending on the pencil);
   Door – more
2. 10
3. 10
4.

cm	dm
150	15
230	23
320	32
90	9
5100	510
400	40
610	61
10	1
780	78

8. 1 dm = 100 mm

Worksheet ME5-4

4. a) 3 000 m
   b) 6 000 m
   c) 7 000 m
   d) 12 000 m
5. 10
7. 2

Worksheet ME5-5

1.

3	4	5	6
30	40	50	60
300	400	500	600
3 000	4 000	5 000	6 000

2. a) 100
   b) 100
   c) 10
3.

m	cm
8	800
70	7 000
m	**mm**
5	5 000
17	17 000
cm	**mm**
4	40
121	1 210
dm	**cm**
32	320
5	50

4. No, since 2 m 23 cm = 223 cm.
5. b) 5 m 14 cm
   c) 6 m 27 cm
   d) 6 m 73 cm
   e) 3 m 81 cm
   f) 2 m 3 cm
6. a) 365 cm
   b) 485 cm
   c) 947 cm
   d) 704 cm
   e) 640 cm
7. b) = 2 m 17 cm = 2.17 m
   c) = 7 m 83 cm = 7.83 m
   d) = 6 m 48 cm = 6.48 m
8. A dollar is 100 cents and a metre is 100 cm.

Worksheet ME5-6

1. 100 mm; 10 cm; 1 dm
   a) largest - dm; smallest - mm
   b) The smaller unit (that is, # of mm > # of dm)
   c) More
2. a) 10
   b) 10
   c) 100
   d) 10
   e) 100
   f) 1 000
3. a) 10 smaller; 10 more; multiply by 10; 0.35 cm
   b) 10 Larger; 10 fewer; divide; 0.27 cm
   c) 10 Smaller; 10 more; multiply; 63 cm
   d) 10 Larger; 10 fewer; divide; 0.3 dm
4. a) 40
   b) 0.13
   c) 0.2
5. Ostrich Fern
   Royal Fern
   Bracken Fern
   Oak Fern
6. 362 mm = 36.2 cm > 20 cm
7. The fence is 32 × 4 = 128 cm > 1 m (100 cm). So the fence is longer than 1 m.
8. 10 cm (1 dm) cost 5¢, so 90 cm will cost 9 × 5¢ = 45¢.
9. 6 m 80 cm = 6.8 m = 680 cm

Worksheet ME5-7

1. a) mm = millimetre → thickness of a fingernail;
   cm = centimetre → length of a finger;
   m = metre → height of a door;
   km = kilometre → distance to Moscow.
   b) mm = millimetre → length of a flea;
   cm = centimetre → length of a pen;
   m = metre → length of a canoe;
   km = kilometre → distance to the moon.
2. a) m
   b) dm
   c) m
3. a) cm
   b) m
   c) cm
   d) cm
4. a) km

b) cm

c) m

d) mm

6. *1.* Red Fox (55 cm)

2. Beaver (40 cm)

3. Grey Squirrel (23 cm)

4. Black Bear (12 cm)

9. a) 553 m; 2 km; 20 years

b) 4 500 km; 5.5 hours; 12 km

Worksheet ME5-8

1.	H1	H2	B1	B2
1	12	60	24	120
2	20	100	39	195
3	20	100	42	210
4	29	145	45	225

2. a) 66 cm; 6.6 dm

b) 100 cm; 10 dm

c) 66 m

d) 225 bricks

3.	H1	H2	B1	B2
1	16	80	21	105
2	18	90	29	145
3	29	145	46	230

Worksheet ME5-9

1. a) 15 cm

b) 15 000 m

2. 12 900 m

3. 1 290 buses

4. 11 000 m

5. 110 m

6. 13, 16 or 17 (depending on rounding selected)

Worksheet ME5-10

1. a) 2 + 2 + 5 + 3 + 1 + 1 = 14 cm

b) 16 cm

c) 14 cm

d) 20 cm

2. *A:* 16 units

B: 22 units

C: 22 units

Worksheet ME5-11

1 a) 10 cm

b) 8 cm

c) 14 cm

2. a) 24 m

b) 28 cm

c) 6 km

d) 30 cm

3. a) P = 18 cm

b) P = 16 cm

4. a) 10 × 1; 2 × 5

b) 12 × 1; 2 × 6; 3 × 4

c) 1 × 7

d) 12 × 1; P = 26

5. a) $4.20

b) Sally could make two different rectangles: 2 × 4 and 1 × 8. The border would be least expensive for the 2 × 4 one, since its perimeter is less (12 m vs. 18 m).

Worksheet ME5-12

1. a) 6

b) 6 m

c) 3 m

2. a) Length = 4 cm

b) Width = 4 cm

c) Length = 3 cm

d) Width = 1 m

3. a) W = 1, L = 2

b) W = 1, L = 5; W = 2, L = 4; W = 3, L = 3.

c) W = 1, L = 7; W = 2, L = 6; W = 3, L = 5; W = 4, L = 4.

d) W = 1, L = 8; W = 2, L = 7; W = 3, L = 6; W = 4, L = 5.

4. To find the perimeter of a rectangle, add its length and width and multiply the sum by 2.

5. a)

Input	Output
1	6
2	8
3	10
4	12
5	14

b) Multiply the INPUT by 2 and add 4.

c) P = 24

6. a) Original Perimeter = 8 units

b) Original Perimeter = 10 units

c) Original Perimeter = 12 units

7. a) Original Perimeter = 5 units

b) Original Perimeter = 7 units

8. a) i) 1, 8; 2, 10; 3, 12

ii) multiply by 2 and add 6

iii) 26

b) i) 1, 8; 2, 10; 3, 12

ii) multiply by 2 and add 6

iii) 26

9. Yes.

Worksheet ME5-13

1. a) 8 cm^2

b) 8 cm^2

c) 9 cm^2

2. a) 8 cm^2

b) 3 cm^2

c) 4 cm^2

3. Area of A = 6 cm^2

Area of B = 4 cm^2

Area of C = 8 cm^2

6. 3 cm × 4 cm rectangle:

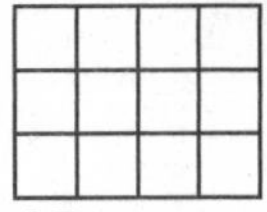

OR

4 cm × 3 cm rectangle:

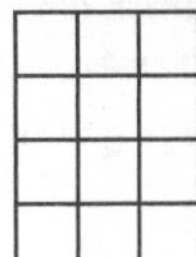

Worksheet ME5-14

1. a) 4 × 3 = 12

b) 2 × 3 = 6

c) 3 × 2 = 6

d) 5 × 3 = 15

2. a) 3 × 7 = 21

b) 3 × 4 = 12

c) 3 × 2 = 6

d) 4 × 6 = 24

3. a) Length = 6 units

Width = 2 units

Area = 12 sq units

b) Length = 3 units

Width = 2 units

Area = 6 sq units

c) Length = 4 units

Width = 3 units

Area = 12 sq units

4. a) 2 cm × 3 cm = 6 cm^2

b) 1 cm × 3 cm = 3 cm^2

c) 2 cm × 4 cm = 8 cm^2

d) 4 cm × 3 cm = 12 cm^2

e) 2 cm × 5 cm = 10 cm^2

5. Area = Length × Width

Worksheet ME5-15

1. a) 2 cm × 5 cm = 10 cm^2

b) 1 cm × 3 cm = 3 cm^2

c) 3 cm × 5 cm = 15 cm^2

2. a) 6 m × 7 m = 42 m^2

No unauthorized copying

b) $3 \text{ m} \times 7 \text{ m} = 21 \text{ m}^2$

c) $4 \text{ cm} \times 8 \text{ cm} = 32 \text{ cm}^2$

3. a) A: $3 \text{ m} \times 7 \text{ m} = 21 \text{ m}^2$

B: $4 \text{ cm} \times 5 \text{ cm} = 20 \text{ cm}^2$

C: $11 \text{ m} \times 6 \text{ m} = 66 \text{ m}^2$

D: $3 \text{ km} \times 2 \text{ km} = 6 \text{ km}^2$

b) D, C, A, B

4. Width = 3 cm (since you can find the width by dividing the area by the length, and $18 \text{ cm}^2 \div 6 \text{ cm}$ is 3 cm)

5. 3 cm

6. 5 cm

7. *OPTION 1* -
Box 1: 2 × 2 = 4;
Box 2: 3 × 6 = 18;
Total Area: 4 + 18 = 22

OPTION 2 -
Box 1: 2 × 5 = 10;
Box 2: 3 × 4 = 12;
Total Area: 10 + 12 = 22

8. Three rectangles have side lengths that are whole numbers: 1 × 20, 2 × 10, and 4 × 5

Worksheet ME5-16

1. a) 3 whole squares
b) 2 whole squares
c) 3 whole squares
d) 3 whole squares

2. a) 7.5 square units
b) 6 square units
c) 7.5 square units

3. a) More:
shaded = 7
unshaded = 5
and 7 > 5

b) Equal:
shaded = 4
unshaded = 4

c) Less:
shaded = 3
unshaded = 4
and 3 < 4

4. a) $\frac{1}{2}$
b) 4 square units
c) 2 square units

5. a) 1 square units
b) 3 square units
c) 3 square units
d) 5 square units

6. a) 3 square units
b) 3 square units
c) 6 square units
d) 2 square units

7. a) 5 square units
b) 2 square units
c) 8 square units
d) 9 square units

8. a) 6 square units
b) 8.5 square units
c) 8.5 square units

9. a) Area: 5 units2
Fraction: $\frac{5}{9}$

b) Area: 1 units2
Fraction: $\frac{1}{4}$

c) Area: 2 units2
Fraction: $\frac{1}{4}$

Worksheet ME5-17

1. a) Area:
5 square units
Perimeter:
14 units

b) Area:
12 square units
Perimeter:
18 units

c) Area:
6 square units
Perimeter:
11 units

2. b) **Shape A**
Old Area: 1 units^2
Old Per: 4 units
New Area: 4 units^2
New Per: 8 units

Shape B
Old Area: 2 units^2
Old Per: 6 units
New Area: 8 units^2
New Per: 12 units

Shape C
Old Area: .5 units^2
Old Per: 3.4 units
New Area: 2 units^2
New Per: 6.8 units

Shape D
Old Area: 1 units^2
Old Per: 4.8 units
New Area: 4 units^2
New Per: 9.6 units

c) The area of the shape quadruples (is multiplied by 4).

Worksheet ME5-18

1.

Shape	P	A
A	12 cm	8 cm^2
B	22 cm	30 cm^2
C	22 cm	18 cm^2
D	20 cm	21 cm^2
E	26 cm	30 cm^2
F	14 cm	10 cm^2
G	22 cm	10 cm^2

2. No

3. D & G

4. E; B, C & G; D; F; A

5. E & B; D; C; F& G; A

6. No

7. Perimeter is the measure of the length along the outside edge of a shape; area is the measure of the space contained *within* the edges of a shape.

Worksheet ME5-19

1. Actual measurements:

R	P	A
A	14 cm	10 cm^2
B	16 cm	12 cm^2
C	16 cm	15 cm^2
D	10 cm	6 cm^2
E	18 cm	14 cm^2
F	12 cm	8 cm^2
G	14 cm	12 cm^2

2. a) 6 cm^2
b) 20 cm^2

3. a) 9 cm^2
b) 25 cm^2

4. a) 5 cm × 2 cm
OR
2 cm × 5 cm
rectangle

b) 4 cm × 2 cm
OR
2 cm × 4 cm
rectangle

5. Stays the same.

Worksheet ME5-20

1. a) 4 m
c) $168

2.

	Length	Width
8 cm^2	1	8
	2	4
	4	2
	8	1
14 cm^2	1	14
	2	7
	7	2
	14	1
18 cm^2	1	18
	2	9
	3	6
	6	3
	9	2
	18	1

4. 3 × 3

5. 4 × 5

6. Width × 2 + Width × 4

Worksheet ME5-21

1. a) 280 cm
b) 175 cm
c) 160 cm

2. a) 15 cm
b) 24 cm
c) 64 cm

3. a) 0.5 m^2
b) 2 m^2
c) 6 m

4. a) Perimeter = 20 m
Area = 25 m^2
b) 10 m^2

5. 12

No unauthorized copying